THE GHIDRA BOOK

The Definitive Guide

by Chris Eagle and Kara Nance

no starch press

San Francisco

THE GHIDRA BOOK.

Copyright © 2020 Chris Eagle and Kara Nance.

Printed in USA

Second printing

25 24 23 22 21   2 3 4 5 6 7 8 9

ISBN-13: 978-1-71850-102-7 (print)
ISBN-13: 978-1-71850-103-4 (ebook)

Publisher: William Pollock
Executive Editor: Barbara Yien
Production Editors: Laurel Chun and Katrina Taylor
Cover Illustration: Gina Redman
Interior Design: Octopod Studios
Project Editor: Dapinder Dosanjh
Developmental Editor: Athabasca Witschi
Technical Reviewer: Brian Hay
Copyeditor: Barton D. Reed
Compositor: Danielle Foster
Proofreader: Sharon Wilkey

For information on distribution, translations, or bulk sales, please contact No Starch Press, Inc. directly:
No Starch Press, Inc.
245 8th Street, San Francisco, CA 94103
phone: 1.415.863.9900; info@nostarch.com
www.nostarch.com

Library of Congress Control Number: 2020938508

[S]

To all those who believe in science and fact-based decision making as well as all of the COVID-19 first responders around the world whose hard work and sacrifice provided a ray of hope in a time of global crisis.

To all girls who are passionate about investigating and understanding technology and the men and women who support and encourage them. Dream big and keep exploring!

About the Authors

Chris Eagle has been reverse engineering software for 40 years. He is the author of *The IDA Pro Book* (No Starch Press) and is a highly sought-after provider of reverse engineering training. He has published numerous reverse engineering tools and given talks at conferences such as Blackhat, Defcon, and Shmoocon.

Kara Nance is a private security consultant. She has been a professor of computer science for many years. She has served on the Honeynet Project Board of Directors and given numerous talks at conferences around the world. She enjoys building Ghidra extensions and regularly provides Ghidra training.

About the Tech Reviewer

Brian Hay has been a reverse engineer, professor, and software developer for many years. He has spoken and taught at many conferences and is currently a senior researcher for a boutique security research company. He specializes in designing and developing virtualized environments for training and testing exciting new tools like Ghidra.

BRIEF CONTENTS

CONTENTS IN DETAIL

3
MEET GHIDRA   33

PART II: BASIC GHIDRA USAGE   39

4
GETTING STARTED WITH GHIDRA   41

5
GHIDRA DATA DISPLAYS   55

6
MAKING SENSE OF A GHIDRA DISASSEMBLY   89

7
DISASSEMBLY MANIPULATION   119

PART III: MAKING GHIDRA WORK FOR YOU   215

11
COLLABORATIVE SRE   217

12
CUSTOMIZING GHIDRA   241

13
EXTENDING GHIDRA'S WORLDVIEW   261

14
BASIC GHIDRA SCRIPTING

285

19
THE GHIDRA DECOMPILER
427

20
COMPILER VARIATIONS
443

PART V: REAL-WORLD APPLICATIONS
467

21
OBFUSCATED CODE ANALYSIS
469

ACKNOWLEDGMENTS

This book would not have been possible without the help and support of the extremely professional staff at No Starch Press. Bill Pollock and Barbara Yien supported our goal of creating a book about Ghidra that aligned with our vision and we deeply appreciate their confidence in us throughout this journey. Athabasca Witschi's initial feedback on chapters provided valuable insight and guidance. Laurel Chun's ongoing support and patience through all our questions helped turn this book into a finished product we are very proud of. We would also like to thank all of the people "behind the scenes" for their hard work in making this dream a reality, including Katrina Taylor, Barton D. Reed, Sharon Wilkey, and Danielle Foster.

We would like to thank our technical editor, Brian Hay, for reviewing our many words and examples. His knowledge and experience with Ghidra has helped to ensure that the technical content in this book is solid, and his teaching experience guided our presentation so that the material is presented in a way that appeals to both new and experienced reverse engineers.

We would like to thank the entire Ghidra development team, past and present, at the National Security Agency for building Ghidra and sharing it with the world as an open source project.

Kara would like to thank Ben for his patience while she learned about technology and Katie for her patience while she wrote about it. She thanks Jen for the inspirational introduction, and Dickie and Lenora for always believing in her. Finally, she would like to thank Brian for his humor and ongoing support every hour of every day. Without the support that you all provided, this book would not have been possible.

INTRODUCTION

Our goal in writing this book is to provide a resource that introduces Ghidra to both current and future reverse engineers. In the hands of a skilled reverse engineer, Ghidra streamlines the analysis process and allows users to customize and extend its capabilities to suit their individual needs and improve their workflows. Ghidra is also very accessible to new reverse engineers, particularly with its included decompiler that can help them more clearly understand the relationships between high-level language and disassembly listings as they begin exploring the world of binary analysis.

Writing a book about Ghidra is a challenging undertaking. Ghidra is a complex open source reverse engineering tool suite that is continually evolving. Our words describe a moving target, as the Ghidra community continues to improve and extend its capabilities. As with many new open source projects, Ghidra has begun its public life with a rapid string of evolutionary releases. A primary goal while writing this book has been to ensure that as Ghidra evolves, the book's content continues to provide readers with a wide and deep foundation of knowledge to understand and effectively utilize current and future Ghidra versions to address their reverse engineering challenges. As much as possible, we have tried to keep the book version-agnostic. Fortunately, new releases of Ghidra are well-documented, with detailed listings of changes that provide version-specific guidance should you encounter any differences between the book and your version of Ghidra.

About This Book

This book is the first comprehensive book about Ghidra. It is intended to be an all-encompassing resource for reverse engineering with Ghidra. It provides introductory content to bring new explorers to the reverse engineering world, advanced content to extend the worldview of experienced reverse engineers, and examples for rookie and veteran Ghidra developers alike to continue to extend Ghidra's extensive capabilities and become contributors to the Ghidra community.

Who Should Read This Book?

This book is intended for aspiring and experienced software reverse engineers. If you don't already have reverse engineering experience, that's okay, as the early chapters provide the background material necessary to introduce you to reverse engineering and enable you to explore and analyze binaries with Ghidra. Experienced reverse engineers who want to add Ghidra to their toolkits might choose to move quickly through the first two parts to gain a basic understanding of Ghidra and then jump to specific chapters of interest. Experienced Ghidra users and developers may choose to focus on the later chapters so that they can create new Ghidra extensions and can apply their experience and knowledge to contribute new content to the Ghidra project.

What's in This Book?

The book is divided into five parts. Part I introduces disassembly, reverse engineering, and the Ghidra project. Part II covers basic Ghidra usage. Part III demonstrates ways you can customize and automate Ghidra to make it work for you. Part IV takes a deeper dive into explaining specific types of Ghidra modules and supporting concepts. Part V demonstrates how Ghidra can be applied to some real-world situations a reverse engineer is likely to encounter.

Part I: Introduction

Chapter 1: Introduction to Disassembly

This introductory chapter walks you through the theory and practice of disassembly and discusses some of the pros and cons associated with the two common disassembly algorithms.

Chapter 2: Reversing and Disassembly Tools

This chapter discusses the major categories of tools available for reverse engineering and disassembly.

Chapter 3: Meet Ghidra

Here you get to meet Ghidra and learn a little bit about its origin and how you can obtain and start using this free open source tool suite.

Part II: Basic Ghidra Usage

Chapter 4: Getting Started with Ghidra

Your journey with Ghidra begins in this chapter. You'll get your first glimpse of Ghidra in action as you create a project, analyze a file, and begin to understand the Ghidra graphical user interface (GUI).

Chapter 5: Ghidra Data Displays

Here you'll be introduced to the CodeBrowser, Ghidra's main tool for file analysis. You'll also explore the primary CodeBrowser display windows.

Chapter 6: Making Sense of a Ghidra Disassembly

This chapter explores the concepts that are fundamental to understanding and navigating Ghidra disassemblies.

Chapter 7: Disassembly Manipulation

In this chapter, you'll learn to supplement Ghidra's analysis and manipulate a Ghidra disassembly as part of your own analysis process.

Chapter 8: Data Types and Data Structures

In this chapter, you will learn how to manipulate and define simple and complex data structures found within compiled programs.

Chapter 9: Cross-References

This chapter provides a detailed look at cross-references, how they support graphing, and the critical role they play in understanding a program's behavior.

Chapter 10: Graphs

This chapter introduces you to Ghidra's graphing capabilities and the use of graphs as binary analysis tools.

Part III: Making Ghidra Work for You

Chapter 11: Collaborative SRE

This chapter presents a unique capability within Ghidra—using Ghidra as a collaborative tool. You will learn how to configure a Ghidra server and share projects with other analysts.

Chapter 12: Customizing Ghidra

Here you begin to see how you can customize Ghidra by configuring projects and tools to support your individual analysis workflows.

Chapter 13: Extending Ghidra's Worldview

This chapter teaches you how to generate and apply library signatures and other specialized content so that Ghidra can recognize new binary constructs.

Chapter 14: Basic Ghidra Scripting

In this chapter, you'll be introduced to the basic Ghidra scripting capabilities in Python and Java using Ghidra's inline editor.

Chapter 15: Eclipse and GhidraDev

This chapter takes your Ghidra scripting to a whole new level by integrating Eclipse into Ghidra and exploring the powerful scripting capabilities that this combination provides, including a worked example of building a new analyzer.

Chapter 16: Ghidra in Headless Mode

You'll be introduced to the use of Ghidra in headless mode, where no GUI is required. You will quickly understand the advantage of this mode for common large-scale repetitive tasks.

Part IV: A Deeper Dive

Chapter 17: Ghidra Loaders

Here you'll take a deep dive into how Ghidra imports and loads files. You will have the opportunity to build new loaders to handle previously unrecognized file types.

Chapter 18: Ghidra Processors

This chapter introduces you to Ghidra's SLEIGH language for defining processor architectures. You will explore the process for adding new processors and instructions to Ghidra.

Chapter 19: The Ghidra Decompiler

Here you'll be provided with a closer look at one of Ghidra's most popular features: the Ghidra Decompiler. You will see how it works behind the scenes and how it can contribute to your analysis process.

Chapter 20: Compiler Variations

This chapter helps you understand the variations you can expect to see in code compiled using different compilers and targeting different platforms.

Part V: Real-World Application

Chapter 21: Obfuscated Code Analysis

You'll learn how to use Ghidra to analyze obfuscated code in a static context so that the code doesn't need to be executed.

Chapter 22: Patching Binaries

This chapter teaches you some methods for using Ghidra to patch binaries during analysis, both within Ghidra itself and to create new patched versions of the original binaries.

Chapter 23: Binary Differencing and Version Tracking

This final chapter provides an overview of the Ghidra features that allow you to identify differences between two binaries as well as a brief introduction to Ghidra's advanced version tracking capabilities.

Appendix: Ghidra for IDA Users

If you are an experienced IDA user, this appendix will provide you with tips and tricks for mapping IDA terminology and usage to similar functionality in Ghidra.

NOTE   *Visit the companion sites,* https://nostarch.com/GhidraBook/ *and* https://ghidrabook.com/, *to access the code listings contained in this book.*

PART I

INTRODUCTION

1

INTRODUCTION TO DISASSEMBLY

You may be wondering what to expect in a book dedicated to Ghidra. While obviously Ghidra-centric, this book is not intended to come across as *The Ghidra User's Manual*. Instead, we intend to use Ghidra as the enabling tool for discussing reverse engineering techniques that you will find useful in analyzing a wide variety of software, ranging from vulnerable applications to malware. When appropriate, we will provide detailed steps in Ghidra for performing specific actions related to the task at hand. As a result, we will take a rather roundabout walk through Ghidra's capabilities, beginning with the basic tasks you will want to perform upon initial examination of a file and leading up to advanced uses and customization of Ghidra for more challenging reverse engineering problems. We make no attempt to cover all of Ghidra's features. We do, however, cover the features you will find most useful in meeting your reverse engineering challenges. This book will help make Ghidra the most potent weapon in your arsenal of tools.

Prior to diving into any Ghidra specifics, we will cover some of the basics of the disassembly process and review other tools available for reverse engineering compiled code. While these tools may not match the complete range of Ghidra's capabilities, each does address specific subsets of Ghidra functionality and offers valuable insight into specific Ghidra features. The remainder of this chapter is dedicated to understanding the disassembly process from a high level.

Disassembly Theory

Anyone who has spent any time at all studying programming languages has probably learned about the various generations of languages, but they are summarized here for those who may have been sleeping:

First-generation languages   These are the lowest form of language, generally consisting of ones and zeros or a shorthand form, such as hexadecimal, and readable only by binary ninjas. Distinguishing data from instructions is difficult at this level because all the content looks the same. First-generation languages may also be referred to as *machine languages*, and in some cases *byte code*, while machine language programs are often referred to as *binaries*.

Second-generation languages   Also called *assembly languages*, second-generation languages are a mere table lookup away from machine language and generally map specific bit patterns, or operation codes (opcodes), to short but memorable character sequences called *mnemonics*. These mnemonics help programmers remember the instructions with which they are associated. An *assembler* is a tool used by programmers to translate their assembly language programs into machine language suitable for execution. In addition to instruction mnemonics, a complete assembly language generally includes *directives* to the assembler that help dictate the memory layout of code and data in the final binary.

Third-generation languages   These languages take another step toward the expressive capability of natural languages by introducing keywords and constructs that programmers use as the building blocks for their programs. Third-generation languages are generally platform independent, though programs written using them may be platform dependent as a result of using features unique to a specific operating system. Often-cited examples of third-generation languages include FORTRAN, C, and Java. Programmers generally use compilers to translate their programs into assembly language or all the way to machine language (or some rough equivalent such as byte code).

Fourth-generation languages   These exist but aren't relevant to this book and are not discussed.

The What of Disassembly

In a traditional software development model, compilers, assemblers, and linkers are used by themselves or in combination to create executable programs. To work our way backward (or reverse engineer programs), we use tools to undo the assembly and compilation processes. Not surprisingly, such tools are called *disassemblers* and *decompilers*, and they do pretty much what their names indicate. A disassembler undoes the assembly process, so we should expect assembly language as the output (and therefore machine language as input). Decompilers aim to produce output in a high-level language when given assembly or even machine language as input.

The promise of "source code recovery" will always be attractive in a competitive software market, and thus the development of usable decompilers remains an active research area in computer science. The following are just a few of the reasons that decompilation is difficult:

The compilation process is lossy. At the machine language level, there are no variable or function names, and variable type information can be determined only by how the data is used rather than explicit type declarations. When you observe 32 bits of data being transferred, you'll need to do some investigative work to determine whether those 32 bits represent an integer, a 32-bit floating point value, or a 32-bit pointer.

Compilation is a many-to-many operation. This means that a source program can be translated to assembly language in many different ways, and machine language can be translated back to source in many different ways. As a result, compiling a file and immediately decompiling it commonly yields a source file that is vastly different from the original.

Decompilers are language and library dependent. Processing a binary produced by a Delphi compiler with a decompiler designed to generate C code can yield very strange results. Similarly, feeding a compiled Windows binary through a decompiler that has no knowledge of the Windows programming API may not yield anything useful.

A nearly perfect disassembly capability is needed in order to accurately decompile a binary. Any errors or omissions in the disassembly phase will almost certainly propagate through to the decompiled code. Disassembled code can be verified for correctness against appropriate processor reference manuals; however, no canonical reference manuals are available to use in verifying the correctness of a decompiler's output.

Ghidra has a built-in decompiler, which is the subject of Chapter 19.

The Why of Disassembly

The purpose of disassembly tools is often to facilitate understanding of programs when source code is unavailable. Common situations in which disassembly is used include the following:

- Analysis of malware
- Analysis of closed source software for vulnerabilities
- Analysis of closed source software for interoperability
- Analysis of compiler-generated code to validate compiler performance or correctness
- Display of program instructions while debugging

The subsequent sections explain each situation in more detail.

Malware Analysis

Unless you are dealing with script-based malware, malware authors seldom do you the favor of providing the source code to their creations. Lacking source code, you are faced with a very limited set of options for discovering exactly how the malware behaves. The two main techniques for malware analysis are dynamic analysis and static analysis. *Dynamic analysis* involves allowing the malware to execute in a carefully controlled environment (sandbox) while recording every observable aspect of its behavior by using any number of system instrumentation utilities. In contrast, *static analysis* attempts to understand the behavior of a program simply by reading through the program code, which, in the case of malware, generally consists solely of a disassembly listing and possibly a decompiler listing.

Vulnerability Analysis

For the sake of simplification, let's break the entire security-auditing process into three steps: vulnerability discovery, vulnerability analysis, and exploit development. The same steps apply whether you have source code or not; however, the level of effort increases substantially when all you have is a binary. The first step in the process is to discover a potentially exploitable condition in a program. This is often accomplished using dynamic techniques such as fuzzing,[1] but it can also be performed (usually with much more effort) via static analysis. Once a problem has been discovered, further analysis is often required to determine whether the problem is exploitable at all and, if so, under what conditions.

Identifying variables that can be manipulated to the attacker's advantage is an important early step in vulnerability discovery. Disassembly listings provide the level of detail required to understand exactly how the compiler has chosen to allocate program variables. For example, it might

---

1. *Fuzzing* is a vulnerability-discovery technique that relies on generating large numbers of unique inputs for programs in the hope that one of those inputs will cause the program to fail in a manner that can be detected, analyzed, and ultimately exploited.

be useful to know that a 70-byte character array declared by a programmer was rounded up to 80 bytes when allocated by the compiler. Disassembly listings also provide the only means to determine exactly how a compiler has chosen to order all of the variables declared globally or within functions. Understanding the spatial relationships among variables is often essential when attempting to develop exploits. Ultimately, by using a disassembler and a debugger together, an exploit may be developed.

Software Interoperability

When software is released in binary form only, it is very difficult for competitors to create software that can interoperate with it or to provide plugin replacements for that software. A common example is driver code released for hardware that is supported on only one platform. When a vendor is slow to support or, worse yet, refuses to support the use of its hardware with alternative platforms, substantial reverse engineering effort may be required in order to develop software drivers to support the hardware. In these cases, static code analysis is almost the only remedy and often must go beyond the software driver to understand embedded firmware.

Compiler Validation

Since the purpose of a compiler (or assembler) is to generate machine language, good disassembly tools are often required to verify that the compiler is doing its job in accordance with any design specifications. Analysts may also be interested in locating additional opportunities for optimizing compiler output and, from a security standpoint, ascertaining whether the compiler itself has been compromised to the extent that it may be inserting backdoors into generated code.

Debugging Displays

Perhaps the single most common use of disassemblers is to generate listings within debuggers. Unfortunately, disassemblers embedded within debuggers tend to lack sophistication. They are generally incapable of batch disassembly and sometimes balk at disassembling when they cannot determine the boundaries of a function. This is one of the reasons it is best to use a debugger in conjunction with a high-quality disassembler to provide better situational awareness and context during debugging.

The How of Disassembly

Now that you're well versed in the purposes of disassembly, it's time to move on to how the process actually works. Consider a typical daunting task faced by a disassembler: *Take these 100KB, distinguish code from data, convert the code to assembly language for display to a user, and please don't miss anything along the way.* We could tack on any number of special requests, such as asking the disassembler to locate functions, recognize jump tables, and identify local variables, making the disassembler's job that much more difficult.

To accommodate all of our demands, any disassembler will need to pick and choose from a variety of algorithms as it navigates through the files we feed it. The quality of the generated disassembly listing will be directly related to the quality of the algorithms utilized and how well they have been implemented.

In this section, we discuss two of the fundamental algorithms in use today for disassembling machine code. As we present these algorithms, we also point out their shortcomings in order to prepare you for situations in which your disassembler appears to fail. By understanding a disassembler's limitations, you will be able to manually intervene to improve the overall quality of the disassembly output.

A Basic Disassembly Algorithm

For starters, let's develop a simple algorithm for accepting machine language as input and producing assembly language as output. In doing so, you will gain an understanding of the challenges, assumptions, and compromises that underlie an automated disassembly process:

1. The first step in the disassembly process is to identify a region of code to disassemble. This is not necessarily as straightforward as it may seem. Instructions are generally mixed with data, and it is important to distinguish between the two. In the most common case, disassembly of an executable file, the file will conform to a common format for executable files such as the *Portable Executable (PE)* format used on Windows and the *Executable and Linkable Format (ELF)* common on many Unix-based systems. These formats typically contain mechanisms (often in the form of hierarchical file headers) for locating the sections of the file that contain code and entry points into that code.[2]

2. Given the address of an instruction, the next step is to read the value or values contained at that address (or file offset) and perform a table lookup to match the binary opcode value to its assembly language mnemonic. Depending on the complexity of the instruction set being disassembled, this may be a trivial process, or it may involve several additional operations such as understanding any prefixes that may modify the instruction's behavior and determining any operands required by the instruction. For instruction sets with variable-length instructions, such as the Intel x86 instruction set, additional instruction bytes may need to be retrieved in order to completely disassemble a single instruction.

3. Once an instruction has been fetched and any required operands decoded, its assembly language equivalent is formatted and output as part of the disassembly listing. It may be possible to choose from more

---

2. A *program entry point* is simply the address of the instruction to which the operating system passes control after a program has been loaded into memory.

than one assembly language output syntax. For example, the two pre-dominant formats for x86 assembly language are the Intel format and the AT&T format.

4. Following the output of an instruction, we need to advance to the next instruction and repeat the previous process until we have disassembled every instruction in the file.

X86 ASSEMBLY SYNTAX: AT&T VS. INTEL

Two main syntaxes are used for assembly source code: AT&T and Intel. Even though they are second-generation languages, the two vary greatly in syntax—from variable, constant, and register access, to segment and instruction size overrides, to indirection and offsets. The AT&T assembly syntax is distinguished by its use of the % symbol to prefix all register names, the use of $ as a prefix for literal constants (also called *immediate operands*), and its operand ordering in which the source operand appears on the left and the destination operand appears on the right. Using AT&T syntax, the instruction to add 4 to the EAX register would be add $0x4,%eax. The GNU Assembler (as) and many other GNU tools, including gcc and gdb, utilize AT&T syntax by default.

Intel syntax differs from AT&T in that it requires no register or literal prefixes, and the operand ordering is reversed such that the source operand appears on the right and the destination appears on the left. The same add instruction using the Intel syntax would be add eax,0x4. Assemblers utilizing Intel syntax include the Microsoft Assembler (MASM) and the Netwide Assembler (NASM).

Various algorithms exist for determining where to begin a disassembly, how to choose the next instruction to be disassembled, how to distinguish code from data, and how to determine when the last instruction has been disassembled. The two predominant disassembly algorithms are linear sweep and recursive descent.

Linear Sweep Disassembly

The *linear sweep* disassembly algorithm takes a very straightforward approach to locating instructions to disassemble: where one instruction ends, another begins. As a result, the most difficult decisions faced are where to begin and when to stop. The usual solution is to assume that everything contained in sections of a program marked as code (typically specified by the program file's headers) represents machine language instructions. Disassembly begins with the first byte in a code section and moves, in a linear fashion, through the section, disassembling one instruction after another until the end of the section is reached. No effort is made to understand the program's control flow through recognition of nonlinear instructions such as branches.

During the disassembly process, a pointer can be maintained to mark the beginning of the instruction currently being disassembled. As part of the disassembly process, the length of each instruction is computed and used to determine the location of the next instruction to be disassembled. Instruction sets with fixed-length instructions (MIPS, for example) are somewhat easier to disassemble, as locating subsequent instructions is straightforward.

The main advantage of the linear sweep algorithm is that it provides complete coverage of a program's code sections. One of the primary disadvantages of the linear sweep method is that it fails to account for data that may be comingled with code. This is evident in Listing 1-1, which shows the output of a function disassembled with a linear sweep disassembler.

```
40123f:    55                          push ebp
401240:    8b ec                       mov ebp,esp
401242:    33 c0                       xor eax,eax
401244:    8b 55 08                    mov edx,DWORD PTR [ebp+8]
401247:    83 fa 0c                    cmp edx,0xc
40124a:    0f 87 90 00 00 00           ja 0x4012e0
401250:    ff 24 95 57 12 40 00        jmp DWORD PTR [edx*4+0x401257]❶
401257:    e0 12                       loopne 0x40126b
401259:    40                          inc eax
40125a:    00 8b 12 40 00 90           add BYTE PTR [ebx-0x6fffbfee],cl
401260:    12 40 00                    adc al,BYTE PTR [eax]
401263:    95                          xchg ebp,eax
401264:    12 40 00                    adc al,BYTE PTR [eax]
401267:    9a 12 40 00 a2 12 40        call 0x4012:0xa2004012
40126e:    00 aa 12 40 00 b2           add BYTE PTR [edx-0x4dffbfee],ch
401274:    12 40 00                    adc al,BYTE PTR [eax]
401277:    ba 12 40 00 c2              mov edx,0xc2004012
40127c:    12 40 00                    adc al,BYTE PTR [eax]
40127f:    ca 12 40                    lret 0x4012
401282:    00 d2                       add dl,dl
401284:    12 40 00                    adc al,BYTE PTR [eax]
401287:    da 12                       ficom DWORD PTR [edx]
401289:    40                          inc eax
40128a:    00 8b 45 0c eb 50           add BYTE PTR [ebx+0x50eb0c45],cl
401290:    8b 45 10                    mov eax,DWORD PTR [ebp+16]
401293:    eb 4b                       jmp 0x4012e0
```

❷ marks 401257:

Listing 1-1: Linear sweep disassembly

This function contains a switch statement, and the compiler used in this case has elected to implement the switch by using a jump table to resolve case label targets. Furthermore, the compiler has elected to embed the jump table within the function itself. The jmp statement ❶ references an address table ❷. Unfortunately, the disassembler treats the address table as if it were a series of instructions and incorrectly generates the following assembly language representation.

If we treat successive 4-byte groups in the jump table ❷ as little-endian values,[3] we see that each represents a pointer to a nearby address that is in fact the destination for one of the various jumps (004012e0, 0040128b, 00401290, . . .). Thus, the loopne instruction ❷ is not an instruction at all. Instead, it indicates a failure of the linear sweep algorithm to properly distinguish embedded data from code.

Linear sweep is used by the disassembly engines contained in the GNU debugger (gdb), Microsoft's WinDbg debugger, and the objdump utility.

Recursive Descent Disassembly

The *recursive descent* disassembly algorithm takes a different approach to locating instructions: it focuses on the concept of control flow, which determines whether an instruction should be disassembled based on whether it is referenced by another instruction. To understand recursive descent, it is helpful to classify instructions according to how they affect the instruction pointer.

Sequential Flow Instructions

Sequential flow instructions pass execution to the instruction that immediately follows. Examples of sequential flow instructions include simple arithmetic instructions, such as add; register-to-memory transfer instructions, such as mov; and stack-manipulation operations, such as push and pop. For such instructions, disassembly proceeds as with linear sweep.

Conditional Branching Instructions

Conditional branching instructions, such as the x86 jnz, offer two possible execution paths. If the condition evaluates to true, the branch is taken, and the instruction pointer must be changed to reflect the target of the branch. However, if the condition is false, execution continues in a linear fashion, and a linear sweep methodology can be used to disassemble the next instruction. As it is generally not possible in a static context to determine the outcome of a conditional test, the recursive descent algorithm disassembles both paths, deferring disassembly of the branch target instruction by adding the address of the target instruction to a list of addresses to be disassembled at a later point.

Unconditional Branching Instructions

Unconditional branches do not follow the linear flow model and therefore are handled differently by the recursive descent algorithm. As with the sequential flow instructions, execution can flow to only one instruction; however, that

---

3. The x86 is a little-endian architecture, meaning that the least significant byte of a multi-byte data value is stored first, at a lower memory address than each subsequent byte of that data item. Big-endian data is stored in reverse order, with the most significant byte of a data value being stored at a lower memory address than each subsequent byte. Processors may be classified as big-endian or little-endian, or in some cases, both.

instruction need not immediately follow the branch instruction. In fact, as seen in Listing 1-1, there is no requirement at all for an instruction to immediately follow an unconditional branch. Therefore, there is no reason to immediately disassemble the bytes that follow an unconditional branch.

A recursive descent disassembler attempts to determine the target of the unconditional jump and continues disassembly at the target address. Unfortunately, some unconditional branches can cause problems for recursive descent disassemblers. When the target of a jump instruction depends on a runtime value, it may not be possible to determine the destination of the jump by using static analysis. The x86 instruction jmp rax demonstrates this problem. The rax register contains a value only when the program is actually running. Since the register contains no value during static analysis, we have no way to determine the target of the jump instruction, and, consequently, we have no way to determine where to continue the disassembly process.

Function Call Instructions

Function call instructions operate similarly to unconditional jump instructions (including the inability of the disassembler to determine the target of instructions such as call rax), with the additional expectation that execution usually returns to the instruction immediately following the call instruction after the function completes. In this regard, they are similar to conditional branch instructions in that they generate two execution paths. The target address of the call instruction is added to a list for deferred disassembly, while the instruction immediately following the call is disassembled in a manner similar to linear sweep.

Recursive descent can fail if programs do not behave as expected when returning from called functions. For example, code in a function can deliberately manipulate the return address of that function so that upon completion, control returns to a location different from the one expected by the disassembler. A simple example is shown in the following incorrect listing, where function badfunc simply adds 1 to the return address before returning to the caller:

```
badfunc proc near
48 FF 04 24  inc qword ptr [rsp] ; increments saved return addr
C3           retn
badfunc endp
; -------------------------------------
label:
E8 F6 FF FF FF   call badfunc
05 48 89 45 F8   add eax, F8458948h❶
```

As a result, control does not actually pass to the add instruction ❶ following the call to badfunc. A proper disassembly appears next:

```
badfunc proc near
48 FF 04 24  inc qword ptr [rsp]
C3           retn
badfunc endp
```

```
;  -------------------------------------
label:
E8 F6 FF FF FF   call badfunc
05               db 5          ;formerly the first byte of the add instruction
48 89 45 F8      mov [rbp-8], rax❶
```

This listing more clearly shows the flow of the program in which function badfunc actually returns to the mov instruction ❶. It is important to
understand that a linear sweep disassembler will also fail to properly disassemble this code, though for slightly different reasons.

Return Instructions

In some cases, the recursive descent algorithm runs out of paths to follow.
A function *return instruction* (x86 ret, for example) offers no information
about which instruction will be executed next. If the program were actually running, an address would be taken from the top of the runtime stack,
and execution would resume at that address. Disassemblers do not have the
benefit of access to a stack. Instead, disassembly abruptly comes to a halt.
It is at this point that the recursive descent disassembler turns to the list of
addresses it has been setting aside for deferred disassembly. An address is
removed from this list, and the disassembly process is continued from this
address. This is the recursive process that lends the disassembly algorithm
its name.

One of the principle advantages of the recursive descent algorithm is its
superior ability to distinguish code from data. As a control flow-based algorithm, it is much less likely to incorrectly disassemble data values as code. The
main disadvantage of recursive descent is the inability to follow indirect code
paths, such as jumps or calls, which utilize tables of pointers to look up a target address. However, with the addition of some heuristics to identify pointers to code, recursive descent disassemblers can provide very complete code
coverage and excellent recognition of code versus data. Listing 1-2 shows the
output of Ghidra's recursive descent disassembler used on the same switch
statement shown earlier in Listing 1-1.

```
0040123f  PUSH   EBP
00401240  MOV    EBP,ESP
00401242  XOR    EAX,EAX
00401244  MOV    EDX,dword ptr [EBP + param_1]
00401247  CMP    EDX,0xc
0040124a  JA     switchD_00401250::caseD_0
          switchD_00401250::switchD
00401250  JMP    dword ptr [EDX*0x4 + ->switchD_00401250::caseD_0] = 004012e0
          switchD_00401250::switchdataD_00401257
00401257  addr   switchD_00401250::caseD_0
0040125b  addr   switchD_00401250::caseD_1
0040125f  addr   switchD_00401250::caseD_2
00401263  addr   switchD_00401250::caseD_3
00401267  addr   switchD_00401250::caseD_4
0040126b  addr   switchD_00401250::caseD_5
0040126f  addr   switchD_00401250::caseD_6
```

```
00401273   addr    switchD_00401250::caseD_7
00401277   addr    switchD_00401250::caseD_8
0040127b   addr    switchD_00401250::caseD_9
0040127f   addr    switchD_00401250::caseD_a
00401283   addr    switchD_00401250::caseD_b
00401287   addr    switchD_00401250::caseD_c
          switchD_00401250::caseD_1
0040128b   MOV     EAX,dword ptr [EBP + param_2]
0040128e   JMP     switchD_00401250::caseD_00040128E
```

Listing 1-2: Recursive descent disassembly

Note that this section of the binary has been recognized as a switch statement and formatted accordingly. An understanding of the recursive descent process will help us recognize situations in which Ghidra may produce less-than-optimal disassemblies and allow us to develop strategies to improve Ghidra's output.

Summary

Is deep understanding of disassembly algorithms essential when using a disassembler? No. Is it useful? Yes! Battling your tools is the last thing you want to spend time doing while reverse engineering. One of the many advantages of Ghidra is that, as an interactive disassembler, it offers you plenty of opportunity to guide and override its decisions. The net result is quite often a disassembly that is both thorough and accurate.

In the next chapter, we review a variety of existing tools that prove useful in many reverse engineering situations. While not directly related to Ghidra, many of these tools have influenced Ghidra, and they help to explain the wide variety of informational displays available in the Ghidra user interface.

2

REVERSING AND DISASSEMBLY TOOLS

With some disassembly background under our belts, and before we begin our dive into the specifics of Ghidra, it will be useful to understand some of the other tools that are used for reverse engineering binaries. Many of these tools predate Ghidra and continue to be useful for quick glimpses into files as well as for double-checking the work that Ghidra does. As we will see, Ghidra rolls many of the capabilities of these tools into its user interface to provide a single, integrated environment for reverse engineering.

Classification Tools

When first confronted with an unknown file, it is often useful to answer simple questions such as, "What is this thing?" The first rule of thumb when attempting to answer that question is to *never* rely on a file extension to determine what a file actually is. That is also the second, third, and fourth rules of thumb. Once you have become an adherent of the *file extensions are meaningless* line of thinking, you may wish to familiarize yourself with one or more of the following utilities.

file

The file command is a standard utility, included with most *nix-style operating systems as well as the Windows Subsystem for Linux (WSL).[1] This command is also available to Windows users by installing either Cygwin or MinGW.[2] The file command attempts to identify a file's type by examining specific fields within the file. In some cases, file recognizes common strings such as #!/bin/sh (a shell script) and <html> (an HTML document).

Files containing non-ASCII content present somewhat more of a challenge. In such cases, file attempts to determine whether the content appears to be structured according to a known file format. In many cases, it searches for specific tag values (often referred to as *magic numbers*)[3] known to be unique to specific file types. The following hex listings show several examples of magic numbers used to identify some common file types.

```
Windows PE executable file
    00000000 4D 5A 90 00 03 00 00 00 04 00 00 00 FF FF 00 00 MZ..............
    00000010 B8 00 00 00 00 00 00 00 40 00 00 00 00 00 00 00 ........@.......
Jpeg image file
    00000000 FF D8 FF E0 00 10 4A 46 49 46 00 01 01 01 00 60 ......JFIF.....`
    00000010 00 60 00 00 FF DB 00 43 00 0A 07 07 08 07 06 0A .`.....C........
Java .class file
    00000000 CA FE BA BE 00 00 00 32 00 98 0A 00 2E 00 3E 08 .......2......>.
    00000010 00 3F 09 00 40 00 41 08 00 42 0A 00 43 00 44 0A .?..@.A..B..C.D.
```

The file command has the capability to identify many file formats, including several types of ASCII text files and various executable and data file formats. The magic number checks performed by file are governed by rules contained in a *magic file*. The default magic file varies by operating system, but common locations include */usr/share/file/magic*, */usr/share/misc /magic*, and */etc/magic*. Please refer to the documentation for file for more information concerning magic files.

---

1. See *https://docs.microsoft.com/en-us/windows/wsl/about/*.

2. For Cygwin, see *http://www.cygwin.com/*. For MinGW, see *http://www.mingw.org/*.

3. A *magic number* is a special tag value required by some file format specifications whose presence indicates conformance to such specifications. In some cases, magic numbers are selected for humorous reasons. The MZ tag in MS-DOS executable file headers represents the initials of Mark Zbikowski, one of the original architects of MS-DOS, while the hex value 0xcafebabe, the well-known magic number associated with Java *.class* files, was chosen because it is an easily remembered sequence of hex digits.

In some cases, file can distinguish variations within a given file type. The following listing demonstrates file's ability to identify not only several variations of ELF binaries but also information pertaining to how the binary was linked (statically or dynamically) and whether the binary was stripped.

```
ghidrabook# file ch2_ex_*
  ch2_ex_x64:        ELF 64-bit LSB shared object, x86-64, version 1 (SYSV),
                     dynamically linked, interpreter /lib64/l, for GNU/Linux
                     3.2.0, not stripped
  ch2_ex_x64_dbg:    ELF 64-bit LSB shared object, x86-64, version 1 (SYSV),
                     dynamically linked, interpreter /lib64/l, for GNU/Linux
                     3.2.0, with debug_info, not stripped
  ch2_ex_x64_static: ELF 64-bit LSB executable, x86-64, version 1 (GNU/Linux),
                     statically linked, for GNU/Linux 3.2.0, not stripped
  ch2_ex_x64_strip:  ELF 64-bit LSB shared object, x86-64, version 1 (SYSV),
                     dynamically linked, interpreter /lib64/l, for GNU/Linux
                     3.2.0, stripped
  ch2_ex_x86:        ELF 32-bit LSB shared object, Intel 80386, version 1
                     (SYSV), dynamically linked, interpreter /lib/ld-, for
                     GNU/Linux 3.2.0, not stripped
  ch2_ex_x86_dbg:    ELF 32-bit LSB shared object, Intel 80386, version 1
                     (SYSV), dynamically linked, interpreter /lib/ld-, for
                     GNU/Linux 3.2.0, with debug_info, not stripped
  ch2_ex_x86_static: ELF 32-bit LSB executable, Intel 80386, version 1
                     (GNU/Linux), statically linked, for GNU/Linux 3.2.0,
                     not stripped
  ch2_ex_x86_strip:  ELF 32-bit LSB shared object, Intel 80386, version 1
                     (SYSV), dynamically linked, interpreter /lib/ld-, for
                     GNU/Linux 3.2.0, stripped
  ch2_ex_Win32:      PE32 executable (console) Intel 80386, for MS Windows
  ch2_ex_x64:        PE32+ executable (console) x86-64, for MS Windows
```

THE WSL ENVIRONMENT

The Windows Subsystem for Linux provides a GNU/Linux command line environment directly within Windows without the need to create a virtual machine. During WSL installation, users choose a Linux distribution and can then run it on the WSL. This provides access to common command line free software (grep, awk), compilers (gcc, g++), interpreters (Perl, Python, Ruby), networking utilities (nc, ssh), and many others. Once WSL has been installed, many programs written for use with Linux can be compiled and executed on Windows systems.

The `file` utility and similar utilities are not foolproof. It is quite possible for a file to be misidentified simply because it happens to bear the identifying marks of a particular file format. You can see this for yourself by using a hex editor to modify the first 4 bytes of any file to the Java magic number sequence: `CA FE BA BE`. The `file` utility will incorrectly identify the newly modified file as *compiled Java class data*. Similarly, a text file containing only the two characters `MZ` will be identified as an *MS-DOS executable*. A good approach to take in any reverse engineering effort is to never fully trust the output of any tool until you have correlated that output with several tools and manual analysis.

STRIPPING BINARY EXECUTABLE FILES

Stripping a binary is the process of removing symbols from the binary file. Binary object files contain symbols as a result of the compilation process. Some of these symbols are utilized during the linking process to resolve references between files when creating the final executable file or library. In other cases, symbols may be present to provide additional information for use with debuggers. Following the linking process, many of the symbols are no longer required. Options passed to the linker can cause the linker to remove the unnecessary symbols at build time. Alternatively, a utility named `strip` may be used to remove symbols from existing binary files. While a stripped binary will be smaller than its unstripped counterpart, the behavior of the stripped binary will remain unchanged.

PE Tools

PE Tools is a collection of tools useful for analyzing both running processes and executable files on Windows systems.[4] Figure 2-1 shows the primary interface offered by PE Tools, which displays a list of active processes and provides access to all of the PE Tools utilities.

From the process list, users can dump a process's memory image to a file or utilize the PE Sniffer utility to determine what compiler was used to build the executable or whether the executable was processed by any known obfuscation utilities. The Tools menu offers similar options for analysis of disk files. Users can view a file's PE header fields by using the embedded PE Editor utility, which also allows for easy modification of any header values. Modification of PE headers is often required when attempting to reconstruct a valid PE from an obfuscated version of that file.

---

4. See *https://github.com/petoolse/petools/*.

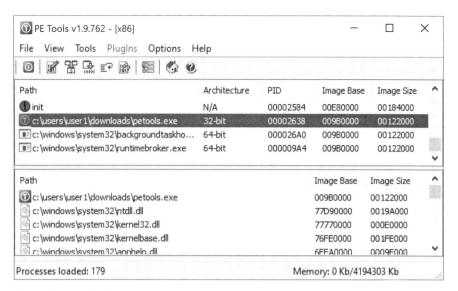

Figure 2-1: The PE Tools utility

BINARY FILE OBFUSCATION

Obfuscation is any attempt to obscure the true meaning of something. When applied to executable files, obfuscation is any attempt to hide the true behavior of a program. Programmers may employ obfuscation for a number of reasons. Commonly cited examples include protecting proprietary algorithms and obscuring malicious intent. Nearly all forms of malware utilize obfuscation in an effort to hinder analysis. Tools are widely available to assist program authors in generating obfuscated programs. Obfuscation tools and techniques and their associated impact on the reverse engineering process are discussed further in Chapter 21.

PEiD

PEiD is another Windows tool whose primary purposes are to identify the compiler used to build a particular Windows PE binary and to identify any tools used to obfuscate a Windows PE binary.[5] Figure 2-2 shows the use of PEiD to identify the tool (ASPack in this case) used to obfuscate a variant of the Gaobot worm.[6]

---

5. See *https://github.com/wolfram77web/app-peid/*.

6. See *https://www.trendmicro.com/vinfo/us/threat-encyclopedia/malware/GAOBOT/*.

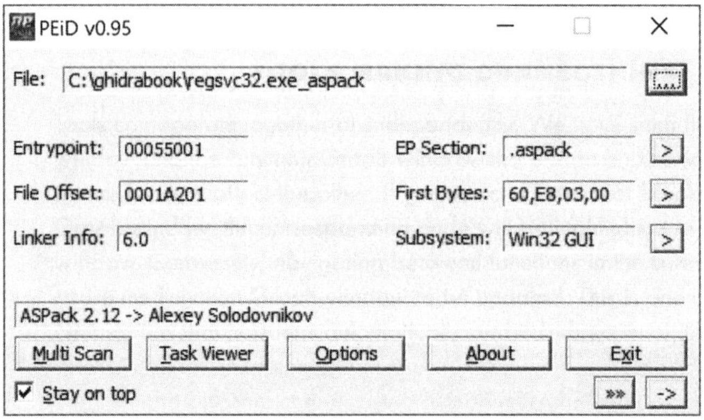

Figure 2-2: The PEiD utility

Many additional capabilities of PEiD overlap those of PE Tools, including the ability to summarize PE file headers, collect information on running processes, and perform basic disassembly.

Summary Tools

Since our goal is to reverse engineer binary program files, we are going to need more sophisticated tools to extract detailed information following initial classification of a file. The tools discussed in this section, by necessity, are far more aware of the formats of the files that they process. In most cases, these tools understand a very specific file format, and the tools are utilized to parse input files to extract very specific information.

nm

When source files are compiled to object files, compilers must embed information regarding the location of any global (external) symbols so that the linker will be able to resolve references to those symbols when it combines object files to create an executable. Unless instructed to strip symbols from the final executable, the linker generally carries symbols from the object files over into the resulting executable. According to the man page, the nm utility "lists symbols from object files."

When nm is used to examine an intermediate object file (a *.o* file rather than an executable), the default output yields the names of any functions and global variables declared in the file. Sample output of the nm utility is shown next:

```
ghidrabook# gcc -c ch2_nm_example.c
ghidrabook# nm ch2_nm_example.o
                 U exit
                 U fwrite
000000000000002e t get_max
                 U _GLOBAL_OFFSET_TABLE_
                 U __isoc99_scanf
```

```
00000000000000a6 T main
0000000000000000 D my_initialized_global
0000000000000004 C my_uninitialized_global
                 U printf
                 U puts
                 U rand
                 U srand
                 U __stack_chk_fail
                 U stderr
                 U time
0000000000000000 T usage
ghidrabook#
```

Here we see that nm lists each symbol, along with information about the symbol. The letter codes are used to indicate the type of symbol being listed. In this example, we see the following letter codes:

U   An undefined symbol (usually an external symbol reference).

T   A symbol defined in the text section (usually a function name).

t   A local symbol defined in the text section. In a C program, this usually equates to a static function.

D   An initialized data value.

C   An uninitialized data value.

NOTE   *Uppercase letter codes are used for global symbols, whereas lowercase letter codes are used for local symbols. More information, including a full explanation of the letter codes, can be found in the man page for nm.*

Somewhat more information is displayed when nm is used to display symbols from an executable file. During linking, symbols are resolved to virtual addresses (when possible), which results in more information being available when nm is run. Truncated sample output from nm used on an executable is shown here:

```
ghidrabook# gcc -o ch2_nm_example ch2_nm_example.c
ghidrabook# nm ch2_nm_example
...
                 U fwrite@@GLIBC_2.2.5
0000000000000938 t get_max
0000000000201f78 d _GLOBAL_OFFSET_TABLE_
                 w __gmon_start__
0000000000000c5c r __GNU_EH_FRAME_HDR
0000000000000730 T _init
0000000000201d80 t __init_array_end
0000000000201d78 t __init_array_start
0000000000000b60 R _IO_stdin_used
                 U __isoc99_scanf@@GLIBC_2.7
                 w _ITM_deregisterTMCloneTable
                 w _ITM_registerTMCloneTable
0000000000000b50 T __libc_csu_fini
0000000000000ae0 T __libc_csu_init
```

```
                        U __libc_start_main@@GLIBC_2.2.5
0000000000009b0  T main
0000000000202010 D my_initialized_global
000000000020202c B my_uninitialized_global
                        U printf@@GLIBC_2.2.5
                        U puts@@GLIBC_2.2.5
                        U rand@@GLIBC_2.2.5
0000000000000870 t register_tm_clones
                        U srand@@GLIBC_2.2.5
                        U __stack_chk_fail@@GLIBC_2.4
0000000000000800 T _start
0000000000202020 B stderr@@GLIBC_2.2.5
                        U time@@GLIBC_2.2.5
0000000000202018 D __TMC_END__
000000000000090a T usage
ghidrabook#
```

At this point, some of the symbols (main, for example) have been assigned virtual addresses, new ones (_libc_csu_init) have been introduced as a result of the linking process, some (my_unitialized_global) have had their symbol type changed, and others remain undefined as they continue to reference external symbols. In this case, the binary we are examining is dynamically linked, and the undefined symbols are defined in the shared C library.

ldd

When an executable is created, the location of any library functions referenced by that executable must be resolved. The linker has two methods for resolving calls to library functions: *static linking* and *dynamic linking*. Command line arguments provided to the linker determine which of the two methods is used. An executable may be statically linked, dynamically linked, or both.[7]

When static linking is requested, the linker combines an application's object files with a copy of the required library to create an executable file. At runtime, there is no need to locate the library code because it is already contained within the executable. Advantages of static linking are that (1) it results in slightly faster function calls and (2) distribution of binaries is easier because no assumptions need be made regarding the availability of library code on users' systems. Disadvantages of static linking include (1) larger resulting executables and (2) greater difficulty upgrading programs when library components change. Programs are more difficult to update because they must be relinked every time a library is changed. From a reverse engineering perspective, static linking complicates matters somewhat. If we are faced with the task of analyzing a statically linked binary, there is no easy way to answer the questions "Which libraries are linked into this binary?" and "Which of these functions is a library function?" Chapter 13 discusses the challenges encountered while reverse engineering statically linked code.

---

7. For more information on linking, consult John R. Levine's *Linkers and Loaders* (Morgan Kaufmann, 1999).

Dynamic linking differs from static linking in that the linker has no need to make a copy of any required libraries. Instead, the linker simply inserts references to any required libraries (often *.so* or *.dll* files) into the final executable, usually resulting in much smaller executable files. Upgrading library code is much easier when dynamic linking is utilized. Since a single copy of a library is maintained and that copy is referenced by many binaries, replacing the single outdated library with a new version results in any new process based on a binary that dynamically links to that library using the updated version. One of the disadvantages of using dynamic linking is that it requires a more complicated loading process. All of the necessary libraries must be located and loaded into memory, as opposed to loading one statically linked file that happens to contain all of the library code. Another disadvantage of dynamic linking is that vendors must distribute not only their own executable file but also all library files upon which that executable depends. Attempting to execute a program on a system that does not contain all the required library files will result in an error.

The following output demonstrates the creation of dynamically and statically linked versions of a program, the size of the resulting binaries, and the manner in which file identifies those binaries:

```
ghidrabook# gcc -o ch2_example_dynamic ch2_example.c
ghidrabook# gcc -o ch2_example_static ch2_example.c -static
ghidrabook# ls -l ch2_example_*
 -rwxrwxr-x 1 ghidrabook ghidrabook  12944 Nov  7 10:07 ch2_example_dynamic
 -rwxrwxr-x 1 ghidrabook ghidrabook 963504 Nov  7 10:07 ch2_example_static
ghidrabook# file ch2_example_*
 ch2_example_dynamic: ELF 64-bit LSB executable, x86-64, version 1 (SYSV),
 dynamically linked, interpreter /lib64/l, for GNU/Linux 3.2.0,
 BuildID[sha1]=e56ed40012accb3734bde7f8bca3cc2c368455c3, not stripped
 ch2_example_static:  ELF 64-bit LSB executable, x86-64, version 1 (GNU/Linux),
 statically linked, for GNU/Linux 3.2.0,
 BuildID[sha1]=430996c6db103e4fe76aea7d578e636712b2b4b0, not stripped
ghidrabook#
```

In order for dynamic linking to function properly, dynamically linked binaries must indicate which libraries they depend on, along with the specific resources required from each of those libraries. As a result, unlike statically linked binaries, it is quite simple to determine the libraries on which a dynamically linked binary depends. The ldd (*list dynamic dependencies*) utility is a tool used to list the dynamic libraries required by any executable. In the following example, ldd is used to determine the libraries on which the Apache web server depends:

```
ghidrabook# ldd /usr/sbin/apache2
  linux-vdso.so.1 =>  (0x00007fffc1c8d000)
  libpcre.so.3 => /lib/x86_64-linux-gnu/libpcre.so.3 (0x00007fbeb7410000)
  libaprutil-1.so.0 => /usr/lib/x86_64-linux-gnu/libaprutil-1.so.0 (0x00007fbeb71e0000)
  libapr-1.so.0 => /usr/lib/x86_64-linux-gnu/libapr-1.so.0 (0x00007fbeb6fa0000)
  libpthread.so.0 => /lib/x86_64-linux-gnu/libpthread.so.0 (0x00007fbeb6d70000)
  libc.so.6 => /lib/x86_64-linux-gnu/libc.so.6 (0x00007fbeb69a0000)
  libcrypt.so.1 => /lib/x86_64-linux-gnu/libcrypt.so.1 (0x00007fbeb6760000)
```

```
libexpat.so.1 => /lib/x86_64-linux-gnu/libexpat.so.1 (0x00007fbeb6520000)
libuuid.so.1 => /lib/x86_64-linux-gnu/libuuid.so.1 (0x00007fbeb6310000)
libdl.so.2 => /lib/x86_64-linux-gnu/libdl.so.2 (0x00007fbeb6100000)
/lib64/ld-linux-x86-64.so.2 (0x00007fbeb7a00000)
ghidrabook#
```

The ldd utility is available on Linux and BSD systems. On macOS systems, similar functionality is available using the otool utility with the -L option: otool -L *filename*. On Windows systems, the dumpbin utility, part of the Visual Studio tool suite, can be used to list dependent libraries: dumpbin /dependents *filename*.

BEWARE YOUR TOOLS!

While ldd may appear to be a simple tool, the ldd man page states that "you should never employ ldd on an untrusted executable, since this may result in the execution of arbitrary code." While this is unlikely in most cases, it provides a reminder that running even apparently simple software reverse engineering (SRE) tools may have unintended consequences when examining untrusted input files. While it is hopefully obvious that executing untrusted binaries is unlikely to be safe, it is wise to take precautions even when statically analyzing untrusted binaries, and to assume that the computer on which you perform SRE tasks, along with any data on it or other hosts connected to it, may be compromised as a result of SRE activities.

---

objdump

Whereas ldd is fairly specialized, objdump is extremely versatile. The purpose of objdump is to "display information from object files."[8] This is a fairly broad goal, and to accomplish it, objdump responds to more than 30 command line options tailored to extract various pieces of information from object files. The objdump tool can be used to display the following data (and much more) related to object files:

Section headers   Summary information for each of the sections in the program file.

Private headers   Program memory layout information and other information required by the runtime loader, including a list of required libraries, such as that produced by ldd.

---

8. See *http://www.sourceware.org/binutils/docs/binutils/objdump.html.*

Debugging information Any debugging information embedded in the program file.

Symbol information Symbol table information, dumped in a manner similar to the nm utility.

Disassembly listing The objdump tool performs a linear sweep disassembly of sections of the file marked as code. When disassembling x86 code, objdump can generate either AT&T or Intel syntax, and the disassembly can be captured as a text file. Such a text file is called a disassembly *dead listing*, and while these files can certainly be used for reverse engineering, they are difficult to navigate effectively and even more difficult to modify in a consistent and error-free manner.

The objdump tool is available as part of the GNU binutils tool suite and can be found on Linux, FreeBSD, and Windows (via WSL or Cygwin).[9] Note that objdump relies on the *Binary File Descriptor library (libbfd)*, a component of binutils, to access object files and thus is capable of parsing file formats supported by libbfd (ELF and PE among others). For ELF-specific parsing, a utility named readelf is also available. The readelf utility offers most of the same capabilities as objdump, and the primary difference between the two is that readelf does not rely upon libbfd.

otool

The otool utility is most easily described as an objdump-like option for macOS, and it is useful for parsing information about macOS Mach-O binaries. The following listing demonstrates how otool displays the dynamic library dependencies for a Mach-O binary, thus performing a function similar to ldd:

```
ghidrabook# file osx_example
  osx_example: Mach-O 64-bit executable x86_64
ghidrabook# otool -L osx_example
  osx_example:
    /usr/lib/libstdc++.6.dylib (compatibility version 7.0.0, current version 7.4.0)
    /usr/lib/libgcc_s.1.dylib (compatibility version 1.0.0, current version 1.0.0)
    /usr/lib/libSystem.B.dylib (compatibility version 1.0.0, current version 1281.0.0)
```

The otool utility can be used to display information related to a file's headers and symbol tables and to perform disassembly of the file's code section. For more information regarding the capabilities of otool, please refer to the associated man page.

dumpbin

The dumpbin command line utility is included with Microsoft's Visual Studio suite of tools. Like otool and objdump, dumpbin is capable of displaying a wide range of information related to Windows PE files. The following listing

---

9. See *http://www.gnu.org/software/binutils/*.

shows how dumpbin displays the dynamic dependencies of the Windows note-pad program in a manner similar to ldd:

```
$ dumpbin /dependents C:\Windows\System32\notepad.exe
Microsoft (R) COFF/PE Dumper
Copyright (C) Microsoft Corporation.  All rights reserved.

Dump of file notepad.exe

File Type: EXECUTABLE IMAGE

  Image has the following delay load dependencies:

    ADVAPI32.dll
    COMDLG32.dll
    PROPSYS.dll
    SHELL32.dll
    WINSPOOL.DRV
    urlmon.dll

  Image has the following dependencies:

    GDI32.dll
    USER32.dll
    msvcrt.dll
    ...
```

Additional dumpbin options offer the ability to extract information from various sections of a PE binary, including symbols, imported function names, exported function names, and disassembled code. Additional information related to the use of dumpbin is available via the Microsoft website.[10]

c++filt

Languages that allow function overloading must have a mechanism for distinguishing among the many overloaded versions of a function since each version has the same name. The following C++ example shows the proto-types for several overloaded versions of a function named demo:

```
void demo(void);
void demo(int x);
void demo(double x);
void demo(int x, double y);
void demo(double x, int y);
void demo(char* str);
```

As a general rule, it is not possible to have two functions with the same name in an object file. To allow overloading, compilers derive unique names for overloaded functions by incorporating information describing the type sequence of the function arguments. The process of deriving unique names

---

10. See *https://docs.microsoft.com/en-us/cpp/build/reference/dumpbin-command-line/*.

for functions with identical names is called *name mangling*.[11] If we use nm to dump the symbols from the compiled version of the preceding C++ code, we might see something like the following (filtered to focus on versions of demo):

```
ghidrabook# g++ -o ch2_cpp_example ch2_cpp_example.cc
ghidrabook# nm ch2_cpp_example | grep demo
  000000000000060b T _Z4demod
  0000000000000626 T _Z4demodi
  0000000000000601 T _Z4demoi
  0000000000000617 T _Z4demoid
  0000000000000635 T _Z4demoPc
  00000000000005fa T _Z4demov
```

The C++ standard does not define a standard name mangling scheme, leaving compiler designers to develop their own. To decipher the mangled variants of demo shown here, we need a tool that understands our compiler's (g++ in this case) name mangling scheme. This is precisely the purpose of c++filt. This utility treats each input word as if it were a mangled name and then attempts to determine the compiler that was used to generate that name. If the name appears to be a valid mangled name, it outputs the demangled version of the name. When c++filt does not recognize a word as a mangled name, it simply outputs the word with no changes.

If we pass the results of nm from the preceding example through c++filt, it is possible to recover the demangled function names, as seen here:

```
ghidrabook# nm ch2_cpp_example | grep demo | c++filt
  000000000000060b T demo(double)
  0000000000000626 T demo(double, int)
  0000000000000601 T demo(int)
  0000000000000617 T demo(int, double)
  0000000000000635 T demo(char*)
  00000000000005fa T demo()
```

It is important to note that mangled names contain additional information about functions that nm does not normally provide. This information can be extremely helpful in reverse engineering situations, and in more complex cases, this extra information may include data regarding class names or function-calling conventions.

Deep Inspection Tools

So far, we have discussed tools that perform a cursory analysis of files based on minimal knowledge of those files' internal structure. We have also seen tools capable of extracting specific pieces of data from files based on very detailed knowledge of a file's structure. In this section, we discuss tools

---

11. For an overview of name mangling, refer to *http://en.wikipedia.org/wiki/Name_mangling*.

designed to extract specific types of information independently of the type of file being analyzed.

strings

It is occasionally useful to ask more generic questions regarding file content—questions that don't necessarily require any specific knowledge of a file's structure. One such question is "Does this file contain any embedded strings?" Of course, we must first answer the question "What exactly constitutes a string?" Let's loosely define a *string* as a consecutive sequence of printable characters. This definition is often augmented to specify a minimum length and a specific character set. Thus, we could specify a search for all sequences of at least four consecutive ASCII printable characters and print the results to the console. Searches for such strings are generally not limited in any way by the structure of a file. You can search for strings in an ELF binary just as easily as you can search for strings in a Microsoft Word document.

The strings utility is designed specifically to extract string content from files, often without regard for the format of those files. Using strings with its default settings (7-bit ASCII sequences of at least four characters) might yield something like the following:

```
ghidrabook# strings ch2_example
  /lib64/ld-linux-x86-64.so.2
  libc.so.6
  exit
  srand
  __isoc99_scanf
  puts
  time
  __stack_chk_fail
  printf
  stderr
  fwrite
  __libc_start_main
  GLIBC_2.7
  GLIBC_2.4
  GLIBC_2.2.5
  _ITM_deregisterTMCloneTable
  __gmon_start__
  _ITM_registerTMCloneTable
  usage: ch4_example [max]
  A simple guessing game!
  Please guess a number between 1 and %d.
  Invalid input, quitting!
  Congratulations, you got it in %d attempt(s)!
  Sorry too low, please try again
  Sorry too high, please try again
  GCC: (Ubuntu 7.4.0-1ubuntu1~18.04.1) 7.4.0
  ...
```

Unfortunately, while we see some strings that look like they might be output by the program, other strings appear to be function names and library names. We should be careful not to jump to any conclusions regarding the behavior of the program. Analysts often fall into the trap of attempting to deduce the behavior of a program based on the output of strings. Remember, the presence of a string within a binary in no way indicates that the string is ever used in any manner by that binary.

Here are some final notes on the use of strings:

- By default, strings gives no indication of where, within a file, a string is located. Use the -t command line argument to have strings print file offset information for each string found.

- Many files utilize alternate character sets. Utilize the -e command line argument to cause strings to search for wide characters such as 16-bit Unicode.

Disassemblers

As mentioned earlier, tools are available to generate dead listing–style disassemblies of binary object files. PE, ELF, and Mach-O binaries can be disassembled using dumpbin, objdump, and otool, respectively. None of those, however, can deal with arbitrary blocks of binary data. You will occasionally be confronted with a binary file that does not conform to a widely used file format, in which case you will need tools capable of beginning the disassembly process at user-specified offsets.

Two examples of such *stream disassemblers* for the x86 instruction set are ndisasm and diStorm.[13] The utility ndisasm is included with the NASM.[14]

---

13. See *https://github.com/gdabah/distorm/*.

14. See *http://www.nasm.us/*.

The following example illustrates the use of ndisasm to disassemble a piece of shellcode generated using the Metasploit framework:[15]

```
ghidrabook#   msfvenom -p linux/x64/shell_find_port -f raw > findport
ghidrabook#   ndisasm -b 64 findport
 00000000  4831FF            xor rdi,rdi
 00000003  4831DB            xor rbx,rbx
 00000006  B314              mov bl,0x14
 00000008  4829DC            sub rsp,rbx
 0000000B  488D1424          lea rdx,[rsp]
 0000000F  488D742404        lea rsi,[rsp+0x4]
 00000014  6A34              push byte +0x34
 00000016  58                pop rax
 00000017  0F05              syscall
 00000019  48FFC7            inc rdi
 0000001C  66817E024A67      cmp word [rsi+0x2],0x674a
 00000022  75F0              jnz 0x14
 00000024  48FFCF            dec rdi
 00000027  6A02              push byte +0x2
 00000029  5E                pop rsi
 0000002A  6A21              push byte +0x21
 0000002C  58                pop rax
 0000002D  0F05              syscall
 0000002F  48FFCE            dec rsi
 00000032  79F6              jns 0x2a
 00000034  4889F3            mov rbx,rsi
 00000037  BB412F7368        mov ebx,0x68732f41
 0000003C  B82F62696E        mov eax,0x6e69622f
 00000041  48C1EB08          shr rbx,byte 0x8
 00000045  48C1E320          shl rbx,byte 0x20
 00000049  4809D8            or rax,rbx
 0000004C  50                push rax
 0000004D  4889E7            mov rdi,rsp
 00000050  4831F6            xor rsi,rsi
 00000053  4889F2            mov rdx,rsi
 00000056  6A3B              push byte +0x3b
 00000058  58                pop rax
 00000059  0F05              syscall
ghidrabook#
```

The flexibility of stream disassembly is useful in many situations. One scenario involves the analysis of computer network attacks in which network packets may contain shellcode. Stream disassemblers can be used to disassemble the portions of the packet that contain shellcode in order to analyze the behavior of the malicious payload. Another situation involves the analysis of ROM images for which no layout reference can be located. Portions of the ROM will contain data, while other portions will contain code. Stream disassemblers can be used to disassemble just those portions of the image thought to be code.

---

15. See *https://metasploit.com/*.

Summary

The tools discussed in this chapter are not necessarily the best of their breed. They do, however, represent tools commonly available for anyone who wishes to reverse engineer binary files. More important, they represent the types of tools that motivated much of the development of Ghidra. In future chapters, we occasionally highlight stand-alone tools that provide functionality similar to that integrated into Ghidra. An awareness of these tools will greatly enhance your understanding of the Ghidra user interface and the many informational displays that Ghidra offers.

3

MEET GHIDRA

Ghidra is a freely available open source SRE tool suite developed by the National Security Agency (NSA). The platform-independent Ghidra environment includes an interactive disassembler and decompiler as well as a plethora of related tools that work together to help you analyze code. It supports a wide variety of instruction set architectures and binary formats and can be run in both stand-alone and collaborative SRE configurations. Perhaps the best feature of Ghidra is that it allows you to customize your work environment and develop your own plugins and scripts to enhance your SRE process and to share your innovations with the Ghidra community at large.

Ghidra Licenses

Ghidra is distributed free of charge and is licensed under the Apache License, Version 2.0. This license provides a lot of freedom to individuals to use Ghidra but does have some associated restrictions. All individuals downloading, using, or editing Ghidra are encouraged to read the Ghidra User Agreement (*docs/UserAgreement.html*) as well as the license files in the *GPL* and *licenses* directories in order to ensure that they are complying with all licensing agreements, as third-party components within Ghidra have their own licenses. In case you ever forget anything in this paragraph, Ghidra helpfully displays the licensing information every time you start Ghidra or select About Ghidra from the Help menu.

Ghidra Versions

Ghidra is available for Windows, Linux, and macOS. While Ghidra is highly configurable, most new users will likely download Ghidra and choose to start with the most current version of Ghidra Core, which includes traditional reverse engineering functionality. The focus of this book is on the Ghidra Core functionality for nonshared projects. In addition, we spend time discussing shared projects and headless Ghidra as well as the Developer, Function ID, and Experimental configurations.

Ghidra Support Resources

Working with a new software suite can be daunting, especially when the intent is to approach a challenging real-world problem by using reverse engineering. As a Ghidra user (or potential developer), you may wonder where you can turn for help when you have Ghidra-related questions. If we do our job well enough, this book will suffice in many situations. When you find yourself needing additional help, though, here are some additional resources you can turn to:

Official help documentation   Ghidra contains a detailed help system that can be activated through the menu or by pressing F1. The help system provides a hierarchical menu as well as search functionality. While the Help menu offers various views, it does not currently provide support for interrogatory questions such as "How can I do x?"

Readme files   In some cases, the Ghidra Help menu will refer you to additional content on a particular topic such as a readme file. Many readme files are included in the documentation to supplement specific plugins, extend topics in the Help menu (such as *support /analyzeHeadlessREADME.html*), assist with various installations (*docs /InstallationGuide.html*), and aid your evolution as a developer (such as *Extensions/Eclipse/GhidraDev/GhidraDev_README.html*) should you choose to pursue that path (and perhaps develop support for interrogatory questions such as "How can I do x?").

Ghidra site   The Ghidra project home page (*https://www.ghidra-sre.org/*) provides options for potential users, current users, developers, and contributors to further their knowledge about Ghidra. Along with detailed download information associated with each Ghidra release, a helpful Installation Guide video walks you through the installation process.

Ghidra *docs* directory   Your installation of Ghidra includes a directory containing helpful Ghidra-related documentation, including a printable guide to menus and hotkeys (*docs/CheatSheet.html*) that can greatly ease your introduction to Ghidra, and much more. Tutorials that cover beginner, intermediate, and advanced features of Ghidra can be found under *docs/GhidraClass*.

Downloading Ghidra

Obtaining your free copy of Ghidra is an easy three-step process:

1. Navigate to *https://ghidra-sre.org/*.
2. Click the big red **Download Ghidra** button.
3. Save the file to the desired location on your computer.

As with many simple three-step processes, there are a couple of points where a few renegades may choose to veer slightly from the recommended path. The following options are for those of you who want something different from the traditional starter pack:

*   If you want to install a different release, just click the **Releases** button and you will have the option to download other released versions. While some functionality may vary, the basics of Ghidra should remain the same.

*   If you wish to install to a server to support collaborative work, hang on until Chapter 11 to find out how to make that important change to your installation (or feel free to jump ahead and give it a try using the information in the *server* directory.) Worst case, it is easy to back out and start again with the simple three-step process and begin with a local Ghidra instance.

*   The truly brave at heart may wish to build Ghidra from source. The Ghidra source code is available on GitHub at *https://github.com /NationalSecurityAgency/ghidra/*.

Let's move ahead with the traditional installation process.

Installing Ghidra

So, what did the magical red download button do when you clicked it and selected a destination on your computer? If everything went as planned, you should now have a *zip* file in your selected directory. For the original Ghidra release, the *zip* file's name was *ghidra_9.0_PUBLIC_20190228.zip*.

We can break down the naming convention. First, *9.0* is the version number. Next, *PUBLIC* is the type of release (there are other release types such as *BETA_DEV* releases). Finally, we have the release date, followed by the *.zip* file extension.

This *zip* file is actually a collection of the over 3400 files that make up the Ghidra framework. If you are happy with the location you saved the file to, unzipping it (for example, by right-clicking and selecting Extract All in Windows) will provide access to the Ghidra hierarchical directory. Note that Ghidra needs to compile some of its internal data files, so a Ghidra user will typically need write access to all Ghidra program subdirectories.

The Ghidra Directory Layout

Familiarity with the contents of your Ghidra installation is by no means a requirement before you start using Ghidra. However, since our attention is on your extracted download for the moment, let's take an initial look at the basic layout. An understanding of the Ghidra directory structure will become more important as you progress to using the more advanced features of Ghidra covered in later chapters. A brief description of each of the subdirectories within the Ghidra installation follows. Figure 3-1 shows the Ghidra directory layout.

Name

- docs
- Extensions
- Ghidra
- GPL
- licenses
- server
- support
- ghidraRun
- ghidraRun.bat
- LICENSE

Figure 3-1: Ghidra directory layout

> **docs** Contains general support documentation about Ghidra and how to use it. Included in this directory are two subdirectories that bear mentioning. First, the *GhidraClass* subdirectory provides educational content to help you learn about Ghidra. Second, the *languages* subdirectory describes Ghidra's processor specification language, SLEIGH. SLEIGH is discussed extensively in Chapter 18.

Extensions Contains useful prebuilt extensions and important content and information for writing Ghidra extensions. This directory is covered more thoroughly in Chapters 15, 17, and 18.

Ghidra Contains the code for Ghidra. You will learn more about the resources and contents in this directory as we begin customizing Ghidra in Chapter 12 and building new capabilities in Chapters 13 through 18.

GPL Some of the components that make up part of the Ghidra framework were not developed by the Ghidra team, but consist of other code distributed under the GNU General Public License (GPL). The *GPL* directory contains files associated with this content, including licensing information.

licenses Contains files outlining the appropriate and legal usage of various third-party components of Ghidra.

server Supports the installation of the Ghidra server, which facilitates collaborative SRE. This directory is discussed in depth in Chapter 11.

support Serves as a catchall for a variety of specialized Ghidra capabilities and functionalities. As a bonus, this is also where the Ghidra icon can be found (*ghidra.ico*) if you want to customize your work environment further (for example, creating a shortcut to your Ghidra startup script). This directory is discussed as needed throughout the text, as we introduce various Ghidra capabilities.

Starting Ghidra

Alongside the subdirectories, files in the root directory allow you to get started on your Ghidra SRE journey. Yet another license file is in this directory (*LICENSE.txt*), but more importantly, you will find the scripts that actually launch Ghidra. The first time you double-click *ghidraRun.bat* (or run the equivalent *ghidraRun* script from the command line on Linux or macOS), you will need to agree to the end-user license agreement (EULA) shown in Figure 3-2, to acknowledge that you plan to use Ghidra in compliance with the Ghidra User Agreement. Once you have agreed, you will not see this window on subsequent startups, but can view the content at any time through the Help menu.

In addition, you may be asked for the path to your Java installation. (If you do not have Java installed, see the Installation Guide in the *docs* subdirectory, which provides supporting documentation in the Java Notes section.) Ghidra requires version 11 or higher of the Java Development Kit (JDK).[1]

---

1. JDK is available at *https://adoptopenjdk.net/releases.html?variant=openjdk11&jvmVariant=hotspot/*.

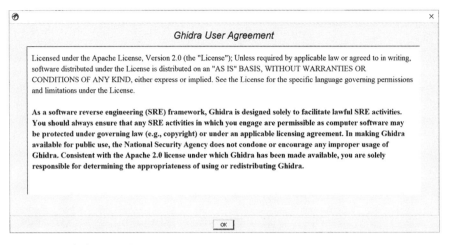

Figure 3-2: Ghidra User Agreement

Summary

Once you are successful in opening Ghidra, you are ready to move on to using it to accomplish something useful. Over the course of the next few chapters, you will discover how to use Ghidra to perform basic file analysis, learn about CodeBrowser and the many common Ghidra display windows, and see how to configure and manipulate those displays to further your understanding of a program's behavior.

PART II

BASIC GHIDRA USAGE

4

GETTING STARTED WITH GHIDRA

It's about time we got down to actually using Ghidra. The remainder of this book is dedicated to various features of Ghidra and how you can leverage them to best meet your reverse engineering needs. In this chapter, we begin by covering the options you are presented with when you launch Ghidra, and then we describe what happens when you open a single binary file for analysis. Finally, we present a quick overview of the user interface to lay the groundwork for the remaining chapters.

Launching Ghidra

Anytime you launch Ghidra, you will be greeted briefly by a splash screen that displays the Ghidra logo, build information, the Ghidra and Java version numbers, and the licensing information. If you wish to thoroughly read the splash screen to learn more about your versions, you can display it at any time by choosing Help ▶ About Ghidra from the Ghidra Project window.

Once the splash screen clears, Ghidra displays the Ghidra Project window behind a Tip of the Day dialog, as shown in Figure 4-1. You can scroll through tips by clicking the Next Tip button. When you are ready to begin working, close the Tip of the Day dialog.

If you prefer not to see the daily tips, feel free to uncheck the Show Tips on Startup? checkbox at the bottom of the dialog. If you uncheck the box and find yourself missing the Tip of the Day dialog, you can easily restore it through the Ghidra Help menu.

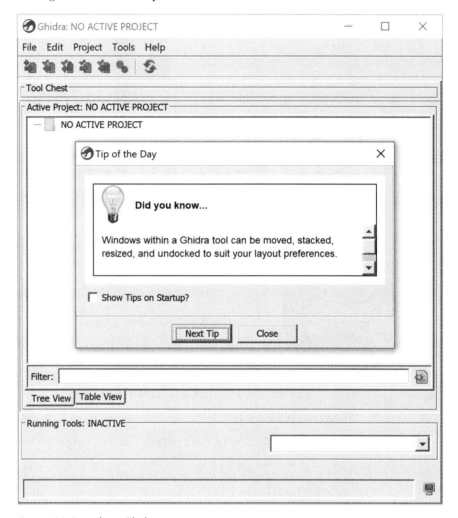

Figure 4-1: Launching Ghidra

If you close the Tip of the Day dialog or uncheck the box and restart Ghidra, you will be presented with the Ghidra Project window. Ghidra uses a project environment to allow you to manage and control the tools and data associated with a file or group of files as you are working with them. This initial introduction focuses on a single file as a component of a nonshared project. More complex project capabilities are discussed in Chapter 11.

Creating a New Project

If this is your first time launching Ghidra, you will need to create a project. If you have launched Ghidra previously, the active project will be the one you used most recently. Choosing File ▶ New Project allows you to specify characteristics of the environment associated with the project. The first step in creating a new project is to choose between a nonshared project and a shared project. In this chapter, we begin with a nonshared project. With that choice out of the way, you will be presented with the dialog in Figure 4-2. Nonshared projects require you to specify a project directory and name.

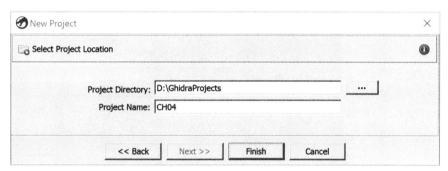

Figure 4-2: Creating a Ghidra project

Once you have entered the project location information, click **Finish** to complete the project creation process. This will return you to the Project window with the newly created project selected, as shown in Figure 4-3.

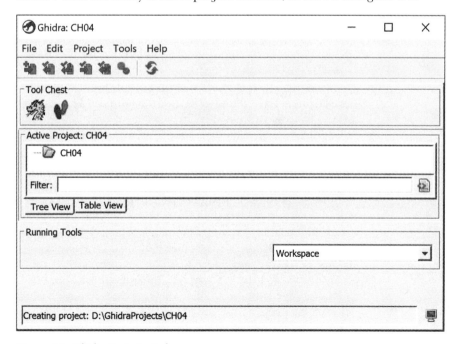

Figure 4-3: Ghidra Project window

Ghidra File Loading

To do any useful work, you will need to add at least one file to your new project. You can open a file either by choosing File ▶ Import File and browsing to the file you wish to import or by dragging and dropping a file directly into a folder in the Project window. After you have selected a file, you will be presented with the Import dialog shown in Figure 4-4.

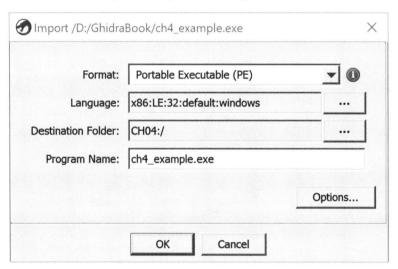

Figure 4-4: Ghidra Import dialog

Ghidra generates a list of potential file types and provides these to you in the Format picklist at the top of the dialog. Clicking the Information button to the right of the Format field will provide you with a list of supported formats, which are described in Chapter 17. The Format picklist provides the subset of Ghidra loaders that are best suited for dealing with the selected file. For this example, two options are provided in the Format picklist: Portable Executable (PE) and Raw Binary. The Raw Binary option will always be present since it is Ghidra's default for loading files that it does not recognize; this provides the lowest-level option for loading any file. When offered the choice of several loaders, it is not a bad strategy to accept the default selections unless you possess specific information that contradicts Ghidra's determination.

The Language field allows you to specify which processor module should be used during the disassembly process. A Ghidra language/compiler specification can consist of a processor type, an endian-ness specification (LE/BE), a bitness value (16/32/64), a processor variant, and a compiler ID (for example, ARM:LE:32:v7:default). For more information, refer to the Language/Compiler Specifications callout in Chapter 13 as well as "Language Definition Files" on page 396. In most cases, Ghidra will choose the proper processor based on information that it reads from the executable file's headers.

The Destination Folder field lets you select the project folder in which the newly imported file will be displayed. The default is to display the top-level project folder, but subfolders can be added to organize imported programs within a project. You can select the extension buttons to the right of the Language and Destination Folder fields to view other options for each. You can also edit the text in the Program Name field. Don't be confused by the change in terminology: Program Name is the name that Ghidra uses to refer to the imported binary within the project, including for display in the project window. It defaults to the name of the imported file but could be changed to something more descriptive, such as "Malware from Starship Enterprise."

In addition to the four fields shown in Figure 4-4, you can access other options to control the loading process via the Options button. These options are dependent on the selected format and processor. The options for *ch4_example.exe*, a PE file for x86, are shown in Figure 4-5, with the default options selected. While moving ahead with the default options is generally a good approach, you may choose other options as you gain experience. For example, you could include the Load External Libraries option if you wanted to have any dependent libraries imported into your project as well.

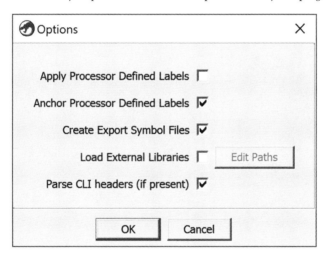

Figure 4-5: Ghidra PE file-loading options

The import options are used to gain finer control over the file-loading process. The options are not applicable to all input file types, and in most cases, you can rely on the default selections. Additional information about options is available in Ghidra Help. More details about Ghidra's import process and loaders are provided in Chapter 17.

When you are happy with your loading options and click OK to close the dialogs, you are presented with an Import Results Summary window, as shown in Figure 4-6. This provides you an opportunity to review the selected import options along with basic information that the loader has extracted from your chosen file. In "Importing Files" on page 262, we discuss ways to modify some of the import results prior to analysis if you have additional information that isn't reflected in the Import Results Summary window.

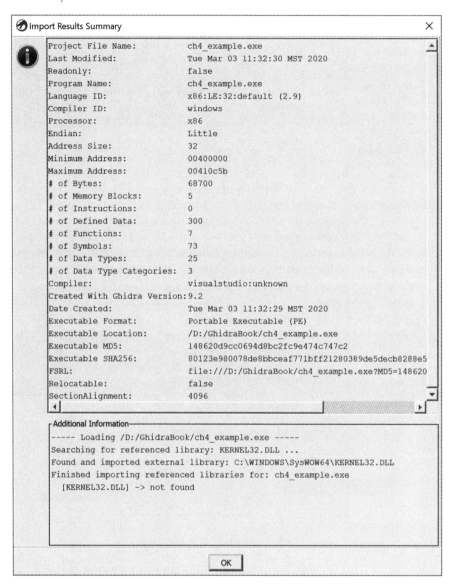

```
 Import Results Summary                                              ×

  Project File Name:          ch4_example.exe
  Last Modified:              Tue Mar 03 11:32:30 MST 2020
  Readonly:                   false
  Program Name:               ch4_example.exe
  Language ID:                x86:LE:32:default (2.9)
  Compiler ID:                windows
  Processor:                  x86
  Endian:                     Little
  Address Size:               32
  Minimum Address:            00400000
  Maximum Address:            00410c5b
  # of Bytes:                 68700
  # of Memory Blocks:         5
  # of Instructions:          0
  # of Defined Data:          300
  # of Functions:             7
  # of Symbols:               73
  # of Data Types:            25
  # of Data Type Categories:  3
  Compiler:                   visualstudio:unknown
  Created With Ghidra Version:9.2
  Date Created:               Tue Mar 03 11:32:29 MST 2020
  Executable Format:          Portable Executable (PE)
  Executable Location:        /D:/GhidraBook/ch4_example.exe
  Executable MD5:             148620d9cc0694d8bc2fc9e474c747c2
  Executable SHA256:          80123e980078de8bbceaf771bff21280389de5decb8288e5
  FSRL:                       file:///D:/GhidraBook/ch4_example.exe?MD5=148620
  Relocatable:                false
  SectionAlignment:           4096

 ┌Additional Information─────────────────────────────────────────────
  ----- Loading /D:/GhidraBook/ch4_example.exe -----
  Searching for referenced library: KERNEL32.DLL ...
  Found and imported external library: C:\WINDOWS\SysWOW64\KERNEL32.DLL
  Finished importing referenced libraries for: ch4_example.exe
    [KERNEL32.DLL] -> not found



                              [   OK   ]
```

Figure 4-6: Ghidra Import Results Summary window

Using the Raw Binary Loader

At times, Raw Binary will be the only entry in the Format picklist. This is Ghidra's way of telling you that none of its loaders recognize the chosen file. Examples of situations that may call for the use of the Raw Binary loader include the analysis of custom firmware images and exploit payloads that may have been extracted from network packet captures or log files. In these cases, Ghidra cannot recognize any file header information to guide the loading process, so it is up to you to step in and perform tasks that loaders often do automatically, like specifying the processor, the bit size, and, in some cases, a particular compiler.

For example, if you know the binary contains x86 code, many choices are available in the Language dialog, as shown in Figure 4-7. Often some research, and occasionally some trial and error, is required to narrow your language choices to something that will work for your binary. Any information you can obtain about the device the file was designed to run on will be useful. If you are confident that the file is not intended for a Windows system, you should select gcc or default (if available) for the Compiler setting.

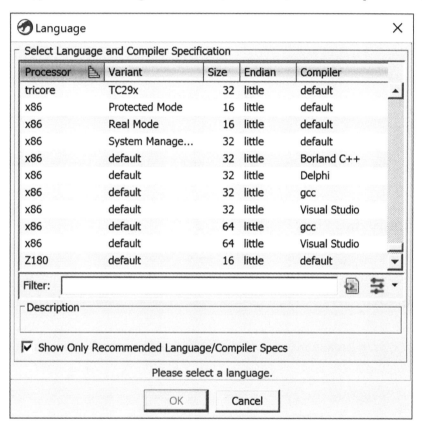

Figure 4-7: Language and compiler selection options

If the binary file contains no header information Ghidra can work with, Ghidra also will not recognize the memory layout of the file. If you know the base address, file offset, or length of the file, you can enter those values into the corresponding loader option fields shown in Figure 4-8, or continue to load the file without entering this additional information. (This information can be provided or adjusted at any point before or after analysis through the Memory Map window discussed in the "The Memory Map Window" on page 85.)

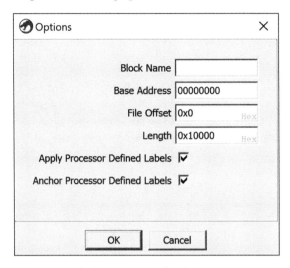

Figure 4-8: Ghidra Raw Binary loader options

Chapter 17 provides a more detailed discussion of manually loading and organizing unrecognized binary files.

Analyzing Files with Ghidra

At its heart, Ghidra is essentially a database application controlled by a library of plugins, each with its own functionality. All project data is stored using a custom database that grows and evolves as the user adds information to the project. The various displays that Ghidra offers are simply views into the database that reveal information in formats useful to the software reverse engineer. Any modifications that users make to the database are reflected in the views and saved into the database, but these changes have no effect on the original executable file. The power of Ghidra lies in the tools it contains to analyze and manipulate the data within the database.

The CodeBrowser anchors the many tools available in Ghidra and has unique functionality to help you keep your windows organized, add and delete tools, rearrange content, and document your process. By default, the CodeBrowser opens with windows for Program Tree, Symbol Tree, Data Type Manager, Listing, Decompiler, and Console. These and other displays are introduced in Chapter 5.

The process just described can be used to create projects and populate them with files, but the real work of analysis has not yet begun. When you double-click a file in the Ghidra Project window, you are presented with the CodeBrowser window, shown in Figure 4-9. If this is your first time selecting one of the files you have imported, you will be presented with an option to allow Ghidra to auto analyze the file. An example of auto analysis using the Analysis Options dialog is shown in Figure 4-10. In the majority of cases involving binaries taken from common platforms and built with commonly available compilers, auto analysis is probably the correct first choice. You can halt the auto analysis process at any time by clicking the red stop button at the bottom-right corner of the CodeBrowser window. (The button is visible only during auto analysis.)

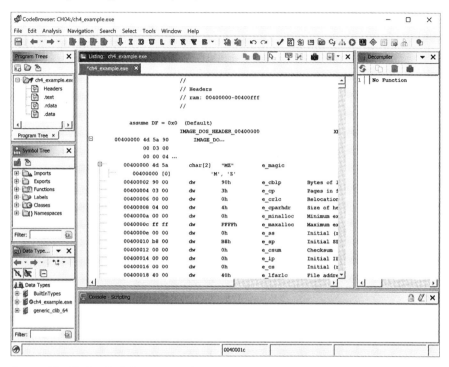

Figure 4-9: Ghidra CodeBrowser window

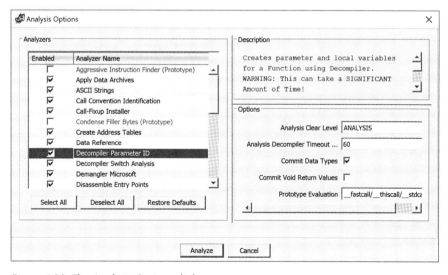

Figure 4-10: The Analysis Options dialog

Keep in mind that if you are not happy with Ghidra's auto analysis, you can always discard your work by closing the CodeBrowser and electing not to save your changes, at which point you may reopen the file and try a different combination of auto analysis options. The most common reasons for modifying your auto analysis options involve unusually structured files such as obfuscated binaries, or binaries built with compilers or on operating systems that may be unknown to Ghidra.

Note that if you are opening an extremely large binary (perhaps 10MB or larger), Ghidra may take minutes to hours to perform its auto analysis. In such cases, you may opt to disable or set an analysis time-out for some of the more demanding analyzers (for example, Decompiler Switch Analysis, Decompiler Parameter ID, and Stack). As shown in Figure 4-10, highlighting an analyzer will display a description of the analyzer, which may include useful warnings about the amount of time the analyzer may take to run. In addition, you will see the Options frame, which provides you an opportunity to control some behavioral aspects of the individual analyzers. Any analysis that you opt to disable or that times out can always be run later using the options available under Ghidra's Analysis menu.

AUTO ANALYSIS WARNINGS

Once a loader begins to analyze a file, it may encounter issues during analysis that it deems important enough to warn you about. One example of this occurs with PE files that have been built without an associated Program Database (PDB) file. In such cases, once analysis is complete, you will be presented with an Auto Analysis Summary dialog that includes a message summarizing any issues encountered (see Figure 4-11).

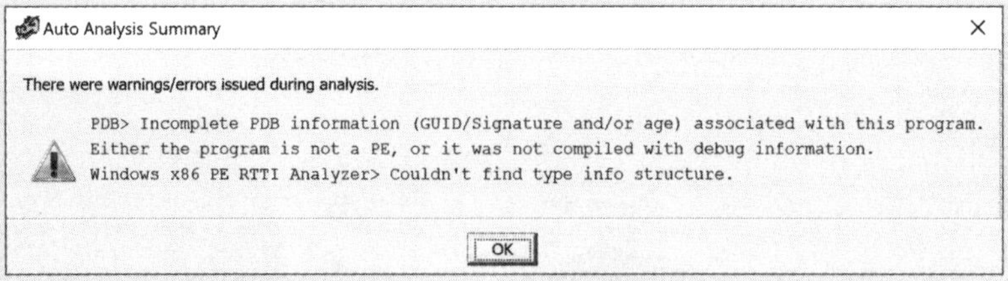

Figure 4-11: Auto Analysis Summary dialog

In most cases, the messages are simply informational. In some cases, the messages are instructional, offering you suggestions for ways to resolve an issue, perhaps by installing an optional, third-party utility for Ghidra to make use of in the future.

After Ghidra has auto analyzed the file, you can see that the import summary information has been supplemented with new information about your file, as shown in Figure 4-12.

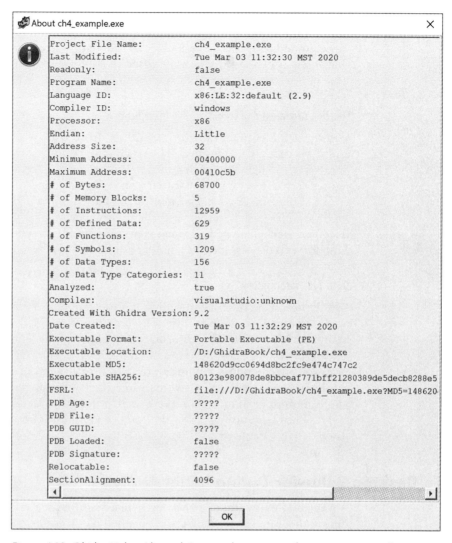

```
About ch4_example.exe                                                    ×

   Project File Name:         ch4_example.exe
   Last Modified:             Tue Mar 03 11:32:30 MST 2020
   Readonly:                  false
   Program Name:              ch4_example.exe
   Language ID:               x86:LE:32:default (2.9)
   Compiler ID:               windows
   Processor:                 x86
   Endian:                    Little
   Address Size:              32
   Minimum Address:           00400000
   Maximum Address:           00410c5b
   # of Bytes:                68700
   # of Memory Blocks:        5
   # of Instructions:         12959
   # of Defined Data:         629
   # of Functions:            319
   # of Symbols:              1209
   # of Data Types:           156
   # of Data Type Categories: 11
   Analyzed:                  true
   Compiler:                  visualstudio:unknown
   Created With Ghidra Version: 9.2
   Date Created:              Tue Mar 03 11:32:29 MST 2020
   Executable Format:         Portable Executable (PE)
   Executable Location:       /D:/GhidraBook/ch4_example.exe
   Executable MD5:            148620d9cc0694d8bc2fc9e474c747c2
   Executable SHA256:         80123e980078de8bbceaf771bff21280389de5decb8288e5
   FSRL:                      file:///D:/GhidraBook/ch4_example.exe?MD5=148620
   PDB Age:                   ?????
   PDB File:                  ?????
   PDB GUID:                  ?????
   PDB Loaded:                false
   PDB Signature:             ?????
   Relocatable:               false
   SectionAlignment:          4096

                              OK
```

Figure 4-12: Ghidra Help ▸ About ch4_example.exe view of import summary information

Auto Analysis Results

Ghidra's auto analysis is carried out by running each of the selected analyzers over your newly loaded binary. The Analysis Options dialog, as well as Ghidra Help, offers descriptions of each analyzer. The default analyzers are chosen because Ghidra users have historically found them to be the most useful across a wide range of file types. In the sections that follow, we discuss some of the most useful information extracted from a binary file during its initial loading and subsequent auto analysis.

Compiler Identification

Identifying the compiler used to build a piece of software can help us understand function-calling conventions used in a binary as well as determine which libraries the binary may be linked with. If the compiler can be identified when a file is loaded, Ghidra's auto analysis will incorporate knowledge of behaviors specific to the identified compiler. Differences that you may observe when using different compilers and different compile time options are the focus of Chapter 20.

Function Argument and Local Variable Identification

Within each identified function (identified from symbol table entries and addresses that are targets of call instructions), Ghidra performs a detailed analysis of the behavior of the stack pointer register in order to both recognize accesses to variables located within the stack and understand the layout of the function's stack frame. Names are automatically generated for such variables based on their use as either local variables within the function or as stack-allocated arguments passed into the function as part of the function call process. Stack frames are discussed further in Chapter 6.

Data Type Information

Ghidra uses its knowledge of common library functions and their associated parameters to identify functions, data types, and data structures used within each function. This information is added to the Symbol Tree and Data Type Manager windows as well as the Listing window. This process saves you a tremendous amount of time by providing information that would otherwise need to be manually retrieved and applied from various application programming interface (API) references. Detailed information about Ghidra's handling of library functions and associated data types is discussed in Chapter 8.

Desktop Behavior During Initial Analysis

A tremendous amount of activity takes place within the CodeBrowser desktop during the initial analysis of a newly opened file. You can gain an understanding of this analysis by watching the analysis updates in the bottom right of the CodeBrowser window. This also keeps you updated on the progress of the analysis. If you are not an expert in speed reading, you can open the associated Ghidra log file and peruse the activities at a more leisurely pace. You can open the log file from the Ghidra Project window by selecting Help ▸ Show Log. (Note that the Show Log menu option is available only in the Ghidra Project ▸ Help menu, not in the CodeBrowser ▸ Help menu.)

The following output is from the log file generated by Ghidra during the auto analysis of *ch4_example.exe* and is representative of messages generated during the auto analysis process. The messages form a narrative of the analysis process and offer insight into the sequence of operations performed by Ghidra as well as the time required for each task during that analysis:

```
2019-09-23 15:38:26 INFO  (AutoAnalysisManager) ----------------------------
        ASCII Strings                       0.016 secs
        Apply Data Archives                 1.105 secs
```

```
Call Convention Identification         0.018 secs
Call-Fixup Installer                   0.000 secs
Create Address Tables                  0.012 secs
Create Function                        0.000 secs
Data Reference                         0.014 secs
Decompiler Parameter ID                2.866 secs
Decompiler Switch Analysis             2.693 secs
Demangler                              0.004 secs
Disassemble Entry Points               0.016 secs
Embedded Media                         0.031 secs
External Entry References              0.000 secs
Function ID                            0.312 secs
Function Start Search                  0.051 secs
Function Start Search After Code       0.006 secs
Function Start Search After Data       0.005 secs
Non-Returning Functions - Discovered   0.062 secs
Non-Returning Functions - Known        0.000 secs
PDB                                    0.000 secs
Reference                              0.025 secs
Scalar Operand References              0.074 secs
Shared Return Calls                    0.000 secs
Stack                                  0.063 secs
Subroutine References                  0.016 secs
Windows x86 PE Exception Handling      0.000 secs
Windows x86 PE RTTI Analyzer           0.000 secs
WindowsResourceReference               0.100 secs
X86 Function Callee Purge              0.001 secs
x86 Constant Reference Analyzer        0.509 secs
-------------------------------------------------------
   Total Time   7 secs
-------------------------------------------------------
2019-09-23 15:38:26 DEBUG (ToolTaskManager)   task finish (8.128 secs)
2019-09-23 15:38:26 DEBUG (ToolTaskManager)   Queue - Auto Analysis
2019-09-23 15:38:26 DEBUG (ToolTaskManager)   (0.0 secs)
2019-09-23 15:38:26 DEBUG (ToolTaskManager)   task Complete (8.253 secs)
```

Even before the auto analysis has completed, you can begin navigating through the various data displays. When the auto analysis is complete, it is safe to make any changes you like to your project file.

Saving Your Work and Exiting

When you need to take a break from your analysis, it is a good idea to save your work. This is easy to accomplish in the CodeBrowser window in any of the following ways:

- Use one of the Save options within the **CodeBrowser File** menu.
- Click the **Save** icon in the **CodeBrowser** toolbar.
- Close the **CodeBrowser** window.
- Save the project in the **Ghidra** window.
- Exit Ghidra through the **Ghidra File** menu.

In each case, you will be prompted to save any modified files. More detailed information about changing the appearance and functionality of CodeBrowser and other Ghidra tools is discussed in Chapter 12.

Ghidra Desktop Tips and Tricks

Ghidra displays a tremendous amount of information, and its desktop can become cluttered. Here are some quick tips for making the best use of your desktop:

- The more screen real estate you dedicate to Ghidra, the happier you will be. Use this fact to justify the purchase of a king-size monitor (or four)!

- Don't forget to use the Window menu in the CodeBrowser as a means of opening new views or restoring data displays that you have inadvertently closed. Many windows can also be opened using tool buttons on the CodeBrowser toolbar.

- When you open a new window, it may appear in front of an existing window. When this happens, look for tabs at the top or bottom of windows that allow you to switch between them.

- You can close any window and reopen it as needed and drag it to a new location in the CodeBrowser desktop.

- The appearance of displays can be controlled using Edit ▶Tool Options and locating the associated Display options.

While these pointers are just the tip of the iceberg, they should be helpful as you begin to navigate the Ghidra CodeBrowser desktop. Additional CodeBrowser tips and tricks, including shortcuts and toolbar options, are discussed in Chapter 5.

Summary

Familiarity with the CodeBrowser desktop will greatly enhance your Ghidra experience. Reverse engineering binary code is difficult enough without having to struggle with your tools. The options you choose during the initial loading phase and the associated analysis performed by Ghidra set the stage for all of the analysis you will do later. At this point, you may be content with the work that Ghidra has accomplished on your behalf, and for simple binaries, this may be all that you need. On the other hand, if you wonder how you can gain additional control over your reverse engineering process, you are now ready to dive deeper into the functionality of Ghidra's many data displays. In the coming chapters, you will be introduced to each of the primary displays, the circumstances under which you will find each one useful, and how to gain mastery of the tools and displays to optimize your workflow.

5

GHIDRA DATA DISPLAYS

At this point, you should have some confidence creating projects, loading binaries into projects, and initiating auto analysis. Once Ghidra's initial analysis phase is complete, it is time for you to take control. As discussed in Chapter 4, when you launch Ghidra, your adventure starts in the Ghidra Project window. When you open a file within one of your projects, a second window opens. This is the Ghidra CodeBrowser, and it's your home base for much of your SRE efforts. You've already used the CodeBrowser to auto analyze your file; now we'll take a deeper dive into the CodeBrowser menu, windows, and basic options to increase your awareness of Ghidra's capabilities and allow you to create an SRE analysis environment that is consistent with your personal workflow. Let's begin with the principal Ghidra data displays.

CodeBrowser

You can open the CodeBrowser window by selecting Tools ▸ RunTool ▸ CodeBrowser from the Ghidra Project window. Although CodeBrowser is generally opened by selecting a file for analysis, we are opening an empty instance so that the functionality and configuration options can be demonstrated without specific file-related content influencing the display, as shown in Figure 5-1. In its default configuration, CodeBrowser has six subwindows. Before we get into the details associated with each of these displays, let's spend a little time looking at the CodeBrowser menu and its associated functionality.

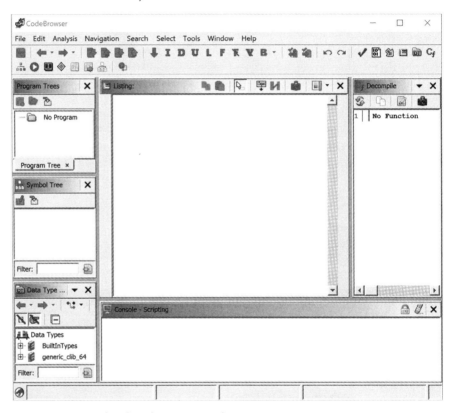

Figure 5-1: Unpopulated CodeBrowser window

At the top of the CodeBrowser window is the main menu with a toolbar immediately below. The toolbar provides one-click shortcuts to some of the most commonly used menu options. As we do not currently have a file loaded, we will focus on the menu options that are not associated with a loaded file in this section. Other menu actions will be demonstrated and explained in context with their applicability to the SRE process.

File   Provides the basic functionality expected in most file manipulation menus, including options for Open/Close, Import/Export, Save, and Print. In addition, some options are specific to Ghidra, such as

Tool options, which allow you to save and manipulate the CodeBrowser tool, and Parse C Source, which can aid in the decompilation process by extracting data type information from C header files. (See "Parsing C Header Files" on page 269.)

Edit   Includes one command that is applicable outside individual sub-windows: the Edit ▸Tool Options command, which opens a new window that allows you to control parameters and options associated with the many tools available from the CodeBrowser. The options related to the console are shown in Figure 5-2. The Restore Defaults button (revert to default settings) is always available at the bottom right.

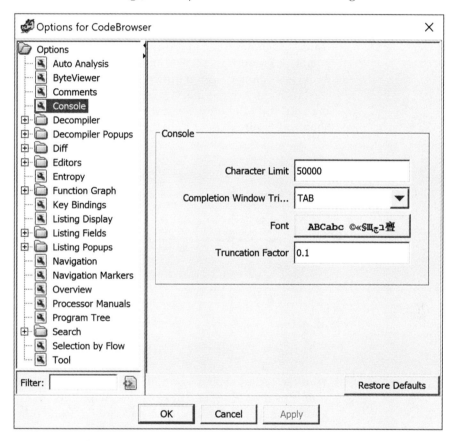

Figure 5-2: CodeBrowser Console edit options

Analysis   Allows you to reanalyze a binary or selectively perform individual analysis tasks. The basic analysis options were introduced in "Analyzing Files with Ghidra" on page 48.

Navigation   Facilitates navigation within files. This menu provides the basic keyboard functionality supported by many applications and adds special navigation options for binaries. While the menu provides one method for moving through a file, you will likely use toolbar options or shortcuts (listed at the right of each menu option) after you gain experience with the many options available for navigation.

Search   Provides search capabilities for memory, program text, strings, address tables, direct references, instruction patterns, and much more. Basic searching functionality is introduced in "Searching" on page 114. More specialized search concepts are presented in context as part of the many examples in subsequent chapters.

Select   Provides the capability to identify a portion of the file to consider for a specific task. Selections can be based on subroutines, functions, control flows, or simply by highlighting a desired portion of the file.

Tools   Includes some interesting features that allow you to place additional SRE resources on your desktop. One of the most useful is the Processor Manual option, which brings up the processer manual associated with the current file. If you attempt to open a missing processor manual, you will be provided with a method to include the manual, as shown in Figure 5-3.

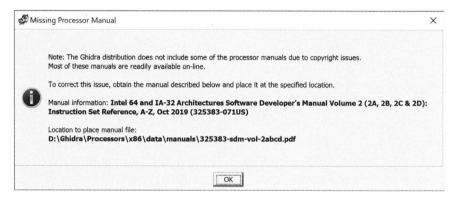

Figure 5-3: Missing Processor Manual message

Window   Allows you to configure your Ghidra work environment for your workflow. We spend most of this chapter introducing and investigating the default Ghidra windows as well as some others that you will find helpful.

Help   Provides rich, well-organized, and very detailed options. The Help window supports searching, different views, favorites, zooming in/out, as well as printing and page setup options.

CodeBrowser Windows

The expanded Window menu can be seen running down the center of Figure 5-4. By default, six of the available windows are opened when CodeBrowser is launched: Program Trees, Symbol Tree, Data Type

Manager, Listing, Console, and Decompiler. The name of each window is displayed at the top left of the associated window. Each of these windows appears as an option on the Window menu, and some also have associated icons on the toolbar directly below the menu. (As an example, we've used arrows in Figure 5-4 to highlight the toolbar option and menu option for opening and accessing the Decompiler window.)

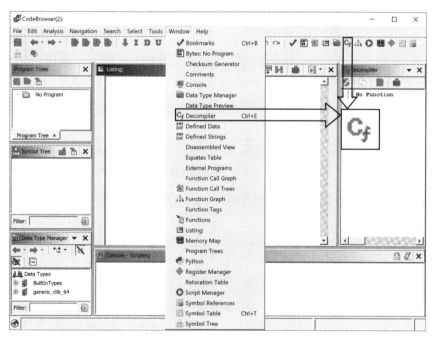

Figure 5-4: CodeBrowser window with options to display Decompiler window emphasized

Let's dive into the six default windows to understand their fundamental importance in the SRE process.

WINDOW INSIDERS AND OUTSIDERS

As you begin exploring the various Ghidra windows, you will notice that, by default, some windows open within the CodeBrowser desktop and others open as new floating windows outside the CodeBrowser desktop. Let's take a minute to talk about these "insiders" and "outsiders" in the context of the Ghidra environment.

The "outsider" windows float outside the CodeBrowser environment and may be connected or independent. These windows allow you to explore their contents side by side with CodeBrowser. Examples of these windows are Function Graph, Comments, and Memory Map.

Next, there are three distinct classes of "insider" windows:

- Windows that open by default in CodeBrowser (for example, Symbol Tree and Listing)
- Windows that are stacked with a default CodeBrowser window (for example, Bytes)
- Windows that create or share space with other CodeBrowser windows (for example, Equates and External Programs)

When you open a window that shares a space with another open window, it appears in front of the existing window. All windows sharing the same space are tabbed to allow rapid navigation between windows. If you want to view two windows that share a space simultaneously, you can click the title bar of the window and drag it outside the CodeBrowser window.

But be careful! Getting windows back into the CodeBrowser window is not as easy as moving them out. (See "Rearranging Windows" on page 242 for more details.)

WHERE'S MY WINDOW?

Ghidra has a lot of windows, and it can be challenging to keep track of where they are at any particular time. This becomes even more complicated as you open more windows and others disappear behind them in CodeBrowser or on your desktop. Ghidra has a unique feature to help you locate those missing windows. Clicking the associated toolbar icon or menu item will move the selected window to the front, but that might not be enough. If you continue clicking the toolbar icon for the window, your missing window will try to catch your attention by vibrating, changing font size or colors, zooming, spinning, and other exciting motions that are sure to catch your eye to help you find it. If you are bored, you can wave back.

The Listing Window

Also known as the Disassembly window, the Listing window will be your primary tool for viewing, manipulating, and analyzing Ghidra-generated disassemblies. The text display presents the entire disassembly listing of a program and provides the primary means for viewing the data regions of a binary.

The CodeBrowser display for *ch5_example1.exe* is shown in its default configuration in Figure 5-5. The margin to the left of the Listing window provides important information about the file as well as your location within the file. There is an additional marker area on the right side of the Listing window (immediately to the right of the vertical scroll bar) that also provides important information and navigational capabilities. The scroll bar indicates your location within the file and can be used for navigation. To the immediate right of the scroll bar are some informational displays, including bookmarks, that provide additional insight into the file.

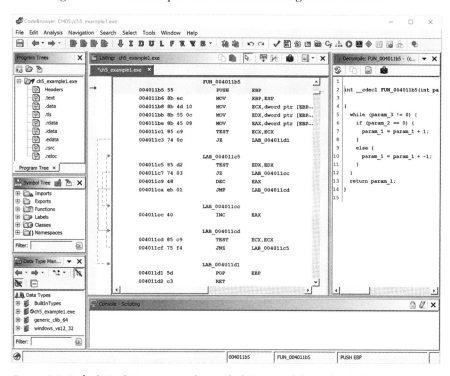

Figure 5-5: Default CodeBrowser window with ch5_example1.exe loaded

YOUR FAVORITE BARS

After a file is auto analyzed, you can use informational margin bars to help you navigate and further analyze the file. By default, only the Navigation bar is displayed. You can choose to add (or hide) the Overview bar and Entropy bar by using the Toggle Overview Margin tool button at the top right of the Listing window (see Figure 5-6). Regardless of which bars are displayed, a navigation marker to the left of all of the bars reminds you of where you are in the file. Left-clicking any location in any of the bars will move you to that location in the file and update the contents of the Listing window.

Now that you know how to control the appearance (and disappearance) of the bars, let's investigate what each bar shows and how you might use it in your SRE process:

Navigation Marker area   Allows you to move through the file, but it also has another very important function: if you right-click the Navigation Marker area, you will see the classes of markers and bookmarks that can be associated with your file. By selecting and deselecting marker types, you can control what is displayed in the Navigation bar. This allows you to easily move through particular types of markers (such as highlights).

Overview bar   Provides you with important visual information about the contents of a file. The horizontal bands in the Overview bar represent color-coded regions of the program. While Ghidra provides default colors associated with common categories, such as functions, external references, data, and instructions, you can control the color scheme through the Edit ▸ Tool Options menu. By default, if you hover over a region, you can view detailed information about that region, including the region type and an associated address, if applicable.

Entropy bar   Provides a unique Ghidra functionality: it "stereotypes" file content based on the file content around it. If there is very little variation within a region, it is assigned a low entropy value. If there is high degree of randomness, the corresponding entropy value is high. Hovering your mouse over a horizontal band in the Entropy bar will give you the entropy value (between 0.0 and 8.0), a type (for example, *.text*), as well as the associated address in the file. The highly configurable Entropy bar can be used to help determine the most likely content in the band. More information about this capability and the mathematics behind it can be discovered in the Ghidra Help menu.

Figure 5-6 provides a breakdown of tool buttons specific to the Listing window. In Figure 5-7, we have expanded and zoomed in on the Listing window to investigate what is shown. The disassembly is presented in linear fashion, with the leftmost column displaying virtual addresses by default.

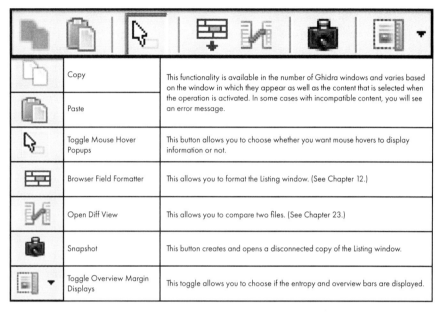

	Copy	This functionality is available in the number of Ghidra windows and varies based on the window in which they appear as well as the content that is selected when the operation is activated. In some cases with incompatible content, you will see an error message.
	Paste	
	Toggle Mouse Hover Popups	This button allows you to choose whether you want mouse hovers to display information or not.
	Browser Field Formatter	This allows you to format the Listing window. (See Chapter 12.)
	Open Diff View	This allows you to compare two files. (See Chapter 23.)
	Snapshot	This button creates and opens a disconnected copy of the Listing window.
	Toggle Overview Margin Displays	This toggle allows you to choose if the entropy and overview bars are displayed.

Figure 5-6: Listing window tool buttons

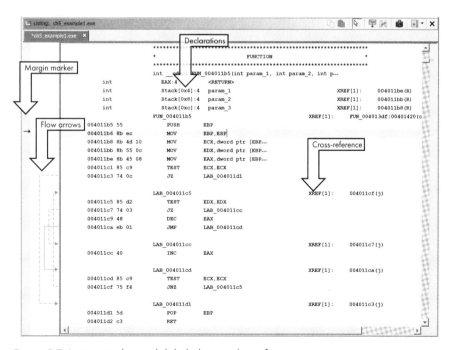

Figure 5-7: Listing window with labeled example artifacts

Within the Listing window are several items that merit your attention. The gray band at the far left of the window is the margin marker. It is used to indicate your current location in the file and includes point markers and area markers, which are described in Ghidra Help. In this example, the current file location (004011b6) is indicated in the margin marker by the small black arrow.

The region immediately to the right of the margin marker is used to graphically depict nonlinear flow within a function.[1] When the source or target address for a control flow instruction is visible in the Listing window, associated flow arrows appear. Solid arrows represent unconditional jumps, while dashed arrows represent conditional jumps. Hovering over a flow line opens a tool tip that displays the start and end address of the flow along with the flow type. When a jump (conditional or unconditional) transfers control to an earlier address in the program, it is often indicative of a loop. This is demonstrated in Figure 5-7 by the flow arrow from address 004011cf to 004011c5. You can easily navigate to the source or destination of any jump by double-clicking the associated flow arrow.

The declarations at the top of Figure 5-7 show Ghidra's best estimate concerning the layout of the function's stack frame.[2] Ghidra computes the structure of a function's stack frame (local variables) by performing detailed analysis of the behavior of the stack pointer and any stack frame pointer used within a function. Stack displays are discussed further in Chapter 6.

Listings generally have numerous data and code *cross-references* indicated by *XREF*, seen on the right side of Figure 5-7. A cross-reference is created anytime one location in the disassembly refers to another location in the disassembly. For example, an instruction at address A jumping to an instruction at address B would result in the creation of a cross-reference from A to B. Hovering over a reference address causes a reference pop-up to appear with the referencing location. The reference pop-up is in the same layout as the Listing window but has a yellow background (similar to a tool tip pop-up). The pop-up window allows you to view the content but does not allow you to follow the references. Cross-references are the subject of Chapter 9.

Creating Additional Disassembly Windows

If you ever find yourself wanting to view a listing of two functions simultaneously, all you need to do is open another disassembly window by using the Snapshot icon in the Listing toolbar (refer to Figure 5-6). The first disassembly

---

1. Ghidra uses the term *flow* to indicate how execution can continue from a given instruction. A *normal* (also called *ordinary*) flow indicates default sequential execution of instructions. A *jump* flow indicates that the current instruction jumps (or may jump) to a nonsequential location. A *call* flow indicates that the current instruction calls a subroutine.

2. A *stack frame* (or *activation record*) is a block of memory, allocated in a program's runtime stack, that contains both the parameters passed into a function and the local variables declared within the function. Stack frames are allocated upon entry into a function and released as the function exits. Stack frames are discussed in more detail in Chapter 6.

CONFIGURING LISTING WINDOWS

A disassembly listing may be decomposed into a number of component fields, including information such as a mnemonic field, an address field, and a comment field. The listings we have seen so far have been composed from a default set of fields that provide important information about the file. However, sometimes the default view does not provide the information you would like to see. Enter the Browser Field Formatter.

The Browser Field Formatter provides you the ability to customize over 30 fields to ensure you have ultimate control over the appearance of your Listing windows. You can activate the Browser Field Formatter by clicking the button in the Listing toolbar (refer to Figure 5-6). This opens a powerful submenu and layout editor, seen in Figure 5-8, at the top of the listing. The Browser Field Formatter allows you to control the appearance of address breaks, plate comments, functions, variables, instructions, data, structures, and arrays. Within each of these categories are fields that you can adjust, tune, and control to create the perfect listing format for you. We stick primarily with the default formats for listings, but you should explore the Browser Field Formatter to determine whether any options improve your understanding of the Listing window contents.

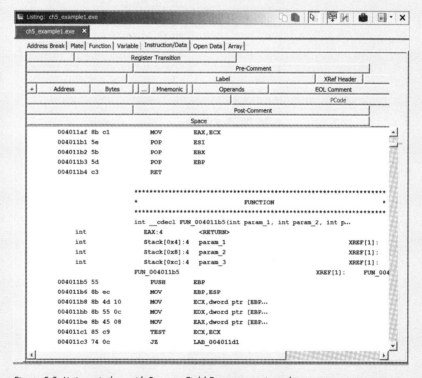

Figure 5-8: Listing window with Browser Field Formatter activated

window opened has the prefix *Listing:* before the filename. All subsequent disassembly windows are titled *[Listing: <filename>]* to indicate that they are disconnected from the primary display. The snapshots are disconnected so you can navigate freely through them without affecting other windows.

Ghidra Function Graph View

While assembly listings are interesting and informative, the flow of the program might be easier to understand by viewing a graph-based display. You can open a Function Graph window associated with the CodeBrowser by choosing Window ▶ Function Graph or clicking the associated icon in the CodeBrowser toolbar. The Function Graph window corresponding to the function in Figure 5-7 is shown in Figure 5-9. Graph views are somewhat reminiscent of program flowcharts in that a function is broken into basic blocks so you can visualize the function's control flow from one block to another.[3]

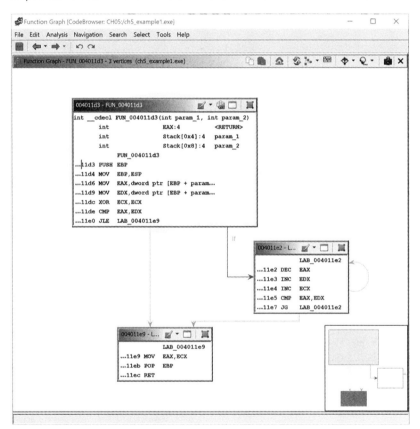

Figure 5-9: Graph view of listing from Figure 5-7

---

3. A *basic block* is a maximal sequence of instructions that executes, without branching, from beginning to end. Each basic block has a single entry point (the first instruction in the block) and a single exit point (the last instruction in the block). The first instruction in a basic block is often the target of a branching instruction, while the last instruction in a basic block is often a branch instruction.

Onscreen, Ghidra uses different-colored arrows to distinguish various types of flows between the blocks of a function. In addition, the flows become animated as you mouse over them to indicate direction. Basic blocks that terminate with a conditional jump generate two possible flows: the *Yes edge* arrow (yes, the tested condition was met) is green by default, and the *No edge* arrow (no, the tested condition was not met) is red by default. Basic blocks that terminate with only one potential successor block use a *Normal edge* (blue by default) to point to the next block to be executed. You can click any arrow to see the associated transition from one block to another. Since the graph and listing tools are synchronized by default, your file location will generally remain consistent when switching between and navigating within the listing view and graph view. Exceptions are discussed in Chapter 10 as well as in Ghidra Help.

In graph mode, Ghidra displays one function at a time. Ghidra facilitates navigation around the graph by using traditional image interaction techniques such as pan and zoom. Large or complex functions may cause the graph to become extremely cluttered, making the graph difficult to navigate, which is where the Satellite View can help you. By default, the Satellite View is positioned at the bottom right of the graph window and can be a valuable aid to provide some situational awareness (see Figure 5-9).

SATELLITE NAVIGATION

The Satellite View always displays the complete block structure of the graph along with a highlighted frame that indicates the region of the graph currently being viewed in the disassembly window. Clicking any block in the Satellite View centers the graph around that block. The highlighted frame acts as a lens and can be dragged around the overview window to rapidly reposition the graph view to any location on the graph. In addition to providing a means to navigate the Function Graph window, this magical window has other powers that can work for or against you as you examine files.

This window consumes valuable space in your Function Graph window and can hide important blocks and contents just when you want to see them. There are two approaches to remedy this situation. You can right-click the Satellite View and uncheck the Dock Satellite View checkbox. This will move the Satellite View and its full functionality outside the Function Graph window. Rechecking the option at any time will move it back to its original location in the Function Graph window.

A second option is to hide the Satellite View, provided you don't need to use it to navigate. This is another checkbox available in the right-click context menu. When you hide the Satellite View, a small icon will appear in the bottom right of the Function Graph window. Clicking this icon will restore the Satellite View.

When visible, the Satellite View can cause the primary view to behave more slowly than desired. Hiding the Satellite View can help to make it more responsive.

In addition to navigating with the Satellite View, you can manipulate the view within the Function Graph window in many ways to suit your needs:

Panning   First, in addition to using the Satellite View to rapidly reposition the graph, you can reposition the graph by clicking and dragging the background to change the graph view.

Zooming   You can zoom in and out using traditional keyboard methods such as CTRL/COMMAND, a mouse scroll, or associated key bindings. If you zoom out too far, you may pass the *painting threshold*, where the block contents are no longer displayed. Each block just becomes a colored rectangle. In some cases, particularly when working side by side with the Listing window, this might be advantageous, as it improves the speed at which the function graph can be rendered.

Rearranging blocks   Individual blocks within the graph can be dragged to new positions by clicking the title bar for the desired block and dragging it to a new position. All links between blocks are preserved as you move the blocks. If at any point you find yourself wishing to revert to the default layout for your graph, you can do so by selecting the Refresh icon in the Function Graph toolbar.

Grouping and collapsing blocks   Blocks can be grouped, either individually or together with other blocks, and collapsed to reduce the clutter in the display. Grouping causes a block to collapse. Collapsing blocks is an easy method to keep track of the blocks you have analyzed. You can collapse any block by choosing the Group icon in the far right of the block toolbar. If you choose this option with multiple blocks selected, they will be collapsed, and the list of associated blocks will be displayed in the stacked window. Some nuances are associated with forming/unforming groups as well as performing actions on the newly formed groups that are explained in Ghidra Help.

CUSTOMIZING YOUR GRAPH DISPLAY

To help you with your analysis, Ghidra provides a menu bar at the top of each node in the Function Graph display that allows you to control the display for that particular node. You can control background/text color for the node, jump to an XREF, view a full window listing of the graph node, and use grouping functionality to combine and collapse nodes. (Note that changing the background for a block in the Function Graph also changes the background in the Listing window.) Some of these features might be unnecessary if you are actively using the Listing window in conjunction with the Function Graph window, but the customization options may be helpful and are certainly worth investigating. These options are discussed further in Chapter 10.

As the graph-based display opens in a window external to CodeBrowser, you can view the two displays side by side. Because the windows have a connection, changing locations in one of the windows moves the location marker in the other window. While many users tend to prefer one view over the other to visualize program flow, you don't have to choose only one. Also, keep in mind that your control over the graph and text views extends far beyond these examples. Additional Ghidra graphing capabilities are covered in Chapter 10, while more information on the manipulation of Ghidra's view options is available in Ghidra Help.

For the next five chapters, we primarily focus on the listing display for examples, supplemented with the graph display in cases where it adds significant clarity. In Chapter 6 we will focus on understanding a Ghidra disassembly, and in Chapter 7, we cover the specifics of manipulating the listing display in order to clean up and annotate a disassembly.

MOVING AROUND

In addition to traditional means of navigating a file (up arrow, down arrow, page up, page down, and so on), Ghidra provides navigation tools specific to the SRE process. The icons in the Navigation toolbar (shown in Figure 5-10) make it easy to move through the program. Let's meet the icons that serve the reverse engineer.

Figure 5-10: CodeBrowser Navigation toolbar

On the far left is the Direction icon. This arrow toggles between up and down and controls the direction for all of the other navigation icons. The next eight icons advance you through the various targets shown in Figure 5-11.

I Instruction

D Data

U Undefined

L Label

F Function

K Instruction not in the function

V Different byte value

B Bookmark (all types)

Figure 5-11: Navigation toolbar definitions

Rather than just advancing you to the next data in the listing, choosing the Data option skips over adjacent data and takes you to the start of the next non-adjacent data. Instruction and Undefined demonstrate the same behavior.

The drop-down arrow at the far right of the Navigation toolbar displays a list that allows you to select among specific bookmark types for quick navigation. While used primarily with the Listing window, these navigation shortcuts work in all windows that are connected to the Listing window. Navigating within any of these windows results in synchronous navigation in all connected windows.

The Program Trees Window

Let's return to our discussion of the default CodeBrowser windows by taking a brief look at the Program Trees window, shown in Figure 5-12.

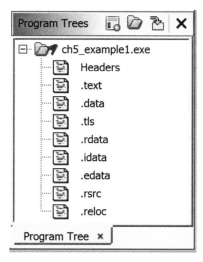

Figure 5-12: Program Trees window

This window shows your program organized into folders and fragments and provides you with the ability to refine the organization that takes place during auto analysis. *Fragment* is a Ghidra term for a contiguous range of addresses. Fragments may not overlap one another. A more traditional name for a fragment is a *program section* (for example, *.text*, *.data*, and *.bss*). Program tree–related operations include the following:

- Create folder/fragment
- Expand/Collapse/Merge folders
- Add/Remove folders/fragments
- Identify content in Listing window and move to a fragment
- Sort by name/address
- Select addresses
- Copy/Cut/Paste fragment/folders
- Reorder folders

The Program Trees window is a connected window, so clicking a fragment in the window navigates you to that location in the Listing window. More information about the Program Trees window can be found in Ghidra Help.

The Symbol Tree Window

When you import a file into a Ghidra project, a Ghidra loader module is selected to load the file content. When present in the binary, the loader is capable of extracting symbol table information (discussed in Chapter 2) for display in the Symbol Tree window shown in Figure 5-13. The Symbol Tree window includes the imports, exports, functions, labels, classes, and namespaces associated with a program. Each of these categories and associated symbol types are discussed in the sections that follow.

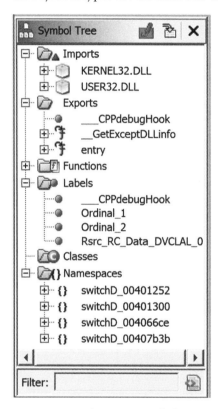

Figure 5-13: CodeBrowser Symbol
Tree window

All six of the Symbol Tree folders can be controlled by the filter at the bottom of the Symbol Tree window. This functionality will become more valuable as you get to know the file that you are analyzing. In addition, you will find the Symbol Tree window offers functionality similar to command line tools such as objdump (-T), readelf (-s), and dumpbin (/EXPORTS).

Imports

The *Imports* folder in the Symbol Tree window lists all functions that are imported by the binary being analyzed. It is relevant only when a binary makes use of shared libraries—statically linked binaries have no external dependencies and therefore no imports. The *Imports* folder lists imported libraries with entries for each item (function or data) imported from that library. Clicking any symbol within the Symbol Tree view jumps all connected displays to the selected symbol. In our sample Windows binary, clicking the GetModuleHandleA in the *Imports* folder would jump the disassembly window to the import address table entry for GetModuleHandleA, which in this example resides at address 0040e108, as shown in Figure 5-14.

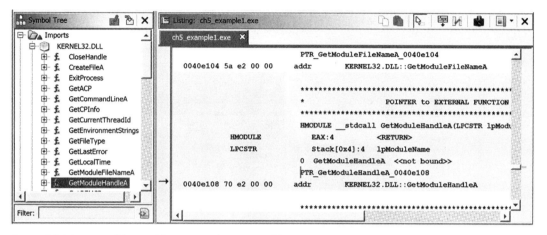

Figure 5-14: Import address table entry and associated location in Listing window

An important point to remember about the Imports category is that it displays only the symbols named in the binary's import table. Symbols that a binary chooses to load on its own using a mechanism such as dlopen/dlsym or LoadLibrary/GetProcAddress will not be listed in the Symbol Tree window.

Exports

The *Exports* folder lists the entry points into the file. These include the program's execution entry point, as specified in its header section, along with any functions and variables that the file exports for use by other files. Exported functions are commonly found in shared libraries such as Windows DLL files. Exported entries are listed by name, and the corresponding virtual address will be highlighted in the Listing window when the export is selected. For executable files, the *Exports* folder always contains at least one entry: the program's execution entry point. Ghidra may name this symbol entry or _start, depending on the binary's type.

Functions

The *Functions* folder contains a list of every function that Ghidra has identified in the binary. Hovering over a function name in the Symbol Tree window generates a pop-up with detailed information about the function, as shown in Figure 5-15. As part of the loading process, the loader utilizes various algorithms, including file structure analysis and byte sequence matching to infer the compiler that was used to create the file. During the analysis phase, the *Function ID* analyzer utilizes the compiler identification information to perform hash-based function body matching in order to identify the presence of library function bodies that may have been linked into the binary. When a hash match is made, Ghidra retrieves the matched function's name from the hash database (contained in Ghidra *.fidbf* files) and adds the name as a function symbol. Hash matching is particularly useful on stripped binaries, as it provides a means of symbol recovery that is independent of the presence of a symbol table. This functionality is discussed in more depth in "Function IDs" on page 272.

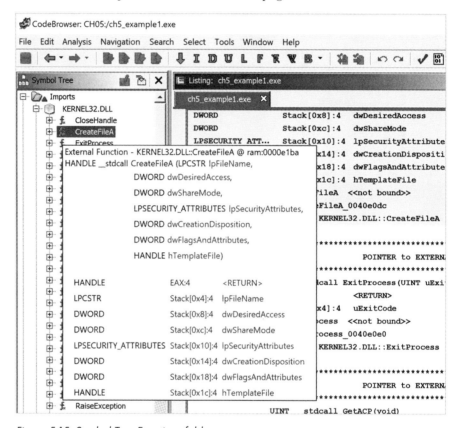

Figure 5-15: Symbol Tree Functions folder pop-up

Labels

The *Labels* folder is the data equivalent of the *Functions* folder. Any data symbols contained in a binary's symbol table will be listed in the *Labels* folder. In addition, anytime you add a new label name to a data address, that label will be added to the *Labels* folder.

Classes

The *Classes* folder contains an entry for each class identified by Ghidra during its analysis phase. Under each, Ghidra lists the identified data and methods that may assist you in understanding the behavior of the class.

C++ classes and the structures that Ghidra uses to populate the classes folder are discussed in more detail in Chapter 8.

Namespaces

In the *Namespaces* folder, Ghidra may create new namespaces to provide organization and ensure that assigned names do not conflict in the binary. For example, a namespace may be created for each identified external library or for each switch statement that uses jump tables (allowing jump table labels to be reused in other switch statements without conflicting).

The Data Type Manager Window

The Data Type Manager window allows you to locate, organize, and apply data types to your file by using a system of data type archives. Archives represent Ghidra's accumulated knowledge of predefined data types gleaned from header files included with most popular compilers. By processing header files, Ghidra understands the data types that are expected by common library functions and can annotate your disassembly and decompiler listings accordingly. Similarly, from these header files, Ghidra understands both the size and layout of complex data structures. All of this information is collected into archive files and applied anytime a binary is analyzed.

Referring back to Figure 5-4, you can see that the root of the BuiltInTypes tree, which contains primitive types like int that cannot be changed, renamed, or moved within a data type archive, is displayed in the Data Type Manager window (bottom left of the CodeBrowser window) even without a program loaded. In addition to the built-in types, Ghidra supports the creation of user-defined data types, including structures, unions, enums, and typedefs. It also supports arrays and pointers as derived data types.

Each file you open has an associated entry in the Data Type Manager window, as shown previously in Figure 5-5. The folder shares the name of the current file and entries within the folder are specific to the current file.

The Data Type Manager window displays nodes for each of the data type archives that are open. Archives can be opened automatically, such as when a program references an archive, or manually by the user. Data types and the Data Type Manager are covered in more detail in Chapters 8 and 13.

The Console Window

The Console window at the bottom of the CodeBrowser window serves as Ghidra's output area for plugins and scripts, including those you develop yourself, and is the place to look for information on tasks Ghidra is performing as you work with a file. Developing scripts and plugins is introduced in Chapters 14 and 15.

The Decompiler Window

The Decompiler window allows you to simultaneously view and manipulate assembly and C representations of your binary through connected windows. The C representation that is generated by the Ghidra decompiler isn't always perfect, but it can be very useful in helping you to understand a binary. Basic functionality provided by the decompiler includes recovery of expressions, variables, function parameters, and structure fields. The decompiler is also often capable of recovering a function's block structure, which tends to get obscured in assembly language, which is not block structured and makes extensive use of goto (or equivalent) statements to appear block structured.

The Decompiler window displays a C representation of a function selected in the Listing window, as shown in Figure 5-16. Depending on your experience with assembly language, the decompiled code may be much easier to understand than the code in the Listing window. Even beginning programmers should be able to identify the infinite loop in the decompiled function. (The while loop condition is dependent on the value of param_3, which is not modified within the loop.)

Figure 5-16: Listing and Decompiler windows

The Decompiler window icons are shown in Figure 5-17. You can use the Snapshot icon to open additional (disconnected) Decompiler windows if you want to compare the decompiled version of multiple functions or continue viewing a particular function while moving elsewhere in the Listing window. The Export icon allows you to save the decompiled function to a C file.

Within the Decompiler window, context menus are available through right-clicking that allow you to perform actions associated with a highlighted item. The options associated with one of the function parameters, param_1, are shown in Figure 5-18.

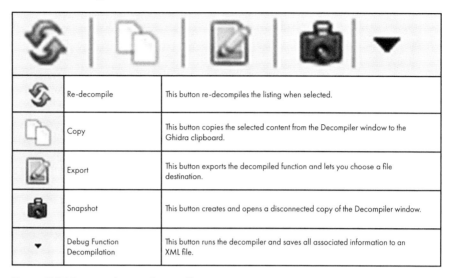

	Re-decompile	This button re-decompiles the listing when selected.
	Copy	This button copies the selected content from the Decompiler window to the Ghidra clipboard.
	Export	This button exports the decompiled function and lets you choose a file destination.
	Snapshot	This button creates and opens a disconnected copy of the Decompiler window.
▼	Debug Function Decompilation	This button runs the decompiler and saves all associated information to an XML file.

Figure 5-17: Decompiler window toolbar

```
Decompile: FUN_004011b5 - (ch5_example1.exe)

1
2  int __cdecl FUN_004011b5(int param_1,int param_2,int param_3)
3
4  {
5    while (param_3 != 0) {
6      if (param_2 == 0) {
7        param_1 = param_1 + 1;
8      }
9      else {
10       param_1 = param_1 + -1;
11     }
12   }
13   return param_1;
14 }
15
```

Edit Function Signature

Rename Variable   L
Retype Variable   Ctrl+L
Auto Create Structure   Shift+Open Bracket

Commit Params/Return P
Commit Locals

Highlight   ▶
Secondary Highlight   ▶

Copy   Ctrl+C

Comments   ▶

Find...   Ctrl+F
References   ▶

Properties

Figure 5-18: Decompiler window options for function parameters

Decompilation is an extraordinarily complicated process, and decompiler theory remains an active research area. Unlike disassembly, whose accuracy can be verified against manufacturers' reference manuals, there are no reference manuals that provide canonical translations of assembly language back to C (or C to assembly for that matter). In fact, while Ghidra's decompiler always generates C source code, it may be the case that the binary the decompiler is analyzing was originally written in a language other than C, and many of the decompiler's C-oriented assumptions may not hold at all.

As with most complex plugins, the decompiler has idiosyncrasies, and the quality of its output depends, to a large extent, on the quality of its input. Many of the issues and irregularities in the Decompiler window can be traced back to issues with the underlying disassembly, so if the decompiled code doesn't make sense, you may need to spend time improving the quality of the disassembly. In most cases, this involves annotating the disassembly with more accurate data type information, which is discussed in Chapters 8 and 13. We continue to explore the decompiler's capabilities in subsequent chapters and discuss it in depth in Chapter 19.

Other Ghidra Windows

In addition to the six default windows, you can open other windows to support your SRE process with alternate or specialized views into the file. The list of available windows is displayed from the Window menu, shown previously in Figure 5-4. The utility of these displays depends on both the characteristics of the binary you are analyzing and your skill with Ghidra. Several of these windows are sufficiently specialized to require more detailed coverage in later chapters, but we introduce some common ones here.

The Bytes Window

The Bytes window provides a raw look at the byte-level content of the file. By default, the Bytes window opens on the upper-right side of the CodeBrowser and provides a standard hex dump display of the program contents with 16 bytes per line. The window doubles as a hex editor and can be configured to display a variety of formats by using the Settings tool in the Bytes window toolbar. In many cases, it might be helpful to add the ASCII display to the Bytes window, as shown in Figure 5-19. The figure also shows the Byte Viewer Options dialog and toolbar icons for editing or snapshotting the byte view.

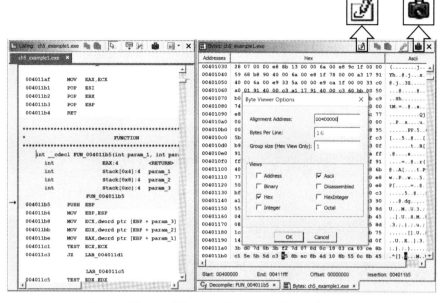

Figure 5-19: Synchronized hex and disassembly views with Toggle and Snapshot icons emphasized

As with the Listing window, several Bytes windows can be opened simultaneously using the Snapshot icon (see Figure 5-19) in the Bytes window toolbar. By default, the first Bytes window has a connection to the Listing window, so scrolling in one window and clicking an element causes the other window to scroll to the same location (same virtual address). Subsequent Bytes windows are disconnected, which allows you to scroll through them independently. When a window is disconnected, the window name appears within square brackets in the window title bar.

To turn the Bytes window into a hex (or ASCII) editor, simply toggle the pencil icon highlighted in Figure 5-19. The cursor will turn red to indicate that you can edit, though you will not be able to edit at addresses that contain an existing code item such as an instruction. When you are finished editing, toggle the icon again and you will be back in read-only mode. (Note that any changes will not be reflected in disconnected Bytes windows.)

If the Hex column displays question marks rather than hex values, Ghidra is telling you that it is not sure what values might occupy a given virtual address range. Such is the case when a program contains a *bss* section,[4] which typically occupies no space within a file but is expanded by the loader to accommodate the program's static storage requirements.

---

4. A *bss* section is created by a compiler to house all of a program's uninitialized, static variables. Since no initial value is assigned to these variables, there is no need to allocate space for them in the program's file image, so the section's size is noted in one of the program's headers. When the program is executed, the loader allocates the required space and initializes the entire block to zero.

The Defined Data Window

The Defined Data window displays a string representation of data defined in the current program, view, or selection, along with the associated address, type, and size, as shown in Figure 5-20. As with most of the columnar windows, you can sort by any column in ascending or descending order by clicking the column header. Double-clicking any row in the Defined Data window causes the Listing window to jump to the address of the selected item.

When used with cross-references (discussed in Chapter 9), the Defined Data window provides the means to rapidly spot an interesting item and to track back to any location in the program that references that item with only a few clicks. For example, you might see the string "SOFTWARE\Microsoft \Windows\Current Version\Run" listed and wonder why an application is referencing this particular key within the Windows registry, and then discover that the program is setting that registry key to automatically start itself when Windows boots.

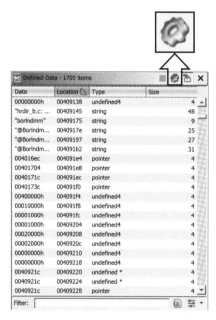

Figure 5-20: Defined Data window with Filter icon emphasized

The Defined Data window has extensive filtering capabilities. In addition to the Filter bar at the bottom of the window, a Filter icon at the top right (emphasized in Figure 5-20) allows you to control additional data type filter options, as shown in Figure 5-21.

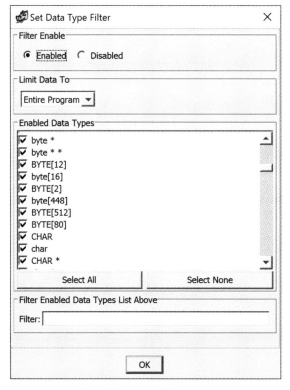

Figure 5-21: Defined data type filter options

Every time you close the Set Data Type Filter dialog by clicking OK, Ghidra will regenerate the Defined Data window contents in accordance with the new settings.

The Defined Strings Window

The Defined Strings window displays strings that have been defined in the binary. An example of this window is shown in Figure 5-22. In addition to the default columns displayed in the figure, you can add columns by right-clicking in the row of column titles. Perhaps one of the most interesting available columns is the Has Encoding Error flag, which can be indicative of an issue with the character set or misidentification of a string. In addition to this window, substantial string search functionality is available in Ghidra. This is discussed in Chapter 6.

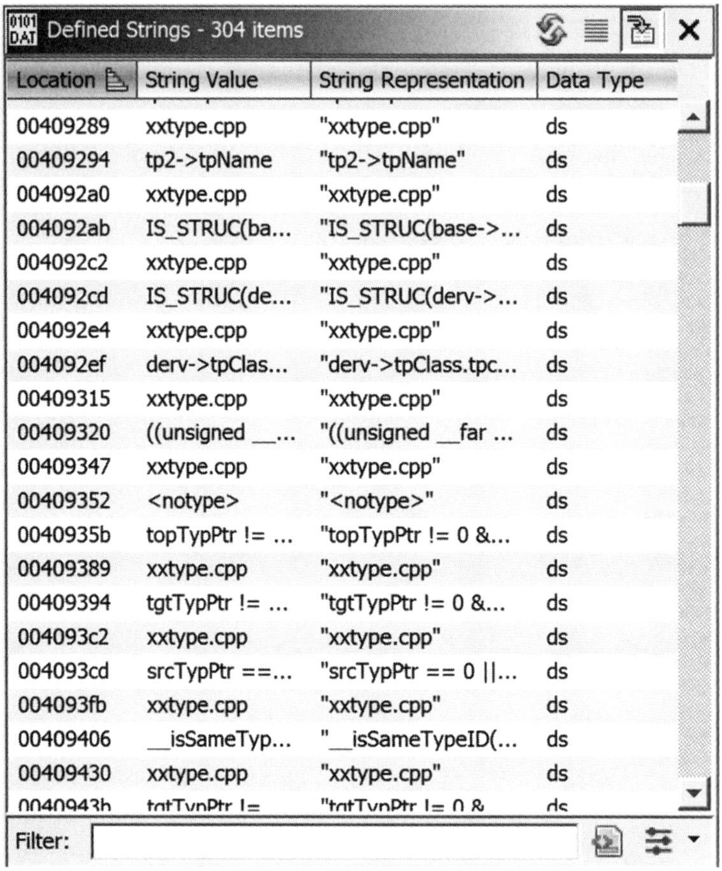

Location	String Value	String Representation	Data Type
00409289	xxtype.cpp	"xxtype.cpp"	ds
00409294	tp2->tpName	"tp2->tpName"	ds
004092a0	xxtype.cpp	"xxtype.cpp"	ds
004092ab	IS_STRUC(ba...	"IS_STRUC(base->...	ds
004092c2	xxtype.cpp	"xxtype.cpp"	ds
004092cd	IS_STRUC(de...	"IS_STRUC(derv->...	ds
004092e4	xxtype.cpp	"xxtype.cpp"	ds
004092ef	derv->tpClas...	"derv->tpClass.tpc...	ds
00409315	xxtype.cpp	"xxtype.cpp"	ds
00409320	((unsigned ___...	"((unsigned __far ...	ds
00409347	xxtype.cpp	"xxtype.cpp"	ds
00409352	<notype>	"<notype>"	ds
0040935b	topTypPtr != ...	"topTypPtr != 0 &...	ds
00409389	xxtype.cpp	"xxtype.cpp"	ds
00409394	tgtTypPtr != ...	"tgtTypPtr != 0 &...	ds
004093c2	xxtype.cpp	"xxtype.cpp"	ds
004093cd	srcTypPtr ==...	"srcTypPtr == 0 ||...	ds
004093fb	xxtype.cpp	"xxtype.cpp"	ds
00409406	__isSameTyp...	"__isSameTypeID(...	ds
00409430	xxtype.cpp	"xxtype.cpp"	ds
0040943b	tgtTypPtr !=	"tgtTypPtr != 0 &	ds

Filter:

Figure 5-22: Defined Strings window

The Symbol Table and Symbol References Windows

The Symbol Table window provides a summary listing of all the global names within a binary. Eight columns are displayed by default, as shown in Figure 5-23. The window is highly configurable, with the capability to add and delete columns in the display as well as to sort in ascending or descending order on any column. The first two default columns are Name and Location. A *name* is nothing more than a symbolic description given to a symbol defined at a *location*.

The Symbol Table is connected to the Listing window but provides the capability to control its interaction with the Listing window. The emphasized icon on the right in Figure 5-23 is a toggle that determines whether a single click on a location in the Symbol Table window causes a related move in the Listing window. Regardless of the toggle selection, double-clicking any Symbol Table location entry will immediately jump the Listing view to display the selected entry. This provides a useful tool for rapidly navigating to known locations within a program listing.

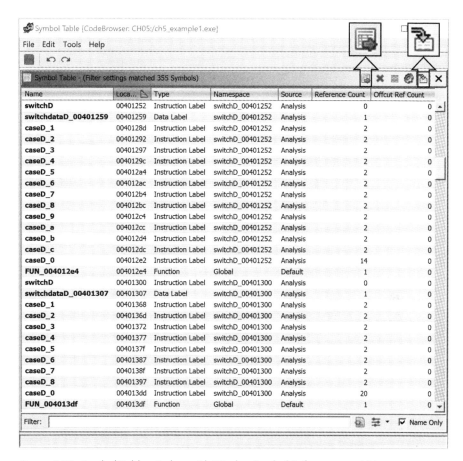

Name	Loca...	Type	Namespace	Source	Reference Count	Offcut Ref Count
switchD	00401252	Instruction Label	switchD_00401252	Analysis	0	0
switchdataD_00401259	00401259	Data Label	switchD_00401252	Analysis	1	0
caseD_1	0040128d	Instruction Label	switchD_00401252	Analysis	2	0
caseD_2	00401292	Instruction Label	switchD_00401252	Analysis	2	0
caseD_3	00401297	Instruction Label	switchD_00401252	Analysis	2	0
caseD_4	0040129c	Instruction Label	switchD_00401252	Analysis	2	0
caseD_5	004012a4	Instruction Label	switchD_00401252	Analysis	2	0
caseD_6	004012ac	Instruction Label	switchD_00401252	Analysis	2	0
caseD_7	004012b4	Instruction Label	switchD_00401252	Analysis	2	0
caseD_8	004012bc	Instruction Label	switchD_00401252	Analysis	2	0
caseD_9	004012c4	Instruction Label	switchD_00401252	Analysis	2	0
caseD_a	004012cc	Instruction Label	switchD_00401252	Analysis	2	0
caseD_b	004012d4	Instruction Label	switchD_00401252	Analysis	2	0
caseD_c	004012dc	Instruction Label	switchD_00401252	Analysis	2	0
caseD_0	004012e2	Instruction Label	switchD_00401252	Analysis	14	0
FUN_004012e4	004012e4	Function	Global	Default	1	0
switchD	00401300	Instruction Label	switchD_00401300	Analysis	0	0
switchdataD_00401307	00401307	Data Label	switchD_00401300	Analysis	1	0
caseD_1	00401368	Instruction Label	switchD_00401300	Analysis	2	0
caseD_2	0040136d	Instruction Label	switchD_00401300	Analysis	2	0
caseD_3	00401372	Instruction Label	switchD_00401300	Analysis	2	0
caseD_4	00401377	Instruction Label	switchD_00401300	Analysis	2	0
caseD_5	0040137f	Instruction Label	switchD_00401300	Analysis	2	0
caseD_6	00401387	Instruction Label	switchD_00401300	Analysis	2	0
caseD_7	0040138f	Instruction Label	switchD_00401300	Analysis	2	0
caseD_8	00401397	Instruction Label	switchD_00401300	Analysis	2	0
caseD_0	004013dd	Instruction Label	switchD_00401300	Analysis	20	0
FUN_004013df	004013df	Function	Global	Default	1	0

Figure 5-23: Symbol Table window with Display Symbol References and Navigation Toggle icons emphasized

There is extensive filtering capability available in the Symbol Table window and several ways to access the filtering options. The cog icon in the toolbar opens the Symbol Table Filter dialog. The dialog (with the Use Advanced Filters box checked) is shown in Figure 5-24. In addition to this dialog, you can use the Filter options at the bottom of the window. Thorough discussions of the symbol table filtering options are available in Ghidra Help.

The emphasized icon on the left in Figure 5-23 is the Display Symbol References icon. Clicking this icon adds the Symbol References window to the Symbol Table window. By default, these two tables will appear side by side. To improve readability, you can drag the Symbol References window below the Symbol Table window, as shown in Figure 5-25. The connection between these two tables is unidirectional, with the Symbol References table being updated when a selection is made in the Symbol Table.

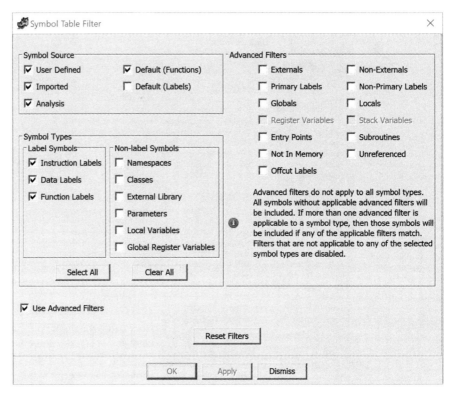

Figure 5-24: Symbol Table Filter dialog

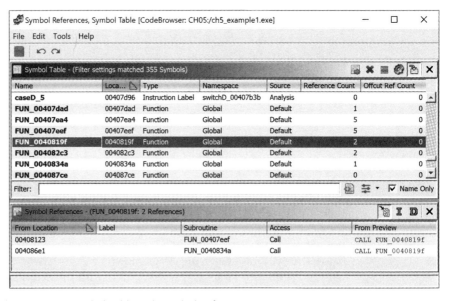

Figure 5-25: Symbol Table with Symbol References

Like the Symbol Table window, the Symbol References window has the same column organization controls. In addition, the content of the Symbol References window is controlled by the three icons (S, I, and D) at the top right of the Symbol References toolbar. These options are mutually exclusive, meaning only one can be selected at a time:

S icon When this icon is selected, the Symbol References window will display all *references to* the symbol that you have selected in the Symbol Table. Figure 5-25 shows a Symbol References window with this option selected.

I icon When this icon is selected, the Symbol References window will display all instruction references from the function that you have selected in the Symbol Table. (This list will be empty if you did not select a function entry point.)

D icon When this icon is selected, the Symbol References window will display all data references from the function that you have selected in the Symbol Table. This list will be empty if you did not select a function entry point or if the function makes no references to any data symbols.

The Memory Map Window

The Memory Map window displays a summary listing of the memory blocks present in the program, as shown in Figure 5-26. Note that what Ghidra terms *memory blocks* are frequently called *sections* when discussing the structure of binary files. Information presented in the window includes the memory block (section) name, start and end addresses, length, permission flags, block type, initialized flag, as well as a space for source filename and user comments. The start and end addresses represent the virtual address range to which the program sections will be mapped at runtime.

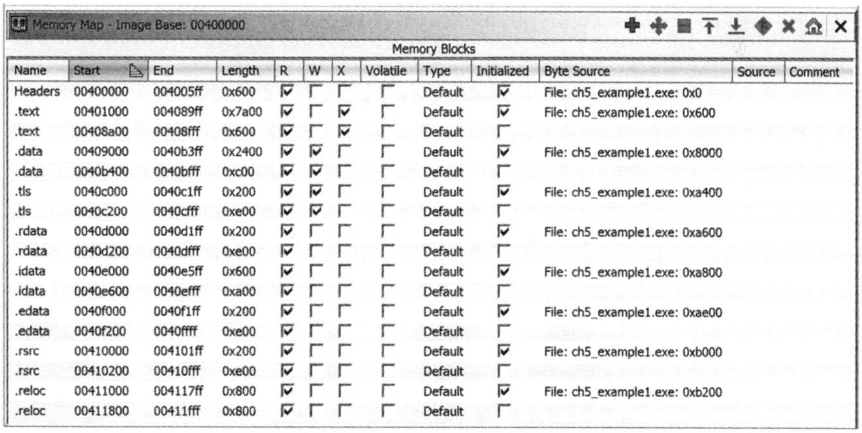

Name	Start	End	Length	R	W	X	Volatile	Type	Initialized	Byte Source	Source	Comment
Headers	00400000	004005ff	0x600	☑	☐	☐	☐	Default	☑	File: ch5_example1.exe: 0x0		
.text	00401000	004089ff	0x7a00	☑	☐	☑	☐	Default	☑	File: ch5_example1.exe: 0x600		
.text	00408a00	00408fff	0x600	☑	☐	☑	☐	Default	☐			
.data	00409000	0040b3ff	0x2400	☑	☑	☐	☐	Default	☑	File: ch5_example1.exe: 0x8000		
.data	0040b400	0040bfff	0xc00	☑	☑	☐	☐	Default	☐			
.tls	0040c000	0040c1ff	0x200	☑	☑	☐	☐	Default	☑	File: ch5_example1.exe: 0xa400		
.tls	0040c200	0040cfff	0xe00	☑	☑	☐	☐	Default	☐			
.rdata	0040d000	0040d1ff	0x200	☑	☐	☐	☐	Default	☑	File: ch5_example1.exe: 0xa600		
.rdata	0040d200	0040dfff	0xe00	☑	☐	☐	☐	Default	☐			
.idata	0040e000	0040e5ff	0x600	☑	☐	☐	☐	Default	☑	File: ch5_example1.exe: 0xa800		
.idata	0040e600	0040efff	0xa00	☑	☐	☐	☐	Default	☐			
.edata	0040f000	0040f1ff	0x200	☑	☐	☐	☐	Default	☑	File: ch5_example1.exe: 0xae00		
.edata	0040f200	0040ffff	0xe00	☑	☐	☐	☐	Default	☐			
.rsrc	00410000	004101ff	0x200	☑	☐	☐	☐	Default	☑	File: ch5_example1.exe: 0xb000		
.rsrc	00410200	00410fff	0xe00	☑	☐	☐	☐	Default	☐			
.reloc	00411000	004117ff	0x800	☑	☐	☐	☐	Default	☑	File: ch5_example1.exe: 0xb200		
.reloc	00411800	00411fff	0x800	☑	☐	☐	☐	Default	☐			

Figure 5-26: Memory Map window

Double-clicking any start or end address in the window jumps the Listing window (and all other connected windows) to the specified address. The Memory Map window toolbar provides options to add/delete blocks, move blocks, split/merge blocks, edit addresses, and set a new image base.

These features are particularly useful when reverse engineering files with nonstandard formats, as the binary's segment structure may not have been detected by the Ghidra loader.

Command line counterparts to the Memory Map window include objdump (-h), readelf (-S), and dumpbin (/HEADERS).

The Function Call Graph Window

In any program, a function can both call and be called by other functions. The Function Call Graph window shows the immediate neighbors of a given function. For our purposes, we will call Y a neighbor of X if Y directly calls X or if X directly calls Y. When you open the Function Call Graph window, Ghidra determines the neighbors of the function in which the cursor is positioned and generates the associated display. This display shows a function in the context it is used in the program file, but it is just a part of the big picture.

Figure 5-27 shows a function named FUN_0040198c that is called from FUN_00401edc and, in turn, makes calls to six other functions. Double-clicking any function in the window immediately jumps the Listing window and other connected windows to the selected function. Ghidra cross-references (XREFs) are the mechanisms that underlie the generation of the Function Call Graph window. XREFs are covered in more detail in Chapter 9.

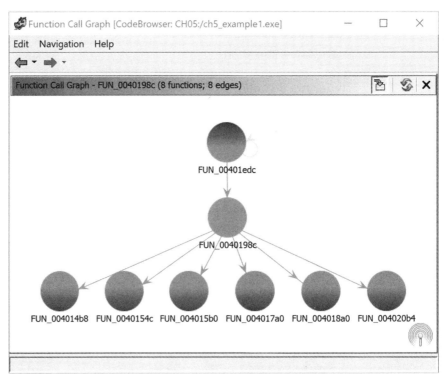

Figure 5-27: Function Call Graph window

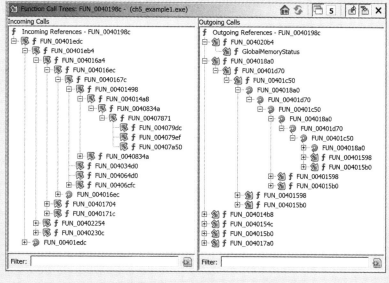

WHO'S CALLING?

While the Function Call Graph window is helpful, sometimes you need the big picture, or at least a bigger picture. The Function Call Trees window (Window ▸ Function Call Trees) allows you to see all calls to and from a selected function. The Function Call Trees window (as shown in Figure 5-28) has two sections: one for incoming calls and one for outgoing calls. Both incoming and outgoing calls can be expanded and collapsed, as desired.

Figure 5-28: The Function Call Trees view

If you open the Function Call Tree window with the entry function selected, you can view a hierarchical representation of the program's function calls.

Summary

At first glance, the number of displays that Ghidra offers can seem overwhelming. You may find it easiest to stick with the default displays until you are comfortable enough to begin exploring the additional display offerings. In any case, you should certainly not feel obligated to use everything that Ghidra throws at you. Not every window will be useful in every reverse engineering scenario.

One of the best ways to familiarize yourself with Ghidra's displays is simply to browse around the various tabbed subwindows that Ghidra populates with data about your binary and also open a few of the other available windows. The efficiency and effectiveness of your reverse engineering sessions will improve as your comfort level with Ghidra increases.

Ghidra is a very complex tool. In addition to the windows covered in this chapter, you may encounter additional dialogs as you endeavor to master Ghidra. We introduce key dialogs as they become relevant throughout the remainder of the book.

At this point, you should be starting to feel more comfortable with the Ghidra interface and the CodeBrowser desktop. In the next chapter, we begin to focus on the many ways that you can manipulate a disassembly to enhance your understanding of its behavior and to generally make your life easier with Ghidra.

6

MAKING SENSE OF A GHIDRA DISASSEMBLY

In this chapter, we cover important basic skills that will help you to better understand the Ghidra disassembly. We start with basic navigational techniques that allow you to move through the assembly and examine the artifacts you encounter. As you navigate from function to function, you will find that you need to decode each function's prototype by using only clues available in the disassembly. Accordingly, we'll discuss techniques for understanding how many parameters a function receives and how we might decode the data types of each parameter we encounter. Since much of the work that a function performs is associated with local variables maintained by the function, we'll also discuss how functions use the stack for local variable storage and how you can, with Ghidra's help, understand exactly how a function makes use of any stack space it may reserve for itself. Whether you find yourself debugging code, analyzing malware, or developing exploits, understanding how to decode a function's stack-allocated variables is an essential skill for understanding the behavior of any program. Finally, we will look at the options

Ghidra provides for searching and how that can contribute to understanding the disassembly.

Disassembly Navigation

In Chapters 4 and 5, we demonstrated that at a basic level, Ghidra combines the features of many common reverse engineering tools into its integrated CodeBrowser display. Navigating around the display is one of the essential skills required to master Ghidra. Static disassembly listings, such as those provided by tools like objdump, offer no inherent navigational capability other than scrolling up and down the listing. Even with the best text editors offering an integrated, grep-style search, such *dead listings* are very difficult to navigate. Ghidra, on the other hand, provides exceptional navigational features. In addition to offering fairly standard search features that you are accustomed to from your use of text editors or word processors, Ghidra develops and displays a comprehensive list of cross-references that behave like web page hyperlinks. The end result is that, in most cases, navigating to locations of interest requires nothing more than a double-click.

Names and Labels

When a program is disassembled, every location in the program is assigned a virtual address. As a result, we can navigate anywhere within a program by providing the virtual address of the location we are interested in visiting. Unfortunately for us, maintaining a catalog of addresses in our heads is not a trivial task. This fact motivated early programmers to assign symbolic names to program locations that they wished to reference, making things a whole lot easier on themselves. The assignment of symbolic names to program addresses was not unlike the assignment of mnemonic instruction names to program opcodes; programs became easier to read and write by making identifiers easier to remember. Ghidra continues this tradition by creating labels for virtual addresses and allowing the user to modify and expand the set of labels. We have already seen the use of names in relation to the Symbol Tree window. Recall that double-clicking a name caused the Listing view (and the Symbol References window) to jump to the referenced location. While there are usage differences between the terms *name* and *label* (for example, functions have names and appear in a separate branch of the Ghidra Symbol Tree from labels), in a navigational context the terms are largely interchangeable because both represent navigational targets.

Ghidra generates symbolic names during the auto analysis phase by using an existing name from the binary (if available) or by automatically generating a name based on how a location is referenced within the binary. In addition to its symbolic purpose, any label displayed in the disassembly window is a potential navigation target similar to a hyperlink on a web page. The two major differences between these labels and standard hyperlinks are that the labels are not highlighted in any way to indicate that they can be followed and that Ghidra generally requires a double-click to follow rather than the single-click required by a traditional hyperlink.

Navigation in Ghidra

In the listing shown in Figure 6-1, each of the symbols indicated by a solid arrow represents a named navigational target. Double-clicking any of them in the Listing window will cause Ghidra to relocate the Listing display (and all connected windows) to the selected location.

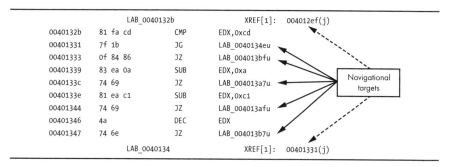

Figure 6-1: Listing showing navigational targets

For navigational purposes, Ghidra treats two additional display entities as navigational targets. First, cross-references (indicated by dashed arrows in Figure 6-1) are treated as navigational targets. Double-clicking the bottom cross-reference address will jump the display to the referencing location (00401331 in this case). Cross-references are covered in more detail in Chapter 9. Hovering over any of these navigable objects will display a pop-up that shows the destination code.

Second, the other type of display entity afforded special treatment in a navigational sense is one that uses hexadecimal values. If a displayed sequence of hexadecimal values represents a valid virtual address within the binary, then the associated virtual address will be displayed to the right, as shown in Figure 6-2. Double-clicking the displayed value will reposition the disassembly window to the associated virtual address. In Figure 6-2, double-clicking any of the values indicated by a solid arrow will jump the display, because each is a valid virtual address within this particular binary. Double-clicking any of the other values will have no effect.

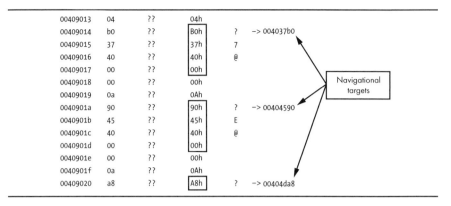

00409013	04	??	04h		
00409014	b0	??	B0h	?	-> 004037b0
00409015	37	??	37h	7	
00409016	40	??	40h	@	
00409017	00	??	00h		
00409018	00	??	00h		
00409019	0a	??	0Ah		
0040901a	90	??	90h	?	-> 00404590
0040901b	45	??	45h	E	
0040901c	40	??	40h	@	
0040901d	00	??	00h		
0040901e	00	??	00h		
0040901f	0a	??	0Ah		
00409020	a8	??	A8h	?	-> 00404da8

Figure 6-2: Listing showing hexadecimal navigational targets

Go To

When you know the address or name you want to navigate to (for example, navigating to *main* in an ELF binary to begin your analysis), you could scroll through the listing to look for the address, scroll through the Functions folder in the Symbol Tree window to find the desired name, or use Ghidra's search features (which are discussed later in this chapter). Ultimately, the easiest way to get to a known address or name is to use the Go To dialog (shown in Figure 6-3), accessed via Navigation ▶ Go To or by using the G hotkey while the disassembly window is active.

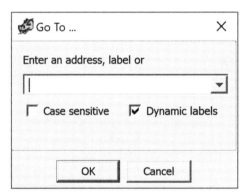

Figure 6-3: The Go To dialog

Navigating to any location in the binary is as simple as specifying a valid address (a case-sensitive symbol name or hex value) and clicking OK, which will immediately jump the display to the desired location. Values entered into the dialog are made available on subsequent use via a drop-down history list, which simplifies returning to previously requested locations.

Navigation History

As a final navigational feature, Ghidra supports forward and backward navigation based on the order in which you navigate the disassembly. Each time you navigate to a new location within a disassembly, your current location is appended to a history list. This list can be traversed from the Go To window or the left and right arrow icons in the CodeBrowser toolbar.

In the Go To window, shown in Figure 6-3, the arrow on the right side of the text box opens a picklist that allows you to choose from previous locations you have entered in the Go To dialog. The CodeBrowser toolbar buttons, seen near the top left in Figure 6-4, provide familiar browser-style forward and backward behavior. Each button is associated with a detailed drop-down history list that provides instant access to any location in the navigation history without having to retrace your steps through the entire list. A sample drop-down list associated with the back arrow is displayed in Figure 6-4.

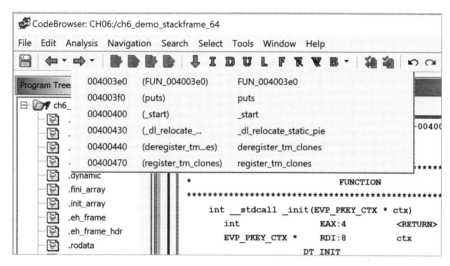

Figure 6-4: Forward and backward navigation arrows with address list

ALT-left arrow (OPTION-left arrow on Mac), for backward navigation, is one of the most useful hotkeys you can commit to memory. Backward navigation is extremely handy when you have followed a chain of function calls several levels deep and you decide that you want to navigate back to your original position within the disassembly. ALT-right arrow (OPTION-right arrow on Mac) moves the disassembly window forward in the history list.

While we now have a much clearer picture regarding navigating a disassembly in Ghidra, we still have not attached meaning to the various destinations we have visited. The next section investigates what makes functions in general, and stack frames in particular, such important navigational targets for a reverse engineer.

Stack Frames

Because Ghidra is a low-level analysis tool, many of its features and displays expect the user to be somewhat familiar with the low-level details of compiled languages, which focus on the specifics of generating machine language and managing the memory used by a high-level program. Ghidra pays particular attention to the manner in which compilers handle local variable declarations and accesses. You may have noticed that a significant number of lines are dedicated to local variables at the beginning of most function listings. These lines result from detailed stack analysis that Ghidra performs on each function, using its Stack analyzer. This analysis is necessary because compilers place a function's local variables (and in some circumstances, the function's incoming arguments) in blocks of memory allocated on the stack. In this section, we review how compilers treat local variable and function arguments to help you better understand the details of Ghidra's Listing view.

Function Call Mechanics

A function invocation may require memory for information passed into the function in the form of parameters (arguments) and for temporary storage space while executing the function. The parameter values, or their corresponding memory addresses, need to be stored somewhere the function can locate them. The temporary space is often allocated by a programmer through the declaration of local variables, which can be used within the function but cannot be accessed after the function has completed. *Stack frames* (also known as *activation records*) are blocks of memory allocated within a program's runtime stack and dedicated to a specific invocation of a function.

Compilers use stack frames to make the allocation and deallocation of function parameters and local variables transparent to the programmer. For calling conventions that pass parameters on the stack, the compiler inserts code to place a function's parameters into the stack frame prior to transferring control to the function itself, at which point the compiler inserts code to allocate enough memory to hold the function's local variables. In some cases, the address to which the function should return is also stored within the new stack frame. Stack frames also enable recursion,[1] as each recursive call to a function is given its own stack frame, neatly segregating each call from its predecessor.

The following operations take place when a function is called:

1. The caller places any parameters required by the function being called into locations dictated by the calling convention employed by the called function. The program stack pointer may change if parameters are passed on the runtime stack.

2. The caller transfers control to the function being called with an instruction such as the x86 CALL, ARM BL, or MIPS JAL. A return address is saved onto the program stack or in a processor register.

---

1. Recursion results when a function, either directly or indirectly, calls itself. Each time a function recursively calls itself, it creates a new stack frame. If there isn't a clearly defined stopping case (or if the stopping case is not reached within a reasonable number of recursive calls), uncontrolled recursion can consume all available stack space and crash the program.

3. If necessary, the called function configures a frame pointer and saves any register values that the caller expects to remain unchanged.[2]

4. The called function allocates space for any local variables that it may require. This is often done by adjusting the program stack pointer to reserve space on the runtime stack.

5. The called function performs its operations, potentially accessing the parameters passed to it and generating a result. If the function returns a result, it is often placed into a specific register or registers that the caller can examine after the function returns.

6. When the function has completed its operations, any stack space reserved for local variables is released. This is often done by reversing the actions performed in step 4.

7. Registers whose values were saved (in step 3) on behalf of the caller are restored to their original values.

8. The called function returns control to the caller. Typical instructions for this include the x86 RET, ARM POP, and MIPS JR. Depending on the calling convention in use, this operation may also clear one or more parameters from the program stack.

9. Once the caller regains control, it may need to remove parameters from the program stack by restoring the program stack pointer to the value that it held prior to step 1.

Steps 3 and 4 are so commonly performed upon entry to a function that together they are called the function's *prologue*. Similarly, steps 6 through 8 make up the function's *epilogue*. All of these operations, except step 5, are part of the overhead associated with calling a function, which may not be obvious in a program's high-level source code, but is quite observable in assembly language.

ARE THEY REALLY GONE?

When we talk about "removing" items from the stack, as well as the removal of entire stack frames, we mean that the stack pointer is adjusted so it points to data lower on the stack and the removed content is no longer accessible through the POP operation. Until that content is overwritten by a PUSH operation, it is still there. From a programming perspective, that qualifies as removal. From a digital forensics perspective, you just have to look a little harder to find the contents. From a variable initialization standpoint, it means that any uninitialized local variables within a stack frame may contain stale values that remain in memory from the last use of a particular range of stack bytes.

---

2. A *frame pointer* is a register that points to a location inside a stack frame. Variables within the stack frame are typically referenced by their relative distance from the location to which the frame pointer points.

Calling Conventions

When passing arguments from caller to callee, the calling function must store parameters exactly as the function being called expects to find them; otherwise, serious problems can arise. A *calling convention* dictates exactly where a caller should place any parameters that a function requires: in specific registers, on the program stack, or in both registers and on the stack. When parameters are passed on the program stack, the calling convention also determines who is responsible for removing them from the stack after the called function has completed: the caller or the callee.

Regardless of what architecture you are reversing for, understanding the code surrounding a function call will be difficult if you don't understand the calling conventions in use. In the sections that follow, we review some of the common calling conventions encountered in compiled C and C++ code.

Stack and Register Arguments

Function arguments may be passed in processor registers, on the program stack, or in a combination of both. When arguments are placed on the stack, the caller performs a memory write (often a PUSH) to place the argument onto the stack, and the called function must then perform a memory read to access the argument. To speed up the function call process, some calling conventions pass arguments in processor registers. When an argument is passed in a register, there is no need to perform the memory write and read operations, as the argument is immediately available to the called function in a designated register. The one shortcoming with register-based calling conventions is that processors have a finite number of registers while function argument lists can be arbitrarily long, so the conventions must properly handle functions that require more arguments than available registers. Excess arguments that "spill" out of available registers are generally placed on the stack.

The C Calling Convention

The *C calling convention* is the default calling convention used by most C compilers when generating function calls. The keyword _cdecl may be used in a function's prototype to force the use of this calling convention in C/C++ programs. The cdecl calling convention specifies that the caller place any stack-allocated parameters to a function on the stack in right-to-left order and that the caller (as opposed to the callee) remove the parameters from the stack after the called function completes. For 32-bit x86 binaries, cdecl passes all arguments on the program stack. For 64-bit x86 binaries, cdecl varies by operating system; on Linux, up to six arguments are placed in registers RDI, RSI, RDX, RCX, R8, and R9, in that order, and any additional arguments spill onto the stack. For ARM binaries, cdecl passes the first four arguments in registers R0 to R3, with arguments five and later spilling onto the stack.

When stack-allocated arguments are placed on the stack in right-to-left order, the leftmost argument will always be on the top of the stack when the function is called. This makes the first argument easy to locate regardless of the number of parameters the function expects, and it makes the cdecl calling convention ideally suited for use with functions that can take a variable number of arguments (such as printf).

Requiring the calling function to remove parameters from the stack means that you will often see instructions that make an adjustment to the program stack pointer immediately following the return from a called function. In the case of functions that can accept a variable number of arguments, the caller knows exactly how many arguments it passed to the function and can easily make the correct adjustment, whereas the called function does not know ahead of time how many parameters it will receive.

In the following examples, we consider calls to functions in a 32-bit, x86 binary, each using a different calling convention. The first function has the following prototype:

```
void demo_cdecl(int w, int x, int y, int z);
```

By default, this function will use the cdecl calling convention, expecting the four parameters to be pushed in right-to-left order and requiring the caller to clean the parameters off the stack. Given the following function call in C:

```
demo_cdecl(1, 2, 3, 4);    // call to demo_cdecl (in C)
```

a compiler might generate the following code:

```
❶ PUSH    4                ; push parameter z
  PUSH    3                ; push parameter y
  PUSH    2                ; push parameter x
  PUSH    1                ; push parameter w
  CALL    demo_cdecl       ; call the function
❷ ADD     ESP, 16          ; adjust ESP to its former value
```

The four PUSH operations ❶ change the program stack pointer (ESP) by 16 bytes (4 * sizeof(int) on a 32-bit architecture), which is undone immediately following the return from demo_cdecl ❷. The following technique, which has been used in some versions of the GNU compilers (gcc and g++), also adheres to the cdecl calling convention while eliminating the need for the caller to explicitly clean parameters off the stack following each call to demo_cdecl:

```
MOV     [ESP+12], 4        ; move parameter z to fourth position on stack
MOV     [ESP+8], 3         ; move parameter y to third position on stack
MOV     [ESP+4], 2         ; move parameter x to second position on stack
MOV     [ESP], 1           ; move parameter w to top of stack
CALL    demo_cdecl         ; call the function
```

In this example, when the parameters for demo_cdecl are placed on the stack, there is no change to the program stack pointer. Note that either method results in the stack pointer pointing to the leftmost stack argument when the function is called.

The Standard Calling Convention

In 32-bit Windows DLLs, Microsoft makes heavy use of a calling convention it has named the *standard calling convention*. In source code, this may be mandated by the use of the _stdcall modifier in a function declaration, as shown here:

```
void _stdcall demo_stdcall(int w, int x, int y);
```

To avoid any confusion surrounding the word *standard*, we refer to this calling convention as the stdcall calling convention for the remainder of the book.

The stdcall calling convention also requires that any stack-allocated function parameters be placed on the program stack in right-to-left order, but the called function is responsible for clearing any stack-allocated arguments from the stack when the function has finished. This is possible only for functions that accept a fixed number of parameters; variable argument functions such as printf cannot use the stdcall calling convention.

The demo_stdcall function expects three integer parameters, occupying a total of 12 bytes on the stack (3 * sizeof(int) on a 32-bit architecture). An x86 compiler can use a special form of the RET instruction to simultaneously pop the return address from the top of the stack and add to the stack pointer to clear the stack-allocated function arguments. In the case of demo_stdcall, we might see the following instruction used to return to the caller:

```
RET 12    ; return and clear 12 bytes from the stack
```

Using stdcall eliminates the need to clean parameters off the stack following every function call, which results in slightly smaller, slightly faster programs. By convention, Microsoft uses the stdcall convention for all fixed-argument functions exported from 32-bit shared library (DLL) files. This is an important point to remember if you are attempting to generate function prototypes or binary-compatible replacements for any shared library components.

The fastcall Convention for x86

The Microsoft C/C++ and GNU gcc/g++ (version 3.4 and later) compilers recognize the fastcall convention, a variation on the stdcall convention where the first two parameters are placed in the ECX and EDX registers, respectively. Any remaining parameters are placed on the stack in right-to-left order, and called functions are responsible for removing parameters from the stack when they return to their caller. The following declaration demonstrates the use of the fastcall modifier:

```
void fastcall demo_fastcall(int w, int x, int y, int z);
```

Given the following function call in C:

```
demo_fastcall(1, 2, 3, 4);      // call to demo_fastcall (in C)
```

a compiler might generate the following code:

```
PUSH    4               ; move parameter z to second position on stack
PUSH    3               ; move parameter y to top position on stack
MOV     EDX, 2          ; move parameter x to EDX
MOV     ECX, 1          ; move parameter w to ECX
Call    demo_fastcall   ; call the function
```

No stack adjustment is required upon return from demo_fastcall, as demo_fastcall is responsible for clearing parameters y and z from the stack as it returns to the caller. It is important to understand that because two arguments are passed in registers, the called function needs to clear only 8 bytes from the stack even though there are four arguments to the function.

C++ Calling Conventions

Nonstatic member functions in C++ classes must make available a pointer to the object used to invoke the function (the this pointer).[3] The address of the object used to invoke the function must be provided by the caller as a parameter, but the C++ language standard does not specify how this should be passed, so it should come as no surprise that different compilers use different techniques.

On x86, Microsoft's C++ compiler utilizes the thiscall calling convention, which passes this in the ECX/RCX register and requires the non-static member function to clean parameters off the stack, as in stdcall. The GNU g++ compiler treats this as the implied first parameter to any nonstatic member function and behaves in all other respects as if the cdecl convention is being used. Thus, for g++-compiled 32-bit code, this is placed on top of the stack prior to calling the nonstatic member function, and the caller is responsible for removing parameters (there will always be at least one) from the stack after the function returns. Additional characteristics of compiled C++ programs are discussed in Chapters 8 and 20.

Other Calling Conventions

Complete coverage of every calling convention would require a book in its own right. Calling conventions are often operating system, language, compiler, and/or processor specific, and some research on your part may be required if you encounter code generated by less-common compilers. A few additional situations deserve special mention, however: optimized code, custom assembly language code, and system calls.

When functions are exported for use by other programmers (such as library functions), it is important that they adhere to well-known calling conventions so that programmers can easily interface to those functions.

---

3. A C++ class may define two types of member functions: static and nonstatic. Nonstatic member functions are used to manipulate the attributes of specific objects and as such, must have some means of knowing exactly what object they are operating on (a this pointer). Static member functions belong to the class at-large and are used to manipulate attributes shared across all instances of the class. They do not require (nor do they receive) a this pointer.

On the other hand, if a function is intended for internal program use only, then the calling convention used by that function need be known only within the program. In such cases, optimizing compilers may choose to use alternate calling conventions to generate faster code. For example, the use of the /GL option with Microsoft C/C++ instructs it to perform "whole program optimization," which may result in optimized use of registers across function boundaries, and the use of the regparm keyword with GNU gcc/g++ allows the programmer to dictate that up to three arguments be passed to registers.

When programmers go to the trouble of writing in assembly language, they gain complete control over how parameters will be passed to any functions that they create. Unless they wish to make their functions available to other programmers, assembly language programmers are free to pass parameters in any way they see fit. As a result, take extra care when analyzing custom assembly code, like obfuscation routines and shellcode.

A *system call* is a special type of function call used to request an operating system service. System calls usually affect a state transition from user mode to kernel mode in order for the operating system kernel to service the user's request. The manner in which system calls are initiated varies across operating systems and processors. For example, 32-bit Linux x86 system calls may be initiated using the INT 0x80 instruction or the sysenter instruction, while other x86 operating systems may use only the sysenter instruction or alternate interrupt numbers, and 64-bit x86 code uses the syscall instruction. On many x86 systems (Linux being an exception), parameters for system calls are placed on the runtime stack, and a system call number is placed in the EAX register immediately prior to initiating the system call. Linux system calls accept their parameters in specific registers and occasionally in memory when there are more parameters than available registers.

Additional Stack Frame Considerations

On any processor, registers are a finite resource that need to be shared, cooperativley, among all functions within a program. When a function (func1) is executing, its world view is that it has complete control over all processor registers. When func1 calls another function (func2), func2 may wish to adopt this same view and make use of all available processor registers according to its own needs, but if func2 makes arbitrary changes to the registers, it may destroy values that func1 depends on.

To address this problem, all compilers follow well-defined rules for register allocation and use. These rules are generally referred to as a platform's *application binary interface (ABI)*. An ABI divides registers into two categories: caller-saved and callee-saved. When one function calls another, the caller needs to save only registers in the caller-saved category to prevent values from being lost. Any registers in the callee-saved category must be saved by the called function (the callee) before that function is allowed to use any of those registers for its own purposes. This typically takes place as part of the function's prologue sequence, with the caller's saved values being restored within the function's epilogue immediately prior to returning. Caller-saved registers are referred to as *clobber* registers because a called function is free to modify their contents without first saving any of them. Conversely, callee-saved registers are referred to as *no-clobber* registers.

The System V ABI for Intel 32-bit processors states that the caller-saved registers include EAX, ECX, and EDX, while the callee-saved registers include EBX, EDI, ESI, EBP, and ESP.[4] In compiled code, you may notice that compilers often prefer to use caller-saved registers within a function because they are relieved from the responsibility of saving and restoring their contents on entry and exit from the function.

Local Variable Layout

Unlike the calling conventions that dictate how parameters are passed into a function, no conventions dictate the memory layout of a function's local variables. When compiling a function, a compiler must compute the amount of space required by a function's local variables, along with space required to save any no-clobber registers, and determine whether those variables can be allocated in processor registers or whether they must be allocated on the program stack. The exact manner in which these allocations are made is irrelevant to both the caller of a function and to any functions that may, in turn, be called, and it is not generally possible to determine a function's local variable layout based solely on examination of the function's source code. One thing is certain with regard to stack frames: the compiler must dedicate at least one register to remember the location of a function's newly allocated stack frame. The most obvious choice for this register is the stack pointer, which, by definition, points at the stack and thus the current function's stack frame.

Stack Frame Examples

When you perform any complex task, such as reverse engineering a binary, you should always strive to make efficient use of your time. When it comes to understanding the behavior of a disassembled function, the less time you spend examining common code sequences, the more time you will have to spend on difficult sequences. Function prologues and epilogues are excellent examples of common code sequences, and it is important that you're able to recognize them, understand them, and rapidly move on to more interesting code that requires more thought.

Ghidra summarizes its understanding of function prologues in the local variable list at the head of each function listing, and while it may make the code more readable, it does nothing to reduce the amount of disassembled code that you need to read. In the following examples, we discuss two common types of stack frames and review the code necessary to create them so that when you encounter similar code in the wild, you can quickly move through it to get to the meat of a function.

---

4. See *https://wiki.osdev.org/System_V_ABI*.

Consider the following function compiled on a 32-bit x86-based computer:

```
void helper(int j, int k);      // a function prototype
void demo_stackframe(int a, int b, int c) {
    int x;
    char buffer[64];
    int y;
    int z;
    // body of function not terribly relevant
    // other than the following function call
    helper(z, y);
}
```

The local variables for demo_stackframe require 76 bytes (three 4-byte integers and a 64-byte buffer). This function could use either stdcall or cdecl, and the stack frame would look the same.

Example 1: Local Variable Access via the Stack Pointer

Figure 6-5 shows one possible stack frame for an invocation of demo_stackframe. In this example, the compiler has elected to utilize the stack pointer anytime it references a variable contained in the stack frame, leaving all other registers available for other purposes. If any instruction causes the value of the stack pointer to change, the compiler must ensure that it accounts for that change in all subsequent local variable accesses.

Variable	Offset
z	[ESP]
y	[ESP+4]
buffer	[ESP+8]
x	[ESP+72]
Saved EIP	[ESP+76]
a	[ESP+80]
b	[ESP+84]
c	[ESP+88]

ESP → (points to z)

Local variables: z, y, buffer, x
Parameters: a, b, c

Figure 6-5: Sample stack frame for a function compiled on a 32-bit x86 computer

The space for this frame is set up on entry to demo_stackframe with the one-line prologue:

```
SUB    ESP, 76        ; allocate sufficient space for all local variables
```

The Offset column in Figure 6-5 indicates the x86 addressing mode (base + displacement in this case) required to reference each of the local variables and parameters in the stack frame. In this case, ESP is being used as the base register, and each displacement is the relative offset from ESP to the start of the variable within the stack frame. However, the displacements shown in Figure 6-5 are correct only as long as the value held in ESP doesn't change. Unfortunately, the stack pointer changes frequently, and the compiler must constantly adapt to ensure that proper offsets are used when referencing any variables within the stack frame. Consider the call made to helper in the function demo_stackframe, the code for which is shown here:

```
❶ PUSH    dword [ESP+4]   ; push y
❷ PUSH    dword [ESP+4]   ; push z
  CALL    helper
  ADD     ESP, 8          ; cdecl requires caller to clear parameters
```

The first PUSH ❶ correctly pushes local variable y per the offset in Figure 6-5. At first glance, it might appear that the second PUSH ❷ incorrectly references local variable y a second time. However, because all variables in the stack frame are referenced relative to ESP and the first PUSH ❶ modifies ESP, all of the offsets in Figure 6-5 must be temporarily adjusted. Therefore, following the first PUSH ❶, the new offset for local variable z becomes [ESP+4]. When examining functions that reference stack frame variables using the stack pointer, you must be careful to note any changes to the stack pointer and adjust all future variable offsets accordingly.

Once demo_stackframe has completed, it needs to return to the caller. Ultimately, a RET instruction will pop the desired return address off the top of the stack into the instruction pointer register (EIP in this case). Before the return address can be popped, the local variables need to be removed from the top of the stack so that the stack pointer correctly points to the saved return address when the RET instruction is executed. For this particular function (assuming the cdecl calling convention is in use), the epilogue becomes the following:

```
ADD     ESP, 76         ; adjust ESP to point to the saved return address
RET                     ; return to the caller
```

Example 2: Give the Stack Pointer a Break

At the expense of dedicating a second register to locating variables with a stack frame, the stack pointer may be allowed to freely change without the need to recompute offsets for each variable within the frame. Of course, the compiler needs to commit to not changing this second register; otherwise, it will need to contend with the same issues raised in the previous example. In this situation, the compiler needs to first select a register for this purpose and then it must generate code to initialize that register on entry to the function.

Any register selected for this purpose is known as a *frame pointer*. In the preceding example, ESP was being used as a frame pointer, and we can say that it was an ESP-based stack frame. The ABI for most architectures suggests which register should be used as a frame pointer. The frame pointer is always considered a no-clobber register because the calling function may already be using it for the same purpose. In x86 programs, the EBP/RBP (extended base pointer) register is typically dedicated for use as a frame pointer. By default, most compilers generate code to use a register other than the stack pointer as a frame pointer, though options typically exist for specifying that the stack pointer should be used instead. (GNU gcc/g++, for example, offers the -fomit-frame-pointer compiler option, which generates functions that do not use a second register as a frame pointer.)

To see what the stack frame for demo_stackframe will look like using a dedicated frame pointer, we need to consider this new prologue code:

```
❶ PUSH    EBP             ; save the caller's EBP value, because it's no-clobber
❷ MOV     EBP, ESP        ; make EBP point to the saved register value
❸ SUB     ESP, 76         ; allocate space for local variables
```

The PUSH instruction ❶ saves the value of EBP currently being used by the caller because EBP is a no-clobber register. The caller's value of EBP must be restored before we return. If any other registers need to be saved on behalf of the caller (ESI or EDI, for example), compilers may save them at the same time EBP is saved, or they may defer saving them until local variables have been allocated. Thus, there is no standard location within a stack frame for the storage of saved registers.

Once EBP has been saved, it can be changed to point to the current stack location with the MOV instruction ❷, which copies the current value of the stack pointer (the only register guaranteed to be pointing into the stack at this moment in time) into EBP. Finally, as in the ESP-based stack frame, space for local variables is allocated ❸. The resulting stack frame layout is shown in Figure 6-6.

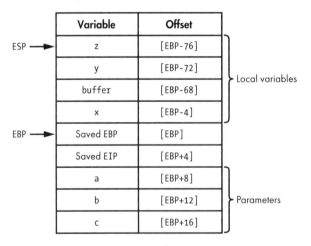

Figure 6-6: An EBP-based stack frame

With a dedicated frame pointer, all variable offsets can now be computed relative to the frame pointer register, as seen in Figure 6-6. It is most often (though not necessarily) the case that positive offsets are used to access any stack-allocated function arguments, while negative offsets are used to access local variables. With a dedicated frame pointer in use, the stack pointer may be freely changed without affecting the offset to any variables within the frame. The call to the function helper can now be implemented as follows:

```
❹ PUSH    dword [ebp-72] ; PUSH y
  PUSH    dword [ebp-76] ; PUSH z
  CALL    helper
  ADD     ESP, 8         ; cdecl requires caller to clear parameters
```

The fact that the stack pointer has changed following the first PUSH ❹ has no effect on the access to local variable z in the subsequent PUSH.

In the epilogue of a function that uses a frame pointer, the caller's frame pointer must be restored prior to returning. If the frame pointer is to be restored using a POP instruction, local variables must be cleared from the stack before the old value of the frame pointer can be popped, but this is made easy by the fact that the current frame pointer points to the location on the stack that holds the saved frame pointer value. In 32-bit x86 programs utilizing EBP as a frame pointer, the following code represents a typical epilogue:

```
MOV    ESP, EBP    ; clears local variables by resetting ESP
POP    EBP         ; restore the caller's value of EBP
RET                ; pop return address to return to the caller
```

This operation is so common that the x86 architecture offers the LEAVE instruction to accomplish the same task:

```
LEAVE              ; copies EBP to ESP AND then pops into EBP
RET                ; pop return address to return to the caller
```

While the names of registers and instructions used will certainly differ for other processor architectures, the basic process of building stack frames will remain the same. Regardless of the architecture, you will want to familiarize yourself with typical prologue and epilogue sequences so that you can quickly move on to analyzing more interesting code within functions.

Ghidra Stack Views

Stack frames are a runtime concept; a stack frame can't exist without a stack and without a running program. While this is true, it doesn't mean that you should ignore the concept of a stack frame when you are performing static analysis with tools such as Ghidra. All of the code required to set up stack frames for each function is present within a binary. Through careful analysis of this code, we can gain a detailed understanding of the structure of any function's stack frame, even though the function is not running. In fact, some of Ghidra's most sophisticated analysis is performed specifically to determine the layout of stack frames for every function that it disassembles.

Ghidra Stack Frame Analysis

During initial analysis, Ghidra goes to great lengths to track the behavior of the stack pointer over the course of a function by making note of every PUSH or POP operation along with any arithmetic operations that may change the stack pointer, such as adding or subtracting constant values. The goal of this analysis is to determine the exact size of the local variable area allocated to a function's stack frame, determine whether a dedicated frame pointer is in use in a given function (by recognizing a PUSH EBP/MOV EBP, ESP sequence, for example), and recognize all memory references to variables within a function's stack frame.

For example, if Ghidra noted the instruction

```
MOV    EAX, [EBP+8]
```

in the body of demo_stackframe, it would understand that the first argument to the function (a in this case) is being loaded into the EAX register (refer to Figure 6-6). Ghidra can distinguish between memory references that access function arguments (those that lie below the saved return address) and references that access local variables (those that lie above the saved return address).

Ghidra takes the additional step of determining which memory locations within a stack frame are directly referenced. For example, while the stack frame in Figure 6-6 is 96 bytes in size, there are only seven variables that we are likely to see referenced (four locals and three parameters). As a result, you can focus your attention on the seven things that Ghidra has identified as important and spend less time thinking about all the bytes that Ghidra has left unnamed. In the process of identifying and naming individual items within a stack frame, Ghidra also recognizes the spatial relationship of variables with respect to one another. This can be tremendously helpful in some use cases, such as exploit development, when Ghidra makes it easy to determine exactly which variables may get overwritten as the result of a buffer overflow. Ghidra's decompiler (discussed in Chapter 19) also relies heavily on stack frame analysis, and it uses the results to infer how many arguments a function receives and what local variable declarations are necessary in the decompiled code.

Stack Frames in Listing View

Understanding the behavior of a function often comes down to understanding the types of data that the function manipulates. When you're reading a disassembly listing, one of the first opportunities you have to understand the data that a function manipulates is to view the breakdown of the function's stack frame. Ghidra offers two views into any function's stack frame: a summary view and a detailed view. To understand these two views, we will refer to the following version of demo_stackframe, which we have compiled using gcc:

```
void demo_stackframe(int i, int j, int k) {
    int x = k;
    char buffer[64];
```

```
    int y = j;
    int z = 10;
    buffer[0] = 'A';
    helper(z, y);
}
```

As local variables exist only while the function is running, any local variable that is not used in the function in a meaningful way is essentially useless. From a high-level view, the following code is a functionally equivalent (you might say optimized) version of demo_stackframe:

```
void demo_stackframe_2(int b) {
    helper(10, b);
}
```

(So, while this function acts like it is doing a lot of work, it's really just trying to look busy to impress the boss.)

In the original version of demo_stackframe, local variables x and y are initialized from parameters k and j, respectively. Local variable z is initialized with the literal value 10, and the first character in the 64-byte local array, named buffer, is initialized to the character 'A'. The corresponding Ghidra disassembly of this function, using the default auto analysis, is shown in Figure 6-7.

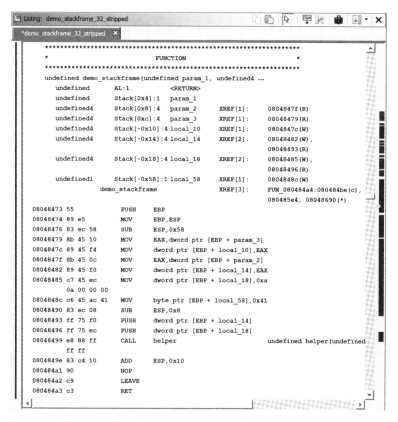

Figure 6-7: Disassembly of the demo_stackframe function

There are many points to cover in this listing as we begin to acquaint ourselves with Ghidra's disassembly notation. In this discussion, we focus on two sections of the disassembly that provide us with particularly useful information. Let's start by zooming in on the stack summary, as shown in the following listing. (You can always refer back to Figure 6-7 to see this summary stack frame in context.) To simplify the discussion, the terms *local variable* and *argument* are used to distinguish between the two types of variables. The term *variable* is used when discussing both collectively.

```
undefined    AL:1             <RETURN>
undefined    Stack[0x4]:1     param_1
undefined4   Stack[0x8]:4     param_2
undefined4   Stack[0xc]:4     param_3
undefined4   Stack[-0x10]:4   local_10
undefined4   Stack[-0x14]:4   local_14
undefined4   Stack[-0x18]:4   local_18
undefined1   Stack[-0x58]:1   local_58
```

Ghidra provides a summary stack view that lists every variable directly referenced within the stack frame, along with important information about each. The meaningful names (in the third column) that Ghidra assigns to each variable provide information about the variables when you see them throughout the disassembly listing: the names of arguments passed to the function begin with a helpful prefix of param_, and local variable names begin with local_. As a result, it is easy to distinguish between the two types of variables.

The variable name prefixes are combined with information about the position or location of a variable. For arguments, like param_3, the number in the name corresponds to the argument's position in the function's parameter list. For local variables, like local_10, the number is a hexadecimal offset representing the variable's location within the stack frame. The location can also be found in the center column of the listing, to the left of the names. This column has two components separated by a colon: Ghidra's estimate of the size of the variable in bytes, and the location of the variable within the stack frame, represented as the offset of that variable from the initial stack pointer value on entry into the function.

A tabular representation of this stack frame is shown in Figure 6-8. As discussed, parameters lie below the saved return address and thus have a positive offset from the return address. Local variables lie above the saved return address and thus have a negative offset. The order of the local variables in the stack do not match the order in which they were declared in the source code shown earlier in this chapter, because the compiler is free to arrange local variables on the stack based on a variety of internal factors, such as byte alignment and placement of arrays relative to other local variables.

Address	Desc	Name
-0x68	helper parameters	
-0x64		
-0x58	buffer	local_58
-0x18	z	local_18
-0x14	y	local_14
-0x10	x	local_10
-0x04	Saved EBP	
0x00	Saved RET	
0x04	i	param_1
0x08	j	param_2
0x0c	k	param_3

Figure 6-8: Sample stack frame image

Decompiler-Assisted Stack Frame Analysis

Remember the functional equivalent of the code that we identified?

```
void demo_stackframe_2(int j) {
    helper(10, j);
}
```

The code that the decompiler generated for this function is shown in Figure 6-9. Ghidra's decompiler-generated code is very similar to our optimized code, as the decompiler includes only the executable equivalent of the original function. (The exception is the inclusion of param_1.)

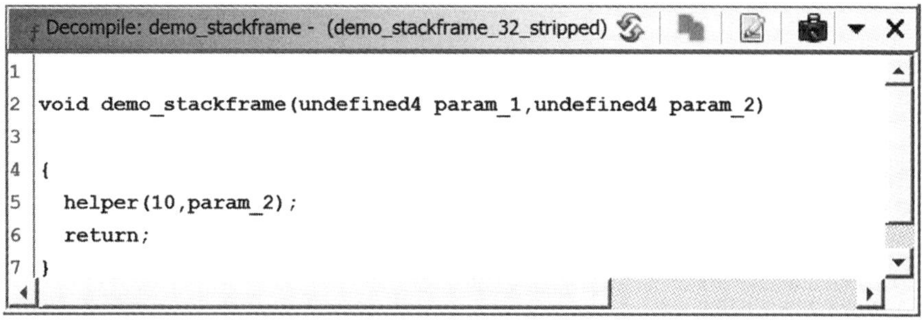

```
Decompile: demo_stackframe - (demo_stackframe_32_stripped)

1
2  void demo_stackframe(undefined4 param_1,undefined4 param_2)
3
4  {
5    helper(10,param_2);
6    return;
7  }
```

Figure 6-9: Decompiler window for demo_stackframe (with Decompiler Parameter ID analyzer)

You may have noticed that the function demo_stackframe accepted three integer parameters, but only two of them (param_1 and param_2) are accounted for in the decompiler listing. Which one is missing and why? It turns out that the Ghidra disassembler and the Ghidra decompiler approach the names a little differently. While both name all of the parameters up to the last one referenced, the decompiler names only the parameters up to the last one that is used in a meaningful way. One of the analyzers that Ghidra can run for you is called the *Decompiler Parameter ID* analyzer. In most cases, this analyzer is not enabled by default (it is enabled for only Windows PE files smaller than 2MB). When the Decompiler Parameter ID analyzer is enabled, Ghidra uses decompiler-derived parameter information to name a function's parameters in the disassembly listing. The following listing shows the variables in the disassembly listing of demo_stackframe when the Decompiler Parameter ID analyzer is enabled:

```
undefined    AL:1                          <RETURN>
undefined    Stack[0x4]:4      param_1
undefined4   Stack[0x8]:4      param_2
undefined4   Stack[-0x10]:4    local_10
undefined4   Stack[-0x14]:4    local_14
undefined4   Stack[-0x18]:4    local_18
undefined1   Stack[-0x58]:1    local_58
```

Note that param_3 no longer appears in the list of function arguments, as the decompiler has determined that it is not used in any meaningful way within the function. This particular stack frame is discussed further in Chapter 8. If you ever want Ghidra to perform Decompiler Parameter ID analysis after opening a binary with that analyzer disabled, you can always choose Analysis ▸ One Shot ▸ Decompiler Parameter ID to run the analyzer after the fact.

Local Variables as Operands

Let's shift our focus to the actual disassembly portion of the following listing:

```
08048473 55            PUSH    EBP❶
08048474 89 e5         MOV     EBP,ESP
08048476 83 ec 58      SUB     ESP,0x58❷
08048479 8b 45 10      MOV     EAX,dword ptr [EBP + param_3]
0804847c 89 45 f4      MOV     dword ptr [EBP + local_10],EAX❸
0804847f 8b 45 0c      MOV     EAX,dword ptr [EBP + param_2]
08048482 89 45 f0      MOV     dword ptr [EBP + local_14],EAX❹
08048485 c7 45 ec      MOV     dword ptr [EBP + local_18],0xa❺
         0a 00 00 00
0804848c c6 45 ac 41   MOV     byte ptr [EBP + local_58],0x41❻
08048490 83 ec 08      SUB     ESP,0x8
08048493 ff 75 f0      PUSH    dword ptr [EBP + local_14]❼
08048496 ff 75 ec      PUSH    dword ptr [EBP + local_18]
```

The function uses a common function prologue ❶ for an EBP-based stack frame. The compiler allocates 88 bytes (0x58 equals 88) of local variable space ❷ in the stack frame. This is slightly more than the estimated 76 bytes and demonstrates that compilers occasionally pad the local variable space with extra bytes in order to maintain a particular memory alignment within the stack frame.

An important difference between Ghidra's disassembly listing and the stack frame analysis that we performed earlier is that in the disassembly listing you don't see memory references similar to [EBP-12] (which you might see with objdump, for example). Instead, Ghidra has replaced all constant offsets with symbolic names corresponding to the symbols in the stack view and their relative offsets from the function's initial stack pointer location. This is in keeping with Ghidra's goal of generating a higher-level disassembly. It is simply easier to deal with symbolic names than numeric constants. It also gives us a name that can be modified to match our understanding of the variable's purpose once known. Ghidra does display the raw form of the current instruction, without any labels, in the extreme, lower-right corner of the CodeBrowser window for reference.

In this example, since we have source code available for comparison, we can map the Ghidra-generated variable names back to the names used in the original source by using a variety of clues available in the disassembly:

1. First, demo_stackframe accepts three parameters, i, j, and k, which correspond to variables param_1, param _2, and param _3, respectively.

2. Local variable x (local_10) is initialized from parameter k (param_3) ❸.

3. Similarly, local variable y (local_14) is initialized from parameter j (param _2) ❹.

4. Local variable z (local_18) is initialized with the value 10 ❺.

5. The first character buffer[0] (local_58) in the 64-byte character array is initialized with *A* (ASCII 0x41) ❻.

6. The two arguments for the call to helper are pushed onto the stack ❼. The 8-byte stack adjustment that precedes these two pushes combines with the two pushes to yield a net stack change of 16 bytes. As a result, the stack maintains any 16-byte alignment achieved earlier in the program.

The Ghidra Stack Frame Editor

In addition to the summary stack view, Ghidra offers a detailed stack frame editor in which every byte allocated to a stack frame is accounted for. The Stack Frame Editor window is accessed by right-clicking and selecting Function ▸ Edit Stack Frame from the context menu when you have selected a function or stack variable within Ghidra's summary stack view for a function. The resulting window for the demo_stackframe function is shown in Figure 6-10.

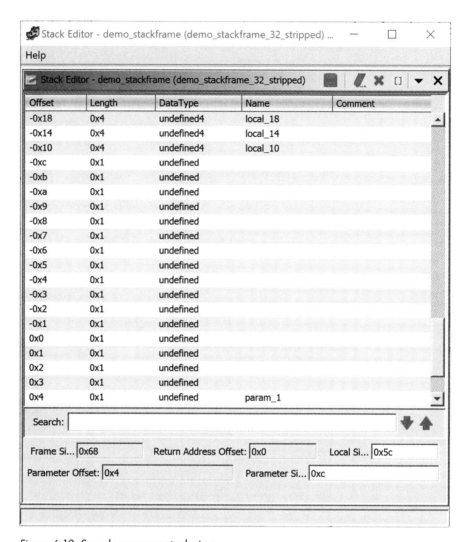

Offset	Length	DataType	Name	Comment
-0x18	0x4	undefined4	local_18	
-0x14	0x4	undefined4	local_14	
-0x10	0x4	undefined4	local_10	
-0xc	0x1	undefined		
-0xb	0x1	undefined		
-0xa	0x1	undefined		
-0x9	0x1	undefined		
-0x8	0x1	undefined		
-0x7	0x1	undefined		
-0x6	0x1	undefined		
-0x5	0x1	undefined		
-0x4	0x1	undefined		
-0x3	0x1	undefined		
-0x2	0x1	undefined		
-0x1	0x1	undefined		
0x0	0x1	undefined		
0x1	0x1	undefined		
0x2	0x1	undefined		
0x3	0x1	undefined		
0x4	0x1	undefined	param_1	

Search:

Frame Si... 0x68   Return Address Offset: 0x0   Local Si... 0x5c

Parameter Offset: 0x4   Parameter Si... 0xc

Figure 6-10: Sample summary stack view

Because the detailed view accounts for every byte in the stack frame, it occupies significantly more space than the summary view. The portion of the stack frame shown in Figure 6-10 spans a total of 29 bytes, which is only a small portion of the entire stack frame. Also in the previous listing, local_10 ❸, local_14 ❹, and local_18 ❺ are directly referenced in the disassembly listing where their contents were initialized using dword (4-byte) writes. Based on the fact that 32 bits of data were moved, Ghidra is able to infer that each of these variables is a 4-byte quantity and labels each as an undefined4 (a 4-byte variable of unknown type).

As this is a Stack Frame Editor, we can use this window to edit fields, change display formats, and add supplemental information if it benefits our process. For example, we could add a name for the saved return address at 0x0.

REGISTER-BASED PARAMETERS

ARM calling conventions use up to four registers to pass parameters to functions without using the stack. Some x86-64 conventions use as many as six registers, and some MIPS conventions use up to eight. Register-based parameters are a little harder to identify than stack-based parameters.

Consider the following two assembly language fragments:

```
stackargs:                  ; An example x86 32-bit function
    PUSH EBP                ; save no-clobber ebp
    MOV  EBP, ESP           ; set up frame pointer
 ❶  MOV  EAX, [EBP + 8]     ; retrieve stack-allocated argument
    MOV  CL, byte [EAX]     ; dereference retrieved pointer argument
    ...
    RET
regargs:                    ; An example x86-64 function
    PUSH RBP                ; save no-clobber rbp
    MOV  RBP, RSP           ; set up frame pointer
 ❷  MOV  CL, byte [RDI]     ; dereference pointer argument
    ...
    RET
```

In the first function, the region of the stack beneath the saved return address is being accessed ❶, and we conclude that the function expects at least one argument. Ghidra, like most high-end disassemblers, performs stack pointer and frame pointer analysis to identify instructions that access members of a function's stack frame.

In the second function, RDI is used ❷ before it has been initialized. The only logical conclusion is that RDI must have been initialized in the caller, in which case RDI is being used to pass information from the caller into the regargs function (that is, it is a parameter). In program analysis terms, RDI is *live* on entry to regargs. To determine the number of register-based parameters the function expects, identify all registers that appear to be live within a function by observing that their contents are read and utilized before the register has been written (initialized) within a function.

Unfortunately, this data flow analysis is usually beyond the capabilities of most disassemblers, including Ghidra. Decompilers, on the other hand, must perform this type of analysis and are generally quite good at identifying the use of register-based parameters. Ghidra's Decompiler Parameter ID analyzer (Edit ▸ Options for <prog> ▸ Properties ▸ Analyzers) can update the disassembly listing based on parameter analysis performed by the decompiler.

The stack editor view offers a detailed look at the inner workings of compilers. In Figure 6-10, it is clear that the compiler has inserted 8 extra bytes between the saved frame pointer -0x4 and the local variable x (local_10). These bytes occupy offsets -0x5 through -0xc in the stack frame. Unless you happen to be a compiler writer yourself or are willing to dig deep into the source code for GNU gcc, all you can do is speculate as to why these extra bytes are allocated in this manner. In most cases, we can chalk up the extra bytes to padding for alignment, and usually the presence of these extra bytes has no impact on a program's behavior. In Chapter 8, we return to the stack editor view and its uses in dealing with more complex data types such as arrays and structures.

Searching

As shown at the start of the chapter, Ghidra makes it easy to navigate through the disassembly to locate artifacts that you know about and to discover new artifacts. It also designs many of its data displays to summarize specific types of information (names, strings, imports, and so on), making them easy to find as well. However, effective analysis of a disassembly listing often requires the ability to search for new clues to inform the disassembly analysis. Fortunately for us, Ghidra has a Search menu that allows us to conduct searches to locate items of interest. The default search menu options are shown in Figure 6-11. In this section, we investigate methods to search the disassembly by using both text and byte search functionality provided in the CodeBrowser.

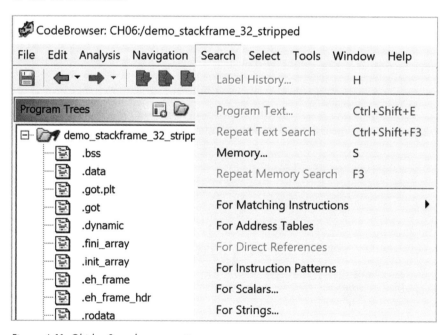

Figure 6-11: Ghidra Search menu options

Search Program Text

Ghidra text searches amount to substring searches through the disassembly listing view. Text searches are initiated via Search ▸ Program Text, which opens the dialog shown in Figure 6-12. Two search types are available: the entire program database, which extends beyond what you see in the CodeBrowser window, and the listing display within the CodeBrowser. Beyond the search type, several self-explanatory options let you select how and what to search.

To navigate between matches, use the Next and Previous buttons at the bottom of the Search Program Text dialog, or select Search All to open the search results in a new window, allowing easy navigation to any match.

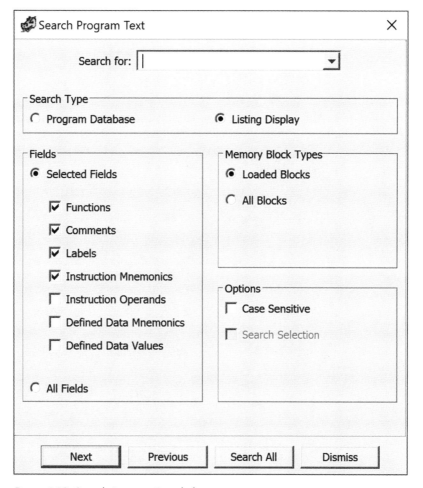

Figure 6-12: Search Program Text dialog

Search Memory

If you need to search for specific binary content, such as a known sequence of bytes, then text searches are not the answer. Instead, you need to use Ghidra's memory search functionality. A memory search can be initiated using Search ▸ Memory, or the associated hotkey S. Figure 6-13 shows the Search Memory dialog. To search for a sequence of hex bytes, the search string should be specified as a space-separated list of two-digit, case-insensitive hex values, such as c9 c3, as shown in Figure 6-13. If you are not sure of the hex sequence, you can use wildcards (* or ?).

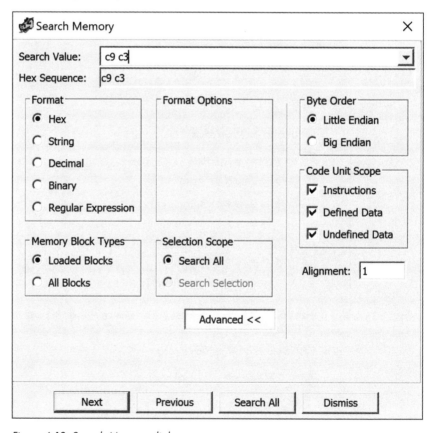

Figure 6-13: Search Memory dialog

The Search Memory results for the bytes c9 c3, run with the Search All option, are shown in Figure 6-14. You can sort on any column, rename the window, or apply a filter. This window also offers some right-click options, including the ability to delete rows and manipulate selections.

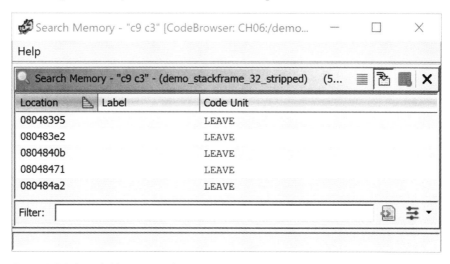

Figure 6-14: Search Memory results

Search values can be input in string, decimal, binary, and regular expression formats as well. String, decimal, and binary each provide context-appropriate format options. Regular expressions let you search for a particular pattern, but only in the forward direction, because of restrictions on how they are processed. Ghidra uses Java's built-in regular expressions grammar, which is described in significant detail in Ghidra Help.

Summary

The intent of this chapter was to provide you with the minimum essential skills for effectively interpreting Ghidra's disassembly listings and navigating your way around them. The overwhelming majority of your interactions with Ghidra will involve the operations that we have discussed so far. However, the ability to perform basic navigation, understand important disassembly constructs like the stack, and search the disassembly are just the tip of the iceberg for a reverse engineer.

With these skills safely under your belt, the logical next step is learning how to use Ghidra to suit your particular needs. In the next chapter, we begin to look at how to make the most basic changes to a disassembly listing as a means of adding new knowledge based on our understanding of a binary's content and behavior.

7

DISASSEMBLY MANIPULATION

After navigation, disassembly modification is the next most significant feature of Ghidra. Ghidra offers the ability to easily manipulate disassemblies to add new information or reformat a listing to suit your particular needs, and because of Ghidra's underlying structure, changes that you make to a disassembly are easily propagated to all associated Ghidra views to maintain a consistent picture of your program. Ghidra automatically handles operations such as context-aware search and replace when it makes sense to do so, and it makes trivial work of reformatting instructions as data, and data as instructions. And perhaps the best feature is that almost anything you do can be undone!

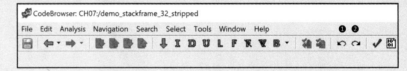

Figure 7-1: Undo and Redo icons in the CodeBrowser toolbar

Manipulating Names and Labels

At this point, we have encountered two categories of identifiers in Ghidra disassemblies: labels (which are identifiers associated with locations) and names (which are identifiers associated with stack frame variables). For the most part, we will refer to both as *names*, as Ghidra is somewhat loose in this distinction also. (If you want to be really precise, labels actually have associated names, addresses, histories, and so on. The name of the label is how we generally reference the label.) We use more specific terms when the distinction makes a critical difference.

To review, stack variable names have one of two prefixes based on whether the variable is a parameter (param_) or a local variable (local_), and locations are assigned names/labels with helpful prefixes during auto analysis (for example, LAB_, DAT_, FUN_, EXT_, OFF_, and UNK_). In most cases, Ghidra will automatically generate names and labels based on its best guess about the use of the associated variable or address, but you will need to analyze the program yourself to understand the purpose of a location or variable.

As you begin to analyze any program, one of the first and most common ways to manipulate a disassembly listing is to change default names into more meaningful names. Fortunately, Ghidra allows you to easily change any name, and it intelligently propagates name changes throughout the entire program. To open a name-change dialog, select the name by clicking it and then use the L hotkey or the Edit Label option on the right-click context menu. From there, the process for stack variables (names) and named locations (labels) varies, as detailed in the following sections.

Renaming Parameters and Local Variables

Names associated with stack variables are not associated with a specific virtual address. As in most programming languages, such names are restricted to the scope of the function to which a given stack frame belongs. Thus, every function in a program can have its own stack variable named param_1, but no function may have more than one variable named param_1, as shown in Figure 7-2.

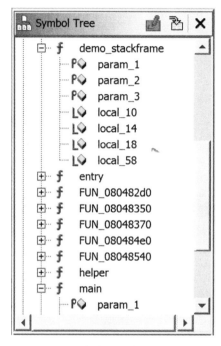

Figure 7-2: Symbol Tree showing reuse of parameter names (param_1)

When you rename a variable in the Listing window, the informative dialog shown in Figure 7-3 will pop up. The type of entity you are changing (variable, function, and so on) appears in the title bar of the window, and the current (about to be changed) name appears in the editable text box and the title bar.

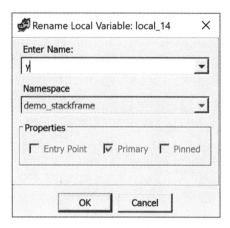

Figure 7-3: Renaming a stack variable
(local_14 to y)

Once a new name is supplied, Ghidra changes every occurrence of the old name in the current function. The following listing shows the result of renaming local_14 to y in demo_stackframe:

```
        ****************************************************************
        *                         FUNCTION                          *
        ****************************************************************
        undefined demo_stackframe(undefined param_1, undefined4
            undefined        AL:1              <RETURN>
            undefined        Stack[0x4]:1       param_1
            undefined4       Stack[0x8]:4       param_2
            undefined4       Stack[0xc]:4       param_3
            undefined4       Stack[-0x10]:4     local_10
            undefined4       Stack[-0x14]:4     y❶
            undefined4       Stack[-0x18]:4     local_18
            undefined1       Stack[-0x58]:1     local_58
        demo_stackframe
08048473 55              PUSH    EBP
08048474 89 e5           MOV     EBP,ESP
08048476 83 ec 58        SUB     ESP,0x58
08048479 8b 45 10        MOV     EAX,dword ptr [EBP + param_3]
0804847c 89 45 f4        MOV     dword ptr [EBP + local_10],EAX
0804847f 8b 45 0c        MOV     EAX,dword ptr [EBP + param_2]
08048482 89 45 f0        MOV     dword ptr [EBP + y],EAX❷
08048485 c7 45 ec        MOV     dword ptr [EBP + local_18],0xa
         0a 00 00 00
0804848c c6 45 ac 41     MOV     byte ptr [EBP + local_58],0x41
08048490 83 ec 08        SUB     ESP,0x8
08048493 ff 75 f0        PUSH    dword ptr [EBP + y]❸
08048496 ff 75 ec        PUSH    dword ptr [EBP + local_18]
08048499 e8 88 ff        CALL    helper
         ff ff
0804849e 83 c4 10        ADD     ESP,0x10
080484a1 90              NOP
080484a2 c9              LEAVE
080484a3 c3              RET
```

These changes ❶❷❸ are also reflected in the Symbol Tree, as shown in Figure 7-4.

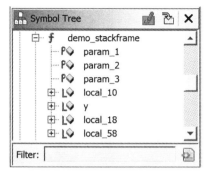

Figure 7-4: Symbol Tree view of renamed stack variable, y

THE FORBIDDEN NAMES

Some interesting rules restrict what you can name variables within a function. Here are some of the more relevant rules for parameters:

- You *can't* use the prefix param_ followed by an integer in a name, even if the resulting name does not conflict with an existing parameter name.

- You *can* use the prefix param_ followed by other characters.

- You *can* use the prefix Param_ followed by an integer, as names are case-sensitive (but it might not be advisable).

- You *can* restore a parameter name to its original Ghidra-assigned name by entering param_ followed by an integer value. If you use the original integer value, Ghidra will revert the name with no complaints. If you use any integer other than the original value, Ghidra will warn "Rename failed – default names may not be used." At this point, clicking Cancel in the Rename Parameter dialog will restore the original name.

- You *can* have two parameters with the names param_1 (named by Ghidra) and Param_1 (named by you). Names are case-sensitive, but it might not be advisable to reuse them.

Local variables are also case-sensitive, and you can use the prefix local_ with a non-numeric suffix.

For all types of variables, you *can't* use a variable name that's already used in that scope (for example, in the same function). Your attempt will be rejected with a reason in the dialog.

Finally, if you are thoroughly confused by your labels, you can see the label history for a variable by pressing the hotkey H, choosing Show All History, and entering the current name (or a past name) of the variable into the text box. (This option is also available through Search ▸ Label History in the main menu.)

Variable names can be changed from the Listing, Symbol Tree, and Decompiler windows; the outcome is the same regardless, but the dialog accessed from the Listing window presents more information. All rules associated with naming variables are enforced when using any of these methods.

Many of the example parameter names in this book were changed in the Listing window using the dialog shown on the left in Figure 7-5. To change a name in the Symbol Tree, right-click the name and select **Rename** from the context menu. In the Decompiler window, use the hotkey L, or use the **Rename Variable** context menu option; the corresponding dialog is shown on the right in Figure 7-5. While the two dialogs provide the same functionality, the right dialog does not include information about the namespace or properties associated with the parameter.

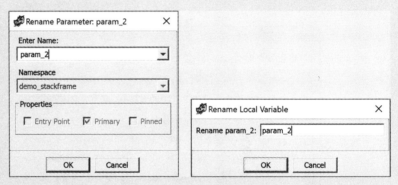

Figure 7-5: Renaming a variable from the Listing window or Symbol Tree (left) or the Decompiler window (right)

In Ghidra, a *namespace* is simply a named scope. Within a namespace, all symbols are unique. The global namespace contains all symbols within a binary. Function namespaces are nested within the global namespace. Within a function namespace, all variable names and labels are unique. Functions may themselves contain nested namespaces, such as a namespace associated with a switch statement (which allows case labels to be reused in separate namespaces; for example, when a function contains two switch statements that each have a case 10).

Renaming Labels

A label is a default or user-assigned name associated with a location. As with stack variables, the name-change dialog is opened with the hotkey L or context option Edit Label. When you change a location's name, you can also change its namespace and properties, as shown in Figure 7-6.

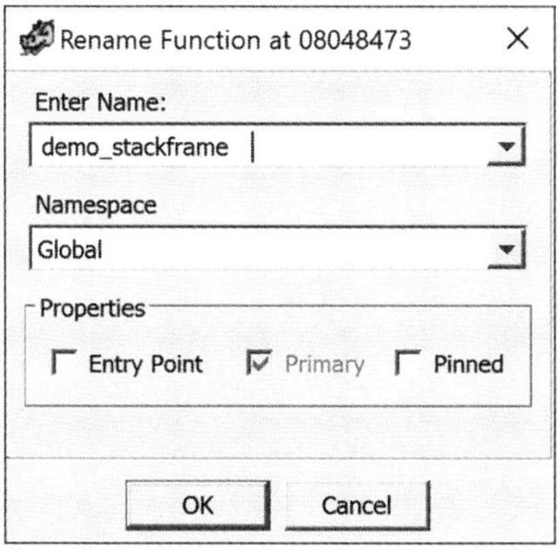

Figure 7-6: Renaming a function

This enhanced dialog shows the entity type and virtual address of the location in the title bar. Under Properties, you can identify the address as an entry point or pin the address (see "Editing Labels" on page 126). As mentioned in Chapter 6, Ghidra limits names to a maximum of 2000 characters, so feel free to use meaningful names or even embed a narrative about the address (without any spaces). The Listing window will display only a portion of the name if the length is excessive, but the Decompiler window shows the entire thing.

Adding a New Label

While Ghidra generates many default labels, you can also add new labels and associate them with any address in the listing. These can be used to annotate your disassembly, although in many cases *comments* (discussed later in this chapter) are a more appropriate mechanism for this. To add a new label, open the Add Label dialog (hotkey L), shown in Figure 7-7, for the address associated with the cursor location. The drop-down list for the name includes a list of names you have used recently, and the Namespace drop-down list lets you choose an appropriate label scope.

Figure 7-7: Add Label dialog

FUN_ WITH PREFIXES

When Ghidra creates labels during auto analysis, it uses meaningful prefixes followed by an address to let you know what to expect at that location. These prefixes are listed next with very general descriptions. More information about the meaning of each prefix can be found in Ghidra Help.

LAB_*address* Code—an auto-generated label (usually a jump target within a function)

DAT_*address* Data—an auto-generated global variable name

FUN_*address* Function—an auto-generated function name

SUB_*address* Target of a call (or equivalent)—probably not a function

EXT_*address* External entry point—probably someone else's function

OFF_*address* An offcut (inside existing data or code)—probably a disassembly error

UNK_*address* Unknown—the purpose of the data here can't be determined

Function labels have the following specific behaviors associated with them:

- If you delete a default function label (such as FUN_08048473) in the Listing window, the FUN_ prefix will be replaced by the SUB_ prefix (in this case, resulting in SUB_08048473).

- Adding a new label to an address that has a default FUN_ label changes the function name rather than creating a new label.

- Labels are case-sensitive, so you can use Fun_ or fun_ as a valid prefix if your desire is to create a confusing disassembly.

You can run into conflicts if you attempt to use one of Ghidra's reserved prefixes when entering a name. If you insist on using a reserved prefix, Ghidra will reject your new label if it believes that a name conflict might arise. This occurs only when Ghidra determines that your suffix looks like an address (in our experience, this means four or more hex digits). For example, Ghidra will allow FUN_zone and FUN_123, but will reject FUN_12345. Also, if you attempt to add a label at the same address as a function that has a default label (for example, FUN_08048473), Ghidra renames the function rather than adding a second label at that location.

Editing Labels

To edit a label, use the hotkey L or context menu option Edit Label. Editing a label presents you with the same dialog as adding a label, except that the fields in the dialog will be initialized with the current values for the existing label. Note that editing labels can have an effect on other labels that share the same address, whether or not they share the same namespace. For example, if you identify a label as an entry point, Ghidra will identify all labels associated with that location as entry points.

The Primary checkbox in Figure 7-7 indicates that this is the label that will be displayed when the address is displayed. By default, this checkbox is disabled for the primary label, so you cannot deselect the primary name. This is necessary to ensure that there is always a name to display. If another label were chosen as the primary, its checkbox would be disabled, and checkboxes for other labels at the same address would be enabled.

Although we have, up to now, associated labels with addresses, in reality labels are most commonly associated with content that happens to have an address. For example, the label main typically denotes the beginning of the block of code that is the main function in a program. Ghidra assigns an address to this location based on file header information. If we were to relocate the entire content of the binary to a new address range, we would expect that the label main would continue to correctly associate with the new address of main and its corresponding, unchanged byte content. When a label is *pinned*, the label's association with the content at its address is severed. If you were to then relocate the binary's content to a new address range, any pinned labels would not move accordingly, but remain fixed to the address that you pinned them to. The most common use of pinned labels is to name reset vectors and memory mapped I/O locations that exist at specific addresses designated by the processor/system designers.

Removing a Label

To remove a label at the cursor, you can use the right-click context option (or hotkey DELETE). Be warned that not all labels are removable. First, it is impossible to delete a default, Ghidra-generated label. Second, if you have renamed a default label and later decide to delete the new label, Ghidra will replace the name you are deleting with the originally assigned, default label (this is a direct result of the previous statement). The finer details associated with removing labels are discussed in Ghidra Help.

Navigating Labels

Labels are associated with navigable locations, so double-clicking a reference to a label will navigate you to that label. While this is discussed more thoroughly in Chapter 9, remember that you can add labels to any location you wish to navigate to in the disassembly. While the same functionality is described in "Annotations" on page 132, sometimes a label (particularly with its 2000-character allowance) is the quickest way to accomplish the same goal.

Comments

Embedding comments into your disassembly and decompiler listings is a particularly useful way to leave notes for yourself regarding your progress and discoveries as you analyze a program. Ghidra offers five categories of comments, each suited for a different purpose. We begin by looking at comments that we can add directly to the disassembly in the Listing window.

While you can navigate to the Set Comment dialog (shown in Figure 7-8) through the right-click context menu, the quickest way is to use the hotkey for comments, which is the semicolon (;) key. (This is a logical choice, as the semicolon is the comment indicator in many flavors of assembly.)

Figure 7-8: Set Comment dialog

The Set Comment dialog opens in association with a particular address: 08048479 in Figure 7-8, as displayed in the title bar. Any content entered into any one of the five comment category tabs (EOL, Pre, Post, Plate, and Repeatable Comments) is associated with that address.

By default, you enter content in the text box, including carriage returns, create a comment that is one or more lines long, and then click **Apply** or **OK**. (Apply allows you to see the comment in context and keeps the Set Comment dialog open for continued editing.) To save time when entering short comments, select the **Enter accepts comment** checkbox in the lower left of the dialog. (You can always deselect the box temporarily if you are writing a particularly informative plate comment.)

THOSE THREE BUTTONS

Of the three buttons at the bottom of the Set Comment dialog (Figure 7-8), the OK and Apply buttons behave as you might expect. Clicking OK closes the dialog and commits your changes. When you click Apply, the listing is updated so that you can examine your changes and approve them or continue editing your comment.

Dismiss, however, is not the same as Cancel, which would exit the dialog with no effect on your listing! The unique term is consistent with the unique behavior. Clicking the Dismiss button exits the window immediately if you have not modified any comments, but lets you decide whether you want to save changes if you did modify comments. Closing the window using the X in the top right exhibits the same behavior. This Dismiss functionality will be encountered in other places within Ghidra.

To delete a comment, clear a comment's text in the Set Comment dialog, or use the hotkey DELETE when the cursor is on a comment in the Listing window. Right-clicking Comments ▸ Show History for Comment can be used to recall the comments associated with a particular address and reinstate them as needed.

End-of-Line Comments

Perhaps the most commonly used type of comment is the *end-of-line (EOL) comment*, placed at the end of existing lines in the Listing window. To add one, open the Set Comment dialog with the semicolon hotkey and select the EOL Comment tab. By default, EOL comments are displayed as blue text and will span multiple lines if you enter multiple lines in the comment text box. Each line will be indented to align at the right side of the disassembly, and existing content will be moved down to make space for the new comments. You can edit your comments at any time by reopening the Set Comment dialog. The quickest method to delete a comment is to click the comment in the Listing window and press DELETE.

Ghidra itself adds many EOL comments during auto analysis. For example, when you load a PE file, Ghidra inserts descriptive EOL comments to describe the fields in the IMAGE_DOS_HEADER section, including the comment Magic number. Ghidra is able to do this only when it has this information associated with a particular data type. This information is typically contained within type libraries, which are displayed in the Data Type Manager window and discussed in depth in Chapter 8 and Chapter 13. Among all the comment types, EOL comments are the most configurable through the Edit ▸ Tool Options ▸ Listing Fields options for each comment type.

Pre and Post Comments

Pre and *post comments* are full-line comments that appear either immediately before or after a given disassembly line. The following listing shows a multi-line pre comment and a truncated single-line post comment, associated with address 08048476. Hovering over a truncated comment will display the complete comment. By default, pre comments are displayed in purple, and post comments are displayed in blue, so that you can easily associate them with the correct address in the listing.

```
08048473  PUSH    EBP
08048474  MOV     EBP,ESP
          ******** Pre Comment - This is a multi-line comment.
          ******** The following statement allocates 88 bytes of local
          ******** variable space in the stack frame.
08048476  SUB     ESP,0x58
          ******** Post Comment - Now that we have allocated the space...
08048479  MOV     EAX,dword ptr [EBP + param_3]
```

Plate Comments

Plate comments allow you to group comments for display anywhere in the Listing window. A plate comment is centered and placed within an asterisk-bounded rectangle. Many of the listings we have examined include a simple plate comment with the word FUNCTION inside the bounding box, as shown in Figure 7-9. This example includes the associated Decompiler window on the right side so you can see that, in this default presentation, a plate comment has been inserted in the Listing window, but no corresponding comment exists in the Decompiler window.

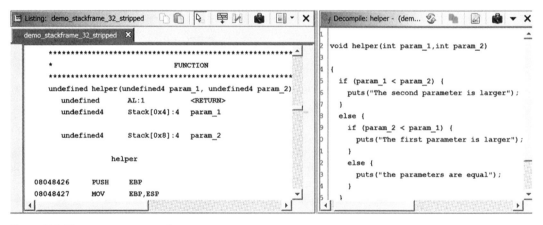

Figure 7-9: Plate comment example

When you open the comment dialog with the first address in the function selected, you have the option to replace this general plate comment with your own, more informative one, as shown in Figure 7-10. In addition to replacing the default plate comment, Ghidra adds your comment as a C-style comment at the top of the Decompiler window. If the cursor were at the top of the Decompiler window when the plate comment was created, the result would have been the same.

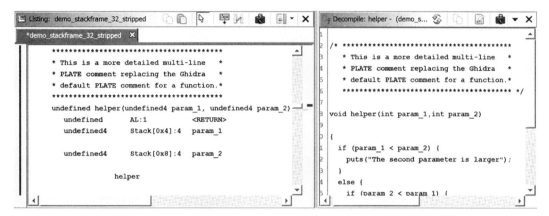

Figure 7-10: Custom plate comment example

NOTE *Only plate and pre comments are displayed in the Decompiler window by default, although you can change this using options in Edit ▶ Tool Options ▶ Decompiler ▶ Display.*

Repeatable Comments

A *repeatable comment* is entered once but may appear automatically in many locations throughout the disassembly. The behavior of repeatable comments is tied to the concept of cross-references, which are discussed in depth in Chapter 9. Basically, a repeatable comment entered at the target of a cross-reference is echoed at the source of a cross-reference. As a result, a single repeatable comment may be echoed at many locations in the disassembly (because cross-references can be many-to-one). In a disassembly listing, the default color is orange for repeatable comments and gray for echoed comments, making them easily distinguishable from other types of comments. The following listing demonstates the use of a repeatable comment.

```
08048432  JGE    LAB_08048446                      Repeatable comment at 08048446❶
08048434  SUB    ESP,0xc
08048437  PUSH   s_The_second_parameter_is_larger
0804843c  CALL   puts
08048441  ADD    ESP,0x10
08048444  JMP    LAB_08048470
         LAB_08048446
08048446  MOV    EAX,dword ptr [EBP + param_2] Repeatable comment at 08048446❷
```

In the listing, a repeatable comment is set at 08048446 ❷ and repeated at 08048432 ❶ because the instruction at 08048432 refers to address 08048446 as a jump target (thus a cross-reference exists from 08048432 to 08048446).

When an EOL comment and a repeatable comment share the same address, only the EOL comment is visible in the listing. Both comments can be viewed and edited in the Set Comment dialog. If you delete the EOL comment, the repeatable comment will become visible in the listing.

Parameter and Local Variable Comments

To associate a comment with a stack variable, select the stack variable and use the semicolon hotkey. Figure 7-11 shows the resulting minimal comment window. The comment will be displayed next to the stack variable in a truncated format similar to an EOL comment. Hovering over the comment will display it in its entirety. The color of the comment matches the default color of the variable type, rather than the blue default for EOL comments.

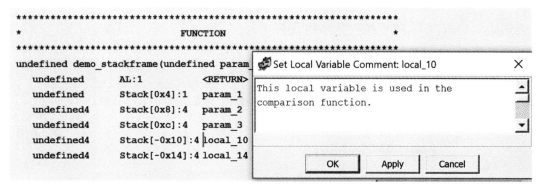

Figure 7-11: Stack variable comment

Annotations

Ghidra provides a powerful capability to annotate comments with links to programs, URLs, addresses, and symbols in its Set Comment dialog. Symbol information in comments will automatically update when symbol names are changed. When you use an annotation to launch a specified executable, you can provide optional parameters to gain even more control (yes, that sounds dangerous to us, too).

For example, the annotation on a plate comment in Figure 7-12 provides a hyperlink to an address in the listing. Additional information about the power of annotations is provided in Ghidra Help.

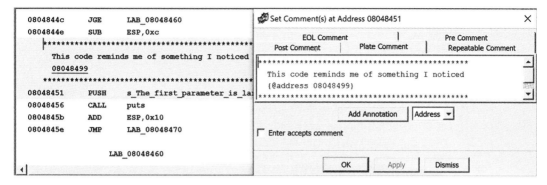

Figure 7-12: Address annotation example

Basic Code Transformations

In many cases, you will be perfectly content with the disassembly listings that Ghidra generates. In some cases, however, you won't. As the types of files that you analyze diverge further and further from ordinary executables generated with common compilers, you may need to take more control of the disassembly analysis and display processes. This will be especially true if you analyze obfuscated code or files that utilize a custom (unknown to Ghidra) file format.

Ghidra facilitates the following code transformations (among others):

- Changing code display options
- Formatting instruction operands
- Manipulating functions
- Converting data into code
- Converting code into data

In general, if a binary is very complex, or if Ghidra is not familiar with the code sequences generated by the compiler used to build the binary, then Ghidra will encounter more problems during the analysis phase, and you will need to make manual adjustments to the disassembled code.

Changing Code Display Options

Ghidra allows very fine-grained control over the formatting of lines within the Listing window. Layout is controlled with the Browser Field Formatter (introduced in Chapter 5). Selecting the Browser Field Formatter icon opens a tabbed display of all the fields associated with your listing, as displayed in Figure 5-8. You can add, delete, and rearrange fields by using a simple drag-and-drop interface that allows you to immediately observe the changes in your listing. The tight association between an item in the listing field and in the associated Browser Field Formatter is very useful. Anytime you move the cursor to a new location in the Listing window, the Browser Field Formatter moves the appropriate tab and associated field so that you can immediately identify options associated with a particular item. See "Special Tool Editing Features" on page 247 for additional discussion of the Browser Field Formatter.

To control the appearance of individual elements within the Listing window, you can select Edit ▶ Tool Options, as described in Chapter 4. The unique submenus for each field in the Listing window allow you to fine-tune each field to your liking. While the capabilities associated with each field vary, in general you can control display colors, associated default values, configurations, and formats. For example, users who love assembly code and read it in their spare time may choose to adjust the default parameters in the EOL Comments Field area, shown in Figure 7-13, to activate the Show Semicolon at Start of Each Line option in order to view the assembly comments in a familiar format.

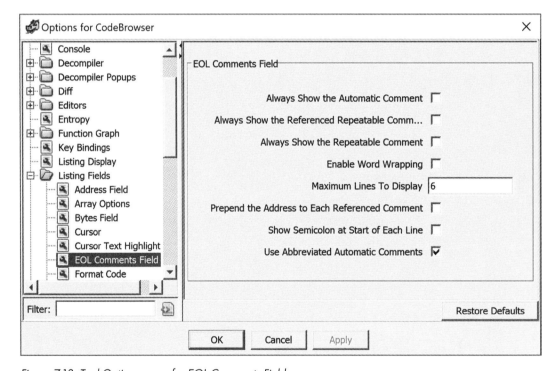

Figure 7-13: Tool Options menu for EOL Comments Field

To color the background for individual lines or larger selections in the Listing window, select the Colors option through the right-click context menu and choose a color. The range of available colors is extensive, and a quick pick option is provided for recently used colors. Through the same menu, you can also clear the background color for a line, a selection, or an entire file.

NOTE   *Clearing options do not appear if no colors are currently set for the listing.*

Formatting Instruction Operands

During the auto analysis process, Ghidra makes many decisions regarding how to format operands associated with each instruction, especially various integer constants used by a wide variety of instruction types. Among other things, these constants can represent relative offsets in jump or call instructions, absolute addresses of global variables, values to be used in arithmetic operations, or programmer-defined constants. To make a disassembly more readable, Ghidra attempts to use symbolic names rather than numbers whenever possible.

In some cases, formatting decisions are made based on the context of the instruction being disassembled (such as a call instruction); in other cases, the decision is based on the data being used (such as access to a global variable or an offset into a stack frame or structure). Often, the exact context in which a constant is used may not be discernable to Ghidra. When this happens, the constant is typically formatted as a hexadecimal value.

If you are not one of the few people in the world who eat, sleep, and breathe hex, then you will welcome Ghidra's operand-formatting features. Assume that you have the following in your disassembly listing:

```
08048485   MOV    dword ptr [EBP + local_18],0xa
0804848c   MOV    byte ptr [EBP + local_58],0x41
```

Right-clicking the hex constant 0x41 opens the context-sensitive menu shown in Figure 7-14. (See Figure 6-7 for this example in context.) The constant can be reformatted in the various numeric representations displayed on the right side of the figure, or as a character constant (since this value also falls within the ASCII printable range). This can be a very helpful feature as you may not realize the many representations that can be associated with a given constant. In all cases, the menu displays the exact text that will replace the operand text should a particular option be selected.

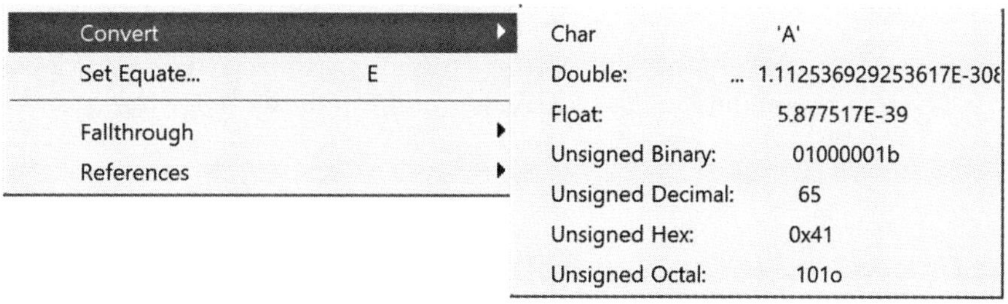

Convert			Char	'A'
Set Equate...	E		Double:	... 1.112536929253617E-30&
			Float:	5.877517E-39
Fallthrough		▶	Unsigned Binary:	01000001b
References		▶	Unsigned Decimal:	65
			Unsigned Hex:	0x41
			Unsigned Octal:	101o

Figure 7-14: Formatting options for constants

In many cases, programmers use named constants in their source code. Such constants may be the result of #define statements (or their equivalent), or they may belong to a set of enumerated constants. Unfortunately, by the time a compiler is finished with the source code, it is no longer possible to determine whether the source used a symbolic constant or a literal, numeric constant. Fortunately, Ghidra maintains a large catalog of named constants associated with many common libraries, such as the C standard library or the Windows API. This catalog is accessible via the Set Equate option (hotkey E) on the context-sensitive menu associated with any constant value. Selecting this option for the constant 0xa opens the Set Equate dialog (Figure 7-15).

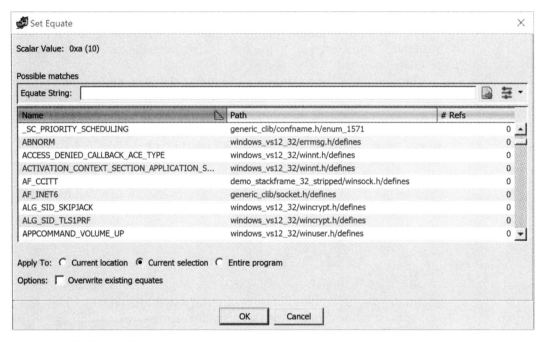

Figure 7-15: Set Equate dialog

The dialog is populated from Ghidra's internal list of constants after filtering according to the value of the constant we are attempting to format. In this case, we can scroll to see all of the constants that Ghidra knows to be equated with the value 0xA. If we determined that the value was being used in conjunction with the creation of an X.25-style network connection, we might select AF_CCITT and end up with the following disassembly line:

```
08048485  MOV    dword ptr [EBP + local_18],AF_CCITT
```

The list of standard constants is useful to determine whether a particular constant may be associated with a known name and can save a lot of time reading through API documentation in search of potential matches.

Manipulating Functions

Ghidra provides the capability to manipulate functions in the disassembly (for example, correcting which code Ghidra identifies as belonging to functions, or changing function attributes), which is especially helpful when you disagree with the results of the auto analysis. In some cases, such as when Ghidra fails to locate a call to a function, functions may not be recognized, as there may be no obvious way to reach them. In other cases, Ghidra may fail to properly locate the end of a function, requiring you to correct the disassembly. Ghidra may have trouble locating the end of a function if a compiler has split the function across several address ranges or when, in the process of optimizing code, a compiler merges common end sequences of two or more functions in order to save space.

Creating New Functions

New functions can be created from existing instructions that do not already belong to a function. You create functions by right-clicking the first instruction to be included in the new function and selecting Create Function (or hotkey F). If you selected a range, that will become the function body. If you did not, Ghidra will follow the control flow to try to determine the bounds of the function body.

Deleting Functions

You can delete existing functions by placing the cursor within the function signature and using the hotkey DELETE. You may wish to delete a function if you believe that Ghidra has erred in its auto analysis or you have erred in creating a function. Note that while the function and its associated attributes will no longer exist, no change occurs to the underlying byte content, so the function can be re-created if desired.

Editing Function Attributes

Ghidra associates several attributes with each function that it recognizes, which can be viewed by selecting the Window ▸ Functions option from the CodeBrowser menu. (While only five attributes are displayed by default, you can add any of 16 additional attributes by right-clicking in a column heading.) To edit the attributes, open the Edit Function dialog from the right-click context menu when the cursor is positioned in the region between a function's plate comment and the last local variable listed before the beginning of the function's disassembled code. An example of the Edit Function dialog is shown in Figure 7-16.

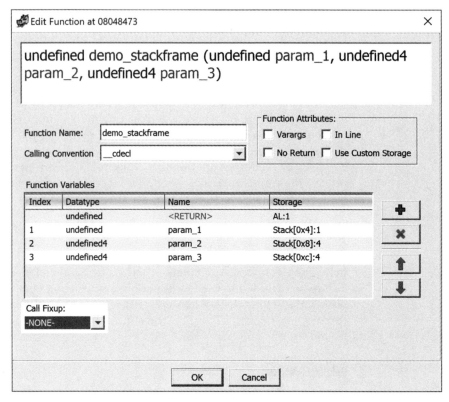

Figure 7-16: Edit Function dialog

Each attribute that can be modified through this dialog is explained here:

Function Name

You can modify the name within the text box at the top of the dialog or within the Function Name field.

Function Attributes

Five optional function attributes can be enabled in this area. The first four attributes, Varargs, In Line, No Return, and Use Custom Storage, are checkboxes that are unchecked by default. The fifth optional attribute, Call Fixup, appears in the bottom left of the dialog, defaults to none, and provides a drop-down menu from which you can choose a value. If you modify any of the function's attributes, Ghidra automatically propagates the function's updated prototype to all locations at which it may be displayed throughout the disassembly.

The Varargs option indicates that a function takes a variable number of arguments (for example, printf). Varargs is also enabled if you edit (in the text field at the top of Figure 7-16) the function's parameter list such that the last argument has an ellipsis (. . .). The In Line option has no effect on disassembly analysis other than to include the inline keyword in the function's prototype. (Keep in mind that if a function were actually inlined by a compiler, you would not see that function as a distinct entity in a disassembly because its body would have been embedded within the body of the functions that call it.) The No Return option is used when it is known that a function will never return (for example, if it uses exit or an opaque predicate to jump to another function). When a function is tagged as No Return, Ghidra will not assume that the bytes following a call to that function are reachable unless it has other evidence to support their reachability, such as a jump instruction targeting those bytes. The Use Custom Storage option allows you to override Ghidra's analysis of parameter and return value storage locations and sizes.

Calling Convention

The Calling Convention drop-down allows you to modify the calling convention used by the function. Modifying the calling convention may change Ghidra's stack pointer analysis, so it is important to get this correct.

Function Variables

The Function Variables area allows you to edit function variables with guidance. As you modify the data in the four columns associated with the variables, Ghidra will provide information to help you change things appropriately. For example, attempts to change the Storage for param_1 will result in a message saying Enable 'Use Custom Storage' to allow editing of Parameter and Return Storage. The four icons on the right allow you to add, delete, and navigate through the variables.

Converting Data to Code (and Vice Versa)

During the automatic analysis phase, data bytes may be incorrectly classified as code bytes and disassembled into instructions, or code bytes may be incorrectly classified as data bytes and formatted as data values. This happens for many reasons, including because some compilers embed data into the code section of programs and because some code bytes are never directly referenced as code and thus Ghidra opts not to disassemble them. Obfuscated programs in particular tend to deliberately blur the distinction between code and data. (See Chapter 21.)

The first option for reformatting anything is to remove its current formatting (code or data). It is possible to undefine functions, code, or data by right-clicking the item you wish to undefine and selecting Clear Code Bytes (hotkey C). Undefining an item causes the underlying bytes to be reformatted as a list of raw byte values. Large regions can be undefined by using a click-and-drag operation to select a range of addresses prior to performing the undefine operation. As an example, consider this simple function listing:

```
004013e0   PUSH   EBP
004013e1   MOV    EBP,ESP
004013e3   POP    EBP
004013e4   RET
```

Undefining this function would yield the series of uncategorized bytes shown here, which we could reformat in virtually any manner:

004013e0	??	55h	U
004013e1	??	89h	
004013e2	??	E5h	
004013e3	??	5Dh	]
004013e4	??	C3h	

To disassemble a sequence of undefined bytes, right-click the first byte to be disassembled and select **Disassemble**. This causes Ghidra to start the recursive descent algorithm at that point. Large regions can be converted to code by using click-and-drag to select a range of addresses prior to performing the code-conversion operation.

Converting code to data is a little more complex. First, you cannot directly convert code to data by using the context menu, unless you first undefine the instructions that you wish to convert to data and then format the bytes appropriately. Basic data formatting is discussed in the following section.

Basic Data Transformations

To understand a program's behavior, properly formatted data can be as important as properly formatted code. Ghidra takes information from a variety of sources and uses an algorithmic approach to determine the most appropriate way to format data within a disassembly. For example:

- Data types and/or sizes can be inferred from the manner in which registers are used. An instruction that loads a 32-bit register from memory implies that the associated memory location holds a 4-byte data type (though we may not be able to distinguish between a 4-byte integer and a 4-byte pointer).

- Function prototypes can be used to assign data types to function parameters. Ghidra maintains a large library of function prototypes for exactly this purpose. Analysis is performed on the parameters passed to functions in an attempt to tie a parameter to a memory location. If such a relationship can be uncovered, a data type can be applied to the associated memory location. Consider a function whose single parameter is a pointer to a CRITICAL_SECTION (a Windows API data type). If Ghidra can determine the address passed in a call to this function, that address can be flagged as a CRITICAL_SECTION object.

- Analysis of a sequence of bytes can reveal likely data types. This is precisely what happens when a binary is scanned for string content. When long sequences of ASCII characters are encountered, it is not unreasonable to assume that they represent character arrays.

In the next few sections, we discuss some basic transformations that you can perform on data within your disassemblies.

Specifying Data Types

Ghidra offers data size and type specifiers. The most commonly encountered specifiers are byte, word, dword, and qword, representing 1-, 2-, 4-, and 8-byte data, respectively. Data types can be set or changed by right-clicking any disassembly line that contains data (that is not an instruction) and selecting the Set Data Type submenu shown in Figure 7-17.

Array...	Open Bracket
Auto Create Structure	Shift+Open Bracket
Choose Data Type...	T
Cycle	▶
TerminatedCString	
TerminatedUnicode	
byte	
char	
double	
dword	
float	
int	
long	
longdouble	
pointer	P
qword	
string	
uint	
ulong	
undefined	
void	V
word	
Last Used: <empty>	Y

Figure 7-17: The Data submenu

This list allows you to immediately change the formatting and data size of the currently selected item by choosing a data type. The Cycle option lets you quickly cycle through a group of associated data types, such as numeric, character, and floating point types, as shown (with associated hotkeys) in Figure 7-18. For example, repeatedly pressing F would cycle you between float and double, as they are the only items in that cycle group.

Cycle: byte,word,dword,qword	B
Cycle: char,string,unicode	Quote
Cycle: float,double	F

Figure 7-18: Cycle groups

Toggling through data types causes data items to grow, shrink, or remain the same size. If an item's size remains the same, the only observable change is in the way the data is formatted. If you reduce an item's size, from ddw (4 bytes) to db (1 byte), for example, any extra bytes (3 in this case) become undefined. If you increase the size of an item, Ghidra will warn you of any conflict and guide you through resolving it. An example involving array dimensioning is shown in Figure 7-19.

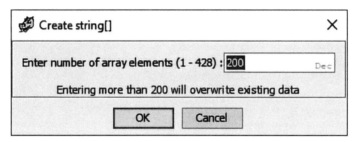

Figure 7-19: Example of an array declaration and warning

Working with Strings

Choosing Search ▸ For Strings brings up the dialog shown in Figure 7-20, where you can set and control the search criteria for a specific string search. While most of the fields in this window are self-explanatory, a unique feature of Ghidra is the ability to associate a *word model* with a search. A word model can be used to determine whether a particular string is considered a word in a given context. Word models are discussed in Chapter 13.

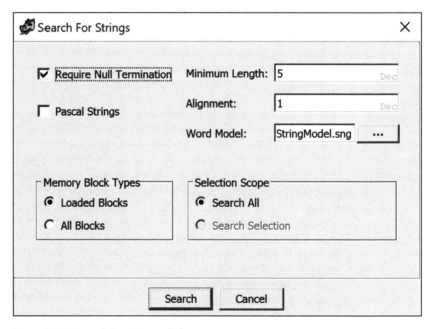

Figure 7-20: Search For Strings dialog

Once a search has been conducted, the results are presented in a String Search window (Figure 7-21). Subsequent searches will be tabbed within the same window, and the window title bar will include timestamps for each search so you can easily order them.

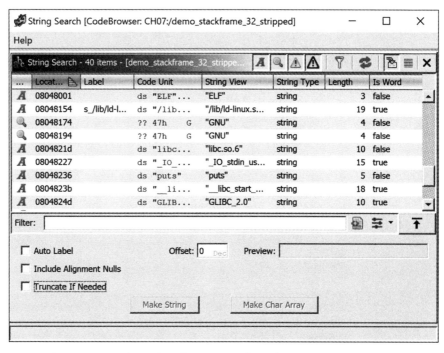

Figure 7-21: String Search window showing search results

The leftmost column of the String Search window contains icons that indicate the string definition status (from undefined to conflicting). The meanings of the icons are shown in Figure 7-22. To show or hide strings in any of the categories, toggle the corresponding icons in the title bar.

Icon	Definition
A	The string is already defined (and thus appears in the Defined Strings window). Such strings are usually the target of a cross-reference.
🔍	The string is not defined. The string is not the target of a cross-reference, and the bytes generally appear as individual hex values.
⚠	Part of the string has been defined. Usually this is a string that has a defined string as a substring.
⚠	The string conflicts (overlaps) with something already defined such as existing instructions or data.

Figure 7-22: String toggle icon definitions

Using the icons allows you to easily identify the items in the listing that are not already defined as strings and make a string or character array from these entries by selecting them and clicking the Make String or Make Char Array button, as appropriate. These newly defined entities will be displayed in the Defined Strings window, which is discussed in "The Defined Strings Window" on page 81.

Defining Arrays

One of the drawbacks to disassembly listings derived from higher-level languages is that they provide very few clues regarding the size of arrays. In a disassembly listing, an array can require a tremendous amount of space if each item in the array is specified on its own line. The following listing shows a sequence of items in a data section. The fact that only the first item in the listing is referenced by any instructions suggests that it may be the first element in an array. Rather than being referenced directly, additional elements within arrays are often referenced using index computations relative to the beginning of the array.

```
          DAT_004195a4                      XREF[1]:  main:00411727(W)
004195a4    undefined4    ??
004195a8      ??          ??
004195a9      ??          ??
004195aa      ??          ??
004195ab      ??          ??
004195ac      ??          ??
004195ad      ??          ??
004195ae      ??          ??
004195af      ??          ??
004195b0      ??          ??
004195b1      ??          ??
004195b2      ??          ??
004195b3      ??          ??
004195b4      ??          ??
004195b5      ??          ??
004195b6      ??          ??
```

Ghidra can group consecutive data definitions into a single array definition. To create an array, select the first element of the array and use the Data ▶ Create Array option in the context menu (hotkey [). You will be prompted for the number of elements in the array, or you can accept the default that Ghidra suggests. (If you have selected a range of data, rather than a single value, Ghidra will use your selection as the array bounds.) By default, the data type and size associated with the array elements are based on the data type of the first element in the selection. The array is presented in a collapsed format, but can be expanded to view the individual elements. The number of elements displayed per line is controlled in the Edit ▶ Tool Options of the CodeBrowser window. Arrays are discussed more thoroughly in Chapter 8.

Summary

Together with the previous chapter, this chapter encompasses the most common operations that Ghidra users will ever need to perform. Disassembly manipulation lets you combine your knowledge with the knowledge imparted by Ghidra during its analysis phase to produce valuable information. As in source code, the effective use of names, assignment of data types, and detailed comments will not only assist you in remembering what you have analyzed but also greatly assist others who make use of your work. In the next chapter, we take a look at how to deal with more complex data structures, such as the C struct, and examine some of the low-level details of compiled C++.

8

DATA TYPES AND DATA STRUCTURES

Understanding the data types and data structures that you encounter as you analyze a binary is foundational to reverse engineering. The data that is being passed into a function is a key to reverse engineering the function's signature (the number, type, and sequence of parameters required by the function). Beyond that, the data types and data structures declared and utilized within functions provide additional clues to what each function is doing. This reinforces the importance of developing a deep understanding of how data types and data structures are represented and manipulated at the assembly language level.

In this chapter, we devote significant time to these topics that are so critical to the success of a reverse engineering effort. We demonstrate how to recognize data structures used in a disassembly and to model those structures in Ghidra. We follow with a demonstration of how Ghidra's rich collection of structure layouts can save you time with your analysis. Since C++ classes are a complex extension of C structures, the chapter concludes with a discussion of reverse engineering compiled C++ programs. So let's begin our discussion of the manipulation and definition of simple and complex data types and structures found within compiled programs.

Making Sense of Data

As a reverse engineer, you want to make sense of the data you see in a disassembly. The simplest method for associating a specific data type with a variable is to observe the use of the variable as a parameter to a function that we know something about. During its analysis phase, Ghidra makes every effort to annotate data types when they can be deduced based on a variable's use with a function for which Ghidra possesses a prototype.

With imported library functions, Ghidra often will already know the prototype of the function. In such cases, you can easily view the prototype by hovering over the function name in the Listing window or the Symbol Tree window. When Ghidra has no knowledge of a function's parameter sequence, it should, at a minimum, know the name of the library from which the function was imported (see the *Imports* folder in the Symbol Tree window). When this happens, your best resources for learning the signature and behavior of the function are any associated man pages or other available API documentation. When all else fails, remember the adage "Google is your friend."

The low-hanging fruit in understanding the behavior of binary programs lies in cataloging the library functions that the program calls. A C program that calls the connect function is creating a network connection. A Windows program that calls RegOpenKey is accessing the Windows registry. Additional analysis is required, however, to gain an understanding of how and why these functions are called.

Discovering how a function is called requires learning about the parameters associated with the function. Let's consider a C program that calls the connect function as part of retrieving an HTML page. To call connect, the program needs to know the IP address and destination port of the server that is hosting the page, which is provided by a library function called getaddrinfo. Ghidra recognizes this as a library function and adds a comment to the call to provide us with additional information in the Listing window, as shown here:

```
00100a30  CALL  getaddrinfo    int getaddrinfo(char * __name, c...
```

You can obtain more information about this call in several ways. Hovering over the abbreviated comment to the right of the instruction shows that Ghidra has provided the complete function prototype to help you understand the parameters that are being passed in the function call. Hovering over the function name in the Symbol Tree displays the function prototype and variables in a pop-up window. Alternatively, choosing Edit Function from the right-click menu provides the same information in an editable format, as shown in Figure 8-1. If you want even more information, you can then use the Data Type Manager window to find information on specific parameters such as the addrinfo data type. If you had clicked getaddrinfo in the preceding listing, you would see that the content shown in Figure 8-1 is replicated within the listing. (This is within a thunk function, which is discussed in "Thunk" on page 212.)

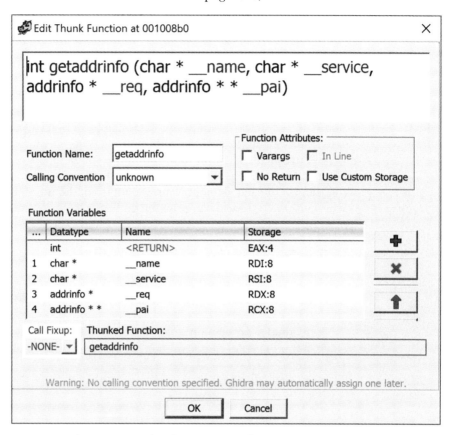

Figure 8-1: Edit Function window for getaddrinfo function

Finally, you aren't required to navigate through the Symbol Tree and Data Type Manager windows to make these observations, as the decompiler has already applied this information in the Decompiler window. If you look at the Decompiler window, you will see that Ghidra has already incorporated member names for the fields contained within the structure (addrinfo) by using information from loaded type libraries. For the same example, in the following excerpt of code from the decompiler, you can see that the member names ai_family and ai_socktype help us understand that local_48 is a structure that is used when getting the information needed for connect. In this case, the ai_family assignment indicates that an IPv4 address is being used (2 equates to the symbolic constant AF_INET), and ai_socktype indicates the use of a stream socket (1 equates to the symbolic constant SOCK_STREAM):

```
local_48.ai_family = 2;
local_48.ai_socktype = 1;
local_10 = getaddrinfo(param_1,"www",&local_48,&local_18);
```

Recognizing Data Structure Use

While primitive data types often fit in a processor's registers or instruction operands, composite data types such as arrays and structures typically require more complex instruction sequences in order to access the individual data items they contain. Before we can discuss Ghidra's features for improving the readability of code that utilizes complex data types, we need to review what that code looks like.

Array Member Access

Arrays are the simplest composite data structures in terms of memory layout. Traditionally, arrays are contiguous blocks of memory that contain consecutive elements of the same data type (a homogeneous collection). The size of an array is the product of the number of elements in the array and the size of each element. Using C notation, the minimum number of bytes consumed by declaring the integer array

```
int array_demo[100];
```

is computed as

```
int bytes = 100 * sizeof(int); // or 100 * sizeof(array_demo[0])
```

Individual array elements can be accessed by supplying an index value, which may be a variable or a constant, as shown in these valid array references:

```
❶ array_demo[20] = 15;              // fixed index into the array
   for (int i = 0; i < 100; i++) {
   ❷ array_demo[i] = i;             // varying index into the array
```

Assuming, for the sake of example, that sizeof(int)is 4 bytes, then the first array access ❶ accesses the integer value that lies 80 bytes into the array, while the second array access ❷ accesses integers at offsets 0, 4, 8, . . . 96 bytes into the array. The offset for the first array access can be computed at compile time as 20 * 4. In most cases, the offset for the second array access must be computed at runtime because the value of the loop counter, i, is not fixed at compile time. Thus, the product i * 4 is computed on each pass through the loop to determine the exact offset into the array.

Ultimately, how an array element is accessed depends not only on the type of index used but also on where the array is allocated within the program's memory space.

Globally Allocated Arrays

When an array is allocated within the global data area of a program (within the .data or .bss section, for example), the compiler knows the base address of the array at compile time, which enables the compiler to compute fixed addresses for any array element that is accessed using a fixed index. Consider the following trivial program, which accesses a global array using both fixed and variable indices.

```
int global_array[3];
int main(int argc, char **argv) {
    int idx = atoi(argv[1]); //not bounds checked for simplicity
    global_array[0] = 10;
    global_array[1] = 20;
    global_array[2] = 30;
    global_array[idx] = 40;
}
```

WHAT IS C REALLY EXPECTING?

For simplicity, we said that C is expecting an integer index as either a variable or a constant. In reality, any expression that can be evaluated to or interpreted as an integer will do. The general guideline is, "anywhere you can use an integer, you can use an expression that evaluates to an integer." Of course, this is not limited to just integers. C is perfectly happy to evaluate any expression you provide and try to make it work for the variable type expected. What if the values are outside the bounds of the array? You have the makings of numerous exploitable vulnerabilities, of course! Values will be read from or written to the resulting out-of-bounds memory region, or the program will simply crash if the computed target address is not valid within the program.

If we disassemble a stripped version of the corresponding binary, the main function contains the following code:

```
          ...
00100657  CALL    atoi
0010065c  MOV     dword ptr [RBP + local_c],EAX
0010065f  MOV     dword ptr [DAT_00301018],10❶
00100669  MOV     dword ptr [DAT_0030101c],20❷
00100673  MOV     dword ptr [DAT_00301020],30❸
0010067d  MOV     EAX,dword ptr [RBP + local_c]
00100680  CDQE
00100682  LEA     RDX,[RAX*4]❹
0010068a  LEA     RAX,[DAT_00301018]❺
00100691  MOV     dword ptr [RDX + RAX*1]=>DAT_00301018,40❻
          ...
```

While this program has only one global variable (the global array), the disassembly lines ❶ ❷❸ seem to indicate three global variables: DAT_00301018, DAT_0030101c, and DAT_00301020, respectively. However, the LEA instruction ❺ loads the address of a global variable seen previously ❶. In

this context, when combined with the computation of an offset (RAX*4) ❹,
and scaled memory access ❺, DAT_00301018 is most likely the base address of a
global array. The annotated operand =>DAT_00301018 ❻ provides us with the
base of the array into which 40 will be written.

WHAT'S A STRIPPED BINARY?

When compilers generate object files, they must include enough information
for the linker to be able to do its job. One of the linker's jobs is to resolve references between object files, such as a call to a function whose body resides in
a different file, utilizing information from a compiler-generated symbol. In many
cases, the linker combines all of the symbol table information from the object
files and includes the consolidated information in the resulting executable file.
This information is not necessary for the executable to run properly, but it is
very useful from a reverse engineering perspective, as Ghidra (and other tools
like debuggers) can use the symbol table information to recover function and
global variable names and sizes.

Stripping a binary means removing portions of an executable file that are
not essential to the runtime operation of the binary. This can be accomplished
by using the command-line strip utility to post-process an executable, or by
providing build options to the compiler and/or linker (-s for gcc/ld) to have
them generate a stripped binary themselves. In addition to symbol table information, strip can remove any debugging symbol information, such as local
variable names and type information, that were embedded in a binary when
it was built. Lacking symbol information, reverse engineering tools must have
algorithms for both identifying and naming functions and data.

Based on the names assigned by Ghidra, we know that the global
array starts with the 12 bytes beginning at address 00301018. During compilation, the compiler used the fixed indices (0, 1, 2) to compute the actual
addresses of the corresponding elements in the array (00301018, 0030101c, and
00301020), which are referenced using the global variables at ❶, ❷, and ❸.
Based on the values being moved into these locations, we can surmise that
we are moving 32-bit integer (dword) values into this array. If we navigate to
the associated data in the listing, we see the following content:

```
        DAT_00301018
00301018      ??        ??
00301019      ??        ??
0030101a      ??        ??
0030101b      ??        ??
        DAT_0030101c
0030101c      ??        ??
0030101d      ??        ??
0030101e      ??        ??
0030101f      ??        ??
```

```
          DAT_00301020
00301020      ??        ??
00301021      ??        ??
00301022      ??        ??
00301023      ??        ??
```

The question marks indicate that this array is probably allocated within the program's .bss section and that no initialization values are present within the file image.

It is easier to recognize an array in disassembly when it is accessed using variable indices. When constant indices are used to access global arrays, the corresponding array elements appear as global variables in the disassembly. However, the use of variable index values reveals the base address of the array at ❺ and the size of the individual elements at ❹, because the offset into the array must be computed using the index. (Such scaling operations are required to convert an integer array index from C to a byte offset for the correct array element in assembly language.)

Using Ghidra's type- and array-formatting operations discussed in the previous chapter (Data ▶ Create Array), we can format DAT_000301018 as a three-element integer array, yielding disassembly lines with a named array accessed with indices rather than offsets:

```
00100660  MOV     dword ptr [INT_ARRAY_00301018],10
0010066a  MOV     dword ptr [INT_ARRAY_00301018[1]],20
00100674  MOV     dword ptr [INT_ARRAY_00301018[2]],30
```

The default array name assigned by Ghidra, INT_ARRAY_00301018, includes the array type as well as the starting address of the array.

UPDATING SYMBOL INFORMATION IN COMMENTS

As you begin identifying data types, changing symbol names, and so on, you can make sure that the valuable comments you have added to your listing don't become outdated, or challenging to follow, by using comment annotations that update automatically. The Symbol annotation option lets you include references to symbols that will be updated as you change the symbols to accurately reflect your findings. (See "Annotations" on page 132.)

Let's look at the Decompiler window before (Figure 8-2) and after (Figure 8-3) the array has been created. In Figure 8-2, the important warning on line 2 is another clue that you might be looking at an array, and the assignment of integer values supports the assumption that the array type is integer.

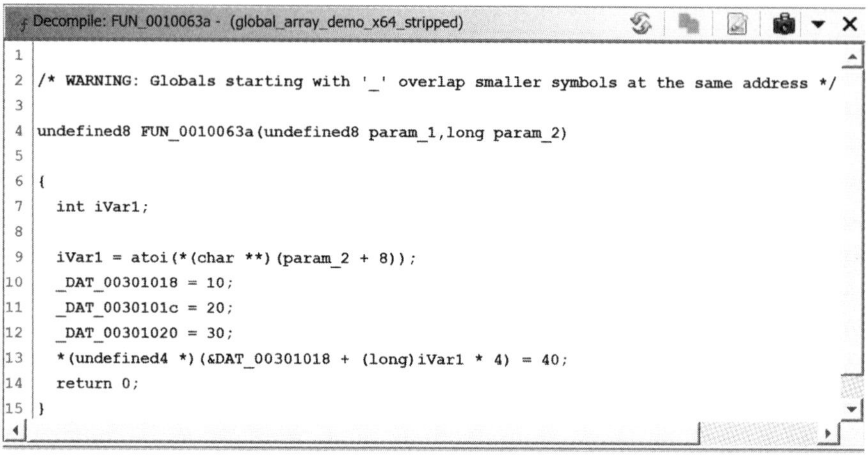

```
 1
 2 /* WARNING: Globals starting with '_' overlap smaller symbols at the same address */
 3
 4 undefined8 FUN_0010063a(undefined8 param_1,long param_2)
 5
 6 {
 7   int iVar1;
 8
 9   iVar1 = atoi(*(char **)(param_2 + 8));
10   _DAT_00301018 = 10;
11   _DAT_0030101c = 20;
12   _DAT_00301020 = 30;
13   *(undefined4 *)(&DAT_00301018 + (long)iVar1 * 4) = 40;
14   return 0;
15 }
```

Figure 8-2: Decompiler view indicating potential array

After the integer array is created, the code in the Decompiler window is updated to use the new array variable, as shown in Figure 8-3.

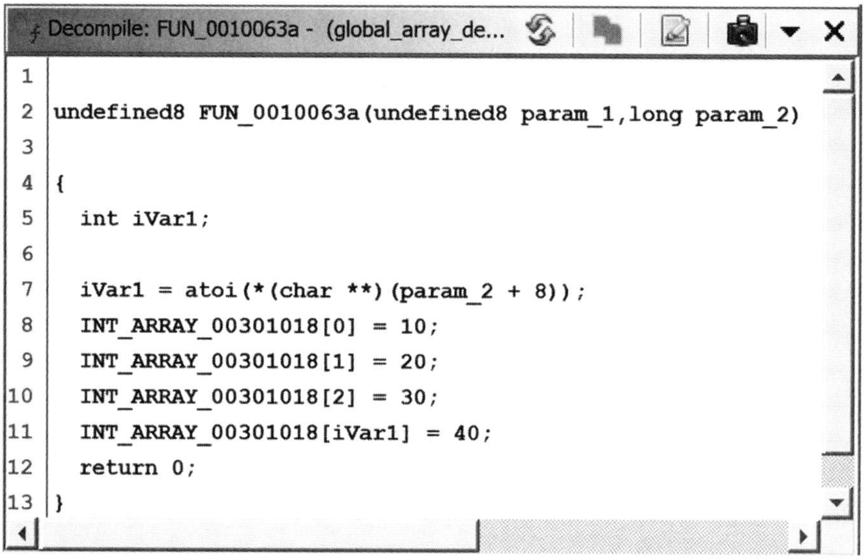

```
 1
 2 undefined8 FUN_0010063a(undefined8 param_1,long param_2)
 3
 4 {
 5   int iVar1;
 6
 7   iVar1 = atoi(*(char **)(param_2 + 8));
 8   INT_ARRAY_00301018[0] = 10;
 9   INT_ARRAY_00301018[1] = 20;
10   INT_ARRAY_00301018[2] = 30;
11   INT_ARRAY_00301018[iVar1] = 40;
12   return 0;
13 }
```

Figure 8-3: Decompiler view after declaring array type

Stack-Allocated Arrays

The compiler can't know the absolute address of an array allocated on the stack as a local variable in a function at compile time, so even accesses that use constant indices require some computation at runtime. Despite the differences, compilers often treat stack-allocated arrays almost identically to globally allocated arrays.

The following program is a variation of the previous example that uses a stack-allocated array rather than a global array:

```
int main(int argc, char **argv) {
    int stack_array[3];
    int idx = atoi(argv[1]); //bounds check omitted for simplicity
    stack_array[0] = 10;
    stack_array[1] = 20;
    stack_array[2] = 30;
    stack_array[idx] = 40;
}
```

The address at which stack_array will be allocated is unknown at compile time, so the compiler cannot precompute the address of stack_array[2] as it did for global_array[2]. The compiler can, however, compute the relative location of any element within the array. For example, element stack_array[2] begins at offset 2*sizeof(int) from the beginning of the array, and the compiler is well aware of this at compile time. If the compiler elects to allocate stack_array at offset EBP-0x18 within the stack frame, it can compute EBP-0x18+2*sizeof(int), which reduces to EBP-0x10 at compile time and avoids the need for additional arithmetic at runtime to access stack_array[2]. This becomes evident in the following listing:

```
      undefined main()
          undefined       AL:1            <RETURN>
          undefined4      Stack[-0xc]:4  local_c❶
          undefined4      Stack[-0x10]:4 local_10
          undefined4      Stack[-0x14]:4 local_14
          undefined4      Stack[-0x18]:4 local_18
          undefined4      Stack[-0x1c]:4 local_1c
          undefined8      Stack[-0x28]:8 local_28
0010063a  PUSH    RBP
0010063b  MOV     RBP,RSP
0010063e  SUB     RSP,0x20
00100642  MOV❷    dword ptr [RBP + local_1c],EDI
00100645  MOV     qword ptr [RBP + local_28],RSI
00100649  MOV     RAX,qword ptr [RBP + local_28]
0010064d  ADD     RAX,0x8
00100651  MOV     RAX,qword ptr [RAX]
00100654  MOV     RDI,RAX
00100657  MOV     EAX,0x0
0010065c  CALL    atoi
00100661  MOV❸    dword ptr [RBP + local_c],EAX
00100664  MOV❹    dword ptr [RBP + local_18],10
0010066b  MOV     dword ptr [RBP + local_14],20
00100672  MOV     dword ptr [RBP + local_10],30
00100679  MOV     EAX,dword ptr [RBP + local_c]
0010067c  CDQE
0010067e  MOV     dword ptr [RBP + RAX*0x4 + -0x10],40❺
00100686  MOV     EAX,0x0
0010068b  LEAVE
0010068c  RET
```

It is even more difficult to detect this array than the global array. This function appears to have six unrelated variables ❶ (local_c, local_10, local_14, local_18, local_1c, and local_28), rather than an array of three integers and an integer index variable. Two of these locals (local_1c and local_28) are the function's two parameters, argc and argv, being saved for later use ❷.

The use of constant index values tends to hide the presence of a stack-allocated array, because you see only assignments to separate local variables ❹. Only the multiplication ❺ hints at the existence of an array with individual elements that are 4 bytes each. Let's break down that statement further: RBP holds the stack frame base pointer address; RAX*4 is the array index (converted by atoi and stored in local_c ❸) multiplied by the size of an array element; -0x10 is the offset to the start of the array from RBP.

The process to convert local variables to an array is a little different from creating an array in the data section of the listing. Because the stack structure information is associated with the first address in the function, you cannot select a subset of the stack variables. Instead, place the cursor on the variable at the start of the array, local_18, select the Set Data Type followed by the Array option from the right-click context menu, and then specify the number of elements in the array. Ghidra will display a warning message about conflict with the local variables that we are pulling into the array definition, as shown in Figure 8-4.

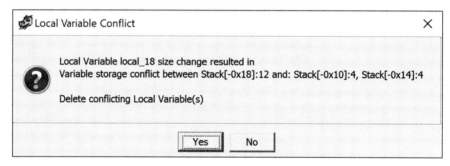

Figure 8-4: Warning about potential conflict when defining stack array

If you proceed, despite the potential conflict, you will see the array in the Listing window, as shown here:

```
        ...
00100664  MOV    dword ptr [RBP + local_18[0]],10
0010066b  MOV    dword ptr [RBP + local_18[1]],20
00100672  MOV    dword ptr [RBP + local_18[2]],30
        ...
```

Even after the array is defined, the decompiler listing in Figure 8-5 doesn't resemble the original source code. The decompiler has omitted the static array assignments because it believes they do not contribute to the result of the function. The call to atoi and resulting assignment remain because Ghidra can't compute the side effects of calling atoi, but Ghidra mistakes the saved result of atoi as the fourth element of the array (local_c in the disassembly, and iVar1 in the decompiler listing).

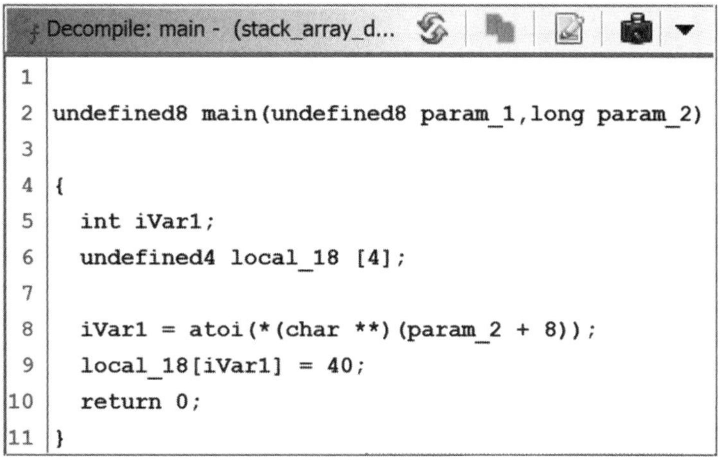

```
 1
 2  undefined8 main(undefined8 param_1,long param_2)
 3
 4  {
 5    int iVar1;
 6    undefined4 local_18 [4];
 7
 8    iVar1 = atoi(*(char **)(param_2 + 8));
 9    local_18[iVar1] = 40;
10    return 0;
11  }
```

Figure 8-5: Decompiler view of function with all stack variables after array is defined

Heap-Allocated Arrays

Heap-allocated arrays are allocated using a dynamic memory allocation function such as malloc (C) or new (C++). From the compiler's perspective, the primary difference in dealing with a heap-allocated array is that the compiler must generate all references into the array based on the address returned from the memory allocation function. The following C program allocates a small array in the program heap:

```
int main(int argc, char **argv) {
    int *heap_array = (int*)malloc(3 * sizeof(int));
    int idx = atoi(argv[1]); //bounds check omitted for simplicity
    heap_array[0] = 10;
    heap_array[1] = 20;
    heap_array[2] = 30;
    heap_array[idx] = 40;
}
```

The corresponding disassembly is a little more complex than the two previous examples:

```
        undefined main()
           undefined      AL:1               <RETURN>
           undefined8     Stack[-0x10]:8     heap_array
           undefined4     Stack[-0x14]:4     local_14
           undefined4     Stack[-0x1c]:4     local_1c
           undefined8     Stack[-0x28]:8     local_28
0010068a   PUSH    RBP
0010068b   MOV     RBP,RSP
0010068e   SUB     RSP,0x20
```

```
00100692    MOV     dword ptr [RBP + local_1c],EDI
00100695    MOV     qword ptr [RBP + local_28],RSI
00100699    MOV     EDI,0xc❶
0010069e    CALL    malloc
001006a3    MOV     qword ptr [RBP + heap_array],RAX❷
001006a7    MOV     RAX,qword ptr [RBP + local_28]
001006ab    ADD     RAX,0x8
001006af    MOV     RAX,qword ptr [RAX]
001006b2    MOV     RDI,RAX
001006b5    CALL    atoi
001006ba    MOV     dword ptr [RBP + local_14],EAX
001006bd    MOV     RAX,qword ptr [RBP + heap_array]
001006c1    MOV     dword ptr [RAX],10❸
001006c7    MOV     RAX,qword ptr [RBP + heap_array]
001006cb    ADD     RAX,0x4❹
001006cf    MOV     dword ptr [RAX],20
001006d5    MOV     RAX,qword ptr [RBP + heap_array]
001006d9    ADD     RAX,0x8❺
001006dd    MOV     dword ptr [RAX],30
001006e3    MOV     EAX,dword ptr [RBP + local_14]
001006e6    CDQE
001006e8    LEA     RDX,[RAX*0x4]❻
001006f0    MOV     RAX,qword ptr [RBP + heap_array]
001006f4    ADD❼    RAX,RDX
001006f7    MOV     dword ptr [RAX],40
001006fd    MOV     EAX,0x0
00100702    LEAVE
00100703    RET
```

The starting address of the array (returned from malloc in the RAX register) is stored in the local variable heap_array ❷. In this example, unlike the previous examples, every access to the array begins with reading the contents of heap_array to obtain the array's base address. The references to heap_array[0], heap_array[1], and heap_array[2] require offsets of 0 ❸, 4 ❹, and 8 bytes ❺, respectively. The variable index array access heap_array[idx] is implemented with multiple instructions to compute the offset into the array by multiplying the array index by the size of an array element ❻, and adding the result to the base address of the array ❼.

Heap-allocated arrays have one particularly nice feature: the number of elements allocated to the array can be computed from the total size of the array and the size of each element. The parameter passed to the memory allocation function (12 passed to malloc ❶) tells you the number of bytes allocated to the array. Dividing this by the size of an element (4 bytes in this example, as observed from the offsets ❸❹❺, which step by 4, and the scale factor ❻) tells us the number of elements in the array. In this example, a three-element array was allocated.

The decompiler was also able to recognize the array, as seen in Figure 8-6. (The name of the array pointer, puVar2, indicates that it is a pointer to an unsigned integer using the prefix pu.)

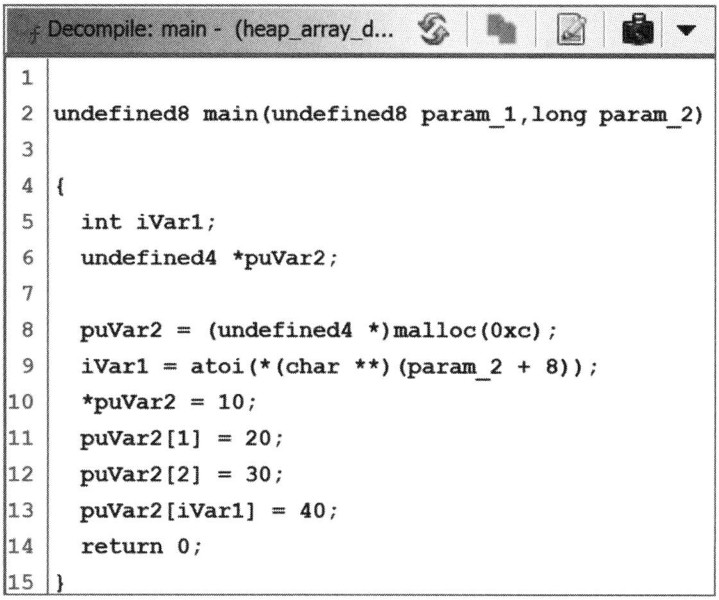

```
  1
  2   undefined8 main(undefined8 param_1,long param_2)
  3
  4   {
  5     int iVar1;
  6     undefined4 *puVar2;
  7
  8     puVar2 = (undefined4 *)malloc(0xc);
  9     iVar1 = atoi(*(char **)(param_2 + 8));
 10     *puVar2 = 10;
 11     puVar2[1] = 20;
 12     puVar2[2] = 30;
 13     puVar2[iVar1] = 40;
 14     return 0;
 15   }
```

Figure 8-6: Decompiler view of heap array function

In this function, unlike the stack-allocated array function, the decompiler listing shows the constant index array assignments, even though it would normally exclude them because the array is not used in other operations or returned from the function. This case is different because the assignments are *not* just manipulating stack variables: the stack variable is actually a pointer to memory that malloc requested from the heap. Writing via that variable does not write to the local stack variable but rather uses the stack variable to locate the allocated memory. The program may lose the pointer (address of the start of the heap array) when the function exits, but the values persist in memory. (This particular example is actually a demonstration of a memory leak. While not a good programming practice, it does allow us to demonstrate the concept of a heap array.)

In conclusion, arrays are easiest to recognize when a variable is used as an index into the array. The array-access operation, which requires the index to be scaled by the size of an array element before adding the resulting offset to the base address of the array, stands out in a disassembly listing.

Structure Member Access

C-style structs, referred to here generically as *structures*, group collections of (often heterogeneous) data items into a composite data type. In source code, the data fields within a structure are accessed by name rather than by index. Unfortunately, these informative field names are converted to numeric offsets by the compiler, so by the time you are looking at a disassembly, structure field access looks remarkably similar to accessing array elements using constant indices.

The following structure definition containing five heterogeneous fields will be used in the upcoming examples:

```
struct ch8_struct {    //Size  Minimum offset  Default offset
    int    field1;     //  4       0               0
    short  field2;     //  2       4               4
    char   field3;     //  1       6               6
    int    field4;     //  4       7               8
    double field5;     //  8      11              16
};                     // Minimum total size: 19 Default size: 24
```

When a compiler encounters a structure definition, the compiler maintains a running total of the number of bytes consumed by the fields of the structure to determine the offset of each field within the structure. The sum of the space required to allocate each field within a structure determines the minimum space required for the structure. However, you should never assume that a compiler utilizes the minimum required space to allocate a structure. By default, compilers align structure fields to memory addresses that allow for the most efficient reading and writing of those fields. For example, 4-byte integer fields will be aligned to offsets that are divisible by four, while 8-byte doubles will be aligned to offsets that are divisible by eight. Depending on the composition of the structure, the compiler may insert padding bytes to meet alignment requirements, meaning the actual size of a structure will be larger than the sum of its component fields. The default offsets and resulting structure size for the sample structure can be seen in the Default offset column in the comments in the preceding structure definition, and they sum to 24 rather than the minimum 19.

Structures can be packed into the minimum required space by using compiler options to request specific member alignments. Microsoft C/C++ and GNU gcc/g++ both recognize the pack pragma for controlling structure field alignment. The GNU compilers additionally recognize the packed attribute for controlling structure alignment on a per-structure basis. Requesting 1-byte alignment for structure fields causes compilers to squeeze the structure into the minimum required space. The offsets and structure size of the sample structure are found in the Minimum offset column. (Note that some processors perform better when data is aligned according to its type, while other processors may generate exceptions if data is *not* aligned on specific boundaries.)

With these facts in mind, let's look at how structures are treated in compiled code. As with arrays, access to structure members is performed by adding the base address of the structure to the offset of the desired member. However, while array offsets can be computed at runtime from a provided index value (because each element in an array has the same size), structure offsets must be computed at compile time and will turn up in compiled code as fixed offsets into the structure, looking nearly identical to array references that make use of constant indices.

Creating structures in Ghidra is more involved than creating arrays, so we cover that in the next section, after we show several examples of disassembled and decompiled structures.

Globally Allocated Structures

As with globally allocated arrays, the addresses of globally allocated structures are known at compile time. This allows the compiler to compute the address of each member of the structure at compile time and eliminates the need to do any math at runtime. Consider the following program that accesses a globally allocated structure:

```
struct ch8_struct global_struct;
int main() {
    global_struct.field1 = 10;
    global_struct.field2 = 20;
    global_struct.field3 = 30;
    global_struct.field4 = 40;
    global_struct.field5 = 50.0;
}
```

If this program is compiled with default structure alignment options, we can expect to see something like the following when we disassemble it:

```
        undefined main()
            undefined      AL:1              <RETURN>
001005fa  PUSH    RBP
001005fb  MOV     RBP,RSP
001005fe  MOV     dword ptr [DAT_00301020],10
00100608  MOV     word ptr [DAT_00301024],20
00100611  MOV     byte ptr [DAT_00301026],30
00100618  MOV     dword ptr [DAT_00301028],40
00100622  MOVSD   XMM0,qword ptr [DAT_001006c8]
0010062a  MOVSD   qword ptr [DAT_00301030],XMM0
00100632  MOV     EAX,0x0
00100637  POP     RBP
00100638  RET
```

This disassembly contains no math whatsoever to access the members of the structure, and, in the absence of source code, it would not be possible to state with any certainty that a structure is being used at all. Because the compiler has performed all of the offset computations at compile time, this program appears to reference five global variables rather than five fields within a single structure. You should be able to note the similarities with the previous example of globally allocated arrays using constant index values.

In Figure 8-2, the uniform offsets coupled with the values allowed us to surmise (accurately) that we were dealing with an array. In this example, we are correct to conclude that we are not dealing with an array because the size of the variables is nonuniform (dword, word, byte, dword, and qword, respectively), but we lack sufficient evidence to assert that we are dealing with a struct.

Stack-Allocated Structures

Like stack-allocated arrays, stack-allocated structures are challenging to recognize based on stack layout alone, and the decompiler doesn't provide additional insight. Modifying the preceding program to use a stack-allocated structure, declared in main, yields the following disassembly:

```
          undefined main()
              undefined       AL:1                    <RETURN>
              undefined8      Stack[-0x18]:8          local_18
              undefined4      Stack[-0x20]:4          local_20
              undefined1      Stack[-0x22]:1          local_22
              undefined2      Stack[-0x24]:2          local_24
              undefined4      Stack[-0x28]:4          local_28
001005fa  PUSH    RBP
001005fb  MOV     RBP,RSP
001005fe  MOV     dword ptr [RBP + local_28],10
00100605  MOV     word ptr [RBP + local_24],20
0010060b  MOV     byte ptr [RBP + local_22],30
0010060f  MOV     dword ptr [RBP + local_20],40
00100616  MOVSD   XMM0,qword ptr [DAT_001006b8]
0010061e  MOVSD   qword ptr [RBP + local_18],XMM0
00100623  MOV     EAX,0x0
00100628  POP     RBP
00100629  RET
```

Again, no math is performed to access the structure's fields since the compiler can determine the relative offsets for each field within the stack frame at compile time, and we are left with the same, potentially misleading picture that five individual variables are being used rather than a single variable that happens to contain five distinct fields. In reality, local_28 should be the start of a 24-byte structure, and each of the other variables should somehow be formatted to reflect the fact that they are fields within the structure.

Heap-Allocated Structures

Heap-allocated structures reveal much more about the size of the structure and the layout of its fields. When a structure is allocated in the program heap, the compiler has no choice but to generate code to compute the proper field address whenever a field is accessed, because the structure's address is unknown at compile time. For globally allocated structures, the compiler is able to compute a fixed starting address. For stack-allocated structures, the compiler can compute a fixed relationship between the start of the structure and the frame pointer for the enclosing stack frame. When a structure has been allocated in the heap, the only reference to the structure available to the compiler is the pointer to the structure's starting address.

To demonstrate heap-allocated structures, we modify the sample program to declare a pointer within main and assign it the address of a block of memory large enough to hold the structure:

```
int main() {
    struct ch8_struct *heap_struct;
    heap_struct = (struct ch8_struct*)malloc(sizeof(struct ch8_struct));
    heap_struct->field1 = 10;
    heap_struct->field2 = 20;
    heap_struct->field3 = 30;
    heap_struct->field4 = 40;
    heap_struct->field5 = 50.0;
}
```

Here is the corresponding disassembly:

```
        undefined main()
            undefined      AL:1              <RETURN>
            undefined8     Stack[-0x10]:8    heap_struct
0010064a  PUSH    RBP
0010064b  MOV     RBP,RSP
0010064e  SUB     RSP,16
00100652  MOV     EDI,24❶
00100657  CALL    malloc
0010065c  MOV     qword ptr [RBP + heap_struct],RAX
00100660  MOV     RAX,qword ptr [RBP + heap_struct]
00100664  MOV     dword ptr [RAX],10❷
0010066a  MOV     RAX,qword ptr [RBP + heap_struct]
0010066e  MOV     word ptr [RAX + 4],20❸
00100674  MOV     RAX,qword ptr [RBP + heap_struct]
00100678  MOV     byte ptr [RAX + 6],30❹
0010067c  MOV     RAX,qword ptr [RBP + heap_struct]
00100680  MOV     dword ptr [RAX + 8],40❺
00100687  MOV     RAX,qword ptr [RBP + heap_struct]
0010068b  MOVSD   XMM0,qword ptr [DAT_00100728]
00100693  MOVSD   qword ptr [RAX + 16],XMM0❻
00100698  MOV     EAX,0x0
0010069d  LEAVE
0010069e  RET
```

In this example, we can discern the exact size and layout of the structure. The structure size can be inferred to be 24 bytes based on the amount of memory requested from malloc ❶. The structure contains the following fields at the indicated offsets:

- A 4-byte (dword) field at offset 0 ❷
- A 2-byte (word) field at offset 4 ❸
- A 1-byte field at offset 6 ❹
- A 4-byte (dword) field at offset 8 ❺
- An 8-byte (qword) field at offset 16 ❻

Based on the use of floating point instructions (MOVSD), we can further deduce that the qword field is actually a double.

The same program compiled to pack structures with a 1-byte alignment yields the following disassembly:

```
0010064a   PUSH    RBP
0010064e   SUB     RSP,16
00100652   MOV     EDI,19
00100657   CALL    malloc
0010065c   MOV     qword ptr [RBP + local_10],RAX
00100660   MOV     RAX,qword ptr [RBP + local_10]
00100664   MOV     dword ptr [RAX],10
0010066a   MOV     RAX,qword ptr [RBP + local_10]
0010066e   MOV     word ptr [RAX + 4],20
00100674   MOV     RAX,qword ptr [RBP + local_10]
00100678   MOV     byte ptr [RAX + 6],30
0010067c   MOV     RAX,qword ptr [RBP + local_10]
00100680   MOV     dword ptr [RAX + 7],40
00100687   MOV     RAX,qword ptr [RBP + local_10]
0010068b   MOVSD   XMM0,qword ptr [DAT_00100728] =
00100693   MOVSD   qword ptr [RAX + 11],XMM0
00100698   MOV     EAX,0x0
0010069d   LEAVE
0010069e   RET
```

The only changes are the smaller structure size (now 19 bytes) and the adjusted offsets to account for the realignment of each structure field.

Regardless of the alignment used when compiling a program, finding structures allocated and manipulated in the program heap is the fastest way to determine the size and layout of a given data structure. However, keep in mind that many functions will not do you the favor of immediately accessing every member of a structure to help you understand the structure's layout. Instead, you may need to follow the use of the pointer to the structure and make note of the offsets used whenever that pointer is dereferenced, and eventually piece together the complete layout of the structure. In "Example 3: Automated Structure Creation" on page 437, you'll see how the decompiler can automate this process for you.

Arrays of Structures

Some programmers say that the beauty of composite data structures is that they allow you to build arbitrarily complex structures by nesting smaller structures within larger structures: arrays of structures, structures within structures, and structures that contain arrays as members, for example. The preceding discussions regarding arrays and structures apply just as well to such nested types. As an example, consider the following simple program in which heap_struct points to an array of five ch8_struct items:

```
int main() {
    int idx = 1;
    struct ch8_struct *heap_struct;
```

```
    heap_struct = (struct ch8_struct*)malloc(sizeof(struct ch8_struct) * 5);
    heap_struct[idx].field1 = 10;
}
```

Underneath the hood, accessing field1 involves multiplying the index value by the size of an array element (in this case, the size of the structure) and then adding the offset to the desired field. The corresponding disassembly is shown here:

```
        undefined main()
            undefined      AL:1              <RETURN>
            undefined4     Stack[-0xc]:4     idx
            undefined4     Stack[-0x18]:8    heap_struct
0010064a  PUSH    RBP
0010064b  MOV     RBP,RSP
0010064e  SUB     RSP,16
00100652  MOV     dword ptr [RBP + idx],1
00100659  MOV❶    EDI,120
0010065e  CALL    malloc
00100663  MOV     qword ptr [RBP + heap_struct],RAX
00100667  MOV     EAX,dword ptr [RBP + idx]
0010066a  MOVSXD  RDX,EAX
0010066d  MOV❷    RAX,RDX
00100670  ADD     RAX,RAX
00100673  ADD     RAX,RDX
00100676  SHL❸    RAX,3
0010067a  MOV     RDX,RAX
0010067d  MOV     RAX,qword ptr [RBP + heap_struct]
00100681  ADD❹    RAX,RDX
00100684  MOV❺    dword ptr [RAX],10
0010068a  MOV     EAX,0
0010068f  LEAVE
00100690  RET
```

The function allocates 120 bytes ❶ in the heap. The array index in RAX is multiplied by 24 using a series of operations ❷, ending with SHL RAX, 3 ❸ before being added to the start address for the array ❹. (If it is not readily apparent to you that the series of operations starting at ❷ is equivalent to multiplication by 24, don't worry. Code sequences such as this are discussed in Chapter 20.) Because field1 is the first member of the struct, no additional offset is required in order to generate the final address for the assignment into field1 ❺.

From these facts, we can deduce the size of an array item (24), the number of items in the array (120 / 24 = 5), and the fact that there is a 4-byte (dword) field at offset 0 within each array element. This short listing does not offer enough information to draw any conclusions about how the remaining 20 bytes within each structure are allocated to additional fields. The size of the array can be even more easily deduced using the same formula from the decompiler listing in Figure 8-7 (0x18 hex is 24 decimal).

```
  ƒ  Decompile: main - (heap_struct_array_demo_x64_stripped)

 1
 2   undefined8 main(void)
 3
 4   {
 5     void *pvVar1;
 6
 7     pvVar1 = malloc(120);
 8     *(undefined4 *)((long)pvVar1 + 0x18) = 10;
 9     return 0;
10   }
```

Figure 8-7: Decompiler view of function with heap-allocated struct array

Creating Structures with Ghidra

In the preceding chapter, you saw how to use Ghidra's array-aggregation capabilities to collapse long lists of data declarations into a single disassembly line representing an array. The next few sections explore Ghidra's facilities for improving the readability of code that manipulates structures. Our goal is to move away from cryptic structure references such as [EDX + 10h] and toward something more readable like [EDX + ch8_struct.field_e].

Whenever you discover that a program is manipulating a data structure, you need to decide whether you want to incorporate structure field names into your disassembly or whether you can make sense of all the numeric offsets sprinkled throughout the listing. In some cases, Ghidra may recognize the use of a structure defined as part of the C standard library or the Windows API and use its knowledge of the exact layout of the structure to convert numeric offsets into symbolic field names. This is the ideal case, as it leaves you with a lot less work to do. We will return to this scenario once you understand a little more about how Ghidra deals with structure definitions in general.

Creating a New Structure

When Ghidra has no layout knowledge for a structure, you can create the structure by selecting the data and using the right-click context menu. When you select Data ▶ Create Structure (or use the hotkey SHIFT-[), you will see the Create Structure window shown in Figure 8-8. Since you have highlighted a block of data (which could be defined or undefined), Ghidra will try to identify existing structures that have a matching format or the same size. You can select one of the existing structures from the window or create a new structure. In this example, we are using the globally allocated structure sample code discussed previously and are creating a new structure called ch8_struct. As soon as you click OK, the structure becomes an official type in the Data Type Manager window and the information is propagated to other CodeBrowser windows.

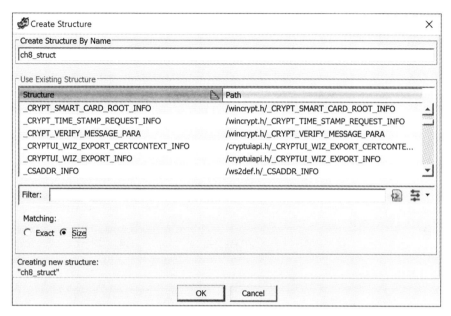

Figure 8-8: Create Structure window

Let's look at the effect of this creation on the associated CodeBrowser windows, starting with the Listing window. As shown earlier in the chapter, the disassembly listing gives you few hints that you might be dealing with a structure, because the code modifies a series of seemingly unrelated global variables:

```
001005fa  PUSH   RBP
001005fb  MOV    RBP,RSP
001005fe  MOV    dword ptr [DAT_00301020],10
00100608  MOV    word ptr [DAT_00301024],20
00100611  MOV    byte ptr [DAT_00301026],30
00100618  MOV    dword ptr [DAT_00301028],40
00100622  MOVSD  XMM0,qword ptr [DAT_001006c8]
0010062a  MOVSD  qword ptr [DAT_00301030],XMM0
00100632  MOV    EAX,0
00100637  POP    RBP
00100638  RET
```

When you navigate to the associated data items, select the range (00301020 through 00301037), and create the associated structure, you see the individual data items in the structure are now associated with a structure called ch8_struct _00301020, and each item in the structure has the name field_ concatenated with its offset from the first element in the structure.

```
00401035  POP    EBP
001005fb  MOV    RBP,RSP
001005fe  MOV    dword ptr [ch8_struct_00301020],10
00100608  MOV    word ptr [ch8_struct_00301020.field_0x4],20
00100611  MOV    byte ptr [ch8_struct_00301020.field_0x6],30
00100618  MOV    dword ptr [ch8_struct_00301020.field_0x8],40
00100622  MOVSD  XMM0,qword ptr [DAT_001006c8]
0010062a  MOVSD  qword ptr [ch8_struct_00301020.field_0x10],XMM0
00100632  MOV    EAX,0
00100637  POP    RBP
00100638  RET
```

This is just one of the windows that changes with the creation of the structure. Recall that the Decompiler window gave us a helpful warning that we might be working with a structure or array. After we create the structure, the warning disappears and the decompiled code more closely resembles the original C code, as shown in Figure 8-9.

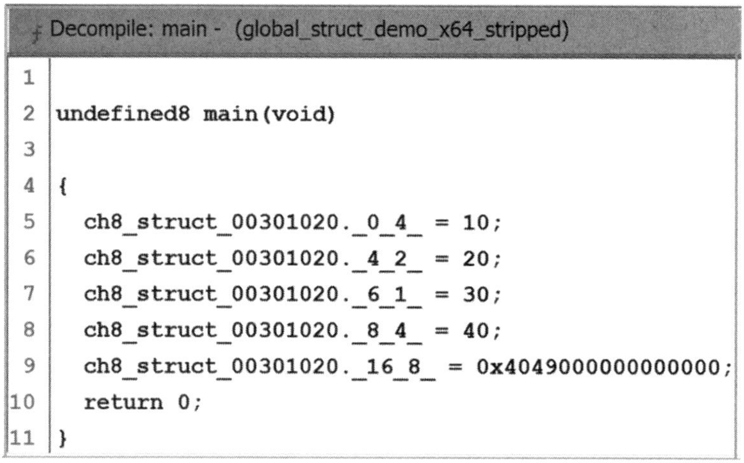

```
Decompile: main - (global_struct_demo_x64_stripped)

 1
 2  undefined8 main(void)
 3
 4  {
 5    ch8_struct_00301020._0_4_ = 10;
 6    ch8_struct_00301020._4_2_ = 20;
 7    ch8_struct_00301020._6_1_ = 30;
 8    ch8_struct_00301020._8_4_ = 40;
 9    ch8_struct_00301020._16_8_ = 0x4049000000000000;
10    return 0;
11  }
```

Figure 8-9: Decompiler view after struct is created

STATE OF THE UNION

A *union* is a construct that is similar to a structure. The major difference between structures and unions is that structure fields have unique offsets and their own dedicated memory space, whereas union fields all overlap one another beginning at offset 0. The result is that all union fields share the same memory space. The Union Editor window in Ghidra looks similar to the Structure Editor window, and the functionality is basically the same.

The new structure also now appears as an entry in the Data Type Manager window in the CodeBrowser. Figure 8-10 shows the new entry in the Data Type Manager window and the associated window showing all uses of ch8_struct.

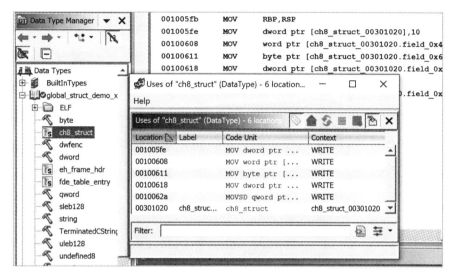

Figure 8-10: Newly declared structure in Data Type Manager and References windows

Editing Structure Members

At this point, Ghidra presents the newly created structure as a contiguous collection of undefined bytes with cross-references at each offset accessed by the example program, instead of a collection of defined data types (which you have identified from the size of each item and the way it is being used). To define the type of each field, you can edit the structure from the Listing window by right-clicking and selecting the appropriate Data option. Alternatively, you can edit the structure from within the Data Type Manager by double-clicking the structure.

If you double-click the newly created structure in the Data Type Manager window (shown in Figure 8-10), the Structure Editor window (shown in Figure 8-11) opens to show 24 elements of undefined type, all with a length of 1. To determine the number, sizes, and types of the individual elements within the structure, you could study the disassembly, or you could let the decompiler listing shown earlier in Figure 8-9 provide the answers.

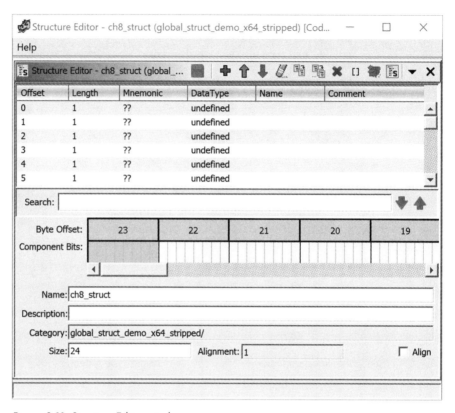

Figure 8-11: Structure Editor window

The original decompiler listing associated with our newly created structure shows that five items are referenced within the same structure, ch8_struct _00301020, using field names containing two integers. The first integer represents the offset from the base address of the structure. The second shows the number of bytes used, which is a good indicator of the size of the item. Using this information (and some meaningful field names), you can update the Structure Editor window, as shown in Figure 8-12. The Byte Offset/ Component Bits scroll bar within the Structure Editor provides a visual representation of the structure. When a structure is edited, the Decompiler window (on the left of Figure 8-12), the Listing window, and other associated windows are also updated.

Because field_c is a character, the decompiler converted the integer 30 into the ASCII character represented by 30 (0x1e), which is an unprintable control character (RS). In the Structure Editor, the padding bytes (indicated by the mnemonic ??) have been included for proper field alignment, and the offsets to each field and the overall size (24 bytes) of the structure match the values seen in the earlier examples.

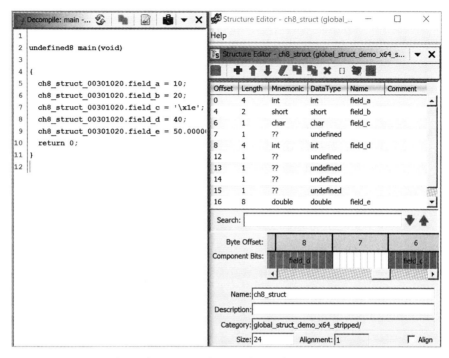

Figure 8-12: Decompiler and Structure Editor windows after editing structure

Applying Structure Layouts

You have seen how to use existing structure definitions and create new ones to associate existing memory with a particular memory layout. You have also seen how that association is propagated through the CodeBrowser windows to make the contents clearer. Vague memory references such as [EBX+8] become more readable by converting numeric structure offsets into symbolic references such as [EBX+ch8_struct.field_d], especially because symbolic references can be given meaningful names. Ghidra's use of a hierarchical notation makes it clear exactly what type of structure, and exactly which field within that structure, is being accessed.

Ghidra's library of known structure layouts has been populated with information gathered by parsing common C header files. The layout of a structure defines its total size, the name and size of each field, and the starting offset of each field within the structure. You can use structure layouts even without associated content in the data section, which is especially helpful when dealing with structure pointers.

Anytime you encounter a memory reference in the form [reg+N] (for example, [RAX+0x12]), where reg is a register name and N is a small constant, reg is being used as a pointer and N represents an offset into the memory that reg points to. This is a common pattern for structure member access, with reg pointing to the beginning of the structure and N selecting the field at structure offset N. Under some circumstances, Ghidra, with your assistance, can clean up this type of memory reference to reflect both the type of structure being pointed to and the specific field within that structure that is being referenced.

Let's look at the 32-bit version of the example from the beginning of the chapter, where we were requesting an HTTP page from a server. The request is made by a function named get_page. In this version of the binary, Ghidra asserts that the function receives three stack-allocated parameters. These parameters appear in the Listing window as follows:

```
undefined get_page(undefined4 param_1, undefined param_2...
    undefined     AL:1                <RETURN>
    undefined4    Stack[0x4]:4        param_1
    undefined     Stack[0x8]:1        param_2
    undefined4    Stack[0xc]:4        param_3
```

The Decompiler window shows that param_3 is used with some offsets in a call to connect:

```
iVar1=connect(local_14,*(sockaddr **)(param_3+20),*(socklen_t*)(param_3+16));
```

Tracing through the calling sequence and the return values from the called functions, we can conclude that param_3 is a pointer to an addrinfo struct and retype param_3 as an addrinfo* (using CTRL-L from the Listing or Decompiler window). The decompiled statement using param_3 will be replaced with the far more informative statement shown here:

```
iVar1 = connect(local_14, param_3->ai_addr, param_3->ai_addrlen);
```

You can see that pointer arithmetic has been replaced by structure field references. Pointer arithmetic in source code is rarely self-explanatory. Any effort you spend updating data types for program variables will be well worth it. You'll have saved your colleagues the time required to deduce the type of param_3 themselves, and you'll thank yourself upon returning from two weeks at the beach that you don't need to reanalyze the code to relearn the type of that variable that you forgot to update.

C++ Reversing Primer

C++ classes are the object-oriented extensions of C structs, so it is somewhat logical to wrap up our discussion of data structures by reviewing the features of compiled C++ code. Detailed coverage of C++ is beyond the scope of this book. Here, we attempt to cover the highlights and a few of the differences between Microsoft's C++ compiler and GNU's g++.

Remember that a solid, fundamental understanding of the C++ language will assist you greatly in understanding compiled C++. Object-oriented concepts such as inheritance and polymorphism are difficult enough to master at the source level. Attempting to dive into these concepts at the assembly level without understanding them at the source level can be an exercise in frustration.

The this Pointer

The this pointer is available in all nonstatic C++ member functions. Whenever such a function is called, this is initialized to point to the object used to invoke the function. Consider the following function calls in C++:

```
// object1, object2, and *p_obj are all the same type.
object1.member_func();
object2.member_func();
p_obj->member_func();
```

In the three calls to member_func, this takes on the values &object1, &object2, and p_obj, respectively.

It is easiest to view this as a hidden first parameter passed in to all non-static member functions. As discussed in Chapter 6, the Microsoft C++ compiler utilizes the thiscall calling convention and passes this in the ECX register (x86) or the RCX register (x86-x64). The GNU g++ compiler treats this exactly as if it were the first (leftmost) parameter to nonstatic member functions. On 32-bit Linux x86, the address of the object used to invoke the function is pushed as the topmost item on the stack prior to calling the function. On Linux x86-64, this is passed in the first register parameter, RDI.

From a reverse engineering point of view, moving an address into the ECX register immediately before a function call is a probable indicator of two things. First, the file was compiled using Microsoft's C++ compiler. Second, the function is possibly a member function. When the same address is passed to two or more functions, we can conclude that those functions all belong to the same class hierarchy.

Within a function, the use of ECX prior to initializing it implies that the caller must have initialized ECX (recall the discussion of *liveness* from "Register-Based Parameters" on page 113) and is a possible sign that the function is a member function (though the function may simply use the fastcall calling convention). Further, when a member function passes this to additional functions, those functions can be inferred to be members of the same class as well.

For code compiled using GNU g++, calls to member functions stand out somewhat less because this looks a lot like any other first parameter. However, any function that does not take a pointer as its first argument can certainly be ruled out as a member function.

Virtual Functions and Vftables

Virtual functions enable polymorphic behavior in C++ programs. For each class (or subclass through inheritance) that contains virtual functions, the compiler generates a table containing pointers to each virtual function in the class. Such tables are called *vftables* (also *vtables*). Every instance of a class that contains virtual functions is given an additional data member that points to the class's vftable. The *vftable pointer* is allocated as the first data member within the class instance, and when an object is created at runtime, its constructor function sets its vftable pointer to point at the appropriate vftable. When that object invokes a virtual function, the correct function is selected by performing a lookup in the object's vftable. Thus, vftables are the underlying mechanism that facilitates runtime resolution of calls to virtual functions.

A few examples may help to clarify the use of vftables. Consider the following C++ class definitions:

```
class BaseClass {
    public:
        BaseClass();
    ❶ virtual void vfunc1() = 0❷;
        virtual void vfunc2();
        virtual void vfunc3();
        virtual void vfunc4();
    private:
        int x;
        int y;
};
class SubClass : public BaseClass❸ {
    public:
        SubClass();
    ❹ virtual void vfunc1();
        virtual void vfunc3();
        virtual void vfunc5();
    private:
        int z;
};
```

In this case, SubClass inherits from BaseClass ❸. BaseClass contains four virtual functions ❶, while SubClass contains five ❹ (four from BaseClass, two of which it overrides, plus the new vfunc5). Within BaseClass, vfunc1 is a *pure virtual function*, indicated by = 0 ❷ in its declaration. Pure virtual functions have no implementation in their declaring class and *must* be overridden in a subclass before the class is considered concrete. In other words, there is no function named BaseClass::vfunc1, and until a subclass provides an implementation, no objects can be instantiated. SubClass provides such an implementation, so SubClass objects can be created. In object-oriented terms, BaseClass::vfunc1 is an *abstract function*, which makes BaseClass an *abstract base class* (that is, an incomplete class that cannot be directly instantiated since it is missing an implementation for at least one function).

At first glance, BaseClass appears to contain two data members, and SubClass three data members. Recall, however, that any class that contains virtual functions, either explicitly or because they are inherited, also contains a vftable pointer. As a result, the compiled implementation of BaseClass has three data members, while instantiated SubClass objects have four data members. In each case, the first data member is the vftable pointer. Within SubClass, the vftable pointer is actually inherited from BaseClass rather than being introduced specifically for SubClass. You can see this in the simplified memory layout in Figure 8-13, in which a single SubClass object has been dynamically allocated. During the creation of the object, the new object's vftable pointer is initialized to point to the correct vftable (SubClass's in this case).

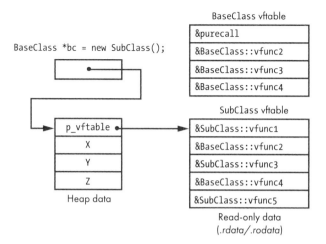

BaseClass *bc = new SubClass();

BaseClass vftable

| &purecall |
| &BaseClass::vfunc2 |
| &BaseClass::vfunc3 |
| &BaseClass::vfunc4 |

SubClass vftable

| &SubClass::vfunc1 |
| &BaseClass::vfunc2 |
| &SubClass::vfunc3 |
| &BaseClass::vfunc4 |
| &SubClass::vfunc5 |

Heap data

Read-only data
(.rdata/.rodata)

Figure 8-13: A simple vftable layout

The vftable for SubClass contains two pointers to functions belonging to BaseClass (BaseClass::vfunc2 and BaseClass::vfunc4) because SubClass does not override either of these functions and instead inherits them from BaseClass. The vftable for BaseClass shows how pure virtual functions are handled. Because there is no implementation for the pure virtual function BaseClass::vfunc1, no address is available to store in the BaseClass vftable slot for vfunc1. In such cases, compilers insert the address of an error-handling function, dubbed purecall in Microsoft libraries and __cxa_pure_virtual in GNU libraries. In theory, these functions should never be called, but in the event that they are, they cause the program to be terminated abnormally.

You must account for the vftable pointer when you manipulate classes within Ghidra. Because C++ classes are extensions of C structures, you can use Ghidra's structure definition features to define the layout of C++ classes. With polymorphic classes, you must include a vftable pointer as the first field within the class as well as account for the vftable pointer in the total size of the object. This is most apparent when observing the dynamic allocation of an object using the new operator, where the size value passed to new includes the space needed by all explicitly declared fields in the class (and any superclasses) as well as any space required for a vftable pointer.

In the following example, a SubClass object is created dynamically and its address saved in a BaseClass pointer. The pointer is then passed to a function (call_vfunc), which uses the pointer to call vfunc3:

```
void call_vfunc(BaseClass *bc) {
    bc->vfunc3();
}
int main() {
    BaseClass *bc = new Subclass();
    call_vfunc(bc);
}
```

Since vfunc3 is a virtual function and bc points to a SubClass object, the compiler must ensure that SubClass::vfunc3 is called. The following disassembly of a 32-bit, Microsoft C++ version of call_vfunc demonstrates how the virtual function call is resolved:

```
undefined __cdecl call_vfunc(int * bc)
        undefined       AL:1            <RETURN>
        int *           Stack[0x4]:4    bc
004010a0  PUSH    EBP
004010a1  MOV     EBP,ESP
004010a3  MOV     EAX,dword ptr [EBP + bc]
004010a6  MOV❶    EDX,dword ptr [EAX]
004010a8  MOV❷    ECX,dword ptr [EBP + bc]
004010ab  MOV❸    EAX,dword ptr [EDX + 8]
004010ae  CALL❹   EAX
004010b0  POP     EBP
004010b1  RET
```

The vftable pointer (the address of SubClass's vftable) is read from the structure and saved in EDX ❶. Next, the this pointer is moved into ECX ❷. Then, the vftable is indexed to read the third pointer (the address of SubClass::vfunc3 in this case) into the EAX register ❸. Finally, the virtual function is called ❹.

The vftable indexing operation ❸ looks very much like a structure reference operation. In fact, it is no different, and it is possible to define new structures for the class and its vftable (right-click in the Data Type Manager window) and then use the defined structures (see Figure 8-14) to make the disassembly and decompilation more readable.

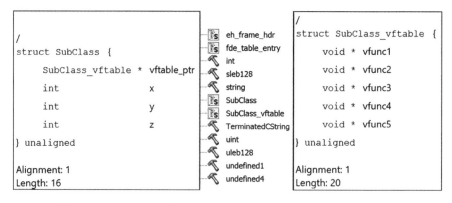

Figure 8-14: Data Manager Window showing new SubClass and SubClass_vftable

The Decompiler window with references to the new structures is shown in Figure 8-15.

```
Decompile: call_vfunc - (call_vfunc.exe)

1
2  void __cdecl call_vfunc(SubClass *bc)
3
4  {
5    (*(code *)bc->vftable_ptr->vfunc3)();
6    return;
7  }
```

Figure 8-15: Decompiler window reflecting defined structures
for SubClass

A class's vftable is referenced directly in only two circumstances: within
the class constructor(s) and destructor. When you locate a vftable, you
can utilize Ghidra's data cross-referencing capabilities (see Chapter 9) to
quickly locate all constructors and destructors for the associated class.

The Object Life Cycle

Understanding the mechanism by which objects are created and destroyed
can help to reveal object hierarchies and nested object relationships as well
as quickly identify class constructor and destructor functions.

WHAT'S A CONSTRUCTOR?

A *class constructor function* is an initialization function that is invoked when
a new object of that class is created. Constructors provide an opportunity to
initialize variables within the class. The inverse of a constructor, a *destructor*, is
called when an object goes out of scope or a dynamically allocated object is
explicitly deleted. Destructor functions perform cleanup activities such as releas-
ing resources like open file descriptors and dynamically allocated memory.
Properly written destructors mitigate the potential for memory leaks.

The storage class of an object determines when its constructor is
called.[1] For global and statically allocated objects (static storage class),
constructors are called during program startup prior to entry into the program's main function. Constructors for stack-allocated objects (automatic
storage class) are invoked when the object comes into scope within the
function in which it is declared. In many cases, this will be immediately

---

1. A variable's storage class roughly defines its lifetime during program execution. The two
most common storage classes in C are static and automatic. The storage space for static variables exists for the duration of the program. Automatic variables are associated with function
invocations and exist only for the duration of a specific function call.

upon entry to the function in which it is declared. However, when an object is declared within a nested block statement, its constructor is not invoked until that block is entered, if it is entered at all. When an object is allocated dynamically in the program heap, its creation is a two-step process: the new operator is invoked to allocate the object's memory and then the constructor is invoked to initialize the object. Microsoft C++ ensures that the result of new is not null prior to invoking the constructor, but GNU's g++ does not.

When a constructor executes, the following sequence of actions takes place:

1. If the class has a superclass, the superclass constructor is invoked.
2. If the class has any virtual functions, the vftable pointer is initialized to point to the class's vftable. This may overwrite a vftable pointer that was initialized in the superclass constructor, which is exactly the desired behavior.
3. If the class has any data members that are themselves objects, the constructor for each of those data members is invoked.
4. Finally, the class constructor is executed. This is the C++ constructor code specified by the programmer of the class.

From a programmer's perspective, constructors do not specify a return type or allow a value to be returned. Some compilers actually return this as a result that they may further utilize in the caller, but this is a compiler implementation detail and C++ programmers cannot access the returned value.

Destructors, as their name implies, are called at the end of an object's lifetime. For global and static objects, destructors are called by cleanup code that is executed after the main function terminates. Destructors for stack-allocated objects are invoked as the objects go out of scope. Destructors for heap-allocated objects are invoked via the delete operator immediately before the memory allocated to the object is released.

The actions performed by destructors mimic those performed by constructors, with the exception that they are performed in roughly reverse order:

1. If the class has any virtual functions, the vftable pointer for the object is restored to point to the vftable for the associated class. This is required in case a subclass had overwritten the vftable pointer as part of its creation process.
2. The programmer-specified code for the destructor executes.
3. If the class has any data members that are themselves objects, the destructor for each of those members is executed.
4. Finally, if the object has a superclass, the superclass destructor is called.

By understanding when superclass constructors and destructors are called, it is possible to trace an object's inheritance hierarchy through the chain of calls to its related superclass functions.

I THINK YOU ARE OVERLOADED

Overloaded functions are functions that share the same name but have different parameters. C++ requires that each version of an overloaded function differ from every other version in the sequence and/or quantity of parameter types that the function receives. In other words, while they share the same function name, each function prototype must be unique, and each overloaded function body can be uniquely identified within the disassembled binary. This is not to be confused with functions, such as printf, that take a variable number of arguments but are associated with a single function body.

Name Mangling

Also called *name decoration, name mangling* is the mechanism C++ compilers use to distinguish among overloaded versions of a function. To generate unique, internal names for overloaded functions, compilers decorate the function name with additional characters that encode various pieces of information about the function: the namespace to which the function (or its owning class) belongs (if any), the class to which the function belongs (if any), and the parameter sequence (type and order) required to call the function.

Name mangling is a compiler implementation detail for C++ programs and, as such, is not part of the C++ language specification. Not unexpectedly, compiler vendors have developed their own, often-incompatible conventions for name mangling. Fortunately, Ghidra understands the name mangling conventions employed by Microsoft's C++ compiler and GNU g++ v3 (and later) as well as some other compilers. Ghidra provides names of the form FUN_*address* in place of the mangled name. Mangled names do carry valuable information regarding the signature of each function, and Ghidra includes this information in the Symbol Table window as well as propagating the information to the disassembly and other related windows. (To determine the signature of a function without a mangled name, you might need to conduct time-consuming analysis of the data flowing into and out of the function.)

Runtime Type Identification

C++ provides operators to determine (typeid) and check (dynamic_cast) an object's data type at runtime. To support these operations, C++ compilers must embed type-specific information, for each polymorphic class, within a program binary. When a typeid or dynamic_cast operation is performed at runtime, library routines reference the type-specific information in order to determine the exact runtime type of the polymorphic object being referenced. Unfortunately, as with name mangling, *Runtime Type Identification (RTTI)* is a compiler implementation detail rather than a language issue, and there is no standard means by which compilers implement RTTI capabilities.

We will take a brief look at the similarities and differences between the RTTI implementations of Microsoft's C++ compiler and GNU g++. Specifically, we'll describe how to locate RTTI information and, from there, how to learn the name of the class to which that information pertains. Readers desiring more detailed discussion of Microsoft's RTTI implementation should consult the references listed at the end of this chapter. In particular, the references detail how to traverse a class's inheritance hierarchy, including how to trace that hierarchy when multiple inheritance is being used.

Consider the following simple program, which uses polymorphism:

```
class abstract_class {
    public:
        virtual int vfunc() = 0;
};
class concrete_class : public abstract_class {
    public:
        concrete_class(){};
        int vfunc();
};
int concrete_class::vfunc() {return 0;}
❶ void print_type(abstract_class *p) {
    cout << typeid(*p).name() << endl;
}
int main() {
    abstract_class *sc = new concrete_class();❷
    print_type(sc);
}
```

The print_type function ❶ prints the type of the object being pointed to by the pointer p. In this case, it must print "concrete_class" since a concrete _class object is created in the main function ❷. How does print_type, and more specifically typeid, know what type of object p is pointing to?

The answer is surprisingly simple. Since every polymorphic object contains a pointer to a vftable, compilers leverage that fact by co-locating class-type information with the class vftable. Specifically, the compiler places a pointer, immediately prior to the class vftable, that points to a structure containing information about the class that owns the vftable. In GNU g++ code, this pointer points to a type_info structure, which contains a pointer to the name of the class. In Microsoft C++ code, the pointer points to a Microsoft RTTICompleteObjectLocator structure, which in turn contains a pointer to a TypeDescriptor structure. The TypeDescriptor structure contains a character array that specifies the name of the polymorphic class.

RTTI information is required only in C++ programs that use the typeid or dynamic_cast operator. Most compilers provide options to disable the generation of RTTI in binaries that do not require it; therefore, you should not be surprised if you encounter compiled binaries that contain no RTTI information even though vftables are present.

For C++ programs built with Microsoft's C++ compiler, Ghidra contains an RTTI analyzer that is enabled by default and that is capable of identifying Microsoft RTTI structures, annotating those structures (if present) in the disassembly listing, and utilizing class names recovered from those RTTI structures in the Symbol Tree's *Classes* folder. Ghidra has no RTTI analyzer for non-Windows binaries. When Ghidra encounters an unstripped, non-Windows binary, if it understands the name mangling scheme employed in the binary, then Ghidra utilizes available name information to populate the Symbol Tree's *Classes* folder. If a non-Windows binary has been stripped, Ghidra will not be able to automatically recover any class names or identify vftables or RTTI information.

Inheritance Relationships

It is possible to unravel inheritance relationships by using a compiler's particular implementation of RTTI, but RTTI may not be present when a program does not utilize the typeid or dynamic_cast operators. Lacking RTTI information, what techniques can be employed to determine inheritance relationships among C++ classes?

The simplest method to determine an inheritance hierarchy is to observe the chain of calls to superclass constructors that are called when an object is created. The single biggest hindrance to this technique is the use of inline constructors. In C/C++, a function declared as inline is usually treated as a macro by the compiler, and the code for the function is expanded in place of an explicit function call. Inline functions hide the fact that a function is being used, since no assembly language call statement will be generated. This makes it challenging to understand that a superclass constructor has in fact been called.

The analysis and comparison of vftables can also reveal inheritance relationships. For example, in comparing the vftables shown in Figure 8-13, we note that the vftable for SubClass contains two of the same pointers that appear in the vftable for `BaseClass`, and we conclude that `BaseClass` and `SubClass` must be related in some way. To understand which one is the base class and which one is the subclass, we can apply the following guidelines, singly or in combination:

- When two vftables contain the same number of entries, the two corresponding classes *may* be involved in an inheritance relationship.

- When the vftable for class X contains more entries than the vftable for class Y, class X *may* be a subclass of class Y.

- When the vftable for class X contains entries that are also found in the vftable for class Y, then one of the following relationships must exist: X is a subclass of Y, Y is a subclass of X, or X and Y are both subclasses of a common superclass Z.

- When the vftable for class X contains entries that are also found in the vftable for class Y and the vftable for class X contains at least one `purecall` entry that is not also present in the corresponding vftable entry for class Y, then class Y is likely to be a subclass of class X.

While the preceding list is by no means all-inclusive, we can use these guidelines to deduce the relationship between `BaseClass` and `SubClass` in Figure 8-14. In this case, the last three rules all apply, but the last rule specifically leads us to conclude, based on vftable analysis alone, that `SubClass` inherits from `BaseClass`.

C++ Reverse Engineering References

Several excellent references exist on reverse engineering compiled C++.[2] While many of the details in each of these articles apply specifically to programs compiled using Microsoft's C++ compiler, many of the concepts apply equally to programs compiled using other C++ compilers.

Summary

You can expect to encounter complex data types in all but the most trivial programs. Understanding how data within data structures is accessed and knowing how to recognize clues to the layout of those data structures is an essential reverse engineering skill. Ghidra provides a wide variety of features designed specifically to deal with data structures. Familiarity with these features will greatly enhance your ability to comprehend what data is being manipulated and spend more time understanding how and why that data is being manipulated. In the next chapter, we continue our discussion of Ghidra's basic capabilities with an in-depth look at cross-references.

---

2. See Igor Skochinsky's article "Reversing Microsoft Visual C++ Part II: Classes, Methods and RTTI," available at *http://www.openrce.org/articles/full_view/23* and Paul Vincent Sabanal and Mark Vincent Yason's paper "Reversing C ++," available at *http://www.blackhat.com/presentations /bh-dc-07/Sabanal_Yason/Paper/bh-dc-07-Sabanal_Yason-WP.pdf*.

9

CROSS-REFERENCES

Two common questions asked while reverse engineering a binary are "Where is this function called from?" and "Which functions access this data?" These and other similar questions seek to identify and catalog the references to and from various resources in a program. The following two examples serve to show the usefulness of such questions.

Example 1

While you are reviewing the large number of ASCII strings in a particular binary, you see a string that seems particularly suspicious: "Pay within 72 hours or the recovery key will be destroyed and your data will remain encrypted forever." On its own, this string is just circumstantial evidence. It in no way confirms that the binary has the capability or intent to execute a crypto ransomware attack. The answer to the question "Where is this string referenced in the binary?" would help you to quickly track down the program location(s) that makes use of the string. This information, in turn, should assist you in locating any related crypto ransomware code that uses the string or to demonstrate that the string, in this context, is benign.

Example 2

You have located a function containing a stack-allocated buffer that can be overflowed, possibly leading to exploitation of the program, and you want to determine if this is actually possible. If you want to develop and demonstrate an exploit, the function is useless to you unless you can get it to execute. This leads to the question "Which functions call this vulnerable function?" as well as additional questions regarding the nature of the data that those functions may pass to the vulnerable function. This line of reasoning must continue as you work your way back up potential call chains to find one that you can influence to demonstrate that the overflow is exploitable.

Referencing Basics

Ghidra can help you analyze both of these cases (and many others) through its extensive mechanisms for displaying and accessing reference information. In this chapter, we discuss the types of references that Ghidra makes available, the tools for accessing reference information, and ways to interpret that information. In Chapter 10, we will use Ghidra's graphing capabilities to examine visual representations of reference relationships.

All references obey the same general traffic rules. Associated with each reference is the notion of a direction. All references are made from one address to another address. If you are familiar with graph theory, you can think of addresses as nodes (or *vertices*) in a directed graph, and references as the *edges* that identify directed connections between the nodes. Figure 9-1 provides a quick refresher on basic graph terminology. In this simple graph, three nodes—A, B, and C—are connected by two directed edges.

Figure 9-1: Directed graph with three nodes and two edges

Directed edges are represented by arrows to indicate the allowable direction of travel along the edge. In Figure 9-1, travel from A to B is possible, but travel from B to A is not, similar to a one-way street. If the arrows were bidirectional, travel in either direction would be acceptable.

Ghidra has two basic categories of references: forward references and back references (each with subcategories as well). The back references are the less complex of the two types and are likely to be used most frequently in reverse engineering. Back references, also referred to as *cross-references*, provide a means to navigate between locations in the listing such as code and data.

Cross-References (Back References)

Back references within Ghidra are often referred to simply as *XREFs*, which is a mnemonic for the term *cross-reference*. Within this text, we use the term *XREF* only when referring to the specific sequence of characters (XREF) in a Ghidra listing, menu item, or dialog. In all other cases, we stick to the more general term *cross-reference* when referring to back references. Let's start by looking at specific examples of XREFs in Ghidra before moving on to a more comprehensive example.

Example 1: Basic XREFs

Let's begin by examining some of the XREFs that we encountered in demo_stackframe (see Chapter 6) and use the following listing to understand the associated format and meaning:

```
*****************************************************************
*                        FUNCTION                             *
*****************************************************************
undefined demo_stackframe(undefined param_1, undefined4. . .
    undefined    AL:1            <RETURN>
    undefined    Stack[0x4]:4    param_1
    undefined4   Stack[0x8]:4    param_2    XREF[1]:❶0804847f❷(R)❸
    undefined4   Stack[0xc]:4    param_3    XREF[1]: 08048479(R)
    undefined4   Stack[-0x10]:4  local_10   XREF[1]: 0804847c(W)
    undefined4   Stack[-0x14]:4  local_14   XREF[2]: 08048482(W),
                                                     08048493(R)
    undefined4   Stack[-0x18]:4  local_18   XREF[2]: 08048485(W),
                                                     08048496(R)
    undefined1   Stack[-0x58]:1  local_58   XREF[1]: 0804848c(W)
demo_stackframe                             XREF[4]: Entry Point(*),
                                                     main:080484be(c)❹,
                                                     080485e4, 08048690(*)
```

Ghidra not only indicates that there is a cross-reference with the indicator XREF ❶ but also shows the number of cross-references with an index value following XREF. This part of the cross-reference (for example, XREF[2]:) is called the *XREF header*. Examining the headers in the listing, we can see that most of the cross-references have only one referring address, but a few have more.

Following the header is the address associated with the cross-reference ❷, which is a navigable object. Following the address, there is a type indicator in parentheses ❸. For data cross-references (which is the case in this example), the valid types are R (indicating that the variable is read at the corresponding XREF address), W (indicating that the variable is being written to), and * (indicating that an address of a location is being taken as a pointer). In summary, *data cross-references* are identified in the listing where the data is declared, and associated XREF entries provide links to the locations where the data is referenced.

FORMATTING XREFS

As with most items you encounter in the Listing window, you can control the attributes associated with the cross-reference display. Selecting Edit ▸Tool Options opens the editable options for the CodeBrowser. Since an XREF is part of the Listing window, the XREFs Field can be found within the Listing Fields folder. When it is selected, it will open the dialog shown in Figure 9-2 (here with default options). If you were to change Maximum Number of XREFs to Display to 2, the header for all cross-references exceeding this number would be displayed as XREF[more]. The option to display nonlocal namespaces allows you to quickly identify all of the cross-references that are not within the current function's body. All of the options are explained in Ghidra Help.

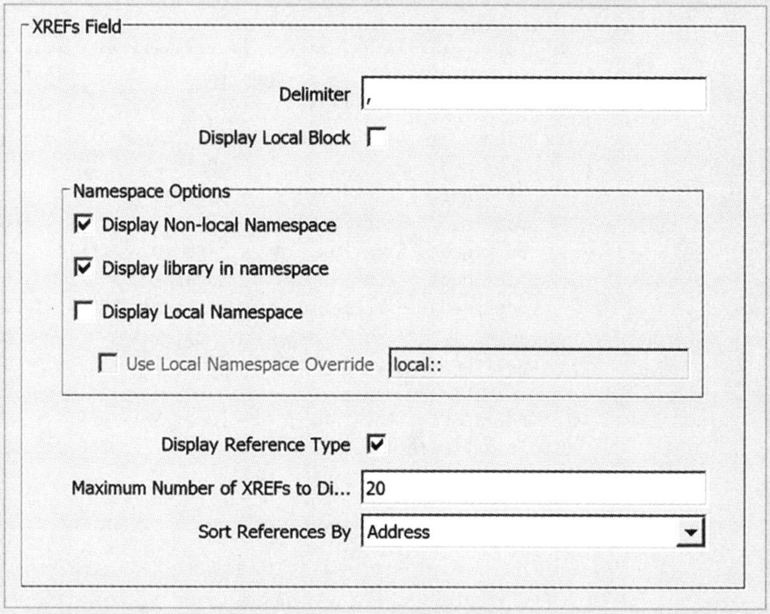

```
┌─XREFs Field────────────────────────────────────────────────┐
│                                                             │
│                         Delimiter  │,                    │  │
│                 Display Local Block  ☐                      │
│                                                             │
│   ┌─Namespace Options──────────────────────────────────┐    │
│   │  ☑ Display Non-local Namespace                      │    │
│   │  ☑ Display library in namespace                     │    │
│   │  ☐ Display Local Namespace                          │    │
│   │       ☐ Use Local Namespace Override  │local::    │  │    │
│   └─────────────────────────────────────────────────────┘    │
│                                                             │
│              Display Reference Type  ☑                      │
│     Maximum Number of XREFs to Di...  │20                 │  │
│               Sort References By  │Address            ▼│    │
│                                                             │
└─────────────────────────────────────────────────────────────┘
```

Figure 9-2: XREFs Field edit window showing defaults

The listing also contains a *code cross-reference* ❹. Code cross-references are a very important concept, as they facilitate Ghidra's generation of function graphs and function call graphs, which are the focus of Chapter 10. A code cross-reference is used to indicate that an instruction transfers or may transfer control to another instruction. The manner in which instructions transfer control is referred to as a *flow*. Flows may be any of three basic types: sequential, jump, or call. Jump and call flows can be further divided according to whether the target address is a near or far address.

A *sequential flow* is the simplest flow type, as it represents linear flow from one instruction to the next. This is the default execution flow for all non-branching instructions such as ADD. There are no special display indicators for sequential flows other than the order in which instructions are listed in the disassembly: if instruction A has a sequential flow to instruction B, then instruction B will immediately follow instruction A in the disassembly listing.

Example 2: Jump and Call XREFs

Let's take a quick look at a new example containing code cross-references that demonstrate jumps and calls. As with data cross-references, code cross-references also have an associated XREF entry in the Listing window. The following listing shows information associated with the function `main`:

```
*******************************************************************
*                            FUNCTION                            *
*******************************************************************
undefined4 __stdcall main(void)
   undefined4   EAX:4            <RETURN>
   undefined4   Stack[-0x8]:4   ptr      ❶ XREF[3]:  00401014(W),
                                                     0040101b(R),
                                                     00401026(R)
   main                                  ❷ XREF[1]:  entry:0040121e(c)
```

You can clearly identify the three XREFs associated with the stack variable ❶ as well as the XREF associated with the function itself ❷. Let's decode the meaning of the XREF, `entry:0040121e(c)`. The address (or in this case, identifier) before the colon indicates the referring (or source) entity. In this case, control is transferred from entry. To the right of the colon is the specific address within entry that is the source of the cross-reference. The suffix (c) indicates that this is a CALL to main. Stated simply, the cross-reference says, "main is called from address `0040121e` within entry."

If we double-click the cross-reference address to follow the link, we are taken to the specified address within entry where we can examine the call. While the XREF is a unidirectional link, we can quickly return to main by double-clicking the function name (main) or using the backward navigation arrow in the CodeBrowser toolbar:

```
0040121e  CALL   main
```

In the following listing, the (j) suffix on the XREF indicates that this labeled location is the target of a JUMP:

```
004011fe  JZ      LAB_00401207 ❶
00401200  PUSH    EAX
00401201  CALL    __amsg_exit
00401206  POP     ECX
          LAB_00401207                          XREF[1]: 004011fe(j) ❷
00401207  MOV     EAX,[DAT_0040acf0]
```

Similar to the previous example, we can double-click the XREF address ❷ to navigate to the statement that transferred control. We can return by double-clicking the associated label ❶.

References Example

Let's walk through an example from source code to disassembly to demonstrate many types of cross-references. The following program, *simple_flows.c*, contains various operations that exercise Ghidra's cross-referencing features, as noted in the comment text:

```
int read_it;        // integer variable read in main
int write_it;       // integer variable written 3 times in main
int ref_it;         // integer variable whose address is taken in main
void callflow() {}  // function called twice from main

int main() {
    int *ptr = &ref_it; // results in a "pointer" style data reference (*)
    *ptr = read_it;     // results in a "read" style data reference (R)
    write_it = *ptr;    // results in a "write" style data reference (W)
    callflow();         // results in a "call" style code reference (c)
    if (read_it == 3) { // results in "jump" style code reference (j)
        write_it = 2;   // results in a "write" style data reference (W)
    }
    else {              // results in an "jump" style code reference (j)
        write_it = 1;   // results in a "write" style data reference (W)
    }
    callflow();         // results in an "call" style code reference (c)
}
```

Code Cross-References

Listing 9-1 shows the disassembly of the preceding program.

```
         undefined4 __stdcall main(void)
            undefined4 EAX:4 <RETURN>
            undefined4 Stack[-0x8]:4 ptr      XREF[3]:  00401014(W),
                                                        0040101b(R),
                                                        00401026(R)
         main                                 XREF[1]:  entry:0040121e(c)
00401010 PUSH    EBP
00401011 MOV     EBP,ESP
00401013 PUSH    ECX
00401014 MOV❶    dword ptr [EBP + ptr],ref_it
0040101b MOV     EAX,dword ptr [EBP + ptr]
0040101e MOV❷    ECX,dword ptr [read_it]
00401024 MOV     dword ptr [EAX]=>ref_it,ECX
00401026 MOV     EDX,dword ptr [EBP + ptr]
00401029 MOV     EAX=>ref_it,dword ptr [EDX]
0040102b MOV     [write_it],EAX
00401030 CALL❸   callflow
00401035 CMP     dword ptr [read_it],3
0040103c JNZ     LAB_0040104a
0040103e MOV     dword ptr [write_it],2
00401048 JMP❹    LAB_00401054


         LAB_0040104a                         XREF[1]:❺0040103c(j)
0040104a MOV     dword ptr [write_it],1
```

```
        LAB_00401054                              XREF[1]:   00401048(j)
00401054  CALL    callflow
00401059  XOR     EAX,EAX
0040105b  MOV     ESP,EBP
0040105d  POP     EBP
0040105e  RET❻
```

Listing 9-1: Disassembly of main in simple_flows.exe

Every instruction other than JMP ❹ and RET ❻ has an associated sequential flow to its immediate successor. Instructions used to invoke functions, such as the x86 CALL instruction ❸, are assigned a *call flow*, indicating transfer of control to the target function. Call flows are noted by XREFs at the target function (the destination address of the flow). The disassembly of the callflow function referenced in Listing 9-1 is shown in Listing 9-2.

```
    undefined __stdcall callflow(void)
        undefined AL:1 <RETURN>
    callflow                                      XREF[4]:   0040010c(*),
                                                             004001e4(*),
                                                             main:00401030(c),
                                                             main:00401054(c)

00401000  PUSH    EBP
00401001  MOV     EBP,ESP
00401003  POP     EBP
00401004  RET
```

Listing 9-2: Disassembly of the callflow *function*

EXTRA XREFS?

Every now and again, you see something in a listing that seems anomalous. Listing 9-2 has two pointer XREFs, 0040010c(*) and 004001e4(*), that are not easily explained. We immediately understood the two XREFs that we could trace back to the calls to callflow in main. What are the other two XREFs? It turns out that these are an interesting artifact of this particular code. This program was compiled for Windows, which results in a PE file, and the two anomalous XREFs take us to the PE header in the Headers section of the listing. The two reference addresses (including the associated bytes) are shown here:

```
0040010c  00 10 00 00 ibo32    callflow            BaseOfCode
                . . .
004001e4  00 10 00 00 ibo32    callflow            VirtualAddress
```

Why is this function referenced in the PE header? A quick Google search can help us understand what is happening: callflow just happens to be the very first thing in the text section, and the two PE fields indirectly reference the start of the text section, hence the unanticipated XREFs associated with the callflow function.

In this example, we see that `callflow` is called twice from `main`: once from address 00401030 and again from address 00401054. Cross-references resulting from function calls are distinguished by the suffix (c). The source location displayed in the cross-references indicates both the address from which the call is being made and the function that contains the call.

A *jump flow* is assigned to each unconditional and conditional branch instruction. Conditional branches are also assigned sequential flows to account for control flow when the branch is not taken; unconditional branches have no associated sequential flow because the branch is always taken. Jump flows are associated with jump-style cross-references displayed at the target of the `JNZ` ❺ in Listing 9-1. As with call-style cross-references, jump cross-references display the address of the referring location (the source of the jump). Jump cross-references are distinguished by the (j) suffix.

BASIC BLOCKS

In program analysis, a *basic block* is a maximal sequence of instructions that executes, without branching, from beginning to end. Each basic block therefore has a single entry point (the first instruction in the block) and a single exit point (the last instruction in the block). The first instruction in a basic block is often the target of a branching instruction, while the last instruction is often a branch instruction. The first instruction may be the target of multiple code cross-references. Other than the first instruction, no other instruction within a basic block can be the target of a code cross-reference. The last instruction of a basic block may be the source of multiple code cross-references, such as a conditional jump, or it may flow into an instruction that is the target of multiple code cross-references (which, by definition, must begin a new basic block).

Data Cross-References

Data cross-references are used to track how data is accessed within a binary. The three most commonly encountered types of data cross-references indicate when a location is being read, when a location is being written, and when the address of a location is being taken. The global variables from the previous sample program are shown in Listing 9-3, as they provide several examples of data cross-references.

```
        read_it                          XREF[2]:   main:0040101e(R),
                                                    main:00401035(R)
0040b720 undefined4    ??
        write_it                         XREF[3]:   main:0040102b(W),
                                                    main:0040103e(W),
                                                    main:0040104a(W)
```

```
0040b724     ??          ??
0040b725     ??          ??
0040b726     ??          ??
0040b727     ??          ??
        ref_it                                    XREF[3]:  main:00401014(*),
                                                            main:00401024(W),
                                                            main:00401029(R)

0040b728 undefined4      ??
```

Listing 9-3: Global variables referenced in simple_flows.c

A *read cross-reference* indicates that the contents of a memory location are being read. Read cross-references can originate only from an instruction address but may refer to any program location. The global variable read_it is read twice in Listing 9-1. The associated cross-reference comments shown in this listing indicate exactly which locations in main are referencing read_it and are recognizable as read cross-references from the (R) suffix. The read performed on read_it ❷ in Listing 9-1 is a 32-bit read into the ECX register, which leads Ghidra to format read_it as an undefined4 (a 4-byte value of unspecified type). Ghidra often attempts to infer the size of a data item based on how the item is manipulated by code throughout a binary.

The global variable write_it is referenced three times in Listing 9-1. Associated *write cross-references* are generated and displayed as comments for the write_it variable, indicating the program locations that modify the contents of the variable. Write cross-references utilize the (W) suffix. In this case, Ghidra did not format write_it as a 4-byte variable even though there seems to be enough information to do so. As with read cross-references, write cross-references can originate only from a program instruction but may reference any program location. Generally, a write cross-reference that targets a program instruction byte is indicative of self-modifying code and is frequently encountered in malware de-obfuscation routines.

The third type of data cross-reference, a *pointer cross-reference*, indicates that the address of a location is being used (rather than the content of the location). The address of global variable ref_it is taken ❶ in Listing 9-1, resulting in the pointer cross-reference at ref_it in Listing 9-3, as indicated by the suffix (*). Pointer cross-references are commonly the result of address derivations either in code or in data. As you saw in Chapter 8, array access operations are typically implemented by adding an offset to the starting address of the array, and the first address in most global arrays can often be recognized by the presence of a pointer cross-reference. For this reason, most string literals (strings being arrays of characters in C/C++) are the targets of pointer cross-references.

Unlike read and write cross-references, which can originate only from instruction locations, pointer cross-references can originate from either instruction locations or data locations. An example of pointers that can originate from a program's data section is any table of addresses (such as a vftable, which results in the generation of a pointer cross-reference from each entry in the table to the corresponding virtual function). Let's see this in context using the `SubClass` example from Chapter 8. The disassembly for the vftable for `SubClass` is shown here:

```
         SubClass::vftable             XREF[1]:  SubClass_Constructor:00401062(*)
  00408148 void * SubClass::vfunc1 vfunc1
❶ 0040814c void * BaseClass::vfunc2 vfunc2
  00408150 void * SubClass::vfunc3 vfunc3
  00408154 void * BaseClass::vfunc4 vfunc4
  00408158 void * SubClass::vfunc5 vfunc5
```

Here you see that the data item at location `0040814c` ❶ is a pointer to `BaseClass::vfunc2`. Navigating to `BaseClass::vfunc2` presents us with the following listing:

```
         ****************************************************************
         *                          FUNCTION                           *
         ****************************************************************
         undefined __stdcall vfunc2(void)
            undefined AL:1 <RETURN>
            undefined4 Stack[-0x8]:4 local_8    XREF[1]:  00401024(W)
         BaseClass::vfunc2                      XREF[2]:  00408138(*)❶,
                                                          0040814c(*)❷
  00401020 PUSH   EBP
  00401021 MOV    EBP,ESP
  00401023 PUSH   ECX
  00401024 MOV    dword ptr [EBP + local_8],ECX
  00401027 MOV    ESP,EBP
  00401029 POP    EBP
  0040102a RET
```

Unlike most functions, this function has no code cross-references. Instead, we see two pointer cross-references indicating that the address of the function is derived in two locations. The second XREF ❷ refers back to the `SubClass` vftable entry discussed earlier. Following the first XREF ❶ would lead us to the vftable for `BaseClass`, which also contains a pointer to this virtual function.

This example demonstrates that C++ virtual functions are rarely called directly and are usually not the target of a call cross-reference. Because of the way vftables are created, all C++ virtual functions will be referred to by at least one vftable entry and will always be the target of at least one pointer cross-reference. (Remember that overriding a virtual function is not mandatory.)

When a binary contains sufficient information, Ghidra is able to locate vftables for you. Any vftables that Ghidra finds are listed as an entry under the vftable's corresponding class entry within the *Classes* folder of the Symbol Tree. Clicking a vftable in the Symbol Tree window navigates you to the vftable location in the program's data section.

Reference Management Windows

By now, you've probably noticed that XREF annotations are quite common in the Listing window. This is no accident, as the links formed by cross-references are the glue that hold a program together. Cross-references tell the story of intra- and inter-functional dependencies, and most successful reverse engineering efforts demand a comprehensive understanding of their behavior. The sections that follow move beyond the basic display and navigational usefulness of cross-references to introduce several options for managing cross-references within Ghidra.

XRefs Window

You can use XREF headers to learn more about a particular cross-reference, as shown in the following listing:

```
undefined4 Stack[-0x10]:4 local_10   XREF[1]:  0804847c(W)
undefined4 Stack[-0x14]:4 local_14   XREF[2]:❶08048482(W),
                                               08048493(R)
```

Double-clicking the XREF[2] header ❶ will bring up the associated XRefs window shown in Figure 9-3 with a more detailed listing of the cross-references. By default, the window shows the location, label (if applicable), referring disassembly, and reference type.

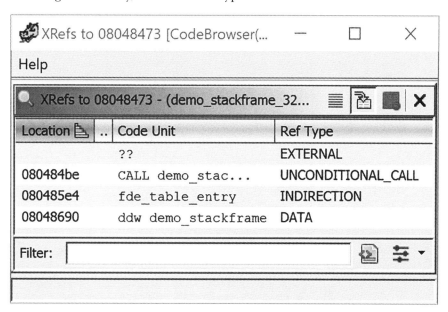

Figure 9-3: XRefs window

References To

Another window that can be helpful in understanding the program flow is the References To window. Right-clicking any address in the Listing window and choosing **References ▸ Show Reference to Address** brings up the window shown in Figure 9-4.

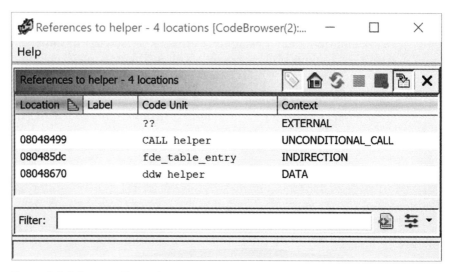

Figure 9-4: References To window

In this example, we have selected the starting address of the helper function. Within this window, you can navigate to the associated location by clicking any entry in the window.

Symbol References

Another reference view that was introduced in "The Symbol Table and Symbol References Windows" on page 82 is the combination of the Symbol Table and Symbol Reference windows. By default, when you choose Window ▸ Symbol References, you get two related windows. One displays every symbol in the entire symbol table. The other displays the associated references to the symbols. Selecting any entry in the Symbol Table window (function, vftable, and so on) causes the associated symbol references to be displayed in the Symbol References window.

Reference lists can be used to rapidly identify every location from which a particular function is called. For example, many people consider the C strcpy function to be dangerous as it copies a source array of characters, up to and including the associated null termination character, to a destination array, with no checks whatsoever that the destination array is large enough to hold all of the characters from the source. You could locate any one call to strcpy in your listing and use the aforementioned method to open the References To window, but if you don't want to take the time to find `strcpy` used somewhere in the binary, you can open the Symbol References window and quickly locate `strcpy` and all associated references.

Advanced Reference Manipulation

At the start of this chapter, we equated the term *back reference* with *cross-reference* and briefly mentioned that Ghidra also has *forward references*, of which there are two types. *Inferred forward references* are generally added to the listing automatically and correspond one-for-one to back references, although inferred forward references are travelled in the opposite direction. In other words, we traverse back references from a target address back to a source address, and we traverse inferred forward references from a source address forward to a target address.

The second type is an *explicit forward reference*. There are several types of explicit forward references, and their management is much more complex than other cross-references. The types of explicit forward references include memory references, external references, stack references, and register references. In addition to viewing references, Ghidra allows you to add and edit a variety of reference types.

You may need to add your own cross-references when Ghidra's static analysis cannot determine jump or call targets that are computed at runtime, but you know the target from other analysis. In the following code, which we last saw in Chapter 8, a virtual function is called.

```
0001072e   PUSH    EBP
0001072f   MOV     EBP,ESP
00010731   SUB     ESP,8
00010734   MOV     EAX,dword ptr [EBP + param_1]❶
00010737   MOV     EAX,dword ptr [EAX]
00010739   ADD     EAX,8
0001073c   MOV     EAX,dword ptr [EAX]
0001073e   SUB     ESP,12
00010741   PUSH    dword ptr [EBP + param_1]
00010744   CALL❷   EAX
00010746   ADD     ESP,16
00010749   NOP
0001074a   LEAVE
0001074b   RET
```

The value held in `EAX` ❷ depends on the value of the pointer passed in `param_1` ❶. As a result, Ghidra does not have enough information to create a cross-reference linking `00010744` (the address of the `CALL` instruction) to the target of the call. Manually adding a cross-reference (to `SubClass::vfunc3` for example) would, among other things, link the target functions into a call graph, thereby improving Ghidra's analysis of the program. Right-clicking the call ❷ and selecting **References ▸ Add Reference from** opens the dialog shown in Figure 9-5. This dialog is also available through the References ▸Add/Edit option.

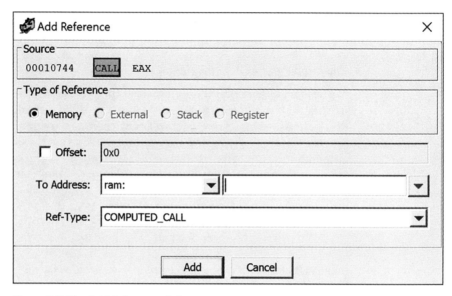

Figure 9-5: The Add Reference dialog

Specify the address of the target function as the To Address setting and make sure that the correct setting for Ref-Type is selected. When you close the dialog with the Add button, Ghidra creates the reference, and a new (c) cross-reference appears at the target address. More information on forward references, including the remaining reference types as well as reference manipulation, can be found in Ghidra Help.

Summary

References are powerful tools to help you understand how artifacts within a binary are related. We discussed cross-references in detail and introduced some other capabilities associated with references that will be visited again in later chapters. In the next chapter, we look at visual representations of references and how the resulting graphs can help us better understand the control flows within functions and the relationships between functions in our binaries.

10

GRAPHS

Visually representing data with graphs, as we did in the previous chapter (see Figure 9-1), provides a concise and clear mechanism to demonstrate the many connections between the nodes within a graph as well as helps us recognize patterns that might otherwise be difficult to discover when operating on a graph as an abstract data type. Ghidra's graph views offer a new perspective (in addition to disassembly and decompiler listings) for viewing the contents of a binary. They let you quickly see the control flow in a function and the relationships between functions in a file, by representing functions and other types of blocks as nodes and by representing flows and cross-references as edges (the lines that connect nodes). With enough practice, you may find that common control structures, such as switch statements and nested if/else structures, are easier to recognize in graph form than in a long text listing. In Chapter 5, we briefly introduced the Function Graph and Function Call Graph windows. In this chapter, we take a deeper dive into Ghidra's graph capabilities.

Because cross-references relate one address to another, they are a natural place to begin graphing our binaries. By restricting ourselves to sequential flows and specific types of cross-references, we can derive a number of useful graphs for analyzing our binaries. While the flows and cross-references serve as the edges in our graphs, the meaning behind nodes can vary. Depending on the type of graph we wish to generate, nodes may contain one or more instructions, or entire functions. Let's start our discussion about graphs by looking at the ways that Ghidra organizes code into *blocks* and then move on to the types of graphs available in Ghidra.

Basic Blocks

In a computer program, a *basic block* is a grouping of one or more instructions with a single entry at the beginning of the block and a single exit from the end of the block. Other than the last instruction, every instruction within a basic block transfers control to exactly one *successor* instruction within the block. Similarly, other than the first instruction, every instruction in a basic block receives control from exactly one *predecessor* instruction within the block. In "Cross-References (Back References)" on page 185, we identified this as *sequential flow*. You may notice, from time to time, a function call being made in the middle of a basic block and think to yourself, "Isn't this precisely the type of instruction, like a jump, that should terminate a block?" For the purposes of basic block determination, the fact that function calls transfer control outside the current block is generally ignored, unless it is known that the function being called does not return normally.

Once the first instruction in a basic block is executed, the remainder of the block is guaranteed to execute to completion. This can factor significantly into runtime instrumentation of a program, since it is no longer necessary to set a breakpoint on every instruction in a program or even single-step the program in order to record which instructions have executed. Instead, breakpoints can be set on the first instruction of each basic block, and as each breakpoint is hit, it can be assumed that every instruction in the associated block will be executed. Let's shift our focus to Ghidra's Function Graph capabilities to provide another perspective on blocks.

Function Graphs

The Function Graph window, introduced in Chapter 5, displays a single function in a graphical format. The following program comprises a single function that is composed of a single basic block, so it's a useful starting point to demonstrate Ghidra's function graphs:

```
int global_array[3];

int main() {
    int idx = 2;
    global_array[0] = 10;
    global_array[1] = 20;
```

```
    global_array[2] = 30;
    global_array[idx] = 40;
}
```

When you open the Function Graph window (Window ▸ Function Graph) with main selected, you are presented with a function graph with only one basic block, as shown in Figure 10-1.

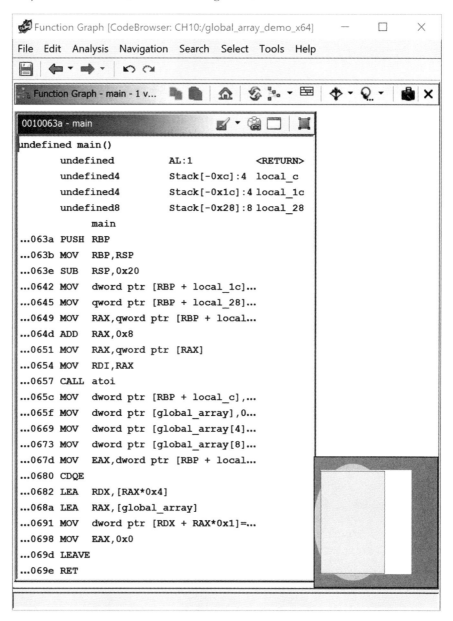

Figure 10-1: A single-block Function Graph window with satellite view at lower right

The Function Graph window and the Listing window have a useful bidirectional link. If you view the windows side by side, the concurrent listing and graphical representation can help you better understand the function's control flow. Changes you make in the Function Graph window (for example, renaming functions, variables, and so on) will be immediately reflected in the Listing window. Changes you make in the Listing window will also be reflected in the Function Graph window, although you may have to refresh the window to see the change.

ARTICULATION

As your functions become more complex, the number of blocks in each will likely increase. When you first generate a function graph, the edges connecting the blocks are articulated. This means that they bend neatly at 90-degree angles so that they are not hidden behind nodes. This results in a neat grid layout where all components of all edges are either horizontal or vertical. If you decide to change the layout of the graph by dragging nodes around, the edges may lose their articulation and revert to straight lines that route behind other nodes in the graph. Figure 10-2 demonstrates the contrast between the articulated representation on the left and the unarticulated version on the right. You can revert to the original layout at any time by refreshing the Function Graph window.

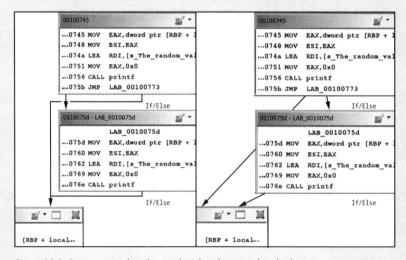

Figure 10-2: Function graph with articulated and unarticulated edges

If you click any line of text in the Function Graph window, the cursor in the Listing window moves to the corresponding location in the disassembly listing. If you double-click data in a function graph, the Listing window will navigate to the associated data in the data section of the listing, while the Function Graph window retains focus on the function. (Although Ghidra does not currently provide graph-based visualization of data or relationships among data components, it does allow you to concurrently view the data in listing view and associated code in graph view.)

Let's look at a quick example to demonstrate the relationship between the Listing window and the Function Graph window. Suppose you see the global_array variable in Figure 10-1 and want to know more about its type. When you navigate to it by double-clicking the name in the graph view, you can see that Ghidra has classified global_array as an array of undefined bytes (undefined1), accessed with indices to the fourth and eighth elements. If you change the array definition in the data section of the Listing window from undefined1[12] to int[3] (respectively shown in the upper and lower halves of Figure 10-3), you can immediately see the effects of the declaration on the disassembly in the Function Graph window (as well as the Decompiler window): the index values change to 1 and 2 to reflect the new 4-byte size of each array element.

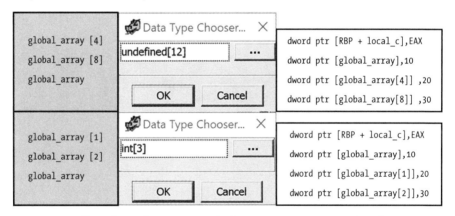

Figure 10-3: Effect of modifying an array declaration on Function Graph and Listing windows

Navigating in the Listing window is flexible, provided you do not click a different function. You can scroll through the entire Listing window contents, click and make changes in the data section, make changes within the function, and so on. If you click within another function, the graph view will be updated to display the graph of the newly selected function.

WHAT IS AN INTERACTION THRESHOLD?

When interacting with the Function Graph window, particularly with a complex function, you may zoom out because you cannot see everything you want to see. When the individual nodes become too small to interact with in a meaningful way, you have passed the *interaction threshold*. Drop shadows on each node in the Function Graph are used to indicate this condition. Virtual addresses may show only the least significant values, and the sheer number of nodes in the graph display can become unwieldy. An attempt to select content within a node ends up selecting the entire block. Don't despair if the complexity of your function pushes you beyond this threshold. You can click any of the nodes to bring them into focus, or double-click a node to zoom in on it.

Figure 10-4 highlights the menus and toolbars available in the Function Graph window.

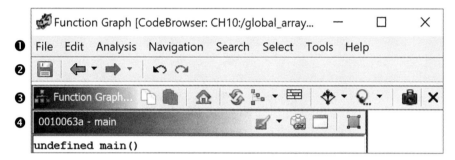

Figure 10-4: Function Graph toolbars

A function graph is really nothing more than a graphical presentation of the Listing window isolated to a single function, so it should not be surprising that all of the menus from the CodeBrowser (with the exception of the Window menu) are available ❶ in the Function Graph window. The available subset of the CodeBrowser toolbar ❷ includes the capability to save the current state of the open file, undo and redo, and navigate forward and backward within the current navigation chain. It is important to note that, since the windows are linked, this may navigate you out of (and back into) the current function, which will change the contents of the Function Graph window.

The Function Graph toolbar icons ❸ and their default behaviors are described in Figure 10-5.

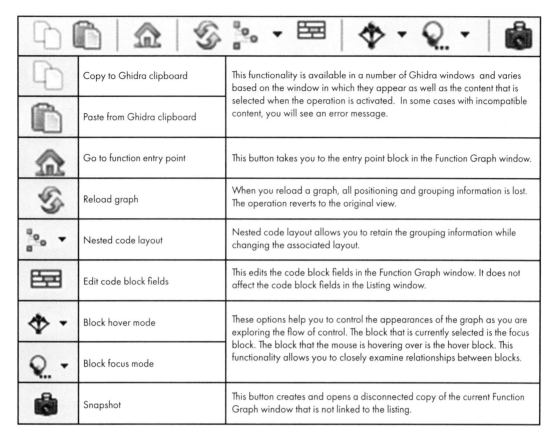

	Copy to Ghidra clipboard	This functionality is available in a number of Ghidra windows and varies based on the window in which they appear as well as the content that is selected when the operation is activated. In some cases with incompatible content, you will see an error message.
	Paste from Ghidra clipboard	
	Go to function entry point	This button takes you to the entry point block in the Function Graph window.
	Reload graph	When you reload a graph, all positioning and grouping information is lost. The operation reverts to the original view.
	Nested code layout	Nested code layout allows you to retain the grouping information while changing the associated layout.
	Edit code block fields	This edits the code block fields in the Function Graph window. It does not affect the code block fields in the Listing window.
	Block hover mode	These options help you to control the appearances of the graph as you are exploring the flow of control. The block that is currently selected is the focus block. The block that the mouse is hovering over is the hover block. This functionality allows you to closely examine relationships between blocks.
	Block focus mode	
	Snapshot	This button creates and opens a disconnected copy of the current Function Graph window that is not linked to the listing.

Figure 10-5: Function Graph toolbar operations

Each basic block also has a toolbar ❹ that lets you modify the block and group it with other blocks by combining several blocks (vertices) into a single block (see Figure 10-6 for an explanation of the toolbar's icons and their default behaviors). This feature is extremely useful for reducing the complexity of graphs that results from highly nested functions. For example, you might elect to collapse all of the blocks nested within a loop statement into a single graph node after you understand the behavior of the loop and feel less need to see the code within the loop. Depending on the number of nested blocks that you group, the readability of the graph may be enhanced significantly. To group nodes, you must select all nodes that will belong to the group by using CTRL-click to select all member nodes, and then click the **Combine vertices** tool of the node you consider to lie at the root of the group. *Restore group* is a particularly helpful button that lets you quickly look inside a group and then re-collapse it.

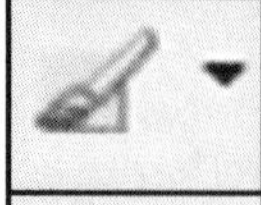	Background color	Select a background color for a block or group of blocks. This color is reflected in the Function Graph window as well as the Listing window.
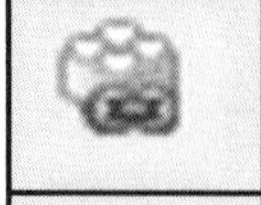	Jump to XREF	This button displays a list of cross-references to the entry point of the function.
	Fullscreen/Graph view	This is a toggle button that allows you to view the graph block in a full window.
	Combine vertices	This button will combine selected vertices into a single group.
	Restore group	This option is displayed only after you have ungrouped vertices, and it provides the option to regroup them.
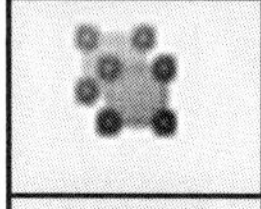	Ungroup vertices	This option is available only if vertices have been grouped and allows you to ungroup the vertices.
	Add vertex to group	This option is available only if vertices have been grouped and allows you to add a vertex to a group.

Figure 10-6: Function Graph basic block toolbar

To see some of the other features associated with a function graph, you will need to look at examples with more than one basic block. The following program is used in the examples that follow:

```
int do_random() {
    int r;
    srand(time(0));
    r = rand();
    if (r % 2 == 0) {
        printf("The random value %d is even\n", r);
    }
    else {
        printf("The random value %d is odd\n", r);
    }
    return r;
}
int main() {
    do_random();
}
```

The do_random function contains control structures (if/else) that result in a graph with four basic blocks, which we have labeled in Figure 10-8. Viewing a function with more than one block makes it more obvious that a function graph is a control flow graph, with edges indicating possible flows from one block to another. Note that Ghidra's layout for function graphs is called *nested code layout* and closely resembles the flow of C code. This makes it easy to view a graphical representation of your Listing and Decompiler windows within the context of a larger program. To maintain this view, we highly recommend changing your graph options to route edges around vertices (Edit ▸ Tool Options ▸ Function Graph ▸ Nested Code Layout ▸ Route Edges Around Vertices). By default, Ghidra has the unfortunate tendency to route edges behind nodes, which can often paint a misleading picture of the relationships between nodes.

THIS GRAPH IS STALE

While some changes in the listing are immediately reflected in the Function Graph window, in other cases the graph can become stale (not synchronized with the listing view). When this happens, Ghidra displays the message shown in Figure 10-7 at the bottom of the graph window.

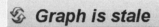

Figure 10-7: Stale graph warning message

The *recycle* icon to the left of the message allows you to refresh the graph without reverting to the original layout. (Of course, you can also choose to refresh and lay out again.)

In the graph shown in Figure 10-8, BLOCK-1 is the single point of entry into the function. This block, like all basic blocks, exhibits sequential flow from instruction to instruction within the block. None of the three function calls within the block (to time, srand, and rand) "break" the basic block, since Ghidra assumes that all of them return to continue sequential execution of the remaining instructions. BLOCK-2 is entered if the JNZ condition at the end of BLOCK-1 evaluates to false, meaning that the random value is even. BLOCK-3 is entered if the JNZ condition evaluates to true, indicating that the random value is odd. The final block, BLOCK-4, is entered following the completion of BLOCK-2 or BLOCK-3. Note that clicking an edge brings it into focus and causes it to appear thicker than the rest of the edges. In the figure, the edge that connects BLOCK-1 and BLOCK-3 is the active edge and appears bolded.

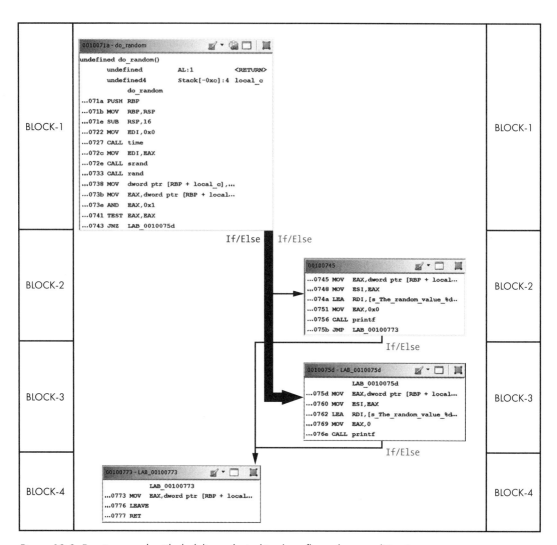

Figure 10-8: Function graph with dark line selected to show flow when condition is met

If you have a particularly long basic block and wish to break it into smaller blocks or wish to visually isolate a section of code for further analysis, you can split a basic block within a function graph by introducing new labels into the block. Using the hotkey L to insert a new label at line 0010072e in BLOCK-1 before the call to srand results in the addition of a fifth block to the function graph in Figure 10-9. The new edge that is introduced represents flow and is not associated with a cross-reference.

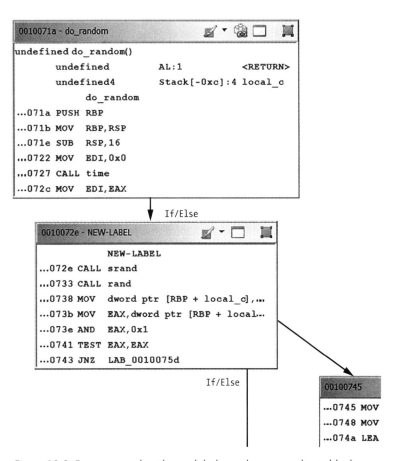

```
0010071a - do_random                    🖉 ▾ 🕸 ▢    🔳

undefined do_random()
        undefined          AL:1                <RETURN>
        undefined4         Stack[-0xc]:4 local_c
                do_random
...071a PUSH  RBP
...071b MOV   RBP,RSP
...071e SUB   RSP,16
...0722 MOV   EDI,0x0
...0727 CALL  time
...072c MOV   EDI,EAX
```

If/Else

```
0010072e - NEW-LABEL                    🖉 ▾   ▢    🔳

                NEW-LABEL
...072e CALL  srand
...0733 CALL  rand
...0738 MOV   dword ptr [RBP + local_c],...
...073b MOV   EAX,dword ptr [RBP + local...
...073e AND   EAX,0x1
...0741 TEST  EAX,EAX
...0743 JNZ   LAB_0010075d
```

If/Else

```
00100745

...0745 MOV
...0748 MOV
...074a LEA
```

Figure 10-9: Function graph with new label introducing new basic block

INTERACTING WITH FUNCTION GRAPHS

While it isn't easy to show in a book, the Function Graph window includes color, animation, and informational pop-ups as you interact with the various components in the graph:

Edges

The edges are colored based on the nature of the transition represented by the edge. You can control the colors through the Edit ▸Tool Options window, as shown in Figure 10-10. By default, a green edge indicates a conditional jump when the condition is true (jump taken), a red edge indicates a fallthrough (jump not taken), and a blue edge indicates an unconditional jump. Clicking an individual edge or set of edges increases the thickness of the edge and changes to a highlighted shade of the same color.

(continued)

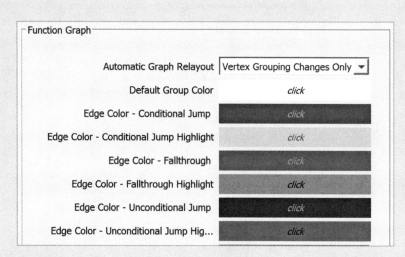

Figure 10-10: Function Graph color customization options

Nodes

The content of each node is a disassembly listing of the corresponding basic block. The way you interact with the listing code is identical to the way you interact with code in the Listing window. For example, hovering over names opens a pop-up that displays disassembly at the named location. When you hover over a node, Ghidra utilizes a path-highlighting animation on associated edges to indicate the control flow direction consistent with the currently selected path highlight options. This functionality can be disabled in Edit ▸ Tool Options.

Satellite

The satellite (a small overview of the graph) has a yellow halo around the block that is currently in focus, as does the Function Graph window. For easy identification, the function's entry block (which contains the function's entry point address) is green in the satellite, and any return blocks (blocks containing a ret, or equivalent) are red. Even if you change the background color of the associated block in the graph, the entry and exit colors don't change in the satellite. All other blocks will mirror the color assigned to them in the Function Graph window.

Function Call Graphs

A function call graph is useful for gaining a quick understanding of the hierarchy of function calls made within a program. Function call graphs are similar to function graphs, but each block represents an entire function body, and each edge represents a call cross-reference from one function to another.

To discuss function call graphs, we make use of the following trivial program that creates a simple hierarchy of function calls:

```
#include <stdio.h>
void depth_2_1() {
    printf("inside depth_2_1\n");
}
void depth_2_2() {
    fprintf(stderr, "inside depth_2_2\n");
}
void depth_1() {
    depth_2_1();
    depth_2_2();
    printf("inside depth_1\n");
}
int main() {
    depth_1();
}
```

After compiling a dynamically linked version of this program using GNU gcc and loading the binary with Ghidra, we can generate a function call graph by using Window ▸ Function Call Graph. By default, this creates a function call graph centered around the function that is currently selected. The function call graph when main is selected is shown in Figure 10-11. (The satellite view is hidden in these examples for clarity. To unhide the satellite view, use the icon in the bottom right of Figure 10-11.)

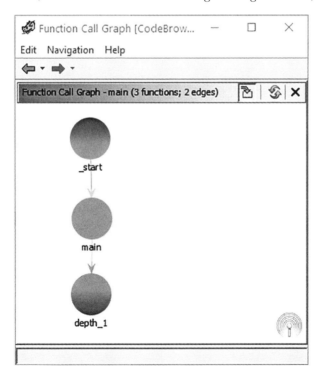

Figure 10-11: Simple function call graph with focus on main

The string *main (3 functions; 2 edges)* in the title bar of the graph lets us know what function we are in, along with the number of functions and edges displayed. Hovering over a node in the graph displays + and/or – icons at the top and/or bottom of the node, as shown in Figure 10-12.

A + icon at the top or bottom means you can display additional incoming or outgoing functions. Conversely, the – icon provides the ability to contract nodes. For instance, clicking a – symbol at the bottom of the function depth_1 when it is expanded will change the function call graph from the one shown in Figure 10-13 to the one in Figure 10-11.

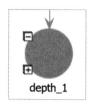

Figure 10-12: Function Call graph node with expand/collapse icons

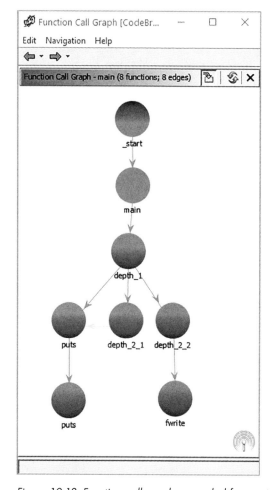

Figure 10-13: Function call graph expanded from main

The right-click context menu associated with each node provides you with options to expand or contract all outgoing edges for all nodes, on the same horizontal level, simultaneously. This is equivalent to clicking the

+ or – icon on all nodes in the same rank at the same time. Finally, double-clicking a node in the graph centers the graph on the selected node and fully expands all incoming and outgoing edges. An option that is disabled by default, but that many find helpful, provides you with the ability to zoom out and back in. This option can be enabled through Edit ▸ Tool Options by checking the Scroll Wheel Pans option. Ghidra maintains a short history of graphs in a cache as you shift focus to retain graph state upon return. This allows you to expand and contract nodes, navigate away, and then return to find your graph just the way you left it to continue your analysis.

Figure 10-14 shows the same program, with the focus on _start rather than main and most nodes fully expanded to show the full extent of the graph. In addition to our main function and associated subroutines, we can see wrapper code that was inserted by the compiler. This code is responsible for library initialization and termination as well as configuring the environment properly prior to transferring control to the main function. (Alert readers may notice that the compiler has substituted calls to puts and fwrite for printf and fprintf, respectively, as they are more efficient when printing static strings.)

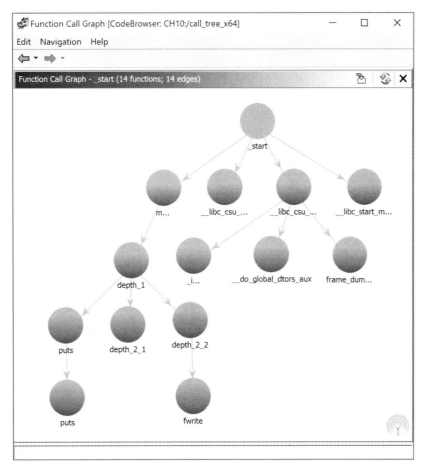

Figure 10-14: Expanded function call graph expanded from _start

THUNK

You may notice that the graph in Figure 10-14 shows multiple (apparently recursive) calls to puts. Welcome to the magical world of thunk functions. A *thunk function* is a compiler device that facilitates calls to functions whose address is unknown at compile time (such as a dynamically linked library function). Ghidra refers to the function whose address is unknown as the *thunked* function. The compiler replaces all calls the program makes to thunked functions with a call to a thunk function stub that the compiler inserts into the executable. The *thunk function stub* typically performs a table lookup to learn the runtime address of the thunked function before transferring control to the thunked function. The table consulted by a thunk stub is populated at runtime after the associated thunked function addresses become known. In Windows executables, this table is typically called the *import table*. In ELF binaries, this table is typically called the *global offset table* (or *got*).

If we navigate to puts from the function depth_1 in the Listing window, we find ourselves in the following listing:

```
*****************************************************************
*                        THUNK FUNCTION                         *
*****************************************************************
        thunk int puts(char * __s)
          Thunked-Function: <EXTERNAL>::puts
   int            EAX:4           <RETURN>
   char *         RDI:8              __s
          puts@@GLIBC_2.2.5
          puts    XREF[2]: puts:00100590(T),
                           puts:00100590(c), 00300fc8(*)
00302008          ??              ??
00302009          ??              ??
0030200a          ??              ??
```

This thunk function listing appears in a program section that Ghidra names EXTERNAL. Ghidra thunked function listings such as this are a consequence of the way in which external libraries are dynamically loaded and linked into processes at runtime, which means the libraries are generally not available during static analysis. While the listing provides you an indication of the function and library being called, the function code is not directly accessible (unless the library is also loaded into Ghidra, which is easily accomplished via the options page during the import process).

Here we also observe a new type of XREF. The (T) suffix on the first XREF indicates that this XREF is a link to the thunked function.

Now, let's revisit a statically linked version of the call_tree program. The initial graph generated from the main function is identical to the dynamically linked version shown in Figure 10-11. However, to get an idea of the potential complexity associated with graphs of statically linked binaries, let's investigate two expansions that seem relatively benign. Figure 10-15 shows the outgoing calls from the puts function. The title bar shows *puts(9 functions; 11 edges)*. Note that the title bar totals may be inaccurate until the program has been fully analyzed.

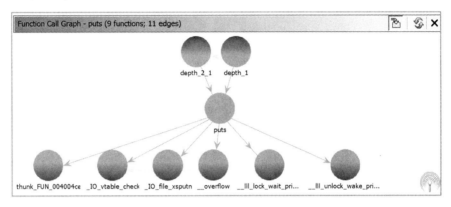

Figure 10-15: Function call graph in a statically linked binary

When we shift the focus to *_lll_lock_wait_private*, we are presented with an overwhelming graph with 70 nodes and over 200 edges, a portion of which is shown in Figure 10-16.

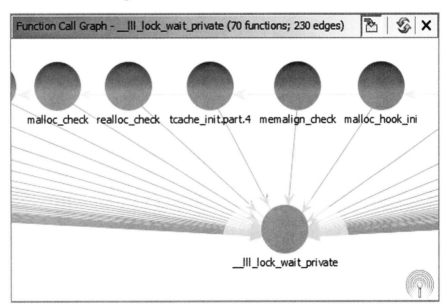

Figure 10-16: Expanded function call graph in a statically linked binary

While statically linked binaries are complex and working with the associated graphs can be challenging, two features make this tenable. First, you can usually locate main by using the hotkey G or by navigating from the program's entry symbol. Second, once you have located main in the listing, you can open and easily control what is displayed in the associated function call graph.

Trees

Ghidra presents many hierarchical concepts associated with a particular binary as a tree-like structure. While not always trees in a pure graph-theoretical sense, these structures provide the capability to expand and collapse nodes and to see the hierarchical relationship between nodes of varying types. When we discussed the CodeBrowser window in Chapter 5, you were introduced to Program Trees, Symbol Tree, Function Call Tree, and the Data Type Manager (which is also presented as a tree). These tree views can be used concurrently with other views to provide additional insight into the binary you are analyzing.

Summary

Graphs are a powerful tool available to assist you in analyzing any binary. If you are accustomed to viewing disassemblies in pure text format, it may take some time to adjust to using a graph-based display. In Ghidra, it is generally a matter of realizing that all of the information that was available in the text display remains available in the graph display; however, it may be formatted somewhat differently. Cross-references, for example, become the edges that connect the blocks in a graph display.

Which graph you view depends on what you want to know about a binary. If you want to know how a particular function is reached, you are probably interested in a function call graph. If you want to know how a specific instruction is reached, you are probably more interested in a function graph. Both can provide valuable insight into how the program works.

Now that you have seen the basic functionality available when running Ghidra as a standalone instance with you as the only reverse engineer, it is time to investigate options for using Ghidra as a collaborative tool. In the next chapter, we look at Ghidra Server and the environment it provides to support collaborative reverse engineering.

PART III

MAKING GHIDRA WORK FOR YOU

11

COLLABORATIVE SRE

At this point, you should be comfortable navigating the Ghidra project environment and the many available tools and windows. You know how to create a project, import files, navigate, and manipulate the disassembly. You understand Ghidra data types, data structures, and cross-references. But do you understand scale? A 200MB binary is likely to generate a disassembly that is millions of lines long and consists of hundreds of thousands of functions. Even with the largest, portrait-oriented monitor you can find, you'll be able to view only a few hundred lines of that disassembly at any one time.

One way to take on such a monumental task is to assign a team of people to it, but that introduces an additional problem: how will you synchronize everyone's efforts so that people aren't walking all over one another with their changes? It's time to extend our discussion of using Ghidra to cover a collaborative team working together on a shared project. Ghidra's support for collaborative reverse engineering alone makes it unique among software analysis tools. In this chapter, we introduce Ghidra's collaboration server, which is included with the standard Ghidra distribution. We discuss its installation, configuration, and use to help you get more eyes focused on your most challenging RE problems.

Teamwork

SRE is a complex process, and few individuals are experts in all of its intricacies. The ability to have analysts with different skill sets simultaneously analyzing a single binary can drastically reduce the amount of time needed to obtain the desired results. A rock star in navigating control flows through a complex program may dread having to analyze and document the associated data structures. An expert in malware analysis may be ill-suited for vulnerability discovery work, and anyone who is pressed for time is less likely to use that time inserting the inevitable plethora of comments that will certainly be useful down the road, but may in the short run keep them from analyzing additional code. Five colleagues may want to individually analyze the same binary but recognize that there are certain steps in the process that they will all need to do. An individual may need to pass off an assignment to a colleague for expert input or while on vacation. Sometimes, it is just helpful to have multiple sets of eyes looking at the same thing for sanity checks. Regardless of the motivation, the shared project capability within Ghidra supports collaborative SRE in many forms.

Ghidra Server Setup

Collaboration in Ghidra is facilitated by a shared Ghidra Server instance. If you are the system administrator responsible for setting up the Ghidra Server, you have a lot of choices to make, like whether to deploy it on a bare-metal server or in a virtual environment for ease of migration and repeatable installation. The deployment we use in this chapter to demonstrate Ghidra's collaborative features is suitable for development and experimentation only. If you are configuring a Ghidra Server for production use, you should carefully read the Ghidra Server documentation and determine an appropriate configuration for your environment and specific use case. (An entire book could be written to describe Ghidra Server setup and all the installation options and associated approaches, but that isn't this book.)

Although Ghidra Server can be configured on all platforms that support Ghidra, we will describe running a Ghidra Server instance in a Linux environment and assume some familiarity with the Linux command line and system administration. We will make a few minor modifications to the Ghidra Server configuration file (specified in *server/server.conf*) to facilitate the concepts that we want to demonstrate in this chapter so that we are not overly reliant on use of the Linux command line interface after we complete the initial installation, configuration, administration, and access control. Modifications include changing the default Ghidra repository directory to one of our own choosing, as recommended in the Ghidra Server documentation, and tuning user management and access control settings.

The following steps walk you through a scripting process to create an environment and initial set of Ghidra users on an Ubuntu host.

1. Define some environment variables used throughout the script including the Ghidra version you are installing:

```
#set some environment variables
OWNER=ghidrasrv
SVRROOT=/opt/${OWNER}
REPODIR=/opt/ghidra-repos
GHIDRA_URL=https://ghidra-sre.org/ghidra_version.zip
GHIDRA_ZIP=/tmp/ghidra.zip
```

2. Install the two packages (*unzip* and *OpenJDK*), which are needed to complete the installation and run the server:

```
sudo apt update && sudo apt install -y openjdk-version-jdk unzip
```

3. Create a nonprivileged user to run the server and create a directory for hosting shared Ghidra repositories outside the directory in which Ghidra Server will be installed. Keeping the server executables and your repositories in separate directories is recommended in the server configuration guide and facilitates future server updates. The Ghidra Server administration tool (svrAdmin) will use the home directory of the server admin user.

```
sudo useradd -r -m -d /home/${OWNER} -s /usr/sbin/nologin -U ${OWNER}
sudo mkdir ${REPODIR}
sudo chown ${OWNER}.${OWNER} ${REPODIR}
```

4. Download Ghidra, unzip it, and move it to the server root directory. Make sure that you grab the latest public release when you are downloading Ghidra (the release date is in the *.zip* filename):

```
wget ${GHIDRA_URL} -O ${GHIDRA_ZIP}
mkdir /tmp/ghidra && cd /tmp/ghidra && unzip ${GHIDRA_ZIP}
sudo mv ghidra_* ${SVRROOT}
cd /tmp && rm -f ${GHIDRA_ZIP} && rmdir ghidra
```

5. Create a backup of the original server configuration file and change the location in which the repositories will be saved:

```
cd ${SVRROOT}/server && cp server.conf server.conf.orig
REPOVAR=ghidra.repositories.dir
sed -i "s@^$REPOVAR=.*\$@$REPOVAR=$REPODIR@g" server.conf
```

6. Add the -u parameter to your Ghidra Server launch parameters, so users can specify a username when connecting, instead of being forced to use their local username. This option allows us to log in as several different users from a single machine for demonstration purposes, and allows us to log in to the same account from several machines. (Some versions of Ghidra expect the repository path to be the last command line parameter, so we changed parameter.2 to parameter.3 and then added the new parameter.2=-u before that updated line.)

```
PARM=wrapper.app.parameter.
sed -i "s/^${PARM}2=/${PARM}3=/" server.conf
sed -i "/^${PARM}3=/i ${PARM}2=-u" server.conf
```

7. Change the ownership of the Ghidra Server process and the Ghidra Server directory to the *ghidrasvr* user. (Because this was just a demonstration server, we left all other parameters unchanged. You are strongly advised to read *server/svrREADME.html* to determine the configurations appropriate for a production deployment.)

```
ACCT=wrapper.app.account
sed -i "s/^.*$ACCT=.*/$ACCT=$OWNER/" server.conf
sudo chown -R ${OWNER}.${OWNER} ${SVRROOT}
```

8. Finally, install the Ghidra Server as a service and add users authorized to connect to the server:

```
sudo ./svrInstall
sudo ${SVRROOT}/server/svrAdmin -add user1
```

```
sudo ${SVRROOT}/server/svrAdmin -add user2
sudo ${SVRROOT}/server/svrAdmin -add user3
```

While a more detailed discussion of access control comes later in the chapter, it is important to mention here since the users need to exist in the authentication system that your Ghidra Server instance uses. This happens on the Ghidra Server itself. By default, each user must log in from a Ghidra client within 24 hours by using the default password *changeme* (which must be changed during the initial login). If a user does not activate their account within 24 hours, the account is locked and must be reset. Ghidra provides the Ghidra Server System Administrator with several options for authentication, ranging from simple passwords to public key infrastructure(PKI). We chose to use a local Ghidra password (which is the default).

If you want to install your own Ghidra Server or just need a more in-depth description of the various installation options, see *server/svrREADME.html* in your Ghidra directory.

THE PROJECT REPOSITORY

One advantage of working together as a team is that multiple people can work on the same binary at the same time. One disadvantage of working together as a team is that multiple people can work on the same binary at the same time. Whenever multiple users are interacting with the same content, there is a potential to introduce race conditions. In a *race condition*, the order in which the operations (such as saving an updated file) are performed can affect the final outcome. Ghidra has a project repository and versioning system to control which changes are committed, when, and by whom.

The Ghidra repository checks files in and out, tracks version history, and lets you see what is currently checked out. When you check out a file, you get a copy of the file. When you have finished working with the file and check the file back in, a new version of the file is created and becomes part of the file's legacy, and if someone else has also checked in a new version of the file, the repository helps resolve any conflicts. We demonstrate interactions with the repository later in the chapter.

Shared Projects

Up to this point, we have created and worked with only standalone Ghidra projects, suitable for use by a single analyst working on a single computer. Now that you have configured and given yourself access to a Ghidra Server, let's walk through the process of creating a shared project. A shared project can be made accessible to any users who are authorized to connect to your Ghidra Server and facilitates collaborative, concurrent access to the project.

Creating a Shared Project

When you create a new project (File ▸ New Project) and select Shared Project, you must specify the server information associated with your Ghidra Server, as shown on the left in Figure 11-1. The default port number (13100) is provided, but you must supply the server's hostname or IP address, and may need to authenticate yourself, depending on the configuration of your Ghidra Server.

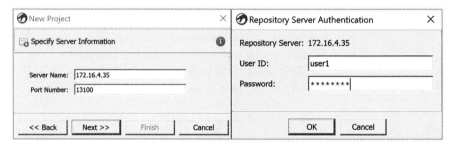

Figure 11-1: Logging in to a Ghidra Server repository

On the right side of the figure, we log in as one of the users created by our installation script (*user1*). If this is the first time logging in as this user, you will need to change the password from *changeme*, as discussed earlier.

Next, select an existing repository or create a new one by entering a new repository name, as shown in Figure 11-2. For this example, we will create a new repository named *CH11*.

🌀 New Project ✕

🗂 Specify Repository Name on 172.16.4.35 ⓘ

┌─ Choose Existing Repository ─────────────────────────────────┐
○ Existing Repository
Repository Names
┌──┐
│   │
│   │
│   │
│   │
└──┘
└──┘

┌─ Create Repository ──┐
● Create Repository
                          Repository Name: ⎸CH11⎹
└──┘

          << Back   Next >>   Finish   Cancel

Figure 11-2: The New Project dialog

Clicking **Next** creates a new repository and a new project and takes you to the now-familiar Project window (Figure 11-3).

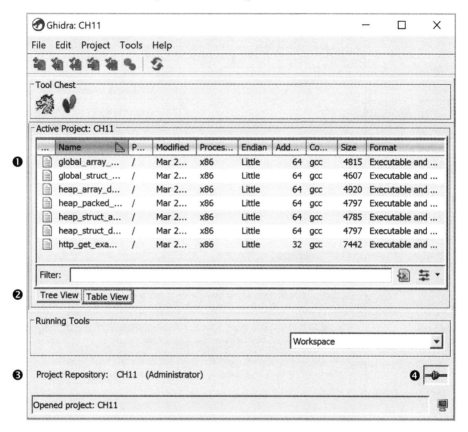

Figure 11-3: Project window for shared project showing Table View

We have imported some files ❶ and are displaying them using a table instead of the default tree structure for project files. The *Table View*, which is one of the tabbed layout choices ❷, provides much more information about each of the project's files. The Project window shows the name of the project repository (*CH11*), your role on the project (Administrator), and an icon to the right to provide information about your connection to the server ❸. In this case, hovering over the icon ❹ displays the message "Connected as user1 to 172.16.4.35." If you were not connected, the icon would be a broken link rather than the connected link shown in the image.

Project Management

Once a project has been created and has an administrator, authorized users can log in to the server and work with the project. A successful login takes you to the Ghidra Project window, where you will have access to your authorized projects.

WHO'S THE BOSS AROUND HERE?

The server administrator is responsible for creating Ghidra Server accounts and configuring an authentication protocol for connections to the server. Server administration is an inherently command line–oriented activity, and there is no requirement for the server administrator to be a Ghidra user themselves. On the client side, any authorized user may create repositories on the Ghidra Server, automatically becoming the administrator of each repository they create. This gives them complete control of the repository, including who can access it and the type of access each user can have. After creation, administrators may grant access to additional authorized users via Ghidra's Project window.

I DON'T WANT TO SHARE

Using a Ghidra Server installation for nonshared projects has advantages as well. Your initial introduction to Ghidra focused on installing Ghidra on a single computer and using that computer to access your projects and files (which were all stored on that computer). This means all analysis work depends on that computer. Ghidra Server facilitates multipoint access to your files from a wide variety of devices. You can require authentication before your files are accessed, and you can convert your projects from nonshared to shared if desired. One limitation is that you need to be connected to the Ghidra Server to check out or check in files.

Project Window Menus

Now that we have created and connected to a Ghidra Server, the options available in the Project window become more meaningful, as some of the previously unavailable options now have a new context. Here, as well as in Chapter 12, we discuss the individual menu components and how they can be used to improve your analysis process.

File

The File menu is shown in Figure 11-4. The first five options in the File menu are pretty standard file-type operations, and their behavior is what you would expect from menu-driven applications. We'll discuss the notable options, marked with numerals, in detail.

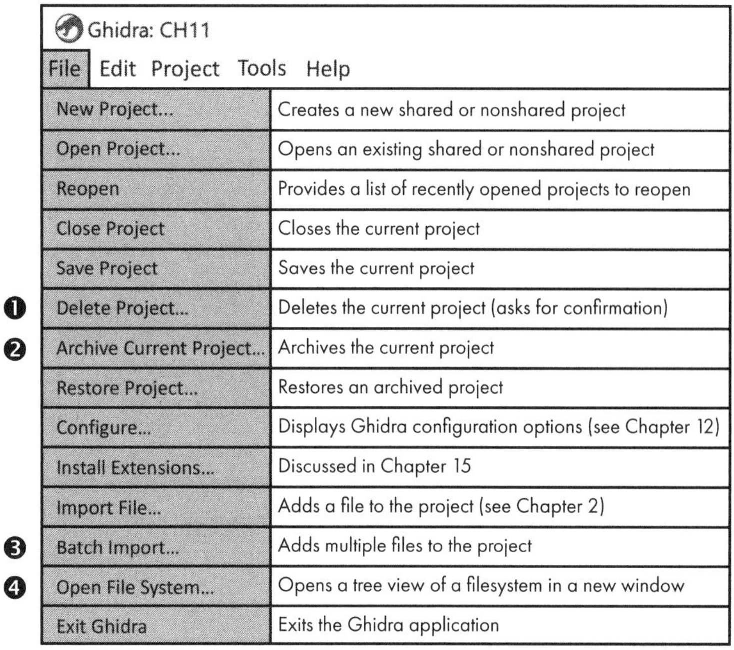

Ghidra: CH11

File Edit Project Tools Help

	Menu Item	Description
	New Project...	Creates a new shared or nonshared project
	Open Project...	Opens an existing shared or nonshared project
	Reopen	Provides a list of recently opened projects to reopen
	Close Project	Closes the current project
	Save Project	Saves the current project
❶	Delete Project...	Deletes the current project (asks for confirmation)
❷	Archive Current Project...	Archives the current project
	Restore Project...	Restores an archived project
	Configure...	Displays Ghidra configuration options (see Chapter 12)
	Install Extensions...	Discussed in Chapter 15
	Import File...	Adds a file to the project (see Chapter 2)
❸	Batch Import...	Adds multiple files to the project
❹	Open File System...	Opens a tree view of a filesystem in a new window
	Exit Ghidra	Exits the Ghidra application

Figure 11-4: File menu

Deleting Projects

Deleting a project ❶ is a permanent action in Ghidra that cannot be undone. Fortunately, it takes effort and requires confirmation. First, you cannot delete your active project. This minimizes the danger of an accidental deletion. To delete a project, you must complete the following three steps:

1. Choose **File ▸ Delete Project** from the menu.
2. Browse to (or enter the name of) the project to be deleted.
3. Confirm that you want to delete the project in the resulting confirmation window.

Deleting a project deletes all of its associated files. For that reason, it may be wise to first archive the project via the Archive Current Project option ❷.

Archiving Projects

Archiving a project allows you to save a snapshot of the project, its associated files, and associated tool configurations. Reasons for archiving a project include the following:

- You are going to delete the project but want to preserve a copy "just in case."
- You want to package a project for migration to another server.

- You want a version you can easily transfer between Ghidra versions.
- You want to create a backup of a project.

Follow these steps to archive a project:

1. Close the CodeBrowser window and all associated tools.
2. Choose **File ▸ Archive Current Project** from the menu.
3. Choose a location and name for the archive file on your local machine.

If you choose the name of an existing file, you will have the opportunity to change the name or overwrite the existing file. Archived files can easily be restored through the Restore Project option.

Batch Import

The Batch Import option (at ❸ in Figure 11-4) allows you to import a collection of files into a project in a single operation. When you choose File ▸ Batch Import, Ghidra presents a file browser window similar to the one shown in Figure 11-5. This window allows you to navigate to the directory containing the files you wish to import.

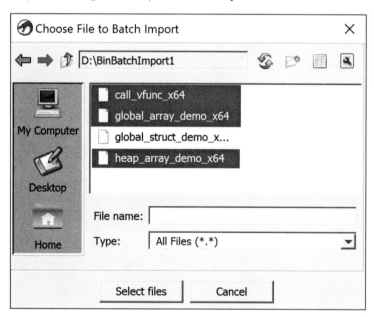

Figure 11-5: Batch file import selection window with files selected

You can select a file (or files) from a single directory, or an entire directory, to add to the batch import list. After you highlight the files and click the Select files button, you are taken to the Batch Import window, which shows you the files you have already selected for import. In Figure 11-6, the files from the directory *BinBatchImport1* were loaded as individual files, and the directory *BinBatchImport2* was added as a directory with five files, as shown to the right of the directory name. You can add/remove files to refine your import list and control several options, including the depth of recursion to search for files in a directory.

To determine the appropriate depth limit in the Batch Import window, or simply to explore the filesystem, use the Open File System menu option (at ❹ in Figure 11-4). This option opens the selected file system container (.*zip* file, .*tar* file, directory, and so on) in a separate window. (It is best to determine the depth beforehand because you would need a second Ghidra instance open to operate both windows simultaneously. Each window blocks access to the other in a single instance.)

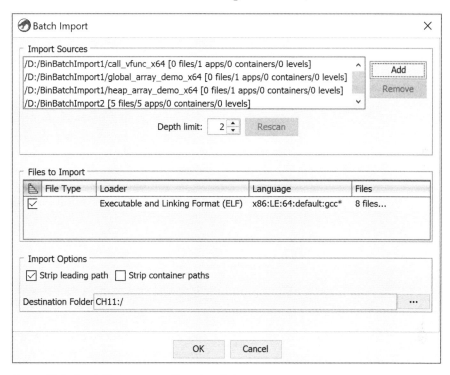

Figure 11-6: Batch file import confirmation dialog

Edit

The Edit menu is shown in Figure 11-7. The Tool Options and Plugin Path options are be discussed in Chapter 12, but the PKI options are related to the Ghidra Server setup and merit discussion in this chapter.

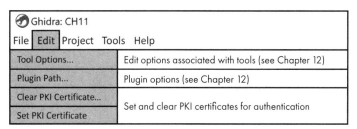

Figure 11-7: Edit menu

PKI Certificates

As mentioned at the start of this chapter, when you set up a Ghidra Server, you can choose from several authentication methods. We set up a simple server that uses a username and password for authentication. PKI certificates are more complex. While PKI implementations can vary, the following example represents a reasonable PKI client authentication process for Ghidra Server:

> *User1* wants to be authenticated so she can work on her Ghidra Server project. She has a client certificate that includes her username and a public cryptographic key. She also has a private cryptographic key corresponding to the public key contained in the certificate, which she keeps safely hidden away for important occasions such as this. Her certificate was cryptographically signed by a certificate authority (CA) that is trusted by the Ghidra Server.
>
> *User1* presents the server with her certificate, from which the server can extract the public key and username. The server runs checks to confirm the certificate is valid (for example, is not on a Certificate Revocation List, is within a valid date range, and has a valid signature from a trusted CA, and possibly others). If all checks pass, the server confirms a valid certificate and binds *User1*'s identity to a public key. Now *User1* needs to prove she has the corresponding private key so the Ghidra Server can verify it against the extracted public key. As long as the private key is truly held by only *User1*, the Ghidra Server correctly validates her certificate, and the server verifies that *User1* actually possesses the private key, so *User1* is considered to be authenticated.

The process for managing PKI certificate authorities is described in the Ghidra Server readme file (*server/svrREADME.html*). The Set PKI Certificate and Clear PKI Certificate menu options enable a user to associate (or disassociate) themselves with a key file (**.pfx*, **.pks*, **.p12*). When setting a PKI certificate, the user will be provided a file navigation window to identify the appropriate keystore. The certificate can be cleared at any time with the Clear PKI Certificate option. Should you choose to enable PKI authentication, Java's keytool utility may be used to manage keys, certificates, and Java keystores.

Project

The Project menu, shown in Figure 11-8, provides facilities for managing project-level activities, including viewing and copying from other projects, changing your password, and managing user access to projects that you administer.

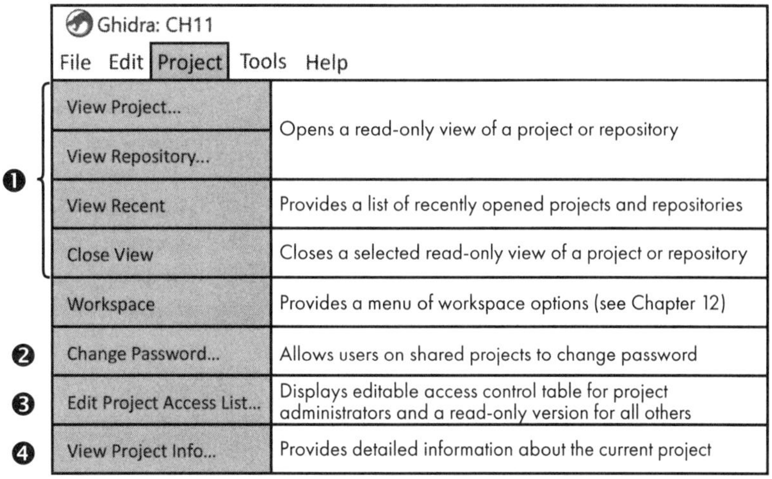

Ghidra: CH11		
File Edit **Project** Tools Help		
❶	View Project... View Repository...	Opens a read-only view of a project or repository
	View Recent	Provides a list of recently opened projects and repositories
	Close View	Closes a selected read-only view of a project or repository
	Workspace	Provides a menu of workspace options (see Chapter 12)
❷	Change Password...	Allows users on shared projects to change password
❸	Edit Project Access List...	Displays editable access control table for project administrators and a read-only version for all others
❹	View Project Info...	Provides detailed information about the current project

Figure 11-8: Project menu

Viewing Projects and Repositories

The first four options ❶ are related to viewing projects and repositories. The first two, View Project and View Repository, open read-only versions of a project (local) or repository (remote server) in a new window adjacent to the Active Project window. In Figure 11-9, the local project *ExtraFiles* has been opened beside the active project. You can explore the read-only project or drag any file or directory from the Read-Only Project Data window to the Active Project window. In Figure 11-9, the three selected files (with the extension *NEW*) have been copied from the Project Data window to the active project: *CH11*.

The next option, View Recent, provides a list of recent projects that can speed up the process of locating a project or repository. Close View closes the read-only view (although in some versions of Ghidra, this option appears to be inactive). A simpler reliable alternative is to click the X at the bottom of the project tab you wish to close, as seen in the bottom right of Figure 11-9.

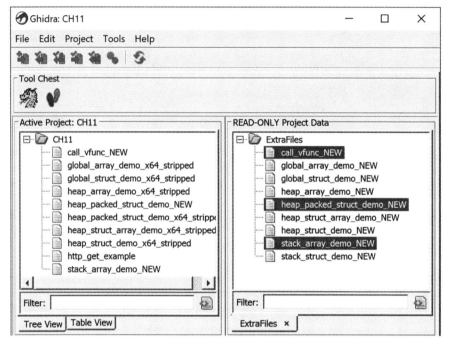

Figure 11-9: Using Project window to view another project

Changing Passwords and Project Access

The Change Password option (at ❷ in Figure 11-8) is available only to users on shared projects, provided that the Ghidra Server is configured with an authentication method that allows a password change. This is a two-step process with an initial confirmation dialog, as shown in Figure 11-10, followed by the same password change option dialog used for the initial mandatory password change.

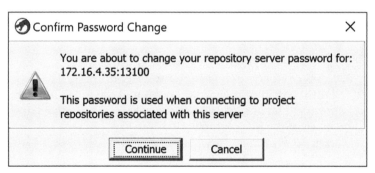

Figure 11-10: Password change initial confirmation dialog

While users can each control their own passwords, shared projects also offer the capability to control who can access a project and what permissions are granted to each user. As mentioned earlier in the chapter, the Ghidra Server system administrator has some control over access. Specifically, an administrator can assign an administrator to a repository and create and delete user accounts.

On the client side, if you are an administrator, you can also control access through the Edit Project Access List option (at ❸ in Figure 11-8) from the Project menu. When it is selected, you will see the dialog shown in Figure 11-11, which allows you to add and remove users from the project and to control their associated permissions. Each user can be placed in exactly one privilege class, from least privileged (Read Only to the left) to most privileged (Admin on the right).

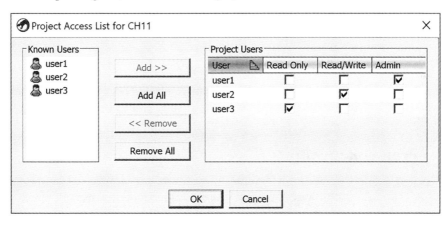

Figure 11-11: Access control window

Viewing Project Information

The final menu option is View Project Info (at ❹ in Figure 11-8). The options available in the resulting dialog depend on the whether the project is hosted on a Ghidra Server. Examples of nonserver-based (left) and server-based (right) project information dialogs are shown in Figure 11-12. While the information displayed is pretty straightforward, buttons at the bottom of each window allow you to convert a nonshared project to a shared project (with the Convert to Shared button) or change project information.

Clicking the Convert to Shared button opens a dialog that asks you to specify the server information and enter the user ID and password for the project administrator. The subsequent steps allow you to specify a repository, add users, set their permissions, and confirm that you want to convert the project. Note that this operation cannot be undone and removes all existing local version history.

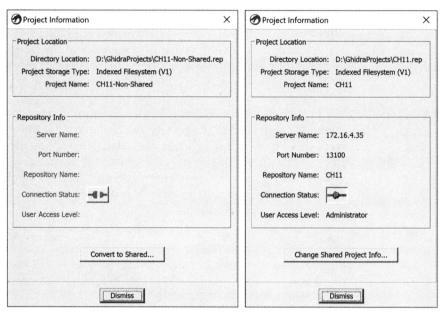

Figure 11-12: Project information windows for nonshared and shared projects

Project Repository

At this point, you may be wondering how projects can be shared while maintaining project integrity. This section covers the process that Ghidra uses to ensure that everyone's work is retained in a shared project that a team can work on concurrently. Before we delve too deeply into the process, let's investigate the file types associated with a shared Ghidra project. We start with discussing the relationship between a project and a repository.

A repository is the key facilitator of the versioning process. When you create a new nonshared project, a project file (*.gpr* file) and a repository directory, with a *.rep* extension, are created to facilitate version control. Additional files are created to control locks, versioning, and so on, but understanding the purpose of each file is not critical to successful Ghidra usage. For nonshared projects, all files reside on your computer within the directories that you specify at project creation time (refer to Chapter 4).

When you create a shared project, you have the option of creating a new repository or selecting from existing repositories, as discussed earlier in the chapter (refer to Figure 11-2). If you create a new project and a new repository at the same time, a one-to-one relationship exists between the project and its repository, and you become the project administrator. If you choose an existing repository, you are creating a new project for which you are not the project administrator (unless you owned the repository). In either case, the *.gpr* file and the *.rep* directory share the same base name. If the repository is named RepoExample, the project file will be named *RepoExample.gpr* and the repository folder will be named *RepoExample.rep*. (Despite having an extension, the repository is a directory rather than a file.)

To sum it up: if you create the repository, you are the project administrator and can choose who else can access your repository. If you use an existing repository, you are a user with the rights and privileges that have been assigned to you by the project administrator. So what happens when multiple users want to make changes to the same project? That's where version control comes into play.

VERSION CONTROL VS. VERSION TRACKING

Ghidra includes two very different versioning systems. In this chapter, we are discussing version control, and hopefully that concept will become quite clear shortly. Ghidra also has a *version tracking* capability. Version tracking is used to identify differences (and similarities) between two binaries. In the SRE community, this process is generally known as *binary differencing*. The goals may include identifying updates in different versions of a binary, identifying functions used by a malware family, identifying signatures, and so on. This functionality can be important given that the associated source code may not be available to allow for source-based diffing. Ghidra version tracking is discussed in more detail in Chapter 23.

Version Control

Version control is an important concept in any system where changes can be made by multiple users or a recorded history of changes is desirable. Version control allows you to manage updates to the system, effectively controlling race conditions. The Project window has a version control toolbar (Figure 11-13). Many of the operations require that the file(s) in question be closed in order to complete the action.

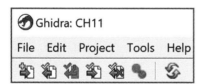

Figure 11-13: Ghidra Project window version control toolbar

The icons are enabled for valid version control operations based on the selected file(s). The basic actions that make up the version control workflow are shown in Figure 11-14. (We have included a column that provides the rough Git equivalents for all the Git fans.)

Icon	Action	Special option(s)	Similar git commands
	Add file to version control	Keep File Checked Out	git add git commit
	Check out file	None	git clone (ish)
	Update checked-out file with latest version	Keep File Checked Out	git pull
		Create .keep file	
	Check in file	Keep File Checked Out	git commit git push
		Create .keep file	
	Undo checkout	Save Copy with .keep extension	git checkout
	Find my checkouts recursively	None	git status

Figure 11-14: Ghidra version control toolbar actions

In addition to using the toolbar icons, you can perform the version control actions via the right-click context menu.

Merging Files

When a collaborative team member decides to check in changes they have made to the project, one of two conditions will be true:

No conflict In this case, no new versions of the file have been checked in since the user checked out the file. Since no potential conflict exists (no committed, conflicting changes that the user is not already aware of), the file that is being checked in will become the new version of the file. The old version will be retained in an archival fashion and the version number incremented to ensure that a continuous chain of versions can be tracked.

Potential conflict In this case, another user has committed new changes while the user had the file checked out. The order in which the files are checked in can affect the resulting "current version." In this case, Ghidra begins a merge process. If no conflicts are introduced by the submissions, Ghidra continues with its automatic merge process. If conflicts are detected, each must be manually resolved by the user.

As an example of a conflict, assume that *user1* and *user2* both have the same file checked out and that *user2* changes the name of FUN_00123456 to hash_something and checks in their change. Meanwhile, *user1* analyzes the same function and renames it to compute_hash. When *user1* finally checks their changes in (after *user2*), they will be informed of a naming conflict

and will be asked to choose the correct name of the function, between hash
_something and compute_hash, before the check-in operation may be completed.
Additional information about this process can be found in Ghidra Help.

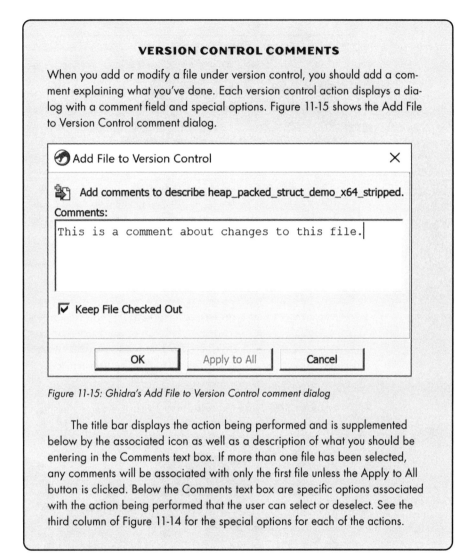

VERSION CONTROL COMMENTS

When you add or modify a file under version control, you should add a comment explaining what you've done. Each version control action displays a dialog with a comment field and special options. Figure 11-15 shows the Add File to Version Control comment dialog.

Add File to Version Control ✕

Add comments to describe heap_packed_struct_demo_x64_stripped.

Comments:

This is a comment about changes to this file.

☑ Keep File Checked Out

OK   Apply to All   Cancel

Figure 11-15: Ghidra's Add File to Version Control comment dialog

The title bar displays the action being performed and is supplemented below by the associated icon as well as a description of what you should be entering in the Comments text box. If more than one file has been selected, any comments will be associated with only the first file unless the Apply to All button is clicked. Below the Comments text box are specific options associated with the action being performed that the user can select or deselect. See the third column of Figure 11-14 for the special options for each of the actions.

Example Scenario

A lot of intricacies, options, and overloaded terminology are associated with shared projects. To clarify some of the concepts associated with Ghidra Server and shared projects, let's walk through an example that demonstrates the concepts we have been discussing, starting with the concept of a project.

A *project* is the local entity that lives on the client machine (like a local Git repo). Shared projects are also associated with a repository on a Ghidra Server (like a Git remote), and that repository is where all of the collaborative analysis effort results are stored. Files are shared after they have been imported and added to version control, and are private before that. Therefore, a user can import files into a project, at which point they are private, and then choose to add them to version control, at which point they are shared.

HELP! MY FILE HAS BEEN HIJACKED!

Ghidra has a special term (and associated Project Data Tree icon) for a situation that can frequently occur in a shared project environment. If you have a private file (imported but not yet added to version control) in your project *and* another user adds a file of the same name to the repository, your file will be *hijacked!* This is such a frequent occurrence that Ghidra provides a right-click context menu option to handle the situation. You will need to close the hijacked file and then select the Undo Hijack option from the context menu. This will provide you with the option to accept the file in the repository and keep a copy of your own file, if desired. Other options for resolving a hijack include renaming the file, moving it to another project, and deleting it.

In reality, project permissions are really repository permissions. If you create a project using an existing repository, you're really saying, "This project locally is backed remotely by that repository on the server" (like a Git clone). Let's walk through a sequence of shared project activities and observe how they affect the shared project environment:

1. *user1* creates a new shared project (and associated new repository) called *CH11-Example*, adds *user2* and *user3*, and assigns them permissions (see Figure 11-16).

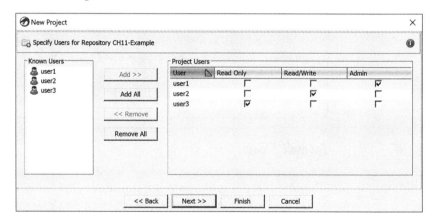

Figure 11-16: Example scenario, step 1

2. *user2* creates a new shared project associated with the existing *CH11-Example* repository (that is, *user2* clones *CH11-Example*). Note that the project is not the same name as *user1*'s project, but the repository (remote) is the same. In addition, *user2*'s permissions for the repository are shown at the bottom of the window (see Figure 11-17).

Figure 11-17: Example scenario, step 2

3. *user1* imports a file and adds it to version control, which *user2* can then also see (roughly equivalent to git add/commit/push). This is shown in Figure 11-18.

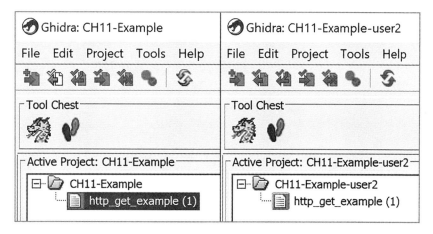

Figure 11-18: Example scenario, step 3

4. *user1* and *user2* then each import the same file to their projects but don't add them to version control. These are private files (see Figure 11-19).

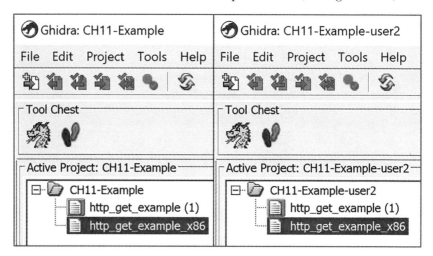

Figure 11-19: Example scenario, step 4

5. *user2* adds this second file to version control (which checks it in). As a result, the file is no longer private. *user1* now sees this as a hijacked file (see Figure 11-20).

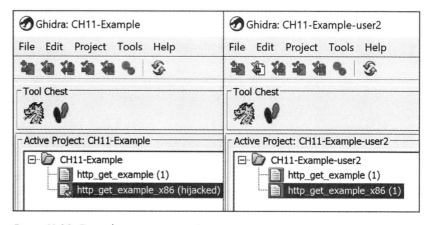

Figure 11-20: Example scenario, step 5

6. *user1* chooses Undo Hijack from the right-click context menu and has the option to replace her file with the version in the repository and keep a copy of her own file if desired. She chooses to accept the repository version and to keep a copy of her own file (which she has moved to another project, and it now has the extension *.keep*). Now everything is good again. In this case, *user1* is now seeing the state of the second file as it was when *user2* added it to version control (see Figure 11-21).

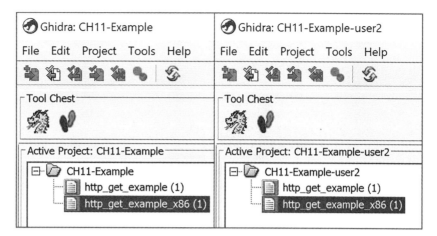

Figure 11-21: Example scenario, step 6

7. *user1* checks out the second file, analyzes it, and then checks it in. Both *user1* and *user2* now see the analyzed version of the file (version 2), as shown in Figure 11-22.

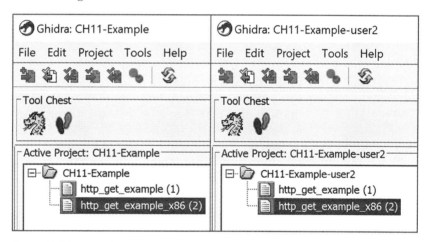

Figure 11-22: Example scenario, step 7

8. *user3* creates a project and associates it with the same repository (see Figure 11-23). *user3* can now see all of the files and can make changes locally (including adding private files), but has no option to commit to the repository, because she was not given write permissions. (The project is noted as "Read Only" at the bottom of the window.)

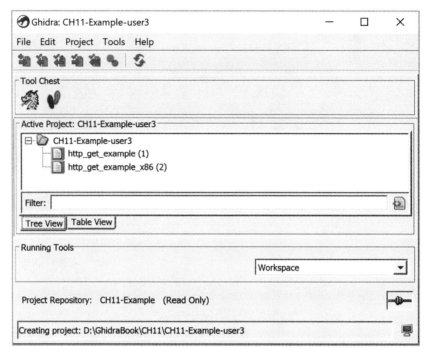

Figure 11-23: Example scenario, step 8

9. *user2* checks in all of her files before leaving work. This is important because she knows that she wants to continue working on her project by using her home computer. Because the project does not exist on her home computer, she needs to log in to the Ghidra Server and create a new project by using the existing repository. This will create the project on her home computer, where she can continue working. (Had she not checked in all of her files before leaving work, she would not have access to her latest work while at home.)

10. The remaining users go home confident that their collaborative Ghidra Server is working as intended.

Summary

Not everyone will require a Ghidra Server or shared projects to facilitate collaborative reverse engineering, but many of the associated capabilities can also be applied to nonshared projects. The remaining chapters focus on nonshared projects, with references to shared projects and Ghidra Server when appropriate. Regardless of the configuration of your Ghidra installation, there is a good chance the default configurations, tools, and views may not be perfect for your workflow. The next chapter focuses on Ghidra configurations, tools, and workspaces and how you can make them work better for you.

12

CUSTOMIZING GHIDRA

After spending time with Ghidra, you may prefer some settings that you wish to use as defaults every time you open a new project or that you want to apply to all files within a particular project. At this point, you may be confused as to why some of the options you have changed carry over from session to session, while other options need resetting every time you load a new project or file. In this chapter, we examine the ways in which you can customize Ghidra's default appearance and behavior to better serve your reverse engineering needs.

To understand the scope of some customizations, it's useful to understand the (fuzzy) distinction between the terms *plugin* and *tool*. In a general sense, the following is true:

Plugin   A plugin is a software component (for example, Byte Viewer, Listing window, and so on) that adds functionality to Ghidra. Plugins frequently present themselves as windows, but many plugins do their work behind the scenes (for example, analyzers).

Tool   A tool can be a single plugin or a set of plugins that work together. They generally present as a useful graphical user interface (GUI) to help users accomplish tasks. A tool that we have been working with extensively, CodeBrowser, is a window that serves as a GUI framework. Function Graph is also a tool.

Don't panic if these definitions are not strictly adhered to. In many cases, distinguishing between the two simply doesn't matter. For example, some menus, such as the Tool Options menu discussed later in this chapter, include options that can be applied to both tools and plugins despite using the term *Tool*. In that context, as well as many others, the distinction is not important, as both are treated the same. You should be able to successfully navigate the customization process even when the usage of the terms varies.

In addition to Ghidra customizations, we'll also discuss Ghidra *workspaces* to round out the chapter. Workspaces couple a tool with a configuration and provide the capability to design and use a personalized virtual desktop.

CodeBrowser

In Chapters 4 and 5, we introduced the CodeBrowser and many of its associated windows. We already covered some of the basic customization options; now we will walk through a more thorough example of customizations in the CodeBrowser before moving on to the Ghidra Project window and workspaces.

Rearranging Windows

The following six basic operations allow you to control where the individual windows appear in relation to the CodeBrowser window:

Open   Windows are generally opened using the CodeBrowser's Window menu. Each window has defaults that determine where it opens.

Close   Windows can be closed by clicking the X in the upper right of the window. (If you reopen a closed window, it will reappear at the same location rather than its original default location.)

Move   Move windows around by dragging and dropping them.

Stack   Use the drag-and-drop functionality to stack and unstack windows.

Resize   Hovering on a border between two windows reveals an arrow that allows to you grow and shrink the windows adjacent to the border.

Undock   You can undock a tool from the CodeBrowser window, but redocking is not as straightforward as you might wish, as shown in Figure 12-1.

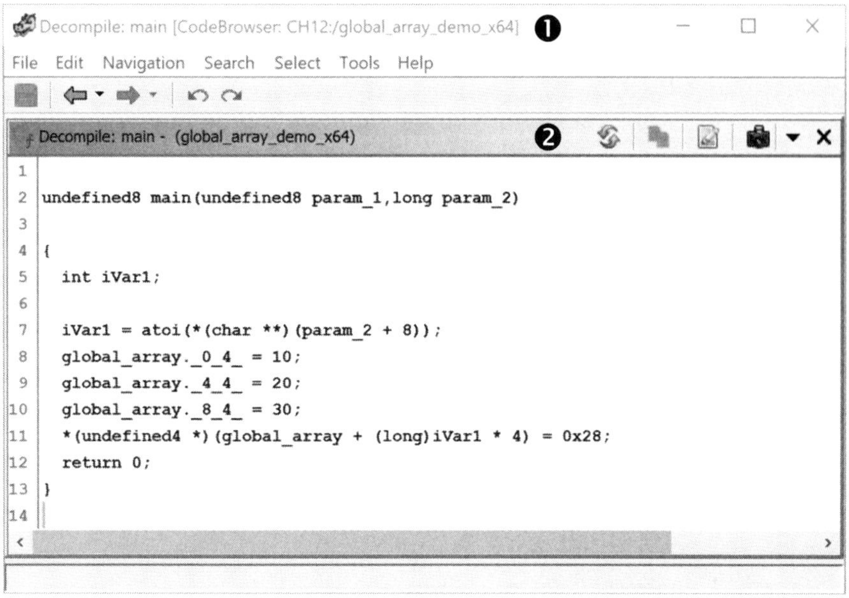

Figure 12-1: Redocking the Decompiler window

To redock a window, you can't click the title bar ❶, as you'll just drag the window around in front of the CodeBrowser. Instead, click the internal title bar ❷ to redock or stack a window. Now that we can rearrange windows, let's customize the windows themselves by using the Edit ▸ Tool Options menu.

Editing Tool Options

When you choose Edit ▸ Tool Options, a CodeBrowser option window opens, as shown in Figure 12-2. This window allows you to control options associated with individual CodeBrowser components.

Available options are determined by the developers of each component, and the significant variability between available options reflects the specific nature of the individual tools. Because describing every available tool option would take up an entire book, we'll look at a few edits that affect tools we have discussed in previous chapters and some that are similar for many tools.

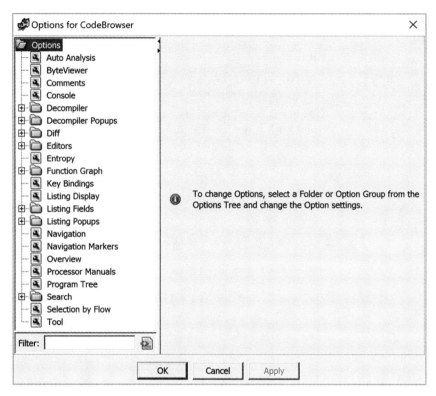

Figure 12-2: Default CodeBrowser Edit ▸Tool Options window

While it may not be apparent when rendered in grayscale, many of the tools use color to identify attributes, and the associated color palette is configurable. Clicking a default color within the Options window opens a standard Color Editor dialog, as shown in the Byte Viewer options panels in Figure 12-3. This provides you with the option to control the color of a plethora of items within your CodeBrowser.

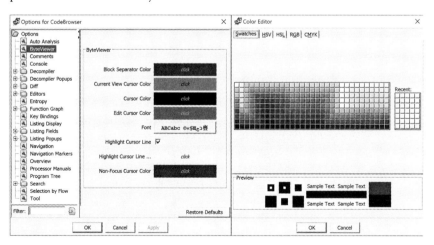

Figure 12-3: Edit ▸Tool Options Color Editor dialog

In Figure 12-3, you can select colors for six items in the Byte Viewer window: Block Separator, Current View Cursor, Cursor, Edit Cursor, Highlight Cursor Line, and Non-Focus Cursor. In addition to customizing color in the Byte Viewer window, you can also select the font and choose to highlight the cursor line. Conveniently, any CodeBrowser tool's option panel includes a Restore Defaults option in the lower right. This enables you to use special color schemes during some analysis steps and then revert to the default color scheme for the tool when done.

Beyond cosmetic changes, many tools provide the ability to set parameters in the edit options. We have hinted at this potential as we introduced new functionality in previous chapters, such as the ability to control which analyzers are included in auto analysis. In general, anytime something has a *default*, there is a way to change it to something else.

The settings for some overarching tools are also accessible and modifiable through the Options window. For example, key bindings are used to specify mappings between Ghidra actions and hotkey sequences, and there are over 550 actions in the default CodeBrowser window for which you can create or reassign a hotkey binding using the Options window. Hotkey reassignment is useful in many instances, including making additional commands available via hotkeys, changing default sequences to sequences that are easier to remember, and changing sequences that might conflict with others in use by the operating system or your terminal application. You might even remap all hotkeys to match those of other disassemblers.

Three fields are associated with each key binding, as shown in Figure 12-4. The first field is Action Name. In some cases, the action name corresponds to a menu command (for example, Analysis ▸Auto Analyze). In other cases, it is a parameter associated with a menu command (for example, Aggressive Instruction Finder within Analysis Options).

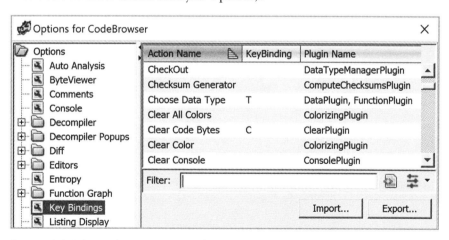

Figure 12-4: Edit ▸Tool Options Key Bindings option

The second column is the actual key binding (hotkey) that is associated with the action. The final column holds the name of the plugin in which the action is implemented.[1] Not all actions have associated hotkeys, but you can easily assign hotkeys by selecting an action and entering the desired hotkey in the text box. A list of all other uses of that hotkey is displayed if the hotkey has already been associated with another action. When you use a hotkey that has multiple key bindings, you will be provided a list of potential actions and will need to choose the appropriate one.

Editing the Tool

At the bottom of the Edit ▸ Tool Options window is an option called Tool. The meaning of Tool changes depending on the tool whose menu was used to reach the Options dialog. Generally this will be either the CodeBrowser or the Project window. Figure 12-5 shows the default configuration options for the CodeBrowser tool. The title bar of the Options dialog provides the most prominent clue that we are looking at the options page for the CodeBrowser.

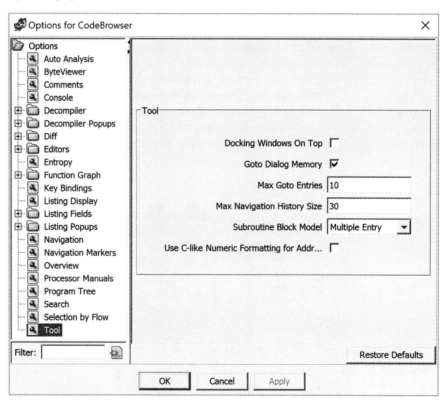

Figure 12-5: Using Edit ▸ Tool Options ▸ Tool to edit CodeBrowser options

---

1. This provides another example of synonymous use of terms when the distinction is not important. Most entries in the Plugin Name column are plugins, but tools such as the Configure tool are also included in the list. In this context also, you can apply a key binding to either.

Special Tool Editing Features

Some tools have editing features integrated within their individual windows so that you can immediately see the effect of the options on the associated contents. The most extensive set of built-in editing features is available in the Listing window. The Listing window contains the textual contents of the disassembly and is highly configurable using the Browser Field Formatter introduced in "Changing Code Display Options" on page 133. Figure 12-6 shows a Listing window with the default Browser Field Formatter open.

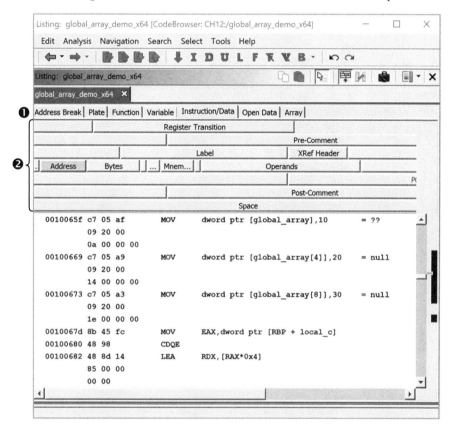

Figure 12-6: Listing window with default Browser Field Formatter open

A row of tabs ❶ representing the various field types present in the disassembly appears at the top of the formatter. In this case, we are looking at instructions, so the Instruction/Data tab is selected. The remainder of the formatter ❷ displays bars for each individual field associated with an address in an Instruction/Data section. In this case, the cursor is on an address within the Listing window, so the Address field is highlighted.

You can use the Browser Field Formatter to change the appearance of the listing. The capabilities are extensive, and each field has its own associated options. We will investigate only some of the simpler capabilities, many of which are similar to editing the appearance of windows in the CodeBrowser. You can rearrange fields by dragging them to new locations;

increase or decrease the width of a field; and add, remove, enable, or disable individual fields.

Figure 12-7 shows the same listing contents after removing the Bytes field. We have removed the Bytes field in many of the listing images in previous chapters to condense the listing and show more content in the available space.

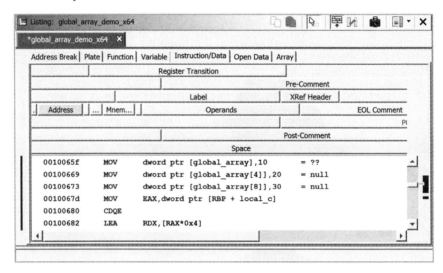

Figure 12-7: Listing window with customized Browser Field Formatter selections

Saving the CodeBrowser Layout

When closing the CodeBrowser, you can save any layout changes associated with a file. Alternatively, you can exit without saving, which generates a warning message to make sure you understand the implications. If you use the File ▸ Save Tool option in the CodeBrowser window, the current CodeBrowser appearance will be associated with the current file within the active project. The next time you open the file, Ghidra will use the saved CodeBrowser layout. When you have multiple CodeBrowser instances open at the same time and have modified some (or all) of them, this can result in conflicting tool configurations. Ghidra will then display a new Save Tool dialog, as shown in Figure 12-8.

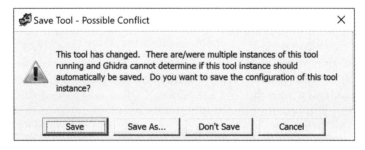

Figure 12-8: Ghidra's Save Tool – Possible Conflict dialog

Later in this chapter, we will show you how to use this and similar customization functionality to create a new powerful suite of tools that are tuned to your individual reverse engineering tasks and tastes.

Ghidra Project Window

Let's switch gears (or windows anyway) and venture back to the Ghidra Project window, shown in Figure 12-9. The main menu was discussed in the preceding chapter. Before we discuss Project window customizations, let's look at two areas of the window that we have not yet discussed.

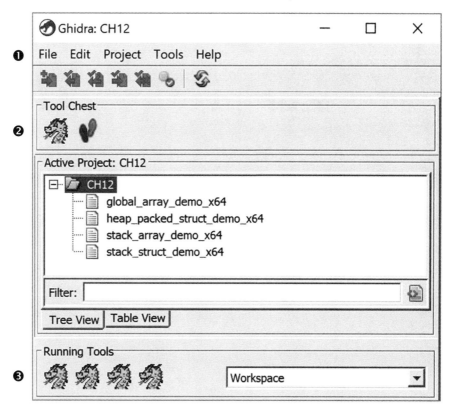

Figure 12-9: Ghidra Project window

The Tool Chest ❷ displays icons for all of the tools capable of operating on the binaries that you have imported into your projects. By default, two tools are available. The dragon icon is the default for the CodeBrowser, and the footprints icon is associated with Ghidra's version control tool. We demonstrate how to supplement the Tool Chest by modifying and importing tools, as well as building our own, a little later in this chapter.

The Running Tools ❸ contains icons for each running tool instance. In this example, we have opened each of the project files in a separate CodeBrowser window. As a result, four instances of CodeBrowser are currently running. Clicking any of the Running Tools icons brings the associated tool to the foreground of your desktop.

Let's return to the Ghidra Project window menu ❶ and look at some of the options to customize the window. We will start by investigating the four Edit ▸ Tool Options actions for the Ghidra project shown in Figure 12-10. Two of the options are the same as in CodeBrowser: Key Bindings and Tool.

In Figure 12-10, the Key Bindings option has been selected. The Ghidra Project tool has significantly fewer actions than the CodeBrowser tool does, and therefore fewer options for key binding. If you're playing along at home, you may notice that most of the actions are associated with the FrontEndPlugin. (The Ghidra Project tool is also called the Ghidra Frontend, and these terms are used interchangeably throughout the Ghidra environment, including Ghidra Help.)

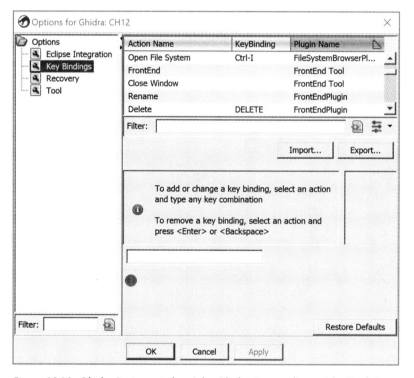

Figure 12-10: Ghidra Project window (aka Ghidra Frontend), via Edit ▸ Tool Options

Eclipse Integration is the focus of Chapter 15, so we will postpone discussion of this particular option for now. Recovery simply allows you to set a frequency for snapshots. The default value is 5 minutes. Setting this value to 0 disables snapshots.

The final option, Tool, can be quite fun to experiment with. As mentioned earlier in the chapter, the generic term *tool*, in this context, refers to the active tool. In this case, it is the Ghidra Project tool. The associated options are shown in Figure 12-11, and we will focus on the Swing Look And Feel and Use Inverted Colors options, which change the appearance of the Ghidra windows.

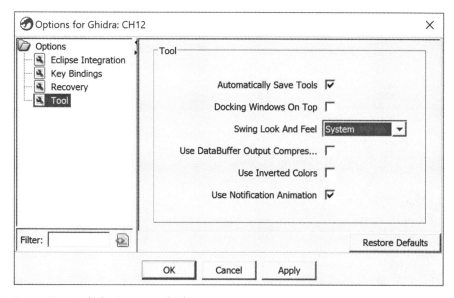

Figure 12-11: Ghidra Project tool edit options

The combination of Use Inverted Colors with the selection of Metal for the Swing Look And Feel results in a dark theme that is popular with many reverse engineers. Your changes will take effect after you restart Ghidra, and the new styles will be used for all Ghidra windows, including the CodeBrowser and Decompiler. A portion of the resulting CodeBrowser window is shown in Figure 12-12.

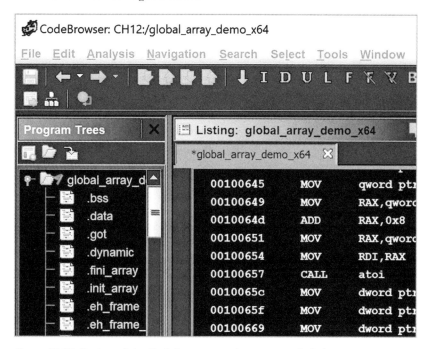

Figure 12-12: Portion of the CodeBrowser window using a dark theme

Now that you know how to change the look and feel of Ghidra to better suit your personality, let's return to the File menu and investigate what configuration means in that context. The File ▶ Configure option displays three categories of Ghidra plugin collections, as shown in Figure 12-13. Each category has a different purpose.

Ghidra Core contains the set of plugins that we have been using in our default Ghidra configuration. These provide the basic functionality that is essential to reverse engineering. The Developer category provides plugins that assist you in the process of developing new plugins. This is a good starting point if you want to learn more about Ghidra development. The final group of plugins is Experimental. These plugins have not been thoroughly tested and could destabilize your Ghidra instance, so use them with caution.

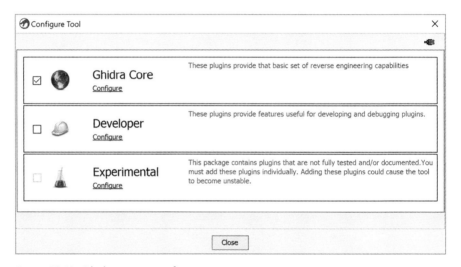

Figure 12-13: Ghidra project configuration options

While only Ghidra Core is enabled as part of the default Ghidra installation, you can check the box next to the other options to enable them as well. Use the Configure option beneath a category to select (or deselect) the individual plugins that appear in the category list. Figure 12-14 displays the Ghidra Core plugins list, including a description and category for each. If you click a Ghidra plugin within this menu, a window at the bottom of the screen will provide additional information about the plugin.

Two additional Ghidra Project menu options are available for Ghidra configuration. The first is File ▶ Install Extensions, which we discuss in Chapter 15. The other option, Edit ▶ Plugin Path, allows you to add, modify, and delete new user plugin paths, which tell Ghidra where to look for additional Java classes beyond its installed defaults. Through this option, you can include additional plugins and classes in your Ghidra instance. Editing the plugin path requires that you restart Ghidra in order to see the results.

Figure 12-14: Ghidra Core configuration window with ImporterPlugin selected

Now that you have seen the potential to modify plugin options, we can move on to extend plugin use. The Tools menu option allows you to perform operations associated with tools, including creating new tools (if none of the existing tools exactly fit your needs). In this case, we will build and work with tools that are collections of existing plugins, rather than coding plugins from scratch.

Tools

Most of the tool options are provided in the Ghidra Project window Tools menu, shown in Figure 12-15. Until now, you have been using and modifying the default tool, CodeBrowser, as your primary analysis tool. We will now demonstrate how you can create custom tools in Ghidra.

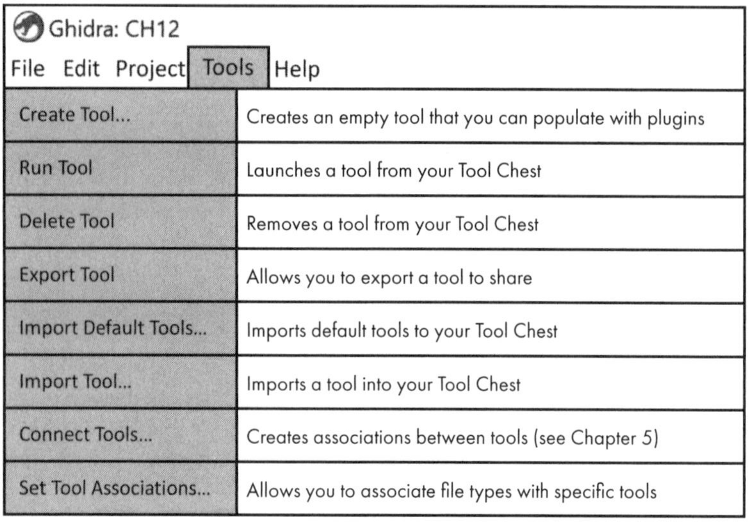

Ghidra: CH12	
File Edit Project **Tools** Help	
Create Tool...	Creates an empty tool that you can populate with plugins
Run Tool	Launches a tool from your Tool Chest
Delete Tool	Removes a tool from your Tool Chest
Export Tool	Allows you to export a tool to share
Import Default Tools...	Imports default tools to your Tool Chest
Import Tool...	Imports a tool into your Tool Chest
Connect Tools...	Creates associations between tools (see Chapter 5)
Set Tool Associations...	Allows you to associate file types with specific tools

Figure 12-15: Ghidra Tools menu options

If you have experimented with modifying the CodeBrowser tool, you may have become frustrated when the default tool is modified for subsequent files you open. Let's consider a specialized case where you want to examine a file, with many function calls, that is complicated to navigate. In Chapter 10, we demonstrated the use of function call graphs and function graphs to help you understand the control flow of a program. Both of these graphs open in their own windows, which can cause challenges if you have many files open. Let's address these challenges with a specialized tool called *ExamineControlFlow* that you can use to analyze the flow of control in a program.

When you choose the Tools ▶ Create Tool... menu option, you are presented with two windows (shown stacked in Figure 12-16). The upper window in the figure presents plugin options similar to those you saw in Figure 12-13, but with one additional category, Function ID, which we discuss in Chapter 13. The lower window in the figure is an empty, untitled tool development window that you can customize to create your tool, ExamineControlFlow.

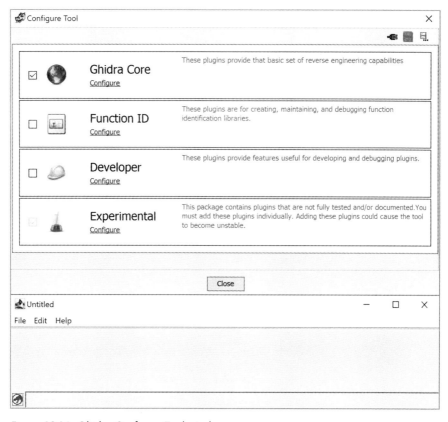

Figure 12-16: Ghidra Configure Tool window

You can compose your new tool by using plugins from Ghidra Core. When you select the Ghidra Core category, your tool development window populates with options from Ghidra Core, as shown in Figure 12-17. The resulting window has a lot in common with the CodeBrowser. This makes sense, as the CodeBrowser is also based on Ghidra Core.

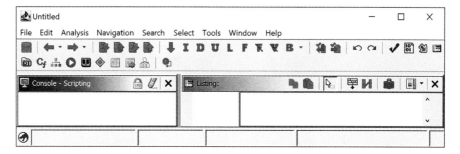

Figure 12-17: New, untitled tool before configuration

You will need to remove some of the plugins that you don't want in your new tool and then specify the windows that you do want. Click the **Configure** option under Ghidra Core and delete the following plugins you don't need (you could remove many others, but we have chosen not to for the sake of brevity):

- Console
- DataTypeManagerPlugin
- EclipseIntegrationPlugin
- ProgramTreePlugin

Each of these is associated with other plugins, so, as you remove each one from your new tool, Ghidra will display a warning message with the list of additional plugins that are being removed. You can add plugins back in by choosing File ▶ Configure from your new tool at any time. An example of the warning message associated with removing DataTypeManagerPlugin is shown in Figure 12-18.

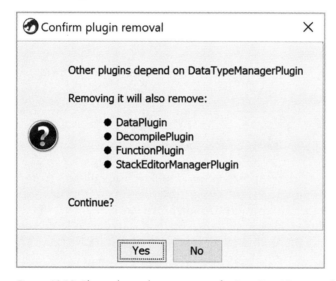

Figure 12-18: Plugin dependency warning for DataTypeManagerPlugin

You can also control the layout of your new tool. In this case, you want to be able to see the Listing, Function Call Graph, and Function Graph windows in the same tool. Using the techniques described in previous chapters, you open the desired windows by using the Window menu in your new tool and then drag them into the desired locations. The new, untitled tool is shown in Figure 12-19.

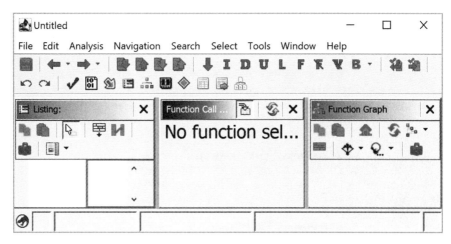

Figure 12-19: New, untitled tool

Since you plan to use this tool frequently and share it with your collaborators, you should save the tool by selecting File ▸ Save Tool As, which presents you with the options to name the tool and associate an icon with it (see Figure 12-20). You can choose from among the provided icons or select your own image file in a supported format (for example, *.jpg*, *.png*, *.gif*, and so on).

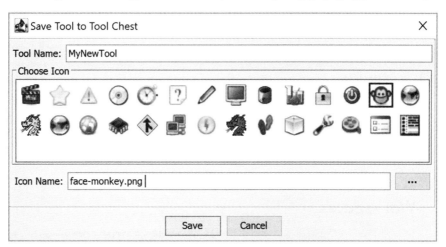

Figure 12-20: Icon options for new tools

This new tool (and other tools you create) becomes part of your Tool Chest and will be displayed as an option in your projects, as shown in Figure 12-21.

To share a new tool with others, export it using Tools ▸ Export Tools. Ghidra will ask you to choose a folder in which to save the tool and then create a *.tool* file containing your tool specification. To import a tool, use the Tools ▸ Import Tool option.

Figure 12-21: New project with new tool options displayed in Tool Chest

While double-clicking a file in the Ghidra Project window opens the file in the CodeBrowser by default, you can choose any tool in your Tool Chest by right-clicking the file and then choosing the tool from the context menu. Alternatively, you can drag the filename and drop it onto a tool.

The more you use Ghidra, the more you will realize that there is no one-size-fits-all Ghidra interface that provides exactly the tools you need for each RE task you undertake. As a reverse engineer, the approach to analyzing a particular file largely depends on the file itself, the goal of the analysis, and the progress toward that goal.

We have devoted much of this chapter and earlier chapters to describing how you might change Ghidra's look and feel as well as the tools available to meet your needs. A final step in customizing Ghidra is the ability to save these configurations you have created so that you can choose the correct configuration based on the analysis project you are undertaking. This is accomplished through the creation and preservation of Ghidra workspaces.

Workspaces

A Ghidra *workspace* can be viewed as a virtual desktop that includes the tools as they are currently configured and the associated files. Imagine that you are analyzing a binary. While you are looking at the file, you notice characteristics that are similar to another file you analyzed last week. You would like to compare the two files to identify the similarities between the two functions, but you also want to continue analyzing the file. These are two unique problems that have a file in common.

One way to proceed down these two paths concurrently is to create a workspace associated with each analysis problem. You can preserve your current analysis by selecting Project ▸ Workspace ▸ Add from the Ghidra Project window and giving the new workspace a name. In this example, we will call this workspace *FileAnalysis*. You can then open another tool from the Tool Chest and perhaps compare the two files using a specialized tool that utilizes the *Diff View* (see Chapter 23), then create a second workspace (*FileComparison*) using the same method. You can now easily switch between the workspaces by selecting the workspace in the pull-down menu shown in Figure 12-22 or by using the Switch option in the Project ▸Workspace menu, which cycles you through the available workspaces.

Figure 12-22: Workspace options within Ghidra Project window

Summary

When starting out with Ghidra, you may be perfectly satisfied with its default behaviors and its default CodeBrowser layout. However, as you become more comfortable with Ghidra's basic features, you are certain to find ways to customize Ghidra for your reverse engineering workflow. While there is no way for a single chapter to provide complete coverage of every possible option Ghidra offers, we have introduced and provided examples for the customization capabilities that you will most likely need at some point in your SRE experience. Discovering additional useful tools and options is left as a matter of exploration for inquisitive readers.

13

EXTENDING GHIDRA'S WORLDVIEW

One of the things we hope for from a high-quality reverse engineering tool is fully automated identification and annotation of as much of a binary as possible. In ideal cases, 100 percent of instructions are identified and grouped into 100 percent of the original functions that compose the binary. Each of these functions would have a name and a full prototype, and all data manipulated by the functions would also be identified to include full understanding of the original data types used by the programmers. This is precisely Ghidra's goal, beginning with the initial import of a binary and continuing through auto analysis, at which point anything that Ghidra was unable to accomplish becomes an exercise for its user.

In this chapter, we look at the techniques Ghidra uses to identify various constructs within binaries and discuss how you can enhance its ability to do so. We begin with a discussion of the initial loading and analysis processes. The choices you make during these steps help determine what resources Ghidra will bring to the table for the file you are analyzing. This is your opportunity to provide Ghidra with information that it may have failed to detect automatically so that Ghidra's analysis stages can make more informed decisions. Following that, we will look at how Ghidra utilizes word models, data types, and function identification algorithms, and how each of these may be enhanced to tailor its performance to your particular RE application.

Importing Files

During the import, the dialog shown in Figure 13-1 presents Ghidra's initial analysis of the file's identity, which will guide the file-loading process. You can override any of the fields or proceed with the recommendations Ghidra has made. The additional options, accessed with the Options . . . button, are specific to the type of file being loaded. Figure 13-1 shows options for a PE file, and Figure 13-2 shows options for loading an ELF binary.

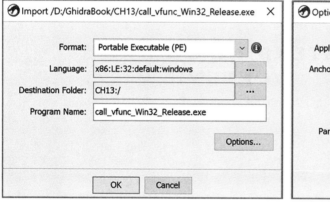 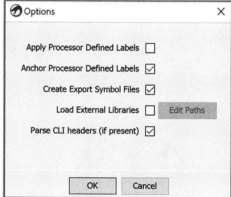

Figure 13-1: Import dialog and options for a PE file

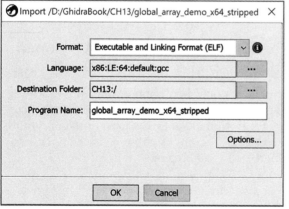 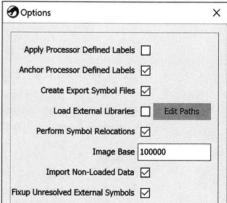

Figure 13-2: Import dialog and options for an ELF binary

LANGUAGE/COMPILER SPECIFICATIONS

The Language field in Figures 13-1 and 13-2 dictates exactly how Ghidra will interpret any bytes recognized as machine code within the file you are loading. The language/compiler specification is composed of three to five colon-separated subfields, as described here:

- The processor name field names the processor type for which the binary was built. It directs Ghidra to a specific subdirectory under *Ghidra/Processors*.

- The endian field indicates the endianness of the binary's processor, which is either little-endian (LE) or big-endian (BE).

- The architecture size (bitness) field usually coincides with the size of a pointer for the chosen processor (16/32/64 bits).

- The processor variant/mode field is used to choose a specific model of the selected processor or identify a specific mode of operation. For example, when the x86 processor is selected, we can choose modes System Management Mode, Real Mode, Protected Mode, or default. For the ARM processor, we can choose models v4, v4T, v5, v5T, v6, Cortex, v7, v8 or v8T, among others.

- When known, the compiler field names the compiler, or in some cases a calling convention, that was used to compile the binary. Valid names include *windows*, *gcc*, *borlandcpp*, *borlanddelphi*, and *default*.

    Figure 13-3 breaks down the language identifier ARM:LE:32:v7:default into its component subfields. One of a loader's most important jobs is to infer a correct language/compiler specification.

Language				Compiler
Processor	Endian	Size	Variant	
ARM	LE	32	v7	Default

Figure 13-3: Language/compiler specification example

The Format option specifies which loader Ghidra will use to import the file. Ghidra relies on a loader's detailed knowledge of a particular file format to identify characteristics of the file and choose the proper plugins to use for analysis. A well-written loader recognizes specific content or structural features to identify the file's type, architecture, and, hopefully, the compiler that was used to create the binary. Information about the compiler can enhance function identification. To fingerprint a compiler, a loader examines the structure of a binary to look for compiler-specific characteristics (like number, name, position, and ordering of program sections) or searches the binary for compiler-specific byte sequences (like blocks of code or strings). For example, it is not uncommon to find version strings in binaries compiled using gcc—for example, *GCC: (Ubuntu 7.3.0-27ubuntu1~18.04) 7.3.0.*

When Ghidra has completed the loading process, an Import Results Summary window is displayed, as shown in Figure 13-4.

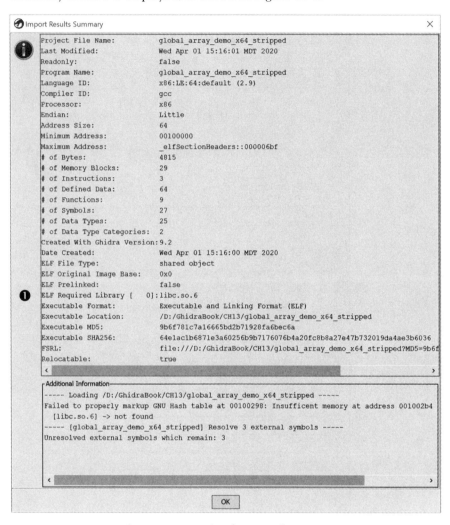

Figure 13-4: Import Results Summary window for an ELF binary

This summary identifies an ELF Required Library, *lib.so.6* ❶. (Note that this library would not be listed as a requirement if the file were statically linked.) More than one library file may be listed when an executable depends on multiple shared libraries. Understanding which libraries a program depends on can help direct you to resources you may need while analyzing the program. For example, if *libssl.so* or *libcrypto.so* appears in the list of required libraries, you might want to locate OpenSSL documentation and possibly source code. We discuss how Ghidra can make use of source code later in this chapter. Once a file has been successfully imported, you can auto analyze the file.

Analyzers

Auto analysis is accomplished by a collection of cooperating analysis tools (analyzers) that are activated either manually (for example, when opening a new file) or automatically when a change that can affect the resulting disassembly is detected. Analyzers run sequentially in a prioritized order based on the type of analyzer because the changes an analyzer makes can affect subsequent analyzers. For example, the stack analyzers cannot look at functions until a function analyzer has looked at all calls and created the functions. We investigate this hierarchy in more detail in Chapter 15 when we build an analyzer.

When you open a new file in the CodeBrowser and choose to auto analyze it, Ghidra presents a list of analyzers that can be run on that file. The list of default and optional analyzers is dependent on file information provided by the loader (which is also displayed to the user as part of the import summary, as shown in Figure 13-4). For example, the Windows x86 PE RTTI Analyzer would not be of much use in analyzing an ELF or ARM binary. Default analyzer selections can be modified using the Edit ▸ Tool Options menu.

Some analyzers are also available as one-shot options by using the Analysis ▸ One Shot menu in the CodeBrowser. An analyzer appears in the list if it supports one-shot use and applies to the type of file being analyzed. One-shot analysis is useful for running analyzers that were not selected during the initial auto analysis, or for rerunning an analyzer after new information has been located that might benefit from additional analysis. For example, if you receive a missing PDB error message during initial analysis, you can locate the PDB file and then run the PDB analyzer.

The Analyze All Open option on the CodeBrowser ▸ Analysis menu analyzes all open files in the project at once, using the list of analyzers selected in Edit ▸ Tool Options. If all of the open files in the project have the same architecture (language/compiler specification), all of the files will be analyzed. Any files that do not match the architecture of the current file will not be included in the analysis. This ensures that the analyzers are consistent with the type of file being analyzed.

Many CodeBrowser tools, including analyzers, rely on various artifacts in order to identify important constructs in a file. Fortunately for us, we can extend many of these artifacts to improve Ghidra's capabilities. We will start with a discussion of word model files and how they are used to identify special strings and types of strings within search results.

Word Models

A *word model* provides a way to identify special strings and types of strings you're interested in searching for, such as known identifiers, email addresses, directory pathnames, file extensions, and so on. When your string search is associated with a word model, the String Search results window will include a column called IsWord that specifies whether the found string is a word according to the word model. Defining strings of interest as valid words and then filtering for valid words is a good way to prioritize strings for further inspection.

At a high level, a word model uses training sets of valid strings to determine that "if trigram X (a sequence of three characters) appears in a sequence Y of length Z, then there is a probability, P, that Y is a word." The resulting probability is used indirectly as a threshold to determine if the string should be considered a valid word during analysis.

StringModel.sng, seen in Figure 13-5, is the default word model file for string searches in Ghidra.

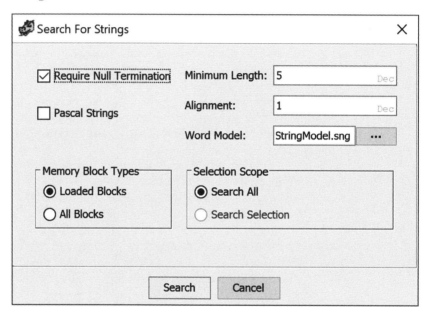

Figure 13-5: Search for Strings dialog

The following excerpt from the *StringModel.sng* file shows the format of a valid word model file:

```
❶ # Model Type: lowercase
❷ # Training file: contractions.txt
  # Training file: uniqueStrings_012615_minLen8.edited.txt
  # Training file: connectives
  # Training file: propernames
  # Training file: web2
  # Training file: web2a
  # Training file: words
❸ # [^] denotes beginning of string
  # [$] denotes end of string
  # [SP] denotes space
  # [HT] denotes horizontal tab
❹ [HT]    [HT]    [HT]    17
  [HT]    [HT]    [SP]    8
  [HT]    [HT]    (   1
```

```
[HT]    [HT]    ;    1
[HT]    [HT]    \    25
[HT]    [HT]    a    2
[HT]    [HT]    b    1
[HT]    [HT]    c    1
```

The first 12 lines in the file are metadata comments about the model. In this example, the model type ❶ is lowercase, which likely means the model does not distinguish between upper- and lowercase letters. The names of the training files used for this model are listed ❷. The names generally indicate the content: *contractions.txt* is likely a file of valid contractions, like *can't*. Four lines ❸ describe the notation for some nonprinting ASCII characters used in the trigrams. The actual trigram list starts ❹, where each entry row contains the three characters in the trigram followed by a value that is used in determining the probability that the trigram is part of a word.

You can supplement or replace the default word model by editing *String Model.sng* or creating new model files and storing them in *Ghidra/Features /Base/data/stringngrams* and then selecting the new file in the Word Model field in the Search for Strings dialog. There are many reasons to modify word models, like including strings specific to known malware families or detecting words in languages other than English. Ultimately, word models provide a powerful means to control the types of strings that Ghidra recognizes as higher priority by tagging them in the Strings window.

In a similar manner, we can edit and extend the data types that Ghidra recognizes.

Data Types

The Data Type Manager allows us to manage all of the data types associated with a file. Ghidra lets you reuse data type definitions by storing them in *data type archive files*. Each root node in the Data Type Manager window is a data type archive. Figure 13-6 shows a Data Type Manager window with three data type archives selected by the Ghidra loader.

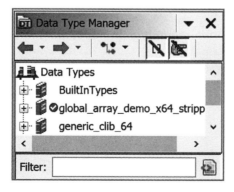

Figure 13-6: Data Type Manager window

The BuiltInTypes archive is always listed. This archive includes all (and only) types that are modeled within Ghidra by Java classes that implement the `ghidra.program.model.data.BuiltInDataType` interface. Ghidra searches for every such class within its classpath in order to populate this archive.

The second archive is specific to the file that is being analyzed, and the archive shares the file's name. In this case, the archive is associated with the file *global_array_demo_x64*. The checkmark next to the archive indicates that it is associated with the active file. Initially, Ghidra populates this archive with data types specific to the file's format (for example, PE- or ELF-related data types). During auto analysis, Ghidra copies additional types, from the other archives, into this one when they are recognized to be in use in the program. In other words, this archive contains the subset of all data types, known to the Data Type Manager, that happen to be in use in the current program. This archive is also the home to any custom data types that you choose to create in Ghidra, as discussed in "Creating Structures with Ghidra" on page 166.

The third archive provides the 64-bit ANSI C function prototypes and C library data types. This particular archive contains information extracted from the standard C library headers of a 64-bit Linux system and is one of several platform-specific archives in a default Ghidra installation. It is present because this particular binary has a library dependency on *libc.so.6*, as indicated in Figure 13-4. A default Ghidra installation has four additional platform-specific data archives, located in the *Ghidra/Features/Base/data/typeinfo* directory under a subdirectory specific to the platform. The filenames indicate the platforms they support: *generic_clib.gdt*, *generic_clib_64.gdt*, *mac_osx.gdt*, *windows_vs12_32.gdt*, and *windows_vs12_64.gdt*. (The *.gdt* extension is used for all Ghidra data type archives.)

In addition to the archives that the Ghidra loader selects automatically, you can add your own data type archives as nodes in the Data Type Manager window. For demonstration purposes, Figure 13-7 shows the Data Type Manager window after all of the default *.gdt* files have been added to the Data Types list. The right side of the figure shows the menu for manipulating archives and data types. Additional archives are loaded using the Open File Archive menu option, which opens a file browser for you to select an archive of interest.

To add new built-in types to the BuiltInTypes archive, add corresponding *.class* files to Ghidra's classpath. If you add types while Ghidra is running, you must Refresh BuiltInTypes (see Figure 13-7) in order for them to appear. The refresh operation causes Ghidra to rescan its classpath to find any newly added `BuiltInDataType` classes. The inquisitive reader may find numerous examples of built-in types in their Ghidra source distribution at *Ghidra/Framework/SoftwareModeling/src/main/java/ghidra/program/model/data*.

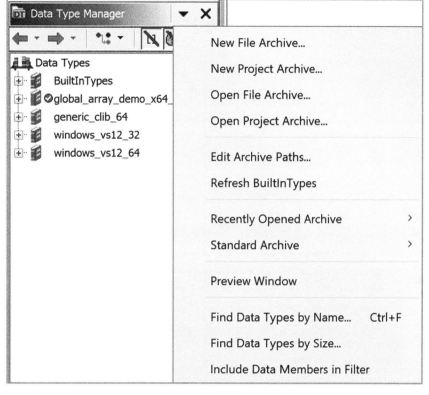

Figure 13-7: Data Type Manager with all standard archives loaded and options menu expanded

Creating New Data Type Archives

It's impossible to anticipate every data type that you may encounter while analyzing binaries. The archives included in your Ghidra distribution include data types culled from the most commonly used libraries on Windows (Windows SDK) and Unix (C library) systems. When Ghidra doesn't contain information on the data types used in a program you're analyzing, it offers you the ability to create new data type archives, populate them in a variety of ways, and share them with others. In the following sections, we discuss the three ways you are likely to create new data type archives.

Parsing C Header Files

One of the most common sources for data type information is C header files. Assuming you have the header files you need, or take the time to create them yourself, you can create your own data type archive by using the C-Parser plugin to extract the information from an existing C header file. For example, if you frequently find yourself analyzing binaries that link against the OpenSSL cryptographic library, you might download the OpenSSL source code and ask Ghidra to parse the included header files to create an archive of OpenSSL data types and function signatures.

This process is not nearly as straightforward as it might seem. Header files are often littered with macros designed to influence the behavior of a compiler based on the compiler being used and the operating system and architecture being targeted. For example, the C structure

```
struct parse_demo {
    uint32_t int_member;
    char    *ptr_member;
};
```

occupies 8 bytes when compiled on a 32-bit system and 16 bytes when compiled on a 64-bit system. This variability poses a problem for Ghidra, which is attempting to act as the universal preprocessor, and it is up to you to guide Ghidra through the parsing process to create a useful archive. When the time comes to use your archive with Ghidra, you must have ensured that the archive was created in a manner compatible with the binary you are analyzing (that is, don't load 64-bit archives to help you analyze a 32-bit file).

To parse one or more C header files, select File ▸ Parse C Source in the CodeBrowser to open the dialog shown in Figure 13-8. The source files to parse section provides an ordered list of header files for the plugin to parse. The order is important, as the data types and preprocessor directives from one file become available for the next file.

The Parse Options box provides a list of options, similar to compiler command line options, that influence the behavior of the C-Parser plugin. The parser recognizes only the -I (include directory) and -D (define a macro) options understood by most compilers. Ghidra offers a number of preprocessor configurations, in the form of .prf files, that you can choose from to provide reasonable defaults for common operating system and compiler combinations. You can also customize any of the available configurations or create your own from scratch and save them to your own .prf for future use. A common change to the parser options is to correctly set the architecture that you want the C-Parser to target, as all of the supplied configurations target x86. For example, you might change -D_X86_ in a Linux-oriented configuration to -D__ARMEL__ if you are analyzing little-endian ARM binaries.

The plugin's output can be merged into the current active file with the Parse to Program button or stored in a separate Ghidra data type archive file (.gdt) with Parse to File. Additional information about the C-Parser can be found in Ghidra Help.

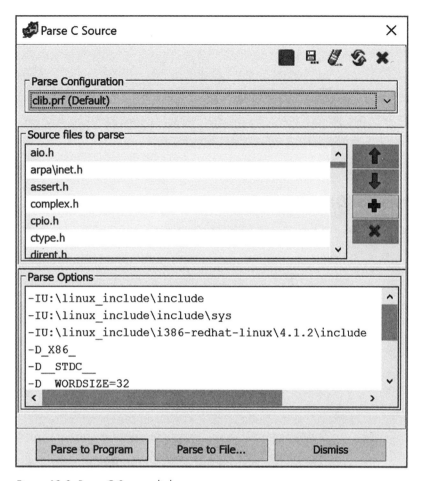

Figure 13-8: Parse C Source dialog

Creating a New File Archive

As an alternative to parsing C headers files, you might want to capture custom data types that you create while analyzing a file into an archive that can be shared with other Ghidra users or used in other Ghidra projects. The Data Type Manager's New File Archive option (refer to Figure 13-7) asks you to select a filename and save location, and then creates a new, empty archive that is listed in the Data Type Manager window. You can add new types to the archive by using the techniques described in "Creating Structures with Ghidra" on page 166. Once your archive is created, you may share it with other Ghidra users or use it in your other Ghidra projects.

Creating a New Project Archive

A project data archive exists only within the project in which it was created. This may be useful if you expect to reuse custom data types in more than one file within a project but never expect to use the data types outside your project. Within the Data Type Manager, the New Project Archive option (refer to Figure 13-7) asks you to select a folder within your project to hold your new archive, and then creates a new, empty archive that is listed in the Data Type Manager window. As with the other data type archives, you can add new types to the archive as needed.

Function IDs

When you set out to reverse engineer any binary, the last thing you want to do is waste time reverse engineering library functions whose behavior you could learn much more easily by simply reading a man page, reading some source code, or doing a little internet research. Unfortunately, statically linked binaries blur the distinction between application code and library code: entire libraries are combined with application code to form a single, monolithic executable file. Fortunately for us, Ghidra has tools to recognize and mark library code, regardless of whether the code was taken from a library archive or is simply the result of code reuse across multiple binaries, allowing us to focus our attention on the unique code within the application. The *Function ID analyzer* recognizes many common library functions using function signatures included with Ghidra, and you can extend the function signature databases by using the Function ID plugin.

The Function ID analyzer works with Function ID databases (FidDbs) that use a hierarchy of hash values to characterize functions. A full hash (which is intended to be resilient against changes that might be introduced by the linker) and a specific hash (which helps differentiate between variants of functions) are computed for each function. The major difference between the two is that the specific hash may include the specific values of any constant operands (based on a heuristic), whereas the full hash does not. The combination of the two hashes coupled with information about any associated parent and child functions forms a fingerprint for each library function, which is recorded in an FidDb. The Function ID analyzer derives the same type of fingerprint for each function in the binary you are analyzing and compares it against all known fingerprints in relevant FidDbs. When a match is found, Ghidra recovers the function's original name from the FidDb, applies the appropriate label to the function under analysis, adds the function to the Symbol Tree window, and updates the function's plate comment. The following is a sample plate comment for the _malloc function:

```
************************************************************
* Library Function - SingleMatch                          *
* Name: _malloc                                           *
* Library: Visual Studio 2005 Release                     *
************************************************************
```

Information about functions in a FidDb are stored hierarchically and include a name, version, and variant. The variant field is used to encode information such as compiler settings, which affect the hashes but aren't part of the version number.

The Function ID analyzer offers several options, accessible when you select the analyzer in the Auto Analysis dialog, to control its behavior, as shown in Figure 13-9. Instruction count threshold is a tunable threshold designed to reduce false positives from random matches against small functions. False positives occur when a function is incorrectly matched to a library function. False negatives occur when a function is not matched to a library function but should be. The threshold roughly represents the minimum number of instructions that a function, its parents, and its children must contain (combined) in order to be considered for a match. Refer to *Scoring and Disambiguation* in Ghidra Help for more information on match scores.

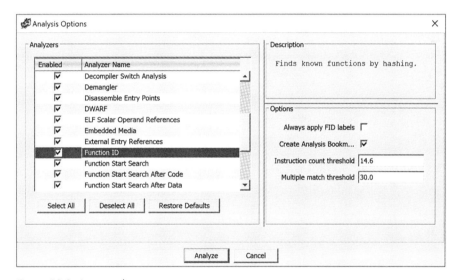

Figure 13-9: Auto analysis options

Since the actual functionality within a binary is generally contained in functions, the ability to extend function signatures is paramount to minimizing duplication of effort, and this work is facilitated by the Function ID plugin.

Function ID Plugin

The *Function ID plugin* (not to be confused with the Function ID analyzer) allows you to create, modify, and control associations for FidDbs. This plugin is not enabled in a default Ghidra installation. To enable it, select **File ▶ Configure** from the CodeBrowser window and then click the checkbox for Function ID. Choose **Configure** within the Function ID description and select the **FidPlugin** to see additional information about actions associated with the plugin, as shown in Figure 13-10.

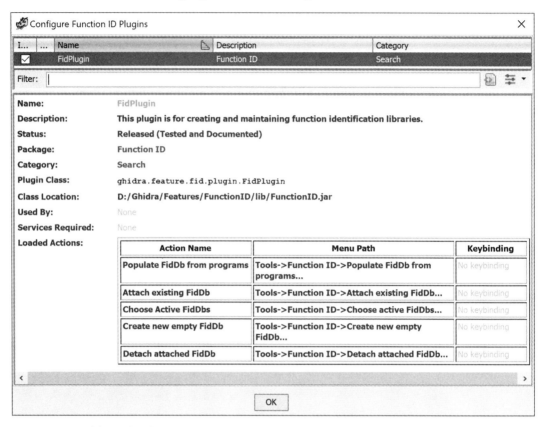

Figure 13-10: FidPlugin details

Once enabled, the Function ID plugin is controlled via the CodeBrowser's Tools ▸ Function ID menu, as shown in Figure 13-11.

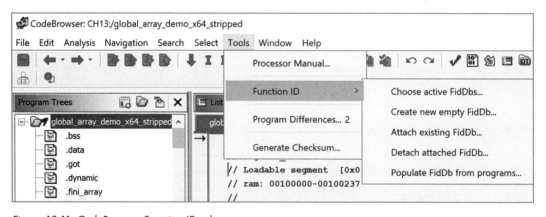

Figure 13-11: CodeBrowser Function ID submenu

Before we walk through an example of using the Function ID plugin to extend Ghidra signatures, let's briefly discuss the five new menu options:

Choose active FidDbs   Displays a list of active Function ID databases. Each may be selected or deselected using an associated checkbox.

Create new empty FidDb   Allows you to create and name a new Function ID database. The new FidDb will be listed when Choose active FidDbs is selected.

Attach existing FidDb   Displays a file chooser dialog that lets you add an existing FidDb to the list of active FidDbs. After you add the FidDb, you can select Choose active FidDbs to see the added FidDb listed.

Detach existing FidDb   Can be applied to only FidDbs that have been manually attached. The operation removes the association between the selected FidDb and the current Ghidra instance.

Populate FidDb from programs   Generates new function fingerprints to add to an existing FidDb. The dialog in Figure 13-12 is used to control this process, and its use will be discussed shortly.

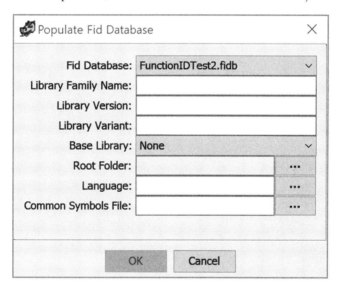

Figure 13-12: Populate Fid Database dialog

Function ID Plugin Example: UPX

When we auto analyze binaries that contain very few functions outside of library functions that Ghidra recognizes, our reverse engineering task is somewhat simplified. We can focus on the subset of functions that Ghidra fails to recognize under the assumption that this is where the new, interesting functionality lies. Our task is much more challenging when Ghidra can't identify any functions. When we (human analysts) recognize functions and extend Ghidra's ability to recognize those same functions in the future, we reduce our future workload. Let's walk through a demonstration of how powerful this sort of extension can be.

Let's assume we load a 64-bit Linux ELF binary into Ghidra and auto analyze the file. The resulting Symbol Tree entries are shown in Figure 13-13. We use the Symbol Tree to navigate to the entry point and examine the code. Our initial analysis leads us to believe that the binary is packed using *the Ultimate Packer for eXecutatbles (UPX)* and that the functions we are seeing were added by the UPX packer to unpack the binary at runtime. We confirm this hypothesis by comparing the bytes we see in entry with published bytes for the UPX entry point function. (Alternatively, we could create our own UPX-packed binary for comparison.) Now, we add this information to our FidDb so that we don't have to perform this same analysis should we ever encounter another UPX-packed 64-bit Linux binary.

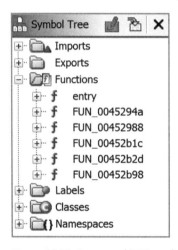

Figure 13-13: Suspected UPX packer functions for upx_demo1_x64_static.upx

Functions you add to an FidDb should have meaningful names. Accordingly, we change the names of the functions in our example to indicate that they are part of a UPX packer, as shown in Figure 13-14, and then add these functions to a new Function ID database so that Ghidra can label the functions appropriately in the future.

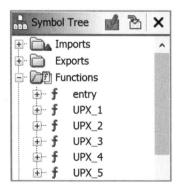

Figure 13-14: Labeled UPX packer functions for upx_demo1_x64_static.upx

We create a new FidDb by selecting **Tools ▸ Function ID ▸ Create new empty FidDb** and then name the new FidDb *UPX.fidb*. Next, we populate our new database with information extracted from the updated binary by selecting **Tools ▸ Function ID ▸ Populate FidDb** from programs. Enter information about the FidDb in the resulting dialog, as shown in Figure 13-15.

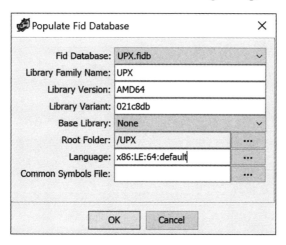

Figure 13-15: Populate Fid Database dialog

The purpose of each field and the values we have entered are described here:

Fid Database   *UPX.fidb* is the name of our new FidDb. The pull-down list allows you to choose from among all of the FidDbs you have created.

Library Family Name   Choose a name that describes the library from which you are extracting function data. In our case, we have input *UPX*.

Library Version   This can be a version number or a platform name or a combination of both. Since UPX is available for many platforms, we chose the library version based on the architecture of the binary.

Library Variant   This field may be used for any additional information that distinguishes this library from others of the same version. In this example, we used the commit ID for this version of UPX from the UPX repository on GitHub (*https://github.com/upx/*).

Base Library   Here you may reference another FidDb that Ghidra will use to establish parent/child relationships. We did not use a base library, as UPX is completely self-contained.

Root Folder   This field names a Ghidra project folder. All files in the chosen folder will be processed during the function ingest process. In this case, we chose */UPX* from the pull-down menu.

Language   This contains the Ghidra language identifier associated with the new FidDb. To be processed from the root folder, a file's language identifier must match this value. This entry is populated from the Imports Results Summary window for the binary, but may be modified using the button to the right of the text box.

Common Symbols File   This field names a file containing a list of functions that should be excluded from the ingest process. This field is unused in this case.

When we click OK, the ingest process begins. When it's complete, we see the results of the FidDb population (Figure 13-16).

```
6 total functions visited
6 total functions added
0 total functions excluded
Breakdown of exclusions:    IS_THUNK: 0
    FAILED_FUNCTION_FILTER: 0
    NO_DEFINED_SYMBOL: 0
    DUPLICATE_INFO: 0
    FAILS_MINIMUM_SHORTHASH_LENGTH: 0
    MEMORY_ACCESS_EXCEPTION: 0
Most referenced functions by name:
1   UPX_1
1   UPX_2
1   UPX_3
1   UPX_4
1   UPX_5
```

                          OK

Figure 13-16: Results window from UPX FidDb population

Once the new FidDb is created, Ghidra can use it to identify functions in any binary you are analyzing. We demonstrate this by loading a new UPX packed 64-bit Linux ELF binary, *upx_demo2_x64_static.upx*, and auto analyze the file *without* the Function ID analyzer. The resulting Symbol Tree, shown in Figure 13-17, shows five unidentified functions, as we expect.

Figure 13-17: Symbol Tree entry for upx_demo2_x64_static.upx before Function ID analyzer

Running Function ID as a one-shot analyzer (Analysis ▸ One Shot ▸ Function ID) results in the Symbol Tree shown in Figure 13-18, which includes the UPX function names.

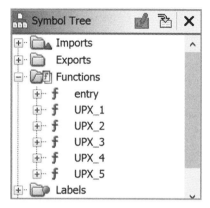

Figure 13-18: Symbol Tree entry for upx_demo2_x64_static.upx after Function ID analyzer

The analyzer also updates the Listing window with new function names and plate comments, like the plate comment for UPX_1 shown next. This plate comment contains the information that we provided when creating the FidDb:

```
**************************************************************
* Library Function - Single Match                           *
* Name: UPX_1                                                *
* Library: UPX AMD64 021c8db                                 *
**************************************************************
                        undefined UPX_1()
    undefined         AL:1              <RETURN>
       UPX_1                            XREF[1]:     UPX_2:00457c08(c)
00457b1a 48 8d 04 2f   LEA    RAX,[RDI + RBP*0x1]
00457b1e 83 f9 05      CMP    ECX,0x5
```

Creating new FidDbs is only the beginning of extending Ghidra's function identification capabilities. You can analyze parameters associated with a function and save them in a Data Type archive. Then, when Function ID correctly identifies the function, you can drag the appropriate Data Type Manager entry onto the function in the Listing window, and the function prototype will be updated with the appropriate parameters.

Function ID Plugin Example: Profiling a Static Library

When you are reverse engineering a statically linked binary, one of the first things you may wish for is an FidDb that matches the functions linked into that binary, so that Ghidra can identify the library code and save you the effort of analyzing it. The following example addresses two important questions: (1) how can you know whether you have such an FidDb, and (2) what can you do if you don't have one? The answer to the first question is simple: Ghidra ships with at least a dozen FidDbs (in the form of *.fidbf* files), all related to Visual Studio library code. If the binary is not a Windows binary and you have not yet created or imported any FidDbs, you'll need to make your own FidDb by using the Ghidra Function ID plugin (which addresses the second question).

The most important thing to understand when populating a new FidDb is that you need an input source that has a high probability of matching against any binaries you plan to apply the FidDb against. In the UPX example, we had a binary that contained code that our intuition told us we might see again in the future. In a common static linking case, we have a binary and we simply want to match as much code in that binary as possible.

There are a variety of ways to recognize that you're dealing with a statically linked binary. Within Ghidra, look at the *Imports* folder within the Symbol Tree. This folder will be empty for a fully statically linked binary with no need for imported functions. A partially statically linked binary may have some imports, so you can look for copyright or version strings from well-known libraries in the Defined Strings window.

On the command line, you can use simple utilities like file and strings:

```
$ file upx_demo2_x64_static_stripped
upx_demo2_x64_static_stripped: ELF 64-bit LSB executable, x86-64,
version 1 (GNU/Linux), statically linked, for GNU/Linux 3.2.0,
BuildID[sha1]=54e3569c298166521438938cc2b7a4dda7ab7f5c, stripped
$ strings upx_demo2_x64_static_stripped | grep GCC
GCC: (Ubuntu 7.4.0-1ubuntu1~18.04.1) 7.4.0
```

The output of file informs us that the binary is statically linked, stripped of any symbols, and from a Linux system. (A stripped binary contains no familiar names to clue us in to the behavior of any of the functions.) Filtering the output of strings using grep GCC identifies the compiler, GCC 7.4.0, as well as the Linux distribution, Ubuntu 18.04.1, used to build the binary. (You can locate the same information with CodeBrowser's Search ▸ Program Text functionality using *GCC* as a qualifier.) It's likely this binary was linked with *libc.a*,[1] so we take a copy of *libc.a* from Ubuntu 18.04.1 and use it as the starting point for recovering symbols in our stripped binary. (Additional strings in the binary might lead us to select additional static libraries for the Function ID analysis; however, we limit this example to *libc.a*.)

To use *libc.a* to populate an FidDb, Ghidra must identify the instructions and functions that it contains. The archive (hence *.a*) file format defines a container for other files, most commonly for object files (*.o*) that a compiler might extract and link into an executable. Ghidra's process for importing container files differs from its process for importing single binaries, so when we import *libc.a* with File ▸ Import, as we usually do when

---

1. An archive of C standard library functions, *libc.a* is used in statically linked binaries on Unix-style systems.

importing a single file, Ghidra offers alternate import modes, as shown in
Figure 13-19. (These other options are also available from the File menu.)

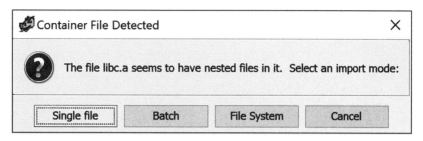

Figure 13-19: Importing a container file

Single File mode asks Ghidra to import the container as if it was a
single file. Since the container is not an executable file, Ghidra is likely
to suggest the Raw Binary format for your import and perform minimal
automated analysis. In File System mode, Ghidra opens a file browser
window (see Figure 13-20) to display the contents of the container file. In
this mode, you may choose any combination of files from the container to
import into Ghidra using options from context menus.

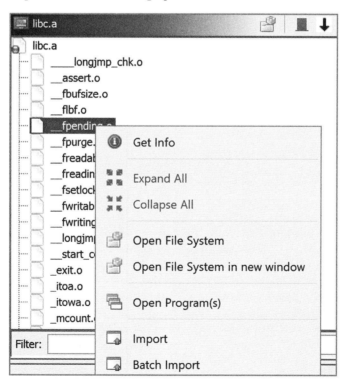

Figure 13-20: File System import mode

In Batch mode, Ghidra automatically imports files in the container without pausing to display individual file information. After initially processing the container's contents, Ghidra displays the Batch Import dialog shown in Figure 13-21. Before clicking OK, you can view information on each file being imported, add more files to the batch import, set import options, and choose the destination folder within your Ghidra project. Figure 13-21 shows that we are about to import 1690 files from the *libc.a* archive into our CH13 project's root directory.

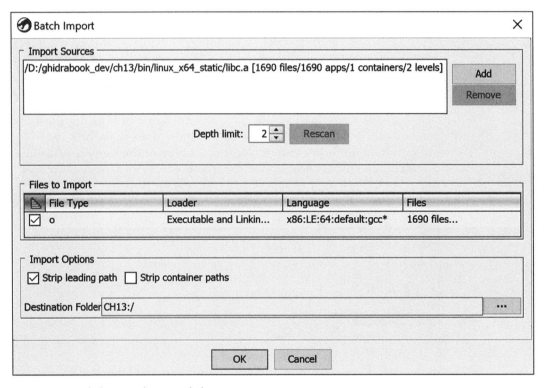

Figure 13-21: Ghidra's Batch Import dialog

Click **OK** to kick off the import process (which may take some time). Once the import is complete, you will be able to browse the newly imported files in the Ghidra Project window. Because *libc.a* is a container file, it will appear as a folder in the Project window, and you can navigate its contents to open and analyze any one of the files contained in the folder.

At this point, we can finally capture fingerprints of each libc function into an FidDb and use that FidDb to perform Function ID analysis against our sample statically linked binary. This process parallels the UPX example, beginning with creating a new empty FidDb that will then be populated from programs. The programs in this case will be the entire contents of our newly import *libc.a* folder. Here we run into a significant challenge.

When we select the files to populate our new FidDb, we must ensure that every file has been properly analyzed by Ghidra to identify functions and their associated instructions (the input to the Function ID hashing process). Up to this point, we have seen Ghidra analyze programs only when we open them in the CodeBrowser, but with *libc.a*, we are faced with the daunting task of analyzing 1690 individual files within the *libc.a* archive. Opening and analyzing them one at a time is not a good use of our time. Even selecting to open all files on import and using Ghidra's Analyze All Open option will still take us a while to work through all 1690 files (and will likely require manual intervention to adjust our tool options and resource allocations to accommodate a task of this size within our Ghidra instance).

If this problem seems unwieldy, you are correct. This is not the sort of task that we should be solving manually through the Ghidra GUI. This is a well-defined repetitive task that shouldn't require human intervention. Fortunately for us, the next three chapters introduce methods we can use to automate this and other tasks. When we get to "Automated FidDb Creation" on page 359, we will revisit this specific task and demonstrate how easily batch processing can be accomplished using Ghidra's headless mode of operation.

Regardless of the method we use to process *libc.a*, once complete, it's a simple matter to return to the Function ID plugin and populate our new FidDb, yielding the following results:

```
FidDb Populate Results

2905 total functions visited
2638 total functions added
267 total functions excluded
Breakdown of exclusions:    FAILS_MINIMUM_SHORTHASH_LENGTH: 234
    DUPLICATE_INFO: 9
    FAILED_FUNCTION_FILTER: 0
    IS_THUNK: 16
    NO_DEFINED_SYMBOL: 8
    MEMORY_ACCESS_EXCEPTION: 0
Most referenced functions by name:
749  __stack_chk_fail
431  free
304  malloc
...
```

Our new FidDb is now available for use and allows the Function ID analyzer to match many of the functions contained in *upx_demo2_x64_static _stripped*, significantly reducing our reverse engineering workload for this particular binary.

Summary

This chapter demonstrated some of the ways that Ghidra can be extended by parsing C source files, extending word models, and extracting function fingerprints using the Function ID plugin. When a binary contains statically linked code or code reused from previously analyzed binaries, matching those functions against Ghidra FidDbs can save you the hassle of manually wading through a mountain of code. Predictably, so many static link libraries exist that it is not possible for Ghidra to include FidDb files that cover every possible use case. The ability to create your own FidDb files when necessary allows you to build up a collection of FidDbs that are tuned to your particular needs. In Chapters 14 and 15, we introduce Ghidra's powerful scripting capabilities to further extend Ghidra's functionality.

14

BASIC GHIDRA SCRIPTING

No application can meet every need of every user. It is just not possible to anticipate every potential use case that may arise. Ghidra's open source model facilitates feature requests and innovative contributions by developers. However, sometimes you need to immediately address a problem at hand and can't wait for someone else to implement new functionality. To support unanticipated use cases and programmatic control of Ghidra's actions, Ghidra includes integrated scripting features.

Uses for scripts are infinite and can range from simple one-liners to full-blown programs that automate common tasks or perform complex analysis. In this chapter, we focus on the basic scripting that is provided through the CodeBrowser interface. We introduce the internal scripting environment, discuss script development using Java and Python, and then move on to other integrated scripting options in Chapter 15.

Script Manager

The Ghidra Script Manager is available through the CodeBrowser menu. Choosing Window ▸ Script Manager opens the window shown in Figure 14-1. The window can also be opened using the Script Manager icon in the CodeBrowser toolbar (a green circle with an arrow inside, also shown in the top left of the Script Manager window).

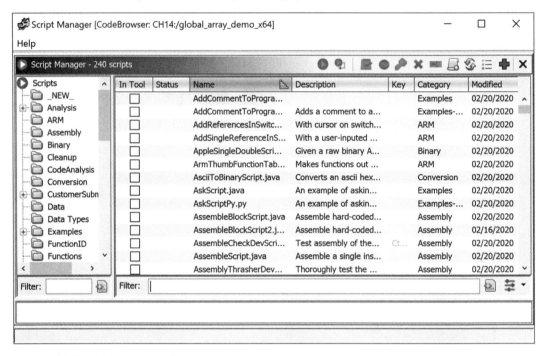

Figure 14-1: Script Manager window

Script Manager Window

In a new Ghidra installation, the Script Manager loads with over 240 scripts organized in a category tree, as seen on the left side of Figure 14-1. Some of the folders contain subfolders to provide even more detailed classification of the scripts. You can expand and collapse the folders to see the organization of the scripts. Selecting an individual folder or subfolder limits the display to the scripts within the selected folder. To populate this window, Ghidra locates and indexes all scripts in subdirectories named *ghidra_scripts* within the Ghidra distribution folder. Ghidra also looks for a *ghidra_scripts* directory within your home directory and indexes any scripts it finds there.

The default set of scripts covers a wide range of functionality. Some of the scripts are intended to demonstrate fundamental scripting concepts. The columns in the script list table provide additional detail about the purpose of each script. As with most Ghidra tables, you can control which columns are displayed as well as the sort order for individual columns. By default, all available fields for the table are displayed except Created and Path. The six information columns provide the following insight into a script:

Status　Indicates the status of the script. The field is generally blank but can contain a red icon to indicate an error in the script. If you have associated a toolbar icon with the script, the icon will appear in this column.

Name　Contains the filename of the script, including its extension.

Description　A description pulled from the metadata comment within the script. This field can be quite lengthy, but you can read the entire contents by hovering over the field. This field is discussed in more depth in "Script Development" on page 289.

Key　Indicates if there is a key binding assigned for running the script.

Category　Specifies the path at which the script will be listed in the Script Manager's topic hierarchy. This is a logical hierarchy, *not* a filesystem directory hierarchy.

Modified　The date the script was last saved. For the default scripts the date is the installation date of the Ghidra instance.

The filter field on the left side of the window searches through the script categories. The filter on the right searches the script names and descriptions. Finally, at the bottom, an additional window is initially empty. This window displays metadata about a selected script in an easy-to-process format that includes the field extracted from the metadata within the script. The format and meaning of the metadata fields are discussed in "Writing Java Scripts (Not JavaScript!)" on page 289.

While the Script Manager provides a significant amount of information, the main power of this window comes from the toolbar it provides. An overview of the toolbar is provided in Figure 14-2.

Script Manager Toolbar

The Script Manager has no menus to help you manage your scripts. Instead, all script management actions are associated with tools on the Script Manager toolbar (Figure 14-2).

While most of the menu options are pretty clear from the descriptions in Figure 14-2, the Edit options merit additional discussion. Editing with Eclipse is covered in Chapter 15, as it facilitates more advanced scripting capabilities. The Edit Script option opens a primitive text editor window with its own toolbar, shown in Figure 14-3. The associated actions provide the basic functionality for editing files. With an editor in hand, we can get down to the business of writing actual scripts.

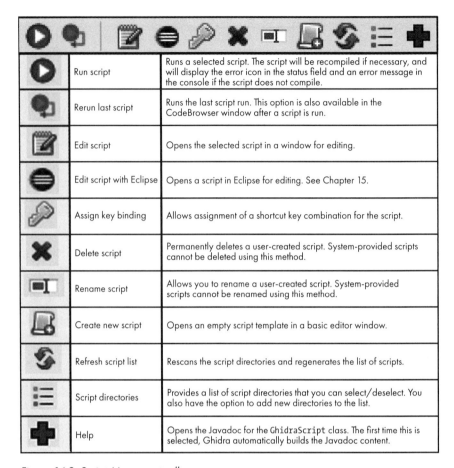

	Run script	Runs a selected script. The script will be recompiled if necessary, and will display the error icon in the status field and an error message in the console if the script does not compile.
	Rerun last script	Runs the last script run. This option is also available in the CodeBrowser window after a script is run.
	Edit script	Opens the selected script in a window for editing.
	Edit script with Eclipse	Opens a script in Eclipse for editing. See Chapter 15.
	Assign key binding	Allows assignment of a shortcut key combination for the script.
	Delete script	Permanently deletes a user-created script. System-provided scripts cannot be deleted using this method.
	Rename script	Allows you to rename a user-created script. System-provided scripts cannot be renamed using this method.
	Create new script	Opens an empty script template in a basic editor window.
	Refresh script list	Rescans the script directories and regenerates the list of scripts.
	Script directories	Provides a list of script directories that you can select/deselect. You also have the option to add new directories to the list.
	Help	Opens the Javadoc for the GhidraScript class. The first time this is selected, Ghidra automatically builds the Javadoc content.

Figure 14-2: Script Manager toolbar

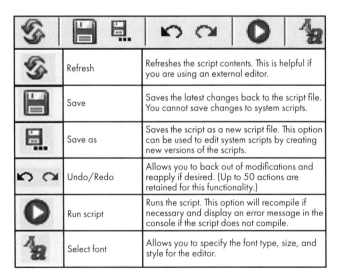

	Refresh	Refreshes the script contents. This is helpful if you are using an external editor.
	Save	Saves the latest changes back to the script file. You cannot save changes to system scripts.
	Save as	Saves the script as a new script file. This option can be used to edit system scripts by creating new versions of the scripts.
	Undo/Redo	Allows you to back out of modifications and reapply if desired. (Up to 50 actions are retained for this functionality.)
	Run script	Runs the script. This option will recompile if necessary and display an error message in the console if the script does not compile.
	Select font	Allows you to specify the font type, size, and style for the editor.

Figure 14-3: Edit Script toolbar

Script Development

There are several methods for developing scripts within Ghidra. In this chapter, we focus on scripting using Java and Python, as these are languages used by the existing scripts in the Script Manager window. Most of the 240+ system scripts are written in Java, so we begin with editing and developing scripts in Java.

Writing Java Scripts (Not JavaScript!)

In Ghidra, a script written in Java is actually a complete class specification designed to be seamlessly compiled, dynamically loaded into your running Ghidra instance, invoked, and finally unloaded. The class must extend the class Ghidra.app.script.GhidraScript, implement a run() method, and be annotated with comments that provide Javadoc-format metadata about the script. We'll show the structure of a script file, describe the metadata requirements, look at some of the system scripts, and then move on to editing existing scripts and building our own scripts.

Figure 14-4 shows the script editor opened when the Create New Script option (refer to Figure 14-2) is selected to create a new Java script. We have named the new script *CH14_NewScript*.

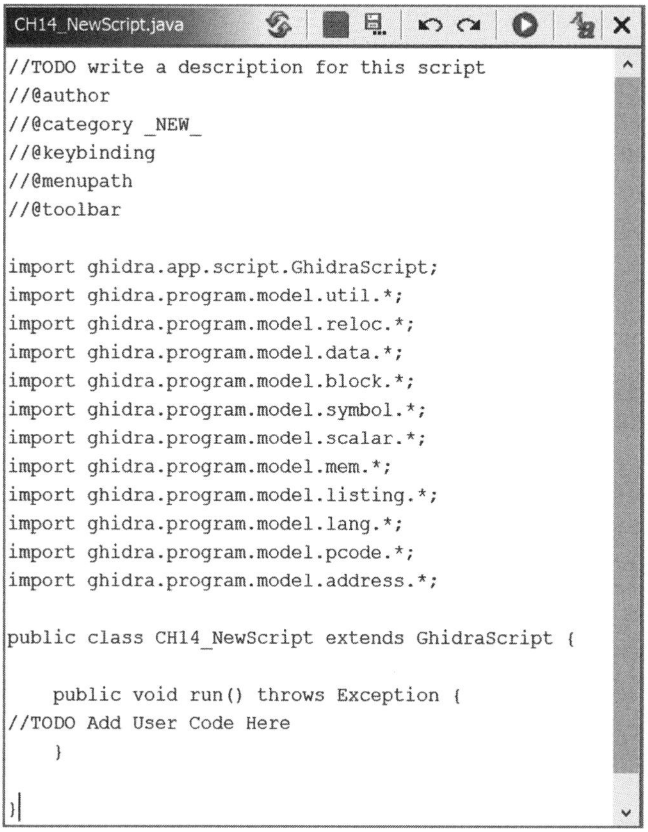

```
CH14_NewScript.java

//TODO write a description for this script
//@author
//@category _NEW_
//@keybinding
//@menupath
//@toolbar

import ghidra.app.script.GhidraScript;
import ghidra.program.model.util.*;
import ghidra.program.model.reloc.*;
import ghidra.program.model.data.*;
import ghidra.program.model.block.*;
import ghidra.program.model.symbol.*;
import ghidra.program.model.scalar.*;
import ghidra.program.model.mem.*;
import ghidra.program.model.listing.*;
import ghidra.program.model.lang.*;
import ghidra.program.model.pcode.*;
import ghidra.program.model.address.*;

public class CH14_NewScript extends GhidraScript {

    public void run() throws Exception {
//TODO Add User Code Here
    }

}
```

Figure 14-4: A new, empty script

At the top of the file are the metadata comments and tags used to produce the expected Javadoc information. This information is also used to populate the fields in the Script Manager window (refer to Figure 14-1). Any comments starting with // before the class, field, or method declarations will become part of the Javadoc Description for the script. Additional comments can be embedded within the script and will not be included in the description. In addition, the following tags within the metadata comments are supported:

@author   Provides information about the author of the script. The information is provided at the discretion of the author and can include any pertinent details (for example, name, contact information, date of creation, and so on).

@category   Determines where the script appears within the category tree. This is the only mandatory tag and must be present in all Ghidra scripts. The period (dot) character acts as a path separator for category names (for example, `@category Ghidrabook.CH14`).

@keybinding   Documents a shortcut for accessing the script from the CodeBrowser window (for example, `@keybinding K`).

@menupath   Defines a period-delimited menu path for the script as well as provides a means to run the script from a CodeBrowser menu (for example, `@menupath File.Run.ThisScript`).

@toolbar   Associates an icon with the script. This icon is displayed as a toolbar button in the CodeBrowser window and may be used to run the script. If Ghidra cannot find the image in the script directory or the Ghidra installation, a default image will be used (for example, `@toolbar myImage.png`).

When confronted with a new API (such as the Ghidra API), it may take some time before you're comfortable writing scripts without constantly consulting available API documentation. Java in particular is very sensitive to classpath issues and the proper inclusion of required support packages. A time- and sanity-saving option is to edit an existing program rather than creating a new program. We adopt this approach in presenting a simple example of a script.

Edit Script Example: Regex Search

Assume that you are tasked with developing a script to accept a regular expression as input from the user and output matching strings to the console. Further, this script needs to appear in the Script Manager for a particular project. While Ghidra offers many ways to accomplish this task, you have been asked to produce a script. To find a script with similar functionality to use as a base, you look through the categories in the Script Manager and check the contents of the Strings and Search categories, and then filter for the term *strings* and find other options. Using filters produces a more comprehensive list of string-related scripts for your consideration. For this example, you will edit the first script in the list that shares some functionality with what you want your script to do—*CountAndSaveStrings.java*.

Open the script in the editor to confirm that it's a good starting point for our new functionality by right-clicking the desired script and selecting **Edit** with basic editor; then save this script with the new name, *FindStringsByRegex.java*, using the **Save As** option. Ghidra does not allow you to edit the system scripts provided as part of your Ghidra installation within the Script Manager window (although you can in Eclipse and other editors). You could also edit the file prior to using Save As since Ghidra prevents you from accidentally writing any modified content to the existing *CountAndSaveStrings.java* script.

The original *CountAndSaveStrings.java* contains the following metadata:

```
❶ /* ###
   * IP: GHIDRA
   *
   * Licensed under the Apache License, Version 2.0 (the "License");
   * you may not use this file except in compliance with the License.
   * You may obtain a copy of the License at
   * http://www.apache.org/licenses/LICENSE-2.0
   * Unless required by applicable law or agreed to in writing, software
   * distributed under the License is distributed on an "AS IS" BASIS,
   * WITHOUT WARRANTIES OR CONDITIONS OF ANY KIND, either express or implied.
   * See the License for the specific language governing permissions and
   * limitations under the License.
   */
❷ //Counts the number of defined strings in the current selection,
   //or current program if no selection is made,
   //and saves the results to a file.
❸ //@category CustomerSubmission.Strings
```

We can leave, modify, or delete the licensing agreement ❶ for the script without impacting the execution of the script or the associated Javadoc. We'll modify the description of the script ❷ so that the information displayed in Javadoc and the Script Manager accurately describes the script. The script author has included only one of the five available tags ❸, so we'll add placeholders for the unpopulated tags and revise the description, as follows:

```
// Counts the number of defined strings that match a regex in the current
// selection, or current program if no selection is made, and displays the
// number of matching strings to the console.
//
//@author Ghidrabook
//@category Ghidrabook.CH14
//@keybinding
//@menupath
//@toolbar
```

The category tag `Ghidrabook.CH14` will be added to the Script Manager's tree display, as shown in Figure 14-5.

The next portion of the original script contains Java `import` statements. Of the long list of imports Ghidra includes when you create a new script, as shown in Figure 14-4, only the following imports are necessary for string searching, so we'll keep the same list as the original *CountAndSaveStrings.java*:

```
import ghidra.app.script.GhidraScript;
import ghidra.program.model.listing.*;
import ghidra.program.util.ProgramSelection;

import java.io.*;
```

Save the new script and then select it in the Script Manager to see the content shown in Figure 14-5. Our new category is included in the script tree, and the script's metadata is displayed in the information window and script table. The table contains only one script, *Ghidrabook.CH14*, as it is the only script in the selected category.

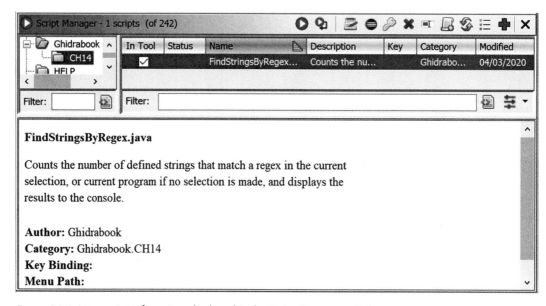

Figure 14-5: New script information displayed in the Script Manager window

As this book is not intended to be a Java tutorial, we summarize the changes we made to the script rather than explaining Java syntax and functionality. The following list describes the behavior of *CountAndSaveStrings.java*:

1. Get the program listing content to search.
2. Get the file to save results to.
3. Open the file.
4. Iterate through the program listing: count the number of qualifying strings and write each qualifying string to the file.
5. Close the file.
6. Write the number of qualifying strings to the console.

The functionality we desire in our modified script is described next:

1. Get the program listing content to search.
2. Ask the user for a regular expression (regex) to search for.
3. Iterate through the program listing: count the number of qualifying strings and write each qualifying string to the console.
4. Write the number of qualifying strings to the console.

Our new script will be significantly shorter than the original script, as there is no need to interact with the filesystem and perform associated error checking. Our implementation follows:

```
public class FindStringsByRegex extends GhidraScript❶ {
  @Override
  public void run() throws Exception {
    String regex =
       askString("Please enter the regex",
       Please enter the regex you're looking to match:);

    Listing listing = currentProgram.getListing();

    DataIterator dataIt;
    if (currentSelection != null) {
       dataIt = listing.getDefinedData(currentSelection, true);
    }
    else {
       dataIt = listing.getDefinedData(true);
    }

    Data data;
    String type;
    int counter = 0;
    while (dataIt.hasNext() && !monitor.isCancelled()) {
       data = dataIt.next();
       type = data.getDataType().getName().toLowerCase();
       if (type.contains("unicode") || type.contains("string")) {
          String s = data.getDefaultValueRepresentation();
          if (s.matches(regex)) {
             counter++;
             println(s);
          }
       }
    }
    println(counter + " matching strings were found");
  }
}
```

All Java scripts that you write for Ghidra must extend (inherit from) an existing class named Ghidra.app.script.GhidraScript ❶. After saving the final version of the script, select it from within the Script Manager and execute it. When the script executes, we see the prompt shown in Figure 14-6. This figure includes the regular expression that we will be searching for to test our script.

Figure 14-6: New script prompt to enter a regex

The CodeBrowser console displays the following content when our new script has completed execution:

```
FindStringsByRegex.java> Running...
FindStringsByRegex.java> "Fatal error: glibc detected an invalid stdio handle\n"
FindStringsByRegex.java> "Unknown error "
FindStringsByRegex.java> "internal error"
FindStringsByRegex.java> "relocation error"
FindStringsByRegex.java> "symbol lookup error"
FindStringsByRegex.java> "Fatal error: length accounting in _dl_exception_create_format\n"
FindStringsByRegex.java> "Fatal error: invalid format in exception string\n"
FindStringsByRegex.java> "error while loading shared libraries"
FindStringsByRegex.java> "Unknown error"
FindStringsByRegex.java> "version lookup error"
FindStringsByRegex.java> "sdlerror.o"
FindStringsByRegex.java> "dl-error.o"
FindStringsByRegex.java> "fatal_error"
FindStringsByRegex.java> "strerror.o"
FindStringsByRegex.java> "strerror"
FindStringsByRegex.java> "__strerror_r"
FindStringsByRegex.java> "_dl_signal_error"
FindStringsByRegex.java> "__dlerror"
FindStringsByRegex.java> "_dlerror_run"
FindStringsByRegex.java> "_dl_catch_error"
FindStringsByRegex.java> 20 matching strings were found
FindStringsByRegex.java> Finished!
```

This simple example demonstrates the low barrier to entry of Ghidra's extensive Java scripting capabilities. Existing scripts can be easily modified and new scripts can be built from the ground up using the Script Manager. We present some more complex Java scripting capabilities in Chapters 15 and 16, but Java is just one of the scripting options provided by Ghidra. Ghidra also allows you to author scripts in Python.

Python Scripts

Of the 240+ scripts in the Script Manager, only a handful are written in Python. You can easily locate the Python scripts by filtering for the *.py* extension in the Script Manager. The majority of the Python scripts can be found in the Examples.Python category in the tree and includes a disclaimer similar to the one shown in Figure 14-7.

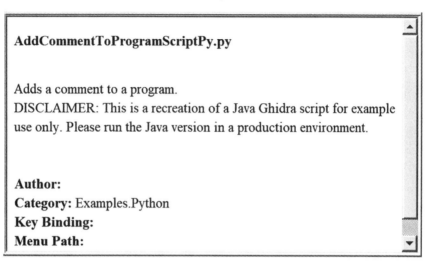

AddCommentToProgramScriptPy.py

Adds a comment to a program.
DISCLAIMER: This is a recreation of a Java Ghidra script for example use only. Please run the Java version in a production environment.

Author:
Category: Examples.Python
Key Binding:
Menu Path:

Figure 14-7: Sample Python script with disclaimer

Of the examples in this directory, the following three provide a good starting point if you prefer to use Python:

ghidra_basic.py   This script includes examples of basic Python scripting as related to Ghidra.

python_basics.py   This is a very basic introduction to many of the Python commands that you might want to use.

jython_basic.py   This extends the basic Python commands to demonstrate content that is specific to Jython.

The Ghidra features demonstrated in these examples barely scratch the surface of the available Ghidra APIs. You'll likely still need to spend some time reading through Ghidra's library of Java examples before you'll be ready to access Ghidra's full Java API from your Python scripts.

In addition to running Python scripts, Ghidra provides the Python Interpreter to allow you to use Python/Jython to directly access the Java objects associated with Ghidra, as shown in Figure 14-8.

GHIDRA'S PYTHON FUTURE

Python is popular for creating scripts because of its simplicity and numerous available libraries. While the majority of the scripts in the Ghidra release are written in Java, the open source RE community likely will use Python as a primary scripting language within Ghidra. Ghidra is reliant on Jython for Python support (which provides the advantage of allowing direct access to Ghidra's Java objects). Jython is compatible with Python 2 (specifically 2.7.1) but not Python 3. Although Python 2 went end-of-life in January 2020, Python 2 scripts will continue to function within Ghidra, and any new Ghidra Python 2 scripts should be written in a way that makes them as portable as possible to Python 3.

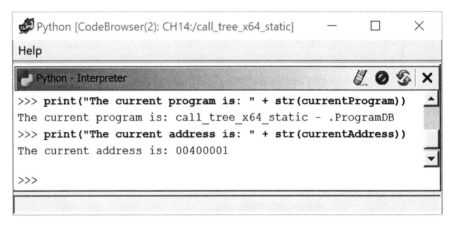

Figure 14-8: Python Interpreter print example

The Python Interpreter is accessible through the CodeBrowser by selecting Windows ▶ Python. For more information about using the interpreter, see Ghidra Help. To get API information when using Python and the Python Interpreter, choose Help ▶ Ghidra API Help at the top left of the Interpreter window shown in Figure 14-8, which opens the Javadoc content on the GhidraScript class. Alternatively, Python has a built-in function, help( ), that has been modified in Ghidra to provide direct access to Ghidra's Javadoc. To use the function, type help(*object*) in the interpreter, as shown in Figure 14-9. For example, help(currentProgram) displays the Ghidra Javadoc content describing the Ghidra API class ProgramDB.

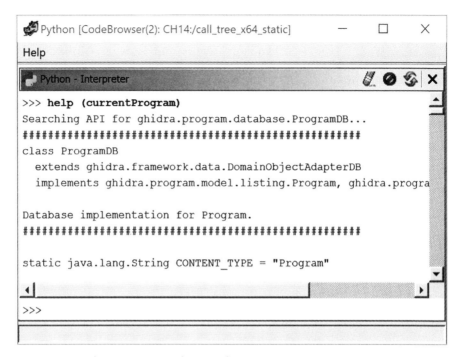

```
Python [CodeBrowser(2): CH14:/call_tree_x64_static]          —    □    ✕

Help

Python - Interpreter                                    🖋 ⊘ 🔄 ✕

>>> help (currentProgram)
Searching API for ghidra.program.database.ProgramDB...
#####################################################
class ProgramDB
  extends ghidra.framework.data.DomainObjectAdapterDB
  implements ghidra.program.model.listing.Program, ghidra.progra


Database implementation for Program.
#####################################################

static java.lang.String CONTENT_TYPE = "Program"

>>>
```

Figure 14-9: Python Interpreter Help example

Support for Other Languages

Finally, Ghidra can support scripts from languages other than Java and
Python, which lets you bring existing scripts from your reverse engineering
toolkit into your Ghidra workflow. This functionality is discussed further in
Ghidra Help.

Introduction to the Ghidra API

At this point, you have all the information required to edit and run Ghidra
scripts. Now it's time to use the Ghidra API to extend your scripting capabilities and interact more directly with Ghidra artifacts. Ghidra exposes its
API in two rather different styles.

The *Program* API defines an object hierarchy, many levels deep, rooted
at the top by the Program class. This API may change from one version of
Ghidra to another. The *Flat* API flattens out the Program API by exposing
all levels of that API from a single class, FlatProgramAPI. The Flat API is often
the most convenient way to access many Ghidra constructs. Additionally, it
is less likely to change from one version of Ghidra to the next.

For the remainder of the chapter, we highlight some of the more useful
Flat API functionality. When necessary, we also provide detail about specific
classes from the Program API. We use Java as the language for this discussion, as it is the native language of Ghidra.

The Ghidra API contains many packages, classes, and associated functions to interface with your Ghidra projects and associated files, all detailed in Javadoc-style documentation supplied with Ghidra that can be accessed by clicking the red plus in the Script Manager window. This documentation, in conjunction with the sample scripts supplied with Ghidra, is your primary reference about the APIs and how to use them. The most common way to figure out how to do something is to browse the Ghidra classes looking for one that, based on its name, appears to do what you need. As you gain more experience with Ghidra, your increased understanding of the naming conventions and file organization will help you identify appropriate classes more quickly.

Ghidra adheres to the Java Swing *model-delegate* architecture in which data values and characteristics are stored in model objects and displayed by user interface delegate objects such as tree, list, and table views. Delegates handle events, such as mouse clicks, to update and refresh data and views. In the overwhelming majority of cases, your scripts will focus on the data encapsulated in the model classes used to represent various program and reverse engineering constructs.

The remainder of this section focuses on commonly used model classes, their relationships to each other, and useful APIs for interacting with them. We make no attempt to cover the entire Ghidra API, and many more functions and classes are available. The authoritative documentation for the entire Ghidra API is the Javadoc that ships with Ghidra, and ultimately the Java source code from which Ghidra is built.

The Address Interface

The Address interface describes a model for an address within an address space. All addresses are represented by an offset up to 64 bits in size. Segmented addresses may be further qualified by a segment value. In many cases, an address's offset is equivalent to a virtual address within a program listing. The getOffset method retrieves the long offset value from an Address instance. Many Ghidra API functions require Address objects as arguments or return an Address object as a result.

The Symbol Interface

The Symbol interface defines properties common to all symbols. At a minimum, a symbol is composed of a name and an address. These attributes may be retrieved with the following member functions:

Address getAddress()
   Returns the address of the Symbol

String getName()
   Returns the name of the Symbol

The Reference Interface

A `Reference` models a cross-reference relationship (as described in Chapter 9) between a source address and a destination address and is characterized by a reference type. Useful functions associated with a `Reference` include these:

`public Address getFromAddress()`
> Returns the source address for this reference

`public Address getToAddress()`
> Returns the destination address for this reference

`public RefType getReferenceType()`
> Returns a `RefType` object that describes the nature of the link between the source and destination addresses

The GhidraScript Class

Although this class doesn't model a specific attribute in a binary, every script that you write must be a subclass of `GhidraScript`, which, in turn, is a subclass of `FlatProgramAPI`. As a result, your scripts have instantaneous access to the entire Flat API and your only obligation is to provide an implementation of

```
protected abstract void run() throws Exception;
```

which, hopefully, makes your script do something interesting. The remainder of the `GhidraScript` class gives you access to the most common resources for interacting with the Ghidra user and the program that is being analyzed. Some of the more useful functions and data members of this class (including some inherited from `FlatProgramAPI`) are summarized in the following sections.

Useful Data Members

The `GhidraScript` class provides convenient access to a number of objects commonly referenced in scripts, including the following:

`protected Program currentProgram;`
> This is the current open program. The `Program` class is discussed later. This data member is likely your gateway to retrieving more interesting information, such as instruction and symbol lists.

`protected Address currentAddress;`
> This is the address of the current cursor location. The `Address` class is discussed later.

`protected ProgramLocation currentLocation;`
> A `ProgramLocation` object that describes the current cursor location, including its address, cursor row, column, and other information.

`protected ProgramSelection currentSelection;`
> A `ProgramSelection` object representing a range of addresses selected in the Ghidra GUI.

`protected TaskMonitor monitor;`
> The `TaskMonitor` class updates the status of long-running tasks and checks to determine whether a long-running task has been cancelled by the user (`monitor.isCancelled()`). Any long-running loops that you write should incorporate a call to `monitor.isCancelled` as an additional termination condition to recognize that the user has attempted to cancel your script.

User Interface Functions

The GhidraScript class provides convenience functions for basic user interface operations, ranging from simple message output to more interactive dialog elements. Some of the more common user interface functions are described here:

`public void println(String message)`
> Prints message followed by a linefeed to Ghidra's console window. This function is useful for printing status messages or results of your scripts in a nonintrusive manner.

`public void printf(String message, Object... args)`
> Uses message as a Java format string and prints the resulting string of formatted args to Ghidra's console window.

`public void popup(final String message)`
> Displays message in a pop-up dialog that requires the user to click OK before script execution can continue. This is a more intrusive way to display status messages to a user.

`public String askString(String title, String message)`
> One of many available ask functions. askString displays a text input dialog, using message as a prompt, and returns the text entered by the user.

`public boolean askYesNo(String title, String question)`
> Uses a dialog to ask the user a yes-or-no question. Returns true for yes, and false for no.

`public Address askAddress(String title, String message)`
> Displays a dialog, using message as a prompt, that parses the user's input into an Address object.

`public int askInt(String title, String message)`
> Displays a dialog, using message as a prompt, that parses the user's input into an int.

```
public File askFile(final String title, final String approveButtonText)
```
Displays a system file chooser dialog and returns a Java File object representing the file selected by the user.

```
public File askDirectory(final String title, final String approveButtonText)
```
Displays a system file chooser dialog and returns a Java File object representing the directory selected by the user.

```
public boolean goTo(Address address)
```
Repositions all connected Ghidra disassembly windows to address. Overloaded versions of this function take a Symbol or a Function argument and navigate the displays accordingly.

Address-Related Functions

For a processor, an address is typically just a number that happens to refer to a memory location. Ghidra models addresses using the Address class. GhidraScript provides a wrapper function that offers easy conversion from numbers to Ghidra Address objects:

```
public Address toAddr(long offset)
```
Convenience function to create an Address object in the default address space

Reading Program Memory

The Memory class represents contiguous ranges of byte values, such as the contents of an executable file loaded into Ghidra. Within a Memory object, every byte value is associated with an address, though addresses may be tagged as uninitialized and have no value to retrieve. Ghidra throws a MemoryAccessException if you attempt to access a location within a memory object with an invalid address. Consult the documentation for the Memory class for a full description of available API functions. The following convenience functions expose some of the Memory class via the Flat API:

```
public byte getByte(Address addr)
```
Returns the single byte value retrieved from addr. Data type byte is a signed type in Java, so this value will be in the range –128..127.

```
public byte[] getBytes(Address addr, int length)
```
Returns length bytes from memory, beginning at addr.

```
public int getInt(Address addr)
```
Returns the 4-byte value, beginning at addr, as a Java int. This function is endianness-aware and respects the binary's underlying architecture when reconstituting the int value.

```
public long getLong(Address addr)
```
Returns the 8-byte value, beginning at addr, as a Java long. This function is endianness-aware and respects the binary's underlying architecture when reconstituting the long value.

Program Search Functions

Ghidra's search capabilities reside within different Program API classes according to the type of item being searched for. The Memory class contains raw byte search functionality. Code units (such as Data and Instruction), comment text, and associated iterators are obtained from the Listing class. Symbols/labels and associated iterators are accessed via the SymbolTable class. The following convenience functions expose some of the available search functionality via the Flat API:

```
public Data getFirstData()
```
Returns the first data item in the program.

```
public Data getDataAfter(Data data)
```
Returns the next data item after data, or null if no such data exists.

```
public Data getDataAt(Address address)
```
Returns the data item at address, or null if no such data exists.

```
public Instruction getFirstInstruction()
```
Returns the first instruction in the program.

```
public Instruction getInstructionAfter(Instruction instruction)
```
Returns the next instruction item after instruction, or null if no such instruction exists.

```
public Instruction getInstructionAt(Address address)
```
Returns the instruction at address, or null if no such instruction exists.

```
public Address find(String text)
```
Searches for a text string within the Listing window. Listing components are searched in the following order:

1. Plate comments
2. Pre comments
3. Labels
4. Code unit mnemonics and operands
5. EOL comments
6. Repeatable comments
7. Post comments

A successful search returns the address containing the match. Note that as a result of the search order, the returned address may *not* represent the first occurrence of text in the disassembly listing when considered in strictly increasing address order.

public Address find(Address start, byte[] values);
Searches memory, beginning at `addr`, for a specified sequence of byte values. When `addr` is `null`, the search begins at the lowest valid address in the binary. A successful search returns the address of the first byte in the matching sequence.

public Address findBytes(Address start, String byteString)
Searches memory, beginning at `addr`, for a specified `byteString` that may contain regular expressions. When `addr` is `null`, the search begins at the lowest valid address in the binary. A successful search returns the address of the first byte in the matching sequence.

Manipulating Label and Symbols

The need to manipulate named locations arises fairly often in scripts. The following functions are available for working with named locations in a Ghidra database:

public Symbol getSymbolAt(Address address)
Returns the `Symbol` associated with the given address, or `null` if the location has no `Symbol`.

public Symbol createLabel(Address address, String name, boolean makePrimary)
Assigns the given `name` to the given `address`. Ghidra allows multiple names to be assigned to a single address. If `makePrimary` is true, the new name will become the primary name associated with `address`.

public List<Symbol> getSymbols(String name, Namespace namespace)
Returns a list of all symbols named `name` in `namespace`. When namespace is `null`, the global namespace is searched. If the result is empty, the named symbol does not exist. If the result contains only one element, the name is unique.

Working with Functions

Many scripts are designed to analyze functions within a program. The following functions can be used to access information about program functions:

public final Function getFirstFunction()
Returns the first `Function` object in the program

```
public Function getGlobalFunctions(String name)
```
Returns the first Function object for the named function, or null if no such function exists

```
public Function getFunctionAt(Address entryPoint)
```
Returns the Function object for the function at entryPoint, or null if no such function exists

```
public Function getFunctionAfter(Function function)
```
Returns the Function object for the successor to function, or null if no such function exists

```
public Function getFunctionAfter(Address address)
```
Returns the Function object for the function that starts after address, or null if no such function exists

Working with Cross-References

Cross-references were covered in Chapter 9. In the Ghidra Program API, the top-level Program object contains a ReferenceManager, which, unsurprisingly, manages the references within the program. As with many other program constructs, the Flat API offers convenience functions for accessing cross-references, some of which are detailed here:

```
public Reference[] getReferencesFrom(Address address)
```
Returns an array of all Reference objects originating from address

```
public Reference[] getReferencesTo(Address address)
```
Returns an array of all Reference objects terminating at address

Program Manipulation Functions

When automating your analysis tasks, you may find yourself wanting to add new information into a program. The Flat API provides a variety of functions for modifying the contents of a program, including the following:

```
public final void clearListing(Address address)
```
Removes any instruction or data defined at address.

```
public void removeFunctionAt(Address address)
```
Removes the function at address.

```
public boolean disassemble(Address address)
```
Performs a recursive descent disassembly beginning at address. Returns true if the operation is successful.

```
public Data createByte(Address address)
```
Converts the item at the specified address into a data byte. Also, createWord, createDword, createQword, and other data creation functions are available.

public boolean setEOLComment(Address address, String comment)
> Adds an EOL comment at the given address. Additional comment-related functions include setPlateComment, setPreComment, and setPostComment.

public Function createFunction(Address entryPoint, String name)
> Creates a function with the given name at entryPoint. Ghidra attempts to automatically identify the end of the function by locating the function's return instruction.

public Data createAsciiString(Address address)
> Creates a null-terminated ASCII string at address.

public Data createAsciiString(Address address, int length)
> Creates an ASCII string of the specified length at address. If length is zero or less, Ghidra attempts to automatically locate the string's null terminator.

public Data createUnicodeString(Address address)
> Creates a null-terminated Unicode string at address.

The Program Class

The Program class represents the root of the Program API hierarchy and outermost layer of the data model of a binary file. You will commonly use a Program object (often currentProgram) to access the binary model. Commonly used Program class member functions include the following:

public Listing getListing()
> Retrieves the Listing object for the current program.

public FunctionManager getFunctionManager()
> Retrieves the program's FunctionManager, which provides access to all of the functions that have been identified within the binary. This class provides the functionality to map an Address back to its containing Function (Function getFunctionContaining (Address addr)). In addition, it provides a FunctionIterator, which is useful when you want to process every function in the program.

public SymbolTable getSymbolTable()
> Retrieves the program's SymbolTable object. Using a SymbolTable, you can work with individual symbols or iterate over every symbol in the program.

public Memory getMemory()
> Retrieves the Memory object associated with this program, which allows you to work with raw program byte content.

```
public ReferenceManager getReferenceManager()
```
Retrieves the program's ReferenceManager object. A ReferenceManager may be used to add and remove references as well as retrieve iterators for many types of references.

```
public Address getMinAddress()
```
Returns the lowest valid address within the program. This is most often the binary's base memory address.

```
public Address getMaxAddress()
```
Returns the highest valid address within the program.

```
public LanguageID getLanguageID()
```
Returns the object representation of the binary's language specification. The language specification itself may then be retrieved using the getIdAsString() function.

The Function Interface

The Function interface defines the required Program API behaviors of function objects. Member functions provide access to various attributes commonly associated with functions and include the following:

```
public String getPrototypeString(boolean formalSignature,
                                 boolean includeCallingConvention)
```
Returns the Function object's prototype as a string. The two arguments influence the format of the returned prototype string.

```
public AddressSetView getBody()
```
Returns the address set that contains the function's body of code. An *address set* is composed of one or more address ranges, and allows for situations in which a function's code is distributed among several non-contiguous ranges of memory. Obtain an AddressIterator to visit all addresses in the set or an AddressRangeIterator to iterate over each range. Note that you must use a Listing object to retrieve the actual instructions contained in the function's body (see getInstructions).

```
public StackFrame getStackFrame()
```
Returns the stack frame associated with the function. The result may be used to retrieve detailed information about the layout of the function's local variables and stack-based arguments.

The Instruction Interface

The Instruction interface defines the required Program API behaviors of instruction objects. Member functions provide access to various attributes commonly associated with instructions and include the following:

```
public String getMnemonicString()
```
Returns the instruction's mnemonic.

```
public String getComment(int commentType)
```
Returns the commentType comment associated with the instruction or null if no comment of the given type is associated with the instruction. A commentType may be one of EOL_COMMENT, PRE_COMMENT, POST_COMMENT, or REPEATABLE_COMMENT.

```
public int getNumOperands()
```
Returns the number of operands associated with this instruction.

```
public int getOperandType(int opIndex)
```
Returns a bitmask of operand type flags defined in class OperandType.

```
public String toString()
```
Returns the string representation of the instruction.

Ghidra Scripting Examples

For the remainder of the chapter, we present some fairly common situations in which a script can be used to answer a question about a program. For brevity, only the body of each script's run function is shown.

Example 1: Enumerating Functions

Many scripts operate on individual functions. Examples include generating the call tree rooted at a specific function, generating the control flow graph of a function, and analyzing the stack frames of every function in a program. Listing 14-1 iterates through every function in a program and prints basic information about each function, including the start and end addresses of the function, the size of the function's arguments, and the size of the function's local variables. All output is sent to the console window.

```java
// ch14_1_flat.java
void run() throws Exception {
    int ptrSize = currentProgram.getDefaultPointerSize();
❶ Function func = getFirstFunction();
    while (func != null && !monitor.isCancelled()) {
        String name = func.getName();
        long addr = func.getBody().getMinAddress().getOffset();
        long end = func.getBody().getMaxAddress().getOffset();
❷      StackFrame frame = func.getStackFrame();
❸      int locals = frame.getLocalSize();
❹      int args = frame.getParameterSize();
        printf("Function: %s, starts at %x, ends at %x\n", name, addr, end);
        printf("  Local variable area is %d bytes\n", locals);
        printf("  Arguments use %d bytes (%d args)\n", args, args / ptrSize);
❺      func = getFunctionAfter(func);
    }
}
```

Listing 14-1: Function enumeration script

The script uses Ghidra's Flat API to iterate over all functions from the first ❶ and advancing through each in succession ❺. A reference to each function's stack frame is obtained ❷, and the size of the local variables ❸ and the stack-based arguments ❹ retrieved. A summary for each function is printed before continuing the iteration.

Example 2: Enumerating Instructions

Within a given function, you may want to enumerate every instruction. Listing 14-2 counts the number of instructions contained in the function identified by the current cursor position:

```
// ch14_2_flat.java
public void run() throws Exception {
   Listing plist = currentProgram.getListing();
❶ Function func = getFunctionContaining(currentAddress);
   if (func != null) {
❷    InstructionIterator iter = plist.getInstructions(func.getBody(), true);
      int count = 0;
      while (iter.hasNext() && !monitor.isCancelled()) {
         count++;
         Instruction ins = iter.next();
      }
❸    popup(String.format("%s contains %d instructions\n",
                         func.getName(), count));
   }
   else {
      popup(String.format("No function found at location %x",
                         currentAddress.getOffset()));
   }
}
```

Listing 14-2: Instruction enumeration script

The function begins by obtaining a reference to the function containing the cursor ❶. If a function is found, the next step is to use the program's Listing object to obtain an InstructionIterator over the function ❷. The iteration loop counts the number of instructions retrieved, and the total is reported to the user with a pop-up message dialog ❸.

Example 3: Enumerating Cross-References

Iterating through cross-references can be confusing because of the number of functions available for accessing cross-reference data and the fact that code cross-references are bidirectional. To get the data you want, you need to access the proper type of cross-reference for your situation.

In our first cross-reference example, shown in Listing 14-3, we retrieve the list of all function calls made within a function by iterating through each instruction in the function to determine if the instruction calls another function. One method of doing this might be to parse the results of the get-MnemonicString function to look for call instructions. This would not be a very portable or efficient solution because the instruction used to call a function varies among processor types, and additional parsing would be required to determine exactly which function was being called. Cross-references avoid each of these difficulties because they are processor-independent and directly inform us about the target of the cross-reference.

```java
// ch14_3_flat.java
void run() throws Exception {
   Listing plist = currentProgram.getListing();
❶ Function func = getFunctionContaining(currentAddress);
   if (func != null) {
      String fname = func.getName();
      InstructionIterator iter = plist.getInstructions(func.getBody(), true);
    ❷ while (iter.hasNext() && !monitor.isCancelled()) {
         Instruction ins = iter.next();
         Address addr = ins.getMinAddress();
         Reference refs[] = ins.getReferencesFrom();
       ❸ for (int i = 0; i < refs.length; i++) {
          ❹ if (refs[i].getReferenceType().isCall()) {
               Address tgt = refs[i].getToAddress();
               Symbol sym = getSymbolAt(tgt);
               String sname = sym.getName();
               long offset = addr.getOffset();
               printf("%s calls %s at 0x%x\n", fname, sname, offset);
            }
         }
      }
   }
}
```

Listing 14-3: Enumerating function calls

DANGEROUS FUNCTIONS

The C functions strcpy and sprintf are considered dangerous to use because they allow unbounded copying into destination buffers. While each may be safely used by programmers who check the size of source and destination buffers, such checks are all too often forgotten by programmers unaware of the dangers of these functions. The strcpy function, for example, is declared as follows:

```c
char *strcpy(char *dest, const char *source);
```

The strcpy function copies all characters up to and including the first null termination character encountered in the source buffer to the given destination buffer (dest). The fundamental problem is that there is no way to determine, at runtime, the size of any array, and strcpy can't determine whether the capacity of the destination buffer is sufficient to hold all of the data to be copied from source. Such unchecked copy operations are a major cause of buffer overflow vulnerabilities.

We begin by obtaining a reference to the function containing the cursor ❶. Next, we iterate through each instruction in the function ❷, and for each instruction, we iterate through each cross-reference from the instruction ❸. We are interested only in cross-references that call other functions, so we must test the return value of getReferenceType ❹ to determine whether isCall is true.

Example 4: Finding Function Calls

Cross-references are also useful for identifying every instruction that references a particular location. In Listing 14-4, we iterate across all of the cross-references *to* a particular symbol (as opposed to *from* in the previous example).

```java
// ch14_4_flat.java
❶ public void list_calls(Function tgtfunc) {
    String fname = tgtfunc.getName();
    Address addr = tgtfunc.getEntryPoint();
    Reference refs[] = getReferencesTo(addr);
❷   for (int i = 0; i < refs.length; i++) {
❸     if (refs[i].getReferenceType().isCall()) {
        Address src = refs[i].getFromAddress();
❹       Function func = getFunctionContaining(src);
        if (func.isThunk()) {
            continue;
        }
        String caller = func.getName();
        long offset = src.getOffset();
❺       printf("%s is called from 0x%x in %s\n", fname, offset, caller);
      }
    }
}
❻ public void getFunctions(String name, List<Function> list) {
    SymbolTable symtab = currentProgram.getSymbolTable();
    SymbolIterator si = symtab.getSymbolIterator();
    while (si.hasNext()) {
      Symbol s = si.next();
      if (s.getSymbolType() != SymbolType.FUNCTION || s.isExternal()) {
        continue;
      }
      if (s.getName().equals(name)) {
        list.add(getFunctionAt(s.getAddress()));
      }
    }
}
public void run() throws Exception {
    List<Function> funcs = new ArrayList<Function>();
    getFunctions("strcpy", funcs);
    getFunctions("sprintf", funcs);
    funcs.forEach((f) -> list_calls(f));
}
```

Listing 14-4: Enumerating a function's callers

In this example, we have written the helper function getFunctions ❻ to collect Function objects associated with our functions of interest. For each function of interest, we call a second helper function, list_calls ❶, to process all cross-references ❷ to the function. If the cross-reference type is determined to be a call-type cross-reference ❸, the calling function is retrieved ❹ and its name is displayed to the user ❺. Among other things, this approach could be used to create a low-budget security analyzer by highlighting all calls to functions such as strcpy and sprintf.

Example 5: Emulating Assembly Language Behavior

There are a number of reasons you might need to write a script that emulates the behavior of a program you are analyzing. For example, the program you are studying may be self-modifying, as many malware programs are, or the program may contain some encoded data that gets decoded when needed at runtime. Without running the program and pulling the modified data out of the running process's memory, how can you understand the behavior of the program?

If the decoding process is not terribly complex, you may be able to quickly write a script that performs the same actions that are performed by the program when it runs. Using a script to decode data in this way eliminates the need to run the program when you don't know what the program does or you don't have access to a platform on which you can run the program. For example, without a MIPS execution environment, you cannot execute a MIPS binary and observe any data decoding it might perform. You could, however, write a Ghidra script to mimic the behavior of the binary and make the required changes within your Ghidra project, all with no need for a MIPS execution environment.

The following x86 code was extracted from a DEFCON Capture the Flag binary:[1]

```
08049ede  MOV    dword ptr [EBP + local_8],0x0
          LAB_08049ee5
08049ee5  CMP    dword ptr [EBP + local_8],0x3c1
08049eec  JA     LAB_08049f0d
08049eee  MOV    EDX,dword ptr [EBP + local_8]
08049ef1  ADD    EDX,DAT_0804b880
08049ef7  MOV    EAX,dword ptr [EBP + local_8]
08049efa  ADD    EAX,DAT_0804b880
08049eff  MOV    AL,byte ptr [EAX]=>DAT_0804b880
08049f01  XOR    EAX,0x4b
08049f04  MOV    byte ptr [EDX],AL=>DAT_0804b880
08049f06  LEA    EAX=>local_8,[EBP + -0x4]
08049f09  INC    dword ptr [EAX]=>local_8
08049f0b  JMP    LAB_08049ee5
```

1. Courtesy of Kenshoto, the organizers of CTF at DEFCON 15. DEFCON Capture the Flag is an annual hacking competition held at DEFCON (*http://www.defcon.org/*).

This code decodes a private key that has been embedded within the program binary. Using the script in Listing 14-5, we can extract the private key without running the program.

```
// ch14_5_flat.java
public void run() throws Exception {
   int local_8 = 0;
   while (local_8 <= 0x3C1) {
      long edx = local_8;
      edx = edx + 0x804B880;
      long eax = local_8;
      eax = eax + 0x804B880;
      int al = getByte(toAddr(eax));
      al = al ^ 0x4B;
      setByte(toAddr(edx), (byte)al);
      local_8++;
   }
}
```

Listing 14-5: Emulating assembly language with a Ghidra script

Listing 14-5 is a fairly literal translation of the preceding assembly language sequence generated according to the following mechanical rules:

- For each stack variable and register used in the assembly code, declare an appropriately typed script variable.

- For each assembly language statement, write a statement that mimics its behavior.

- Emulate reading and writing stack variables by reading and writing the corresponding variable declared in your script.

- Emulate reading from a nonstack location using the getByte, getWord, getDword, or getQword function, depending on the amount of data being read (1, 2, 4, or 8 bytes).

- Emulate writing to a nonstack location using the setByte, setWord, setDword, or setQword function, depending on the amount of data being written.

- If the code contains a loop for which the termination condition is not immediately obvious, begin with an infinite loop such as while(true){...} and then insert a break statement when you encounter statements that cause the loop to terminate.

- When the assembly code calls functions, things get complicated. To properly simulate the behavior of the assembly code, you must mimic the behavior of the function that has been called, including providing a return value that makes sense within the context of the code being simulated.

As the complexity of the assembly code increases, it becomes more challenging to write a script that emulates all aspects of an assembly language sequence, but you don't have to fully understand how the code you are emulating works. Translate one or two instructions at a time. If each instruction has been correctly translated, the script as a whole should properly mimic the complete functionality of the original assembly code. After the script has been completed, you can use the script to better understand the underlying assembly. You will see this approach, and more generic emulation functionality, used again in Chapter 21 when we discuss the analysis of obfuscated binaries.

For example, once we translate the sample algorithm and spend some time considering how it works, we can shorten the emulation script as follows:

```
public void run() throws Exception {
    for (int local_8 = 0; local_8 <= 0x3C1; local_8++) {
        Address addr = toAddr(0x804B880 + local_8);
        setByte(addr, (byte)(getByte(addr) ^ 0x4B));
    }
}
```

Once the script executes, you can see the decoded private key starting at address 0x804B880. If you don't want to modify the Ghidra database when emulating code, replace the setByte function call with a call to printf, which will output the results to the CodeBrowser console, or write the data to a disk file for binary data. Don't forget that in addition to Ghidra's Java API, you have access to all of the standard Java API classes as well as any other Java packages that you've chosen to install on your system.

Summary

Scripting provides a powerful means for automating repetitive tasks and extending Ghidra's capabilities. This chapter has introduced Ghidra's functionality for editing and building new scripts using both Java and Python. The integrated ability to build, compile, and run Java-based scripts within the CodeBrowser environment lets you extend Ghidra's capabilities without requiring an in-depth understanding of the underlying intricacies of the Ghidra development environment. Chapters 15 and 16 introduce Eclipse integration and the ability to run Ghidra in headless mode.

15

ECLIPSE AND GHIDRADEV

The scripts that are distributed with Ghidra and the scripts we created in Chapter 14 are relatively simple. The coding required was minimal, which greatly simplified the development and testing phases. The basic script editor provided by Ghidra's Script Manager is fine for quick-and-dirty work, but it lacks the sophistication to manage complex projects. For more substantial tasks, Ghidra provides a plugin that facilitates development using the Eclipse development environment. In this chapter, we look at Eclipse and the role it can play in the development of more advanced Ghidra scripts. We also show how Eclipse can be used to create new Ghidra modules and revisit this topic in later chapters as we expand Ghidra's inventory of loaders and discuss the inner workings of Ghidra processor modules.

Eclipse

Eclipse is an integrated development environment (IDE) that is used by many Java developers, which makes it a natural fit for Ghidra development. While it is possible to run both Eclipse and Ghidra on the same machine without any interaction between them, the integration of the two can greatly simplify Ghidra development. Without integration, Eclipse would just be another script editing option outside the Ghidra environment. By integrating Eclipse with Ghidra, you suddenly have a rich IDE that includes Ghidra-specific functionality, resources, and templates to facilitate your Ghidra development process. Integrating Eclipse and Ghidra does not require significant effort; you just need to provide each with some information about the other so that they can be used together.

Eclipse Integration

In order for Ghidra to work with Eclipse, Eclipse needs to have the GhidraDev plugin installed. You can integrate the two applications from within either Ghidra or Eclipse. Instructions for both integration approaches are included in the *GhidraDev_README.html* document found in the *Extensions/Eclipse/GhidraDev* directory of your Ghidra installation.

While the written documentation does walk you through the details of the process, the easiest starting point is to select a Ghidra action that requires Eclipse, such as Edit Script with Eclipse (refer to Figure 14-2). If you select this option and have not previously integrated Eclipse and Ghidra, you will be prompted for the directory information required to make the connection. Depending on your configuration, you may need to provide the path to your Eclipse installation directory, your Eclipse workspace directory, your Ghidra installation directory, your Eclipse drop-in directory, and possibly the port number used to communicate with Eclipse for script editing.

Ghidra's documentation will help you overcome any obstacles that you encounter during the integration process. The truly adventurous can explore the integration plugins in the *Ghidra/Features/Base/src/main/java /ghidra/app/plugin/core/eclipse* directory in Ghidra's source repository.

Starting Eclipse

Once Ghidra and Eclipse are successfully integrated, you can use them for writing Ghidra scripts and plugins. The first time you launch Eclipse after it has been integrated with Ghidra, you are likely to see the dialog shown in Figure 15-1, requesting to establish a communication path between your Ghidra instance and your Eclipse GhidraDev instance.

Venturing onward, you will see the Eclipse IDE welcome screen, as shown in Figure 15-2. This instance of Eclipse has a new addition on the menu bar: GhidraDev. This is the menu we will use to create more complex scripts and Ghidra tools.

The landing page for Ghidra Eclipse, the Welcome to the Eclipse IDE for Java Developers workbench, includes links to numerous tutorials, documentation, and information about the Eclipse IDE and Java that should provide the necessary background support to users new to Eclipse as well as an optional refresher for experienced users. To move ahead with Ghidra, we will focus our discussion on how the GhidraDev menu can be used to augment Ghidra's existing capabilities, build new capabilities, and customize Ghidra to improve our reverse engineering workflow.

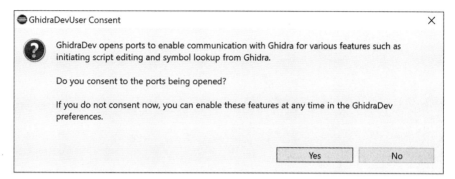

Figure 15-1: GhidraDevUser Consent dialog

Figure 15-2: Eclipse IDE welcome screen

Editing Scripts with Eclipse

Once the GhidraDev plugin has been installed in Eclipse, you are ready to create new scripts, or edit existing ones using the Eclipse IDE. As we migrate from using Ghidra's Script Manager to create and edit scripts, to using Eclipse, it's worth remembering that while it is possible to launch Eclipse from Script Manager, it is possible to do so only to edit an existing script (see Figure 14-2). If you want to edit a new script using Eclipse, you'll need to first launch Eclipse and then use the GhidraDev menu to create the new script. Whether you launch Eclipse yourself, or arrive in Eclipse via Ghidra's Script Manager, for the remainder of this chapter, we use Eclipse rather than the Script Manager's basic editor to create and modify scripts and modules for Ghidra.

To edit the first script we created in "Edit Script Example: Regex Search" on page 290, select **File ▸ Open File** from the Eclipse menu and navigate to the script *FindStringByRegex.java*. This opens the script in the

Eclipse IDE, and you can begin using Eclipse's rich set of editing options. Figure 15-3 shows the first few lines of the script with the comments and imports collapsed. Collapsing lines is a default feature of the Eclipse IDE that could cause some confusion if you are switching between the basic editor provided by Ghidra and Eclipse.

```
FindStringsByRegex.java ⊠
  2⊕  * IP: GHIDRA⬚
 25
26⊕ import ghidra.app.script.GhidraScript;⬚
 31
 32  public class FindStringsByRegex extends GhidraScript {
 33
 34⊖      @Override
 35      public void run() throws Exception {
 36          String regex =
 37              askString("Please enter the regex",
 38                  "Please enter the regex you're looking to match:");
```

Figure 15-3: Eclipse editor presentation of FindStringsByRegex

Only one line of comments is displayed by default. You can click an icon to expand (the + icon at the left of line 2) the content and display all of the comments as well as to collapse (the – icon at the left of line 34) the content if desired. The same is true on line 26 with the import statements. Hovering over the icon for any section that is collapsed displays the hidden content in a pop-up window.

Before we can start building examples that expand Ghidra's capabilities, you need to understand more about the GhidraDev menu and the Eclipse IDE. Let's shift our focus back to the GhidraDev menu and investigate the various options and how they can be used in context.

GhidraDev Menu

The expanded GhidraDev menu is shown in Figure 15-4 and includes five options that you can use to control your development environment and work with files. In this chapter, we focus on developing in Java, although Python is an option in several of the windows.

Figure 15-4: GhidraDev menu options

GhidraDev ▸ New

The GhidraDev ▸ New menu provides you with three submenu options, as shown in Figure 15-5. All three of the options launch wizards that guide you through an associated creation process. We start with the simplest option, which is to create a new Ghidra script. This is an alternative path to creating scripts from that discussed in Chapter 14.

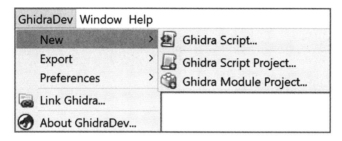

Figure 15-5: GhidraDev ▸ New submenu

Creating a Script

Creating a new script using GhidraDev ▸ New ▸ Ghidra Script results in a dialog that allows you to enter information about your new script. An example of the dialog populated with content is shown in Figure 15-6. In addition to the directory and file information, the dialog collects the same metadata that we manually entered into our script files in the Script Manager's basic editor.

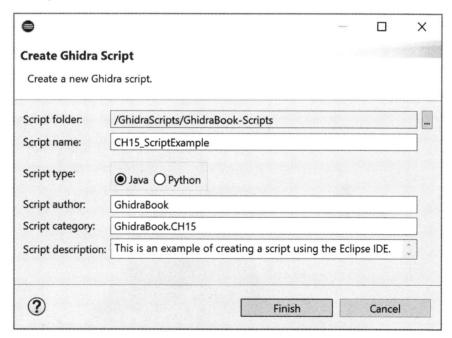

Figure 15-6: Create Ghidra Script dialog

The Finish button at the bottom of the dialog produces the script template shown in Figure 15-7. The metadata entered in Figure 15-6 is included in the comment section at the top of the script. This content is in the same format as the metadata we saw in Chapter 14 (see the top of Figure 14-4). When you edit this script in Eclipse, the task tag (clipboard icon, seen on the left side of line 14 in Figure 15-7) associated with each TODO item in the script identifies locations where there is work to be done. You can delete and insert task tags at will.

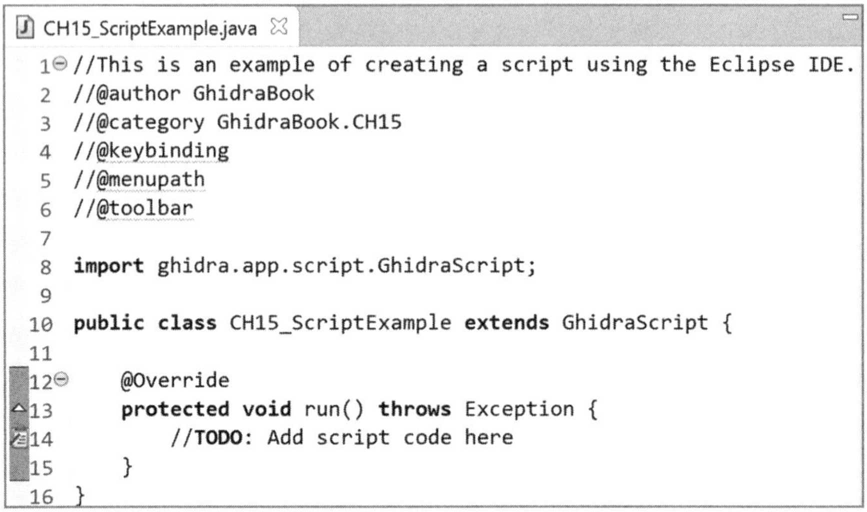

```
📄 CH15_ScriptExample.java  ☒

 1⊖ //This is an example of creating a script using the Eclipse IDE.
 2  //@author GhidraBook
 3  //@category GhidraBook.CH15
 4  //@keybinding
 5  //@menupath
 6  //@toolbar
 7
 8  import ghidra.app.script.GhidraScript;
 9
10  public class CH15_ScriptExample extends GhidraScript {
11
12⊖     @Override
13      protected void run() throws Exception {
14          //TODO: Add script code here
15      }
16  }
```

Figure 15-7: GhidraDev ▸ NewScript script shell

Eclipse does not preload your script with the list of import statements like the Ghidra basic editor does (refer to Figure 14-4). Not to worry. Eclipse helps you to manage your import statements by letting you know when you use something that requires an associated import statement. For example, if we replace the TODO comment in Figure 15-7 with the declaration of a Java ArrayList, Eclipse adds an error tag to the line and underlines ArrayList in red. Hovering over the error tag or ArrayList displays a pop-up window suggesting quick fixes to solve the issue, as shown in Figure 15-8.

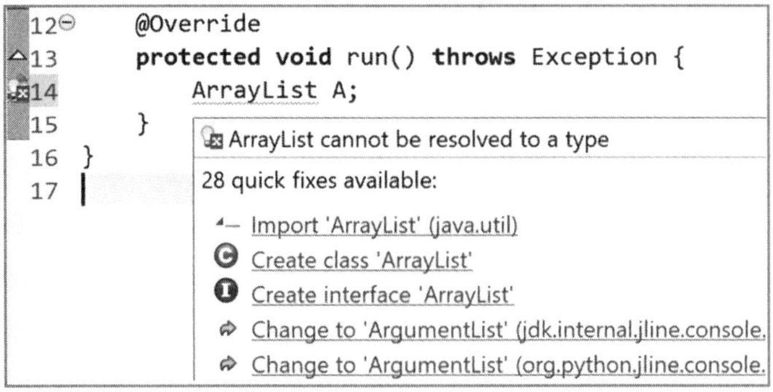

```
12⊖     @Override
13      protected void run() throws Exception {
14          ArrayList A;
15      }
16  }
17  |
```

     🔲 ArrayList cannot be resolved to a type

     28 quick fixes available:

       ◂─ Import 'ArrayList' (java.util)
       © Create class 'ArrayList'
       ❶ Create interface 'ArrayList'
       ⇗ Change to 'ArgumentList' (jdk.internal.jline.console.
       ⇗ Change to 'ArgumentList' (org.python.jline.console.

Figure 15-8: Eclipse Quick Fix options

Choosing the first option in the suggestion list instructs Eclipse to add the selected `import` statement to the script, as shown in Figure 15-9. While it was helpful to have the list of potential `import` statements loaded when creating a new script in the CodeBrowser Script Manager, it is not as essential in Eclipse.

```
 8⊖ import java.util.ArrayList;
 9
10  import ghidra.app.script.GhidraScript;
11
12  public class CH15_ScriptExample extends GhidraScript {
13
14⊖     @Override
15      protected void run() throws Exception {
16          ArrayList A;
17      }
```

Figure 15-9: Eclipse after Quick Fix import is applied

Creating a Script Project

The second option in the GhidraDev ▸ New menu creates a new script project, as shown in Figure 15-10. We name our first script project *CH15_ProjectExample_linked* and place it in the default directory that we have set up for Eclipse. The Create run configuration checkbox allows you to create a *run configuration*, which provides Eclipse with the necessary information (command line arguments, directory paths, and so on) to launch Ghidra and allows us to use Eclipse to run and debug the script in Ghidra. Leave this checkbox in its default state, selected. Click **Finish** to complete creation of the script using the default format, which links the script project to your home directory.

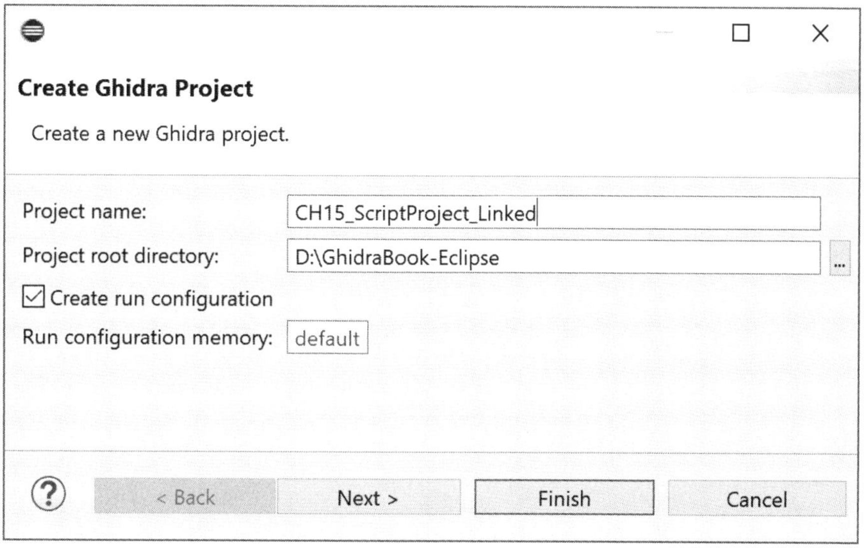

Create Ghidra Project

Create a new Ghidra project.

Project name:	CH15_ScriptProject_Linked
Project root directory:	D:\GhidraBook-Eclipse

☑ Create run configuration

Run configuration memory: default

?	< Back	Next >	Finish	Cancel

Figure 15-10: Eclipse Ghidra Script Project dialog

We will create a second script project *CH15_ProjectExample* and this time will choose the Next button. Choosing Next yields the dialog with two Link options that are set by default (hence the *_linked* extension on our first project name). The first option creates a link to your home script directory. The second lets you link to the Ghidra installation script directories. *Link*, in this case, is a way of saying that folders representing your home script directory and/or Ghidra's own script directories will be added to your new project, making any script in those directories easily accessible to you while working on your project.

The results of selecting or deselecting these options and then clicking the Finish button will become clear later in the chapter when we discuss the Eclipse Package Explorer. For this second script project, de-select the first link checkbox as shown in Figure 15-11.

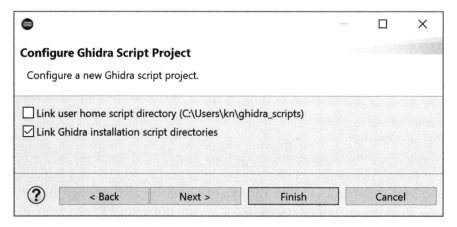

Figure 15-11: Eclipse configuration options for script projects

Creating a Module Project

The final option in the GhidraDev ▸ New menu creates a Ghidra module project.[1] Not to be confused with a Ghidra module (for example, analyzer, loader, and so on), a *Ghidra module project* aggregates code for a new Ghidra module with associated help files, documentation, and other resources, such as icons. Further, it allows you some control over how your new module interacts with the other modules within Ghidra. We demonstrate Ghidra modules in context in this and future chapters.

Choosing New ▸ Ghidra Module Project displays the dialog shown in Figure 15-12, which should be familiar because it is exactly the same as the Script Project dialog. We name our new project *CH15_ModuleExample* to make it easy to identify in the Package Explorer.

---

1. Both types of Ghidra modules are distinct from Java modules, which were introduced in Java 9 as a means to encapsulate packages and other resources and provide the capability to keep packages private or choose to share individual packages with select other modules, effectively allowing modules to control the sharing of services. Additional documentation about modules and other Java topics is available at *https://www.oracle.com/technetwork/java/javase/java-tutorial-downloads-2005894.html*.

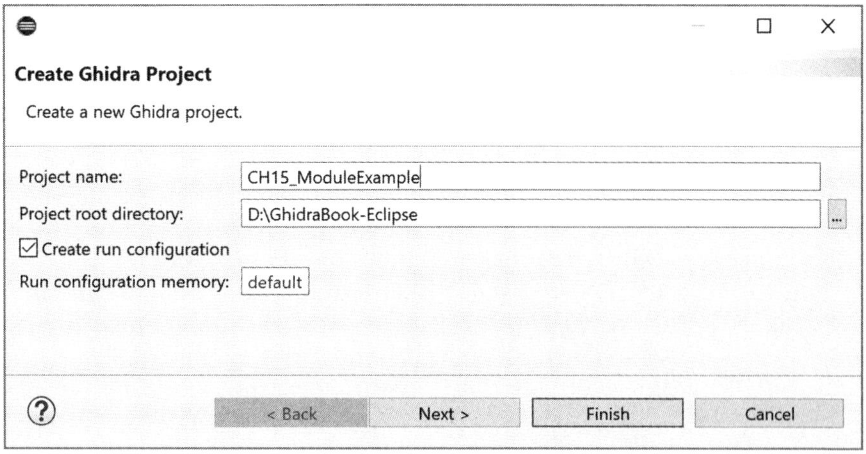

Figure 15-12: Eclipse Module Project dialog

Clicking Next at this point allows you to base your module on existing Ghidra templates, as shown in Figure 15-13. By default, all of the options are selected. You can change this to include none, some, or all of the templates, depending on your development goals. Any of the options you choose will be grouped together in a project within the Package Explorer. In our case, we have deselected all of the options.

While most of the selections will produce an associated source code template with task tags, there are two exceptions. First, if you do not select any of the module templates, you will not have a template file. In addition, the processor module does not produce a template file but does generate other supporting content. (Processor modules are discussed in Chapter 18.)

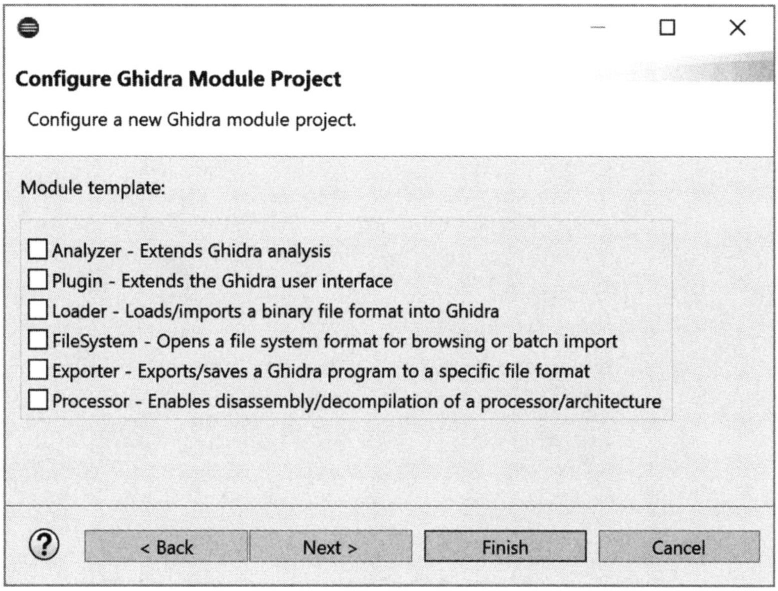

Figure 15-13: Template options for Ghidra module projects

Now that you know how to create Ghidra scripts, script projects, and module projects, let's shift our focus to the Eclipse Package Explorer to better understand how we can work with our new creations.[2]

Navigating the Package Explorer

Eclipse's Package Explorer is the gateway to the Ghidra files you need to complete your Ghidra extension. Here, we present the hierarchical organization and then drill down into examples of Ghidra projects and modules created through the GhidraDev menu. Figure 15-14 displays a sample Eclipse Package Explorer window containing the items we created earlier in this chapter as well as a few others we created to demonstrate the effect of various options on the resulting Package Explorer contents.

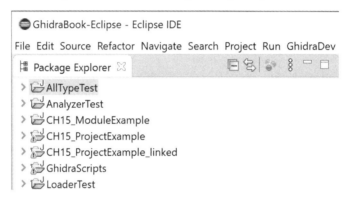

Figure 15-14: Package Explorer populated with example modules and project

We start by looking at the two script projects. *CH15_ProjectExample _linked* is the script project we created with both link options checked (refer to Figure 15-11). Immediately below it, we see a similar project, *CH15_ProjectExample*, but in this case, neither link option was checked. A partially expanded Package Explorer entry for *CH15_ProjectExample* is shown in Figure 15-15.

The following four components are included in this script project:

JUnit4 This is an open source unit-testing framework for Java. More information is available at *https://junit.org/junit4/index.html*.

JRE System Library This is the Java Runtime Environment System Library.

Referenced Libraries These are referenced libraries that are not part of the JRE System Library, but are part of our Ghidra installation.

Ghidra This is the directory for your current Ghidra installation. We have expanded this directory so that you can see the familiar file structure introduced in Chapter 3 (see Figure 3-1) and used throughout this book.

---

2. Package Explorer has been around for a while, whereas modules are a more recent addition to Java. In the default configuration, Package Explorer can be thought of as a project explorer for the Java project you have created or imported.

CH15_ProjectExample
JUnit 4
JRE System Library [jdk11.0.6_10]
Referenced Libraries
Ghidra
docs
Extensions
Ghidra
GPL
licenses
server
support
ghidraRun
ghidraRun.bat
LICENSE

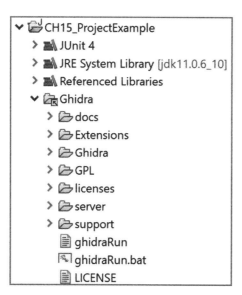

Figure 15-15: Package Explorer script project entries without *links*

Compare the contents of Figure 15-15 with the expanded contents from *CH15_ProjectExample_linked* shown in Figure 15-16. For this script project, we selected both link options. Linking the user home script directory results in the *Home scripts* entry in the project hierarchy and provides us easy access to the scripts we have previously written to use as examples or to modify.

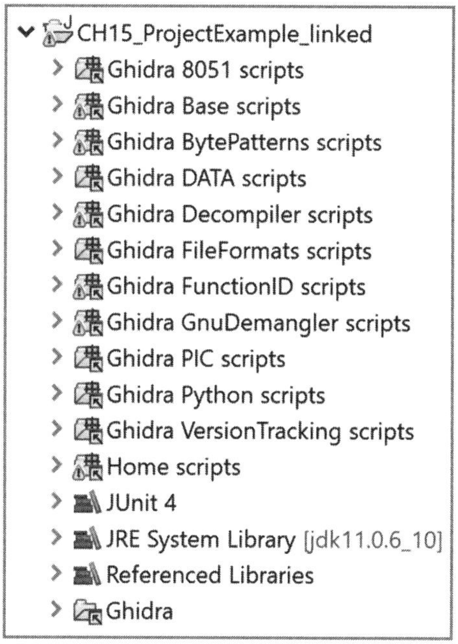

CH15_ProjectExample_linked
Ghidra 8051 scripts
Ghidra Base scripts
Ghidra BytePatterns scripts
Ghidra DATA scripts
Ghidra Decompiler scripts
Ghidra FileFormats scripts
Ghidra FunctionID scripts
Ghidra GnuDemangler scripts
Ghidra PIC scripts
Ghidra Python scripts
Ghidra VersionTracking scripts
Home scripts
JUnit 4
JRE System Library [jdk11.0.6_10]
Referenced Libraries
Ghidra

Figure 15-16: Package Explorer script project entries with *links*

Linking Ghidra installation script directories results in all of the folders in Figure 15-16 that start with *Ghidra* and end with *scripts*. Each one of these corresponds to a script directory within in the *Ghidra/Features* directory in your Ghidra installation.[3] Expanding any of these folders provides access to the source code for each of the scripts included in your Ghidra installation. Like the home scripts, these can serve as examples to modify or use as a base for creating new scripts. While you are not permitted to overwrite these scripts from within the Ghidra Script Manager basic editor, you can edit them in Eclipse and other editors outside of the Ghidra Project environment. When you have finished creating or editing a new script, you can save it in the appropriate script directory within your script project, and it will be available to use the next time you open the Ghidra Script Manager.

Now that we have looked at scripts within the Eclipse Package Explorer, let's see how the Ghidra module project we built is represented. The partially expanded content of our project in the Package Explorer is shown in Figure 15-17.

Figure 15-17: Package Explorer hierarchy for
CH15_ModuleExampleModule

---

3. The location of a script within Eclipse Package Explorer (and *Ghidra/Features* directory) does not necessarily coincide with the organization of the scripts within the Script Manager. This is to be expected as the scripts within the *Ghidra/Features* directory are organized into folders that share a common functionality. The organization of scripts within the Ghidra Script Manager is based on the category metadata within each script.

ARE WE BUILDING THAT SCRIPT AGAIN?

In Chapter 14, we presented a toy example within the Ghidra Script Manager environment where we modified the existing script *CountAndSaveStrings* and used it to build a new script called *FindStringsByRegex*. The following steps do the same task within the Eclipse IDE:

1. Search for *CountAndSaveStrings.java* in Eclipse (CTRL-SHIFT-R).
2. Double-click to open the file in the Eclipse editor.
3. Replace the existing class and comments with the new class and comments.
4. Save the file (*EclipseFindStringByRegex.java*) in the recommended *ghidra_scripts* directory.
5. Run the new script from the Script Manager window in Ghidra.

You can launch Ghidra manually to get access to the Script Manager window. Alternatively, you can select the Run As option in the Eclipse IDE, which will show the dialog in Figure 15-18. The first option launches Ghidra for you. The second option launches a non-GUI version of Ghidra, which is the topic of Chapter 16.

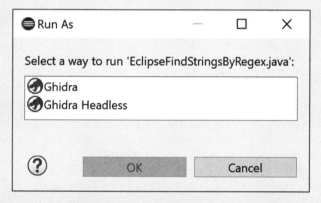

Figure 15-18: Eclipse Run As options

Once Ghidra has been launched, you can run your script from the Script Manager and edit it using Eclipse.

Module projects include the following new elements:

src/main/java   This is the location for the source code. If you created a module type that has a template available, the associated *.java* files are placed in this directory.

src/main/help   When you create or extend content, you have the opportunity to add useful information to Ghidra Help by using the files and information in this directory.

src/main/resources   As with many of the other entries in the *src/main* directory, expanding this content will lead you to a *README.txt* file that provides additional information about the purpose of the directory and how it should be used. For example, the *src/main/resources /images/ README.txt* file lets you know that it is the location in which any image or icon files associated with the module should be stored.

ghidra_scripts   This is where Ghidra scripts that are specific to this module are stored.

data   This folder holds any independent data files that are used with this module. (While not prohibited from use with other module types, this folder is primarily used with processor modules and is discussed in Chapter 18.)

lib   Any *.jar* files required by the module should be stored in this folder.

os   There are subdirectories within this folder for linux64, oxs64, and win64 to hold any native binaries that the module may depend upon.

src   This directory is used to hold unit test cases.

build.gradle   Gradle is an open source build system. This file is used to build your Ghidra extension.

extension.properties   This file stores metadata about the extension.

Module.manifest   You can enter information about the module such as configuration information in this file.

You may have noticed in Figure 15-14 that we created additional *Test* modules (*AnalyzerTest*, *AllTypeTest*, and *LoaderTest*). Each was created using a different combination of Module Template options (see Figure 15-13), which results in a different set of files being instantiated for each project. When using these templates as a starting point for your projects, it's useful to know just how much work Eclipse and Ghidra have done for you—and how much work is left for you to complete.

Let's begin by looking in the *AnalyzerTest* directory that we created to demonstrate an analyzer template. Expand the *src/main/java* directory to find a file called *AnalyzerTestAnalyzer.java*. The name is a concatenation of the module name (*AnalyzerTest*) with the template type (*Analyzer*). Double-click this file to open it in the editor and see the code shown in Figure 15-19. Like the script templates earlier in the chapter, the Eclipse IDE provides task tags with associated comments to guide us through building our analyzer as well as the options to expand and collapse content. The *LoaderTest* module contains the template for building a loader, which is discussed further in Chapter 17. The remaining module, *AllTypeTest*, is the default module that results when you bypass the module template options. This populates the *src/main/java* directory with all of the templates, as shown in Figure 15-20.

Now that we have seen how helpful Ghidra and Eclipse can be when we create new modules, let's use this information to build a new analyzer.

```
 2⊕ * IP: GHIDRA⬚
16 package analyzertest;
17
18⊕import ghidra.app.services.AbstractAnalyzer;⬚
26
27⊖/**
28   * TODO: Provide class-level documentation that describes what this analyzer does.
29   */
30 public class AnalyzerTestAnalyzer extends AbstractAnalyzer {
31
32⊕     public AnalyzerTestAnalyzer() {⬚
38
40⊕     public boolean getDefaultEnablement(Program program) {⬚
46
48⊕     public boolean canAnalyze(Program program) {⬚
55
57⊕     public void registerOptions(Options options, Program program) {⬚
64
66⊕     public boolean added(Program program, AddressSetView set, TaskMonitor monitor, MessageLog log)⬚
74 }
```

Figure 15-19: Default analyzer template for a module (comments, imports, and functions collapsed)

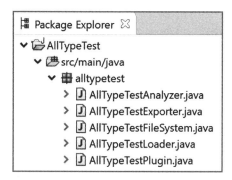

Figure 15-20: Sample default module source code content

Example: Ghidra Analyzer Module Project

With the Eclipse integration basics behind us, let's walk through building a simple Ghidra analyzer to identify potential ROP gadgets in our listing. We will use a simplified software development process, as this is just a simple demonstration project. Our process includes the following steps:

1. Define the problem.
2. Create the Eclipse module.
3. Build the analyzer.
4. Add the analyzer to our Ghidra installation.
5. Test the analyzer from our Ghidra installation.

WHAT'S A ROP GADGET AND WHY DO WE CARE?

For those unfamiliar with exploit development, ROP stands for *return-oriented programming*. One software security mitigation that aims to defeat raw shellcode injection is to ensure that no memory region that is writable is, at the same time, also executable. Such mitigations are often referred to as *NoneXecutable (NX)* or *Data Execution Prevention (DEP))* because it becomes impossible to inject shellcode into memory (must be writable) and then transfer control to that shellcode (must be executable).

ROP techniques aim to hijack a program's stack (often through a stack-based buffer overflow) to place a carefully crafted sequence of return addresses and data into the stack. At some point after the overflow, the program begins using the attacker-supplied return addresses rather than return addresses placed on the stack by normal program execution. The return addresses the attacker places on the stack point to program memory locations that already contain code as a result of normal program and library loading operations. Because the original author of the exploited program did not design the program to do the attacker's work for them, the attacker often needs to pick and choose small portions of this existing code to sequence together.

A *ROP gadget* is a single one of these code fragments, and the sequencing mechanism often relies on the gadget terminating in a return (hence return-oriented) instruction, which retrieves an address from the now attacker-controlled stack to transfer control to the next gadget. A gadget often performs a very simple task such as loading a register from the stack. The following simple gadget could be used to initialize RAX on an x86-64 system:

```
POP RAX  ; pop the next item on the attacker-controlled stack into RAX
RET      ; transfer control to the address contained in the next stack item
```

Because every exploitable program is different, attackers can't depend on a specific set of gadgets being present in any given binary. Automated gadget finders are tools that search a binary for instruction sequences that may be used as gadgets and present these gadgets to the attacker, who must decide which ones are useful in crafting their attack. The most sophisticated gadget finders infer the semantics of a gadget and automatically sequence gadgets to perform a specified action, saving the attacker the trouble of doing it themselves.

Step 1: Define the Problem

Our task is to design and develop an instruction analyzer that will identify simple ROP gadgets within a binary. The analyzer needs to be added to Ghidra and be available as a selectable analyzer in the Ghidra Analyzer menu.

Step 2: Create the Eclipse Module

We use GhidraDev ▸ New ▸ Ghidra Module Project to create a module called *SimpleROP* using the analyzer module template. This creates a file called *SimpleROPAnalyzer.java* in the *src/main/java* folder within the *SimpleROP* module. The resulting Package Explorer view is shown in Figure 15-21.

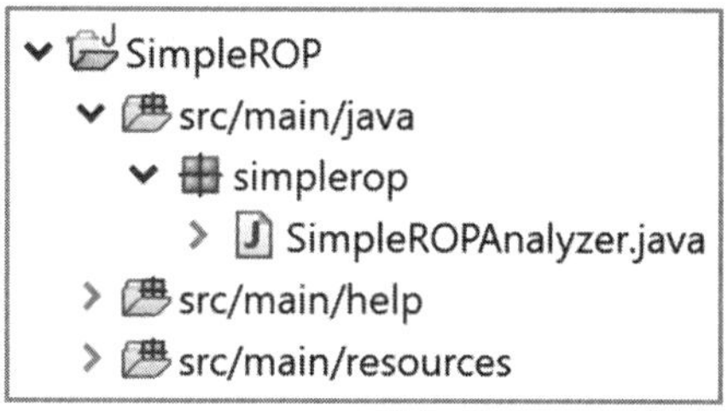

```
✓ 📂 SimpleROP
    ✓ 📁 src/main/java
        ✓ 🏢 simplerop
            > 🗾 SimpleROPAnalyzer.java
    > 📁 src/main/help
    > 📁 src/main/resources
```

Figure 15-21: Package Explorer src/main entries for SimpleROP

Step 3: Build the Analyzer

A portion of the generated *SimpleROPAnalyzer.java* code is shown in Figure 15-22. The functions have been collapsed so that we can see all of the analyzer methods that are provided. Eclipse will recommend imports if we need them as we develop our code so we can jump right into coding the tasks we need to perform and add the recommended `import` statements when Eclipse detects that we need them.

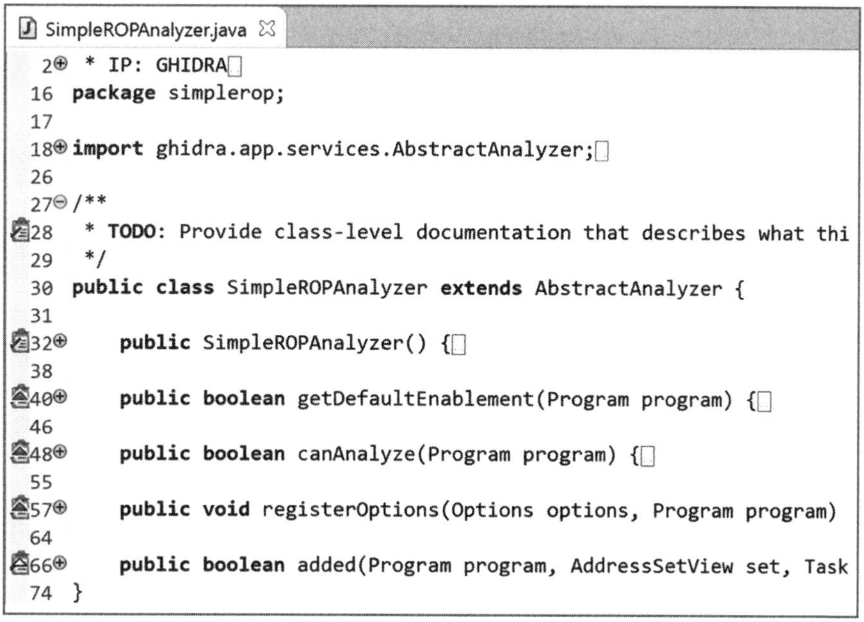

```
🗾 SimpleROPAnalyzer.java  ⨯
 2⊕  * IP: GHIDRA□
16  package simplerop;
17
18⊕ import ghidra.app.services.AbstractAnalyzer;□
26
27⊖ /**
28    * TODO: Provide class-level documentation that describes what thi
29    */
30  public class SimpleROPAnalyzer extends AbstractAnalyzer {
31
32⊕     public SimpleROPAnalyzer() {□
38
40⊕     public boolean getDefaultEnablement(Program program) {□
46
48⊕     public boolean canAnalyze(Program program) {□
55
57⊕     public void registerOptions(Options options, Program program)
64
66⊕     public boolean added(Program program, AddressSetView set, Task
74  }
```

Figure 15-22: SimpleROPAnalyzer template

The six task tags (to the left of the line numbers) in Figure 15-22 indicate where we should start our development. We will expand the associated sections as we address each task and include the before and after content associated with each task. (Note that some content will be wrapped or reformatted for readability and comments minimized to conserve space.)

For functionality, we will rely on the following class-level declarations:

```
    private int gadgetCount = 0;        // Counts the number of gadgets
    private BufferedWriter outFile;     // Output file
// List of "interesting" instructions
    private List<String> usefulInstructions = Arrays.asList(
        "NOP", "POP", "PUSH", "MOV", "ADD", "SUB", "MUL", "DIV", "XOR");
// List of "interesting" instructions that don't have operands
    private List<String> require0Operands = Arrays.asList("NOP");
// List of "interesting" instructions that have one operand
    private List<String> require1RegOperand = Arrays.asList("POP", "PUSH");
// List of "interesting" instructions for which we want the first
// parameter to be a register
    private List<String> requireFirstRegOperand = Arrays.asList(
        "MOV", "ADD", "SUB", "MUL", "DIV", "XOR");
// List of "start" instructions that have ZERO operands
    private List<String> startInstr0Params = Arrays.asList("RET");
// List of "start" instructions that have ONE register operand
    private List<String> startInstr1RegParam = Arrays.asList("JMP", "CALL");
```

Comments associated with each declaration describe the purpose of each variable. The various List variables contain the instructions from which our gadgets will be composed and classify those instructions based on the number and type of operands they require, and whether the instruction is a legal start instruction for one of our gadgets. Because our gadget construction algorithm works its way backward in memory, *start* here actually means a starting point for our algorithm. At runtime, these same start instructions would actually be the last instructions executed in a given gadget.

Step 3-1: Document the Class

When we expand the first task tag, we see the following task description:

```
/**
 * TODO: Provide class-level documentation that describes what this
 * analyzer does.
 */
```

Replace the existing TODO comments with comments that describe what the analyzer does:

```
/**
 * This analyzer searches through a binary for ROP gadgets.
 * The address and contents of each gadget are written to a
 * file called inputfilename_gadgets.txt in the user's home directory.
 */
```

Step 3-2: Name and Describe Our Analyzer

Expanding the next task tag provides us with a TODO comment and the line of code that we need to edit. Within the Eclipse IDE, the code to be modified appears in purple font and has a name indicative of the associated task. The second task contains the following:

```
// TODO: Name the analyzer and give it a description.
public SimpleROPAnalyzer() {
    super("My Analyzer",
        "Analyzer description goes here",
        AnalyzerType.BYTE_ANALYZER);
}
```

The two strings need to be replaced with meaningful content. In addition, the analyzer type needs to be specified. To facilitate dependency resolution across analyzers, Ghidra groups analyzers into the following categories: byte, data, function, function modifiers, function signatures, and instruction. In this case, we are building an instruction analyzer. The resulting code is as follows:

```
public SimpleROPAnalyzer() {
    super("SimpleROP",
        "Search a binary for ROP gadgets",
        AnalyzerType.INSTRUCTION_ANALYZER);
}
```

Step 3-3: Determine If Our Analyzer Should Be a Default Analyzer

The third task asks us to return true if the analyzer should be enabled by default:

```
public boolean getDefaultEnablement(Program program) {
    // TODO: Return true if analyzer should be enabled by default
    return false;
}
```

We do not want this analyzer enabled by default; therefore, no code modifications are required.

Step 3-4: Determine If the Input Is Appropriate for This Analyzer

The fourth task requires us to determine whether our analyzer is compatible with the program content:

```
public boolean canAnalyze(Program program) {
    // TODO: Examine 'program' to determine of this analyzer
    // should analyze it.
    // Return true if it can.
    return false;
}
```

Since this analyzer is only for demonstration purposes, we assume that the input file is compatible with our analysis and simply return true. In reality, we would add code to verify compatibility of the analysis file prior to using our analyzer. For example, we might return true only after we have determined that file is an x86 binary. Worked examples of this verification can be found in most analyzers included in your Ghidra installation (*Ghidra/Features/Base/lib/Base-src/Ghidra/app/analyzers*), accessible through your module directory within Eclipse:

```
public boolean canAnalyze(Program program) {
    return true;
}
```

Step 3-5: Register Analyzer Options

The fifth task offers us the opportunity to specify any special options we wish to present to users of our analyzer:

```
public void registerOptions(Options options, Program program) {
    // TODO: If this analyzer has custom options, register them here
    options.registerOption("Option name goes here", false, null,
                            "Option description goes here");
}
```

Since this analyzer is only for demonstration purposes, we will not add any options. Options might include user-controlled choices (for example, choose output file, optionally annotate the listing, and so on). Options for each analyzer are displayed in the Analyzer window when an individual analyzer is selected:

```
public void registerOptions(Options options, Program program) {
}
```

Step 3-6: Perform the Analysis

The sixth task highlights the function that gets called when our analyzer gets invoked:

```
public boolean added(Program program, AddressSetView set, TaskMonitor
                    monitor, MessageLog log) throws CancelledException {
    // TODO: Perform analysis when things get added to the 'program'.
    // Return true if the analysis succeeded.
    return false;
}
```

This is the part of the module that does the work. Four methods are used by this module, each of which is detailed next:

```
//***********************************************************************
//  This method is called when the analyzer is invoked.
//***********************************************************************
❶ public boolean added(Program program, AddressSetView set, TaskMonitor
                       monitor, MessageLog log) throws CancelledException {
     gadgetCount = 0;
     String outFileName = System.getProperty("user.home") + "/" +
                          program.getName() + "_gadgets.txt";
     monitor.setMessage("Searching for ROP Gadgets");
     try {
        outFile = new BufferedWriter(new FileWriter(outFileName));
     } catch (IOException e) {/* pass */}
     // iterate through each instruction in the binary
     Listing code = program.getListing();
     InstructionIterator instructions = code.getInstructions(set, true);
❷    while (instructions.hasNext() && !monitor.isCancelled()) {
        Instruction inst = instructions.next();
❸       if (isStartInstruction(inst)) {
           // We found a "start" instruction.  This will be the last
           // instruction in the potential ROP gadget so we will try to
           // build the gadget from here
           ArrayList<Instruction> gadgetInstructions =
              new ArrayList<Instruction>();
           gadgetInstructions.add(inst);
           Instruction prevInstr = inst.getPrevious();
❹          buildGadget(program, monitor, prevInstr, gadgetInstructions);
        }
     }
     try {
        outFile.close();
     } catch (IOException e) {/* pass */}
     return true;
  }
//***********************************************************************
//  This method is called recursively until it finds an instruction that
//  we don't want in the ROP gadget.
//***********************************************************************
  private void buildGadget(Program program, TaskMonitor monitor,
                           Instruction inst,
                           ArrayList<Instruction> gadgetInstructions) {
     if (inst == null || !isUsefulInstruction(inst)❺ ||
        monitor.isCancelled()) {
        return;
     }
     gadgetInstructions.add(inst);
❻    buildGadget(program, monitor, inst.getPrevious()❼, gadgetInstructions);
     gadgetCount += 1;
```

```
❽ for (int ii = gadgetInstructions.size() - 1; ii >= 0; ii--) {
      try {
          Instruction insn = gadgetInstructions.get(ii);
          if (ii == gadgetInstructions.size() - 1) {
              outFile.write(insn.getMinAddress() + ";");
          }
          outFile.write(insn.toString() + ";");
      } catch (IOException e) {/* pass */}
  }
  try {
      outFile.write("\n");
  } catch (IOException e) {/* pass */}
  // Report count to monitor every 100th gadget
  if (gadgetCount % 100 == 0) {
      monitor.setMessage("Found " + gadgetCount + " ROP Gadgets");
  }
  gadgetInstructions.remove(gadgetInstructions.size() - 1);
}
//*****************************************************************************
//  This method determines if an instruction is useful in the context of
//  a ROP gadget
//*****************************************************************************
private boolean isUsefulInstruction(Instruction inst) {
    if (!usefulInstructions.contains(inst.getMnemonicString())) {
        return false;
    }
    if (require0Operands.contains(inst.getMnemonicString())) {
        return true;
    }
    if (require1RegOperand.contains(inst.getMnemonicString()) &&
        inst.getNumOperands() == 1) {
        Object[] opObjects0 = inst.getOpObjects(0);
        for (int ii = 0; ii < opObjects0.length; ii++) {
            if (opObjects0[ii] instanceof Register) {
                return true;
            }
        }
    }
    if (requireFirstRegOperand.contains(inst.getMnemonicString()) &&
        inst.getNumOperands() >= 1) {
        Object[] opObjects0 = inst.getOpObjects(0);
        for (int ii = 0; ii < opObjects0.length; ii++) {
            if (opObjects0[ii] instanceof Register) {
                return true;
            }
        }
    }
    return false;
}
//*****************************************************************************
//  This method determines if an instruction is the "start" of a
//   potential ROP gadget
//*****************************************************************************
```

```
private boolean isStartInstruction(Instruction inst) {
    if (startInstr0Params.contains(inst.getMnemonicString())) {
        return true;
    }
    if (startInstr1RegParam.contains(inst.getMnemonicString()) &&
        inst.getNumOperands() >= 1) {
        Object[] opObjects0 = inst.getOpObjects(0);
        for (int ii = 0; ii < opObjects0.length; ii++) {
            if (opObjects0[ii] instanceof Register) {
                return true;
            }
        }
    }
    return false;
}
```

Ghidra invokes an analyzer's added method ❶ to initiate analysis. Our algorithm tests every instruction ❷ in the binary to determine whether the instruction is a valid "start" point ❸ for our gadget builder. Each time a valid start instruction is found, our gadget creation function, buildGadget, is invoked ❹. Gadget creation is a recursive ❻ walk backward ❼ through the instruction list that continues as long as an instruction is considered useful ❺ to us. Finally, each gadget is printed, by iterating over its instructions ❽, as it is completed.

Step 4: Test the Analyzer Within Eclipse

During the development process, it is common to test and modify code frequently. As you are building your analyzer, you can test its functionality within Eclipse by using the Run As option and choosing Ghidra. This opens Ghidra with the current version of the module temporarily installed. If the results are not what you expect when you test the module, you can edit the file within Eclipse and retest. When you are satisfied with your result, you should move on to step 5. Using this method to test your code within Eclipse can be a great time-saver during the development process.

Step 5: Add the Analyzer to Our Ghidra Installation

To add this analyzer to our Ghidra installation, we need to export our module from Eclipse and then install the extension in Ghidra. Exporting is accomplished by selecting **GhidraDev ▸ Export ▸ Ghidra Module Extension**, choosing your module, and clicking **Next**. In the next window, select the **Gradle Wrapper** option shown in Figure 15-23 if you do not have a local Gradle installation (note that an internet connection is required in order for the wrapper to reach out to *gradle.org*). Click **Finish** to complete the export process. If this is your first time exporting the module, a *dist* directory will be added to your module within Eclipse and a *.zip* file of the exported content will be saved to the folder.

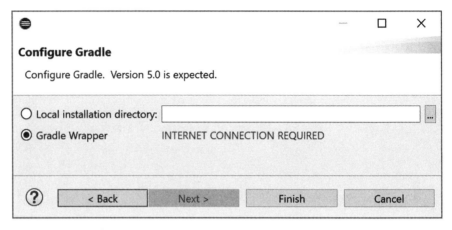

Figure 15-23: Configure Gradle dialog

In the Ghidra Project window, add the new analyzer by selecting **File ▸ Install Extensions**. A window similar to that shown in Figure 15-24 will be displayed showing all of the existing extensions that have not been installed.

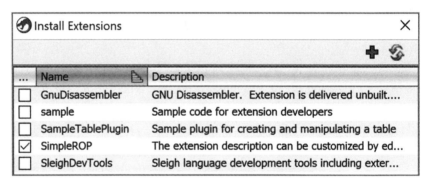

Figure 15-24: Install Extensions window

Add the new analyzer *SimpleROP* by selecting the + icon at the top right and navigating to our newly created *.zip* file in the associated *dist* directory. Once our analyzer appears in the list, we can select it and click OK (not shown). Restart Ghidra to use the new functionality from the Analysis menu.

Step 6: Test the Analyzer Within Ghidra

As with our limited development plan, we used a limited scope test plan just to demonstrate functionality. *SimpleROP* passed acceptance testing as the analyzer met the following criteria:

1. (Pass) *SimpleROP* appears in the Analysis Options in the CodeBrowser ▸ Analysis menu.

2.   (Pass) The description of *SimpleROP* appears in the Analysis Options
     description window when selected.

     Test cases 1 and 2 passed, as shown in Figure 15-25. (Had we chosen to
     register and program associated options in step 3-5, they would have
     been displayed in the Options panel on the right side of the window).

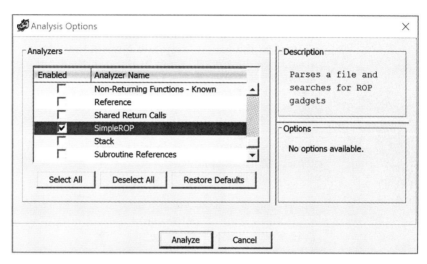

Figure 15-25: Analysis Options window

3.   (Pass) *SimpleROP* executes when selected.

     In this case, we ran *SimpleROP* on an analyzed file, and as part of auto
     analysis. Running *SimpleROP* on an unanalyzed file would not yield
     any results, as INSTRUCTION_ANALYZER extensions require instructions to
     have been previously identified (a default part of auto analysis). When
     SimpleROP is run as part of the auto analysis, it is prioritized appropri-
     ately because of the analyzer type we assigned in step 3-2. Figure 15-26
     shows the Ghidra Log confirmation that the *SimpleROP* analyzer ran.

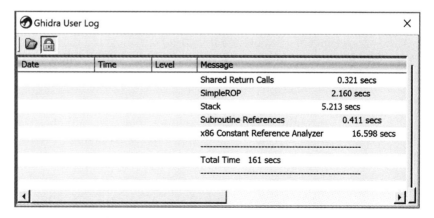

Figure 15-26: Ghidra User Log window showing analysis confirmation

4. (Pass) *SimpleROP* writes each gadget to a file called *fileZZZ_gadgets.txt* when analyzing *fileZZZ*.

The following excerpt from the file *call_tree_x64_static_gadgets.txt* shows that many of the gadgets are taken from the portion of the *call_tree_x64_static* listing shown in Figure 15-27:

```
00400412;ADD RSP,0x8;RET;
004004ce;NOP;RET;
00400679;ADD RSP,0x8;POP RBX;POP RBP;POP R12;POP R13;POP R14;POP R15;RET;
0040067d;POP RBX;POP RBP;POP R12;POP R13;POP R14;POP R15;RET;
0040067e;POP RBP;POP R12;POP R13;POP R14;POP R15;RET;
0040067f;POP R12;POP R13;POP R14;POP R15;RET;
00400681;POP R13;POP R14;POP R15;RET;
00400683;POP R14;POP R15;RET;
00400685;POP R15;RET;
00400a8b;POP RBP;MOV EDI,0x6babd0;JMP RAX;
00400a8c;MOV EDI,0x6babd0;JMP RAX;
00400a98;POP RBP;RET;
```

```
                    LAB_00400672
00400672    MOV      qword ptr
00400679    ADD      RSP,0x8
0040067d    POP      RBX
0040067e    POP      RBP
0040067f    POP      R12
00400681    POP      R13
00400683    POP      R14
00400685    POP      R15
00400687    RET
```

Figure 15-27: CodeBrowser listing of call_tree_x64_static

Summary

In Chapter 14, we introduced scripting as a means of extending Ghidra's capabilities. In this chapter, we introduced Ghidra extension modules along with Ghidra's Eclipse integration capabilities. While Eclipse is not your only option for editing Ghidra extensions, the integration of Ghidra and the Eclipse IDE provides an incredibly powerful environment for developers extending Ghidra's capabilities. The development wizards and templates lower the bar for authoring extensions as they present coders with a guided approach to modifying existing content and building new extensions. In Chapter 16, we take a look at headless Ghidra, an option that appeared in Figure 15-18. Subsequent chapters build on the integration of Ghidra and the Eclipse IDE to further extend Ghidra's capabilities and provide a solid foundation for making Ghidra into the optimal tool for your reverse engineering workflow.

16

GHIDRA IN HEADLESS MODE

In earlier chapters, we focused on exploring a single file within a single project, facilitated by the Ghidra GUI. In addition to the GUI, Ghidra has a command line interface called the *Ghidra headless analyzer.* The headless analyzer provides some of the same capabilities as the Ghidra GUI, including the ability to work with projects and files, but it's better suited for batch processing and scripted control of Ghidra. In this chapter, we discuss Ghidra's headless mode and how it can help you perform repetitive tasks across a larger number of files. We start with a familiar example and then expand our discussion to more complex options.

Getting Started

Let's start by recalling our first use of Ghidra in Chapter 4. We successfully accomplished the following steps:

1. Launch Ghidra.
2. Create a new Ghidra project.
3. Identify a location for the project.
4. Import a file to the project.
5. Auto analyze the file.
6. Save and exit.

Let's replicate these tasks using the Ghidra headless analyzer's command line interface. The headless analyzer (*analyzeHeadless* or *analyzeHeadless.bat*) as well as a helpful file called *analyzeHeadlessREADME.html* can be found in the *support* directory of your Ghidra installation. To simplify file paths, we have temporarily placed the file *global_array_demo_x64* in the same directory. First, we will identify the commands and parameters needed for each of the individual tasks and then we will put them all together to accomplish our goal. While it hasn't made a significant difference in previous chapters, there are more distinctions between the three Ghidra platforms when we are operating from the command line. In our examples, we use the Windows installation and make note of significant differences on other platforms.

TO SLASH OR BACKSLASH?

A major difference among the operating system platforms that support Ghidra is the manner in which they identify filesystem paths. While the syntax is consistent, different platforms use different directory separators. Windows uses a backward slash, whereas Linux and macOS use a forward slash. A path looks like this in Windows:

```
D:\GhidraProjects\ch16\demo_stackframe_32
```

And it looks like this in Linux and macOS:

```
/GhidraProjects/ch16/demo_stackframe_32
```

This syntax can be even more confusing for Windows users as forward slashes are used in URLs and command line switches (and Ghidra documentation). Operating systems recognize this issue and try to accept either, but not always in a predictable manner. For the examples in this chapter, we use the Windows convention so readers can enjoy being backward compatible with DOS.

Step 1: Launch Ghidra

This step is accomplished using the analyzeHeadless command. All additional steps will be accomplished using the parameters and options associated with this command. Running analyzeHeadless without any parameters displays a usage message with the command's syntax and options, as shown in Figure 16-1. To launch Ghidra, we need to add some of these parameters to the command.

```
Headless Analyzer Usage: analyzeHeadless
         <project_location> <project_name>[/<folder_path>]
            | ghidra://<server>[:<port>]/<repository_name>[/<folder_path>]
         [[-import [<directory>|<file>]+] | [-process [<project_file>]]]
         [-preScript <ScriptName>]
         [-postScript <ScriptName>]
         [-scriptPath "<path1>[;<path2>...]"]
         [-propertiesPath "<path1>[;<path2>...]"]
         [-scriptlog <path to script log file>]
         [-log <path to log file>]
         [-overwrite]
         [-recursive]
         [-readOnly]
         [-deleteProject]
         [-noanalysis]
         [-processor <languageID>]
         [-cspec <compilerSpecID>]
         [-analysisTimeoutPerFile <timeout in seconds>]
         [-keystore <KeystorePath>]
         [-connect <userID>]
         [-p]
         [-commit ["<comment>"]]
         [-okToDelete]
         [-max-cpu <max cpu cores to use>]
         [-loader <desired loader name>]

Please refer to 'analyzeHeadlessREADME.html' for detailed usage examples and notes.
```

Figure 16-1: Headless analyzer syntax

Steps 2 and 3: Create a New Ghidra Project in a Specified Location

In headless mode, Ghidra creates a project for you if the project does not already exist. If the project already exists in the specified location, Ghidra opens the existing project. As a result, two parameters are required: the project location and the project name. The following command creates a project named *CH16* in our *D:\GhidraProjects* directory:

```
analyzeHeadless D:\GhidraProjects CH16
```

This is a minimal launch of headless Ghidra to open a project and accomplishes nothing more. In fact, the response message from Ghidra tells you exactly that:

```
Nothing to do...must specify -import, -process, or prescript and/or postscript.
```

Step 4: Import a File to the Project

To import a file, Ghidra requires the -import option and the name of the file to import. We will import *global_array_demo_x64*, which we have used in the past. As mentioned, for simplicity in this initial example, we have placed the file in the *support* directory. Alternatively, we could specify the full path to the file on the command line. We add the -import option to our command:

```
analyzeHeadless D:\GhidraProjects CH16 -import global_array_demo_x64
```

Steps 5 and 6: Auto Analyze the File, Save, and Exit

In headless mode, auto analysis and saving happen by default, so the command in step 4 accomplishes everything we want. An option is required to *not* analyze the file (-noanalysis), and there are options available to control how the project and associated files are saved.

Here is our completed command to accomplish our six objectives:

```
analyzeHeadless D:\GhidraProjects CH16 -import global_array_demo_x64
```

As with many console commands, you may be asking yourself, "How can I be sure anything has happened?" Your first sign of success (or failure) is the messages displayed at the console. Informational messages that start with the prefix INFO provide progress reports as the headless analyzer starts its work. Error messages start with the prefix ERROR. Listing 16-1 includes a subset of the messages, including an error message.

```
❶ INFO  HEADLESS Script Paths:
      C:\Users\Ghidrabook\ghidra_scripts
   ❷ D:\ghidra_PUBLIC\Ghidra\Extensions\SimpleROP\ghidra_scripts
      D:\ghidra_PUBLIC\Ghidra\Features\Base\ghidra_scripts
      D:\ghidra_PUBLIC\Ghidra\Features\BytePatterns\ghidra_scripts
      D:\ghidra_PUBLIC\Ghidra\Features\Decompiler\ghidra_scripts
      D:\ghidra_PUBLIC\Ghidra\Features\FileFormats\ghidra_scripts
      D:\ghidra_PUBLIC\Ghidra\Features\FunctionID\ghidra_scripts
      D:\ghidra_PUBLIC\Ghidra\Features\GnuDemangler\ghidra_scripts
      D:\ghidra_PUBLIC\Ghidra\Features\Python\ghidra_scripts
      D:\ghidra_PUBLIC\Ghidra\Features\VersionTracking\ghidra_scripts
      D:\ghidra_PUBLIC\Ghidra\Processors\8051\ghidra_scripts
      D:\ghidra_PUBLIC\Ghidra\Processors\DATA\ghidra_scripts
      D:\ghidra_PUBLIC\Ghidra\Processors\PIC\ghidra_scripts(HeadlessAnalyzer)
   INFO  HEADLESS: execution starts (HeadlessAnalyzer)
   INFO  Opening existing project: D:\GhidraProjects\CH16 (HeadlessAnalyzer)
❸ ERROR Abort due to Headless analyzer error:
      ghidra.framework.store.LockException:
      Unable to lock project! D:\GhidraProjects\CH16 (HeadlessAnalyzer)
      java.io.IOException: ghidra.framework.store.LockException:
      Unable to lock project! D:\GhidraProjects\CH16
      ...
```

Listing 16-1: Headless analyzer with error condition

The script paths used in headless mode are listed ❶. Later in the chapter, we show how to use additional scripts with our headless commands. The extension we created in the preceding chapter, SimpleROP, is included in the script path ❷ because every extension adds a new path to the script path. The LockException ❸ is perhaps the most common error associated with the headless analyzer. The headless analyzer fails if you attempt to run it on a project that you already have open in another Ghidra instance. When this occurs, the headless analyzer is unable to lock the project for its own, exclusive use, so the command fails.

To fix the error, close any running Ghidra instance that has the *CH16* project open and run the command again. Figure 16-2 shows the tail end of the output for successful execution of our command, which is similar to the pop-up windows that we see when analyzing files in the Ghidra GUI.

```
INFO  -------------------------------------------------------
    ASCII Strings                           0.883 secs
    Apply Data Archives                     0.590 secs
    Call Convention Identification          0.137 secs
    Call-Fixup Installer                    0.004 secs
    Create Address Tables                   0.012 secs
    Create Function                         0.005 secs
    DWARF                                   0.020 secs
    Data Reference                          0.010 secs
    Decompiler Switch Analysis              0.473 secs
    Demangler GNU                           0.050 secs
    Disassemble Entry Points                0.105 secs
    ELF Scalar Operand References           0.010 secs
    Embedded Media                          0.014 secs
    External Entry References               0.001 secs
    Function ID                             0.051 secs
    Function Start Search                   0.043 secs
    Function Start Search After Code        0.002 secs
    Function Start Search After Data        0.001 secs
    GCC Exception Handlers                  0.076 secs
    Non-Returning Functions - Discovered    0.013 secs
    Non-Returning Functions - Known         0.004 secs
    Reference                               0.025 secs
    Shared Return Calls                     0.005 secs
    Stack                                   0.054 secs
    Subroutine References                   0.007 secs
    Subroutine References - One Time        0.000 secs
    x86 Constant Reference Analyzer         0.093 secs
-----------------------------------------------------------
    Total Time    2 secs
```

Figure 16-2: Headless analyzer results displayed to the console

To verify the results in the Ghidra GUI, open the project and confirm that the file has been loaded, as shown in Figure 16-3, and then open the file in the CodeBrowser to confirm analysis.

Ghidra: CH16
File Edit Project Tools Help
Tool Chest
Active Project: CH16
CH16
global_array_demo_x64
Filter:
Tree View
Table View
Running Tools
Workspace
Opening project: D:\GhidraProjects\CH16

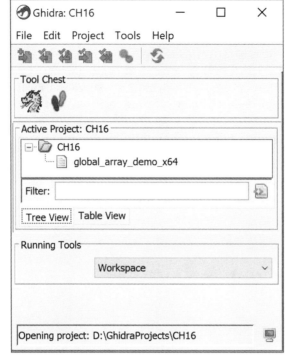

Figure 16-3: Ghidra GUI confirmation that the project has been created and the file loaded

Now that we have replicated our earlier analysis using Ghidra in headless mode, let's investigate some situations where headless mode has an advantage over the GUI. To create a project and load and analyze all of the files shown in Figure 16-4 using the Ghidra GUI, we could create the project and then load each file individually, or select files to include in a batch import operation, as discussed in "Batch Import" on page 226. Headless Ghidra allows us to name a directory and analyze all contained files.

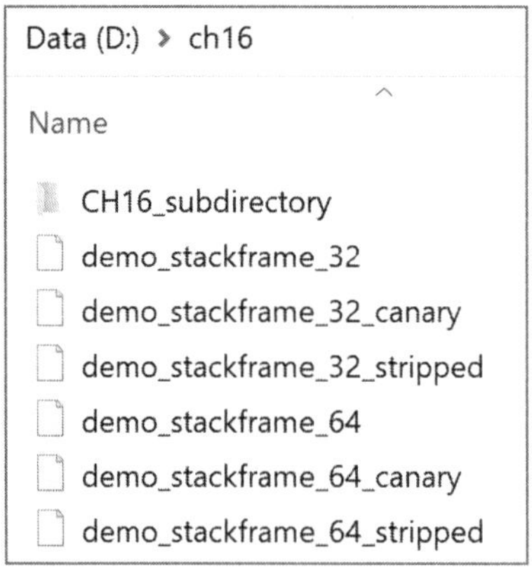

Data (D:) > ch16
Name
CH16_subdirectory
demo_stackframe_32
demo_stackframe_32_canary
demo_stackframe_32_stripped
demo_stackframe_64
demo_stackframe_64_canary
demo_stackframe_64_stripped

Figure 16-4: Input directory for headless Ghidra examples

The following command tells the headless analyzer to open or create a project named *CH16* in the *D:\GhidraProjects* directory and import and analyze all of the files in the *D:\ch16* directory:

```
analyzeHeadless D:\GhidraProjects CH16 -import D:\ch16
```

After the command is executed, we can load the new project into the Ghidra GUI and see its associated files, as shown in Figure 16-5. The subdirectory *D:\ch16\CH16_subdirectory* does not appear in the project, nor do any of the files within the subdirectory. We will come back to this when we discuss additional options and parameters that can be used with headless Ghidra in the following section.

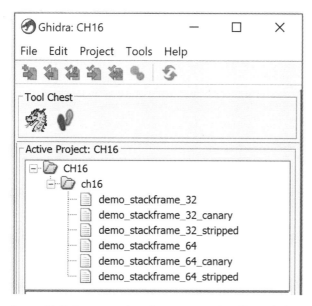

Figure 16-5: Project resulting from pointing headless Ghidra at a directory

Options and Parameters

The simple examples of using headless Ghidra to create a project, load and analyze a single file, and use batch processing to import an entire directory are just the beginning of what is possible. While we will not be able to discuss all capabilities of headless Ghidra, we will provide a brief introduction to each of the options currently available.

General Options

The following are brief descriptions with related examples of additional options that we could use to further control what is happening in our simple examples. (Wrapped lines are indented.) When encountered, common error conditions are discussed. Specialized error conditions are left as an exercise for the reader in the comfort of the Ghidra Help file.

-log *logfilepath*

Many things can go wrong (and right) when executing from the command line. Fortunately, Ghidra plugins provide continuous feedback as to what is happening while Ghidra is running. While this feedback is less vital in the Ghidra GUI (because you have visual cues as to what is happening), it is important in headless Ghidra.

By default, a logfile is written to *.ghidra/.ghidra_<VER>_PUBLIC /application.log* in the user's home directory. You may select a new location by adding the -log option to your command line. To create a directory, *CH16-logs*, and write a logfile to *CH16-logfile*, use the following command:

```
analyzeHeadless D:\GhidraProjects CH16 -import global_array_demo_x64
  -log D:\GhidraProjects\CH16-logs\CH16-Logfile
```

-noanalysis

This option instructs Ghidra not to analyze any files that you import from the command line. Opening the file *global_array_demo_x64* in the Ghidra GUI after the following statement is executed would present you with a loaded, but not analyzed, version of the file within the *CH16* project:

```
analyzeHeadless D:\GhidraProjects CH16 -import global_array_demo_x64
  -noanalysis
```

-overwrite

In Listing 16-1, we saw an error condition when Ghidra tried to open a project that was already open. A second common error occurs when Ghidra tries to import a file into a project and the file has already been imported. To import a new version of the file, or overwrite the existing file regardless of contents, use the -overwrite option. Without this option, running the following headless command twice would result in an error during the second execution. With this option, we can rerun the command as many times as we wish:

```
analyzeHeadless D:\GhidraProjects CH16 -import global_array_demo_x64
  -overwrite
```

-readOnly

To import a file without saving the file in the project, use the -readOnly option. If you use this option, the -overwrite option will be ignored (if present). This option also has meaning when used with the -process option rather than the -import command. The -process option is covered later in the chapter.

```
analyzeHeadless D:\GhidraProjects CH16 -import global_array_demo_x64
  -readOnly
```

-deleteProject

This option instructs Ghidra not to save any project being created with the -import option. This option can be used with any of the other options but is assumed (even if omitted) when using -readOnly. The newly created project is deleted after analysis is complete. This option will not delete an existing project:

```
analyzeHeadless D:\GhidraProjects CH16 -import global_array_demo_x64
  -deleteProject
```

-recursive

By default, Ghidra does not recurse into subdirectories when asked to process an entire directory. Use this option when you do want Ghidra to perform recursive directory processing (that is, process any subdirectories it finds along the way). To demonstrate this functionality, we will point Ghidra at the same *ch16* directory we processed earlier, but this time will use the -recursive option:

```
analyzeHeadless D:\GhidraProjects CH16 -import D:\ch16 -recursive
```

Opening the project, *CH16*, after running this command results in the project structure shown in Figure 16-6. In contrast to Figure 16-5, the *CH16_subdirectory* is included in the project as well as its associated file, and the directory hierarchy is retained within the project hierarchy.

Figure 16-6: Headless Ghidra project resulting from the -recursive option

WILDCARDS!

Wildcards provide an easy method to select multiple files for headless Ghidra without listing each one separately. In short, an asterisk (*) matches any sequence of characters, and a question mark (?) matches a single character. To load and analyze only the 32-bit files from Figure 16-7, use a wildcard as follows:

```
analyzeHeadless D:\GhidraProjects CH16 -import D:\ch16\demo_stackframe_32*
```

This creates the CH16 project and loads and analyzes all of the 32-bit files in the *ch16* directory. The resulting project is shown in Figure 16-7. See *analyzeHeadlessREADME.html* for detailed information about using wildcards to specify files for import and processing. You will also see wildcards in future headless Ghidra scripting examples.

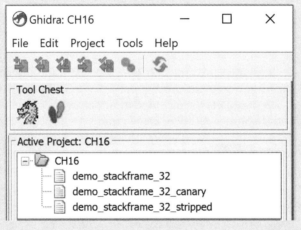

Figure 16-7: Project files resulting from the wildcard *demo_stackframe_32**

-analysisTimeoutPerFile *seconds*

As you have analyzed (or sat and watched Ghidra analyze) files, you may have noticed several factors that impact the analysis time, like the size of the file, whether it's statically linked, and the decompiler analysis options. Regardless of the file contents and options, you can't know in advance exactly how long it may take to analyze a file.

In headless Ghidra, particularly when you are processing a large number of files, you can use the -analysisTimeoutPerFile option to ensure that your task ends in a reasonable amount of time. With this option, you specify a time-out in seconds, and analysis will be interrupted should time expire. For example, our existing headless Ghidra command takes a little over one second to analyze on our system (refer to

Figure 16-2). If we had *really* limited time to execute this script, the following headless command would stop analysis after one second:

```
analyzeHeadless D:\GhidraProjects CH16 -import global_array_demo_x64
  -analysisTimeoutPerFile 1
```

This would result in the console display shown in Figure 16-8.

```
    Non-Returning Functions - Known      0.004 secs
    Reference                            0.025 secs
    Shared Return Calls                  0.004 secs
    Subroutine References                0.008 secs
    Subroutine References - One Time     0.000 secs
    x86 Constant Reference Analyzer      0.092 secs
-------------------------------------------------------
    Total Time   1 secs
-------------------------------------------------------
(AutoAnalysisManager)
ERROR REPORT: Analysis timed out at 1 seconds. Processing not completed
(HeadlessAnalyzer)
```

Figure 16-8: Console warning that analysis timed out

-processor *languageID* and -cspec *compilerSpecID*

As shown in previous examples, Ghidra is generally quite good at identifying information about a file and making import recommendations. A sample window showing the recommendations for a particular file is shown in Figure 16-9. This window is displayed every time you use the GUI to import a file into a project.

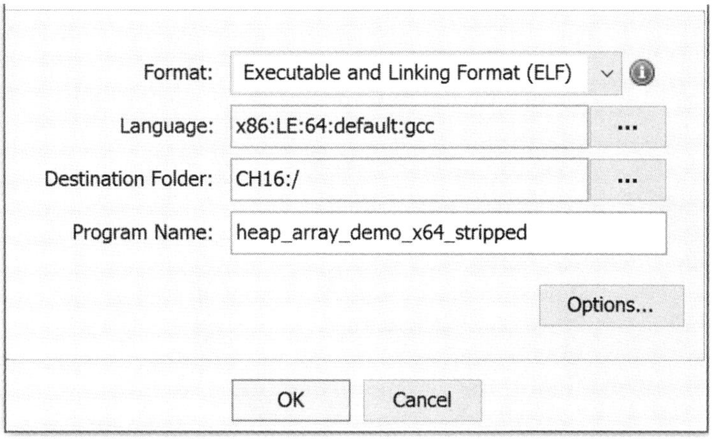

Figure 16-9: Ghidra GUI import confirmation dialog

If you feel that you have additional insight into the appropriate language or compiler, you can expand the box to the right of the Language specification. This presents you with the window shown in Figure 16-10, which gives you the opportunity to select a language and compiler specification.

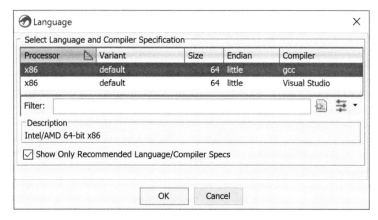

Figure 16-10: Ghidra language/compiler specification selection window

To do the same in headless Ghidra, use the -cspec and/or processor options, as shown next. You cannot use the -cspec option without using the -processor option. You can use the -processor option without the -cspec option, in which case Ghidra will choose the default compiler associated with the processor.

```
analyzeHeadless D:\GhidraProjects CH16 -import global_array_demo_x64
  -processor "x86:LE:64:default" -cspec "gcc"
```

-loader *loadername*

The -loader option can be the most complex of the headless Ghidra options. The *loadername* argument names one of Ghidra's loader modules (discussed in Chapter 17) that will be used to import a new file into the named project. Sample loader names include PeLoader, ElfLoader, and MachoLoader. Each loader module may recognize additional command line arguments of its own. These additional arguments are discussed in *support/analyzeHeadlessREADME.html*.

-max-cpu *number*

This option allows to you to put an upper limit on the number of processor (CPU) cores used to process the headless Ghidra command. The option requires an integer value as an argument. If the value is less than 1, the maximum number of cores is set to 1.

```
analyzeHeadless D:\GhidraProjects CH16 -import global_array_demo_x64
  -max-cpu 5
```

Server Options

Some commands are used only when interacting with a Ghidra Server. As this is not the focus of this book, we will mention these commands only briefly. Additional information can be found in *analyzeheadlessREADME.html*.

`ghidra://server[:port]/repository_name[/folder_path]`

> The previous examples have all specified a project location or project name. This alternative allows you to specify a Ghidra Server repository and optional folder path.

`-p`

> With Ghidra Server, this option forces a password prompt via the console.

`-connect [userID]`

> This option provides a *userID* to override the default *userID* when connecting to a Ghidra Server.

`-keystore path`

> This option allows you to specify a private keystore file when using PKI or SSH authentication.

`-commit ["comment"]`

> While commit is enabled by default, this option allows you to associate a comment with a commit.

Script Options

Perhaps the most powerful applications for headless Ghidra are associated with Ghidra's scripting abilities. Chapters 14 and 15 both demonstrated how scripts can be created and used with the Ghidra GUI. After we present script options, we will demonstrate how powerful headless Ghidra can be in a scripting context.

`-process [project_file]`

> This option processes select files (as opposed to importing them). If you do not specify a file, all files in the project folder will be processed. All specified files will also be analyzed unless you use the -noanalysis option. Ghidra accepts two wildcard characters (* and ?) for the -process option in order to simplify selection of multiple files. For this option, unlike with the -import option, you are naming Ghidra imported project files, *not* local filesystem files, so you need to quote any filenames that contain these wildcards in order to prevent your shell from expanding them prematurely.

`-scriptPath "path1[;path2...]"`

> By default, headless Ghidra includes many default script paths as well as script paths for imported extensions, as seen in Listing 16-1. To extend the list of paths that Ghidra searches for available scripts, use the -scriptPath option, which requires a quoted path list argument. Within the quotes, multiple paths must be separated using a semicolon. Two special prefix designators are recognized in path components:

$GHIDRA_HOME and $USER_HOME. $GHIDRA_HOME refers to the Ghidra installation directory, and $USER_HOME refers to the user's home directory. Note that these are not environment variables and that your command shell may require you to escape the leading $ character in order for it to be passed to Ghidra. The following example adds the *D:\GhidraScripts* directory to the script path:

```
analyzeHeadless D:\GhidraProjects CH16 -import global_array_demo_x64
  -scriptPath "D:\GhidraScripts"
```

After you run the command, the new script directory, *D:\GhidraScripts*, is included in the script path:

```
INFO  HEADLESS Script Paths:
  D:\GhidraScripts
  C:\Users\Ghidrabook\ghidra_scripts
  D:\ghidra_PUBLIC\Ghidra\Extensions\SimpleROP\ghidra_scripts
  D:\ghidra_PUBLIC\Ghidra\Features\Base\ghidra_scripts
  D:\ghidra_PUBLIC\Ghidra\Features\BytePatterns\ghidra_scripts
  D:\ghidra_PUBLIC\Ghidra\Features\Decompiler\ghidra_scripts
  D:\ghidra_PUBLIC\Ghidra\Features\FileFormats\ghidra_scripts
  D:\ghidra_PUBLIC\Ghidra\Features\FunctionID\ghidra_scripts
  D:\ghidra_PUBLIC\Ghidra\Features\GnuDemangler\ghidra_scripts
  D:\ghidra_PUBLIC\Ghidra\Features\Python\ghidra_scripts
  D:\ghidra_PUBLIC\Ghidra\Features\VersionTracking\ghidra_scripts
  D:\ghidra_PUBLIC\Ghidra\Processors\8051\ghidra_scripts
  D:\ghidra_PUBLIC\Ghidra\Processors\DATA\ghidra_scripts
  D:\ghidra_PUBLIC\Ghidra\Processors\PIC\ghidra_scripts (HeadlessAnalyzer)
INFO  HEADLESS: execution starts (HeadlessAnalyzer)
```

-preScript

This option names a script to be run before analysis. The script may contain an optional list of arguments.

-postScript

This option names a script to be run after analysis. The script may contain an optional list of arguments.

-propertiesPath

This option specifies the path to any property files associated with a script. Property files provide input to scripts that are run in headless mode. Examples of scripts and their associated property files are included in the headless analyzer documentation.

-okToDelete

As scripts can do whatever their creators intend, it is possible for a script to delete (or try to delete) files within a Ghidra project. To prevent this as an undesired side-effect, headless Ghidra will not allow deletion of files by a script unless the `-okToDelete` option is included when the script is invoked. Note: This parameter is not required when running in `-import` mode.

Writing Scripts

Now that you understand the basic components of a headless Ghidra command, let's build some scripts to run from the command line.

HeadlessSimpleROP

Recall the SimpleROP analyzer that we wrote in Chapter 15. We wrote the module using the Eclipse IDE and then imported the extension into Ghidra so we could run it on any file we imported. Now we want to point SimpleROP at a directory and have it identify ROP gadgets in every file (or select files) in the directory. In addition to the SimpleROP output file with ROP gadgets for each existing binary, we also want a summary file that lists each file and the number of identified ROP gadgets in each.

For a job like this, running SimpleROP through the Ghidra GUI would introduce a time penalty for actions like opening and closing the CodeBrowser to display each file in the listing window, and so on. We do not need to see any of the files in the CodeBrowser window to accomplish our new goal. Why can't we just write a script to find the gadgets independent of the GUI completely? This is exactly the kind of use case appropriate for headless Ghidra.

While we could modify the functionality of SimpleROP to accomplish our goal, we do not want to lose the utility of an existing Ghidra extension that other users may find useful. (We realize that we just introduced it in the preceding chapter . . . but it might have gone viral.) Instead, we will use some of the code from SimpleROP as a base to create our new script, *HeadlessSimpleROP*, which finds all ROP gadgets in *<filename>* and creates and writes them to *<filename>_gadgets.txt*, then appends *<path>/<filename>* and the count of ROP gadgets to a *HeadlessSimpleROP* summary file called *gadget_summary.txt*. All other functionality required (parsing directories, files, and so on) will be provided by headless Ghidra using the options we discussed earlier in this chapter.

To simplify development, we create a new script using the Eclipse ▶ GhidraDev approach presented in Chapter 15 and then copy the *SimpleROP Analyzer.java* source code into the new script template and edit the code as needed. Finally, we will run the script using the `-postScript` option so that it is invoked following the analysis phase for each opened file.

Creating the HeadlessSimpleROP Script Template

Begin by creating a template. From the GhidraDev menu, choose **New ▶ GhidraScript** and fill in the information shown in the dialog in Figure 16-11. While we could place the script in any folder, we will place it in the *ghidra _scripts* folder within our existing SimpleROP module in Eclipse.

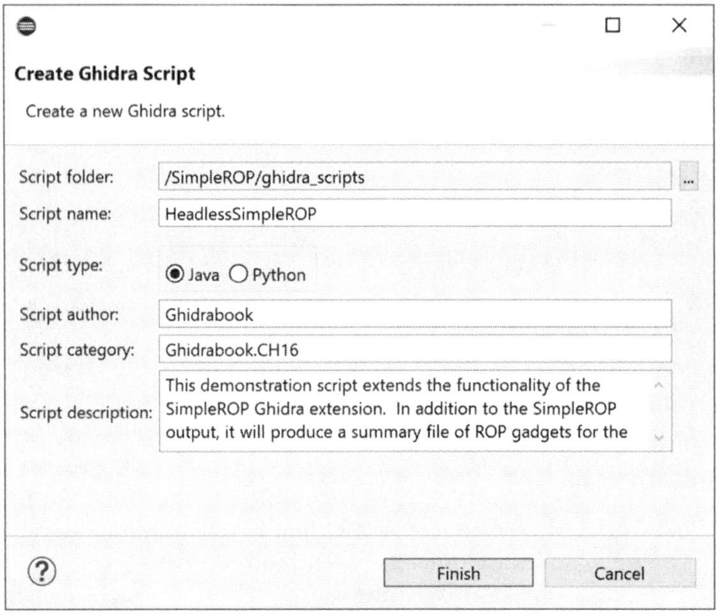

Figure 16-11: Create Ghidra Script dialog

Click **Finish** to see the new script template, complete with metadata, as shown in Figure 16-12. The task tag on line 14 shows you where to get started.

```
 1 //This demonstration script extends the functionality of
 2 //@author Ghidrabook
 3 //@category Ghidrabook.CH16
 4 //@keybinding
 5 //@menupath
 6 //@toolbar
 7
 8 import ghidra.app.script.GhidraScript;
 9
10 public class HeadlessSimpleROP extends GhidraScript {
11
12     @Override
13     protected void run() throws Exception {
14         //TODO: Add script code here
15     }
16 }
```

Figure 16-12: New HeadlessSimpleROP *script template*

To convert the SimpleROP analyzer into the *HeadlessSimpleROP* script, we need to do the following:

1. Remove the unneeded import statements.
2. Remove the analyzer public methods.

3. Duplicate the functionality of the added method that is called when the SimpleROPAnalyzer is invoked with the run method, which is called when the *HeadlessSimpleROP* script is invoked.

4. Add the functionality to append the filename and number of gadgets found to the summary file, *gadget_summary.txt*.

We will place our script, *HeadlessSimpleROP*, in the *D:\GhidraScripts* directory and use the headless analyzer to demonstrate its functionality. In the next sections, we will run a series of tests invoking the *HeadlessSimpleROP* script using items in the directory structure shown in Figure 16-6. These tests also demonstrate some of the options associated with headless Ghidra.

Test Scenario 1: Load, Analyze, and Process a Single File

In the following listing, we use headless Ghidra to import, analyze, and invoke our script to generate a gadget report for a single file (the ^ character is the line-continuation character in a Windows command shell):

```
analyzeHeadless D:\GhidraProjects CH16_ROP ^
    -import D:\ch16\demo_stackframe_32 ^
    -scriptPath D:\GhidraScripts ^
    -postScript HeadlessSimpleROP.java
```

When executed, the Ghidra headless analyzer creates a project called *CH16_ROP* in the *GhidraProjects* directory, then imports the file *demo_stackframe_32*, which will also be loaded and analyzed. We indicate the directory in which our script resides using scriptPath. Finally, after analysis, our script is run on the imported and analyzed file.

Once the command has completed, we check the contents of the *gadget_summary.txt* and *demo_stackframe_32_gadgets.txt* files to determine if our script worked correctly. The *demo_stackframe_32_gadgets.txt* contains 16 potential ROP gadgets:

```
080482c6;ADD ESP,0x8;POP EBX;RET;
080482c9;POP EBX;RET;
08048343;MOV EBX,dword ptr [ESP];RET;
08048360;MOV EBX,dword ptr [ESP];RET;
08048518;SUB ESP,0x4;PUSH EBP;PUSH dword ptr [ESP + 0x2c];PUSH dword ptr [ESP + 0x2c];
        CALL dword ptr [EBX + EDI*0x4 + 0xfffffff0c];
0804851b;PUSH EBP;PUSH dword ptr [ESP + 0x2c];PUSH dword ptr [ESP + 0x2c];
        CALL dword ptr [EBX + EDI*0x4 + 0xfffffff0c];
0804851c;PUSH dword ptr [ESP + 0x2c];PUSH dword ptr [ESP + 0x2c];
        CALL dword ptr [EBX + EDI*0x4 + 0xfffffff0c];
08048520;PUSH dword ptr [ESP + 0x2c];CALL dword ptr [EBX + EDI*0x4 + 0xfffffff0c];
08048535;ADD ESP,0xc;POP EBX;POP ESI;POP EDI;POP EBP;RET;
08048538;POP EBX;POP ESI;POP EDI;POP EBP;RET;
08048539;POP ESI;POP EDI;POP EBP;RET;
0804853a;POP EDI;POP EBP;RET;
0804853b;POP EBP;RET;
```

```
0804854d;ADD EBX,0x1ab3;ADD ESP,0x8;POP EBX;RET;
08048553;ADD ESP,0x8;POP EBX;RET;
08048556;POP EBX;RET;
```

Here is the associated entry in *gadget_summary.txt*:

```
demo_stackframe_32: Found 16 potential gadgets
```

Test Scenario 2: Load, Analyze, and Process All Files in a Directory

In this test, we import an entire directory, rather than a file with the import statement:

```
analyzeHeadless D:\GhidraProjects CH16_ROP ^
    -import D:\ch16 ^
    -scriptPath D:\GhidraScripts ^
    -postScript HeadlessSimpleROP.java
```

When the headless analyzer is complete, the following contents are found in *gadget_summary.txt*:

```
demo_stackframe_32: Found 16 potential gadgets
demo_stackframe_32_canary: Found 16 potential gadgets
demo_stackframe_32_stripped: Found 16 potential gadgets
demo_stackframe_64: Found 24 potential gadgets
demo_stackframe_64_canary: Found 24 potential gadgets
demo_stackframe_64_stripped: Found 24 potential gadgets
```

These are the six files in the root directory shown in Figure 16-6. In addition to the gadget summary file, we also produced individual gadget files listing the potential ROP gadgets associated with each file. In the remaining examples, we will concern ourselves only with the gadget summary file.

Test Scenario 3: Load, Analyze, and Process All Files in a Directory Recursively

In this test, we add the -recursive option. This extends the import operation to recursively visit all files in all subdirectories within the *ch16* directory:

```
analyzeHeadless D:\GhidraProjects CH16_ROP ^
    -import D:\ch16   ^
    -scriptPath D:\GhidraScripts ^
    -postScript HeadlessSimpleROP.java ^
    -recursive
```

When the headless analyzer is complete, the following contents are found in *gadget_summary.txt*, with the subdirectory file appearing at the top of the list:

```
demo_stackframe_32_sub: Found 16 potential gadgets
demo_stackframe_32: Found 16 potential gadgets
demo_stackframe_32_canary: Found 16 potential gadgets
demo_stackframe_32_stripped: Found 16 potential gadgets
```

```
demo_stackframe_64: Found 24 potential gadgets
demo_stackframe_64_canary: Found 24 potential gadgets
demo_stackframe_64_stripped: Found 24 potential gadgets
```

Test Scenario 4: Load, Analyze, and Process All 32-bit Files in a Directory

In this test, we use an * as a shell wildcard to restrict the import contents to the files with the 32-bit designator:

```
analyzeHeadless D:\GhidraProjects CH16ROP ^
    -import D:\ch16\demo_stackframe_32* ^
    -recursive ^
    -postScript HeadlessSimpleROP.java ^
    -scriptPath D:\GhidraScripts
```

The resulting *gadget_summary* file contains the following:

```
demo_stackframe_32: Found 16 potential gadgets
demo_stackframe_32_canary: Found 16 potential gadgets
demo_stackframe_32_stripped: Found 16 potential gadgets
```

If you know in advance that you're interested in only the generated gadget files, use the -readOnly option. This option instructs Ghidra not to save imported files into the project named in the command, and is useful for avoiding project clutter from batch-processing many files.

Automated FidDb Creation

In Chapter 13, we started creating a Function ID database (FidDb) populated with fingerprints of functions taken from a static version of *libc*. Using the GUI and Ghidra's batch file import mode, we imported 1,690 object files from a *libc.a* archive. However, we ran into a roadblock when it came to analyzing the files because the GUI has minimal support for batch analysis. Now that you are familiar with headless Ghidra, we can use it to complete our new FidDb.

Batch Import and Analysis

Importing and analyzing 1,690 files from an archive once seemed a daunting task, but the preceding examples have shown us everything we need to know to make short work of this task. We consider two cases here and provide command line examples for each.

If *libc.a* has not yet been imported into a Ghidra project, we extract the contents of our *libc.a* into a directory and then use headless Ghidra to process the entire directory:

```
$ mkdir libc.a && cd libc.a
$ ar x path\to\archive && cd ..
$ analyzeHeadless D:\GhidraProjects CH16 -import libc.a ^
    -processor x86:LE:64:default -cspec gcc -loader ElfLoader ^
    -recursive
```

The command results in thousands of lines of output as Ghidra reports its progress on the 1,690 files it processes, but once the command has completed, you will have a new *libc.a* folder in your project that contains 1,690 analyzed files.

If we've used the GUI to batch import *libc.a*, but had not processed any of the 1,690 imported files, the following command line would take care of the analysis:

```
$ analyzeHeadless D:\GhidraProjects CH16\libc.a -process
```

With the entire static archive efficiently imported and analyzed, we can now use the features of the Function ID plugin to create and populate an FidDb, as detailed in Chapter 13.

Summary

While GUI Ghidra remains the most straightforward and fully featured version, running Ghidra in headless mode offers tremendous flexibility in creating complex tools built around Ghidra's automated analysis. At this point, we have covered all of Ghidra's most commonly used features and examined ways that you can make Ghidra work for you. It is time to move on to more advanced features.

Over the course of the next few chapters, we will look at approaches for some of the more challenging problems that arise while reverse engineering binaries, including dealing with unknown file formats and unknown processor architectures by building sophisticated Ghidra extensions. We'll also spend some time investigating Ghidra's decompiler and discuss some of the ways that compilers can vary in their generation of code to improve your fluency in reading disassembly listings.

PART IV

A DEEPER DIVE

17

GHIDRA LOADERS

Except for a brief example demonstrating the Raw Binary loader in Chapter 4, Ghidra has identified the file type and happily loaded and analyzed all of the files we have thrown at it. This will not always be the case. At some point, you are likely to be confronted with a dialog like the one shown in Figure 17-1. (This particular file is shellcode, which Ghidra is unable to recognize, as there is no defined structure, meaningful file extension, or magic number.)

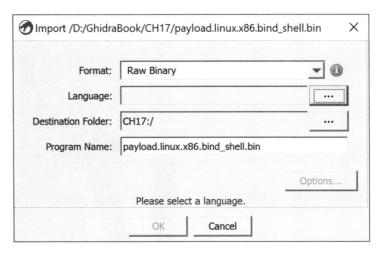

Figure 17-1: Raw Binary loader example

So what happened when we tried to import this file? Let's start with a high-level view of Ghidra's process for loading a file:

1. In the Ghidra Project window, the user specifies a file to load into a project.

2. The Ghidra Importer polls all of the Ghidra loaders, and each loader tries to identify the file. Each then responds with a list of load specifications to populate the Import dialog if it can load the file. (An empty list means "I can't load this file.")

3. The Importer collects responses from all of the loaders, builds a list of loaders that recognize the file, and presents a populated Import dialog to the user.

4. The user chooses a loader and associated information for loading the file.

5. The Importer invokes the user-selected loader that then loads the file.

For the file in Figure 17-1, none of the format-specific loaders responded with a "yes." As a result, the task was passed to the only loader willing to take any file at any time—the Raw Binary loader. This loader performs almost no work, shifting the analysis burden to the reverse engineer. If you ever find yourself analyzing similar files that all appear to have the "raw" format, it may be time to build a specialized loader to help you with some or all of the loading process. Several tasks need to be undertaken to create a new loader that Ghidra can use to load a file in a new format.

In this chapter, we first walk you through analysis of a file whose format is not recognized by Ghidra. This will help you understand the process of analyzing an unknown file and also make a strong case for building a loader, which is how we will spend the second half of the chapter.

Unknown File Analysis

Ghidra includes loader modules to recognize many of the more common executable and archive file formats, but there is no way that Ghidra can accommodate the ever-increasing number of file formats for storing executable code. Binary images may contain executable files formatted for use with specific operating systems, ROM images extracted from embedded systems, firmware images extracted from flash updates, or simply raw blocks of machine language, perhaps extracted from network packet captures. The format of these images may be dictated by the operating system (executable files), the target processor and system architecture (ROM images), or nothing at all (exploit shellcode embedded in application layer data).

Assuming that a processor module is available to disassemble the code contained in the unknown binary, it will be your job to properly arrange the file image within Ghidra before informing Ghidra which portions of the binary represent code and which portions of the binary represent data. For most processor types, the result of loading a file using the raw format is simply a list of the contents of the file piled into a single segment, beginning at address zero, as shown in Listing 17-1.

00000000	4d	??	4Dh	M
00000001	5a	??	5Ah	Z
00000002	90	??	90h	
00000003	00	??	00h	
00000004	03	??	03h	
00000005	00	??	00h	
00000006	00	??	00h	
00000007	00	??	00h	

Listing 17-1: Initial lines of an unanalyzed PE file loaded using the Raw Binary loader

In some cases, depending on the sophistication of the selected processor module, some disassembly takes place. For example, a selected processor for an embedded microcontroller can make specific assumptions about the memory layout of ROM images, or an analyzer with knowledge of common code sequences associated with a specific processor can optimistically format any matches as code.

When you are faced with an unrecognized file, arm yourself with as much information about the file as you can get your hands on. Useful resources might include notes on how and where the file was obtained, processor references, operating system references, system design documentation, and any memory layout information obtained through debugging or hardware-assisted analysis (such as via logic analyzers).

In the following section, for the sake of example, we assume that Ghidra does not recognize the Windows PE file format. PE is a well-known file format that many readers may be familiar with. More importantly, documents detailing the structure of PE files are widely available, which makes dissecting an arbitrary PE file a relatively simple task.

Manually Loading a Windows PE File

When you can find documentation on the format of a particular file, your life will be significantly easier as you attempt to use Ghidra to help you make sense of the binary. Listing 17-1 shows the first few lines of an unanalyzed PE file loaded into Ghidra using the Raw Binary loader and x86:LE:32:default:windows as its language/compiler specification.[1] The PE specification states that a valid PE file begins with an MS-DOS header structure, beginning with the 2-byte signature, 4Dh 5Ah (MZ), which we see in the first two lines of Listing 17-1.[2] The 4-byte value located at offset 0x3C in the file contains the offset to the next header we need to find: the PE header.

Two strategies for breaking down the fields of the MS-DOS header are (1) to define appropriately sized data values for each field in the MS-DOS header and (2) to use Ghidra's Data Type Manager functionality to define and apply an IMAGE_DOS_HEADER structure in accordance with the PE file specification. We will look at the challenges associated with option 1 in an example later in the chapter. In this case, option 2 requires significantly less effort.

When using the Raw Binary loader, Ghidra does not load the Data Type Manager with the Windows data types, so we can load the archive containing MS-DOS types, *windows_vs12_32.gdt*, ourselves. Locate the IMAGE_DOS_HEADER either by navigating to it within the archive or choosing CTRL-F to find it in the Data Type Manager window; then drag and drop the header onto the start of the file. You can also place the cursor on the first address in the listing and choose Data ▶ Choose Data Type (or hotkey T) from the right-click context menu and enter, or navigate to, the data type in the resulting Data Type Chooser dialog. Any of these options yields the following listing, with descriptive end-of-line comments describing each field:

```
00000000 4d 5a         WORD      5A4Dh     e_magic
00000002 90 00         WORD      90h       e_cblp
00000004 03 00         WORD      3h        e_cp
00000006 00 00         WORD      0h        e_crlc
00000008 04 00         WORD      4h        e_cparhdr
0000000a 00 00         WORD      0h        e_minalloc
0000000c ff ff         WORD      FFFFh     e_maxalloc
0000000e 00 00         WORD      0h        e_ss
00000010 b8 00         WORD      B8h       e_sp
00000012 00 00         WORD      0h        e_csum
00000014 00 00         WORD      0h        e_ip
00000016 00 00         WORD      0h        e_cs
00000018 40 00         WORD      40h       e_lfarlc
0000001a 00 00         WORD      0h        e_ovno
0000001c 00 00 00      WORD[4]             e_res
         00 00 00
         00 00
```

---

1. Choosing *Visual Studio* as your compiler results in *windows* being inserted in your language/compiler specification. For most other compilers, the selection name more closely matches the display name.

2. Please see *https://docs.microsoft.com/en-us/windows/win32/debug/pe-format*.

```
00000024 00 00       WORD       0h       e_oemid
00000026 00 00       WORD       0h       e_oeminfo
00000028 00 00 00    WORD[10]            e_res2
         00 00 00
         00 00 00
0000003c d8 00 00    LONG       D8h      e_lfanew
```

The e_lfanew field in the final line of the previous listing has a value of D8h, indicating that a PE header should be found at offset D8h (216 bytes) into the binary. Examining the bytes at offset D8h should reveal the magic number for a PE header, 50h 45h (PE), which indicates that we should apply an IMAGE_NT_HEADERS structure at offset D8h into the binary. Here is a portion of the resulting expanded Ghidra listing:

```
000000d8     IMAGE_NT_HEADERS
   000000d8        DWORD            4550h      Signature
   000000dc     IMAGE_FILE_HEADER             FileHeader
      000000dc        WORD          14Ch       Machine❶
      000000de        WORD          5h         NumberOfSections❷
      000000e0        DWORD         40FDFD     TimeDateStamp
      000000e4        DWORD         0h         PointerToSymbolTable
      000000e8        DWORD         0h         NumberOfSymbols
      000000ec        WORD          E0h        SizeOfOptionalHeader
      000000ee        WORD          10Fh       Characteristics
   000000f0     IMAGE_OPTIONAL_HEADER32       OptionalHeader
      000000f0        WORD          10Bh       Magic
      000000f2        BYTE          '\u0006'   MajorLinkerVersion
      000000f3        BYTE          '\0'       MinorLinkerVersion
      000000f4        DWORD         21000h     SizeOfCode
      000000f8        DWORD         A000h      SizeOfInitializedData
      000000fc        DWORD         0h         SizeOfUninitializedData
      00000100        DWORD         14E0h      AddressOfEntryPoint❸
      00000104        DWORD         1000h      BaseOfCode
      00000108        DWORD         1000h      BaseOfData
      0000010c        DWORD         400000h    ImageBase❹
      00000110        DWORD         1000h      SectionAlignment❺
      00000114        DWORD         1000h      FileAlignment❻
```

At this point, we have revealed a number of interesting pieces of information that will help us to further refine the layout of the binary. First, the Machine field ❶ in a PE header indicates the target processor type for which the file was built. The value 14Ch indicates that the file is for use with x86 processor types. Had the machine type been something else, such as 1C0h (ARM), we would need to close the CodeBrowser, right-click our file in the Project window to select the Set Language option, and choose the correct language setting.

The ImageBase field ❹ indicates the base virtual address for the loaded file image. Using this information, we can incorporate some virtual address information into the CodeBrowser. Using the Window ▸ Memory Map menu option, we are shown the list of memory blocks (Figure 17-2) that make up the current program. In this case, a single memory block contains all of the program's content. The Raw Binary loader has no means of determining appropriate memory addresses for any of our program's content, so it places all of the content in a single memory block starting at address zero.

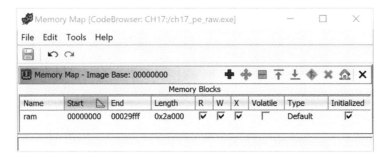

Figure 17-2: The Memory Map window

The Memory Map window's tool buttons, shown in Figure 17-3, are used to manipulate memory blocks. In order to properly map our image into memory, the first thing we need to do is set the base address specified in the PE header.

➕	Add Block	This button displays the Add Memory Block dialog to allow you to add information needed to create a new memory block.
✥	Move Block	When a memory block is selected, this option allows you to modify the start of the end address of the block, effectively moving it.
⊟	Split Block	When a memory block is selected, this option allows you to split the memory block into two memory blocks.
⊤	Expand Up	When a memory block is selected, this option allows you to append additional bytes before the memory block.
⊥	Expand Down	When a memory block is selected, this option allows you to append additional bytes after the memory block.
◈	Merge Blocks	When two (or more) memory blocks are selected, this option merges them into one.
✖	Delete Block	Deletes all selected memory blocks.
⌂	Set Image Base	This option allows you to choose (or modify) the base address of a program.

Figure 17-3: Memory Map window tools

The ImageBase field ❹ tells us that the correct base address for this binary is 00400000. We can use the Set Image Base option to adjust the image base from the default to this value. Once we click OK, all Ghidra windows will be updated to reflect the new memory layout of the program, as shown in Figure 17-4. (Be careful using this option after you already have multiple memory blocks defined; it will shift every memory block the same distance as the base memory block.)

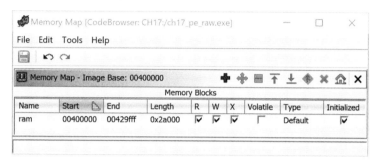

Figure 17-4: Memory Map after setting image base

The AddressOfEntryPoint field ❸ specifies the relative virtual address (RVA) of the program entry point. In the PE file specification, an RVA is a relative offset from the program's base virtual address, while the program entry point is the address of the first instruction within the program file that will be executed. In this case, an entry point RVA of 14E0h indicates that the program will begin execution at virtual address 4014E0h (400000h + 14E0h). This is our first indication of where we should begin looking for code within the program. Before we can do that, however, we need to properly map the remainder of the program to appropriate virtual addresses.

The PE format uses sections to describe the mapping of file content to memory ranges. By parsing the section headers for each section in the file, we can complete the basic virtual memory layout of the program. The NumberOfSections field ❷ indicates the number of sections contained in a PE file (in this case, five). According to the PE specification, an array of section header structures immediately follows the IMAGE_NT_HEADERS structure. Individual elements in the array are IMAGE_SECTION_HEADER structures, which we define in the Ghidra structures editor and apply (five times, in this case) to the bytes following the IMAGE_NT_HEADERS structure. Alternatively, you can select the first byte of the first section header and set its type to IMAGE_SECTION_HEADER[*n*], where *n* is 5 in this example, to collapse the entire array into a single Ghidra display line.

The FileAlignment field ❻ and the SectionAlignment field ❺ indicate how the data for each section is aligned within the file and how that same data will be aligned when mapped into memory. In our example, both fields are set to align on 1000h byte offsets.[3] In the PE format, there is no requirement

---

3. Alignment describes the starting address or offset of a block of data. The address or offset must be an even multiple of the alignment value. For example, when data is aligned to a 200h (512) byte boundary, it must begin at an address (or offset) that is divisible by 200h.

that these two numbers be the same. The fact that they are the same does make our lives easier, however, as it means that offsets to content within the disk file are identical to offsets to the corresponding bytes in the loaded memory image of the file. Understanding how sections are aligned is important in helping us avoid errors when we manually create sections for our program.

After structuring each of the section headers, we have enough information to create additional segments within the program. Applying an IMAGE_SECTION_HEADER template to the bytes immediately following the IMAGE_NT_HEADERS structure yields the first section header in our Ghidra listing:

004001d0	IMAGE_SECTION_HEADER		
004001d0	BYTE[8]	".text"	Name❶
004001d8	_union_226		Misc
004001d8	DWORD	20A80h	PhysicalAddress
004001d8	DWORD	20A80h	VirtualSize
004001dc	DWORD	1000h	VirtualAddress❷
004001e0	DWORD	21000h	SizeOfRawData❸
004001e4	DWORD	1000h	PointerToRawData❹
004001e8	DWORD	0h	PointerToRelocations
004001ec	DWORD	0h	PointerToLinenumbers
004001f0	WORD	0h	NumberOfRelocations
004001f2	WORD	0h	NumberOfLinenumbers

The Name field ❶ informs us that this header describes the .text section. All of the remaining fields are potentially useful in formatting the listing, but we will focus on the three that describe the layout of the section. The PointerToRawData field ❹ (1000h) indicates the file offset at which the content of the section can be found. Note that this value is a multiple of the file alignment value, 1000h. Sections within a PE file are arranged in increasing file offset (and virtual address) order. Since this section begins at file offset 1000h, the first 1000h bytes of the file contain file header data and padding (if there are fewer than 1000h bytes of header data, the section must be padded to a 1000h byte boundary). Therefore, even though the header bytes do not, strictly speaking, constitute a section, we can highlight the fact that they are logically related by grouping them into a memory block in the Ghidra listing.

Ghidra offers two ways to create new memory blocks, both accessed through the Memory Map window from Figure 17-2. The Add Block tool (refer to Figure 17-3) opens the dialog shown in Figure 17-5, which is used to add new memory blocks that do not overlap with any existing memory block. The dialog asks for the name of the new memory block, its start address, and its length. The block may be initialized with a constant value (zero-filled, for example), initialized with content from the current file (you indicate the file offset from which the content is taken), or left uninitialized.

The second way to create a new block is to split an existing block. To split a block in Ghidra, you must first select the block to split in the Memory Map window and then use the Split Block tool (refer to Figure 17-3) to open the dialog shown in Figure 17-6. We are just starting out, so we have only one block to split. We start by splitting the file at the beginning of the .text section to carve the program headers off of the beginning of the existing block. When we enter the length (1000h) of our block to split (the header section), Ghidra automatically computes the remaining address and length fields. All that is left is to provide a name for the new block being created at the split point. Here, we use the name contained in the first section header: .text.

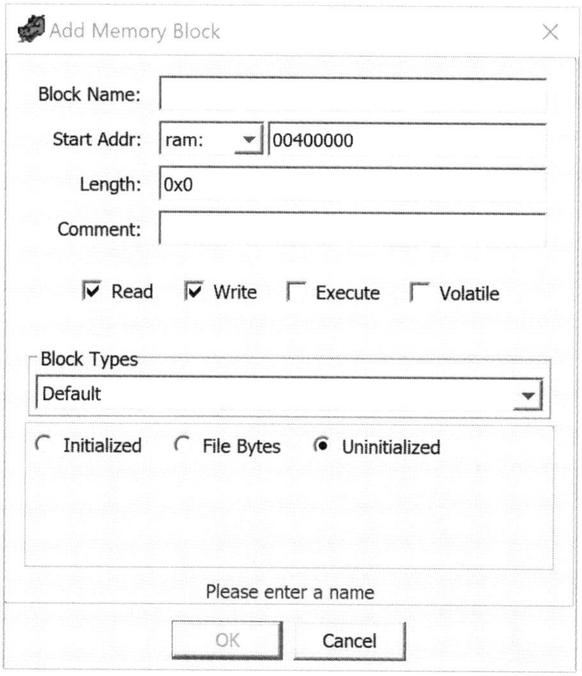

Figure 17-5: The Add Memory Block dialog

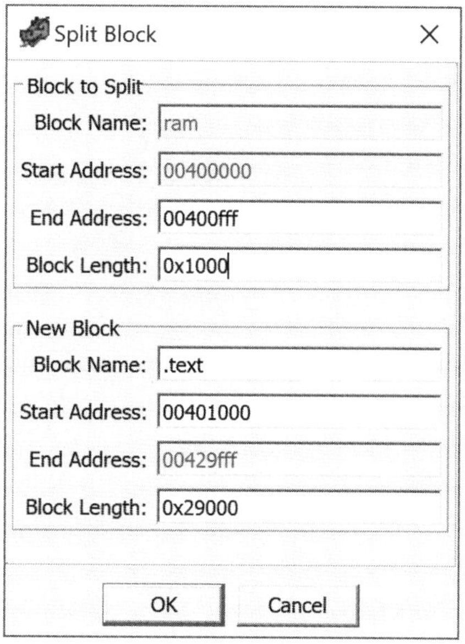

Figure 17-6: The Split Block dialog

We now have two blocks in our memory map. The first block contains the correctly sized program headers. The second block contains the correctly named, but not correctly sized, .text section. This situation is reflected in Figure 17-7, where we can see that the size of the .text section is 0x29000 bytes.

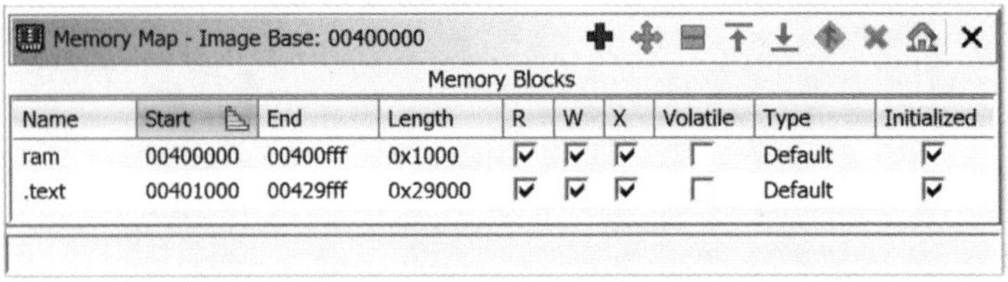

Memory Map - Image Base: 00400000									
Memory Blocks									
Name	Start	End	Length	R	W	X	Volatile	Type	Initialized
ram	00400000	00400fff	0x1000	☑	☑	☑	☐	Default	☑
.text	00401000	00429fff	0x29000	☑	☑	☑	☐	Default	☑

Figure 17-7: Memory Map window after splitting a block

Returning to the header for the .text section, we see that the Virtual Address field ❷ (1000h) is an RVA that specifies the memory offset (from ImageBase) at which the section content begins and that the SizeOfRawData field ❸ (21000h) indicates how many bytes of data are present in the file. In other words, this particular section header tells us that the .text section is created by mapping the 21000h bytes from file offsets 1000h-21FFFh to virtual addresses 401000h-421FFFh.

Because we split the original memory block at the beginning of the .text section, the newly created .text section temporarily contains all remaining sections, since its current size of 0x29000 is greater than the correct size of 0x21000. By consulting the remaining section headers and repeatedly splitting the last memory block, we make progress toward a correct final memory map for the program. However, a problem arises when we reach the following pair of section headers:

```
00400220    IMAGE_SECTION_HEADER
    00400220        BYTE[8]         ".data"     Name
    00400228        _union_226                  Misc
        00400228    DWORD           5624h       PhysicalAddress
        00400228    DWORD           5624h       VirtualSize❶
    0040022c        DWORD           24000h      VirtualAddress❷
    00400230        DWORD           4000h       SizeOfRawData❸
    00400234        DWORD           24000h      PointerToRawData
    00400238        DWORD           0h          PointerToRelocations
    0040023c        DWORD           0h          PointerToLinenumbers
    00400240        WORD            0h          NumberOfRelocations
    00400242        WORD            0h          NumberOfLinenumbers
    00400244        DWORD           C0000040h   Characteristics
00400248    IMAGE_SECTION_HEADER
    00400248        BYTE[8] ".idata" Name
    00400250        _union_226 Misc
        00400250    DWORD           75Ch        PhysicalAddress
        00400250    DWORD           75Ch        VirtualSize
```

00400254	DWORD	2A000h	VirtualAddress❹
00400258	DWORD	1000h	SizeOfRawData
0040025c	DWORD	28000h	PointerToRawData❺
00400260	DWORD	0h	PointerToRelocations
00400264	DWORD	0h	PointerToLinenumbers
00400268	WORD	0h	NumberOfRelocations
0040026a	WORD	0h	NumberOfLinenumbers
0040026c	DWORD	C0000040h	Characteristics

The .data section's virtual size ❶ is larger than its file size ❸. What does this mean and how does it impact our memory map? The compiler has concluded that the program requires 5624h bytes of runtime static data, but supplies only 4000h bytes to initialize that data. The remaining 1624h bytes of runtime data will not be initialized with content from the executable file, as they are allocated for uninitialized global variables. (It is not uncommon to see such variables allocated within a dedicated program section named .bss.)

To finalize our memory map, we must choose an appropriate size for the .data section and ensure that subsequent sections are correctly mapped as well. The .data section maps 4000h bytes of file data from file offset 24000h to memory address 424000h ❷ (ImageBase + VirtualAddress). The next section (.idata) maps 1000h bytes from file offset 28000h ❺ to memory address 42A000h ❹. If you're paying close attention, you may have noticed that the .data section appears to occupy 6000h bytes in memory (42A000h–424000h), and in fact it does. The reasoning behind this size is that the .data section requires 5624h bytes, but this is not an even multiple of 1000h, so the section will be padded up to 6000h bytes so that the .idata section properly adheres to the section alignment requirement specified in the PE header. In order to finish our memory map, we must carry out the following actions:

1. Split the .data section using a length of 4000h. The resulting .idata section will, for the moment, start at 428000h.

2. Move the .idata section to address 42A000h by clicking the Move Block icon (Figure 17-3) and setting the start address to 42A000h.

3. Split off, and, if necessary, move any remaining sections to achieve the final program layout.

4. Optionally, expand any sections whose virtual size aligns to a higher boundary than their file size. In our example, the .data section's virtual size, 5624h, aligns to 6000h, while its file size, 4000h, aligns to 4000h. Once we have created room by moving the .idata section to its proper location, we will expand the .data section from 4000h to 6000h bytes.

To expand the .data section, highlight the .data section in the Memory Map window and then select the **Expand Down** tool (refer to Figure 17-3) to modify the end address (or length) of the section. The Expand Block Down dialog is shown in Figure 17-8. (This operation will add the *.exp* extension to the section name.)

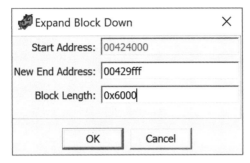

Figure 17-8: The Expand Block Down dialog

Our final memory map, obtained after the series of block moves, splits, and expansions, appears in Figure 17-9. In addition to the section name, start and end addresses, and length columns, read (R), write (W), and execute (X) permissions are shown for each section in the form of checkboxes. For PE files, these values are specified via bits in the Characteristics field of each section header. Consult the PE specification for information on parsing the Characteristics field to properly set permissions for each section.

Name	Start	End	Length	R	W	X	Volatile	Type	Initialized
ram	00400000	00400fff	0x1000	☑	☑	☑	☐	Default	☑
.text	00401000	00421fff	0x21000	☑	☑	☑	☐	Default	☑
.rdata	00422000	00423fff	0x2000	☑	☑	☑	☐	Default	☑
.data.exp	00424000	00429fff	0x6000	☑	☑	☐	☐	Default	☑
.idata	0042a000	0042afff	0x1000	☑	☑	☑	☐	Default	☑
.reloc	0042b000	0042bfff	0x1000	☑	☑	☑	☐	Default	☑

Memory Map - Image Base: 00400000 — Memory Blocks

Figure 17-9: Final Memory Map window after creating all sections

With all program sections properly mapped, we need to locate some bytes that have a high likelihood of being code. The AddressOfEntryPoint (RVA 14E0h, or virtual address 4014E0h) leads us to the program's entry point, which is known to be code. Navigating to this location, we see the following raw byte listing:

```
004014e0   ??   55h   U
004014e1   ??   8Bh
004014e2   ??   ECh
...
```

Using the context menu to disassemble (hotkey D) from address 004014e0 starts the recursive descent process (whose progress may be tracked in the lower-right corner of the Code Browser) and causes the bytes above to be reformatted as the code seen here:

```
           FUN_004014e0
004014e0   PUSH   EBP
```

```
004014e1   MOV    EBP,ESP
004014e3   PUSH   -0x1
004014e5   PUSH   DAT_004221b8
004014ea   PUSH   LAB_004065f0
004014ef   MOV    EAX,FS:[0x0]
004014f5   PUSH   EAX
```

At this point, we would hope that we had enough code to perform a comprehensive analysis of the binary. If we had fewer clues regarding the memory layout of the binary, or the separation between code and data within the file, we would need to rely on other sources of information to guide our analysis. Some potential approaches to determining correct memory layout and locating code include the following:

- Use processor reference manuals to understand where reset vectors may be found.

- Search for strings in the binary that might suggest the architecture, operating system, or compiler used to build the binary.

- Search for common code sequences such as function prologues associated with the processor for which the binary was built.

- Perform statistical analysis over portions of the binary to find regions that look statistically similar to known binaries.

- Look for repetitive data sequences that might be tables of addresses (for example, many nontrivial 32-bit integers that all share the same upper 12 bits).[4] These may be pointers and may provide clues regarding the memory layout of the binary.

In rounding out our discussion of loading raw binaries, consider that you would need to repeat each step covered in this section every time you open a binary with the same format that remains unknown to Ghidra. Along the way, you might automate some of your actions by writing scripts that perform some of the header parsing and segment creation for you. This is exactly the purpose of a Ghidra loader module! In the next section, we'll write a simple loader module to introduce Ghidra's loader module architecture, before moving on to more sophisticated loader modules that perform some common tasks associated with loading files that adhere to a structured format.

Example 1: SimpleShellcode Loader Module

At the beginning of this chapter, we tried to load a shellcode file into Ghidra and were referred to the Raw Binary loader. In Chapter 15, we used Eclipse and GhidraDev to create an analyzer module and then added it as an extension

---

4. Trivial numbers typically have very few significant digits, and include –1, 0, and other small integers. Interesting numbers tend to have many significant digits, usually on the order of an architecture's bit size, and as such are more likely to yield more relevant search results.

to Ghidra. Recall that one of the module options provided by Ghidra was to create a loader module. In this chapter, we will build a simple loader module as an extension to Ghidra to load shellcode. As in our Chapter 15 example, we will use a simplified software development process, as this is just a simple demonstration project. Our process will include the following steps:

1. Define the problem.
2. Create the Eclipse module.
3. Build the loader.
4. Add the loader to our Ghidra installation.
5. Test the loader from our Ghidra installation.

WHAT IS SHELLCODE AND WHY DO WE CARE?

To be pedantic, *shellcode* is raw machine code whose sole purpose is to spawn a user space shell process (for example, */bin/sh*), most often by communicating directly with the operating system kernel using system calls. The use of system calls eliminates any dependencies on user space libraries such as *libc*. The term *raw* in this case should not be confused with a Ghidra Raw Binary loader. Raw machine code is code that has no packaging in the form of file headers and is quite compact when compared to a compiled executable that carries out the same actions. Compact shellcode for x86-64 on Linux may be as small as 30 bytes, but a compiled version of the following C program, which also spawns a shell, is still over 6000 bytes, even after it has been stripped:

```
#include <stdlib.h>
int main(int argc, char **argv, char **envp) {
    execve("/bin/sh", NULL, NULL);
}
```

The drawback to shellcode is that it can't be run directly from the command line. Instead, it is typically injected into an existing process, and action is taken to transfer control to the shellcode. Attackers may attempt to place shellcode into a process's memory space, in conjunction with other input consumed by the process, and then trigger a control flow hijack vulnerability that allows the attacker to redirect the process's execution to their injected shellcode. Because shellcode is often embedded within other input intended for a process, shellcode may be observed in network traffic intended for a vulnerable server process, or within a file meant to be opened by a vulnerable viewing application.

Over time, the term *shellcode* has come to be used generically to describe any raw machine code incorporated into an exploit, regardless of whether the execution of that machine code spawns a user space shell on the target system.

Step 0: Take a Step Back

Before we can even start to define the problem, we need to understand (a) what Ghidra currently does with a shellcode file and (b) what we would like Ghidra to do with a shellcode file. Basically, we have to load and analyze a shellcode file as a raw binary and then use the information we discover to inform the development of our shellcode loader (and potentially an analyzer). Fortunately for us, most shellcode is not nearly as complicated as a PE file. Let's take a deep breath and dive into the world of shellcode.

Let's start by analyzing the shellcode file we tried to load at the beginning of the chapter. We loaded the file and were referred to the Raw Binary loader as our only option, as shown earlier in Figure 17-1. There was no recommendation for a language as the Raw Binary loader just "inherited" our file because none of the other loaders wanted it. Let's select a relatively common language/compiler specification, x86:LE:32:default:gcc, as shown in Figure 17-10.

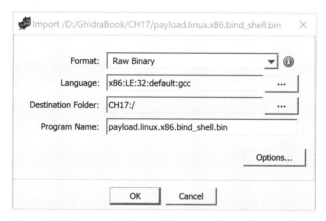

Figure 17-10: Import dialog with language/compiler specification

We click **OK** and get an Import Results Summary window that includes the content shown in Figure 17-11.

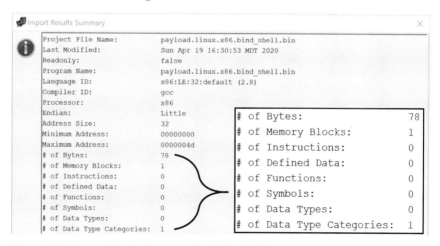

Figure 17-11: Import Results Summary for shellcode file

Based on the contents of the enlarged block in the summary, we know that there are only 78 bytes in the file in one memory/data block, and that is about all the help we get from the Raw Binary loader. If we open the file in the CodeBrowser, Ghidra will offer to auto analyze the file. Regardless of whether or not Ghidra auto analyzes the file, the Listing window in the CodeBrowser displays the content shown in Figure 17-12. Note that there is only one section in Program Trees, the Symbol Tree is empty, and the Data Type Manager has no entries in the folder specific to the file. In addition, the Decompiler window remains empty, as no functions have been identified in the file.

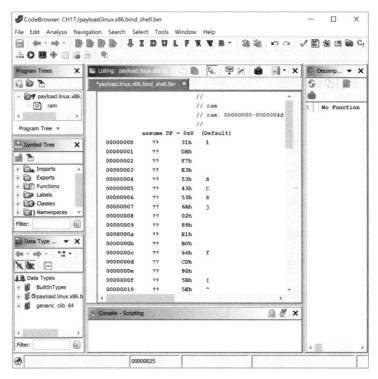

Figure 17-12: CodeBrowser window after loading (or analyzing) the shellcode file

Right-click the first address in the file and choose **Disassemble** (hotkey D) from the context menu. In the Listing window, we now see something we can work with—a list of instructions! Listing 17-2 shows the instructions after disassembly and after we have done some analysis on the file. The end-of-line comments document some of the analysis of this short file.

```
0000002b  INC   EBX
0000002c  MOV   AL,0x66        ; 0x66 is Linux sys_socketcall
0000002e  INT   0x80           ; transfers flow to kernel to
                               ; execute system call
```

```
00000030   XCHG   EAX,EBX
00000031   POP    ECX
           LAB_00000032                 XREF[1]:  00000038(j)
00000032   PUSH   0x3f          ; 0x3f is Linux sys_dup2
00000034   POP    EAX
00000035   INT    0x80          ; transfers flow to kernel to
                                ; execute system call
00000037   DEC    ECX
00000038   JNS    LAB_00000
0000003a   PUSH   0x68732f2f    ; 0x68732f2f converts to "//sh"
0000003f   PUSH   0x6e69622f    ; 0x6e69622f converts to "/bin"
00000044   MOV    EBX,ESP
00000046   PUSH   EAX
00000047   PUSH   EBX
00000048   MOV    ECX,ESP
0000004a   MOV    AL,0xb        ; 0xb is Linux sys_execve which
                                ; executes a specified program
0000004c   INT    0x80          ; transfers flow to kernel to
                                    ; execute system call
```

Listing 17-2: Disassembled 32-bit Linux shellcode

Based on our analysis, the shellcode invokes the Linux *execve* system call (at 0000004c) to launch */bin/sh* (which was pushed onto the stack at 0000003a and 000003f). The fact that these instructions have meaning to us indicates that we likely chose an appropriate language and disassembly starting point.

We now know enough about the loading process to define our loader. (We also have enough information to build a simple shellcode analyzer, but that is a task for another day.)

Step 1: Define the Problem

Our task is to design and develop a simple loader that will load shellcode into our Listing window and set the entry point, which will facilitate auto analysis. The loader needs to be added to Ghidra and be available as a Ghidra Loader option. It also needs to be able to respond to the Ghidra Importer poll in an appropriate manner: the same way as the Raw Binary loader does. This will make our new loader a second catchall loader option. As a side note, all of the examples will utilize the FlatProgramAPI. While the FlatProgramAPI is not generally used for building extensions, its use will reinforce the scripting concepts presented in Chapter 14 that you are likely to use when developing Ghidra scripts in Java.

Step 2: Create the Eclipse Module

As discussed in Chapter 15, use **GhidraDev ▸ New ▸ Ghidra Module Project** to create a module called SimpleShellcode that uses the Loader Module template. This will create a file called *SimpleShellcodeLoader.java* in the *src /main/java* folder within the SimpleShellcode module. This folder hierarchy is shown in context in Figure 17-13.

Figure 17-13: SimpleShellcode hierarchy

Step 3: Build the Loader

A partial image of the loader template *SimpleShellcodeLoader.java* is shown in Figure 17-14. The functions have been collapsed so that you can see all of the loader methods provided in the loader template. Recall that Eclipse will recommend imports if you need them as you develop your code, so you can jump right into coding and accept the recommended import statements when Eclipse detects that you need them.

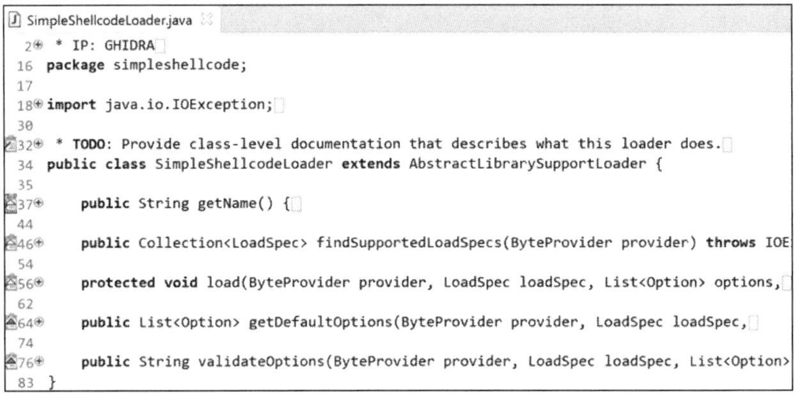

```
SimpleShellcodeLoader.java
 2    * IP: GHIDRA
16  package simpleshellcode;
17
18  import java.io.IOException;
30
32    * TODO: Provide class-level documentation that describes what this loader does.
34  public class SimpleShellcodeLoader extends AbstractLibrarySupportLoader {
35
37      public String getName() {
44
46      public Collection<LoadSpec> findSupportedLoadSpecs(ByteProvider provider) throws IOE
54
56      protected void load(ByteProvider provider, LoadSpec loadSpec, List<Option> options,
62
64      public List<Option> getDefaultOptions(ByteProvider provider, LoadSpec loadSpec,
74
76      public String validateOptions(ByteProvider provider, LoadSpec loadSpec, List<Option>
83  }
```

Figure 17-14: SimpleShellcodeLoader *template*

Within the loader template in Figure 17-14 are six *task tags* to the left of the line numbers that indicate where you should start your development. We will expand each section as we address specific tasks and include the before and after content associated with each task so you will understand how you need to modify the template. (Some content will be wrapped or reformatted for readability and comments minimized to conserve space.) Unlike the analyzer module you wrote in Chapter 15, this module does not require any obvious class member variables, so you can jump right into the tasks at hand.

Step 3-1: Document the Class

When you expand the first task tag, you see the following task description:

```
/**
 * TODO: Provide class-level documentation that describes what this
 * loader does.
 */
```

This task involves replacing the existing TODO comments with comments that describe what the loader does:

```
/*
 * This loader loads shellcode binaries into Ghidra,
 * including setting an entry point.
 */
```

Step 3-2: Name and Describe the Loader

Expanding the next task tag reveals a TODO comment and the string you need to edit. This makes it easy to identify where you should start working. The second task contains the following:

```
public String getName() {
    // TODO: Name the loader.  This name must match the name
    // of the loader in the .opinion files
    return "My loader"❶;
}
```

Change the string ❶ to something meaningful. You don't need to worry about matching the name in the *.opinion* files, as they are not applicable to loaders that will accept any files. You will see *.opinion* files when you get to the third example. Ignoring the *.opinion* file comment in the template results in the following code:

```
public String getName() {
    return "Simple Shellcode Loader";
}
```

Step 3-3: Determine If the Loader Can Load This File

The second step in the loading process we described at the beginning of the chapter involved the Importer loader poll. This task requires you to determine if your loader can load the file and provide a response to the Importer through your method's return value:

```
public Collection<LoadSpec> findSupportedLoadSpecs(ByteProvider provider)
                            throws IOException {
    List<LoadSpec> loadSpecs = new ArrayList<>();

    // TODO: Examine the bytes in 'provider' to determine if this loader
    // can load it.  If it can load it, return the appropriate load
    // specifications.
    return loadSpecs;
}
```

Most loaders do this by examining the content of the file to find a magic number or header structure. The ByteProvider input parameter is a Ghidra-provided read-only wrapper around an input file stream. We are going to simplify our task and adopt the LoadSpec list that the Raw Binary loader uses, which ignores file content and simply lists all possible LoadSpecs. We will then give our loader a lower priority than the Raw Binary loader so that if a more specific loader exists, it will automatically have a higher priority in the Ghidra Import dialog.

```
public Collection<LoadSpec> findSupportedLoadSpecs(ByteProvider provider)
                                                throws IOException {

    // The list of load specs supported by this loader
    List<LoadSpec> loadSpecs = new ArrayList<>();
    List<LanguageDescription> languageDescriptions =
        getLanguageService().getLanguageDescriptions(false);
    for (LanguageDescription languageDescription : languageDescriptions) {
        Collection<CompilerSpecDescription> compilerSpecDescriptions =
            languageDescription.getCompatibleCompilerSpecDescriptions();

        for (CompilerSpecDescription compilerSpecDescription :
                compilerSpecDescriptions) {
            LanguageCompilerSpecPair lcs =
                new LanguageCompilerSpecPair(languageDescription.getLanguageID(),
                compilerSpecDescription.getCompilerSpecID());
            loadSpecs.add(new LoadSpec(this, 0, lcs, false));
        }
    }
    return loadSpecs;
}
```

Every loader has an associated tier and tier priority. Ghidra defines four tiers of loaders, ranging from highly specialized (tier 0) to format agnostic (tier 3). When multiple loaders are willing to accept a file, Ghidra sorts the loader list displayed to the user in increasing tier order. Loaders within the same tier are further sorted in increasing tier priority order (that is, tier priority 10 is listed before tier priority 20).

For example, the PE loader and the Raw Binary loader are both willing to load PE files, but the PE loader is a better choice to load this format (its tier is 1), so it will appear before the Raw Binary loader (tier 3, tier priority 100) in the list. We set the Simple Shellcode Loader's tier to 3 (LoaderTier. UNTARGETED_LOADER) and priority to 101, so it will be given the lowest priority by the Importer when populating the Import window with candidate loaders. To accomplish this, add the following two methods to your loader:

```
@Override
public LoaderTier getTier() {
    return LoaderTier.UNTARGETED_LOADER;
}
@Override
public int getTierPriority() {
    return 101;
}
```

Step 3-4: Load the Bytes

The following method shown before and after we edit the content does the heavy lifting of loading content from the file being imported into our Ghidra project (in this case, it loads the shellcode):

```
protected void load(ByteProvider provider, LoadSpec loadSpec,
            List<Option> options, Program program, TaskMonitor monitor,
            MessageLog log) throws CancelledException, IOException {

    // TODO: Load the bytes from 'provider' into the 'program'.
}
```

```
protected void load(ByteProvider provider, LoadSpec loadSpec,
            List<Option> options, Program program, TaskMonitor monitor,
            MessageLog log) throws CancelledException, IOException {
❶ FlatProgramAPI flatAPI = new FlatProgramAPI(program);
    try {
        monitor.setMessage("Simple Shellcode: Starting loading");
        // create the memory block we're going to load the shellcode into
        Address start_addr = flatAPI.toAddr(0x0);
❷      MemoryBlock block = flatAPI.createMemoryBlock("SHELLCODE",
        start_addr, provider.readBytes(0, provider.length()), false);
        // make this memory block read/execute but not writeable
❸      block.setRead(true);
        block.setWrite(false);
        block.setExecute(true);
        // set the entry point for the shellcode to the start address
❹      flatAPI.addEntryPoint(start_addr);
        monitor.setMessage( "Simple Shellcode: Completed loading" );
    } catch (Exception e) {
        e.printStackTrace();
        throw new IOException("Failed to load shellcode");
    }
}
```

Note that, unlike the scripts in Chapters 14 and 15, which inherit from GhidraScript (and ultimately FlatProgramAPI), our loader class has no direct access to the Flat API. Therefore, to simplify our access to some commonly used API classes, we instantiate our own FlatProgramAPI object ❶. Next, we create a MemoryBlock named SHELLCODE at address zero ❷ and populate it with the entire contents of the input file. We take the time to set some reasonable permissions ❸ on the new memory region before adding an entry point ❹ that informs Ghidra where it should begin its disassembly.

Adding an entry point is a very important step for a loader. The presence of entry points is the primary means by which Ghidra locates addresses known to contain code (as opposed to data). As it parses the input file, the loader is ideally suited to discover any entry points and identify them to Ghidra.

Step 3-5: Register Custom Loader Options

Some loaders offer users the option to modify various parameters associated with the loading process. You may override the `getDefaultOptions` function to provide Ghidra with a list of custom options available for your loader:

```
public List<Option> getDefaultOptions(ByteProvider provider, LoadSpec
        loadSpec,DomainObject domainObject, boolean isLoadIntoProgram) {
    List<Option> list = super.getDefaultOptions(provider, loadSpec,

                    domainObject, isLoadIntoProgram);
    // TODO: If this loader has custom options, add them to 'list'
    list.add(new Option("Option name goes here",
                    Default option value goes here));
    return list;
}
```

Since this loader is just for demonstration purposes, we will not add any options. Options for a loader might include setting an offset into the file at which to start reading, and setting the base address at which to load the binary. To view the options associated with any loader, click the **Options . . .** button on the bottom right of the Import dialog (refer to Figure 17-1).

```
public List<Option> getDefaultOptions(ByteProvider provider, LoadSpec
        loadSpec,DomainObject domainObject, boolean isLoadIntoProgram) {
    // no options
    List<Option> list = new ArrayList<Option>();
    return list;
}
```

Step 3-6: Validate Options

The next task is to validate the options:

```
public String validateOptions(ByteProvider provider, LoadSpec loadSpec,
                    List<Option> options, Program program) {

    // TODO: If this loader has custom options, validate them here.
    // Not all options require validation.
    return super.validateOptions(provider, loadSpec, options, program);
}
```

As we do not have any options, we just return null:

```
public String validateOptions(ByteProvider provider, LoadSpec loadSpec,
                    List<Option> options, Program program) {

    // No options, so no need to validate
    return null;
}
```

Step 4: Add the Loader to Our Ghidra Installation

After confirming that this module functions correctly, export the Ghidra module extension from Eclipse and then install the extension in Ghidra, just as we did with the SimpleROPAnalyzer module in Chapter 15. Select **GhidraDev ▸ Export ▸ Ghidra Module Extension**, choosing the **SimpleShellcode** module, and follow the same click-through process that you did in Chapter 15.

To import the extension into Ghidra, choose **File ▸ Install Extensions** from the Ghidra Project window. Add the new loader to the list and select it. Once you restart Ghidra, the new loader should be available as an option, but you should test to be sure.

Step 5: Test the Loader Within Ghidra

Our simplified test plan is just to demonstrate functionality. SimpleShellcode passed an acceptance test consisting of the following criteria:

1. (Pass) SimpleShellcode appears as a loader option with lower priority than Raw Binary.
2. (Pass) SimpleShellcode loads a file and sets the entry point.

Test case 1 passed, as shown in Figure 17-15. A second confirmation is shown in Figure 17-16, where the PE file analyzed earlier in the chapter is being loaded. In both cases, we see that the Simple Shellcode Loader option has the lowest priority in the Format list.

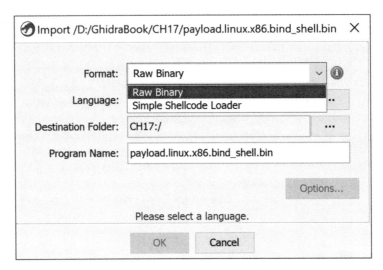

Figure 17-15: Import window with our new loader listed as an option

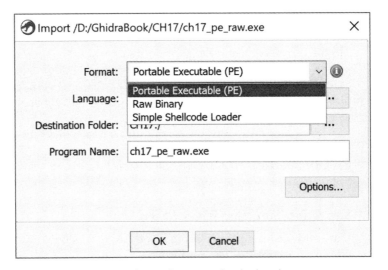

Figure 17-16: Import window with our new loader listed as an option
for a PE file

Choose the language specification based on the information available
about the binary and how it was obtained. Let's assume that the shellcode
was captured from packets headed for an x86 box. In that case, selecting
x86:LE:32:default:gcc for our language/compiler specification is probably
a good starting point.

After we select a language and click OK for the file shown in Figure 17-15, the binary will be imported into our Ghidra project. We can then open the program in the CodeBrowser, and Ghidra will provide us an option to analyze the file. If we accept the analysis, we will see the following listing:

```
undefined FUN_00000000()
    undefined  AL:1 <RETURN>
    undefined4 Stack[-0x10]:4 local_10  XREF[1]: 00000022(W)
  FUN_00000000                                   XREF[1]: Entry Point(*)❶
00000000 31 db          XOR     EBX,EBX
00000002 f7 e3          MUL     EBX
00000004 53             PUSH    EBX
00000005 43             INC     EBX
00000006 53             PUSH    EBX
00000007 6a 02          PUSH    0x2
00000009 89 e1          MOV     ECX,ESP
0000000b b0 66          MOV     AL,0x66
0000000d cd 80          INT     0x80
0000000f 5b             POP     EBX
00000010 5e             POP     ESI
00000011 52             PUSH    EDX
00000012 68 02 00 11 5c PUSH    0x5c110002
```

An entry point ❶ is identified, so Ghidra is able to provide us with a disassembly to begin our analysis.

SimpleShellcodeLoader was a trivial example, as shellcode is generally found embedded within some other data. For demonstration purposes, we will use our loader module as a base to create a loader module that extracts shellcode from C source files and loads the shellcode for analysis. This may, for example, allow us to build shellcode signatures that Ghidra can recognize in other binaries. We will not go into great depth for each step, as we are just augmenting the capabilities of our existing shellcode loader.

Example 2: Simple Shellcode Source Loader

Since modules provide a way to organize code, and the SimpleShellcode module you created has everything required to create a loader, you don't need to create a new module. Simply choose **File ▶ New ▶ File** from the Eclipse menu and add a new file (*SimpleShellcodeSourceLoader.java*) to your SimpleShellcode *src/main/java* folder. By doing this, all of your new loaders will be included in your new Ghidra extension.

To make life simple, paste the contents of your existing *SimpleShellcodeLoader.java* into this new file and update the comments about what the loader does. The following steps highlight the parts of the existing loader that you need to change to make the new loader work as expected. For the most part, you will be adding onto the existing code.

Update 1: Modify the Response to the Importer Poll

The simple source loader is going to make its decision based strictly on the file extension. If the file does not end in *.c*, the loader will return an empty loadSpecs list. If the file does end with *.c*, it will return the same loadSpecs list that it did for the previous loader. To make this work, you need to add the following test to the findSupportLoadSpecs method:

```
// The list of load specs supported by this loader
List<LoadSpec> loadSpecs = new ArrayList<>();
// Activate loader if the filename ends in a .c extension
if (!provider.getName().endsWith(".c")) {
   return loadSpecs;
}
```

We've also decided that our loader deserves a higher priority than the Raw Binary loader because ours identifies a particular type of file to accept and is better suited for that type of file. This is done by returning a higher priority (lower value) from our getTierPriority method:

```
public int getTierPriority() {
   // priority of this loader
   return 99;
}
```

Update 2: Find the Shellcode in the Source Code

Recall that shellcode is just raw machine code that does something useful for us. The individual bytes in the shellcode will lie in the range 0..255, and many of these values fall outside the range of ASCII printable characters. Therefore, when shellcode is embedded into a source file, much of it must be represented using hex escape sequences such as \xFF. Strings of this sort are rather unique, and we can build a regular expression to help our loader identify them. The following instance variable declaration describes the regular expression that all of the functions in our loader may use to find shellcode bytes with the selected C file:

```
private String pattern = "\\\\x[0-9a-fA-F]{1,2}";
```

Within the load method, the loader parses the file looking for patterns that match the regular expression to help calculate the amount of memory needed when loading the file into Ghidra. As shellcode is frequently not contiguous, the loader should parse the entire file looking for shellcode regions to load from the file.

```
// set up the regex matcher
CharSequence provider_char_seq =
      new String(provider.readBytes(0, provider.length())❶, "UTF-8");
Pattern p = Pattern.compile(pattern);
Matcher m = p.matcher(provider_char_seq)❷;
```

```
// Determine how many matches (shellcode bytes) were found so that we can
// correctly size the memory region, then reset the matcher
int match_count = 0;
while (m.find()) {
❸ match_count++;
}
m.reset();
```

After loading the entire contents of the input file ❶, we count all of the matches ❸ against our regular expression ❷.

Update 3: Convert Shellcode to Byte Values

The load() method next needs to convert the hex escape sequences into byte values and put them in a byte array:

```
byte[] shellcode = new byte[match_count];
// convert the hex representation of bytes in the source code to actual
// byte values in the binary we're creating in Ghidra
int ii = 0;
while (m.find()) {
    // strip out the \x
    String hex_digits = m.group().replaceAll("[^0-9a-fA-F]+", "")❶;
    // parse what's left into an integer and cast it to a byte, then
    // set current byte in byte array to that value
    shellcode[ii++]❷ = (byte)Integer.parseInt(hex_digits, 16)❸;
}
```

The hex digits are extracted from each matching string ❶ and converted into byte values ❸ that get appended to our shellcode array ❷.

Update 4: Load Converted Byte Array

Finally, because the shellcode is in a byte array, the load() method needs to copy it from the byte array into the program's memory. This is the actual loading step and the last required step for your loader to accomplish the goal:

```
// create the memory block and populate it with the shellcode
Address start_addr = flatAPI.toAddr(0x0);
MemoryBlock block =
      flatAPI.createMemoryBlock("SHELLCODE", start_addr, shellcode, false);
```

Results

To test our new loader, we create a C source file that contains the following escaped representation of x86 shellcode:

```
unsigned char buf[] =
    "\x31\xdb\xf7\xe3\x53\x43\x53\x6a\x02\x89\xe1\xb0\x66\xcd\x80"
    "\x5b\x5e\x52\x68\x02\x00\x11\x5c\x6a\x10\x51\x50\x89\xe1\x6a"
    "\x66\x58\xcd\x80\x89\x41\x04\xb3\x04\xb0\x66\xcd\x80\x43\xb0"
```

```
"\x66\xcd\x80\x93\x59\x6a\x3f\x58\xcd\x80\x49\x79\xf8\x68\x2f"
"\x2f\x73\x68\x68\x2f\x62\x69\x6e\x89\xe3\x50\x53\x89\xe1\xb0"
"\x0b\xcd\x80";
```

Because our source file's name ends in *.c*, our loader appears in the list as the top selection, with higher priority than the Raw Binary and Simple Shellcode loaders, as shown in Figure 17-17.

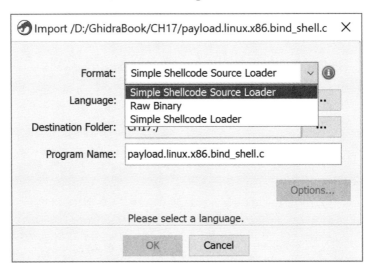

Figure 17-17: Import dialog for shellcode source file

Selecting this loader, using the same default compiler/language specification as the previous example (x86:LE:32:default:gcc), and letting Ghidra auto analyze the file yields the following function in the disassembly listing:

```
**************************************************************
*                        FUNCTION                          *
**************************************************************
undefined  FUN_00000000()
   undefined AL:1 <RETURN>
   undefined4 Stack[-0x10]:4 local_10
 FUN_00000000                      XREF[1]: Entry Point(*)
00000000  XOR    EBX,EBX
00000002  MUL    EBX
00000004  PUSH   EBX
00000005  INC    EBX
00000006  PUSH   EBX
```

Scrolling down through the listing leads us to the familiar content (see Listing 17-2) shown here (with comments added for clarity):

```
        LAB_00000032
00000032  PUSH   0x3f
00000034  POP    EAX
```

```
00000035  INT   0x80
00000037  DEC   ECX
00000038  JNS   LAB_00000
0000003a  PUSH  0x68732f2f         ; 0x68732f2f converts to "//sh"
0000003f  PUSH  0x6e69622f         ; 0x6e69622f converts to "/bin"
```

Most reverse engineering efforts focus on binaries. In this case, we have stepped outside that box and used Ghidra to load shellcode for analysis as well as to extract shellcode from C source files. Our goal was to demonstrate the flexibility and simplicity of creating loaders for Ghidra. Now, let's step back into that box and create a loader for a structured file format.

Assume that our target shellcode is contained within an ELF binary and that, for the sake of this example, Ghidra does not recognize ELF binaries. Further, none of us have ever heard of an ELF binary. Let the adventure begin.

Example 3: Simple ELF Shellcode Loader

Congratulations! You are now the resident RE expert on shellcode, and colleagues are reporting what they suspect is shellcode contained in binaries and are being referred by Ghidra to the Raw Binary loader. Since this does not appear to be a one-off problem, and you think there is a good chance you will see more binaries with similar characteristics, you decide to build a loader that will handle this new type of file. As discussed in Chapter 13, you can use tools internal or external to Ghidra to capture information about the file. If you once again turn to the command line, file provides helpful information to start building your loader:

```
$ file elf_shellcode_min
  elf_shellcode_min: ELF 32-bit LSB executable, Intel 80386, version 1 (SYSV),
  statically linked, corrupted section header size
$
```

The file command provides information about a format you have never heard of before, ELF. Your first step is to do some research to see if you can locate any information about this type of binary. Your friend Google will happily point you to several references about the ELF format, which you can use to locate the information you need to build your loader. Anything that provides enough accurate information to solve the problem works.[5]

As this is a bigger challenge than the previous two loader examples, we will break this into sections associated with the individual files within your Eclipse SimpleShellcode module that you will need to create/modify/delete to complete your new *SimpleELFShellcodeLoader*. We will start off with some simple housekeeping.

---

5. While man pages usually provide a definitive resource, in this case Wikipedia also provides the needed information. Use the resources at hand to answer the questions at hand.

Housekeeping

The first step is to create a *SimpleELFShellcodeLoader.java* file within the SimpleShellcode module in Eclipse. As you don't want to start from nothing, you should use Save As with *SimpleShellcodeLoader.java* to create this new file. Once you have done this, there are a few minor modifications to make to the new file before you can start focusing on the new challenge:

- Change the name of the class to `SimpleELFShellcodeLoader`.
- Modify the getTier method return value from `UNTARGETED_LOADER` to `GENERIC_TARGET_LOADER`.
- Delete the getTierPriority method.
- Modify the getName method to return `"Simple ELF Shellcode Loader"`.

Once you have completed the housekeeping tasks, let's apply the information you learned from your research about the new header format.

ELF Header Format

While researching this new format, you discover that the ELF format contains three types of headers: the file header (or ELF header), the program header(s), and the section header(s). You can start by focusing on the ELF header. Associated with each field in the ELF header is an offset as well as other information about the field. Since you need to access only a few of these fields and you won't be modifying the offsets, declare the following constants as instance variables within your loader class to help your loader correctly parse this new header format:

```
private final byte[] ELF_MAGIC            = {0x7f, 0x45, 0x4c, 0x46};
private final long EH_MAGIC_OFFSET         = 0x00;
private final long EH_MAGIC_LEN            = 4;

private final long EH_CLASS_OFFSET         = 0x04;
private final byte EH_CLASS_32BIT          = 0x01;

private final long EH_DATA_OFFSET          = 0x05;
private final byte EH_DATA_LITTLE_ENDIAN   = 0x01;

private final long EH_ETYPE_OFFSET         = 0x10;
private final long EH_ETYPE_LEN            = 0x02;
private final short EH_ETYPE_EXEC          = 0x02;

private final long EH_EMACHINE_OFFSET      = 0x12;
private final long EH_EMACHINE_LEN         = 0x02;
private final short EH_EMACHINE_X86        = 0x03;

private final long EH_EFLAGS_OFFSET        = 0x24;
private final long EN_EFLAGS_LEN           = 4;

private final long EH_EEHSIZE_OFFSET       = 0x28;
private final long EH_PHENTSIZE_OFFSET     = 0x2A;
private final long EH_PHNUM_OFFSET         = 0x2C;
```

With a description of the ELF header in hand, the next step is to determine how to respond to the Importer poll to ensure that the new ELF loader is capable of loading only files that adhere to the ELF format. In the previous two examples, the shellcode loaders did not look at file contents to determine if they could load a file. This simplified coding these examples significantly. Now things are a bit more complicated. Fortunately, the ELF documentation provides important clues to help determine the appropriate loader specifications.

Find Supported Load Specifications

The loader can't load anything that isn't in the right format and can reject any file by returning an empty loadSpecs list. Within the findSupportedLoad Specs() method, immediately eliminate all binaries that don't have the expected magic number by using the following code:

```
byte[] magic = provider.readBytes(EH_MAGIC_OFFSET, EH_MAGIC_LEN);
if (!Arrays.equals(magic, ELF_MAGIC)) {
    // the binary is not an ELF
    return loadSpecs;
}
```

Once the undesirables have been eliminated, the loader can check the bit width and endianness to see if the architecture is reasonable for an ELF binary. For this demonstration, let's further limit the types of binaries the loader will accept to 32-bit little-endian:

```
byte ei_class = provider.readByte(EH_CLASS_OFFSET);
byte ei_data = provider.readByte(EH_DATA_OFFSET);
if ((ei_class != EH_CLASS_32BIT) || (ei_data != EH_DATA_LITTLE_ENDIAN)) {
    // not an ELF we want to accept
    return loadSpecs;
}
```

To round out the verification process, the following code checks if this is an ELF executable file (as opposed to a shared library) for the x86 architecture:

```
byte[] etyp = provider.readBytes(EH_ETYPE_OFFSET, EH_ETYPE_LEN);
short e_type =
    ByteBuffer.wrap(etyp).order(ByteOrder.LITTLE_ENDIAN).getShort();
byte[] emach = provider.readBytes(EH_EMACHINE_OFFSET, EH_EMACHINE_LEN);
short e_machine =
    ByteBuffer.wrap(emach).order(ByteOrder.LITTLE_ENDIAN).getShort();
if ((e_type != EH_ETYPE_EXEC) || (e_machine != EH_EMACHINE_X86)) {
    // not an ELF we want to accept
    return loadSpecs;
}
```

Now that you have limited your file types, you can query the opinion service for matching language and compiler specifications. Conceptually, you query the opinion services with values extracted from the file you are loading (for example, the ELF header e_machine field), and in response you receive a list of language/compiler specifications that your loader is willing to accept. (The "behind the scenes" actions that take place when you query the opinion service are described in more detail in the following sections.)

```
byte[] eflag = provider.readBytes(EH_EFLAGS_OFFSET, EN_EFLAGS_LEN);
int e_flags = ByteBuffer.wrap(eflag).order(ByteOrder.LITTLE_ENDIAN).getInt();
List<QueryResult> results =
    QueryOpinionService.query(getName(), Short.toString(e_machine),
                              Integer.toString(e_flags));
```

Let's assume that the opinion service is likely to yield more results than you want to handle with this loader. You can pare the list further by excluding results based on the attributes specified in the associated language/compiler specifications. The following code filters out a compiler and a processor variant:

```
for (QueryResult result : results) {
   CompilerSpecID cspec = result.pair.getCompilerSpec().getCompilerSpecID();
   if (cspec.toString().equals("borlanddelphi"❶)) {
      // ignore anything created by Delphi
      continue;
   }
   String variant = result.pair.getLanguageDescription().getVariant();
   if (variant.equals("System Management Mode"❷)) {
      // ignore anything where the variant is "System Management Mode"
      continue;
   }
   // valid load spec, so add it to the list
❸ loadSpecs.add(new LoadSpec(this, 0, result));
}
return loadSpecs;
```

The above examples (which you are free to include in your loader) specifically exclude the *Delphi compiler* ❶ and *x86 system management mode* ❷. You can exclude others if you wish. All of the results you have not excluded need to be added to your loadSpecs list ❸.

Load File Content into Ghidra

The load() method of your simplified loader assumes the file consists of a minimal ELF header and a short program header, followed by the shellcode in a text section. You need to determine the total length of the header to allocate the correct amount of space for it. The following code determines the required size by using the EH_EEHSIZE_OFFSET, EH_PHENTSIZE_OFFSET, and EH_PHNUM_OFFSET fields from the ELF header:

```
// Get some values from the header needed for the load process
//
// How big is the ELF header?
```

```
byte[] ehsz = provider.readBytes(EH_EEHSIZE_OFFSET, 2);
e_ehsize = ByteBuffer.wrap(ehsz).order(ByteOrder.LITTLE_ENDIAN).getShort();

// How big is a single program header?
byte[] phsz = provider.readBytes(EH_PHENTSIZE_OFFSET, 2);
e_phentsize =
      ByteBuffer.wrap(phsz).order(ByteOrder.LITTLE_ENDIAN).getShort();

// How many program headers are there?
byte[] phnum = provider.readBytes(EH_PHNUM_OFFSET, 2);
e_phnum = ByteBuffer.wrap(phunm).order(ByteOrder.LITTLE_ENDIAN).getShort();

// What is the total header size for our simplified ELF format
// (This includes the ELF Header plus program headers.)
long hdr_size = e_ehsize + e_phentsize * e_phnum;
```

Now that you know the size, create and populate the memory blocks for the ELF header section and the text section as follows:

```
// Create the memory block for the ELF header
long LOAD_BASE = 0x10000000;
Address hdr_start_adr = flatAPI.toAddr(LOAD_BASE);
MemoryBlock hdr_block =
      flatAPI.createMemoryBlock(".elf_header", hdr_start_adr,
                                provider.readBytes(0, hdr_size), false);
// Make this memory block read-only
hdr_block.setRead(true);
hdr_block.setWrite(false);
hdr_block.setExecute(false);

// Create the memory block for the text from the simplified ELF binary
Address txt_start_adr = flatAPI.toAddr(LOAD_BASE + hdr_size);
MemoryBlock txt_block =
      flatAPI.createMemoryBlock(".text", txt_start_adr,
              provider.readBytes(hdr_size, provider.length() - hdr_size),
              false);

// Make this memory block read & execute
txt_block.setRead(true);
txt_block.setWrite(false);
txt_block.setExecute(true);
```

Format Data Bytes and Add an Entry Point

A few more steps, and you will be done. Loaders often apply data types and create cross-references for information derived from file headers. It is also the loader's job to identify any entry points in the binary. Creating a list of entry points at load time provides the disassembler with a list of locations it should consider code. Our loader follows these practices:

```
// Add structure to the ELF HEADER
❶ flatAPI.createData(hdr_start_adr, new ElfDataType());
```

```
   // Add label and entry point at start of shellcode
❷ flatAPI.createLabel(txt_start_adr, "shellcode", true);
❸ flatAPI.addEntryPoint(txt_start_adr);

   // Add a cross reference from the ELF header to the entrypoint
   Data d = flatAPI.getDataAt(hdr_start_adr).getComponent(0).getComponent(9);
❹ flatAPI.createMemoryReference(d, txt_start_adr, RefType.DATA);
```

First, the Ghidra ELF header data type is applied at the start of the ELF headers ❶.[6] Second, a label ❷ and an entry point ❸ are created for the shellcode. Finally, we create a cross-reference between the entry point field in the ELF header and the start of the shellcode ❹.

Congratulations! You are done writing the Java code for your loader, but we need to address a couple of issues to ensure that you understand all of the dependencies between your new loader and some important related files in order for your loader to operate as expected.

This example leverages an existing processor architecture (x86), and some work was done behind the scenes that helped this loader work correctly. Recall that the Importer polled the loaders and magically produced acceptable language/compiler specifications. The following two files provided information critical to the loader. The first of these files is the x86 language definition file *x86.ldefs*, is a component of the x86 processor module.

Language Definition Files

Every processer has an associated language definition file. This is an XML-formatted file that includes all of the information required to generate language/compiler specifications for the processor. Language definitions from the *x86.ldefs* file that meet the requirements for a 32-bit ELF binary are shown in the following listing:

```
<language processor="x86"
          endian="little"
          size="32"
          variant="default"
          version="2.8"
          slafile="x86.sla"
          processorspec="x86.pspec"
          manualindexfile="../manuals/x86.idx"
          id="x86:LE:32:default">
   <description>Intel/AMD 32-bit x86</description>
   <compiler name="Visual Studio" spec="x86win.cspec" id="windows"/>
   <compiler name="gcc" spec="x86gcc.cspec" id="gcc"/>
   <compiler name="Borland C++" spec="x86borland.cspec" id="borlandcpp"/>
❶ <compiler name="Delphi" spec="x86delphi.cspec" id="borlanddelphi"/>
</language>
```

---

6. If this were truly a new format, you would probably have to create this structure within Ghidra based on your research. For this example, use the one in the Ghidra Data Type Manager window.

```
<language processor="x86"
          endian="little"
          size="32"
  ❷ variant="System Management Mode"
          version="2.8"
          slafile="x86.sla"
          processorspec="x86-16.pspec"
          manualindexfile="../manuals/x86.idx"
          id="x86:LE:32:System Management Mode">
  <description>Intel/AMD 32-bit x86 System Management Mode</description>
  <compiler name="default" spec="x86-16.cspec" id="default"/>
</language>
```

This file is used to populate the recommended language/compiler specs presented as import options. In this case, there are five recommended specifications (each starting with the `compiler` tag), which will be returned based on information associated with the ELF binary, but our loader eliminates two from consideration based on the compiler ❶ and the variant ❷.

Opinion Files

Another type of support file is the *.opinion* file. This is an XML-formatted file that contains constraints associated with your loader. To be recognized by the opinion query service, each loader must have an entry in an opinion file. The following listing shows a suitable opinion file entry for the loader you just built:

```
<opinions>
  <constraint loader="Simple ELF Shellcode Loader" compilerSpecID="gcc">
    <constraint❶ primary❷="3" processor="x86"  endian="little" size="32" />
    <constraint primary="62" processor="x86"  endian="little" size="64" />
  </constraint>
</opinions>
```

Everything in the entry should be familiar, except possibly the `primary` field ❷. This field is the primary key for a search that identifies the machine as defined in the ELF header. Within the ELF header, the value 0x03 in the e_machine field means x86, and 0x3E in the e_machine field means amd64. A `<constraint>` tag ❶ defines an association between a primary key ("3"/x86) and the remaining attributes of the `<constraint>` tag. This information is used by the query service to locate the appropriate entries in the language definition files.

Our only remaining task is to place our opinion data in an appropriate place where Ghidra will find it. The only opinion files that ship with Ghidra reside in the *data/languages* subdirectory of a Ghidra processor module. Although you could insert your opinion data into an existing opinion file, it's a good idea to avoid modifying any processor opinion files, as your modifications will need to be reapplied anytime you upgrade your Ghidra installation.

Instead, create a new opinion file containing our opinion data. You can name the file anything you wish, but *SimpleShellcode.opinion* seems reasonable. Our Eclipse Loader Module template contains its own *data* subdirectory. Save your opinion file in this location so it will be associated with your loader module. Ghidra will locate it when looking for opinion files, and any upgrades to the Ghidra installation should not affect your module.

Now that you understand what is going on behind the scenes, it is time to test your loader and see if it behaves as anticipated.

Results

To demonstrate the success of the new simplified ELF loader (one program header and no sections), let's walk through the loading process and observe how the loader performs at each step of the process.

From the Ghidra Project window, import a file. The importer will poll all of Ghidra's loaders, including yours, to see which are willing to load this file. Recall that your loader is expecting a file that fits the following profile:

- ELF magic number at the start of the file
- 32-bit little endian
- ELF executable for the x86 architecture
- Cannot have been compiled by Delphi
- Cannot have the variant "System Management Mode"

If you load a file that fits that profile, you should see an Import dialog similar to the one in Figure 17-18 that displays a prioritized list of the loaders willing to process this file.

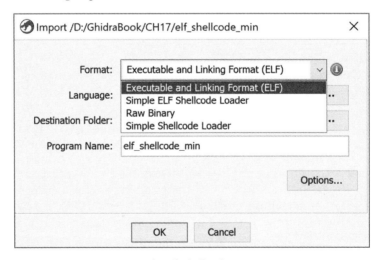

Figure 17-18: Import options for elf_shellcode_min

The loader with the highest priority is Ghidra's ELF loader. Let's compare the language/compiler specifications that it will accept (top of Figure 17-19) with the ones that your new loader will accept at the bottom of the figure.

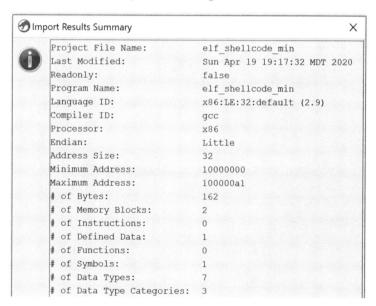

Figure 17-19: Acceptable language/compiler specifications for two different loaders

The Delphi compiler and the System Management Mode variant are accepted by the stock ELF loader but not by your loader, as they have been filtered out. When you select your loader for the file *elf_shellcode_min*, you should see a summary similar to Figure 17-20.

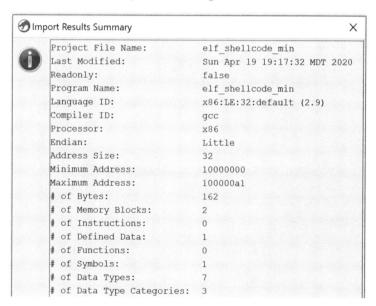

```
Import Results Summary                                           X

    Project File Name:        elf_shellcode_min
    Last Modified:            Sun Apr 19 19:17:32 MDT 2020
    Readonly:                 false
    Program Name:             elf_shellcode_min
    Language ID:              x86:LE:32:default (2.9)
    Compiler ID:              gcc
    Processor:                x86
    Endian:                   Little
    Address Size:             32
    Minimum Address:          10000000
    Maximum Address:          100000a1
    # of Bytes:               162
    # of Memory Blocks:       2
    # of Instructions:        0
    # of Defined Data:        1
    # of Functions:           0
    # of Symbols:             1
    # of Data Types:          7
    # of Data Type Categories: 3
```

Figure 17-20: Import Results Summary window for the new ELF Shellcode Loader

If you open the file in the CodeBrowser and allow Ghidra to auto ana-lyze the file, you should see the following ELF header definition at the top of the file:

```
10000000 7f              db     7Fh        e_ident_magic_num
10000001 45 4c 46        ds     "ELF"      e_ident_magic_str
10000004 01              db     1h         e_ident_class
10000005 01              db     1h         e_ident_data
10000006 01              db     1h         e_ident_version
10000007 00 00 00 00 00  db[9]             e_ident_pad
         00 00 00 00
10000010 02 00           dw     2h         e_type
10000012 03 00           dw     3h         e_machine
10000014 01 00 00 00     ddw    1h         e_version
10000018 54 00 00 10     ddw    shellcode❶ e_entry
1000001c 34 00 00 00     ddw    34h        e_phoff
10000020 00 00 00 00     ddw    0h         e_shoff
10000024 00 00 00 00     ddw    0h         e_flags
10000028 34 00           dw     34h        e_ehsize
```

Within the listing, the shellcode label ❶ is clearly associated with the entry point. Double-clicking the shellcode label takes you to a function, named shellcode, that contains the same shellcode contents we've seen in our previous two examples, including the following:

```
1000008c  JNS    LAB_10000086
1000008e  PUSH   "//sh"
10000093  PUSH   "/bin"
10000098  MOV    EBX,ESP
1000009a  PUSH   EAX
```

Now that you have confirmed that your new loader works, you can add it as an extension to your Ghidra installation and share it with your colleagues who have been anxiously awaiting this functionality.

Summary

In this chapter, we focused on the challenges associated with dealing with unrecognized binary files. We walked through examples of the loading and analysis processes that we can use within Ghidra to help us with these chal-lenging reverse engineering scenarios. Finally, we extended our module creation capabilities to the world of Ghidra loaders.

While the examples that we built were trivial, they provided the founda-tion and introduced all of the components required to write more complex loader modules in Ghidra. In the next chapter, we round out our discussion of Ghidra modules with an introduction to processor modules—the compo-nents most responsible for the overall formatting of a disassembled binary.

18

GHIDRA PROCESSORS

Processor modules, the most complex of Ghidra's module types, are responsible for all of the disassembly operations that take place within Ghidra. Beyond the obvious conversion of machine language opcodes into their assembly language equivalents, processor modules also support the creation of functions, cross-references, and stack frames.

While the number of processors supported by Ghidra is impressive and increases with every major release, development of a new Ghidra processor module is required in some circumstances. The obvious case for developing a processor module is reverse engineering a binary for which no processor module exists in Ghidra. Among other things, such a binary might represent a firmware image for an embedded microcontroller or an executable image pulled from handheld or Internet of Things (IoT) devices. A less-obvious use for a processor module is to disassemble the instructions of a custom virtual machine embedded within an obfuscated x86 executable. In such cases, the existing Ghidra x86 processor module would help you understand only the virtual machine itself, not the virtual machine's underlying byte code.

Should you undertake this arduous task, we want to be sure you have a strong foothold to help support you in this endeavor. Each of our previous module examples (analyzer and loader) required modifying a single Java file. If you created these modules within the Eclipse GhidraDev environment, you were given a module template and task tags within each template to help you complete your task. Processor modules are more complex, and relationships between different files must be maintained for the processor module to work correctly. While we will not build a processor module from scratch in this chapter, we will provide you with a solid foundation to help you understand Ghidra processor modules and demonstrate creating and modifying components within those modules.

WHO IS LIKELY TO AUGMENT GHIDRA?

Based on a thoroughly unscientific study, we strongly suspect that the following categories exist:

Category 1 A small percentage of people who use Ghidra will modify or write a script to customize or automate some functionality related to Ghidra.

Category 2 Of the people in Category 1, a small percentage will choose to modify or develop a plugin to customize some functionality related to Ghidra.

Category 3 Of the people in Category 2, an even smaller percentage will choose to modify or write an analyzer to extend Ghidra's analysis capabilities.

Category 4 Of the people in Category 3, a small percentage will choose to modify or write a loader for a new file format.

Category 5 A *very* small percentage of the people in Category 4 will choose to modify or write a Ghidra processor module because the number of instruction sets that require decoding is much smaller than the number of file formats that make use of those instruction sets. Thus, the demand for new processor modules is comparatively low.

As you get deeper into the list of categories, the nature of the associated tasks tends to become more and more specialized. However, just because you don't currently envision yourself authoring a Ghidra processor module doesn't mean there isn't some utility in learning how they are built. Processor modules form the foundation on which Ghidra's disassembly, assembly, and decompilation capabilities are built, and having some insight into their inner workings just might elevate you to Ghidra wizard status in the eyes of your colleagues.

Understanding Ghidra Processor Modules

Creating a processor module for a real-world architecture is a highly specialized, time-consuming effort and is beyond the scope of this book. However, some fundamental understanding of how processors and their associated instruction sets are represented in Ghidra will help you identify where to look so that you have the right resources at your fingertips when you need information about a Ghidra processor module.

Eclipse Processor Modules

We will start in somewhat familiar territory. When you use Eclipse ▸ GhidraDev to create a processor module, the resulting folder structure is basically the same as every other module type, but a processor module does not provide a Java source file, complete with comments, task tags, and a TODO list, in the *src/main/java* folder, as seen in Figure 18-1.

Figure 18-1: Processor module contents

Instead, the *data* folder (expanded in the figure) contains a lot more than the brief *README.txt* provided in the data folder for other module types. Let's briefly meet the nine files contained in the *data* folder with a focus on their file extensions. (The *skel* prefix lets us know we are working with a skeleton.)

skel.cspec   This is an XML-formatted, initially overwhelming compiler specification file.

skel.ldefs   This is an XML-formatted language definition file. The skeleton has a commented-out template for defining a language..

skel.opinion   This is an XML-formatted importer opinion file. The skeleton has a commented-out template for defining a language/compiler specification.

skel.pspec   This is an XML-formatted processor specification file.

skel.sinc   This is generally a SLEIGH file for language instructions.[1]

skel.slaspec   This is a SLEIGH specification file.

buildLanguage.xml   This XML file describes the build process for the files in the *data/languages* directory.

README.txt   This file is the same in all of the modules, but within this module it finally makes sense as it focuses on the contents of the *data/* directory.

sleighArgs.txt   This file holds SLEIGH compiler options.

The *.ldefs* and *.opinion* files were used in Chapter 17 when building your ELF shellcode loader. Other file extensions will be seen in context as you work through examples. You will learn how to work with these files to modify a processor module, but first let's discuss a new term specific to processor modules—SLEIGH.

SLEIGH

SLEIGH is a language specific to Ghidra that describes microprocessor instruction sets to support the Ghidra disassembly and decompilation processes.[2] Files within the *languages* directory (see Figure 18-1) are either written in SLEIGH or presented in XML format, so you will definitely need to learn a little about SLEIGH to create or modify a processor module.

The specification of how instructions are encoded and how they are interpreted by a processor is contained in a *.slaspec* file (somewhat analogous to the role of a *.c* file). When a processor family has a number of distinct variants, each variant may have its own *.slaspec* file, while common behaviors across variants may be factored out into separate *.sinc* files (similar to the

---

1. For large instruction sets, such as the x86 instruction set, the *.sinc* file may be broken into multiple *.sinc* files. In this case, some of the files may be used as header files with definitions and include statements.

2. Detailed information about the SLEIGH language can be found in your Ghidra installation in *docs/languages/html/sleigh.html*.

role of *.h* files), which may be included in many *.slaspec* files. Ghidra's ARM processor is an excellent example of this, with over a dozen *.slaspec* files, each referencing one or more of five *.sinc* files. These files constitute the SLEIGH source code for a processor module, and it is the SLEIGH compiler's job to compile them into a *.sla* file suitable for use by Ghidra.

Rather than taking a deep dive into SLEIGH from a theoretical perspective, we will introduce various components of the SLEIGH language as we encounter and require them in our examples, but first let's look at the sort of information that a SLEIGH file contains about instructions.

To see additional information associated with an instruction in a CodeBrowser listing, right-click and select **Instruction Info** from the context menu. The displayed information is derived from SLEIGH file specifications for the selected instruction. Figure 18-2 shows the Instruction Info window for an x86-64 PUSH instruction.

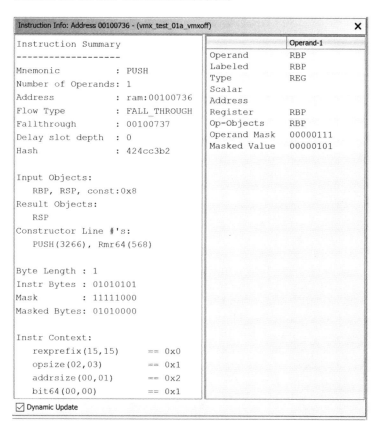

Figure 18-2: Instruction Info window for x86-64 PUSH instruction

The Instruction Info window combines information about the PUSH instruction from the SLEIGH file with details about the specific use of PUSH at address 00100736. Later in the chapter, we will work with instruction definitions within a SLEIGH file and will revisit this window in the context of the instructions we are working with.

Processor Manuals

The documentation provided by the manufacturer of a processor is an important resource for obtaining information about the instruction set. While these copyrighted materials cannot be included within your Ghidra distribution, you can easily incorporate them through a right-click context menu option in the Listing window. If you right-click any instruction and select Processor Manual, you are likely to see a message similar to that shown in Figure 18-3, informing you that the manual for the current processor is not available in the expected location.

Figure 18-3: Missing Processor Manual dialog

Here, Ghidra provides you the information needed to resolve the missing manual situation. In this particular example, you first need to locate the x86 manual online and then save it with the specified name and location.

NOTE *There are many processor manuals associated with the x86. Find the correct manual online by searching for the identifier provided at the end of the manual information: 325383-060US.*

Once you have a manual properly installed, selecting Processor Manual will display the manual. Since processor manuals tend to be large (this particular manual for the x86 processor weighs in at almost 2,200 pages), Ghidra helpfully includes the capability to process index files that map an instruction to a specific page in a manual. Fortunately, the index for this specific x86 manual has already been created for you.

Processor manuals should be placed in the *Ghidra/Processors/<proc> /data/manuals* directory appropriate for your processor. Index files should reside in the same directory as their associated manual. The format of an index file is relatively straightforward. The first few lines of Ghidra's *x86.idx* file are shown in the following listing:

```
@Intel64_IA32_SoftwareDevelopersManual.pdf [Intel 64 and IA-32 Architectures
    Software Developer's Manual Volume 2 (2A, 2B, 2C & 2D): Instruction Set
    Reference, A-Z, Sep 2016 (325383-060US)]
AAA, 120
AAD, 122
BLENDPS, 123
AAM, 124
```

The first line in the file (which has been wrapped across three lines in this listing) pairs the manual's local filename with descriptive text displayed to the user when the manual is not present on the system. The format of the line is as follows:

```
@FilenameInGhidraManualDirectory [Description of manual file]
```

Each additional line is of the form *INSTRUCTION, page*. The instruction must be uppercase, and the page number is counted from the first page of the *.pdf* file. (This is not necessarily the page number that appears on any given page of the document.)

Several manuals can be referenced in a single *.idx* file. Simply use additional @ directives to delineate each additional manual's instruction map. More information about processor manual index files may be found in *docs/languages/manual_index.txt* in your Ghidra installation directory.

Once you have a manual saved and indexed, selecting Processor Manual for any instruction in the Listing window should take you to its corresponding page within the manual. If the manual does not appear, you may need to choose Edit ▸ Tools Options ▸ Processor Manuals to configure an appropriate viewer application for your manual. A sample viewer setting to open the manual using Firefox is shown in Figure 18-4.

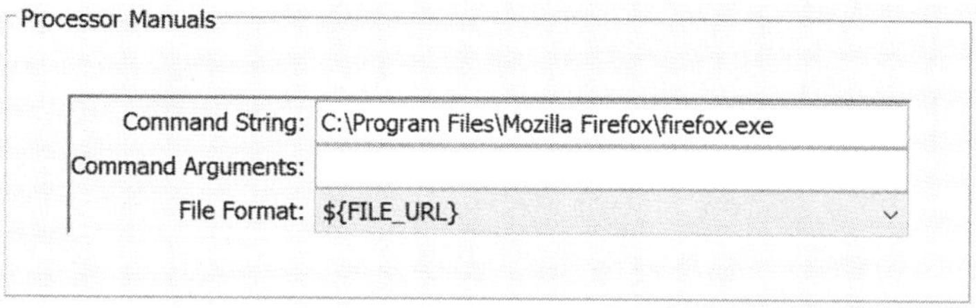

Figure 18-4: Processor Manuals tool options

Now that you have some basic processor module terminology under your belt, it's time to dive into the internals of a processor module implementation.

Modifying a Ghidra Processor Module

Building a processor module from scratch is a significant undertaking. Rather than jumping in headfirst, we are going to start, as we did in in previous examples, by modifying an existing module. Since we want to demonstrate concepts related to real-world problems, we will start by identifying a hypothetical issue regarding Ghidra's x86 processor module. We will walk through some examples that address the issue and then use what we have learned to create a big picture view of how all of the various components work together to form a complete Ghidra processor module.

Problem Statement

A quick search of the *Ghidra/Processors* directory in your local installation shows that the x86 processor module includes many instructions but appears to be missing a hypothetical virtual machine extension (VMX) management instruction for the IA32 and IA64 architectures.[3] This instruction (which we just invented for this example) is called VMXPLODE. Its behavior is similar to the VMXOFF instruction, which Ghidra does support. While the existing VMXOFF instruction causes the processor to leave VMX operation, VMXPLODE leaves with a flourish! We will walk you through adding this very important instruction to the existing Ghidra x86 processor module in order

---

3. Section 30-1 of the following describes the existing VMCS-maintenance instructions: *https://www.intel.com/content/dam/www/public/us/en/documents/manuals/64-ia-32-architectures -software-developer-vol-3c-part-3-manual.pdf.*

to introduce some of the concepts associated with building and modifying a processor module.

Example 1: Adding an Instruction to a Processor Module

Our first goal is to locate the files we need to modify to support the VMXPLODE instruction. The *Ghidra/Processors* directory contains subdirectories for all processors supported by Ghidra, one of which is the x86. You can open the x86 processor module (or any other processor module) directly in Eclipse using File ▸ Open Projects from File System or Archive and providing the path to the processor folder (*Ghidra/Processors/x86*). This will link your Eclipse instance to Ghidra's x86 processor module, meaning that changes you make within Eclipse will be directly reflected in your Ghidra processor module.

A partially expanded version of the x86 module in Eclipse, which exactly reflects the associated Ghidra directory structure, is shown in Figure 18-5. The processor manual you downloaded is present along with the x86 index file.

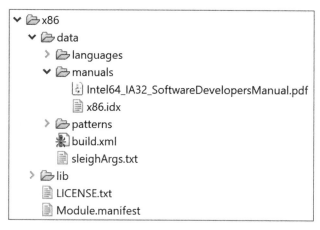

Figure 18-5: x86 processor module in Eclipse Package Explorer

The *x86* folder contains a *data* folder, like the one you saw in the processor module we created using Eclipse ▸ GhidraDev. Within this folder is the *languages* folder, which contains over 40 files, including 19 *.sinc* files that define language instructions. Because the x86 instruction set is rather large, the instruction set is broken up into files grouping similar instructions. Instead of creating a new *.sinc* file for our instruction, we'll add it to an existing x86 *.sinc* file. If we were adding a new group of instructions to Ghidra (for example, the x86 SGX instruction set), we might create a new *.sinc* file to group them all together. (In fact, the SGX instructions are grouped in a common file called *sgx.sinc*. That accounts for one of the many *.sinc* files!)

By searching the *.sinc* files, we find that *ia.sinc* contains the definitions of the existing VMX instruction set. We'll use the definition of VMXOFF in *ia.sinc* as a model to define VMXPLODE. VMXOFF is referenced in two different sections within *ia.sinc*. The first section is the definitions for the Intel IA hardware-assisted virtualization instructions:

```
# MFL: definitions for Intel IA hardware assisted virtualization instructions
define pcodeop invept;   # Invalidate Translations Derived from extended page
                         # tables (EPT); opcode 66 0f 38 80
# -----CONTENT OMITTED HERE-----
define pcodeop vmread;   # Read field from virtual-machine control structure;
                         # opcode 0f 78
define pcodeop vmwrite;  # Write field to virtual-machine control structure;
                         # opcode 0f 79
define pcodeop vmxoff;   # Leave VMX operation; opcode 0f 01 c4
define pcodeop vmxon;    # Enter VMX operation; opcode f3 0f C7 /6
```

Each entry in the definitions section defines a pcodeop, which is a new microcode operation for the x86 architecture.

The definition includes a name and, in this case, a comment that includes a description and an opcode. We will need to populate the comment for our new command. A quick, alt-reality, web search (with a side of testing) confirms that the opcode 0f 01 c5 has long been reserved for VMXPLODE. We now have the information necessary to add our new instruction to the file. The following shows our new definition in context:

```
define pcodeop vmxoff;   # Leave VMX operation; opcode 0f 01 c4
define pcodeop vmxplode; # Explode (Fake) VMX operation; opcode 0f 01 c5
define pcodeop vmxon;    # Enter VMX operation; opcode f3 0f C7 /6
```

The second location we encounter VMXOFF within *ia.sinc* (and where we will insert our new instruction) is the opcode definition section. (We omitted part of this content for clarity and wrapped some instruction definition lines for readability.) While we won't completely dissect the 8,000+ lines of code in the *ia.sinc* file, there are several interesting points to make regarding the following listing:

```
# Intel hardware assisted virtualization opcodes
# -----CONTENT OMITTED HERE-----
# TODO: invokes a VM function specified in EAX❶
:VMFUNC EAX     is vexMode=0 & byte=0x0f; byte=0x01; byte=0xd4 & EAX     { vmfunc(EAX); }
# TODO: this launches the VM managed by the current VMCS. How is the
#       VMCS expressed for the emulator?  For Ghidra analysis?
:VMLAUNCH       is vexMode=0 & byte=0x0f; byte=0x01; byte=0xc2          { vmlaunch(); }
# TODO: this resumes the VM managed by the current VMCS. How is the
#       VMCS expressed for the emulator?  For Ghidra analysis?
:VMRESUME       is vexMode=0 & byte=0x0f; byte=0x01; byte=0xc3          { vmresume(); }
# -----CONTENT OMITTED HERE-----
:VMWRITE Reg32, rm32 is vexMode=0 & opsize=1 & byte=0x0f; byte=0x79;❷
        rm32 & Reg32 ... & check_Reg32_dest ... { vmwrite(rm32,Reg32); build check_Reg32_dest; }
@ifdef IA64❸
:VMWRITE Reg64, rm64 is vexMode=0 & opsize=2 & byte=0x0f;  byte=0x79;
        rm64 & Reg64 ...    { vmwrite(rm64,Reg64); }
@endif
:VMXOFF         is vexMode=0 & byte=0x0f; byte=0x01; byte=0xc4          { vmxoff(); }❹
```

```
:VMXPLODE        is vexMode=0 & byte=0x0f; byte=0x01; byte=0xc5        { vmxplode(); }❺
# -----CONTENT OMITTED HERE-----
#END of changes for VMX opcodes
```

TODO comments ❶, found in many Ghidra files, identify tasks that have yet to be done. Searching for TODO tasks in Ghidra files is a great way to identify opportunities to contribute to this open source project.

Next, we see the VMWRITE instruction for 32-bit ❷ and 64-bit architectures. The 64-bit instruction is surrounded by a test ❸ to ensure it is included in only the 64-bit *.sla* file. While 32-bit instructions are valid in a 64-bit world (for example, EAX is the 32 least-significant bits of RAX), the converse is not true. The conditional statement ensures that instructions that operate on 64-bit registers are included for only 64-bit builds.

The VMXOFF instruction ❹ doesn't directly involve registers, so there is no need to distinguish between 32- and 64-bit versions of the instruction. The constructor for our new instruction, VMXPLODE ❺, complete with its new opcode, is very similar to the constructor for VMXOFF. Let's break this into the components that make up the line:

:VMXPLODE

This is the instruction being defined and is displayed in the disassembly listing.

is vexMode=0 & byte=0x0f; byte=0x01; byte=0xc5

These are the bit patterns associated with the instruction and provide a constraint for the instruction. The & represents a logical AND operation. The semicolons serve a dual purpose of concatenation and logical AND. This part says, "If we are not in VEX mode and the opcode is these 3 bytes in this order, then this constraint is met." [4]

{ vmxplode(); }

Curly brackets enclose the semantic actions section of an instruction. The SLEIGH compiler translates these actions into an internal Ghidra form known as p-code (discussed later in this chapter). Defining an instruction requires understanding SLEIGH operators and syntax. This portion of the constructor, where the real work associated with most instructions is done, can quickly become a complex sequence of multiple statements separated by semicolons. In this case, since we have defined VMXPLODE as a new p-code operation (define pcodeop vmxplode;), we can invoke the instruction here. In future examples, we will add additional SLEIGH semantic actions to this section.

The largest x86 *.sinc* file is *ia.sinc* because a lot of instructions are defined within this file (including our new VMXPLODE instruction) and a significant amount of content to define the attributes of the x86 processor

---

4. The VEX coding scheme is described in section 2.3 of *https://www.intel.com/content/dam /www/public/us/en/documents/manuals/64-ia-32-architectures-software-developer-instruction-set -reference-manual-325383.pdf*.

(for example, endianness, registers, contexts, tokens, variables, and so on). Much of this x86-specific content within *ia.sinc* is not replicated in the other *.sinc* files in this directory, since all the *.sinc* files are, in turn, included in a SLEIGH specification (*.slaspec*) file.

The two *.slaspec* files for x86, *x86.slaspec* and *x86-64.slaspec*, each contain include statements for the required *.sinc* files. (Note that you could forego the use of *.sinc* files and directly include the content in the *.slaspec* file, which might make sense for a processor with a small instruction set.) The contents of *x86-64.slaspec* are shown in the following listing:

```
  @define IA64 "IA64"         # Only in x86-64.slaspec
❶ @include "ia.sinc"
  @include "avx.sinc"
  @include "avx_manual.sinc"
  @include "avx2.sinc"
  @include "avx2_manual.sinc"
  @include "rdrand.sinc"       # Only in x86-64.slaspec
  @include "rdseed.sinc"       # Only in x86-64.slaspec
  @include "sgx.sinc"          # Only in x86-64.slaspec
  @include "adx.sinc"
  @include "clwb.sinc"
  @include "pclmulqdq.sinc"
  @include "mpx.sinc"
  @include "lzcnt.sinc"
  @include "bmi1.sinc"
  @include "bmi2.sinc"
  @include "sha.sinc"
  @include "smx.sinc"
  @include "cet.sinc"
  @include "fma.sinc"          # Only in x86-64.slaspec
```

We have added EOL comments to denote the content that is unique to the *x86-64.slaspec* file. (The *x86.slaspec* file is a subset of the *x86-64.slaspec* file.) Among the included files is *ia.sinc* ❶, in which we defined VMXPLODE, so we don't need to add anything. If you create a new *.sinc* file, you need to add an include statement in both *x86.slaspec* and *x86-64.slaspec* in order for the instruction to be recognized in both 32- and 64-bit binaries.

To test if Ghidra can recognize the new instruction when it is used in a binary, we construct a test file. The file will first verify that the VMXOFF instruction is still recognized and then verify that VMXPLODE has been added successfully. The C source file for testing VMXOFF contains the following:

```
#include <stdio.h>

// The following function declares an assembly block and tells the
// compiler that it should execute the code without moving or changing it.

void do_vmx(int v) {
    asm volatile (
        "vmxon %0;"        // Enable hypervisor operation
        "vmxoff;"          // Disable hypervisor operation
        "nop;"             // Tiny nop slide to accommodate examples
```

```
        "nop;"
        "nop;"
        "nop;"
        "nop;"
        "nop;"
        "nop;"
        "vmxoff;"          // Disable hypervisor operation
        :
        :"m"(v)            // Holds the input variable
        :
    );
}
int main() {
    int x;
    printf("Enter an int: ");
    scanf("%d", &x);
    printf("After input, x=%d\n", x);
    do_vmx(x);
    printf("After do_vmx, x=%d\n", x);
    return 0;
}
```

When we load the compiled binary into Ghidra, we see the following body of the function do_vmx in the Listing window:

```
  0010071a 55              PUSH    RBP
  0010071b 48 89 e5        MOV     RBP,RSP
  0010071e 89 7d fc        MOV     dword ptr [RBP + local_c],EDI
  00100721 f3 0f c7        VMXON   qword ptr [RBP + local_c]
           75 fc
❶ 00100726 0f 01 c4        VMXOFF
  00100729 90              NOP
  0010072a 90              NOP
  0010072b 90              NOP
  0010072c 90              NOP
  0010072d 90              NOP
  0010072e 90              NOP
  0010072f 90              NOP
❷ 00100730 0f 01 c4        VMXOFF
  00100733 90              NOP
  00100734 5d              POP RBP
  00100735 c3              RET
```

The bytes displayed for the opcode (0f 01 c4) in the two calls to VMXOFF ❶❷ match the opcode we observed in *ia.sinc* for this command. The following listing from the Decompiler window is consistent with what we know about the source code and the associated disassembly:

```
void do_vmx(undefined4 param_1)
{
    undefined4 unaff_EBP;

    vmxon(CONCAT44(unaff_EBP,param_1));
```

```
    vmxoff();
    vmxoff();
    return;
}
```

To test that Ghidra detects the VMXPLODE instruction, we replace the first occurrence of VMXOFF in the do_vmx test function with VMXPLODE. However, the VMXPLODE instruction is missing not only from Ghidra's processor definition, but also from our compiler's knowledge base. In order for the assembler to accept our code, we hand-assembled the instruction using a data declaration instead of using the instruction mnemonic directly so that the assembler can process the new instruction:

```
//"vmxoff;"                   // replace this line
".byte 0x0f, 0x01, 0xc5;"     // with this hand assembled one
```

When you load your updated binary into Ghidra, you see the following in the Listing window:

```
  0010071a 55 PUSH RBP
  0010071b 48 89 e5 MOV RBP,RSP
  0010071e 89 7d fc MOV dword ptr [RBP + local_c],EDI
  00100721 f3 0f c7 VMXON qword ptr [RBP + local_c]
           75 fc
❶ 00100726 0f 01 c5 VMXPLODE
  00100729 90 NOP
  0010072a 90 NOP
  0010072b 90 NOP
  0010072c 90 NOP
  0010072d 90 NOP
  0010072e 90 NOP
  0010072f 90 NOP
  00100730 0f 01 c4 VMXOFF
  00100733 90 NOP
  00100734 5d POP RBP
  00100735 c3 RET
```

Your new instruction ❶ appears along with the opcode (0f 01 c5) that we have assigned to it. The Decompiler window also shows the new instruction:

```
void do_vmx(undefined4 param_1)
{
    undefined4 unaff_EBP;

    vmxon(CONCAT44(unaff_EBP,param_1));
    vmxplode();
    vmxoff();
    return;
}
```

So, what work has Ghidra undertaken in the background to add our new instruction to its x86 processor instruction set? When Ghidra is restarted (as it needs to be for these changes to take effect), it detects that the underlying *.sinc* file changed and generates a new *.sla* file when one is needed.

In this example, when we were loading the original compiled 64-bit binary file, Ghidra detected the change in the *ia.sinc* file and displayed the window shown in Figure 18-6 while it was recompiling the *ia.sinc* file. (Note that it recompiles only when needed, not automatically on restart.) Because we loaded a 64-bit file, only *x86-64.sla* was updated, and not *x86.sla*. Later, when we loaded the updated file, complete with the VMXPLODE command, Ghidra did *not* recompile, as no changes were made to any underlying SLEIGH source files since the previous load.

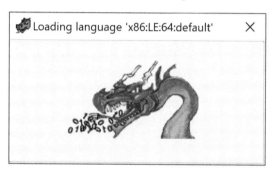

Figure 18-6: Ghidra window displayed while recompiling a language file

Here is a summary of the steps to add a new instruction to a processor module:

1. Locate the *languages* directory for the target processor (for example, *Ghidra/Processor/<<targetprocessor>>/data/languages*).

2. Add the instruction to a selected processor *.sinc* file, or create a new *.sinc* file (for example, *Ghidra/Processor/<targetprocessor>/data/languages /<targetprocessor>.sinc*).

3. If you created a new *.sinc* file, make sure it is included in the *.slaspec* file (for example, *Ghidra/Processor/<targetprocessor>/data/languages /<targetprocessor>.slaspec*).

Example 2: Modifying an Instruction in a Processor Module

We have now successfully added an instruction to the Ghidra x86 processor module, but we have not yet accomplished our goal of making VMXPLODE leave with a *flourish*. Currently, it just exits without any excitement whatsoever. While it is challenging to make an assembly language instruction do anything that would qualify as a flourish, we can make our instruction *dab* when it exits.[5] In this example, we will step through three options for making VMXPLODE dab for us. For our first option, we will exit after setting EAX to a hardcoded value: 0xDAB.

Option 1: Set EAX to a Constant Value

Having the VMXPLODE instruction set the value of EAX to 0xDAB prior to exiting requires only a minor modification to one instruction in the same file (*ia.sinc*) that we worked with in Example 1. The following listing shows the VMXOFF and VMXPLODE instructions as we left them after Example 1:

```
:VMXOFF      is vexMode=0 & byte=0x0f; byte=0x01; byte=0xc4    { vmxoff(); }
:VMXPLODE    is vexMode=0 & byte=0x0f; byte=0x01; byte=0xc5    { vmxplode(); }
```

Within the instruction contents, add the assignment to EAX immediately before the vmxplode action, as shown in the following listing:

```
:VMXOFF      is vexMode=0 & byte=0x0f; byte=0x01; byte=0xc4    { vmxoff(); }
:VMXPLODE    is vexMode=0 & byte=0x0f; byte=0x01; byte=0xc5    { EAX=0xDAB; vmxplode(); }
```

When we reopen Ghidra and load our test file, Ghidra once again displays the window shown in Figure 18-6 to let us know that it has detected a change in an associated language file and is regenerating *x86-64.sla*. The Listing window doesn't show any changes after Ghidra auto analyzes the file, but the difference is apparent in the Decompiler window:

```
undefined4 do_vmx(undefined4 param_1)
{
    undefined4 unaff_EBP;

    vmxon(CONCAT44(unaff_EBP,param_1));
    vmxplode();
    vmxoff();
    return 0xdab;
}
```

In the Decompiler window, the return statement now returns the contents of EAX (0xDAB). This is interesting because we know this is a void function and doesn't have a return value. The Listing window entry for the new instruction doesn't show that the VMXPLODE command has changed in any way:

```
00100726 0f 01 c5      VMXPLODE
```

---

5. A *dab* (or *dabbing*) was a celebratory dance move used by international sports figures starting in 2012. It was chosen for this example as it is one of the few dance moves that can be spelled correctly using only hexadecimal digits.

An important distinction between decompilers and disassemblers is that decompilers understand and incorporate the full semantic behavior of each instruction as part of their analysis, while disassemblers are focused largely on the proper syntactic representation of each instruction. In this example, VMXPLODE takes no operands and is correctly displayed by the disassembler, providing no visual cue that EAX has changed. When reading a disassembly, it is entirely your responsibility to understand the semantic behavior of each instruction. This example also demonstrates the value of the decompiler, which, understanding the full semantics of VMXPLODE, is able to recognize that EAX is changed as a side effect of the instruction. The decompiler also recognizes that EAX is not used for the remainder of the function and assumes that the value is intended to be returned to the calling function.

Ghidra offers you the opportunity to dive a little deeper into how instructions work and allows you to detect and test subtle differences in instructions like this one. First, let's look at the some of the instruction information associated with VMXPLODE, shown in Figure 18-7.

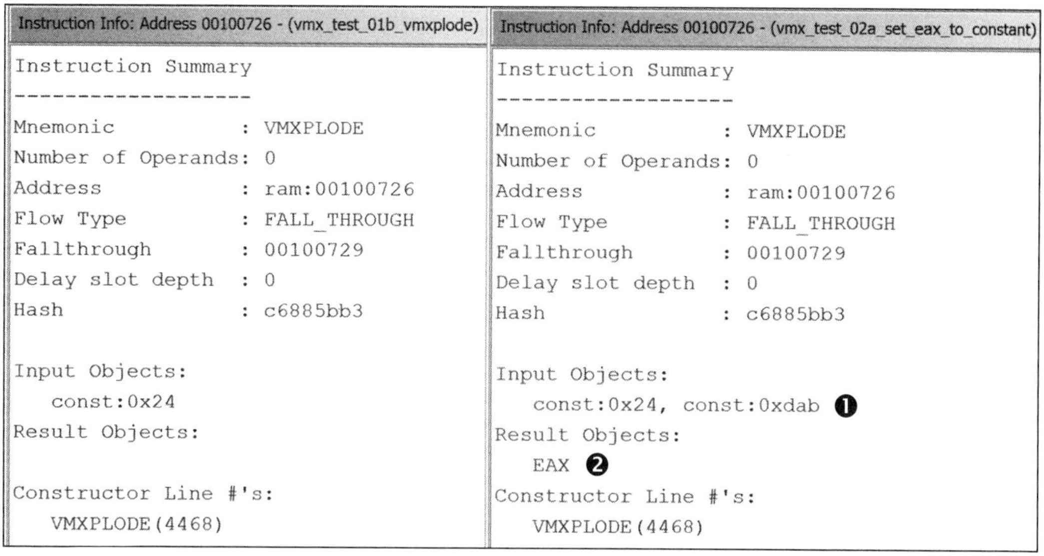

```
Instruction Info: Address 00100726 - (vmx_test_01b_vmxplode)   Instruction Info: Address 00100726 - (vmx_test_02a_set_eax_to_constant)

Instruction Summary                          Instruction Summary
-------------------                          -------------------
Mnemonic           : VMXPLODE                Mnemonic           : VMXPLODE
Number of Operands: 0                        Number of Operands: 0
Address            : ram:00100726            Address            : ram:00100726
Flow Type          : FALL_THROUGH            Flow Type          : FALL_THROUGH
Fallthrough        : 00100729                Fallthrough        : 00100729
Delay slot depth   : 0                       Delay slot depth   : 0
Hash               : c6885bb3                Hash               : c6885bb3

Input Objects:                               Input Objects:
   const:0x24                                   const:0x24, const:0xdab ❶
Result Objects:                              Result Objects:
                                                EAX ❷
Constructor Line #'s:                        Constructor Line #'s:
   VMXPLODE(4468)                               VMXPLODE(4468)
```

Figure 18-7: VMXPLODE instruction info

On the left is our original VMXPLODE instruction, and on the right is the modified version, with 0xdab listed in the Input Objects ❶ section and EAX under Result Objects ❷. We can obtain additional insight about any instruction by looking at underlying information, called p-code, that we haven't looked at previously.[6] The p-code associated with an instruction can be very informative about what exactly an instruction does.

---

6. P-code appears without the hyphen (pcode) in Ghidra Help, and with the hyphen in most other locations including the p-code documentation. If you are having trouble finding information about p-code within Ghidra, try searching for *pcode* without the hyphen.

P-CODE: HOW LOW CAN YOU GO?

The Ghidra documentation describes p-code as a "register transfer language designed for reverse engineering applications." A *register transfer language (RTL)* is an architecture-independent, assembly-language-like language often used as an intermediate representation (IR, or IL for intermediate language) between a high-level language such as C and a target assembly language such as x86 or ARM. Compilers are often composed of a language-specific frontend that translates source code into an IR, and an architecture-specific backend that translates IR into a specific assembly language. This modularity allows a C frontend to be combined with an x86 backend to create a C compiler that produces x86 code and offers the flexibility to replace the backend with an ARM module to instantly have a C compiler that generates ARM code. Swap out the C frontend for a FORTRAN frontend and now you have a FORTRAN compiler for ARM.

Working at the IR level allows us to build tools that operate on our IR rather than maintaining a set of C-specific or ARM-specific tools that are useless to us with other languages or architectures. For example, once we have an optimizer that operates on IR, we can reuse that optimizer with any of our frontend/backend combinations without rewriting the optimizer in each case.

A reverse engineering toolchain, not unsurprisingly, runs in the opposite direction of a traditional software build chain. An RE frontend needs to translate machine code to IR (a process often called *lifting*), while an RE backend translates IR to a high-level language such as C. A pure disassembler doesn't qualify as a frontend under this definition as it gets us only from machine code to assembly language. Ghidra's decompiler is an IR-to-C backend. Ghidra processor modules are machine-code-to-IR frontends.

When you build or modify a Ghidra processor module in SLEIGH, one of the first things you do is let the SLEIGH compiler know about any new p-code operations that you need to introduce in order to describe the semantic actions of any new or modified instructions. For example, the operation definition

```
define pcodeop vmxplode
```

that we added to our *ia.sinc* file instructs the SLEIGH compiler that vmxplode is a valid semantic action available for describing the behavior of any instruction in our architecture. One of the most difficult challenges that you will face is describing each new or changed instruction using a sequence of syntactically correct SLEIGH statements that correctly describe the actions associated with the instruction. All of this information is captured in the *.slaspec* and included *.sinc* files that make up your processor. If you do a good enough job, Ghidra will hand you the decompiler backend for free.

To view the p-code within the Listing window, open the **Browser Field Formatter** and choose the **Instruction/Data** tab, right-click the **P-code** bar, and enable the field. Once the Listing window displays the p-code associated with each instruction, we can compare the previous two listings to observe any differences. With p-code enabled, our first implementation of VMXPLODE appears as follows with the p-code displayed after each instruction:

```
0010071b 48 89 e5       MOV      RBP,RSP
                                  RBP = COPY RSP
                                  $U620:8 = INT_ADD RBP, -4:8
                                  $U1fd0:4 = COPY EDI
                                  STORE ram($U620), $U1fd0
00100721 f3 0f c7 75 fc VMXON    qword ptr [RBP + local_c]

                                  $U620:8 = INT_ADD RBP, -4:8
                                  $Ua50:8 = LOAD ram($U620)
                                  CALLOTHER "vmxon", $Ua50
00100726 0f 01 c5       VMXPLODE
                                  CALLOTHER "vmxplode"
00100729 90             NOP
```

And here is the modified VMXPLODE:

```
00100726 0f 01 c5       VMXPLODE
                              ❶ EAX = COPY 0xdab:4
                                  CALLOTHER "vmxplode"
```

The associated p-code now shows the constant value (0xdab) being moved into EAX ❶.

Option 2: Set a Register (Determined by an Operand) to a Constant Value

Instruction sets are typically made up of a mix of instructions that operate on zero or more operands. As the number and types of operands associated with an instruction increase, so does the level of difficulty in describing the instruction's semantics. In this example, we'll extend the behavior of VMXPLODE to require a single register operand, which will be made to dab. This will require us to visit sections of the *ia.sinc* file that we have not previously encountered. This time, let's start with a modified version of the instruction and then work backward. The following listing shows the modifications we need to make to our instruction definition to accept an operand that will identify the register that ultimately will hold 0xDAB:

```
:VMXPLODE   Reg32❶ is vexMode=0 & byte=0x0f; byte=0x01; byte=0xc5; Reg32❷
        { Reg32=0xDAB❸; vmxplode(); }
```

Here, Reg32 ❶ is declared as a local identifier and then concatenated with the opcode ❷ to become part of the constraints associated with the instruction. Rather than assigning 0xDAB directly into EAX as we did previously, the instruction now assigns the value into Reg32 ❸. To accomplish our goal, we will need to determine a way to associate the value in Reg32 with the x86 register of our choosing. Let's investigate other components within *ia.sinc* to help us understand how to correctly map an operand to a specific x86 general-purpose register.

Near the start of *ia.sinc*, we see all of the definitions that will be needed by the entire specification, as shown in Listing 18-1.

```
# SLA specification file for Intel x86
@ifdef IA64❶
@define SIZE     "8"
@define STACKPTR "RSP"
@else
@define SIZE     "4"
@define STACKPTR "ESP"
@endif
define endian=little;❷
define space ram type=ram_space size=$(SIZE) default;
define space register type=register_space size=4;
# General purpose registers❸
@ifdef IA64
define register offset=0 size=8 [ RAX    RCX    RDX    RBX    RSP    RBP    RSI    RDI ]❹;
define register offset=0 size=4   [ EAX _ ECX _ EDX _ EBX _ ESP _ EBP _ ESI _ EDI ];
define register offset=0 size=2   [ AX _ _ CX _ _ _ DX _ _ _ BX];        # truncated
define register offset=0 size=1   [ AL AH _ _ _ _ _ _ CL CH _ _ _ _ _ _]; # truncated y
define register offset=0x80 size=8 [ R8    R9    R10    R11    R12    R13    R14    R15 ]❺;
define register offset=0x80 size=4 [ R8D _ R9D _ R10D _ R11D _ R12D _ R13D _ R14D _ R15D ];
define register offset=0x80 size=2 [ R8W _ _ R9W _ _ _ R10W _ _ _ R11W ]; # truncated
define register offset=0x80 size=1 [ R8B _ _ _ _ _ _ _ R9B _ _ _ _ _ _ _ ]; # truncated
@else
define register offset=0 size=4   [ EAX ECX EDX EBX ESP EBP ESI EDI ];
define register offset=0 size=2   [ AX _ CX _ DX _ BX _ SP _ BP _ SI _ DI ];
define register offset=0 size=1   [ AL AH _ _ CL CH _ _ DL DH _ _ BL BH ];
@endif
```

Listing 18-1: Partial SLEIGH specification for x86 registers (adapted from ia.sinc)

At the top of the file, we see the name and size of the stack pointer for 32- and 64-bit builds ❶, as well as the endianness ❷ for the x86. A comment ❸ introduces the start of the definitions of the general-purpose registers. As with all its other components, SLEIGH has a special convention for naming and defining registers: registers reside in a special address space named register, and every register (which may span 1 or more bytes) is assigned an offset within the address space. A SLEIGH register definition indicates the offset at which a list of registers begins within the register address space. All registers in a register list are contiguous unless an underscore is used to create space between them. The address space layout of the 64-bit RAX and RCX registers ❹ is shown in more detail in Figure 18-8.

size	offset															
	0	1	2	3	4	5	6	7	8	9	10	11	12	13	14	15
8	RAX								RCX							
4	EAX				_				ECX				_			
2	AX		_		_		_		CX		_		_		_	
1	AL	AH	_	_	_	_	_	_	CL	CH	_	_	_	_	_	_

Figure 18-8: Register layout for x86-64 RAX and RCX registers

The register named AL occupies exactly the same location as the least significant byte of RAX, EAX, and AX (since x86 is a little-endian). Similarly, EAX occupies the low 4 bytes of RAX. An underscore indicates that no name is associated with a given range of bytes for the given size. In this case, there is no name for the 4-byte block at offsets four to seven, although these bytes are synonymous with the upper half of the RAX register. Listing 18-1 describes a separate block of registers beginning with R8 at offset 0x80 ❺. The 1-byte register at offset 0x80 is known as R8B, and the 1-byte register at offset 0x88 is known as R9B. Hopefully, the similarity between the textual register definition in Listing 18-1 and the tabular representation in Figure 18-8 are obvious, since the register definitions in a SLEIGH file are nothing more than the textual representation of an architecture's register address space.

If you are writing a SLEIGH description of an architecture that is entirely unsupported by Ghidra, it will be your job to lay out the register address space for that architecture, ensuring no overlap between registers unless the architecture requires it (such as RAX, EAX, AX, AH, AL in the x86-64 architecture).

Now that you understand how registers are represented in SLEIGH, let's return to our objective of choosing a register to *dab*! In order for our instruction to function properly, it needs to map the identifier Reg32 to a general-purpose register. To accomplish this task, we can use an existing definition in *ia.sinc* that is found within the following lines of code:

```
❶ define token modrm (8)
        mod          = (6,7)
        reg_opcode   = (3,5)
        reg_opcode_hb = (5,5)
        r_m          = (0,2)
        row          = (4,7)
        col          = (0,2)
        page         = (3,3)
        cond         = (0,3)
        reg8         = (3,5)
        reg16        = (3,5)
  ❷ reg32           = (3,5)
        reg64        = (3,5)
        reg8_x0      = (3,5)
```

The define statement ❶ is declaring an 8-bit token called modrm. A SLEIGH token is a syntactic element used to represent byte-sized components that make up the instructions being modeled.[7] SLEIGH allows the definition of any number of bitfields (a range of one or more contiguous bits) within a token. When you're defining instructions in SLEIGH, these bitfields provide a convenient, symbolic means of specifying the associated operands. In this listing, a bitfield named reg32 ❷ spans bits 3 through 5 of modrm. This 3-bit field can take on the values 0 to 7 and can be used to choose one of the eight 32-bit x86 registers.

If we move to the next reference of reg32 in the file, we see the following interesting lines of code:

```
# attach variables fieldlist registerlist;
  attach variables [ r32   reg32   base    index ]   [ EAX  ECX  EDX  EBX  ESP  EBP  ESI  EDI ];
#                                                       0    1    2    3    4    5    6    7
```

The first and last lines of the listing contain comments that show the SLEIGH syntax for this statement and the ordinal values for each register. The attach variables statement associates the field with a list (in this case, a list of the x86 general-purpose registers). A rough interpretation of the line of code, taking the preceding modrm definition into account, is the following: The value of reg32 is determined by looking at bits 3 to 5 of the token modrm. The resulting value (0 to 7) is then used as an index to select a register from the list.

We now have a way to identify the general-purpose registers to target for 0xDAB. Our next encounter with Reg32 within the file finds the following code, which contains the constructor for Reg32 for both 32- and 64-bit registers, and now we can see the association between reg32 and Reg32:[8]

```
Reg32:    reg32  is rexRprefix=0 & reg32    { export reg32; } #64-bit Reg32
Reg32:    reg32  is reg32                   { export reg32; } #32-bit Reg32
```

Let's return to the command that started this little adventure:

```
:VMXPLODE Reg32❶ is vexMode=0 & byte=0x0f; byte=0x01; byte=0xc5; Reg32❷
                                            { Reg32=0xDAB; vmxplode(); }
```

We are going to include an operand with our call to VMXPLODE that will determine which register gets the value 0xDAB. We will update our test binary further by removing the first NOP and appending the value 0x08 to our hand-assembled instruction. The first 3 bytes are the opcode (0f 01 c5), and the following byte (08) will be the operand that specifies the register to use:

```
".byte 0x0f, 0x01, 0xc5, 0x08;"            // hand assembled with operand
```

---

7. This concept is described in detail in the Tokens and Fields (6) section of the SLEIGH documentation.

8. This concept is described in detail in the Constructors (7) section of the SLEIGH documentation.

Figure 18-9 demonstrates the step-by-step translation from the operand through to the determination of the register based on the information in the *ia.sinc* file.

❶	Operand	08							
❷	Value	0	0	0	0	1	0	0	0
❸	modrm bits	7	6	5	4	3	2	1	0
❹	Reg32	001							
❺	Ordinals	0	1	2	3	4	5	6	7
❻	Registers	EAX	ECX	EDX	EBX	ESP	EBP	ESI	EDI

Figure 18-9: Translation path from operand to register

The original operand value, shown in the first row, is 0x08 ❶. The value is decoded into its binary ❷ form and overlaid with the fields of the modrm token ❸. Bits 3 to 5 are extracted, yielding the Reg32 value 001 ❹. This value is used to index the ordinal map ❺ to select the ECX register ❻. Therefore, the operand 0x08 specifies that ECX will get the value 0xDAB.

When we save the updated *ia.sinc* file, restart Ghidra, and then load and analyze the file, the following listing is generated, showing the use of our new instruction. As expected, ECX is the register selected to hold 0xDAB:

```
00100721 f3 0f c7 75 fc VMXON    qword ptr [RBP + local_c]

                                    $U620:8 = INT_ADD RBP, -4:8
                                    $Ua50:8 = LOAD ram($U620)
                                    CALLOTHER "vmxon", $Ua50
00100726 0f 01 c5 08    VMXPLODE ECX

                                    ECX = COPY 0xdab:4
                                    CALLOTHER "vmxplode"

0010072a 90 NOP
```

The value 0xDAB no longer appears in the Decompiler window because the decompiler assumes that the return value is in EAX. In this case, we are using ECX so the decompiler does not identify a return value.

Now that we can make a selected register dab, let's add a 32-bit immediate value as a second operand. This will double our celebratory potential.

Option 3: The Register and Value Operands

To extend the syntax of our instruction to take two operands (a destination register and a source constant), update the definition of VMXPLODE as shown here:

```
:VMXPLODE Reg32,imm32 is vexMode=0 & byte=0x0f; byte=0x01; byte=0xc5;
        Reg32; imm32                        { Reg32=imm32; vmxplode(); }
```

The addition of an immediate 32-bit constant to the instruction requires 4 additional bytes to encode. Accordingly, we replace the next four NOPs with values that correctly encode our imm32 in little-endian order, as seen here:

```
".byte 0x0f, 0x01, 0xc5, 0x08, 0xb8, 0xdb, 0xee, 0x0f;"
"nop;"
"nop;"
```

When we reload the file, VMXPLODE exits with another flourish. As shown in the following listing (with p-code displayed), ECX now has the value 0xFEEDBB8 (which might be a more appealing exit flourish for science fiction fans):

```
00100726 0f 01 c5        VMXPLODE ECX,0xfeedbb8
         08 b8 db
         ee 0f
                                 ECX = COPY 0xfeedbb8:4
                                 CALLOTHER "vmxplode"
```

Example 3: Adding a Register to a Processor Module

We close out our processor module examples by extending an architecture with two entirely new registers.[9] Recall the definition of the 32-bit general-purpose registers from earlier in the chapter:

```
define register offset=0  size=4  [EAX ECX EDX EBX ESP EBP ESI EDI];
```

The definition of a register requires an offset, a size, and the list of registers. We chose a starting offset into the registry memory address space after reviewing the currently allocated offsets and finding the space we need for two 4-byte registers. We can use this information to define two new 32-bit registers in the *ia.sinc* file called VMID and VMVER, as shown in the following listing:

```
# Define VMID and VMVER
define register offset=0x1500 size=4 [ VMID VMVER ];
```

Our instructions need a means to identify which new register (VMID or VMVER) they are operating on. In the previous example, we used a 3-bit field to select one of eight registers. To select between the two new registers requires only a single bit. The following statement defines a 1-bit field within the modrm token and associates the field with vmreg:

```
# Associate vmreg with a single bit in the modrm token.
vmreg = (3, 3)
```

---

9. This concept is described in detail starting in the Naming Registers (4.4) section of the SLEIGH documentation.

The following statement attaches vmreg to the ordinal set containing the two registers, with 0 representing VMID and 1 representing VMVER:

```
attach variables [ vmreg ]    [ VMID  VMVER ];
```

Instruction definitions may refer to vmreg when any of the attached registers are valid within the instruction, while assembly language programmers may refer to VMID and VMER as operands in any instruction that allows a vmreg operand. Let's compare the following two definitions of VMXPLODE. The first is from our previous example, where we chose the register from among the general-purpose registers, and the second selects one of our two registers rather than any of the general-purpose registers:

```
:VMXPLODE Reg32,imm32 is vexMode=0 & byte=0x0f; byte=0x01; byte=0xc5;
          Reg32, imm32                      { Reg32=imm32; vmxplode(); }
:VMXPLODE vmreg,imm32 is vexMode=0 & byte=0x0f; byte=0x01; byte=0xc5;
          vmreg, imm32                       { vmreg=imm32; vmxplode(); }
```

Reg32 is replaced with vmreg in the second listing. If we use the same input file with test instruction vmxplode 0x08,0xFEEDBB8, the immediate operand 0xFEEDBB8 will be loaded into VMVER, since the input value 0x08 maps to an ordinal value of 1 (because bit 3 is set), as we show in Figure 18-10, and VMVER is register 1 in vmreg. After loading the test file (after saving *ia.sinc* and restarting Ghidra), we see that the p-code in the Listing window shows that the immediate operand is loaded into VMVER:

```
00100726 0f 01 c5        VMXPLODE     VMVER,0xfeedbb8
         08 b8 db
         ee 0f

                                      VMVER = COPY 0xfeedbb8:4
                                      CALLOTHER "vmxplode"
```

The associated instruction information, shown in Figure 18-10, confirms the change as well.

Figure 18-10: Instruction Info for VMXPLODE with new register VMVER selected

Summary

While we introduced only a small fraction of the x86 processor file contents in this chapter, we looked at the major components of a processor module, including instruction definitions, register definitions, and tokens, as well as how the Ghidra-specific language, SLEIGH, can be used to build, modify, and augment Ghidra processor modules. If you have a desire (or need) to add a new processor to Ghidra, we highly recommend looking at some of the more recent processors added to Ghidra. (The *SuperH4.sinc* file is particularly well-documented and the processor is significantly less complex than the x86 processor.)

We cannot emphasize enough the role that patience and experimentation play in any processor-development situation. The hard work more than pays off when you are able to reuse your processor module with each new binary you collect and potentially contribute the module back to the Ghidra project for the benefit of other reverse engineers.

In the next chapter, we take a deep dive into the functionality associated with the Ghidra Decompiler.

19

THE GHIDRA DECOMPILER

Until now, we've focused our reverse engineering analysis on the Listing window and presented Ghidra's features through the disassembly listing lens. In this chapter, we shift our focus to the Decompiler window and investigate how we can accomplish familiar analysis tasks (and some new ones) with the Decompiler and its associated functionality. We start with a brief overview of the decompilation process before moving on to the functionality available in the Decompiler window. We then walk through some examples to help you identify ways that the Decompiler window can be used to improve your reverse engineering process.

Decompiler Analysis

It's logical to assume that the content in the Decompiler window is derived from the Listing window, but, surprisingly, the contents of the Listing window and Decompiler window are derived independently, which is why they sometimes disagree and why both should be evaluated in context when you're trying to determine ground truth. The main function of Ghidra's Decompiler is to convert machine language instructions into p-code (see Chapter 18) and then to convert the p-code to C and present it in the Decompiler window.

In a simplified view, the decompilation process includes three distinct phases. In the first phase, the Decompiler uses the SLEIGH specification file to create a draft of the p-code and derive associated basic blocks and flows. The second phase focuses on simplification: unneeded content such as unreachable code is eliminated, and then control flows are adjusted and tuned in response to the changes. In the wrap-up phase, finishing touches are added, some final checks are made, and the final results are sent through a pretty-printing algorithm before being presented in the Decompiler window. Of course, this greatly simplifies a very complex process, but the main takeaways are the following:[1]

- The Decompiler is an analyzer.
- It starts its work with the binary and produces p-code.
- It converts the p-code to C.
- The C code and any associated messages are displayed in the Decompiler window.

We discuss some of these steps in more detail as we navigate through Ghidra's decompilation functionality. Let's start our investigation with the analysis process and the primary capabilities it unleashes.

Analysis Options

During the auto analysis process, there are several analyzers that pertain to the Decompiler window. Decompiler analysis options are managed through the Edit ▶ Tool Options menu, shown in Figure 19-1 with defaults selected.

We discuss two of these options, Eliminate unreachable code and Simplify predication, next. For the remaining options, you can experiment with their results or refer to Ghidra Help.

---

1. The Ghidra decompilation workflow is broken into 15 steps that include subcomponents. The comprehensive internal documentation for the Ghidra Decompiler can be extracted using Doxygen.

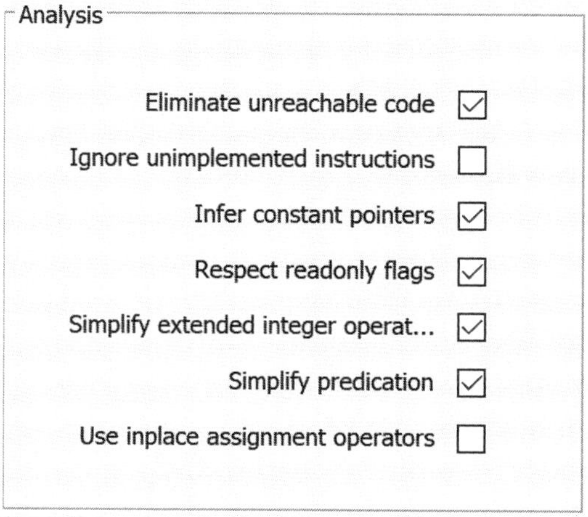

Figure 19-1: Ghidra Decompiler analysis options with defaults selected

Eliminate Unreachable Code

The Eliminate unreachable code option excludes unreachable code from the Decompiler listing. For example, the following C function has two conditions that can never be met, which makes the corresponding conditional blocks unreachable:

```
int demo_unreachable(volatile int a) {
    volatile int b = a ^ a;
❶ if (b) {
        printf("This is unreachable\n");
        a += 1;
    }
❷ if (a - a > 0) {
        printf("This should be unreachable too\n");
        a += 1;
    } else {
        printf("We should always see this\n");
        a += 2;
    }
    printf("End of demo_unreachable()\n");
    return a;
}
```

The variable b is initialized to zero in a perhaps less than obvious manner. When b is tested ❶, its value can never be non zero, and the body of the corresponding if statement will never be executed. Similarly a - a can never be greater than zero, and the condition in the second if statement ❷ can also never evaluate to true. When the Eliminate unreachable code option is selected, the Decompiler window displays warning messages to let us know it has removed unreachable code.

```
/* WARNING: Removing unreachable block (ram,0x00100777) */
/* WARNING: Removing unreachable block (ram,0x0010079a) */
ulong demo_unreachable(int param_1)
{
  puts("We should always see this");
  puts("End of demo_unreachable()");
  return (ulong)(param_1 + 2);
}
```

Simplify Predication

This option optimizes if/else blocks by merging blocks that share the same condition. In the following listing, the first two if statements share the same condition:

```
int demo_simppred(int a) {
    if (a > 0) {
        printf("A is > 0\n");
    }
    if (a > 0) {
        printf("Yes, A is definitely > 0!\n");
    }
    if (a > 2) {
        printf("A > 2\n");
    }
    return a * 10;
}
```

With Simplify predication enabled, the resulting Decompiler listing shows the combined blocks:

```
ulong demo_simppred(int param_1)
{
  if (0 < param_1) {
    puts("A is > 0");
    puts("Yes, A is definitely > 0!");
  }
  if (2 < param_1) {
    puts("A > 2");
  }
  return (ulong)(uint)(param_1 * 10);
}
```

The Decompiler Window

Now that you understand how the Decompiler Analysis Engine populates the Decompiler window, let's see how you can use the window to facilitate your analysis. Navigating the Decompiler window is relatively easy, as it displays only one function at a time. To move between functions or see the function in context, it is helpful to correlate with the Listing window. Because the

Decompiler window and the Listing window are linked by default, you can navigate both by using the available options in the CodeBrowser toolbar.

The function displayed in the Decompiler window helps with analysis, but it may not be so easy to read at first. Any lack of information about the data types used by the functions that it decompiles requires Ghidra to infer those data types itself. As a result, the decompiler may overuse type casts, as you can see in the following sample statements:

```
printf("a=%d, b=%d, c=%d, d=%d, e=%d, f=%d, g=%d\n", (ulong)param_1,
    (ulong)param_2,(ulong)uVar1,(ulong)uVar2,(ulong)(uVar1 + param_1),
    (ulong)(uVar2 * 100),(ulong)uVar4);

uStack44 = *(undefined4 *)**(undefined4 **)(iStack24 + 0x10);
```

As you provide more accurate type information using the Decompiler editing options, you will notice that the Decompiler relies less and less on type casts, and the generated C code become easier to read. In the examples that follow, we'll discuss some of the Decompiler window's most useful features to clean up the generated source code. The ultimate goal is readable source code that is easier to comprehend, which reduces the amount of time needed to understand the behavior of the code.

Example 1: Editing in the Decompiler Window

Consider a program that accepts two integer values from the user and then calls the following function:

```
int do_math(int a, int b) {

    int c, d, e, f, g;
    srand(time(0));

    c = rand();
    printf("c=%d\n", c);

    d = a + b + c;
    printf("d=%d\n", d);

    e = a + c;
    printf("e=%d\n", e);

    f = d * 100;
    printf("f=%d\n", f);

    g = rand() - e;
    printf("g=%d\n", g);

    printf("a=%d, b=%d, c=%d, d=%d, e=%d, f=%d, g=%d\n", a, b, c, d, e, f, g);

    return g;
}
```

The function uses two integer parameters with five local variables to generate its output. The interdependencies can be summed up as follows:

- Variable c depends on the rand() return value, influences d and e directly, and influences f and g indirectly.
- Variable d depends on a, b, and c, and influences f directly.
- Variable e depends on a and c, and influences g directly.
- Variable f depends on d directly and on a, b, and c indirectly, and influences nothing.
- Variable g depends on e directly and on a and c indirectly, and influences nothing.

When the associated binary is loaded into Ghidra and the function is analyzed, you see the following representation of the do_math function in the Decompiler window:

```
ulong do_math(uint param_1,uint param_2)
{
  uint uVar1;
  uint uVar2;
  int iVar3;
  uint uVar4;
  time_t tVar5;

  tVar5 = time((time_t *)0x0);
  srand((uint)tVar5);
  uVar1 = rand();
  printf("c=%d\n");
  uVar2 = uVar1 + param_1 + param_2;
❶ printf("d=%d\n");
  printf("e=%d\n");
  printf("f=%d\n");
  iVar3 = rand();
  uVar4 = iVar3 - (uVar1 + param_1);
  printf("g=%d\n");
  printf("a=%d, b=%d, c=%d, d=%d, e=%d, f=%d, g=%d\n", (ulong)param_1,
        (ulong)param_2,(ulong)uVar1,(ulong)uVar2,(ulong)(uVar1 + param_1),
        (ulong)(uVar2 * 100),(ulong)uVar4);
  return (ulong)uVar4;
}
```

If you want to do your analysis using the Decompiler, you'll want to make sure the code the Decompiler is generating is as accurate as possible. Usually, this is done by providing as much information as possible about data types and function prototypes. Functions that accept a variable number of arguments, such as printf, are especially tricky for the Decompiler since the Decompiler would need to fully understand the semantics of the required arguments in order to estimate the number of supplied optional arguments.

Overriding Function Signatures

You can see a number of `printf` statements ❶ that don't look quite right. Each one has a format string but no additional arguments. Since `printf` takes a variable number of arguments, you can override the function signature at each calling location and (based on the format string) indicate that the `printf` statement should take one integer argument.[2] To make this change, right-click a `printf` statement and choose **Override Signature** from the context menu to open the dialog shown in Figure 19-2.

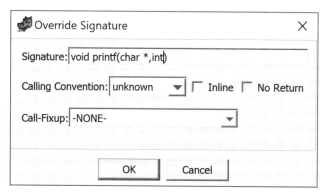

Figure 19-2: The Override Signature dialog

Adding the second parameter type, `int`, to the signature (as shown in the figure) for each of the `printf` statements results in the following listing:

```
ulong do_math(uint param_1,uint param_2)
{
❶ uint uVar1;
   uint uVar2;
   uint uVar3;
   int iVar4;
   uint uVar5;
   time_t tVar6;

   tVar6 = time((time_t *)0x0);
   srand((uint)tVar6);
   uVar1 = rand();
   printf("c=%d\n",uVar1);
   uVar2 = uVar1 + param_1 + param_2;
   printf("d=%d\n",uVar2);
❷ uVar3 = uVar1 + param_1;
   printf("e=%d\n",uVar3);
   printf("f=%d\n",uVar2 * 100);
   iVar4 = rand();
❸ uVar5 = iVar4 - uVar3;
   printf("g=%d\n",uVar5);
❹ printf("a=%d, b=%d, c=%d, d=%d, e=%d, f=%d, g=%d\n", (ulong)param_1,
```

---

2. For functions that do not have a variable number of arguments, you should change the function signature rather than overriding it from the call.

```
        (ulong)param_2,(ulong)uVar1,(ulong)uVar2,(ulong)(uVar1 + param_1),
        (ulong)(uVar2 * 100),(ulong)uVar4);
  return (ulong)uVar4;
}
```

In addition to the updated calls to printf with the correct arguments, two new lines have been added to the Decompiler listing as a result of overriding the printf function ❷❸. These statements weren't included previously because Ghidra believed the results were not used. Once the Decompiler understands that the results are used in each printf, the statements become meaningful and are displayed in the Decompiler window.

Editing Variable Types and Names

After correcting the function calls, you can continue cleaning up the listing by renaming (hotkey L) and retyping (hotkey CTRL-L) the parameters and the variables ❶ based on the names found in the printf format strings. As an aside, format strings are an extremely valuable source of information regarding the type and purpose of variables in any program.

After these changes have been completed, the final printf statement ❹ is still a bit cumbersome:

```
printf("a=%d, b=%d, c=%d, d=%d, e=%d, f=%d, g=%d\n", (ulong)a,
    (ulong)(uint)b, (ulong)(uint)c, (ulong)(uint)d, (ulong)(uint)e,
    (ulong)(uint)(d * 100),(ulong)(uint)g);
```

Right-clicking this statement allows you to override the function signature. The first argument in this printf statement is the format string, and it doesn't need to be modified. Changing the rest of the arguments to type int results in the following cleaner code (Listing 19-1) in the Decompiler window.

```
int do_math(int a, int b)
{
  int c;
  int d;
  int e;
  int g;
  time_t tVar1;

  tVar1 = time((time_t *)0x0);
  srand((uint)tVar1);
  c = rand();
  printf("c=%d\n",c);
  d = c + a + b;
  printf("d=%d\n",d);
  e = c + a;
  printf("e=%d\n",e);
  printf("f=%d\n",d * 100);
  g = rand();
  g = g - e;
  printf("g=%d\n",g);
```

```
printf("a=%d, b=%d, c=%d, d=%d, e=%d, f=%d, g=%d\n",a,b,c,d,e,d * 100❶,g);
    return g;
}
```

Listing 19-1: Decompiled function with updated signatures

This is very similar to our original source code and much easier to read than the original Decompiler listing as the modifications of the function arguments have been propagated throughout the listing. One difference between the Decompiler listing and our original source code is that the variable f has been replaced by an equivalent expression ❶.

Highlighting Slices

Now that you have a more understandable Decompiler window, you can begin further analysis. Suppose that you want to know how individual variables affect and are affected by other variables. A *program slice* is a collection of statements that contribute to the value of a variable (*backward slice*) or are affected by a variable (*forward slice*). In vulnerability analysis scenarios, this might manifest as "I have control of this variable; where does its value get used?"

Ghidra provides five options in its right-click context menu to highlight relationships between variables and instructions in a function. If you right-click a variable in the Decompiler window, you can choose from the following options:

Highlight Def-use   This option highlights all uses of the variable within the function. (You can use a middle mouse click to get the same effect.)

Highlight Forward Slice   This option highlights everything that is impacted by the value in the selected variable. For example, if you select variable b in Listing 19-1 and choose this option, all occurrences of b and d will be highlighted in the listing, because a change in the value of b could also result in a change in the value of d.

Highlight Backward Slice   This is the inverse of the previous option and highlights all of the variables that contribute to a particular value. If you right-click variable e in the final printf statement in Listing 19-1 and choose this option, all of the variables that affect the value of e (in this case e, a, and c) will be highlighted. Changing a or c could also change the value of e.

Highlight Forward Inst Slice   This option highlights the entire statement associated with the Highlight Forward Slice option. In Listing 19-1, if you use this option while variable b is selected, all statements in which b or d appear will be highlighted.

Highlight Backward Inst Slice   This option highlights the entire statement associated with the Highlight Backward Slice option. In Listing 19-1, selecting this option while highlighting variable e in the final printf statement will cause all statements in which a, c, or e appear to be highlighted.

Now that we have a general understanding of some approaches to work with the Decompiler window and use it in our analysis, let's look at a more specific example.

Example 2: Non-Returning Functions

In general, Ghidra can safely assume function calls return and therefore treat function calls as if they exhibit sequential flow within basic blocks. However, some functions, such as those marked with the noreturn keyword in source code, or ended with an obfuscated jump instruction in malware, do not return, and Ghidra may generate inaccurate disassembled or decompiled code. Ghidra offers three approaches for dealing with non-returning functions: two non-returning function analyzers and the capability to edit function signatures manually.

Ghidra can identify non-returning functions based on a list of known noreturn functions such as exit and abort using the Non-Returning Functions-Known analyzer. This analyzer is selected by default as part of auto analysis, and its job is straightforward: if a function name appears in its list, it marks the function as non-returning and does its best to correct any associated issues (for example, set associated calls to non-returning, find flows that might need repairing, and so on).

The Non-Returning Functions-Discovered analyzer looks for clues that might indicate that a function doesn't return (for example, data or bad instructions right after the call). What it does with the information is largely controlled by the three options associated with the analyzer, as shown in Figure 19-3.

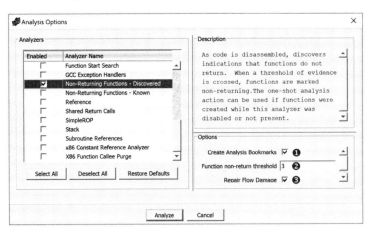

Figure 19-3: Analysis options for Non-Returning Functions-Discovered

The first option ❶ allows the automatic creation of analysis bookmarks (which appear on the Listing window's bookmark bar). The second option ❷ allows you to specify a threshold that determines whether to designate a function as non-returning based on a series of checks for characteristics that are likely to indicate a non-returning function. Finally, there is a checkbox ❸ to repair the associated flow damage.

When Ghidra is unable to identify a non-returning function, you have the option to edit the function signature yourself. If you complete analysis and have error bookmarks, which are used to flag bad instructions, then that is a good indication that something is not quite right with Ghidra's own analysis. If the bad instruction follows a CALL, as in

```
00100839                    CALL        noReturnA
0010083e                    ??          FFh
```

then you are likely to see an associated post-comment warning you about the situation in the Decompiler window, like this:

```
noReturnA(1);
/* WARNING: Bad instruction - Truncating control flow here */
halt_baddata();
```

If you click the function name (noReturnA in this case) in the Decompiler window and then choose Edit Function Signature, you will have the option to modify attributes associated with the function, as shown in Figure 19-4.

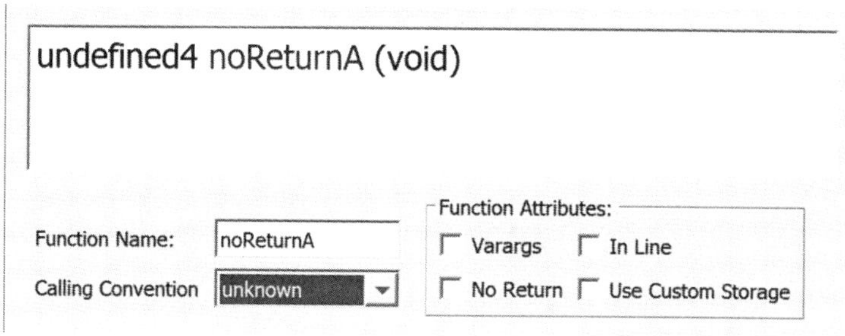

Figure 19-4: Editing function attributes

Check the No Return box to mark the function as non-returning. Ghidra then inserts a pre comment, shown next, in the Decompiler window as well as a post comment in the Listing window:

```
/* WARNING: Subroutine does not return */
noReturnA(1);
```

With this error corrected, you can move on to other issues.

Example 3: Automated Structure Creation

When analyzing decompiled C source code, you're likely to come across statements that appear to contain structure field references. Ghidra helps you create a structure and populate it based on the associated references that the Decompiler has detected. Let's walk through an example starting with the source code and Ghidra's initial decompilation of the code.

Suppose you have source code that defines two struct types and then creates a global instance of each:

```
❶ struct s1 {
      int a;
      int b;
      int c;
  };

❷ typedef struct s2 {
      int x;
      char y;
      float z;
  } s2_type;

  struct s1 GLOBAL_S1;
  s2_type GLOBAL_S2;
```

One structure ❶ contains homogeneous elements, and the other ❷ contains a heterogeneous collection of types. The source code also contains three functions, one of which (do_struct_demo) declares a local instance of each structure type:

```
void display_s1(struct s1* s) {
    printf("The fields in s1 = %d, %d, and %d\n", s->a, s->b, s->c);
}

void update_s2(s2_type* s, int v) {
    s->x = v;
    s->y = (char)('A' + v);
    s->z = v * 2.0;
}

void do_struct_demo() {
    s2_type local_s2;
    struct s1 local_s1;

    printf("Enter six ints: ");
    scanf("%d %d %d %d %d %d", (int *)&local_s1, &local_s1.b, &local_s1.c,
        &GLOBAL_S1.a, &GLOBAL_S1.b, &GLOBAL_S1.c);

    printf("You entered: %d and %d\n", local_s1.a, GLOBAL_S1.a);
    display_s1(&local_s1);
    display_s1(&GLOBAL_S1);

    update_s2(&local_s2, local_s1.a);
}
```

The decompiled version of do_struct_demo appears in Listing 19-2.

```
void do_struct_demo(void)
{
  undefined8 uVar1;
  uint local_20;
  undefined local_1c [4];
  undefined local_18 [4];
  undefined local_14 [12];

  uVar1 = 0x100735;
  printf("Enter six ints: ");
  __isoc99_scanf("%d %d %d %d %d %d", &local_20, local_1c, local_18,
                 GLOBAL_S1,0x30101c,0x301020,uVar1);
  printf("You entered: %d and %d\n",(ulong)local_20,(ulong)GLOBAL_S1._0_4_);
❶ display_s1(&local_20);
❷ display_s1(GLOBAL_S1);
  update_s2(local_14,(ulong)local_20,(ulong)local_20);
  return;
}
```

Listing 19-2: Initial decompilation of do_struct_demo

Navigating to the display_s1 function from either function call ❶❷ by
double-clicking it in the Decompiler window yields the following:

```
void display_s1(uint *param_1)
{
  printf("The fields in s1 = %d, %d, and %d\n", (ulong)*param_1,
         (ulong)param_1[1],(ulong)param_1[2]);
  return;
}
```

Because you suspect the argument to display_s1 might be a structure
pointer, you can ask Ghidra to automate the process of creating a struct for
you by right-clicking param_1 in the function's argument list and selecting
Auto Create Structure from the context menu. In response, Ghidra tracks
all uses of param_1, treats all arithmetic performed on the pointer as referencing a member of a struct, and automatically creates a new struct type
containing fields at each referenced offset. This changes a few things in the
Decompiler listing:

```
void display_s1(astruct *param_1)
{
  printf("The fields in s1 = %d, %d, and %d\n",(ulong)param_1->field_0x0,
         (ulong)param_1->field_0x4,(ulong)param_1->field_0x8);
  return;
}
```

The type of the parameter has changed and is now astruct*, and the call to printf now contains field references. The new type has also been added to the Data Type Manager, and hovering over the structure name displays the field definitions, as shown in Figure 19-5.

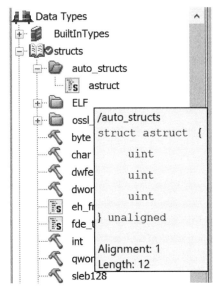

Figure 19-5: Automatic structs in the Data Type Manager

You can update the type for local_20 and GLOBAL_S1 to astruct by using the Retype Variable option from the right-click context menu. The results are shown in the following listing:

```
void do_struct_demo(void)
{
  undefined8 uVar1;
❶ astruct local_20;
  undefined local_14 [12];

  uVar1 = 0x100735;
  printf("Enter six ints: ");
  __isoc99_scanf("%d %d %d %d %d %d", &local_20, &local_20.field_0x4❷,
        ❸ &local_20.field_0x8, &GLOBAL_S1, 0x30101c, 0x301020, uVar1);
  printf("You entered: %d and  %d\n", (ulong)local_20.field_0x0,
      ❹ (ulong)GLOBAL_S1.field_0x0);
  display_s1(&local_20);
  display_s1(&GLOBAL_S1);
  update_s2(local_14,(ulong)local_20.field_0x0,(ulong)local_20.field_0x0);
  return;
}
```

Comparing this with Listing 19-2 shows the modification of the type for local_20 ❶ and the addition of field references for both local_20 ❷❸ and GLOBAL_S1 ❹.

Let's shift focus to the decompilation of the third function, update_s2, shown in Listing 19-3.

```
void update_s2(int *param_1,int param_2)
{
  *param_1 = param_2;
  *(char *)(param_1 + 1) = (char)param_2 + 'A';
  *(float *)(param_1 + 2) = (float)param_2 + (float)param_2;
  return;
}
```

Listing 19-3: Initial decompilation of update_s2

You can use the previous approach to automatically create a structure for param_1. Simply right-click param_1 in the function and choose **Auto Create Structure** from the context menu.

```
void update_s2(astruct_1 *param_1,int param_2)
{
  param_1->field_0x0 = param_2;
  param_1->field_0x4 = (char)param_2 + 'A';
  param_1->field_0x8 = (float)param_2 + (float)param_2;
  return;
}
```

The Data Type Manager now has a second struct definition associated with this file, as shown in Figure 19-6.

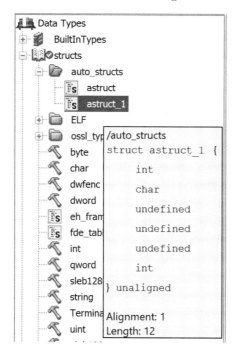

Figure 19-6: Additional automatic structs in the Data Type Manager window

This structure has an int, a char, three undefined bytes (likely padding inserted by the compiler), and a float. To edit the structure, right-click astruct_1 and choose Edit from the context menu, which opens the Structure Editor window. If we choose to name the int field x, the char field y, and the float field z, and then save the changes, the new field names will be reflected in the Decompiler listing:

```
void update_s2(astruct_1 *param_1,int param_2)
{
  param_1->x = param_2;
  param_1->y = (char)param_2 + 'A';
  param_1->z = (float)param_2 + (float)param_2;
  return;
}
```

This listing is much easier to read and understand than the original decompilation in Listing 19-3.

Summary

The Decompiler window, like the Listing window, provides you with a view into a binary, and each has its associated strengths and weaknesses. The Decompiler provides a higher-level view that can help you understand the general structure and functionality of a single function more quickly than looking at the disassembly (particularly for those who do not have years of experience reading disassembly listings). The Listing window provides a lower-level view of the entire binary, with all of the available detail, but this can make it more difficult to gain insight into the big picture.

Ghidra's Decompiler can be used effectively with the Listing window and all of the other tools we have introduced throughout the book to aid you in your reverse engineering process. In the end, it is the reverse engineer's role to determine the best approach to solving the problem at hand.

This chapter focused on the Decompiler window and issues associated with decompilation. Many of challenges can be traced to the wide variety of compilers and associated compiler options that directly influence the resulting binary. In the next chapter, we take a look at some compiler-specific behaviors and compiler build options to better understand the resulting binaries.

20

COMPILER VARIATIONS

At this point, if we have done our job properly, you now possess the essential skills to use Ghidra effectively and, more importantly, to bend it to your will. The next step is to learn to adapt to the challenges that binaries (as opposed to Ghidra) will throw at you. Depending on your motives for staring at assembly language, either you may be very familiar with what you are looking at or you may never know what you are going to be faced with. If you spend all of your time examining code that was compiled using gcc on a Linux platform, you'll become quite familiar with the style of code that it generates, but you may be baffled by a debug version of a program compiled using the Microsoft C/C++ compiler. If you are a malware analyst, you may see code created using gcc, clang, Microsoft's C++ compiler, Delphi, and others, all in the same afternoon.

Like you, Ghidra is more familiar with the output of some compilers than other compilers, and familiarity with code generated by one compiler in no way guarantees that you will recognize high-level constructs compiled using an entirely different compiler (or even different versions of the same compiler family). Rather than relying entirely on Ghidra's analysis capabilities to recognize commonly used code and data constructs, you should always be prepared to utilize your own skills: your familiarity with a given assembly language, your knowledge of compilers, and your research skills to properly interpret a disassembly.

In this chapter, we cover some of the ways that compiler differences manifest themselves in disassembly listings. We primarily use compiled C code for our examples, as the variability of C compilers and target platforms provides foundational concepts that can be extended to other compiled languages.

High-Level Constructs

In some cases, the differences between compilers may just be cosmetic, but in other cases, they are much more significant. In this section, we look at high-level language constructs and demonstrate how different compilers and compiler options may significantly impact the resulting disassembly listing. We begin with switch statements and the two mechanisms most commonly employed to resolve switch case selection. Following that, we look at the way that compiler options affect code generation for common expressions before moving on to discuss how different compilers implement C++-specific constructs and handle program startup.

switch Statements

The C switch statement is a frequent target for compiler optimizations. The goal of these optimizations is to match the switch variable to a valid case label in the most efficient manner possible, but the distribution of the switch statement's case labels constrains the type of search that can be used.

Since the efficiency of a search is measured by the number of comparisons required to find the correct case, we can trace the logic a compiler might use to determine the best way to represent a switch table. A constant time algorithm, such as a table lookup, is the most efficient.[1] At the other end of the continuum is linear search, which, in the worst case, requires comparing the switch variable against every case label before finding a match or resolving to the default and thus is the least efficient.[2] The efficiency of a binary search is much better, on average, than linear search but introduces additional constraints, as it requires a sorted list.[3]

In order to select the most efficient implementation for a particular switch statement, it helps to understand how the case label distribution affects the compiler's decision-making process. When case labels are closely clustered, as in the source code in Listing 20-1, compilers generally resolve

---

1. For you algorithm analysis fans, the use of a table lookup allows the target case to be found in a constant number of operations regardless of the size of the search space—which, as you may recall from your algorithms class, is also called *constant time*, or *O(1)*.

2. Linear time algorithms are $O(n)$ and fortunately are not used in switch statements.

3. Binary search is $O(\log n)$.

the switch variable by performing a table lookup to match the switch variable to the address of its associated case—specifically by using a jump table.

```
switch (a) {
/** NOTE: case bodies omitted for brevity **/
    case 1:  /*...*/ break;
    case 2:  /*...*/ break;
    case 3:  /*...*/ break;
    case 4:  /*...*/ break;
    case 5:  /*...*/ break;
    case 6:  /*...*/ break;
    case 7:  /*...*/ break;
    case 8:  /*...*/ break;
    case 9:  /*...*/ break;
    case 10: /*...*/ break;
    case 11: /*...*/ break;
    case 12: /*...*/ break;
}
```

Listing 20-1: A switch statement with consecutive case labels

A *jump table* is an array of pointers, with each pointer in the array referencing a possible jump target. At runtime, a dynamic index into the table chooses one of the many potential jumps each time the jump table is referenced. Jump tables work well when switch case labels are closely spaced (dense), with most of the cases falling into a consecutive number sequence. Compilers take this into account when deciding whether to utilize a jump table. For any switch statement, we can compute the minimum number of entries an associated jump table will contain as follows:

```
num_entries = max_case_value - min_case_value + 1
```

The *density*, or utilization rate, of the jump tables can then be computed as follows:

```
density = num_cases / num_entries
```

A completely contiguous list with every value represented would have a density value of 100 percent (1.0). Finally, the total amount of space required to store the jump table is as follows:

```
table_size = num_entries * sizeof(void*)
```

A switch statement with 100 percent density will be implemented using a jump table. A set of cases with a density of 30 percent might not be implemented using a jump table, since jump table entries would still need to be allocated for the absent cases, which would be 70 percent of the jump table. If num_entries is 30, the jump table would contain entries for 21 unreferenced case labels. On a 64-bit system, this is 168 of the 240 bytes allocated to the table, which is not a lot of overhead, but if num_entries jumps to 300, then the overhead becomes 1680 bytes, which may not be worth the trade-off for

90 possible cases. A compiler that is optimizing for speed may favor jump table implementations, while a compiler that is optimizing for size may choose an alternative implementation with lower memory overhead: binary search.

Binary search is efficient when the case labels are widely spread (low density), as seen in Listing 20-2 (density 0.0008).[4] Because binary search works only on sorted lists, the compiler must ensure that the case labels are ordered before it begins the search with the median value. This may result in the reordering of case blocks when viewed in a disassembly, as compared to the order they appear in the corresponding source.[5]

```
switch (a) {
/** NOTE: case bodies omitted for brevity **/
    case 1:    /*...*/ break;
    case 211:  /*...*/ break;
    case 295:  /*...*/ break;
    case 462:  /*...*/ break;
    case 528:  /*...*/ break;
    case 719:  /*...*/ break;
    case 995:  /*...*/ break;
    case 1024: /*...*/ break;
    case 8000: /*...*/ break;
    case 13531: /*...*/ break;
    case 13532: /*...*/ break;
    case 15027: /*...*/ break;
}
```

Listing 20-2: Sample switch statement with nonconsecutive case labels

Listing 20-3 shows an outline for a non-iterative binary search through a fixed number of constant values. This is the rough framework that the compiler uses to implement the switch from Listing 20-2.

```
if (value < median) {
    // value is in [0-50) percentile
    if (value < lower_half_median) {
        // value is in [0-25) percentile
        // ... continue successive halving until value is resolved
    } else {
        // value is in [25-50) percentile
        // ... continue successive halving until value is resolved
    }
} else {
    // value is in [50-100) percentile
    if (value < upper_half_median) {
        // value is in [50-75) percentile
```

---

4. For those analyzing algorithms at home, this means that the switch variable is matched after at most $\log_2 N$ comparisons, where N is the number of cases contained in the switch statement. This is $O(\log n)$.

5. While the complexity of sorting is very high compared with the complexity of searching, it is important to note the sorting would occur only once at compilation time, whereas the search would take place every time the switch statement is used during execution.

```
        // ... continue successive halving until value is resolved
    } else {
        // value is in [75-100) percentile
        // ... continue successive halving until value is resolved
    }
}
```

Listing 20-3: Non-iterative binary search through a fixed number of constant values

Compilers are also capable of performing more fine-grained optimizations across a range of case labels. For example, when confronted with the case labels

```
label_set = [1, 2, 3, 4, 5, 6, 7, 8, 50, 80, 200, 500, 1000, 5000, 10000]
```

a less aggressive compiler might see a density of 0.0015 here and generate a binary search through all 15 cases. A more aggressive compiler might emit a jump table to resolve cases 1 to 8, and a binary search for the remaining cases, achieving optimal performance for over half of the cases.

Before we look at the disassembled versions of Listings 20-1 and 20-2, let's look at the Ghidra Function Graph windows corresponding to the listings, shown side by side in Figure 20-1.

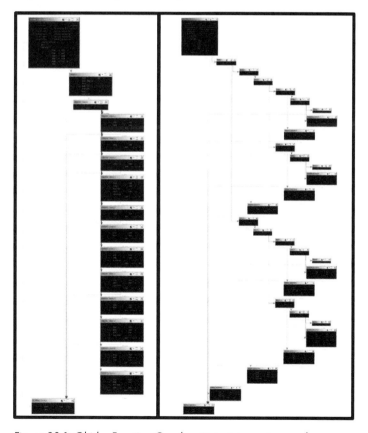

Figure 20-1: Ghidra Function Graph switch statement examples

On the left, the graph for Listing 20-1 shows a nice vertical stack of cases. Each stacked code block resides at the same nesting depth, as is true for cases in a switch statement. The stack suggests that we can use an index to quickly select one block from the many (think array access). This is precisely how jump table resolution works, and the left-hand graph provides us with a visual hint that this is the case, even before we have looked at a single line of the disassembly.

The right-hand graph is Ghidra's result based solely on its understanding of the disassembly of Listing 20-2. The lack of a jump table makes it much more challenging to identify this as a switch statement. What you are seeing is a visual representation of the switch statement using Ghidra's Nested Code Layout. This is the default layout for function graphs in Ghidra and is intended to represent the flow structures in a program. The horizontal branching in this graph suggests conditional execution (if/else) branching to mutually exclusive alternatives. The vertical symmetry suggests that the alternative execution paths have been very carefully balanced to place equal numbers of blocks in each vertical half of the graph. Finally, the distance that the graph traverses horizontally is an indicator of the depth reached by the search, which in turn is dictated by the total number of case labels present in the switch. For a binary search, this depth will always be on the order of $log_2(num\_cases)$. The similarity between the indentation of the graphical representation and the algorithm outlined in Listing 20-3 is easily observable.

Turning our attention to the Decompiler window, Figure 20-2 shows the partial decompilation of the functions displayed in Figure 20-1. On the left is the decompiled version of Listing 20-1. As with the graph, the presence of a jump table in the binary helps Ghidra identify the code as a switch statement.

On the right is the decompiled version of Listing 20-2. The decompiler has presented the switch statement as a nested if/else structure consistent with a binary search, and similar in structure to Listing 20-3. You can see that first comparison is against 719, the median value in the list, and that subsequent comparisons continue to divide the search space in half. Referring to Figure 20-1 (as well as Listing 20-3), we can again observe that the graphical representations of each function closely correspond to the indentation patterns observed in the Decompiler window.

Now that you have an idea of what is happening from a high level, let's look inside the binaries and investigate what is happening at a low level. Since our objective in this chapter is to observe differences between compilers, we present this example as a series of comparisons between two compilers, gcc and Microsoft C/C++.[6]

---

6. <gcc> accepts a large number of command line arguments, and each may affect the resulting generated code. For our starting point, the following gcc command was used to compile the example: <gcc switch_demo_1.c -m32 -fno-pie -fno-pic -fno-stack-protector -o switch_demo_1_x86>. The Microsoft C/C++ example is an unmodified x86 debug build. Additional options will be introduced in subsequent examples.

Decompile: switch1 - (switch_demo_1_x86_gcc)	Decompile: switch4 - (switch_demo_1_x86_gcc)

```
 1
 2   int switch1(int a,int b,int c,int d)
 3
 4   {
 5     int result;
 6
 7     result = 0;
 8     switch(a) {
 9     case 1:
10       result = b + a;
11       break;
12     case 2:
13       result = c + a;
14       break;
15     case 3:
16       result = d + a;
17       break;
18     case 4:
19       result = c + b;
20       break;
21     case 5:
22       result = d + b;
23       break;
24     case 6:
```

```
 1
 2   int switch4(int a,int b,int c,int d)
 3
 4   {
 5     int result;
 6
 7     result = 0;
 8     if (a == 719) {
 9       result = d + c;
10     }
11     else {
12       if (a < 720) {
13         if (a == 295) {
14           result = d + 0x127;
15         }
16         else {
17           if (a < 296) {
18             if (a == 1) {
19               result = b + 1;
20             }
21             else {
22               if (a == 211) {
23                 result = c + 0xd3;
24               }
```

Figure 20-2: Ghidra decompiled switch statement examples

Example: Comparing gcc with Microsoft C/C++ Compiler

In this example, we compare two 32-bit x86 binaries generated for Listing 20-1 by two distinct compilers. We will attempt to identify components of a switch statement in each binary, locate the associated jump table in each binary, and point out significant differences between the two binaries. Let's start by looking at the switch-related components for Listing 20-1 in the binary built with gcc:

```
0001075a   CMP❶     dword ptr [EBP + value],12
0001075e   JA       switchD_00010771::caseD_0❷
00010764   MOV      EAX,dword ptr [EBP + a]
00010767   SHL      EAX,0x2
0001076a   ADD      EAX,switchD_00010771::switchdataD_00010ee0      = 00010805
0001076f   MOV      EAX,dword ptr [EAX]=>->switchD_00010771::caseD_0 = 00010805
           switchD_00010771::switchD
00010771   JMP      EAX
           switchD_00010771::caseD_1❸              XREF[2]:     00010771(j), 00010ee4(*)
```

```
00010773   MOV    EDX,dword ptr [EBP + a]
00010776   MOV    EAX,dword ptr [EBP + b]
00010779   ADD    EAX,EDX
0001077b   MOV    dword ptr [EBP + result],EAX
0001077e   JMP    switchD_00010771::caseD_0
;--content omitted for remaining cases--
        switchD_00010771::switchdataD_00010ee0❹   XREF[2]: switch_version_1:0001076a(*),
                                                            switch_version_1:0001076f(R)

00010ee0   addr   switchD_00010771::caseD_0❺
00010ee4   addr   switchD_00010771::caseD_1
00010ee8   addr   switchD_00010771::caseD_2
00010eec   addr   switchD_00010771::caseD_3
00010ef0   addr   switchD_00010771::caseD_4
00010ef4   addr   switchD_00010771::caseD_5
00010ef8   addr   switchD_00010771::caseD_6
00010efc   addr   switchD_00010771::caseD_7
00010f00   addr   switchD_00010771::caseD_8
00010f04   addr   switchD_00010771::caseD_9
00010f08   addr   switchD_00010771::caseD_a
00010f0c   addr   switchD_00010771::caseD_b
00010f10   addr   switchD_00010771::caseD_c
```

Ghidra recognizes the switch bounds test ❶, the jump table ❹, and individual case blocks by value, such as the one at switchD_00010771::caseD_1 ❸. The compiler generated a jump table with 13 entries, although Listing 20-1 contained only 12 cases. The additional case, case 0 (the first entry ❺ in the jump table), shares a target address with every value outside the range 1 to 12. In other words, case 0 is part of the default case. While it may seem that negative numbers are being excluded from the default, the CMP, JA sequence works as a comparison on unsigned values; thus, -1 (0xFFFFFFFF) would be seen as 4294967295, which is much larger than 12 and therefore excluded from the valid range for indexing the jump table. The JA instruction directs all such cases to the default location: switchD_00010771::caseD_0 ❷.

Now that we understand the basic components of the code generated by the gcc compiler, let's shift our focus to the same components in code generated by the Microsoft C/C++ compiler in debug mode:

```
00411e88   MOV    ECX,dword ptr [EBP + local_d4]
00411e8e   SUB❶   ECX,0x1
00411e91   MOV    dword ptr [EBP + local_d4],ECX
00411e97   CMP❷   dword ptr [EBP + local_d4],11
00411e9e   JA     switchD_00411eaa::caseD_c
00411ea4   MOV    EDX,dword ptr [EBP + local_d4]
        switchD_00411eaa::switchD
00411eaa   JMP    dword ptr [EDX*0x4 + ->switchD_00411eaa::caseD   = 00411eb1
        switchD_00411eaa::caseD_1              XREF[2]: 00411eaa(j), 00411f4c(*)
00411eb1   MOV    EAX,dword ptr [EBP + param_1]
00411eb4   ADD    EAX,dword ptr [EBP + param_2]
```

```
00411eb7  MOV    dword ptr [EBP + local_c],EAX
00411eba  JMP    switchD_00411eaa::caseD_c
;--content omitted for remaining cases--
        switchD_00411eaa::switchdataD_00411f4c    XREF[1]: switch_version_1:00411eaa(R)
00411f4c  addr   switchD_00411eaa::caseD_1 ❸
00411f50  addr   switchD_00411eaa::caseD_2
00411f54  addr   switchD_00411eaa::caseD_3
00411f58  addr   switchD_00411eaa::caseD_4
00411f5c  addr   switchD_00411eaa::caseD_5
00411f60  addr   switchD_00411eaa::caseD_6
00411f64  addr   switchD_00411eaa::caseD_7
00411f68  addr   switchD_00411eaa::caseD_8
00411f6c  addr   switchD_00411eaa::caseD_9
00411f70  addr   switchD_00411eaa::caseD_a
00411f74  addr   switchD_00411eaa::caseD_b
00411f78  addr   switchD_00411eaa::caseD_c
```

Here, the switch variable (local_d4 in this case) is decremented ❶ to shift the range of valid values from 0 to 11 ❷, eliminating the need for a dummy table entry for the value 0. As a result, the first entry (or 0 index entry) in the jump table ❸ actually refers to the code for switch case 1.

Another, perhaps more subtle difference between the two listings is the location of the jump table within the file. The gcc compiler places switch jump tables in the read-only data (.rodata) section of the binary, providing a logical separation between the code associated with the switch statement and the data required to implement the jump table. The Microsoft C/C++ compiler, on the other hand, inserts jump tables into the .text section, immediately following the function containing the associated switch statement. Positioning the jump table in this manner has little effect on the behavior of the program. In this example, Ghidra is able to recognize the switch statements for both compilers and uses the term switch within the associated labels.

One of the key points here is that there is no single correct way to compile source to assembly. As a result, you cannot assume that something is not a switch statement simply because Ghidra fails to label it as such. Understanding the switch statement characteristics that factor into the compiler implementation can help you make a more accurate inference about the original source code.

Compiler Build Options

A compiler converts high-level code that solves a particular problem into low-level code that solves the same problem. Multiple compilers may solve the same problem in rather different ways. Further, a single compiler may solve a problem very differently based on the associated compiler options. In this section, we look at the assembly language code that results from using different compilers and different command line options. (Some differences will have a clear explanation; others will not.)

Microsoft's Visual Studio can build either debug or release versions of program binaries.[7] To see how the two versions are different, compare the build options specified for each. Release versions are generally optimized, while debug versions are not, and debug versions are linked with additional symbol information and debugging versions of the runtime library, while release versions are not.[8] Debugging-related symbols allow debuggers to map assembly language statements back to their source code counterparts and to determine the names of local variables (such information is otherwise lost during the compilation process). The debugging versions of Microsoft's runtime libraries have also been compiled with debugging symbols included, optimizations disabled, and additional safety checks enabled to verify that some function parameters are valid.

When disassembled using Ghidra, debug builds of Visual Studio projects look significantly different from release builds. This is a result of compiler and linker options specified only in debug builds, such as basic runtime checks (/RTCx), which introduce extra code into the resulting binary.[9] Let's jump right in and look at some of these differences in disassemblies.

Example 1: Modulo Operator

We begin our examples with a simple mathematical operation, modulo. The following listing contains the source code for a program whose only goal is to accept an integer value from the user and demonstrate integer division and the modulo operator:

```
int main(int argc, char **argv) {
    int x;
    printf("Enter an integer: ");
    scanf("%d", &x);
    printf("%d %% 10 = %d\n", x, x % 10);
}
```

Let's investigate how the disassembly varies across compilers for the modulo operator in this example.

---

7. Other compilers, such as gcc, also offer the ability to insert debugging symbols during the compilation process.

8. Optimization generally involves elimination of redundancy in code or selection of faster but potentially larger sequences of code in order to satisfy a developer's desire to create either faster or smaller executable files. Optimized code may not be as straightforward to analyze as unoptimized code and may therefore be considered a bad choice for use during a program's development and debugging phases.

9. Please see *https://docs.microsoft.com/en-us/cpp/build/reference/rtc-run-time-error-checks*.

Modulo with Microsoft C/C++ Win x64 Debug

The following listing shows the code that Visual Studio generates when configured to build a debug version of the binary:

```
1400119c6 MOV     EAX,dword ptr [RBP + local_f4]
1400119c9 CDQ
1400119ca MOV     ECX,0xa
1400119cf IDIV❶  ECX
1400119d1 MOV     EAX,EDX
1400119d3 MOV❷   R8D,EAX
1400119d6 MOV     EDX,dword ptr [RBP + local_f4]
1400119d9 LEA     RCX,[s_%d_%%_10_=_%d_140019d60]
1400119e0 CALL    printf
```

A straightforward x86 IDIV instruction ❶ leaves the quotient in EAX and the remainder of the division in EDX. The result is then moved to lower 32 bits of R8 (R8D) ❷, which is the third argument in the call to printf.

Modulo with Microsoft C/C++ Win x64 Release

Release builds optimize software for speed and size in order to enhance performance and minimize storage requirements. When optimizing for speed, compiler writers may resort to non-obvious implementations of common operations. The following listing shows us how Visual Studio generates the same modulo operation in a release binary:

```
140001136 MOV     ECX,dword ptr [RSP + local_18]
14000113a MOV     EAX,0x66666667
14000113f IMUL❶  ECX
140001141 MOV     R8D,ECX
140001144 SAR     EDX,0x2
140001147 MOV     EAX,EDX
140001149 SHR     EAX,0x1f
14000114c ADD     EDX,EAX
14000114e LEA     EAX,[RDX + RDX*0x4]
140001151 MOV     EDX,ECX
140001153 ADD     EAX,EAX
140001155 LEA     RCX,[s_%d_%%_10_=_%d_140002238]
14000115c SUB❷   R8D,EAX
14000115f CALL❸  printf
```

In this case, multiplication ❶ is used rather than division, and after a long sequence of arithmetic operations, what must be the result of the modulo operation ends up in R8D ❷ (again the third argument in the call to printf ❸). Intuitive, right? An explanation of this code follows our next example.

Modulo with gcc for Linux x64

We've seen how differently one compiler can behave simply by changing the compile-time options used to generate a binary. We might expect that a completely unrelated compiler would generate entirely different code yet again. The following disassembly shows us the gcc version of the same modulus operation, and it turns out to look somewhat familiar:

```
00100708   MOV    ECX,dword ptr [RBP + x]
0010070b   MOV    EDX,0x66666667
00100710   MOV    EAX,ECX
00100712   IMUL❶  EDX
00100714   SAR    EDX,0x2
00100717   MOV    EAX,ECX
00100719   SAR    EAX,0x1f
0010071c   SUB    EDX,EAX
0010071e   MOV    EAX,EDX
00100720   SHL    EAX,0x2
00100723   ADD    EAX,EDX
00100725   ADD    EAX,EAX
00100727   SUB    ECX,EAX
00100729   MOV❷   EDX,ECX
```

The code is very similar to the assembly produced by the Visual Studio release version. We again see multiplication ❶ rather than division followed by a sequence of arithmetic operations that eventually leaves the result in EDX ❷ (where it is eventually used as the third argument to printf).

The code is using a multiplicative inverse to perform division by multiplying because hardware multiplication is faster than hardware division. You may also see multiplication implemented using a series of additions and arithmetic shifts, as each of these operations is significantly faster in hardware than multiplication.

Your ability to recognize this code as modulo 10 depends on your experience, patience, and creativity. If you've seen similar code sequences in the past, you are probably more apt to recognize what's taking place here. Lacking that experience, you might instead work through the code manually with sample values, hoping to recognize a pattern in the results. You might even take the time to extract the assembly language, wrap it in a C test harness, and do some high-speed data generation to assist you. Ghidra's decompiler can be another useful resource for reducing complex or unusual code sequences to their more recognizable C equivalents.

As a last resort, or first resort (don't be ashamed), you might turn to the internet for answers. But what should you be searching for? Usually, unique, specific searches yield the most relevant results, and the most unique feature in the sequence of code is the integer constant 0x66666667. When we searched for this constant, the top three results were all helpful, but one in particular was worth bookmarking: *http://flaviojslab.blogspot.com /2008/02/integer-division.html*. Unique constants are also used rather frequently in cryptographic algorithms, and a quick internet search may be all it takes to identify exactly what crypto routine you are staring at.

Example 2: The Ternary Operator

The ternary operator evaluates an expression and then yields one of two possible results, depending on the boolean value of that expression. Conceptually, the ternary operator can be thought of as an if/else statement (and can even be replaced with an if/else statement). The following intentionally unoptimized source code demonstrates the use of this operator:

```
int main() {
    volatile int x = 3;
    volatile int y = x * 13;
 ❶ volatile int z = y == 30 ? 0 : -1;
}
```

NOTE *The* volatile *keyword asks the compiler not to optimize code involving the associated variables. Without its use here, some compilers will optimize away the entire body of this function since none of the statements contribute to the function's result. This is one of the challenges you might face when coding examples for yourself or for others.*

As for the behavior of the unoptimized code, the assignment into variable z ❶ could be replaced with the following if/else statement without changing the semantics of the program:

```
if (y == 30) {
    z = 0;
} else {
    z = -1;
}
```

Let's see how the ternary operator code is handled by different compilers and different compiler options.

Ternary Operator with gcc on Linux x64

gcc, with no options, generated the following assembly for the initialization of z:

```
00100616  MOV    EAX,dword ptr [RBP + y]
00100619  CMP❶   EAX,0x1e
0010061c  JNZ    LAB_00100625
0010061e  MOV    EAX,0x0
00100623  JMP    LAB_0010062a
          LAB_00100625
00100625  MOV    EAX,0xffffffff
          LAB_0010062a
0010062a  MOV❷   dword ptr [RBP + z],EAX
```

This code uses the if/else implementation. Local variable y is compared to 30 ❶ to decide whether to set EAX to 0 or 0xffffffff in opposing branches of the if/else before assigning the result into z ❷.

Ternary Operator with Microsoft C/C++ Win x64 Release

Visual Studio yields a very different implementation of the statement containing the ternary operator. Here, the compiler recognizes that a single instruction can be used to conditionally generate either 0 or -1 (and no other possible value) and uses this instruction in lieu of the if/else construct we saw earlier:

```
140001013 MOV    EAX,dword ptr [RSP + local_res8]
140001017 SUB❶   EAX,0x1e
14000101a NEG❷   EAX
14000101c SBB❸   EAX,EAX
14000101e MOV    dword ptr [RSP + local_res8],EAX
```

The SBB instruction ❸ (*subtract with borrow*) subtracts the second operand from the first operand and then subtracts the carry flag, CF (which can be only 0 or 1). The equivalent arithmetic expression to SBB EAX,EAX is EAX − EAX − CF, which reduces to 0 − CF. This, in turn, can result only in 0 (when CF == 0) or -1 (when CF == 1). For this trick to work, the compiler must set the carry properly prior to executing the SBB instruction. This is accomplished by comparing EAX to the constant 0x1e (30) ❶ using a subtraction that leaves EAX equal to 0 only when EAX was initially 0x1e. The NEG instruction ❷ then sets the carry flag for the SBB instruction that follows.[10]

Ternary Operator with gcc on Linux x64 (Optimized)

When we ask gcc to try a little harder by optimizing its code (-O2), the result is not unlike the Visual Studio code in the previous example:

```
00100506 MOV     EAX,dword ptr [RSP + y]
0010050a CMP     EAX,0x1e
0010050d SETNZ❶ AL
00100510 MOVZX   EAX,AL
00100513 NEG❷    EAX
00100515 MOV❸    dword ptr [RSP + z],EAX
```

In this case, gcc uses SETNZ ❶ to conditionally set the AL register to either 0 or 1 based on the state of the zero flag resulting from the preceding comparison. The result is then negated ❷ to become either 0 or -1 before assignment into variable z ❸.

---

10. The NEG instruction clears the carry flag (CF) when its operand is zero and sets the carry flag in all other cases.

Example 3: Function Inlining

When a programmer marks a function inline, they are suggesting to the compiler that any calls to the function should be replaced with a copy of the entire function body. The intent is to speed up the function call by eliminating parameter and stack frame setup and teardown. The trade-off is that many copies of an inlined function make the binary larger. Inlined functions can be very difficult to recognize in binaries because the distinctive call instruction is eliminated.

Even when the inline keyword has not been used, compilers may elect to inline a function on their own initiative. In our third example, we are making a call to the following function:

```
int maybe_inline() {
    return 0x12abcdef;
}
int main() {
    int v = maybe_inline();
    printf("after maybe_inline: v = %08x\n", v);return 0;
}
```

Function Call with gcc on Linux x86

After building a Linux x86 binary using gcc with no optimizations, we disassemble it to see the following listing:

```
00010775   PUSH   EBP
00010776   MOV    EBP,ESP
00010778   PUSH   ECX
00010779   SUB    ESP,0x14
0001077c   CALL❶  maybe_inline
00010781   MOV    dword ptr [EBP + local_14],EAX
00010784   SUB    ESP,0x8
00010787   PUSH   dword ptr [EBP + local_14]
0001078a   PUSH   s_after_maybe_inline:_v_=_%08x_000108e2
0001078f   CALL   printf
```

We can clearly see the call ❶ to the maybe_inline function in this disassembly, even though it is just a single line of code returning a constant value.

Optimized Function Call with gcc on Linux x86

Next, we look at an optimized (-O2) version of the same source code:

```
0001058a   PUSH   EBP
0001058b   MOV    EBP,ESP
0001058d   PUSH   ECX
0001058e   SUB    ESP,0x8
00010591   PUSH❶  0x12abcdef
00010596   PUSH   s_after_maybe_inline:_v_=_%08x_000108c2
0001059b   PUSH   0x1
0001059d   CALL   __printf_chk
```

Contrasting this code with the unoptimized code, we see that the call to maybe_inline has been eliminated, and the constant value ❶ returned by maybe_inline is pushed directly onto the stack to be used as an argument for the call to printf. This optimized version of the function call is identical to what you would see if the function had been designated inline.

Having examined some of the ways that optimizations can influence the code generated by compilers, let's turn our attention to the different ways that compiler designers choose to implement language-specific features when language designers leave implementation details to the compiler writers.

Compiler-Specific C++ Implementation

Programming languages are designed by programmers for programmers. Once the dust of the design process has settled, it's up to compiler writers to build the tools that faithfully translate programs written in the new high-level language into semantically equivalent machine language programs. When a language permits a programmer to do A, B, and C, it's up to the compiler writers to find a way to make these things possible.

C++ gives us three excellent examples of behaviors required by the language, but whose implementation details were left to the compiler writer to sort out:

- Within a nonstatic member function of a class, programmers may refer to a variable named this, which is never explicitly declared anywhere. (See Chapters 6 and 8 for compilers' treatment of this.)
- Function overloading is allowed. Programmers are free to reuse function names as often as they like, subject to restrictions on their parameter lists.
- Type introspection is supported through the use of the dynamic_cast and typeid operators.

Function Overloading

Function overloading in C++ allows programmers to name functions identically, with the caveat that any two functions that share a name must have different parameter sequences. Name mangling, introduced in Chapter 8, is the under-the-hood mechanism that allows overloading to work by ensuring that no two symbols share the same name by the time the linker is asked to do its job.

Often, one of the earliest signs that you are working with a C++ binary is the presence of mangled names. The two most popular name mangling schemes are Microsoft's and the Intel Itanium ABI.[11] The Intel standard

---

11. See *https://docs.microsoft.com/en-us/cpp/build/reference/decorated-names* for Microsoft and *https://itanium-cxx-abi.github.io/cxx-abi/abi.html#mangling* for Intel.

has been widely adopted by other Unix compilers such as g++ and clang. The following shows a C++ function name and the mangled version of that name under both the Microsoft and Intel schemes:

Function   `void SubClass::vfunc1()`

Microsoft scheme   `?vfunc1@SubClass@@UAEXXZ`

Intel scheme   `_ZN8SubClass6vfunc1Ev`

Most languages that permit overloading, including Objective-C, Swift, and Rust, incorporate some form of name mangling at the implementation level. A passing familiarity with name-mangling styles can provide you with clues about a program's original source language as well as the compiler used to build the program.

RTTI Implementations

In Chapter 8, we discussed C++ Runtime Type Identification (RTTI) and the lack of a standard for implementing RTTI by a compiler. In fact, runtime type identification is not mentioned anywhere in the C++ standard, so it should be no surprise that implementations differ. To support the `dynamic_cast` operator, RTTI data structures record not only a class's name, but its entire inheritance hierarchy, including any multiple inheritance relationships. Locating RTTI data structures can be extremely useful in recovering the object model of a program. Automatic recognition of RTTI-related constructs within a binary is another area in which Ghidra's capabilities vary across compilers.

Microsoft C++ programs contain no embedded symbol information, but Microsoft's RTTI data structures are well understood, and Ghidra will locate them when present. Any RTTI-related information Ghidra does locate will be summarized in the Symbol Tree's *Classes* folder, which will contain an entry for each class that Ghidra locates using its RTTI analyzer.

Programs built with g++ include symbol table information unless they have been stripped. For unstripped g++ binaries, Ghidra relies exclusively on the mangled names it finds in the binary, and it uses those names to identify RTTI-related data structures and the classes they are associated with. As with Microsoft binaries, any RTTI-related information will be included in the Symbol Tree's *Classes* folder.

One strategy for understanding how a specific compiler embeds type information for C++ classes is to write a simple program that uses classes containing virtual functions. After compiling the program, you can load the resulting executable into Ghidra and search for instances of strings that contain the names of classes used in the program. Regardless of the compiler used to build a binary, one thing that RTTI data structures have in common is that they all reference, in some manner, a string containing the mangled name of the class that they represent. Using extracted strings and data cross-references, it should be possible to locate candidate RTTI-related data structures within the binary. The last step is to link a candidate RTTI structure back to the associated class's vftable, which is best accomplished by following data cross-references backward from the candidate RTTI structure until a table of function pointers (the vftable) is reached. Let's walk through an example that uses this method.

Example: Locating RTTI Information in a Linux x86-64 g++ Binary

To demonstrate these concepts, we created a small program with a BaseClass, a SubClass, a SubSubClass, and a collection of virtual functions unique to each. The following listing shows part of the main program we used to reference our classes and functions:

```
BaseClass *bc_ptr_2;
srand(time(0));
if (rand() % 2) {
    bc_ptr_2 = dynamic_cast<SubClass*>(new SubClass());
}
else {
    bc_ptr_2 = dynamic_cast<SubClass*>(new SubSubClass());
}
```

We compiled the program using g++ to build a 64-bit Linux binary with symbols. After we analyze the program, the Symbol Tree provides the information shown in Figure 20-3.

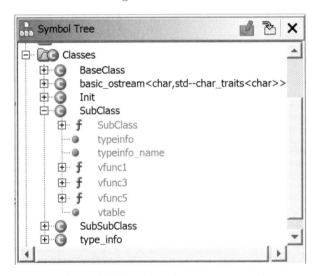

Figure 20-3: Symbol Tree classes for an unstripped binary

The *Classes* folder contains entries for all three of our classes. The expanded *SubClass* entry reveals additional information that Ghidra has uncovered about it. The stripped version of the same binary contains a lot less information, as shown in Figure 20-4.

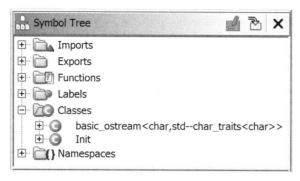

Figure 20-4: Symbol Tree classes for a stripped binary

In this case, we might, incorrectly, assume that the binary contains no C++ classes of interest, although it is likely a C++ binary based on the reference to a core C++ class (basic_ostream). Since stripping removes only symbol information, we may still be able to find RTTI information by searching for class names in the program's strings and walking our way back to any RTTI data structure. A string search yields the results shown in Figure 20-5.

Defi...	Location	String View	String Type	Length	Is Word
A	001017e8	"P8SubClass"	string	11	true
A	001017f8	"P9BaseClass"	string	12	true
A	00101808	"11SubSubClass"	string	14	true
A	00101818	"8SubClass"	string	10	true
A	00101828	"9BaseClass"	string	11	true
⚠	00101947	";*3$\""	string	6	false

Figure 20-5: String Search results revealing class names

If we click the "8SubClass" string, we are taken to this portion of the Listing window:

```
        s_8SubClass_00101818                    XREF[1]:   00301d20(*)
00101818  ds "8SubClass"
```

In g++ binaries, RTTI-related structures contain references to the corresponding class name string. If we follow the cross-reference on the first line to its source, we arrive at the following section of the disassembly listing:

```
          PTR___gxx_personality_v0_00301d18  XREF[2]: FUN_00101241:00101316(*)❶,
                                                       00301d10(*)❷
❸ 00301d18  addr   __gxx_personality_v0            = ??
❹ 00301d20  addr   s_8SubClass_00101818            = "8SubClass"
  00301d28  addr   PTR_time_00301d30               = 00303028
```

The source of the cross-reference ❹ is the second field within SubClass's typeinfo structure, which starts at address 00301d18 ❸. Unfortunately, unless you are willing to dive into the source code for g++, structure layouts like this are just something you need to learn by experience. Our last remaining task is to locate SubClass's vtable. In this example, if we follow the lone cross-reference to the typeinfo structure that originates from a data region ❷ (the other cross-reference ❶ originates from a function and can't possibly be the vtable), we hit a dead end. A little math tells us that the cross-reference originates from the location immediately preceding the typeinfo struct (00301d18 − 8 == 00301d10). Under normal circumstances, a cross-reference would exist from the vtable to the typeinfo structure; however, lacking symbols, Ghidra fails to create that reference. Since we know that another pointer to our typeinfo structure must exist somewhere, we can ask Ghidra for help. With the cursor positioned at the start of the structure ❸, we can use the menu option Search ▸ For Direct References, which asks Ghidra to find the current address in memory for us. The results are shown in Figure 20-6.

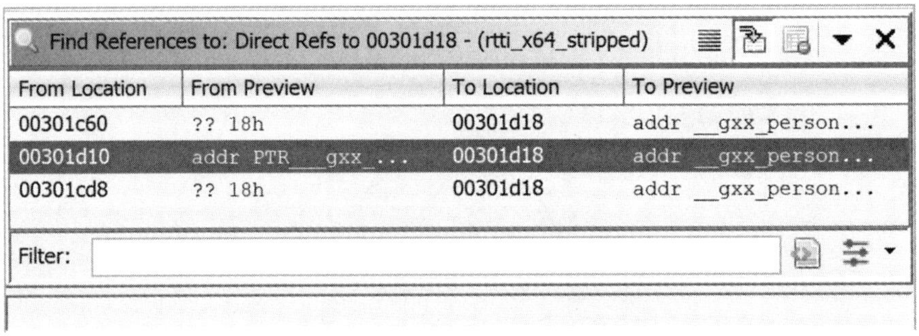

From Location	From Preview	To Location	To Preview
00301c60	?? 18h	00301d18	addr __gxx_person...
00301d10	addr PTR __gxx ...	00301d18	addr __gxx_person...
00301cd8	?? 18h	00301d18	addr __gxx_person...

Find References to: Direct Refs to 00301d18 - (rtti_x64_stripped)

Filter:

Figure 20-6: Results of direct reference search

Ghidra has found two additional references to this typeinfo structure. Investigating each of them finally leads us to a vtable:

```
❶ 00301c60      ??      18h              ?❷ -> 00301d18
  00301c61      ??      1Dh
  00301c62      ??      30h              0
  00301c63      ??      00h
  00301c64      ??      00h
  00301c65      ??      00h
  00301c66      ??      00h
  00301c67      ??      00h
              PTR_FUN_00301c68            XREF[2]:  FUN_00101098:001010b0(*),
                                                    FUN_00101098:001010bb(*)
❸ 00301c68  addr   FUN_001010ea
  00301c70  addr   FUN_00100ff0
  00301c78  addr   FUN_00101122
  00301c80  addr   FUN_00101060
  00301c88  addr   FUN_0010115a
```

Ghidra has not formatted the source ❶ of the `typeinfo` cross-reference as a pointer (which explains the lack of a cross-reference), but it does provide an EOL comment that hints at it being a pointer ❷. The vftable itself begins 8 bytes later ❸ and contains five pointers to virtual functions belonging to `SubClass`. The table contains no mangled names because the binary has been stripped.

In the next section, we apply this "follow the bread crumbs" analysis technique to help identify the `main` function in C binaries generated by several compilers.

Locating the main Function

From a programmer's perspective, program execution typically begins with the `main` function, so it's not a bad strategy to start analyzing a binary from the `main` function. However, compilers and linkers (and the use of libraries) add code that executes before `main` is reached. Thus, it's often inaccurate to assume that the entry point of a binary corresponds to the `main` function written by the program's author. In fact, the notion that all programs have a `main` function is a C/C++ compiler convention rather than a hard-and-fast rule for writing programs. If you have ever written a Windows GUI application, you may be familiar with the `WinMain` variation on `main`. Once you step away from C/C++, you may find that other languages use other names for their primary entry-point function. We refer to this function generically as the `main` function.

If there is a symbol named `main` in your binary, you can simply ask Ghidra to take you there, but if you happen to be analyzing a stripped binary, you will be dropped at the file header and have to find `main` on your own. With a little understanding of how executables operate, and a little experience, this shouldn't prove too daunting a task.

All executables must designate an address within the binary as the first instruction to execute after the binary file has been mapped into memory. Ghidra refers to this address as entry or _start, depending on the file type and the availability of symbols. Most executable file formats specify this address within the file's header region, and Ghidra loaders know exactly how to find it. In an ELF file, the entry point address is specified in a field named e_entry, while PE files contain a field named `AddressOfEntryPoint`. A compiled C program, regardless of the platform the executable is running on, has code at the entry point, inserted by the compiler, to make the transition from a brand-new process to a running C program. Part of this transition involves ensuring that arguments and environment variables provided to the kernel at process creation are gathered and provided to `main` utilizing the C calling convention.

NOTE *Your operating system kernel neither knows nor cares in what language any executable was written. Your kernel knows exactly one way to pass parameters to a new process, and that way may not be compatible with your program's entry function. It is the compiler's job to bridge this gap.*

Now that we know that execution begins at a published entry point and eventually reaches the main function, we can take a look at some compiler-specific code for effecting this transition.

Example 1: _start to main with gcc on Linux x86-64

By examining the start code in an unstripped executable, we can learn exactly how main is reached for a given compiler on a given operating system. Linux gcc offers one of the simpler approaches for this:

```
        _start
004003b0  XOR    EBP,EBP
004003b2  MOV    R9,RDX
004003b5  POP    RSI
004003b6  MOV    RDX,RSP
004003b9  AND    RSP,-0x10
004003bd  PUSH   RAX
004003be  PUSH   RSP=>local_10
004003bf  MOV    R8=>__libc_csu_fini,__libc_csu_fini
004003c6  MOV    RCX=>__libc_csu_init,__libc_csu_init
004003cd  MOV    RDI=>main,main❶
004003d4  CALL❷  qword ptr [->__libc_start_main]
```

The address of main is loaded into RDI ❶ immediately before a call ❷ is made to a library function named __libc_start_main, which means that the address of main is passed as the first argument to __libc_start_main. Armed with this knowledge, we can easily locate main in a stripped binary. The following listing shows the lead-up to the call to __libc_start_main in a stripped binary:

```
004003bf  MOV    R8=>FUN_004008a0,FUN_004008a0
004003c6  MOV    RCX=>FUN_00400830,FUN_00400830
004003cd  MOV    RDI=>FUN_0040080a,FUN_0040080a❶
004003d4  CALL   qword ptr [->__libc_start_main]
```

Though the code contains references to three generically named functions, we conclude that FUN_0040080a must be main because it is being passed as the first argument to __libc_start_main ❶.

Example 2: _start to main with clang on FreeBSD x86-64

On current versions of FreeBSD, clang is the default C compiler, and the _start function is somewhat more substantial and harder to follow than the simple Linux _start stub. To keep things simple, we'll use Ghidra's decompiler to look at the tail end of _start.

```
//~40 lines of code omitted for brevity
atexit((__func *)cleanup);
handle_static_init(argc,ap,env);
argc = main((ulong)pcVar2 & 0xffffffff,ap,env);
                /* WARNING: Subroutine does not return */
exit(argc);
}
```

In this case, main is the penultimate function called in _start, and the return value from main is immediately passed to exit to terminate the program. Using Ghidra's decompiler on a stripped version of the same binary yields the following listing:

```
// 40 lines of code omitted for brevity
atexit(param_2);
FUN_00201120(uVar2 & 0xffffffff,ppcVar5,puVar4);
__status = FUN_00201a80(uVar2 & 0xffffffff,ppcVar5,puVar4)❶;
                /* WARNING: Subroutine does not return */
exit(__status);
}
```

Once again, we can pick main ❶ out of the crowd, even when the binary has been stripped. If you are wondering why this listing shows two function names that have not been stripped, the reason is that this particular binary is dynamically linked. The functions atexit and exit are not symbols in the binary; they are external dependencies. These external dependencies remain, even after stripping, and continue to be visible in the decompiled code. The corresponding code for a statically linked, stripped version of this binary is shown here:

```
FUN_0021cc70();
FUN_0021c120(uVar2 & 0xffffffff,ppcVar13,puVar11);
uVar7 = FUN_0021caa0(uVar2 & 0xffffffff,ppcVar13,puVar11);
                /* WARNING: Subroutine does not return */
FUN_00266d30((ulong)uVar7);
}
```

Example 3: _start to main with Microsoft's C/C++ compiler

The Microsoft C/C++ compiler's startup stub is a bit more complicated because the primary interface to the Windows kernel is via *kernel32.dll* (rather than *libc* on most Unix systems), which provides no C library functions. As a result, the compiler often statically links many C library functions directly into executables. The startup stub uses these and other functions to interface with the kernel to set up your C program's runtime environment.

However, in the end, the startup stub still needs to call main and exit after it returns. Tracking down main among all of the startup code is usually a matter of identifying a three-argument function (main) whose return value is passed to a one-argument function (exit). The following excerpt from this type of binary contains calls to the two functions we are looking for:

```
140001272 CALL    _amsg_exit❶
140001277 MOV     R8,qword ptr [DAT_14000d310]
14000127e MOV     qword ptr [DAT_14000d318],R8
140001285 MOV     RDX,qword ptr [DAT_14000d300]
14000128c MOV     ECX,dword ptr [DAT_14000d2fc]
140001292 CALL❷   FUN_140001060
140001297 MOV     EDI,EAX
140001299 MOV     dword ptr [RSP + Stack[-0x18]],EAX
14000129d TEST    EBX,EBX
14000129f JNZ     LAB_1400012a8
1400012a1 MOV     ECX,EAX
1400012a3 CALL❸   FUN_140002b30
```

Here, FUN_140001060 ❷ is the three-argument function that turns out to be main, and FUN_140002b30 ❸ is the one-argument exit. Note that Ghidra has been able to recover the name ❶ of one of the statically linked functions called by the startup stub because the function matches an FidDb entry. We can use clues provided by any identified symbols to save some time in our search for main.

Summary

The sheer volume of compiler-specific behaviors is too numerous to cover in a single chapter (or even a single book, for that matter). Among other behaviors, compilers differ in the algorithms they select to implement various high-level constructs and the manner in which they optimize generated code. Because a compiler's behavior is heavily influenced by the arguments supplied to the compiler during the build process, it is possible for one compiler to generate radically different binaries when fed the same source with different build options selected.

Unfortunately, coping with all of these variations only comes with experience, and it is often very difficult to search for help on specific assembly language constructs, as it is very difficult to craft search expressions that will yield results applicable to your particular case. When this happens, your best resource is generally a forum dedicated to reverse engineering in which you can post code and benefit from the knowledge of others who have had similar experiences.

PART V

REAL-WORLD APPLICATIONS

21

OBFUSCATED CODE ANALYSIS

Even under ideal circumstances, comprehending a disassembly listing is a difficult task. High-quality disassemblies are essential for anyone trying to understand the inner workings of a binary, which is precisely why we have spent the last 20 chapters discussing Ghidra and its associated capabilities. It can be argued that Ghidra is so effective at what it does that it has lowered the barrier for entry into the binary analysis field. While certainly not attributable to Ghidra alone, recent advances in binary reverse engineering are not lost on anyone who does not want their software to be analyzed. Thus, over the last several years, an arms race of sorts has been taking place between programmers who wish to keep their code secret and reverse engineers

In this chapter, we examine Ghidra's role in this arms race and discuss some of the measures that have been taken to protect code, along with approaches to defeating those measures. We wrap up the chapter by introducing Ghidra's Emulator class and provide examples of how emulation scripts can give us an edge in this arms race.

Anti-Reverse Engineering

Anti–reverse engineering is an umbrella topic that covers all techniques that software developers might employ to make reverse engineering their products more challenging. Many tools and techniques exist to assist developers with this goal, with more appearing every day. The RE/anti-RE ecosystem is similar to the escalating dynamic that plays out between malware authors and antivirus vendors.

As a reverse engineer, you are likely to encounter techniques ranging from trivial to nearly impossible to defeat. The approaches that you will be required to use will also vary depending on the nature of the anti-reversing techniques you encounter, and may require some level of comfort with both static and dynamic analysis techniques. In the sections that follow, we discuss some of the more common anti-reversing techniques, why they are employed, and approaches for defeating them.

Obfuscation

Various dictionary definitions will inform you that *obfuscation* is the act of making something obscure, perplexing, confusing, or bewildering in order to prevent others from understanding the obfuscated item. In the context of this book and the use of Ghidra, the items being obfuscated are binary executable files (as opposed to source files or silicon chips, for example).

Obfuscation, by itself, is too broad to be considered an anti–reverse engineering technique. It also fails to cover all known anti–reverse engineering techniques. Specific, individual techniques can often be described as obfuscating or non-obfuscating techniques and, where applicable, we point these out in the sections that follow. It is important to note that there is no one correct way to categorize techniques, as the general categories often overlap in their descriptions. In addition, new anti–reverse engineering techniques are under continuous development, and it is not possible to provide a single all-inclusive list.

Because Ghidra is primarily a static analysis tool, we find it more useful to divide our discussion of techniques into two, broad categories: *anti–static analysis* and *anti–dynamic analysis*. Both categories may contain obfuscating techniques, but the former is more likely to confound static tools, while the latter generally targets debuggers and other runtime analysis tools.

Anti–Static Analysis Techniques

Anti–static analysis techniques aim to prevent an analyst from understanding the nature of a program without actually running the program. These are precisely the types of techniques that target disassemblers such as Ghidra and are thus of greatest concern whenever you are using Ghidra to reverse engineer binaries. Several types of anti–static analysis techniques are discussed here.

Disassembly Desynchronization

One of the older techniques designed to frustrate the disassembly process involves the creative use of instructions and data to prevent the disassembler from finding the correct starting address for one or more instructions. Forcing the disassembler to lose track of itself usually results in a failed or, at a minimum, incorrect disassembly listing. Listing 21-1 shows Ghidra's efforts to disassemble a portion of the Shiva anti–reverse engineering tool.[1]

```
0a04b0d1 e8 01 00 00 00 CALL❶  FUN_0a04b0d7
0a04b0d6 c7              ??     C7h❷
         ***********************************************************
         *                      FUNCTION                          *
         ***********************************************************
         undefined FUN_0a04b0d7()
             undefined AL:1 <RETURN>
         FUN_0a04b0d7                         XREF[1]: FUN_0a04b0c4:0a04b0d1(c)
0a04b0d7 58              POP❸   EAX
0a04b0d8 8d 40 0a        LEA❹   EAX,[EAX + 0xa]
         LAB_0a04b0db+1                       XREF[0,1]: 0a04b0db(j)
❺ 0a04b0db eb ff         JMP    LAB_0a04b0db+1
  0a04b0dd e0            ??❻    E0h
```

Listing 21-1: Sample of initial Shiva disassembly

This example executes a `CALL` ❶ that is immediately followed by a `POP` ❸. This sequence is not uncommon in self-modifying code and is used by the code to discover where it is running memory. The return address ❷ for the call instruction is `0a04b0d6` and sits on the top of the stack as execution arrives at the `POP` instruction. The `POP` instruction removes the return address from the stack and loads it into `EAX`, while the `LEA` that follows ❹ immediately adds `0xa` (10) to `EAX` so that `EAX` now holds `0a04b0e0` (keep this value handy, as we'll use it in a few moments).

The called function is unlikely to ever return to the original call point, as the original return address is no longer on top of the stack (it would need to be replaced in order to `RET` to the original return location), and Ghidra cannot form an instruction at the return address ❷ because `C7h` is not a valid start byte for an instruction.

So far, the code may be a little unusual or difficult to follow, but Ghidra is presenting a correct disassembly. This all changes when the `JMP` ❺ instruction is reached. This jump instruction is 2 bytes long, its address is `0a04b0db`, and the jump target is `LAB_0a04b0db+1`. The +1 suffix in the label is new to us. The address component of the label is the same as the address of the jump itself. The +1 is telling you that the jump target is 1 byte past `LAB_0a04b0db`. In other words, the jump lands right in the middle of the 2-byte jump instruction. While the processor doesn't care about this unusual situation (it will happily fetch whatever the instruction pointer points to), Ghidra

---

1. Several presentations related to Shiva have been given over the years, beginning with this one: *http://cansecwest.com/core03/shiva.ppt*.

just can't make it work. Ghidra has no means to concurrently display the byte at 0a04b0db (ff) as both the second byte of the jump and the first byte of another instruction. As a result, Ghidra is suddenly unable to continue with the disassembly, as indicated by the undefined data value at 0a04b0dd ❻. (This behavior is not restricted to Ghidra: virtually all disassemblers, whether they utilize a recursive descent algorithm or a linear sweep algorithm, fall victim to this technique.)

Ghidra makes note of any problems it encounters during disassembly by creating *error bookmarks* in the disassembly. Figure 21-1 shows two such bookmarks (X icon to the left of the offending addresses) in the left margin of the Listing window. Hovering over an error bookmark displays an associated detail message. In addition, you can open a listing of all bookmarks in the current binary by using Window ▸ Bookmarks.

Ghidra's message for the first error is "Unable to resolve constructor at 0a04b0d6 (flow from 0a04b0d1)," which means roughly "I think an instruction is supposed to exist at 0a04b0d6, but I couldn't create one." Ghidra's message for the second error is "Failed to disassemble at 0a04b0dc due to conflicting instruction at 0a04b0db (flow from 0a04b0db)," which means roughly "I cannot disassemble an instruction within an existing instruction."

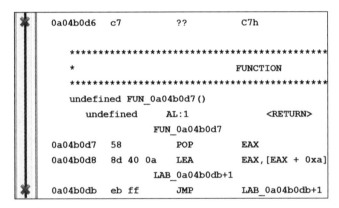

Figure 21-1: Ghidra error bookmarks

As a Ghidra user, you have no solution for the first error. A byte sequence is either a valid instruction or it isn't. With a bit of effort on your part, you can deal with the second error. The proper way to deal with this situation is to undefine the instruction that contains the bytes that are the target of the call and then define an instruction at the call target address in an attempt to resynchronize the disassembly. You will lose the original instruction, but you can leave yourself a comment to remind you of what the original instruction was. The following portion of the previous listing contains the overlapping instruction error:

```
      LAB_0a04b0db+1                          XREF[0,1]:   0a04b0db(j)
❶ 0a04b0db eb ff     JMP     LAB_0a04b0db+1
  0a04b0dd e0        ??      E0h
```

Right-clicking the JMP instruction ❶ and selecting Clear Code Bytes (hot-key C) from the context menu yields the following listing of undefined bytes:

```
   0a04b0db eb         ??      EBh
❶  0a04b0dc ff         ??      FFh
   0a04b0dd e0         ??      E0h
```

The byte that is the target ❶ of the JMP is now accessible for reformatting. Raw bytes are changed to code by right-clicking the start byte of an instruction and selecting Disassemble (hotkey D). The listing is now updated to the following:

```
❶  0a04b0dc ff e0      JMP     EAX
   0a04b0de 90         ??      90h
   0a04b0df c7         ??      C7h
```

The target of the jump instruction turns out to be yet another jump instruction ❶. In this case, however, the jump is impossible for a disassembler (and potentially confusing to the human analyst) to follow, as the target of the jump is contained in a register (EAX) and computed at runtime. This is an example of another type of anti–static analysis technique, discussed in the following section, "Dynamically Computed Target Addresses." We previously determined that EAX contains the value 0a04b0e0 by the time we reach this jump, and this is the address at which we must resume the disassembly process. Lather, rinse, repeat.

Referring back to Listing 21-1, as an alternative to manually moving to address 0a04b0e0 to resume the disassembly, you can set the value of EAX to the known value by right-clicking the address ❸ and selecting Set Register Values. Ghidra will then add a special markup called a *register transition* around the instruction to indicate the *assumed* value of the JMP target, EAX. Subsequent clearing (hotkey C) and disassembling (hotkey D) from this location will restart the recursive descent disassembly process from the JMP to the target, 0a04b0e0, and beyond (including creating the XREFs between those code blocks).

An advantage of this approach is that the code is annotated to show the target of the JMP, allowing other analysts to easily follow the effective control flow through this section. (This is even clearer when combined with an override to the fallthrough for the LEA instruction at 0a04b0d8 in Listing 21-1). This alternative approach results in the following listing:

```
0a04b0d7 58            POP     EAX
0a04b0d8 8d 40 0a LEA        EAX,[EAX + 0xa]
                    -- Fallthrough Override: 0a04b0dc
0a04b0db eb            ??      EBh
           assume EAX = 0xa04b0e0
      LAB_0a04b0dc                              XREF[1]:      0a04b0d8
0a04b0dc ff e0         JMP     EAX=>LAB_0a04b0e0
           assume EAX = <UNKNOWN>
0a04b0de 90            ??      90h
0a04b0df c7            ??      C7h
```

```
            LAB_0a04b0e0                            XREF[1]:      0a04b0dc(j)
0a04b0e0 58          POP     EAX 0a04b0e0 POP EAX
```

Another example of desynchronization taken from a different binary demonstrates how processor flags may be utilized to turn conditional jumps into absolute jumps. The following disassembly demonstrates the use of the x86 Z flag for just such a purpose:

```
00401000  XOR❶   EAX,EAX
00401002  JZ❷    LAB_00401009+1
00401004  MOV    EBX,dword ptr [EAX]
00401006  MOV    dword ptr [param_1 + -0x4],EBX
      ❸ LAB_00401009+1                           XREF[0,1]: 00401002(j)
❹ 00401009  CALL   SUB_adfeffc6
0040100e  FICOM  word ptr [EAX + 0x59]
```

Here, the XOR instruction ❶ is used to zero the EAX register and set the x86 Z flag. The programmer, knowing that the Z flag is set, utilizes a jump-on-zero (JZ) instruction ❷, which will always be taken, to attain the effect of an unconditional jump. As a result, the instructions between the jump ❷ and the jump target ❸ will never be executed and serve only to confuse any analyst who fails to realize this fact. This example also obscures the actual jump target by jumping into the middle of the CALL instruction at 00401009 ❹. Properly disassembled, the code should read as follows:

```
00401000  XOR    EAX,EAX
00401002  JZ     LAB_0040100a
00401004  MOV    EBX,dword ptr [EAX]
00401006  MOV    dword ptr [param_1 + -0x4],EBX
❶ 00401009  ??     E8h
          LAB_0040100a                           XREF[1]: 00401002(j)
❷ 0040100a  MOV    EAX,0xdeadbeef
0040100f  PUSH   EAX
00401010  POP    param_1
```

The actual target of the jump ❷ has been revealed, as has the extra byte ❶ that caused the desynchronization in the first place. It is certainly possible to use far more roundabout ways of setting and testing flags prior to executing a conditional jump. The level of difficulty for analyzing such code increases with the number of operations that may affect the processor flag bits prior to testing their value.

Dynamically Computed Target Addresses

The phrase *dynamically computed* simply means that an address to which execution will flow is computed at runtime. In this section, we discuss several ways in which such an address can be derived. The intent of such techniques is to hide (obfuscate) the actual control flow path that a binary will follow from the prying eyes of the static analysis process.

One example of this technique was shown in the preceding section. The example used a call instruction to place a return address on the stack.

The return address was popped directly off the stack into a register, and a constant value was added to the register to derive the final target address, which was ultimately reached by performing a jump to the location specified by the register contents.

An infinite number of similar code sequences can be developed for deriving a target address and transferring control to that address. The following code, also used in Shiva, demonstrates an alternate method for dynamically computing target addresses:

```
0a04b3be  MOV   ECX,0x7f131760          ; ECX = 7F131760
0a04b3c3  XOR   EDI,EDI                 ; EDI = 00000000
0a04b3c5  MOV   DI,0x1156               ; EDI = 00001156
0a04b3c9  ADD   EDI,0x133ac000          ; EDI = 133AD156
0a04b3cf  XOR   ECX,EDI                 ; ECX = 6C29C636
0a04b3d1  SUB   ECX,0x622545ce          ; ECX = 0A048068
0a04b3d7  MOV   EDI,ECX                 ; EDI = 0A048068
0a04b3d9  POP   EAX
0a04b3da  POP   ESI
0a04b3db  POP   EBX
0a04b3dc  POP   EDX
0a04b3dd  POP   ECX
❶ 0a04b3de  XCHG  dword ptr [ESP],EDI    ; TOS =   0A048068
0a04b3e1  RET                           ; return to 0A048068
```

The comments to the right of the semicolons document the changes being made to various processor registers at each instruction. The process culminates in a derived value being moved into the top position of the stack (TOS) ❶, which causes the return instruction to transfer control to the computed location (0A048068 in this case). An analyst must essentially run the code by hand to determine the actual control flow path taken in the program.

Obfuscated Control Flow

Much more complex methods to hide control flow have been developed and utilized in recent years. In the most complex cases, a program will use multiple threads or child processes to compute control flow information and receive that information via some form of interprocess communication (for child processes) or synchronization primitives (for multiple threads).

In such cases, static analysis can become extremely difficult, as it becomes necessary to understand not only the behavior of multiple executable entities but also the exact manner by which those entities exchange information. For example, one thread may wait on a shared semaphore object, while a second thread computes values or modifies code that the first thread will make use of after the second thread signals its completion via the semaphore.[2]

---

2. Think of a *semaphore* as a token that must be in your possession before you can enter a room to perform an action. While you hold the token, no other person may enter the room. When you have finished with your task in the room, you may leave and give the token to someone else, who may then enter the room and take advantage of the work you have done (without your knowledge because you are no longer in the room). Semaphores are often used to enforce mutual exclusion locks around code or data in a program.

Another technique, frequently used within Windows malware, involves configuring an exception handler,[3] intentionally triggering an exception, and then manipulating the state of the process's registers while handling the exception. The following example is used by the tElock anti–reverse engineering tool to obscure the program's actual control flow:

```
❶ 0041d07a  CALL   LAB_0041d07f
            LAB_0041d07f                          XREF[1]: 0041d07a(j)
❷ 0041d07f  POP    EBP
❸ 0041d080  LEA    EAX,[EBP + 0x46]
❹ 0041d083  PUSH   EAX
  0041d084  XOR    EAX,EAX
❺ 0041d086  PUSH   dword ptr FS:[EAX]
❻ 0041d089  MOV    dword ptr FS:[EAX],ESP
❼ 0041d08c  INT    3
  0041d08d  NOP
  0041d08e  MOV    EAX,EAX
  0041d090  STC
  0041d091  NOP
  0041d092  LEA    EAX,[EBX*0x2 + 0x1234]
  0041d099  CLC
  0041d09a  NOP
  0041d09b  SHR    EBX,0x5
  0041d09e  CLD
  0041d09f  NOP
  0041d0a0  ROL    EAX,0x7
  0041d0a3  NOP
  0041d0a4  NOP
❽ 0041d0a5  XOR    EBX,EBX
❾ 0041d0a7  DIV    EBX
  0041d0a9  POP    dword ptr FS:[0x0]
```

The sequence begins by using a CALL ❶ to the next instruction ❷; the CALL instruction pushes 0041d07f onto the stack as a return address, which is promptly popped off the stack into the EBP register ❷. Next, the EAX register ❸ is set to the sum of EBP and 46h, or 0041d0c5, and this address is pushed onto the stack ❹ as the address of an exception handler function. The remainder of the exception handler setup takes place at ❺ and ❻, which complete the process of linking the new exception handler into the existing chain of exception handlers referenced by FS:[0].[4]

The next step is to intentionally generate an exception ❼, in this case an INT 3, which is a software trap (interrupt) to the debugger. (In x86 programs, the INT 3 instruction is used by debuggers to implement a software breakpoint.) Normally at this point, an attached debugger would gain control, as debuggers are given the first opportunity to handle the exception.

---

3. For more information on Windows Structured Exception Handling (SEH), see *http://bytepointer.com/resources/pietrek_crash_course_depths_of_win32_seh.htm.*

4. Windows configures the FS register to point to the base address of the current thread's environment block (TEB). The first field in a TEB is the head of a linked list of pointers to exception handler functions, which are called as appropriate when an exception is raised in a process.

In this case, the program fully expects to handle the exception, so any attached debugger must be instructed to pass the exception along to the program. Not allowing the program to handle the exception may cause the program to operate incorrectly or crash. Without understanding how the INT 3 exception is handled, it is impossible to know what may happen next in this program. If we assume that execution simply resumes following the INT 3, then it appears that a divide-by-zero exception will eventually be triggered by instructions ❽ and ❾.

The decompiled version of the exception handler associated with the preceding code begins at address 0041d0c5. The first portion of this function is shown here:

```
int FUN_0041d0c5(EXCEPTION_RECORD *param_1,void *frame,❶ CONTEXT *ctx) {
  DWORD code;

❷ ctx->Eip = ctx->Eip + 1;
❸ code = param_1->ExceptionCode;
❹ if (code == EXCEPTION_INT_DIVIDE_BY_ZERO) {
    ctx->Eip = ctx->Eip + 1;
❺ ctx->Dr0 = 0;
    ctx->Dr1 = 0;
    ctx->Dr2 = 0;
    ctx->Dr3 = 0;
    ctx->Dr6 = ctx->Dr6 & 0xffff0ff0;
    ctx->Dr7 = ctx->Dr7 & 0xdc00;
  }
```

The third argument to the exception handler function ❶ is a pointer to a Windows CONTEXT structure (defined in the Windows API header file *winnt.h*). The CONTEXT structure is initialized with the contents of all processor registers as they existed at the time of the exception. An exception handler has the opportunity to inspect and, if desired, modify the contents of the CONTEXT structure. If the exception handler feels that it has corrected the problem that led to the exception, it can notify the operating system that the offending thread should be allowed to continue. At this point, the operating system reloads the processor registers for the thread from the CONTEXT structure that was provided to the exception handler, and execution of the thread resumes as if nothing had ever happened.

In the preceding example, the exception handler begins by accessing the thread's CONTEXT in order to increment the instruction pointer ❷, to allow execution to resume at the instruction following the one that generated the exception. Next, the exception's type code (a field within the provided EXCEPTION_RECORD) is retrieved ❸ in order to determine the nature of the exception. This portion of the exception handler handles the divide-by-zero error ❹, generated in the previous example, by zeroing ❺ all of the x86 hardware debugging registers and disabling hardware breakpoints.[5]

---

5. In the x86 architecture, debug registers 0 to 7 (DR0–DR7) are used to control the use of hardware-assisted breakpoints. DR0 to DR3 are used to specify breakpoint addresses, while DR6 and DR7 are used to enable and disable specific hardware breakpoints.

Without examining the remainder of the tElock code, it is not immediately apparent why the debug registers are being cleared. In this case, tElock is clearing values from a previous operation in which it used the debug registers to set four breakpoints in addition to the INT 3 seen previously. In addition to obfuscating the true flow of the program, clearing or modifying the x86 debug registers can wreak havoc for software debuggers such as OllyDbg or GDB. Such anti-debugging techniques are discussed in "Anti–Dynamic Analysis Techniques" on page 487.

Opcode Obfuscation

While the techniques described to this point may provide—in fact, are intended to provide—a hindrance to understanding a program's control flow, none prevent you from observing the correct disassembled form of a program you are analyzing. Desynchronization had the greatest impact on the disassembly, but it was easily defeated by reformatting the disassembly to reflect the correct instruction flow.

A more effective technique for preventing correct disassembly is to encode or encrypt the actual instructions when the executable file is being created. The obfuscated instructions must be deobfuscated back to their original form before they are fetched for execution by the processor. Therefore, at least some portion of the program must remain unencrypted in order to serve as the startup routine, which, in the case of an obfuscated program, is usually responsible for deobfuscating some or all of the remainder of the program. A very generic overview of the obfuscation process is shown in Figure 21-2.

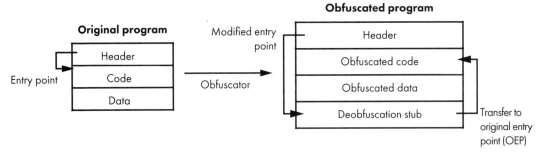

Figure 21-2: Generic obfuscation process

As shown, the input to the process is a program to be obfuscated. In many cases, the input program is written using standard programming languages and build tools (editors, compiler, and the like) with little thought required about the obfuscation to come. The resulting executable file is fed into an obfuscation utility that transforms the binary into a functionally equivalent, yet obfuscated, binary. As depicted, the obfuscation utility is responsible for obfuscating the original program's code and data sections and adding additional code (a deobfuscation stub) that performs the task of deobfuscating the code and data before the original functionality can be accessed at runtime. The obfuscation utility also modifies the program headers to redirect the program entry point to the deobfuscation stub, ensuring that execution begins with the deobfuscation process. Following deobfuscation, execution typically transfers to the entry point of the original program, which begins execution as if it had never been obfuscated at all.

This oversimplified process varies widely based on the obfuscation utility that is used to create the obfuscated binary. An ever-increasing number of utilities are available to handle the obfuscation process. Such utilities offer features ranging from compression to anti-disassembly and anti-debugging techniques. Examples include programs such as UPX (compressor, also works with ELF; *https://upx.github.io/*), ASPack (compressor; *http://www.aspack .com/*), ASProtect (anti–reverse engineering by the makers of ASPack), and tElock (compression and anti–reverse engineering; *http://www.softpedia.com /get/Programming/Packers-Crypters-Protectors/Telock.shtml.*) for Windows PE files. The capabilities of obfuscation utilities have advanced to the point that some anti–reverse engineering tools such as VMProtect integrate with the entire build process, allowing programmers to integrate anti–reverse engineering features at every stage of development, from source code through post-processing the compiled binary file (*https://vmpsoft.com/*).

SANDBOX ENVIRONMENTS

The purpose of a *sandbox environment* for reverse engineering is to allow you to execute programs in a manner that allows observation of the program's behavior without allowing that behavior to adversely impact critical components of your reverse engineering platform or anything it is connected to. Sandbox environments are commonly constructed using platform virtualization software, but they may be constructed on dedicated systems that are capable of being restored to a known-good state following the execution of any malware.

Sandbox systems are typically heavily instrumented in order to observe and collect information on the behavior of programs run within the sandbox. Collected data may include information on the filesystem activity of a program, the registry activity of a (Windows) program, and information about any networking activity generated by the program. One example of a complete sandbox environment is Cuckoo (*https://cuckoosandbox.org/*), a popular open source sandbox specifically oriented toward malware analysis.

As with any offensive technology, defensive measures have been developed to counter many anti–reverse engineering tools. In most cases, the goal of such tools is to recover the original, unprotected executable file (or a reasonable facsimile), which can then be analyzed using more traditional tools such as disassemblers and debuggers.

One such tool designed to deobfuscate Windows executables is called QuickUnpack (*http://qunpack.ahteam.org/?p=458*; site is in Russian). QuickUnpack, like many other automated unpackers, operates by functioning as a debugger and allowing an obfuscated binary to execute through its deobfuscation phase and then capturing the process image from memory. Beware that this type of tool actually runs potentially malicious programs in the hope of intercepting the execution of those programs after they have unpacked or deobfuscated themselves but before they have a chance to do anything malicious. Thus, you should always execute such programs in a sandbox-type environment.

Using a purely static analysis environment to analyze obfuscated code is a challenging task. Without being able to execute the deobfuscation stub, the obfuscated portions of the binary must be unpacked or decrypted before disassembly can begin. The Ghidra Address Type overview bar, at right in Figure 21-3, shows the layout of an executable that has been packed using the UPX packer. Ghidra color-codes content in the overview bar to give you an indication of the associated content in the binary. The general categories for the overview bar include the following:

- Function
- Uninitialized
- External Reference
- Instruction
- Data
- Undefined

Focusing on the overview bar in the figure, we can see Ghidra's preliminary assessment of various parts of the binary. Hovering over any of the sections in the overview bar will provide additional information about the corresponding region of the binary. The unusual appearance of this particular navigation bar is a tip-off that this binary has been obfuscated in some manner. Let's take a closer look at some of the sections in the overview bar.

Ghidra has identified a data section ❶ at the start of the file. Examining this content reveals the headers for the file along with informative content that is indicative of the type of obfuscation used on this file:

```
This file is packed with the UPX executable packer http://upx.tsx.org
UPX 1.07 Copyright (C) 1996-2001 the UPX Team. All Rights Reserved.
```

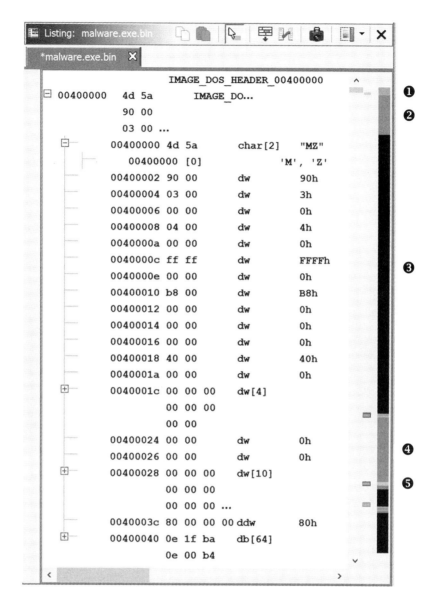

```
      Listing: malware.exe.bin                           ▾  ✕

  *malware.exe.bin  ✕

                        IMAGE_DOS_HEADER_00400000
  ⊟ 00400000   4d 5a         IMAGE_DO...                       ❶
               90 00                                           ❷
               03 00 ...
     ⊟         00400000 4d 5a        char[2]    "MZ"
               00400000 [0]                     'M', 'Z'
               00400002 90 00        dw         90h
               00400004 03 00        dw         3h
               00400006 00 00        dw         0h
               00400008 04 00        dw         4h
               0040000a 00 00        dw         0h
               0040000c ff ff        dw         FFFFh          ❸
               0040000e 00 00        dw         0h
               00400010 b8 00        dw         B8h
               00400012 00 00        dw         0h
               00400014 00 00        dw         0h
               00400016 00 00        dw         0h
               00400018 40 00        dw         40h
               0040001a 00 00        dw         0h
     ⊞         0040001c 00 00 00     dw[4]
                        00 00 00
                        00 00
               00400024 00 00        dw         0h
               00400026 00 00        dw         0h             ❹
     ⊞         00400028 00 00 00     dw[10]
                        00 00 00                                ❺
                        00 00 00 ...
               0040003c 80 00 00 00 ddw         80h
     ⊞         00400040 0e 1f ba     db[64]
                        0e 00 b4

  <                                              >
```

Figure 21-3: Ghidra Listing window and Address Type overview bar for a binary packed using UPX

This section is followed by a block of undefined content ❷ similar to the following, which appears in the Listing window:

004008a3	72	??	72h	r
004008a4	85	??	85h	
004008a5	6c	??	6Ch	l

The largest section ❸ contains uninitialized data, which appears as follows in the Listing window:

```
004034e3  ??        ??
004034e4  ??        ??
```

A little farther in the file, Ghidra has identified another block of undefined content ❹. At the end of this data is a region that Ghidra has identified as a function ❺. This function is easily recognizable as the UPX decompression stub, which Ghidra has identified as the entry point for the binary, as shown in the Listing window on the left in Figure 21-3. The undefined content segments we observed ❷❹ are the result of the UPX compression process. The job of the decompression stub is to unpack that data into the uninitialized region ❸ before finally transferring control to the unpacked code.

The information presented by the Address Type overview bar can be correlated with the properties of each segment within the binary to determine whether the information presented in each display is consistent. The memory map for this binary is shown in Figure 21-4.

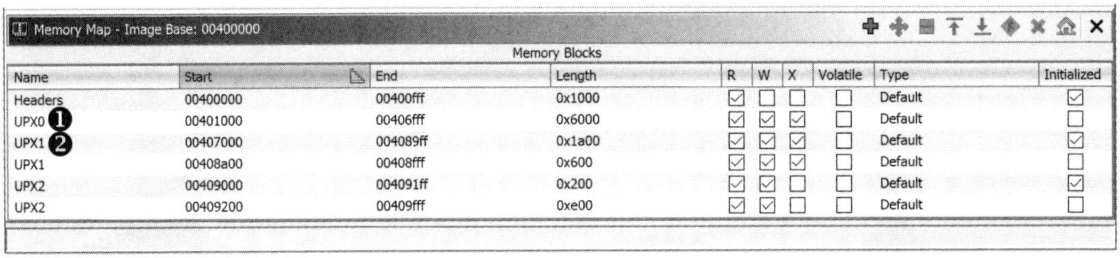

Name	Start	End	Length	R	W	X	Volatile	Type	Initialized
Headers	00400000	00400fff	0x1000	☑	☐	☐	☐	Default	☑
UPX0 ❶	00401000	00406fff	0x6000	☑	☑	☑	☐	Default	☐
UPX1 ❷	00407000	004089ff	0x1a00	☑	☑	☑	☐	Default	☑
UPX1	00408a00	00408fff	0x600	☑	☑	☑	☐	Default	☐
UPX2	00409000	004091ff	0x200	☑	☑	☐	☐	Default	☑
UPX2	00409200	00409fff	0xe00	☑	☑	☐	☐	Default	☐

Memory Map - Image Base: 00400000

Memory Blocks

Figure 21-4: Memory map of a UPX packed binary

In this particular binary, the entire range of addresses contained in segment UPX0 ❶ and segment UPX1 ❷ (00401000–00408fff) is marked as executable (the X flag is set). Given this fact, we should expect to see the entire Address Type overview bar colorized to represent functions. The fact that we do not, coupled with the fact that the entire range of UPX0 is uninitialized and writable, should be considered highly suspicious and provides valuable clues about the binary and how we might proceed with analysis.

Techniques for using Ghidra to perform the decompression operation in a static context (without actually executing the binary) on files such as this one are discussed in "Static Deobfuscation of Binaries Using Ghidra" on page 491.

Imported Function Obfuscation

Anti–static analysis techniques may also hide which shared libraries and library functions a binary uses in order to avoid leaking information about potential actions that the binary may perform. In most cases, it is possible to render tools such as dumpbin, ldd, and objdump ineffective for the purposes of listing library dependencies.

The effect of such obfuscations on Ghidra is most obvious in the Symbol Tree. The entire Symbol Tree for our earlier tElock example is shown in Figure 21-5.

Figure 21-5: Symbol Tree for obfuscated binary

Only two imported functions are referenced: GetModulehandleA (from *kernel32.dll*) and MessageBoxA (from *user32.dll*). Virtually nothing about the behavior of the program can be inferred from this short list. Here again the techniques are varied but essentially boil down to the fact that the program itself must load any additional libraries that it depends on, and once the libraries are loaded, the program must locate any required functions within those libraries. In most cases, these tasks are performed by the deobfuscation stub prior to transferring control to the deobfuscated program. The end goal is for the program's import table to have been properly initialized, just as if the process had been performed by the operating system's own loader.

For Windows binaries, a simple approach is to use the LoadLibrary function to load required libraries by name and then use the GetProcAddress function to perform function address lookups within each library. To use these functions, a program must either be explicitly linked to them or have an alternate means of looking them up. The Symbol Tree for the tElock example does not include either of these functions, while the Symbol Tree for the UPX example, shown in Figure 21-6, includes both.

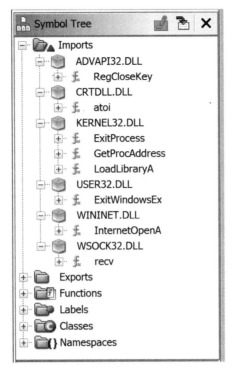

Figure 21-6: Symbol Tree for UPX example

The actual UPX code responsible for rebuilding the import table is shown in Listing 21-2.

```
          LAB_0040886c                              XREF[1]: 0040888e(j)
0040886c  MOV     EAX,dword ptr [EDI]
0040886e  OR      EAX,EAX
00408870  JZ      LAB_004088ae
00408872  MOV     EBX,dword ptr [EDI + 0x4]
00408875  LEA     EAX,[EAX + ESI*0x1 + 0x8000]
0040887c  ADD     EBX,ESI
0040887e  PUSH    EAX
0040887f  ADD     EDI,0x8
00408882  CALL❶   dword ptr [ESI + 0x808c]=>KERNEL32.DLL::LoadLibraryA
00408888  XCHG    EAX,EBP
          LAB_00408889                              XREF[1]: 004088a6(j)
00408889  MOV     AL,byte ptr [EDI]
0040888b  INC     EDI
0040888c  OR      AL,AL
0040888e  JZ      LAB_0040886c
00408890  MOV     ECX,EDI
00408892  PUSH    EDI
00408893  DEC     EAX
00408894  SCASB.REPNE ES:EDI
00408896  PUSH    EBP
00408897  CALL❷   dword ptr [ESI + 0x8090]=>KERNEL32.DLL::GetProcAddress
0040889d  OR      EAX,EAX
```

```
0040889f    JZ      LAB_004088a8
004088a1    MOV❸    dword ptr [EBX],EAX ; save to import table
004088a3    ADD     EBX,0x4
004088a6    JMP     LAB_00408889
```

Listing 21-2: Import table reconstruction in UPX

This example contains an outer loop responsible for calling LoadLibrary ❶ and an inner loop responsible for calling GetProcAddress ❷. Following each successful call to GetProcAddress, the newly retrieved function address is stored into the reconstructed import table ❸.

These loops are executed as the last portion of the UPX deobfuscation stub, because each function takes string pointer parameters that point to either a library name or a function name, and the associated strings are held within the compressed data region to avoid detection by the strings utility. As a result, library loading in UPX cannot take place until the required strings have been decompressed.

Returning to the tElock example, a different problem presents itself. With only two imported functions, neither of which is LoadLibrary or GetProcAddress, how can the tElock utility perform the function-resolution tasks that were performed by UPX? All Windows processes depend on *kernel32.dll*, which means that it is present in memory for all processes. If a program can locate *kernel32.dll*, a relatively straightforward process may be followed to locate any function within the DLL, including LoadLibrary and GetProcAddress. As shown previously, with these two functions in hand, it is possible to load any additional libraries required by the process and locate all required functions within those libraries.

In his paper "Understanding Windows Shellcode," Skape discusses techniques for doing exactly this.[6] While tElock does not use the exact techniques detailed by Skape, there are many parallels, and the net effect is to obscure the details of the loading and linking process. Without carefully tracing the program's instructions, it is extremely easy to overlook the loading of a library or the lookup of a function address. The following small code fragment illustrates the manner in which tElock attempts to locate the address of LoadLibrary:

```
0041d1e4    CMP     dword ptr [EAX],0x64616f4c
0041d1ea    JNZ     LAB_0041d226
0041d1ec    CMP     dword ptr [EAX + 0x4],0x7262694c
0041d1f3    JNZ     LAB_0041d226
0041d1f5    CMP     dword ptr [EAX + 0x8],0x41797261
0041d1fc    JNZ     LAB_0041d226
```

It is immediately obvious that several comparisons are taking place in rapid succession. What may not be immediately clear is the purpose of these comparisons. Reformatting the operands (right-click and then choose **Convert ▶ Char Sequence**) used in each comparison sheds a little light on the code, as seen in the following listing.

---

6. See *http://www.hick.org/code/skape/papers/win32-shellcode.pdf*, specifically Chapter 3, "Shellcode Basics," and Section 3.3, "Resolving Symbol Addresses."

```
0041d1e4   CMP    dword ptr [EAX],"Load"
0041d1ea   JNZ    LAB_0041d226
0041d1ec   CMP    dword ptr [EAX + 0x4],"Libr"
0041d1f3   JNZ    LAB_0041d226
0041d1f5   CMP    dword ptr [EAX + 0x8],"aryA"
0041d1fc   JNZ    LAB_0041d226
```

Each hexadecimal constant is actually a sequence of four ASCII characters, which Ghidra is capable of displaying as quoted ASCII and, together, spell LoadLibraryA.[7] If the three comparisons succeed, tElock has located the export table entry for LoadLibraryA and in a few short operations will obtain the address of this function for loading additional libraries. tElock's approach to function lookup is somewhat resistant to string analysis because the 4-byte constants embedded directly in the program's instructions do not look like standard, null-terminated strings and thus do not get included in the list of strings generated by Ghidra unless you change the defaults (for example, unchecking the Require Null Termination option during your string search).

Manually reconstructing a program's import table through careful analysis of the program's code is made easier in the case of UPX and tElock because, ultimately, both contain ASCII character data that you can use to determine exactly which libraries and which functions are being referenced. Skape's paper details a function-resolution process in which no strings at all appear within the code. The basic idea discussed in the paper is to precompute a unique hash value for the name of each function that you need to resolve.[8] To resolve each function, you can search through a library's exported names table. Each name in the table is hashed, and you can compare the resulting hash against the precomputed hash value for the desired function. If the hashes match, you have located the desired function, and can easily locate its address in the library's export address table.

To statically analyze binaries obfuscated in this manner, you need to understand the hashing algorithm used for each function name and apply that algorithm to all the names exported by the library the program is searching. With a complete table of hashes in hand, you can do a simple lookup of each hash you encounter in the program to determine which function the hash references. A portion of such a table, generated for *kernel32.dll*, might look like this:

❶ GetProcAddress : 8A0FB5E2
  GetProcessAffinityMask : B9756EFE
  GetProcessHandleCount : B50EB87C
  GetProcessHeap : C246DA44

---

7. Many Windows functions that accept string arguments come in two versions: one that accepts ASCII strings and one that accepts Unicode strings. The ASCII versions of these functions carry an A suffix, while the Unicode versions carry a W suffix.

8. A *hash function* is a mathematical process that can derive a fixed-size result (4 bytes, for example) from an arbitrary-sized input (such as a string).

```
GetProcessHeaps : A18AAB23
GetProcessId : BE05ED07
```

Note that the hash values are specific to the hash function being used within a particular binary and are likely to vary from one binary to another. Using this particular table, if the hash value 8A0FB5E2 ❶ were encountered within a program, you could quickly determine that the program was attempting to look up the address of the GetProcAddress function.

Skape's use of hash values to resolve function names was originally developed and documented for use in exploit payloads for Windows vulnerabilities; however, they have been adopted for use in obfuscated programs as well.

Anti–Dynamic Analysis Techniques

None of the anti–static analysis techniques covered in the past few sections have any effect whatsoever on whether a program will actually execute. In fact, while anti–static analysis techniques may make it difficult for you to comprehend the true behavior of a program using static analysis techniques alone, they can't prevent the program from executing, or they would render a program useless from the start and therefore eliminate the need to analyze the program at all.

Given that a program must run in order to do any useful work, dynamic analysis aims to observe the behavior of a program in motion (while it is running) rather than observe the program at rest (using static analysis while the program is not running). In this section, we briefly summarize some of the more common anti–dynamic analysis techniques. For the most part, these techniques have little effect on static analysis tools; however, where there is overlap, we point this out.

Detecting Virtualization

Sandbox environments commonly use virtualization software, such as VMware, to provide an execution environment for malicious software (or any other software of interest). The advantage of such environments is that they typically offer checkpoint and rollback capabilities that facilitate rapid restoration of the sandbox to a known-clean state. The primary disadvantage is that malware may be able to detect the sandbox. Under the assumption that virtualization equates to observation, many programs that want to remain undetected simply shut after once they determine that they are running within a virtual machine. Given the widespread use of virtualization for production purposes, this assumption is less valid today than it has been historically.

The following list describes a few of the techniques that have been used by programs running in virtualized environments to determine that they are running within a virtual machine rather than on native hardware:

Detection of virtualization-specific software
 Users often install helper applications within virtual machines to facilitate communications between a virtual machine and its host operating system or simply to improve performance within the virtual machine.

The VMware Tools collection is one example of this kind of software. The presence of such software is easily detected by programs running within the virtual machine. For example, when VMware Tools is installed into a Microsoft Windows virtual machine, it creates Windows registry keys that can be read by any program. Malware detecting these keys may elect to shut down before exhibiting any noteworthy behaviors. On the other hand, virtualization is so widely used today that a VMware image found without VMware Tools installed might be considered equally suspicious in the eyes of a piece of malware.

Detection of virtualization-specific hardware
Virtual machines use virtual hardware abstraction layers to provide the interface between the virtual machine and the host computer's native hardware. Characteristics of the virtual hardware are often easily detectable by software running within the virtual machine. For example, VMware has been assigned its own organizationally unique identifiers (OUIs) for its virtualized network adapters.[9] Observing a VMware-specific OUI is a good indication that a program is running within a virtual machine. Software that shuts down for this reason may be coaxed into executing by modifying the MAC address assigned to any virtual network adapters associated with the virtual machine.

Detection of processor-specific behavioral changes
Perfect virtualization is difficult to achieve. Ideally, a program should not be able to detect any difference between a virtualized environment and native hardware. However, this is seldom the case. Joanna Rutkowska developed her Red Pill VMware-detection technique after observing behavioral differences between the operation of the x86 sidt instruction on native hardware and the same instruction executed within a virtual machine environment.[10]

Detecting Instrumentation

Following creation of your sandbox environment and prior to executing any program you want to observe, you need to ensure that instrumentation is in place to properly collect and record information about the behavior of the program you are analyzing. A wide variety of tools exist for performing such monitoring tasks. Two widely used examples are *Process Monitor* from the Sysinternals group at Microsoft and *Wireshark*.[11] Process Monitor is a utility capable of monitoring certain activities associated with any running Windows process, including accesses to the Windows registry and filesystem

---

9. An OUI makes up the first 3 bytes of a network adapter's factory-assigned MAC address.

10. See *https://web.archive.org/web/20041130172213/http://invisiblethings.org/papers/redpill.html*.

11. See *https://docs.microsoft.com/en-us/sysinternals/downloads/procmon/* for Process Monitor and *http://www.wireshark.org/* for Wireshark.

activity. Wireshark is a network packet capture and analysis tool often used to analyze network traffic generated by malicious software.

Malware authors with a sufficient level of paranoia may program their software to search for running instances of such monitoring programs. Techniques that have been employed range from scanning the active process list for process names associated with such monitoring software to scanning the title bar text for all active Windows applications to search for known strings. Deeper searches can be performed, with some software going so far as to search for specific characteristics associated with Windows GUI components used within certain instrumentation software.

Detecting Debuggers

Moving beyond simple observation of a program, a debugger allows an analyst to take complete control of the execution of a program that requires analysis. Debuggers are commonly used to run an obfuscated program just long enough to complete any decompression or decryption tasks, and then the debuggers' memory-access features are used to extract the deobfuscated process image from memory. In most cases, standard static analysis tools and techniques can be used to complete the analysis of the extracted process image.

The authors of obfuscation utilities are well aware of such debugger-assisted deobfuscation techniques and so have developed measures to attempt to defeat the use of debuggers for execution of their obfuscated programs. Programs that detect the presence of a debugger often choose to terminate rather than proceed with any operations that might allow an analyst to determine the behavior of the program.

Techniques for detecting the presence of debuggers range from simple queries to the operating system via well-known API functions such as the Windows `IsDebuggerPresent` function, to lower-level checks for memory or processor artifacts resulting from the use of a debugger. An example of the latter includes detecting that a processor's trace (single step) flag is set.

As long as you know what to look for, there is nothing terribly tricky about trying to detect a debugger, and attempts to do so are easily observed during static analysis (unless anti–static analysis techniques are employed simultaneously). For more information on debugger detection, please consult the article "Anti Debugging Detection Techniques with Examples," which provides a comprehensive overview of Windows anti-debugging techniques.[12]

Preventing Debugging

Even an undetectable debugger can be thwarted using additional techniques that attempt to confound the debugger by introducing spurious breakpoints, clearing hardware breakpoints, hindering disassembly to make selection of appropriate breakpoint addresses difficult, or preventing the debugger from attaching to a process in the first place. Many of the

---

12. See *https://www.apriorit.com/dev-blog/367-anti-reverse-engineering-protection-techniques-to-use-before-releasing-software.*

techniques discussed in the previously referenced anti-debugging article are geared toward preventing debuggers from operating correctly.

Intentionally generating exceptions is one way a program may attempt to hinder debugging. In most cases, an attached debugger will catch the exception, and the user of the debugger must analyze why the exception occurred and whether to pass the exception along to the program being debugged. In the case of a software breakpoint such as the x86 INT 3, it may be difficult to distinguish a software interrupt generated by the underlying program from one that results from an actual debugger breakpoint. This confusion is exactly the effect that is desired by the creator of the obfuscated program. In such cases, it's possible, though harder, to understand the true program flow by using careful analysis of the disassembly listing.

Encoding portions of a program has the dual effect of hindering static analysis because disassembly is not possible and hindering debugging because placing breakpoints is difficult. Even if the start of each instruction is known, software breakpoints cannot be placed until the instructions have actually been decoded, as altering the instructions by inserting a software breakpoint is likely to result in a failed decryption of the obfuscated code and then a crash of the program when execution reaches the intended breakpoint.

The Shiva ELF obfuscation tool for Linux uses a technique called *mutual ptrace* as a means of preventing the use of a debugger in analyzing Shiva's behavior.

PROCESS TRACING

The *ptrace*, or process tracing, API available on many Unix-like systems provides a mechanism for one process to monitor and control the execution of another process. The GNU debugger (gdb) is one of the more well-known applications that uses the ptrace API. Using the ptrace API, a ptrace parent process may attach to and control the execution of a ptrace child process. To begin controlling a process, a parent process must first *attach* to the child process that it seeks to control. Once the parent process is attached, the child process is stopped anytime it receives a signal, and the parent is notified of this fact via the POSIX wait function, at which point the parent may choose to alter or inspect the state of the child process before instructing the child process to continue execution. Once a parent process has attached to a child process, no other process may attach to the same child process until the tracing parent chooses to detach from the child process.

Shiva takes advantage of the fact that only one other process may be attached to a process at any given time. Early in its execution, the Shiva process forks to create a copy of itself. The original Shiva process immediately performs a ptrace attach operation on the newly forked child. The newly forked child process, in turn, immediately attaches to its parent process. If either attach operation fails, Shiva terminates under the assumption that a debugger is being used to monitor the Shiva process. If both operations succeed, no other debugger can attach to the running Shiva pair, and Shiva can continue to run without fear of being observed. While operating in this manner, either Shiva process may alter the state of the other, making it difficult to determine, using static analysis techniques, what the exact control flow path is through the Shiva binary.

Static Deobfuscation of Binaries Using Ghidra

At this point, you may be wondering how, given all of the anti–reverse engineering techniques available, it is possible to analyze software that a programmer is intent on keeping secret. Given that these techniques target both static analysis tools and dynamic analysis tools, what is the best approach to take in revealing a program's hidden behavior? Unfortunately, no single solution fits all cases equally well.

In most cases, the solution depends on your skill set and the tools available to you. If your analysis tool of choice is a debugger, you will need to develop strategies for circumventing debugger detection and prevention protections. If your preferred analysis tool is a disassembler, you will need to develop strategies for obtaining an accurate disassembly and, in cases in which self-modifying code is encountered, for mimicking the behavior of that code in order to properly update your disassembly listings.

In this section, we discuss two techniques for dealing with self-modifying code in a static analysis environment (that is, without executing the code). Static analysis may be your only option when you are unwilling (because of hostile code) or unable (because of lack of hardware) to analyze a program while controlling it with a debugger. If these concepts make you feel like you are going down a rabbit hole, don't be discouraged. Ghidra has secret (or not-so-secret) weapons that we can leverage in the static deobfuscation arms race.

Script-Oriented Deobfuscation

Because Ghidra can be used to disassemble binaries for an ever-increasing set of processors, it is not uncommon to analyze a binary developed for an entirely different platform than the one on which you are running Ghidra. For example, you may be asked to analyze a Linux x86 binary even though you happen to be running Ghidra on macOS, or you may be asked to analyze a MIPS or ARM binary even though you are running Ghidra on an x86 platform.

In such cases, you may not have access to appropriate tools, such as debuggers, for dynamically analyzing the binary. When such a binary has been obfuscated by encoding portions of the program, you may have no other option than to create a Ghidra script that will mimic the deobfuscating stage of the program in order to properly decode the program and disassemble the decoded instructions and data.

This may seem like a daunting task; however, in many cases, the decoding stages of an obfuscated program use only a small subset of a processor's instruction set, so familiarizing yourself with the necessary operations may not require understanding the entire instruction set for the target processor.

Chapter 14 presented an algorithm for developing scripts that emulate the behavior of portions of a program. In the following example, we will utilize those steps to develop a simple Ghidra script to decode a program that has been encrypted with the Burneye ELF encryption tool. In our sample program, execution begins with the instructions in Listing 21-3.

```
❶ 05371035  PUSH    dword ptr [DAT_05371008]
❷ 0537103b  PUSHFD
❸ 0537103c  PUSHAD
❹ 0537103d  MOV     ECX,dword ptr [DAT_05371000]
  05371043  JMP     LAB_05371082
  ...
            LAB_05371082                    XREF[1]:     05371043(j)
❺ 05371082  CALL    FUN_05371048
  05371087  SHL     byte ptr [EBX + -0x2b],1
  0537108a  PUSHFD
  0537108b  XCHG    byte ptr [EDX + -0x11],AL
  0537108e  POP     SS
  0537108f  XCHG    EAX,ESP
  05371090  CWDE
  05371091  AAD     0x8e
  05371093  PUSH    ECX
❻ 05371094  OUT     DX,EAX
  05371095  ADD     byte ptr [EDX + 0xa81bee60],BH
  0537109b  PUSH    SS
  0537109c  RCR     dword ptr [ESI + 0xc],CL
  0537109f  PUSH    CS
  053710a0  SUB     AL,0x70
  053710a2  CMP     CH,byte ptr [EAX + 0x6e]
  053710a5  CMP     dword ptr [DAT_cbd35372],0x9c38a8bc
  053710af  AND     AL,0xf4
  053710b1  SBB     EBP,ESP
  053710b4  POP     DS
❼ 053710b5  ??      C6h
```

Listing 21-3: Burneye startup sequence and obfuscated code

The program begins by pushing the contents of memory location 05371008h onto the stack ❶ before pushing the processor flags ❷ and all processor registers ❸. The purpose of these instructions is not immediately clear, so we simply file this information away for later. Next, the ECX register is loaded with the contents of memory location 05371000h ❹. According to the algorithm presented in Chapter 14, we need to declare a variable named ECX at this point and initialize it from memory by using Ghidra's getInt function, as shown here:

```
int ECX = getInt(toAddr(0x5371000));    // from instruction 0537103d
```

Following an absolute jump, the program calls function FUN_05371048 ❺, which pushes address 05371087h (the return address) onto the stack. The disassembled instructions that follow the CALL instruction begin to make less and less sense. The OUT instruction ❻ is not generally encountered in userspace code, and Ghidra is unable to disassemble an instruction at address 053710B5h ❼. These are both indications that something is not quite right with this binary (that and the fact that the Symbol Tree lists only two functions: entry and FUN_05371048).

At this point, analysis needs to continue with the call to function FUN_05371048, which is shown in Listing 21-4.

```
FUN_05371048                                    XREF[1]:     entry:05371082(c)
❶ 05371048  POP    ESI
❷ 05371049  MOV    EDI,ESI
❸ 0537104b  MOV    EBX,dword ptr [DAT_05371004] = C09657B0h
  05371051  OR     EBX,EBX
❹ 05371053  JZ     LAB_0537107f
❺ 05371059  XOR    EDX,EDX
      ❻ LAB_0537105b                            XREF[1]:  0537107d(j)
  0537105b  MOV    EAX,0x8
      ❼ LAB_05371060                            XREF[1]:  05371073(j)
  05371060  SHRD   EDX,EBX,0x1
  05371064  SHR    EBX,1
  05371066  JNC    LAB_05371072
  0537106c  XOR    EBX,0xc0000057
        LAB_05371072                            XREF[1]:  05371066(j)
  05371072  DEC    EAX
  05371073  JNZ    LAB_05371060
  05371075  SHR    EDX,0x18
  05371078  LODSB  ESI
  05371079  XOR    AL,DL
  0537107b  STOSB  ES:EDI
  0537107c  DEC    ECX
  0537107d  JNZ    LAB_0537105b
        LAB_0537107f                            XREF[1]:  05371053(j)
  0537107f  POPAD
  05371080  POPFD
  05371081  RET
```

Listing 21-4: Main Burneye decoding function

This is not a typical function: it begins by immediately popping the return address off the stack into the ESI register ❶. Recalling that the saved return address was 05371087h, and taking into account the initialization of EDI ❷, EBX ❸, and EDX ❺, our script grows to the following:

```
int ECX = getInt(toAddr(0x5371000));   // from instruction 0537103D
int ESI = 0x05371087;                    // from instruction 05371048
int EDI = ESI;                            // from instruction 05371049
int EBX = getInt(toAddr(0x5371004));   // from instruction 0537104B
int EDX = 0;                              // from instruction 05371059
```

Following these initializations, the function performs a test on the value contained in the EBX register ❹ before entering an outer loop ❻ and an inner loop ❼. The remaining logic of the function is captured in the following completed script. Within the script, comments are used to relate script actions to the corresponding actions in the preceding disassembly listing.

```
public void run() throws Exception {
   int ECX = getInt(toAddr(0x5371000));   // from instruction 0537103D
   int ESI = 0x05371087;                  // from instruction 05371048
   int EDI = ESI;                         // from instruction 05371049
   int EBX = getInt(toAddr(0x5371004));   // from instruction 0537104B

   if (EBX != 0) {                        // from instructions 05371051
                                          //    and 05371053
      int EDX = 0;                        // from instruction 05371059
      do {
         int EAX = 8;                     // from instruction 0537105B
         do {
                                          // mimic x86 shrd instruction
                                          //    using several operations
            EDX = EDX >>> 1;              // unsigned shift right one bit
            int CF = EBX & 1;             // remember the low bit of EBX
            if (CF == 1) {                // CF represents the x86 carry flag
               EDX = EDX | 0x80000000;    // shift in low bit of EBX if it's 1
            }
            EBX = EBX >>> 1;              // unsigned shift right one bit
            if (CF == 1) {                // from instruction 05371066
               EBX = EBX ^ 0xC0000057;    // from instruction 0537106C
            }
            EAX--;                        // from instruction 05371072
         } while (EAX != 0);              // from instruction 05371073
         EDX = EDX >>> 24;                // unsigned shift right 24 bits
❶       EAX = getByte(toAddr(ESI));      // from instruction 05371078
         ESI++;
         EAX = EAX ^ EDX;                 // from instruction 05371079
         clearListing(toAddr(EDI));       // clear byte so we can change it
❷       setByte(toAddr(EDI), (byte)EAX); // from instruction 0537107B
         EDI++;
         ECX--;                           // from instruction 0537107C
      } while (ECX != 0);                 // from instruction 0537107D
   }
}
```

Whenever you are trying to emulate an instruction, you should pay particular attention to data sizes and register aliasing. In this example, we need to select an appropriate data size and variable to properly implement the x86 LODSB (load string byte) and STOSB (store string byte) instructions. These instructions write to (LODSB) and read from (STOSB) the low-order 8 bits of the EAX register,[13] leaving the upper 24 bits unchanged. In Java, there

---

13. The low-order 8 bits of the EAX register are also referred to as the AL register.

is no way to partition a variable into bit-sized portions other than using various bitwise operations to mask off and recombine portions of the variable. Specifically, in the case of the LODSB instruction ❶, a more faithful emulation would read as follows:

```
EAX = (EAX & 0xFFFFFF00) | (getByte(toAddr(ESI)) & 0xFF);
```

This example first clears the low 8 bits of the EAX variable and then merges in the new value for the low 8 bits using an OR operation. In the Burneye decoding example, the entire EAX register is set to 8 at the beginning of each outer loop, which has the effect of zeroing the upper 24 bits of EAX. As a result, we have elected to simplify our implementation of LODSB ❶ by ignoring the effect of the assignment on the upper 24 bits of EAX. No thought need be given to our implementation of STOSB ❷, as the setByte function requires us to cast the second argument to a byte.

Following execution of the Burneye decoding script, our disassembly would reflect all of the changes that would normally not be observable until the obfuscated program was executed on a Linux system. If the deobfuscation process was carried out properly, we are very likely to see many more legible strings within Ghidra's Search ▶ "For Strings... option". To observe this fact, you may need to select the Refresh icon in the String Search window.

Remaining tasks include (1) determining where the decoding function will return to, given that it popped its return address in the very first instruction of the function, and (2) coaxing Ghidra to properly display the decoded byte values as instructions or data as appropriate. The Burneye decoding function ends with the following three instructions:

```
0537107f   POPAD
05371080   POPFD
05371081   RET
```

Recall that the function began by popping its own return address, which means that the remaining stack values were set up by the caller. The POPAD and POPFD instructions used here are the counterparts to the PUSHAD and PUSHFD instructions used at the beginning of Burneye's start routine, as shown here:

```
        entry
❶ 05371035   PUSH    dword ptr [DAT_05371008]
  0537103b   PUSHFD
  0537103c   PUSHAD
```

The net result is that the only value that remains on the stack is the one that was pushed at the first line of entry ❶. It is to this location that the Burneye decoding routine returns, and it is at this location that further analysis of the Burneye protected binary would need to continue.

The preceding example may make it seem like writing a script to decode or unpack an obfuscated binary is a relatively easy thing to do. This is true in the case of Burneye, which does not use a terribly sophisticated initial obfuscation algorithm. The deobfuscation stub of more sophisticated utilities such as ASPack and tElock would require somewhat more effort to implement using Ghidra.

Advantages to script-based deobfuscation include that the binary being analyzed need never be executed and that it is possible to create a functional script without ever developing a complete understanding of the exact algorithm used to deobfuscate the binary. This latter statement may seem counterintuitive, as it would seem that you would need to have a complete understanding of the deobfuscation before you could emulate the algorithm using a script. Using the development process described here and in Chapter 14, however, all you really need is a complete understanding of each processor instruction involved in the deobfuscation process. By faithfully implementing each processor action using Ghidra and properly sequencing each action according to the disassembly listing, you will have a script that mimics the program's actions even if you do not fully comprehend the higher-level algorithm that those actions, as a whole, implement.

Disadvantages of using a script-based approach include that the scripts are rather fragile. If a deobfuscation algorithm changes as a result of an upgrade to a deobfuscation tool or through the use of alternate command line settings supplied to the obfuscation tool, a script that had been effective against that tool will likely need to be modified accordingly. For example, it is possible to develop generic unpacking scripts for use with binaries packed using UPX, but such scripts require constant tuning as UPX evolves.

Finally, scripted deobfuscation suffers from the lack of a one-size-fits-all solution to deobfuscation. There is no mega-script capable of deobfuscating all binaries. In a sense, scripted deobfuscation suffers from many of the same shortcomings as signature-based intrusion detection and antivirus systems. A new script must be developed for each new type of packer, and subtle changes in existing packers are likely to break existing scripts. Let's shift focus and look at a more generic approach to deobfuscation.

Emulation-Oriented Deobfuscation

A recurring theme encountered when creating scripts to perform deobfuscation tasks is the need to emulate a processor's instruction set in order to behave identically to the program being deobfuscated. Instruction emulators allow us to shift some or all of the work performed by these scripts over to the emulator and drastically reduce the amount of time required for Ghidra to deobfuscate. Emulators can fill the void between scripts and debuggers and can be more flexible than debuggers. An emulator can, for example, emulate a MIPS binary on an x86 platform or emulate instructions from a Linux ELF binary on a Windows platform.

Emulators vary in capabilities. At a minimum, an emulator requires a stream of instruction bytes and sufficient memory to dedicate to stack operations and processor registers. More sophisticated emulators may provide access to emulated hardware devices and operating system services.

Ghidra's Emulator Class

Fortunately, Ghidra provides a rich `Emulator` class as well as an `EmulatorHelper`, which provides a higher-level abstraction of common emulator functionality and facilitates the quick-and-easy creation of emulation scripts. In Chapter 18, we introduced p-code as an intermediate representation of the underlying assembly and described how this allows the decompiler to work against a variety of target architectures. Similarly, p-code supports emulator functionality as well, and Ghidra's `ghidra.pcode.emulate.Emulate` class provides the ability to emulate a single p-code instruction.

We can use Ghidra's emulator-related classes to build emulators that allow us to emulate a wide variety of processors. As with other Ghidra packages and classes, this functionality is documented in the Javadoc supplied with Ghidra and can be pulled up as a reference by clicking the red plus tool in the Script Manager window. If you are interested in writing emulators, we encourage you to check out the Javadoc associated with the emulator methods used in the following example.

CRACKME, CRACK YOURSELF

A *crackme* is a puzzle built by reverse engineers, for reverse engineers. The name derives from cracking a piece of software to bypass copy or usage restrictions—one of the more nefarious uses of reverse engineering skills. Crackmes provide a legal means to practice these skills as well as provide both the author of the crackme and the person analyzing the crackme a chance to show off their talent.

A common style of crackme receives a user input, transforms that input in some way, and then compares the result of the transformation to a precomputed output. When you attempt to solve a crackme, you are generally given only a compiled executable that contains both the code that performs the transformation and the final output for an unknown input. The crackme is solved when you derive the input that was used to generate the output contained in the binary, which typically requires understanding the transformation so well that you can derive the inverse transformation function.

Example: SimpleEmulator

Assume that we have a binary associated with the following crackme challenge, including some encoded content at the start of the file that eventually serves as the body of a function. In this example, we build an emulator script to automate the process of decoding the information needed to solve the crackme:

❶ unsigned char check_access[] = {
```
    0xf0, 0xed, 0x2c, 0x40, 0x2c, 0xd8, 0x59, 0x26, 0xd8,
    0x59, 0xc1, 0xaa, 0x31, 0x65, 0xaa, 0x13, 0x65, 0xf8, 0x66
};
```

```
unsigned char key = 0xa5;
void unpack() {
    for (int ii = 0; ii < sizeof(check_access); ii++) {
      ❷ check_access[ii] ^= key;
    }
}
void do_challenge() {
    int guess;
    int access_allowed;
    int (*check_access_func)(int);
  ❸ unpack();
    printf("Enter the correct integer: ");
    scanf("%d", &guess);
    check_access_func = (int (*)(int))check_access;
    access_allowed = check_access_func(guess)❹;
    if (access_allowed) {
        printf("Access granted!\n");
    } else {
        printf("Access denied!\n");
    }
}
int main() {
    do_challenge();
    return 0;
}
```

Even with the source code available, this crackme would require some
effort to solve because of the encoded content ❶. Ghidra's decompiler is frequently an awesome partner for solving crackme challenges, but this one
has interesting characteristics that complicate the process. Ghidra sees only
the encoded function body, but we need to know the function's actual purpose before we can solve the challenge. At runtime, the unpack ❸ function
call results in the decoding of the check_access ❷ function before check_access
is called ❹. The answer to this crackme is obfuscated, and we can build an
emulator script in Ghidra to help us attack this challenge. Unlike the previous example, this emulator will not just solve the problem for this specific
case, but will be capable of emulating somewhat arbitrary code.

Step 1: Define the Problem

Our task is to design and develop a simple emulator that will allow us to
choose a region of a disassembly and will emulate the instructions in that
region. The emulator needs to be added to Ghidra and be available as a
script. For example, if we select the unpack function for the crackme challenge
and run the script, our emulator should use the key to unpack the check_access
array and let us know the solution to the crackme challenge. The script will
write the unpacked code bytes into the program's memory in Ghidra.

Step 2: Create the Eclipse Script Project

We can create a project called *SimpleEmulator* using GhidraDev ▸ New ▸ Ghidra
Script Project. This gives us a *SimpleEmulator* folder in Eclipse with a folder

called *Home scripts* (refer to Figure 15-16 on page 325) waiting for our new script. We still need to create the actual script and enter the associated metadata to ensure that our script is documented and can be catalogued. The metadata collected in the script creation dialog is included in the file and, as Figure 21-7 shows, we have only one thing to do: Add script code here.

```java
//SimpleEmulator is a simplified emulator for Ghidra that
//emulates instructions and then displays the state of the
//program (to include registers, the stack, and local variables
//in the function that the emulation ends in.)
//@author KN
//@category Emulator
//@keybinding
//@menupath
//@toolbar

import ghidra.app.script.GhidraScript;

public class SimpleEmulator extends GhidraScript {

    @Override
    protected void run() throws Exception {
        //TODO: Add script code here
    }
}
```

Figure 21-7: Script template for SimpleEmulator

Step 3: Build the Emulator

We know that Eclipse will recommend imports if we need them as we develop our code, so we can jump right into the coding tasks we need to perform and add the recommended import statements when Eclipse detects that we need them. For functionality, we will rely on the following instance variable declarations throughout our SimpleEmulator class:

```java
private EmulatorHelper emuHelper;       // EmulatorHelper member variable object
private Address executionAddress;       // Initially the start of the selection
private Address endAddress;             // End of the selected region
```

Comments associated with each declaration describe the purpose of each variable. The executionAddress will initially be set to the start of the selected range, but will also be used to advance through the selection.

Step 3-1: Set Up the Emulator

The first thing we will do in our script's run method is instantiate our emulator helper object and activate the tracking of any memory written in the emulator so that we can write updated values back into the current program. The instantiation acts as a lock, similar to the lock that the CodeBrowser places on an open binary:

```
emuHelper = new EmulatorHelper(currentProgram);
emuHelper.enableMemoryWriteTracking(true);
```

Step 3-2: Select the Address Range to Be Emulated

Since we want the user to choose the section of code to be emulated, we need to ensure they have selected something in the Listing window. Otherwise, we will generate an error message.

```
if (currentSelection != null) {
    executionAddress = currentSelection.getMinAddress();
    endAddress = currentSelection.getMaxAddress().next();
} else {
    println("Nothing selected");
    return;
}
```

Step 3-3: Get Ready to Emulate

Within the selection, we want to ensure we are looking at an instruction in order to establish the initial processor context, initialize the stack pointer, and set up a breakpoint at the end of the selected region. The continuing flag indicates whether we are just starting the emulation or continuing the emulation, and determines which version of emuHelper.run is called in step 3-4:

```
Instruction executionInstr = getInstructionAt(executionAddress);
if (executionInstr == null) {
    printerr("Instruction not found at: " + executionAddress);
    return;
}
long stackOffset = (executionInstr.getAddress().getAddressSpace().
                    getMaxAddress().getOffset() >>> 1) - 0x7fff;
emuHelper.writeRegister(emuHelper.getStackPointerRegister(), stackOffset);
// Setup breakpoint at the end address
emuHelper.setBreakpoint(endAddress);
// Set continuing to false as we are just starting the emulation
boolean continuing = false;;
```

Step 3-4: Perform Emulation

In this section, you should recognize the use of some Ghidra API functions introduced in Chapter 14 (such as monitor.isCancelled). We need a loop to drive the emulation until a termination condition that we define is reached:

```
❶ while (!monitor.isCancelled() &&
         !emuHelper.getExecutionAddress().equals(endAddress)) {
      if (continuing) {
```

```
        emuHelper.run(monitor);
    } else {
        emuHelper.run(executionAddress, executionInstr, monitor);
    }
❷ executionAddress = emuHelper.getExecutionAddress();

    // determine why the emulator stopped, and handle each possible reason
❸ if (emuHelper.getEmulateExecutionState() ==
        EmulateExecutionState.BREAKPOINT) {
        continuing = true;
    } else if (monitor.isCancelled()) {
        println("Emulation cancelled at 0x" + executionAddress);
        continuing = false;
    } else {
        println("Emulation Error at 0x" + executionAddress +
                ": " + emuHelper.getLastError());
        continuing = false;
    }
❹ writeBackMemory();
    if (!continuing) {
        break;
    }
}
}
```

For this example, emulation continues as long as the monitor hasn't detected a user cancellation, we haven't reached the end of the selected range of instructions, or an error condition hasn't been triggered ❶. When the emulator stops, we need to update the current execution address ❷ and then handle the stop condition appropriately ❸. The final step is to call the writeBackMemory()method ❹.

Step 3-5: Write Memory Back to the Program

The implementation of writeBackMemory() ❹ is shown here. This emulator is going to be tested on an unpack routine, which ultimately changes the bytes in memory. The memory changes that the emulator has made exist only in its working memory. The content needs to be written back to the binary in order to allow the listing and other user interfaces to accurately reflect the changes that result from executing the instructions in the unpack routine. Ghidra provides functionality within its emulatorHelper to facilitate this process.

```
private void writeBackMemory() {
    AddressSetView memWrites = emuHelper.getTrackedMemoryWriteSet();
    AddressIterator aIter = memWrites.getAddresses(true);
    Memory mem = currentProgram.getMemory();
    while (aIter.hasNext()) {
        Address a = aIter.next();
        MemoryBlock mb = getMemoryBlock(a);
        if (mb == null) {
            continue;
        }
```

```
    if (!mb.isInitialized()) {
        // initialize memory
        try {
            mem.convertToInitialized(mb, (byte)0x00);
        } catch (Exception e) {
            println(e.toString());
        }
    }
    try {
        mem.setByte(a, emuHelper.readMemoryByte(a));
    } catch (Exception e) {
        println(e.toString());
    }
}
}
```

Step 3-6: Clean Up Resources

In this step, we need to clean up resources and release the lock that we have on the current program. Both can be accomplished in one easy statement:

```
emuHelper.dispose();
```

Since this emulator is only for demonstration purposes, we took some liberties in what was included in the script. To conserve space, we minimized the comments, functionality, error checking, and error handling that we would normally include in a production script. All that remains is to confirm that our emulator script is able to accomplish our goal.

Step 4: Add the Script to Our Ghidra Installation

Adding a script to our Ghidra installation just requires dropping it somewhere that Ghidra will find it. If you set up the script project as a linked project, Ghidra knows where to find it already. If you did not link your script project (or if you created your emulator script in another editor), you need to save it in one of Ghidra's script directories, as discussed in Chapter 14.

Step 5: Test the Script Within Ghidra

To test the script, we will load the binary associated with the crackme challenge source code. When we load the binary and navigate to the unpack function, we note that it contains references to the check_access label:

```
0010077d 48 8d 05 8c 08 20 00   LEA    RAX,[check_access]
```

The code in the Decompiler window contains the following, which does not get us any closer to solving our crackme:

```
check_access[(int)local_c] = check_access[(int)local_c] ^ key;
```

Double-clicking `check_access` within the Listing window leads us to address 00301010, which does not look like instructions within a function.

```
00301010 f0 ed 2c 40 2c d8 59    undefined1[19]
         26 d8 59 c1 aa 31 65
         aa 13 65 f8 66
```

If we chose to disassemble this content, we would receive a bad data error in Ghidra. The Decompiler window also provides no help for this location. So let's use our script to see if we can emulate the unpack function. We select the instructions that make up the unpack function and open the Script Manager and run our script. We see no observable change in the unpack function or in the Decompiler window. But if we navigate to check_access (00301010), the content has changed!

```
00301010 55 48 89 e5 89 7d    undefined1[19]
         fc 83 7d fc 64 0f
         94 c0 0f b6 c0 5d c3
```

We can clear these code bytes (hotkey C) and then disassemble (hotkey D) and obtain the following results:

```
         check_access
00301010 55                    PUSH    RBP
00301011 48 89 e5              MOV     RBP,RSP
00301014 89 7d fc              MOV     dword ptr [RBP + -0x4],EDI
00301017 83 7d fc 64           CMP     dword ptr [RBP + -0x4],100
0030101b 0f 94 c0              SETZ    AL
0030101e 0f b6 c0              MOVZX   EAX,AL
00301021 5d                    POP     RBP
00301022 c3                    RET
```

Here is the corresponding code in the Decompiler window:

```
ulong UndefinedFunction_00301010(int param_1)
{
  return (ulong)(param_1 == 100);
}
```

This was just a proof-of-concept script to demonstrate the use of emulators to aid in code deobfuscation, but it does show how a relatively general-purpose emulator can be built within Ghidra by using its emulator support classes. There are other situations where developing and using emulators are an appropriate course of action. An immediate advantage of emulation over debugging is that potentially malicious code is never actually executed by an emulator, whereas debugger-assisted deobfuscation must allow at least some portion of the malicious program to execute in order to obtain the deobfuscated version of the program.

Summary

Obfuscated programs are the rule rather than the exception when it comes to malware these days. Any attempts to study the internal operations of a malware sample are almost certain to require some type of deobfuscation. Whether you take a debugger-assisted, dynamic approach to deobfuscation or you prefer not to run potentially malicious code and instead choose to use scripts or emulation to deobfuscate your binaries, the ultimate goal is to produce a deobfuscated binary that can be fully disassembled and properly analyzed.

In most cases, this final analysis will be performed using a tool such as Ghidra. Given this ultimate goal (of using Ghidra for analysis), it makes sense to attempt to use Ghidra from start to finish. The techniques presented in this chapter are intended to demonstrate that Ghidra is capable of far more than simply generating disassembly listings, and we build on this in the next chapter as we look at how we can use Ghidra to patch our disassembly listings.

22

PATCHING BINARIES

Occasionally when reverse engineering a binary, you may decide that you want to modify the behavior of the original binary. Behavioral modification is usually accomplished by patching the binary to insert, remove, or modify existing instructions. Many motivations exist for making such modifications—some more controversial than others—including the following:

- Modifying a malware sample to eliminate anti-debug techniques that prevent the malware from being studied
- Patching vulnerabilities in software for which you have no source code
- Customizing an application's splash screen or string content
- Modifying game logic for the purposes of cheating
- Unlocking hidden features
- Bypassing licensing checks or other anti-piracy protections

In this chapter, we have no intention of teaching you how to do anything unethical, but we discuss the high-level challenges of modifying a binary to reflect any changes that you have made within Ghidra. Chapter 14 introduced the setByte API function, and Chapter 21 showed how different styles of emulation scripts were able to modify the content of a program loaded into Ghidra. These techniques modify the content that has been imported into Ghidra and have no effect whatsoever on the original binary file that Ghidra processed during the import process. To complete the patching process, you'll learn how to get Ghidra to write changes back to a file on disk. We also discuss the challenges that different types of patches might pose.

Planning Your Patch

The patching process typically involves the following steps:

1. Determine the type of patch you intend to make. This will often be determined by your rationale for patching, as discussed previously.
2. Identify the exact program location(s) that needs to be patched. This typically involves some amount of research and analysis of the program to be patched.
3. Plan the content of your patch. Content changes may require new data, new machine code, or both. In any case, your changes must be well thought out to prevent the program from exhibiting any unintended behavior.
4. Use Ghidra to replace existing program content (data or code) with your replacement content.
5. Use Ghidra to verify that your changes appear to be correctly implemented.
6. Use Ghidra to export your changes into a new binary file.
7. Verify that the new binary file behaves as intended, repeating from step 2 as necessary.

In some patching scenarios, many of these steps will be almost trivial; in others, they will be much more challenging. In the sections that follow, we review those steps that Ghidra can help you with and discuss situations that may push you or Ghidra to your limits. We'll start with step 2 and review some of the ways that Ghidra helps you locate items of interest in a patching context.

Finding Things to Change

The exact nature of your patch will dictate what you need to patch. Customizing splash screens or strings requires that you locate the original data that needs changing. Changing the logic of a program requires modifying or inserting code to change the program's behavior. In this case, a significant amount of reverse engineering may be required just to find any program locations that need to be modified. Many of Ghidra's capabilities that facilitate these activities have been covered in previous chapters. Let's review some of the capabilities useful for patching.

Searching Memory

When your patch involves modifying program data, your primary means of identifying where to apply your patches will be some form of memory search. The most general memory search is the CodeBrowser's Search ▸ Memory menu option (hotkey S), shown in Figure 22-1 (with Advanced options expanded). The Search Memory dialog was previously discussed in Chapter 6.

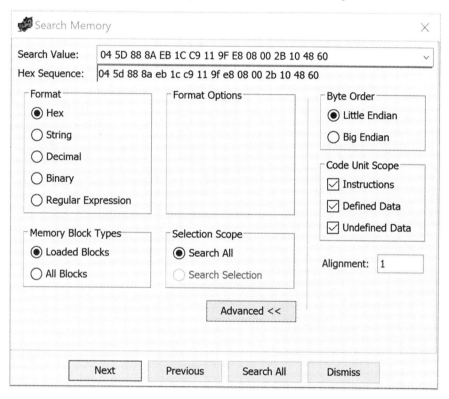

Figure 22-1: The Search Memory dialog

The Search Memory dialog is most useful in a patching context when you are searching for specific, known data within the binary, such as known strings or hex sequences. A successful search will reposition all linked displays to the location of the matching bytes, or in the case of Search All, open a new dialog containing a list of all addresses at which the matched content may be found. For very large binaries, it may be useful to limit the scope of your search to specific regions (Instructions, Defined Data, Undefined Data, and so on) within the program that are likely to contain a match by deselecting any uninteresting code unit types.

While Search ▸ Memory provides the most configurable general-purpose search capability in Ghidra, it is a search across the raw byte content of the database, and other search types may be more suited to the type of data you are looking for. For example, Search ▸ Memory is the wrong choice if you want to search within the body of comments that you have entered into the program. Refer to "Search Program Text" on page 115 for more information on searching within the disassembly listing itself.

Searching for Direct References

In Chapter 20, we used Search ▸ For Direct References to scan the program's binary content for all occurrences of a specific address. The most common use for this search type is to locate pointers to interesting data when Ghidra has failed to create a cross-reference to the data. In a patching context, this is most often used to fully understand and update all references to a data or code location to maintain proper relationships between code and data in the patched binary.

Searching for Instruction Patterns

Ghidra's Search ▸ For Instruction Patterns feature finds a specific sequence of instructions by matching a pattern. When defining an instruction pattern, you need to strike a delicate balance between patterns that are too specific and patterns that are too general. Let's look at an example to illustrate this idea. Assume we have a listing that includes a cleanup_and_exit function that exits the program:

```
int test_even(int v) {
    return (v % 2 == 0);
}
int test_multiple_10(int v) {
    return (v % 10 == 0);
}
int test_lt_100(int v) {
    return v < 100;
}
int test_gte_20(int v) {
    return v >= 20;
}
❶ void cleanup_and_exit(int rv, char* s) {
    printf("Result: %s\n", s);
    exit(rv);
}
void do_testing() {
    int v;
    srand(time(0));
    v = rand() % 150;
    printf("Testing %d\n", v);
  ❷ if (!test_even(v)) {
        cleanup_and_exit(-1, "failed even test");
    }
    if (test_multiple_10(v)) {
        cleanup_and_exit(-2, "failed not multiple of 10 test");
```

```
    }
    if (!test_lt_100(v)) {
        cleanup_and_exit(-3, "failed <100 test");
    }
    if (!test_gte_20(v)) {
        cleanup_and_exit(-4, "failed > 20 test");
    }
    // all tests passed so do interesting work here
❸  system("/bin/sh");
    cleanup_and_exit(0, "success!");
}
int main() {
    do_testing();
    return 0;
}
```

The function do_testing conducts a series of tests ❷. If any of the tests fail, the cleanup_and_exit function ❶ is called and execution ends. If all tests succeed, some very interesting code ❸ will execute. Our patching challenge is to determine where we need to patch to ensure that all of the tests pass so that we can reach the interesting code.

If we load the binary into Ghidra, we can search for all calls to cleanup _and_exit to determine what we need to patch in order for all of the tests to pass regardless of the number of tests. We have several options to consider:

- We could just go to that function and patch it to return so that a failed test doesn't exit the program but rather continues. This isn't an optimal solution because the function is also used for a legitimate exit at the end of the program after it completes the interesting work.

- We could use search functionality or XREFs to cleanup_and_exit. This would give us all of the calls, but we wish to patch only some of them.

- We could identify an instruction pattern that the calls have in common and use Search ▸ For Instruction Patterns to find the correct calls to patch.

To use this search functionality, we need to identify a useful pattern. Each test we are trying to pass takes the following form in the Listing window:

```
001008af  CALL  test_even
001008b4  TEST  EAX,EAX
001008b6  JNZ   LAB_001008c9
001008b8  LEA   RSI,[s_failed_even_test_00100a00]
001008bf  MOV   EDI,0xffffffff
001008c4  CALL  cleanup_and_exit
```

Let's try searching for that sequence by selecting the instruction sequence and Search ▸ For Instruction Patterns. This automatically populates the Instruction Pattern Search dialog, as shown in Figure 22-2.

Mnemonic	Operand 1	Operand 2	Search String Preview
CALL	0x001007aa		e8 f6 fe ff ff
TEST	EAX	EAX	85 c0
JNZ	0x001008c9		75 11
LEA	RSI	[0x100a00]	[01001...] 8d 35 41 01 00 00
MOV	EDI	0xffffffff	bf ff ff ff ff
CALL	0x0010081b		e8 52 ff ff ff

Selection Scope
⦿ Entire Program ◯ Search Selection

Search Direction
⦿ Forward ◯ Backward

Search   Search All   Cancel

Figure 22-2: Instruction Pattern Search dialog with all fields selected

If we click Search All, we see only one result (the specific location that we selected when we started the search), as shown in Figure 22-3.

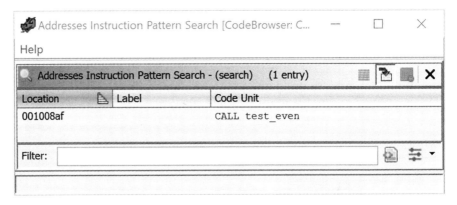

Figure 22-3: Instruction pattern search results from all fields selected

Our issue is that we are including operands that do not remain constant between the test cases. For example, the operand to the first call is the address of a specific test function. We can deselect individual components (mnemonics and operands) of any instruction in the pattern to make it more general, as shown in Figure 22-4. Anything that has been deselected is treated as a wildcard in subsequent searches.

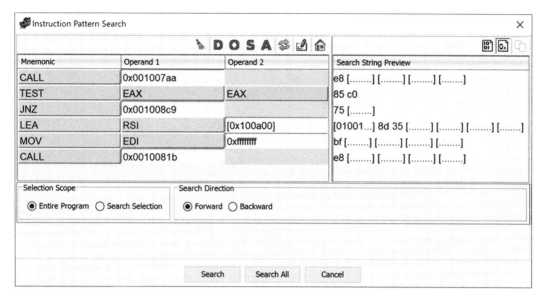

Figure 22-4: Instruction Pattern Search dialog with some operands deselected

If we click Search All with operand fields disabled, we see the three results shown in Figure 22-5.

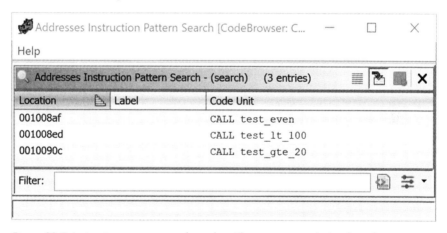

Figure 22-5: Instruction pattern search results with some operands deselected

The search still fails to identify the call to test_multiple_10, which uses a JZ rather than a JNZ instruction. Deselecting the mnemonic field for the JNZ instruction and rerunning the search yields the results shown in Figure 22-6, which includes the four calls we wish to patch and does not include the final call to cleanup_and_exit that we do not want to patch.

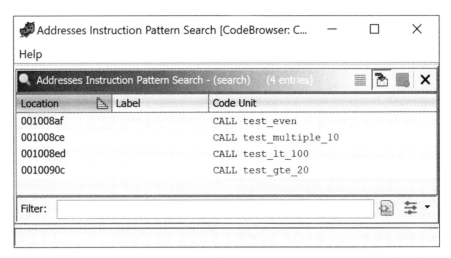

Figure 22-6: Instruction pattern search results with JNZ and some operands deselected

This search functionality has a number of uses beyond locating candidate instruction patterns for patching. It can be used for vulnerability analysis, finding specific functionality, and other searches to identify instruction patterns important to reverse engineers.

Finding Specific Behaviors

A program's behavior is defined by the instructions that it executes combined with the data on which it executes. When your patching task involves modifying a program's behavior, locating the exact behavior that you want to modify is usually much more difficult than locating data that you wish to change. Because we can never predict the exact instruction sequence that a compiler might generate for any source code, it is challenging to use Ghidra's automated search features to pinpoint an exact location to apply a code patch. Locating specific behaviors boils down to plain-old analysis of the functions in the program using techniques covered throughout this book.

Other than a careful analysis of all functions in the binary or a careful traversal of the call tree, beginning with a well-known function such as main, the two most common techniques for identifying functions of interest are relying on the function's name (assuming the binary has symbols) and using cross-references from "interesting" data to backtrack to potentially interesting functions. For example, if we are interested in locating the authentication-related functions within a binary, we might search for common strings associated with authentication such as "Please enter your password:" and "Authentication failed". Strings similar to these often bookend an authentication process, and locating functions that reference these strings may significantly reduce our search space for other authentication-related functions.

Here again, the nature of the data that might lead you to find interesting functions will depend on your particular patching scenario. Regardless of the approaches you use to locate a function that is a candidate for your patch, you should always verify that the function does in fact implement the behavior you wish to modify. In particular, you should always be wary of the names that programmers assign to functions, as there is no requirement for a function's behavior to match its name.

Applying Your Patch

At long last, your hard work and perseverance have paid off, and you have located the code or data that you wish to modify. What now? Assuming you have already developed the replacement content that you intend to patch into the binary, and know precisely where you want to place it, it's time to exercise the Ghidra features that modify the program.

The first thing you need to consider is the size of your new content relative to the content you are replacing. If the new content's size is less than or equal to the original content's size, you are in good shape because your patch will fit within the memory footprint of the original content. However, things get a bit tricky when your patch is larger than the original content, and we will dedicate some time to this case shortly.

Making Basic Changes

Whether you have a pile of bytes in hand or need some help from an assembler, you'll eventually need to get your content into Ghidra. For short runs of bytes, you may find it easier to use Ghidra's built-in byte editor or assembler. For longer runs, you'll probably want to automate. The next few sections describe some of Ghidra's byte-level editing features.

Byte Viewer

The Ghidra Byte Viewer (Window ▶ Bytes), shown in Figure 22-7, provides a standard hex dump view of the raw byte content at the current listing location, synchronized with every other linked window.

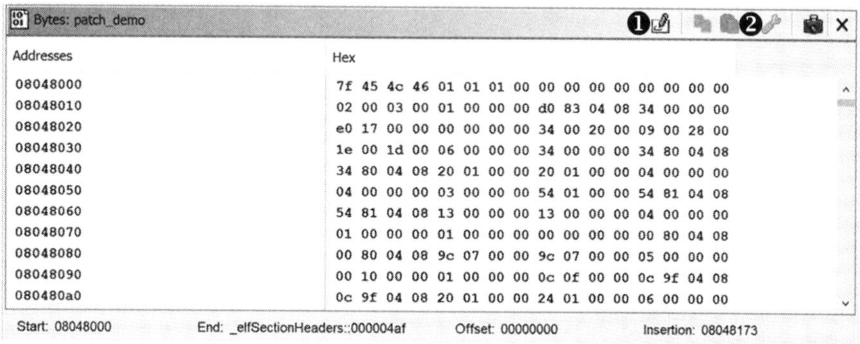

Figure 22-7: The Ghidra Byte Viewer

The Byte Viewer can also double as a hex editor by toggling the Edit Mode tool ❶, and it's a convenient option when you need to change a few bytes at a time.

Inconveniently, Ghidra will not allow you to edit any bytes that are part of an existing instruction. The workaround for this limitation is to clear the associated instruction in the Listing window (right-click Clear Code Bytes or press hotkey C). The Byte Viewer Options tool ❷ is used to open the dialog shown in Figure 22-8, which allows you to customize your Byte Viewer display.

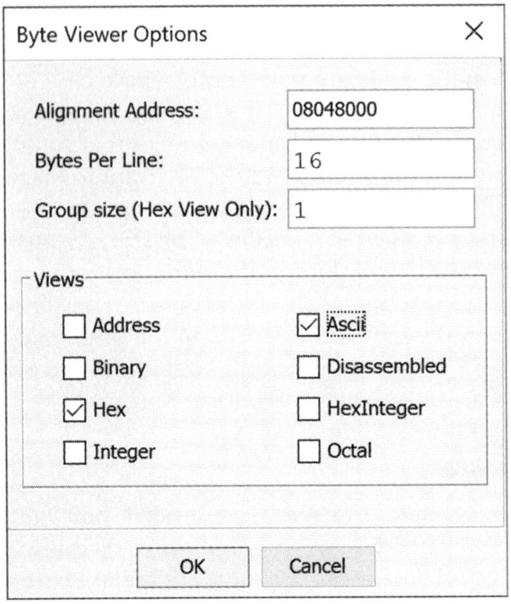

Figure 22-8: Byte Viewer Options dialog

Selecting the Ascii option adds an ASCII dump to the Byte Viewer (see Figure 22-9), which then doubles as an ASCII editor while in edit mode.

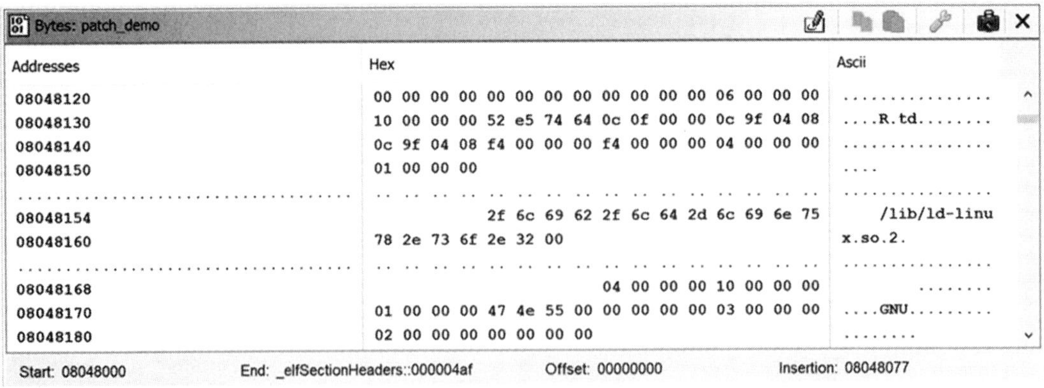

Figure 22-9: Byte Viewer with ASCII dump enabled

Once you have finished entering your new values, you should toggle out of Edit Mode and return to the Listing window to verify that your changes are correct.

Scripting Your Changes

Unless your patch is very short, the most efficient means of modifying the original bytes in Ghidra is to have a script do it for you. Given a patch in the form of a byte array, and the start address of the patch, the following function applies the patch within Ghidra:

```
public void patchBytes(Address start, byte[] patch) throws Exception {
    Address end = start.add(patch.length);
 ❶ clearListing(start, end);
    setBytes(start, patch);
}
```

You may include this function in a script that creates the array of patch bytes from a source of your choosing (for example, by declaring an initialized array or by loading the contents of a file). The clearListing call ❶ is necessary as Ghidra will not allow you to modify bytes that are part of an existing instruction or data item. Once the script completes, you will need to manually format the patched bytes as either code or data and verify the correctness of your patch.

Using the Assembler

When you want to patch the code in a binary, you will most likely find yourself thinking in terms of replacing one assembly language instruction with another (for example, replacing CALL _exit with NOP), which is not necessarily incorrect but tends to gloss over some of the complexities associated with patching code. When the time comes to actually apply your patch to the program, you can't paste in your replacement assembly language statements; instead, you must paste in the corresponding machine code bytes, which means you'll probably want to use an assembler to generate machine code versions of all your replacement instructions.

One approach is to use an external editor to write your replacement assembly statements, assemble them with an external assembler (for example, nasm or as), extract the raw machine code,[1] and finally patch them into the program, perhaps using a script as discussed earlier. An alternative approach is to use Ghidra's built-in assembler capability, which is accessed by right-clicking any instruction and selecting the Patch Instruction menu option.

Just as SLEIGH specifications tell Ghidra how to translate machine code into assembly language, they also enable Ghidra to perform assembly-to-machine-code translations—that is, act like an assembler. The first time you choose the Patch Instruction option for a given architecture, Ghidra will build an assembler based on that architecture's SLEIGH specification. You will initially be presented with a message similar to the one shown in Figure 22-10.

---

1. When using nasm, the -f bin option instructs nasm to emit raw machine code with no file headers. When using as, a second utility such as objcopy is required to extract the raw bytes from the resulting object file.

Figure 22-10: The Assembler Rating dialog

The Ghidra developers have run tests on the accuracy of Ghidra-generated assemblers. If a processor's assembler has been tested, it is assigned one of the following ratings (in decreasing order of accuracy): platinum, gold, silver, bronze, and poor. Any untested assemblers are marked *unrated*. More information about Ghidra assembler ratings, along with the current rating for all available assemblers, may be found in Ghidra Help.

Once you dismiss the Assembler Rating dialog, Ghidra builds the required assembler capability from the current processor's SLEIGH specification. While you wait for the assembler to be built, Ghidra displays the informative wait dialog similar to the one shown in Figure 22-11.

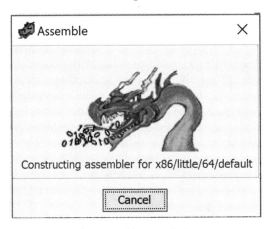

Figure 22-11: The Assemble wait dialog

Once your assembler has been built, Ghidra replaces the selected instruction in the Listing window with two text input boxes (see Figure 22-12) that allow you to edit the instruction's mnemonic and operands. The ESC key discards your changes before they are assembled, while the ENTER key assembles your new instruction and replaces the old instruction's machine code bytes with those of the new instruction.

```
004006ae      MOV      RAX,qword ptr [RBP + local_10]
004006b2      MOV      RDI,RAX
004006b5      CALL     0x004004d0
004006ba      MOV      EAX,0x0
004006bf      LEAVE
004006c0      RET
```

Figure 22-12: Assembling a new instruction

Because they derive from the same specification as the corresponding disassembler, Ghidra's assemblers recognize the same assembly syntax used in the Ghidra Listing window. Ghidra's assemblers are case sensitive and provide auto-completion options as you enter your new instructions. After you enter an instruction, Ghidra returns you to the normal Listing window view, and you can reselect Patch Instruction if there are additional instructions you want to modify. For short patches, Ghidra's assembler offers a convenient way to simultaneously assemble your instructions and modify the program.

Instruction Replacement Pitfalls

While Ghidra's assembler makes quick work of modifying a single instruction, the new replacement instruction can be shorter, longer, or the same size as the old instruction. The third case, in which the replacement and original instructions are the same size, is not interesting. (The first two problems can arise only on architectures without a fixed instruction size, such as x86.)

Consider the first case, in which your replacement instruction is shorter than the original instruction, as reflected in the following listing:

```
;BEFORE:
0804851b  83 45 f4 01   ADD❶  dword ptr [EBP + local_10],0x1
0804851f  83 45 f0 01   ADD   dword ptr [EBP + local_14],0x1

;AFTER
0804851b  66❷ 90        NOP❸
0804851d  f4            ??❹  F4h
0804851e  01            ??   01h
0804851f  83 45 f0 01   ADD   dword ptr [EBP + local_14],0x1

;FIXED:
0804851b  66 90         NOP
0804851d  90            NOP❺
0804851e  90            NOP
0804851f  83 45 f0 01   ADD   dword ptr [EBP + local_14],0x1
```

In this case, a 4-byte ADD instruction ❶ is being replaced by a 2-byte NOP ❸. Ghidra's assembler has done its best to fill the available space by inserting an x86 prefix byte (66) ❷ ahead of the x86 opcode for NOP (90). Unfortunately, the replacement instruction is still too short to account for the two remaining bytes ❹ of the original instruction, one of which translates to a HLT (use the hotkey D to disassemble it), and the other that Ghidra can't disassemble, indicating that it does not represent a valid instruction. If you were to patch the original binary in this way and run it, it would almost certainly crash upon reaching this location.

Ghidra provides no clues—other than the ?? characters that appear in the listing—that a problem may exist, as Ghidra does not understand your motivation for making this change and the "correct" solution depends on your particular use case. If you are modifying instructions within the listing without the intention to export, you could use Ghidra's fallthrough override option from the right-click context menu to bypass the unneeded bytes.[2] Alternatively, you can ask Ghidra to disassemble the undefined bytes, but it's highly unlikely that they will disassemble into an instruction that you will find useful. The most common solution in this situation is to replace all excess bytes from the original instruction with NOPs ❺ to pad to the start of the next instruction.

When your replacement instruction is longer than the original instruction, it introduces a new set of challenges, as shown here:

```
;BEFORE:
08048502 6a 01          PUSH❶  0x1
08048504 ff 75 f0       PUSH❷  dword ptr [EBP + local_14]
08048507 ff 75 08       PUSH   dword ptr [EBP + param_1]
0804850a e8 51 fe ff ff CALL   read


;AFTER:
08048502 68 00 01 00 00 PUSH❸  0x100
08048507 ff 75 08       PUSH   dword ptr [EBP + param_1]
0804850a e8 51 fe ff ff CALL   read
```

In this case, the goal of the patch is to read 256 (0x100) bytes rather than 1 byte. The original, 2-byte PUSH instruction ❶ that places the third argument to read (the length argument) onto the stack is replaced by a 5-byte PUSH ❸ to push a larger constant. The additional bytes in the replacement instruction completely overwrite the instruction that was responsible for the second argument to read (the read buffer) ❷.

The resulting code not only fails to provide read with enough arguments, but also passes an integer where a pointer is expected. As with the previous example, this will almost certainly cause the patched program to crash. Potential solutions to this particular patching problem are nontrivial and are discussed in the next section.

---

2. Fall-through also has an additional option that allows you to bypass portions of a disassembly by identifying start and end addresses to bypass.

Making Nontrivial Changes

The moment the size of your patch grows larger than the instruction(s) or data that you are replacing, your life gets more complicated. In most cases, this doesn't mean that your patch will be impossible to implement, but considerably more thought and effort will be needed to implement the patch properly. In this section, we discuss several approaches for handling this "patch is too large" problem, based on whether the patch contains code or data.

Oversized Code Patches

When your patch is too big to fit on top of the instructions you want to modify, you have no choice but to locate or create an unused region of sufficient size, patch your code into this empty region, and then insert a jump (known as a *hook*) at the original patch location to transfer control to your actual patch. In most cases, you will also need to append a jump to your replacement code to transfer control back to an appropriate location in the hooked function. Figure 22-13 shows the notional flow of a patched function with a jump hook installed.

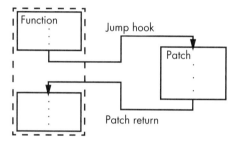

Figure 22-13: Function with installed patch

The available unused space for your oversized code patch must

- Be at least as large as your patch
- Reside at an address that will be executable at runtime
- Be initialized from file content; otherwise, your patch won't get loaded at runtime

The easiest place to begin your search for large, unused, executable blocks of bytes is with any *code caves* that may be present in the binary. A code cave exists when an executable section in a binary, such as the .text section, is padded to adhere to section alignment requirements mandated by the executable file's format. Code caves are very common in Windows PE binaries, as they frequently require every section of the binary to be a multiple of 512 bytes in size.

The first place to look for a code cave is usually the end of the .text section. You can easily navigate to the end of the .text section (or any other section) by double-clicking the section name in the CodeBrowser's Program Trees window and then scrolling to the end of the Listing window.

In our sample PE binary, the Listing window shows the following at the end of the .text section:

```
140012df8 ??      00h
140012df9 ??      00h
140012dfa ??      00h
140012dfb ??      00h
140012dfc ??      00h
140012dfd ??      00h
140012dfe ??      00h
140012dff ??      00h
```

The listing tells us the following:

- The bytes are unclassified by Ghidra (??).
- The bytes are initialized to 00h.
- The .text section ends at address 140012dff, which satisfies the file alignment requirement that the section is a multiple of 512 bytes in size (140012e00 is a multiple of 0x200).

Navigating to the previous instruction by scrolling up (or choosing the I tool in the CodeBrowser with search direction set to Up), we arrive at the following:

```
140012cbd POP    RBP
140012cbe RET❶
140012cbf ??     CCh
140012cc0 ??     00h
```

The RET ❶ is the last meaningful instruction in this particular binary, and we can now compute the size of this binary's code cave as 0x140012e00 - 0x140012cbf = 0x141 (or 321 bytes). This means that we can easily patch as many as 321 bytes of new code into this binary. Assuming that we patched our new code in at address 0x140012cbf, we would need to patch a jump to 0x140012cbf somewhere in the binary's existing code to ensure that execution flow eventually reaches our patch.

When a code cave can't be found, or isn't large enough to hold your patch, you will need to get a little creative in order to find enough space to fit your patch. Depending on the compiler options used to build the binary, you may be able to spread your patch across space gathered from *inter-function alignment gaps*. Inter-function alignment gaps exist when compilers choose to align the start of every function to an address that is a multiple of 2 (often 16). When function alignment is being forced, there will be an average of align / 2 bytes and as many as align – 1 bytes of padding inserted between each function in the binary. The following listing shows an optimal (from a patching perspective) alignment gap (align = 16) between two adjacent functions:

```
     1400010a0 RET
❶    1400010a1 ??     CCh
```

```
    1400010a2 ??      CCh
    1400010a3 ??      CCh
    1400010a4 ??      CCh
    1400010a5 ??      CCh
    1400010a6 ??      CCh
    1400010a7 ??      CCh
    1400010a8 ??      CCh
    1400010a9 ??      CCh
    1400010aa ??      CCh
    1400010ab ??      CCh
    1400010ac ??      CCh
    1400010ad ??      CCh
    1400010ae ??      CCh
❷  1400010af ??      CCh
             **************************************************************
             *                           FUNCTION                        *
             **************************************************************
```

All of the bytes from 1400010a1 ❶ through 1400010af ❷ may be safely overwritten with patch code.

Additional methods exist for squeezing patch code into a binary—some involving expanding existing program sections or injecting entirely new ones. Any technique that manipulates sections in such a manner also requires you to update the binary's section headers to make sure they remain consistent with any modifications that have been made. Accordingly, these techniques are very file-format specific and require a detailed understanding of file header data structures.

Oversized Data Patches

Patching data is easier than patching code in some respects, and more difficult in others. For structured data types, your primary concerns are correct size and byte ordering of each member of the structure, and since the size of a structure is determined at compile time, you don't need to worry about oversized replacement structures. When patching string data, it is recommended that any replacement data fit entirely within the footprint of the original string. If your new string is larger than the original string, you may be fortunate to find a few bytes of padding between the end of the string and the next data item, but you must be careful not to corrupt any data that the program depends upon. If your data simply does not fit into the memory footprint of the original data, you will be forced to find a new location for it, but moving data properly can be difficult.

All global data items are referred to by their offsets from the program's code or data sections. To relocate a data item, in addition to finding sufficient unused space, you'll need to locate every reference to the original data item and patch it to refer to the new data item. Ghidra cross-references go a long way toward identifying every reference to a global, but will fail to identify derived pointers (pointers resulting from pointer arithmetic).

Once all of your patches have been entered in Ghidra and you're happy with the resulting program listing, you'll want to push your changes into the original binary to verify that your patches behave as expected.

Exporting Files

To confirm that any of your changes will have the desired effect on the binary's behavior, you'll need to update the original binary to reflect your changes. In this section, we discuss some of Ghidra's export features as they relate to patching.

Ghidra's File ▸ Export Program menu option offers the capability to export a program's information in any of several formats. The resulting Export dialog is shown in Figure 22-14.

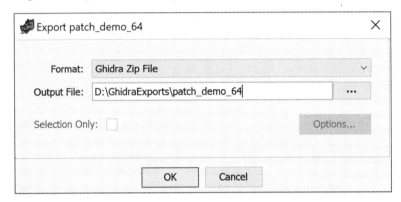

Figure 22-14: The Ghidra Export dialog

The Export dialog is also accessible from the Project Manager by right-clicking the file you wish to export and selecting Export from the context menu. In the dialog, you are asked to specify the export format and the output file location, and to indicate whether you wish to limit the scope of your export to a range you have selected in the CodeBrowser. Some export formats offer additional options for more fine-grained control over the export process.

Ghidra Export Formats

Ghidra supports the following export formats, though only one (binary) is particularly useful for binary patching:

Ascii   The Ascii export format can be used to save a textual representation of the program, similar to what is displayed in the Listing window, with options to choose which fields to include in the output file.

Binary   The Binary export format, which produces a binary file, is the most useful for patching applications and is discussed in its own section.

C/C++   The C/C++ export format is used to save the Decompiler-generated source representation of the program along with declarations for all types known to the Data Type Manager. This option is also available from the Decompiler window.

Ghidra Zip File   A Ghidra *zip* file is a serialized Java object representation of your program suitable for import into other Ghidra instances.

HTML The HTML export format generates an HTML representation of the program listing. Options similar to those available in the Ascii exporter allow you to choose which fields to include in the output file. Labels and cross-references are represented as hyperlinks to provide a basic navigational capability throughout the generated output.

Intel Hex The Intel Hex format defines an ASCII representation for binary data, commonly used for programming EEPROM.

XML The XML exporter outputs the contents of the program in a structured XML format, with options to choose which program constructs should be included in the generated file. This functionality is also available for individual functions in the Decompiler window to facilitate debugging function decompilation. Although Ghidra includes a corresponding XML loader, this exporter includes the following warning: "Warning: XML is lossy and intended only for transferring data to external tools. GZF is the recommended format for saving and sharing program data."

The Binary Export Format

Ghidra's Binary export is used to write a program's underlying binary content to a file. All of the program's initialized memory blocks (see Window ▶ Memory Map) are concatenated to form the output file. Whether the output file is identical to the original file that was imported depends on the loader module used to import the file. The Raw Binary loader is guaranteed to re-create the original input file because it loads every byte of the original file into a single memory block. Other loaders may or may not load every file byte (for example, the PE loader does, while the ELF loader does not).

When it comes time to apply any changes you have made with Ghidra, you need to ensure that the file you generate contains your patches and that it will execute. If you are patching a PE file, a Binary export will generate a patched version of the original binary. Similarly, if you imported your program using the Raw Binary loader, a Binary export will generate a patched version of the original binary. Of course, as discussed in Chapter 17, when using the Raw Binary loader, you may need to perform most of the memory layout for the program manually, so there is a trade-off. Fortunately, it's possible to script up a solution that works with any loader.

Script-Assisted Export

Rather than performing an exhaustive test of every Ghidra loader to understand whether the memory blocks created by the loader span the entire range of file bytes, we can create a Ghidra script that will save a patched version of our program for us. This script provides a loader-agnostic capability for generating patched files with Ghidra. It will always process the entire range of original file bytes regardless of the current memory map layout known to Ghidra.

```
public void run() throws Exception {
    Memory mem = currentProgram.getMemory();
❶   java.util.List<FileBytes> fbytes = mem.getAllFileBytes();
    if (fbytes.size() != 1) {
        return;
    }
❷   FileBytes fb = fbytes.get(0);
❸   File of = askFile("Choose output file", "Save");
    FileOutputStream fos = new FileOutputStream(of, false);
    writePatchFile(fb, fos);
    fos.close();
}
```

The script begins by obtaining the program's list of FileBytes ❶. A FileBytes object encapsulates all of the bytes from the imported program file and tracks both the original and modified value of each byte in the file. As Ghidra allows you to import several files into a single program, this script processes only the bytes from the first file you imported into the program (first range of file bytes) ❷.

After prompting for an output file ❸, the FileBytes object and open OutputStream are passed to our writePatchFile function to handle the finer details of generating the patched executable.

To present a mapped memory view of a program, Ghidra loaders may process a program's relocation table entries in a manner similar to a runtime loader. The result of this processing is that program locations marked for fixup (locations that have relocation table entries) are modified by Ghidra from their original file values to proper relocated values. When we generate the patched version of the binary, we do not want to include any bytes that Ghidra has modified for relocation purposes.

The writePatchFile function, shown next, begins by generating the set of addresses that are patched at runtime (and by Ghidra) in accordance with the program's relocation table:

```
public void writePatchFile(FileBytes fb, OutputStream os) throws Exception {
    Memory mem = currentProgram.getMemory();
    Iterator<Relocation> relocs;
❶   relocs = currentProgram.getRelocationTable().getRelocations();
    HashSet<Long> exclusions = new HashSet<Long>();
    while (relocs.hasNext()) {
        Relocation r = relocs.next();
❷       AddressSourceInfo info = mem.getAddressSourceInfo(r.getAddress());
        for (long offset = 0; offset < r.getBytes().length; offset++) {
❸           exclusions.add(info.getFileOffset() + offset);
        }
    }
❹   saveBytes(fb, os, exclusions);
}
```

After obtaining an iterator over the program's relocation table ❶, the AddressSourceInfo for each relocation entry is obtained ❷.

An AddressSourceInfo object provides a mapping of a program address to the disk file and the offset into that file from which the corresponding program byte was loaded. The file offset of each relocation byte is added to a set of offsets ❸ to be ignored when generating the final patched file. The function concludes by calling the saveBytes function ❹ to write the final patched version of the current program file. The saveBytes function is shown in the following listing:

```
public void saveBytes(FileBytes fb, OutputStream os, Set<Long> exclusions)
                      throws Exception {
    long begin = fb.getFileOffset();
    long end = begin + fb.getSize();
❶ for (long offset = begin; offset < end; offset++) {
❷     int orig = fb.getOriginalByte(offset) & 0xff;
❸     int mod = fb.getModifiedByte(offset) & 0xff;
        if (!exclusions.contains(offset) && orig != mod) {
❹         os.write(mod);
        }
        else {
❺         os.write(orig);
        }
    }
}
```

The function iterates over the entire range of file bytes ❶ to determine whether to save the original or modified byte to the output file.

At each file offset, methods of the FileBytes class are used to obtain the original byte value ❷, loaded from the imported file, and the current byte value ❸, which may have been modified by Ghidra or the Ghidra user. If the original value differs from the current value *and* the byte is not associated with a relocation entry, the modified byte is written to the output file ❹; otherwise, the original byte is written to the output file ❺.

To wrap up this section, let's look at an example of patching a binary and confirming that the patch runs as we expect it to.

Example: Patching a Binary

Let's look at an example that demonstrates patching in context. Assume that you have a piece of malware that checks for a debugger and, if one is present, exits without allowing you to examine its behavior. The following source code outlines that functionality in a trivial program:

```
int is_debugger_present() {
    return ptrace(PTRACE_TRACEME, 0, 0, 0) == -1;
}
void do_work() {
❶ if (is_debugger_present()) {
        printf("No debugging allowed - exiting!\n\n");
        exit(-1);
    }
```

```
        // do interesting things here
        printf("Confirmed that there is no debugger, so do\n"
               "interesting things here that we don't want\n"
               "analysts to see!\n\n");
    }
    int main() {
        do_work();
        return 0;
    }
```

The code checks for a debugger ❶ and exits if it finds one. Otherwise, it goes about its nefarious business. The following shows the output of the program running alone (without a debugger):

```
# ./debug_check_x64
  Confirmed that there is no debugger, so do
  interesting things here that we don't want
  analysts to see!
```

When the program runs under a debugger, we see a different response:

```
# gdb ./debug_check_x64
  Reading symbols from ./debug_check_x64...(no debugging symbols found)...done.
  (gdb) run
  Starting program: /ghidrabook/CH22/debug_check_x64
  No debugging allowed - exiting!
  [Inferior 1 (process 434) exited with code 0377]
  (gdb)
```

If we load the binary into Ghidra, we see the following in the Listing window:

```
        undefined do_work()
            undefined  AL:1 <RETURN>
001006f8 PUSH   RBP
001006f9 MOV    RBP,RSP
001006fc MOV    EAX,0x0
00100701 CALL   is_debugger_present
00100706 TEST   EAX,EAX
00100708 JZ     LAB_00100720
0010070a LEA    RDI,[s_No_debugging_allowed_-_exiting!_001007d8]
00100711 CALL   puts
00100716 MOV    EDI,0xffffffff
0010071b CALL   exit
    -- Flow Override: CALL_RETURN (CALL_TERMINATOR)
        LAB_00100720
00100720 LEA    RDI,[s_Confirmed_that_there_is_no_debug_001008
00100727 CALL   puts
0010072c NOP
0010072d POP    RBP
0010072e RET
```

The Decompiler window provides the following corresponding code:

```
void do_work(void)
{
  int iVar1;

  iVar1 = is_debugger_present();
  if (iVar1 != 0) {
    puts("No debugging allowed - exiting!\n");
                    /* WARNING: Subroutine does not return */
    exit(-1);
  }
  puts("Confirmed that there is no debugger, so do\n"
      "interesting things here that we don't want\n"
      "analysts to see!\n"
      );
  return;
}
```

To patch this binary to bypass the check, you could NOP the call to the is_debugger_present function, change the test condition, or change the contents of the is_debugger_present function. If you use the Patch Instruction option from the right-click context menu, it is easy to replace the JZ with a JNZ (effectively flipping the condition to run only if it is being debugged), as shown in Figure 22-15.

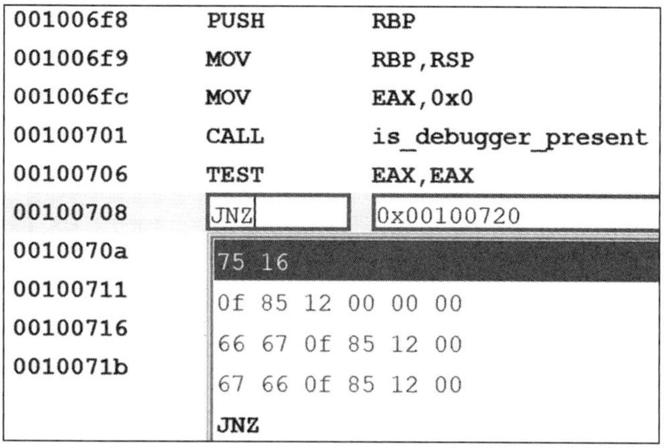

001006f8	PUSH	RBP
001006f9	MOV	RBP,RSP
001006fc	MOV	EAX,0x0
00100701	CALL	is_debugger_present
00100706	TEST	EAX,EAX
00100708	JNZ	0x00100720
0010070a	75 16	
00100711	0f 85 12 00 00 00	
00100716	66 67 0f 85 12 00	
0010071b	67 66 0f 85 12 00	
	JNZ	

Figure 22-15: Patch Instruction option after replacing JZ with JNZ

This would result in the following code in the Decompiler window:

```
void do_work(void)
{
  int iVar1;

  iVar1 = is_debugger_present();
  if (iVar1 == 0) {
    puts("No debugging allowed - exiting!\n");
                    /* WARNING: Subroutine does not return */
```

```
        exit(-1);
    }
    puts("Confirmed that there is no debugger, so do\n"
         "interesting things here that we don't want\n"
         "analysts to see!\n"
        );
    return;
}
```

If we then export the file as a binary using our export script and run it again, we see the following two listings, which demonstrate the behavior we were hoping to accomplish with our patch:

```
# ./debug_check_x64.patched
 No debugging allowed - exiting!

# gdb ./debug_check_x64.patched
 Reading symbols from ./debug_check_x64.patched...(no debugging symbols found)...done.
 (gdb) run
 Starting program: /ghidrabook/CH22/debug_check_x64.patched
 Confirmed that there is no debugger, so do
 interesting things here that we don't want
 analysts to see!

 [Inferior 1 (process 445) exited normally]
 (gdb)
```

While there are many external tools (for example, VBinDiff) available to confirm that only 1 byte was changed within the file for this example, you can also use Ghidra's internal tools to reach the same conclusion. The next chapter focuses on methods to accomplish this goal.

Summary

Regardless of your particular motivation for patching a binary, your patch will require careful planning and deployment. Ghidra provides everything you need to plan your patch; to draft your patch using hex editing, Ghidra's built-in assembler, or scripting; to view the effects of each change; and to possibly revert changes using Undo before generating a patch version of your original binary. The next chapter demonstrates how you can use Ghidra to compare the unpatched and patched versions of your binaries as well as discusses Ghidra's capabilities for more advanced binary differencing and version tracking.

23

BINARY DIFFERENCING AND VERSION TRACKING

We have spent the previous chapters introducing you to ways that Ghidra can assist your reverse engineering analysis efforts. Throughout this journey, we have introduced many ways to transform and annotate your work to document and facilitate understanding of the binary.

In this chapter, we introduce binary differencing and Ghidra's Version Tracking tool to help you identify similarities and differences between files and functions and facilitate the application of previous analysis results to new files. We also discuss file differences from three perspectives: binary differencing, function comparison, and version tracking.

Binary Differencing

In the preceding chapter, we patched a binary to modify the flow of a function to bypass a call to exit by changing a single byte in a single instruction: JZ (74) to JNZ (75). To confirm the change and document exactly what was changed, we could use an external tool such as VBinDiff or WinDiff to compare the two files at the byte level. However, to compare files at the instruction level, we need a much more sophisticated tool: the Program Diff tool available in Ghidra's Listing window. Once the differences have been computed, they can be viewed using custom displays designed to emphasize the differences, facilitate understanding of each change, and provide opportunities to take action based on the type of difference.

To compare two files that have been imported to a project and are in the same state (for example, both analyzed or neither analyzed), open one of the files in the CodeBrowser and then choose **Tools ▶ Program Differences** and select another file within the current project for comparison. Alternatively, you can use the Listing window tool icon shown in Figure 23-1. This icon serves as a toggle to open or close the Program Diff tool.

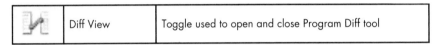

| | Diff View | Toggle used to open and close Program Diff tool |

Figure 23-1: CodeBrowser Diff View toggle icon

For this example, we will start by opening the unpatched version of the file, selecting the Diff View icon, and choosing the patched version of the file. This opens the Determine Program Differences dialog shown in Figure 23-2.

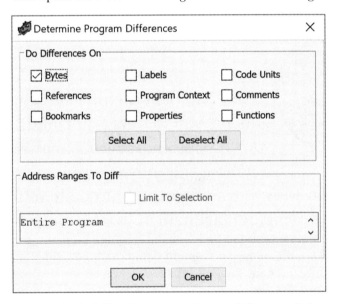

Figure 23-2: The Diff tool's Determine Program Differences dialog

While all available differences fields will be selected by default, in this case Bytes is the appropriate choice to confirm that the patch worked correctly, so it is the only difference option selected. When you click OK, you can see the two binaries in the Listing window, which has been split into side-by-side listings, with one file displayed in each. By default, the listings are synchronized, so navigating in one also navigates the other. There are several ways to navigate the detected differences within this tool, which we present later in the chapter.

When you open two files for diffing, Ghidra initially positions the Listing view at the beginning of each file. The down arrow tool on the Listing window toolbar (or CTRL-ALT-N) may be used to navigate to the first difference between the two files. To call your attention to the differing code, changes are indicated with color-highlighted disassembly lines in each file's Listing window as well as in the Decompiler window if the difference is within a function. (The Decompiler window is synchronized with the first of the two files.) Navigating to the first detected difference reveals the single byte that is JZ (74) in the original listing and JNZ (75) in the second listing.

To view more details, choose **Window ▸ Diff ▸ Diff Details**. You will see the following report in the Diff Details window at the bottom of the CodeBrowser window:

```
Diff address range 1 of 1.
Difference details for address range: [ 00100708 - 00100709 ]

Byte Diffs :
    Address    Program1  Program2
    00100708   0x74      0x75

Code Unit Diffs :
    Program1 CH23:/DiffDemo/debug_check_x64 :
        00100708 - 00100709    JZ 0x00100720
                               Instruction Prototype hash = 16af243b
    Program2 CH23:/DiffDemo/debug_check_x64.patched :
        00100708 - 00100709    JNZ 0x00100720
                               Instruction Prototype hash = 176d4e0c
```

The first line indicates the number of address ranges that contain differences. In this case, only one range in the file contains differences, so you can be confident that the two programs differ by only a single byte. This simple example barely scratches the surface of the capabilities associated with Ghidra's Program Diff tool, so let's take some time to investigate other capabilities that this tool provides.

Program Diff Tool

The nine options at the top of Figure 23-2 form the basis of your comparison, and you can select any or all of them. By default, the Program Diff tool operates on the entire program for each file. If you wish to limit your comparison to a specific address range, you must highlight the range in the first file before opening the tool. Once you have made your selections and clicked OK, the split Listing window you see is called a Program Diff.

Program Diff

Program Diff View lets you view both files simultaneously. Basically, the Listing window now has two listings, one on the left side and one on the right. When you open the Diff Details window, it opens at the bottom of the CodeBrowser window. Within the Diff Details window, the left file is considered Program1 (the file you opened originally), while the right file is considered Program2 (the file you chose to compare to Program1). The Decompiler window reflects the contents of Program1. When you are comparing two files, Ghidra can compute the differences in either direction. It is up to you to remember which file is which as you use the Program Diff tool.

A common workflow is to begin analyzing a file and then realize that some or all of the code looks familiar, which may prompt you to open a file you have previously analyzed in order to begin diffing. Fortunately, Program Diff maintains alignment between the two files by inserting blank lines when necessary. Differences are highlighted, and the Program Diff toolbar provides you navigational capability and the means to determine how you wish to handle the differences.

Program Diff Toolbar

The Program Diff toolbar extends the Listing window toolbar options by adding the tools shown in Figure 23-3.

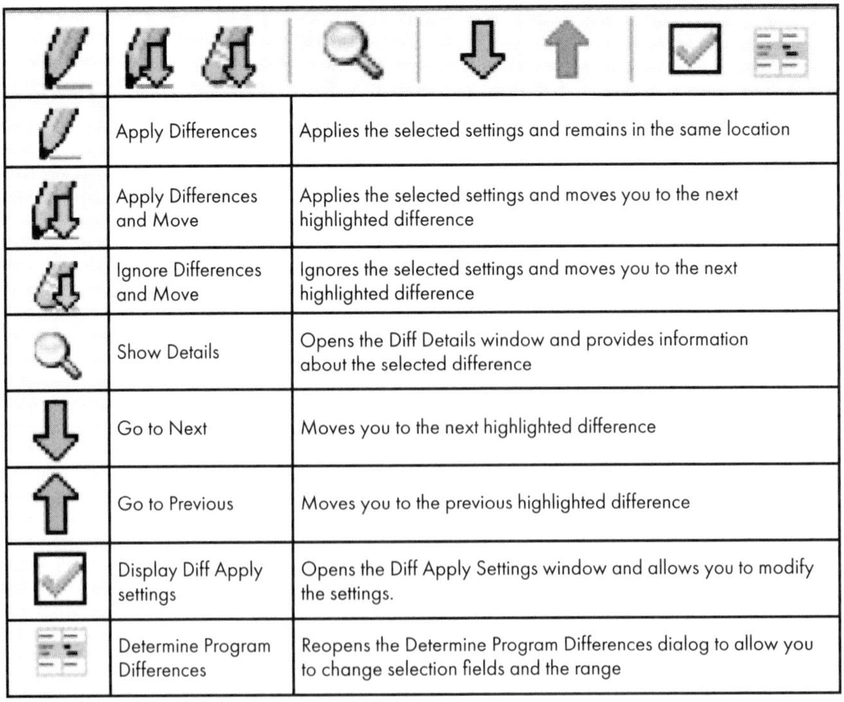

✓	Apply Differences	Applies the selected settings and remains in the same location
	Apply Differences and Move	Applies the selected settings and moves you to the next highlighted difference
	Ignore Differences and Move	Ignores the selected settings and moves you to the next highlighted difference
🔍	Show Details	Opens the Diff Details window and provides information about the selected difference
⬇	Go to Next	Moves you to the next highlighted difference
⬆	Go to Previous	Moves you to the previous highlighted difference
☑	Display Diff Apply settings	Opens the Diff Apply Settings window and allows you to modify the settings.
	Determine Program Differences	Reopens the Determine Program Differences dialog to allow you to change selection fields and the range

Figure 23-3: Program Diff toolbar options

Diff Apply Settings

The Diff Apply Settings define the actions that you would like to take when there is a difference between the two files. Choosing the Display Diff Apply Settings option displays the window shown in Figure 23-4.

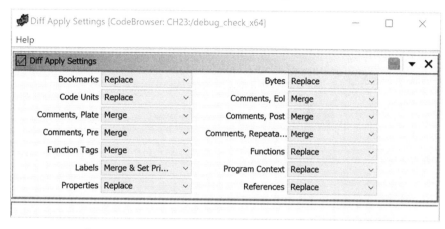

Figure 23-4: Diff Apply Settings window

Each setting specifies a default action you would like to apply from the second program to the first program you opened and how you would like that option applied. The following four options are available from each drop-down:

Ignore   Do not change the first program (available for all cases).

Replace   Change the first program's content to match the second program's content (available for all cases).

Merge   Add the difference from the second program to the first program. If applied to a label, this will not change which label is set to primary (available for only Comments and Labels).

Merge & Set Primary   The action is the same as Merge, but the primary label is set to the second program label if that is possible (available for only Labels).

At the top of Figure 23-4, there are two toolbar icons. The Save as Default icon saves the current Diff Apply Settings. The arrow opens a menu that allows you to make changes to all of the settings at one time by choosing one of the options shown in Figure 23-5.

Figure 23-5: Diff Apply Settings pull-down menu

If you select the Set Merge option and Merge is not a valid choice for a particular setting, it will be changed to Set Replace. For labels, it will be changed to Merge & Set Primary.

Choose Apply Differences from the toolbar if you wish to apply all of the default changes. When you have finished with the Program Diff tool, toggle the Diff View icon in the Listing window and you will see the dialog displayed in Figure 23-6.

Figure 23-6: Close Diff Session confirmation dialog

Confirming that you wish to close the current diff session will close the display of the second file and return you to a normal Listing window with the first file (and all of the changes that you have selected from the diff analysis) displayed.

The Program Diff tool was designed for two primary use cases: first, to compare files analyzed by two different users who don't share a Ghidra Server instance; second, to compare code generated from different versions of the same source code base (for example, unpatched and patched versions of a shared library). In the following example, we walk through the process of using this tool to reconcile two copies of the same binary, each of which was analyzed independently.

Example: Merging Two Analyzed Files

Assume that you are analyzing a binary that contains a crypto routine. A colleague mentions that she is midway through analyzing a binary that also appears to have a crypto routine and is likely from the same malware family. She agrees to provide you with her project so that you can compare the two files. When you look at the files in Diff View, you immediately notice that the two of you appear to be analyzing the same binary.

The challenge is that you have each made progress and have modified the contents of the file based on your individual analysis. You need to merge the two analyzed files so that you can each benefit from the other's analysis. You have agreed to take on this responsibility and have opened your binary in the CodeBrowser and initiated a Program Diff session, adding your colleague's binary for comparison.

Choosing the down arrow on the Program Diff toolbar takes you to the first difference in this file. At this point, you can open the Diff Details window by choosing the option from the Program Diff toolbar (or hotkey

F5). This provides you with the following listing (broken into two sections to facilitate discussion). In the first section at the top of the Diff Details, you see the following:

```
Diff address range 1 of 4. ❶
Difference details for address: 0010075a ❷

Function Diffs : ❸
  Program1 CH23:/Crypto/diff_sample1 :
    Signature: void encrypt_rot13(char * inbuffer, char * outbuffer) ❹
    Thunk? : no
    Stack Frame:
      Parameters: ❺
        DataType    Storage         FirstUse Name        Size Source
        /char *     RDI:8           0x0      inbuffer     8   USER_DEFINED
        /char *     RSI:8           0x0      outbuffer    8   USER_DEFINED
      Local Variables: ❻
        DataType    Storage         FirstUse Name        Size Source
        /int        EAX:4           0xc0     length       4   USER_DEFINED
        /int        Stack[-0x1c]:4  0x0      idx          4   USER_DEFINED
        /char       Stack[-0x1d]:1  0x0      curr_char    1   USER_DEFINED
  Program2 CH23:/Crypto/diff_sample1a : ❼
    Signature: void encrypt(char * param_1, long param_2)
    Thunk? : no
    Stack Frame:
      Parameters:
        DataType    Storage         FirstUse Name        Size Source
        /char *     RDI:8           0x0      param_1      8   DEFAULT
        /long       RSI:8           0x0      param_2      8   DEFAULT
      Local Variables:
        DataType    Storage         FirstUse Name        Size Source
        /undefined4 Stack[-0x1c]:4  0x0      local_1c     4   DEFAULT
        /undefined1 Stack[-0x1d]:1  0x0      local_1d     1   DEFAULT
```

The first of four identified difference address ranges ❶ in this file is being displayed and is associated with the current address, 0010075a ❷. The listing begins by detailing a difference in the function headers of the two binaries ❸. For your binary, you have provided a meaningful name for the function and the parameters in the function signature ❹. Further, each parameter has an appropriately defined type ❺. Likewise, the local variables have been given meaningful names and types ❻. In the second program ❼, the analyst did not make any changes to the default Ghidra header for the corresponding function.

You want to retain your version of the changes for the function definition and local variables. You could use the toolbar icon to reject the change, but this would reject all of the differences associated with this address. Since you have not yet reviewed all of the differences, just scroll down to the next difference in the Diff Details window.

The next section of the differences associated with the first address range contains the label and comment differences.

```
❶ Label Diffs :
    Program1 CH23:/Crypto/diff_sample1 at 0010075a :
      0010075a is an External Entry Point.
        Name            Type            Primary  Source         Namespace
      ❷ encrypt_rot13   Function        yes      USER_DEFINED   Global


    Program2 CH23:/Crypto/diff_sample1a at 0010075a :
      0010075a is an External Entry Point.
        Name            Type            Primary  Source         Namespace
      ❸ encrypt         Function        yes      USER_DEFINED   Global


❹ Plate-Comment Diffs :
  ❺ Program1 CH23:/Crypto/diff_sample1 at 0010075a :
      ***************************************************************
      *                         FUNCTION                          *
      * This is a crypto function originally named cryptor. Renamed *
      * to use our standard format encrypt_rot13. Changed the      *
      * function parameters to char *. Added meaningful variable   *
      * names. Function first seen in fileC13d by Ken H            *
      ***************************************************************
    Program2 CH23:/Crypto/diff_sample1a at 0010075a :
      No Plate-Comment.


❻ EOL-Comment Diffs :
    Program1 CH23:/Crypto/diff_sample1 at 0010075a :
      No EOL-Comment.
  ❼ Program2 CH23:/Crypto/diff_sample1a at 0010075a :
      This looks like an encryption routine. TODO: Analyze to get more information.
```

Within the label differences ❶, the only difference is the name of the function ❷❸, which has already been discussed. In the Plate-Comment section ❹, your file has a detailed comment ❺, but the other file has no plate comments. In the EOL-Comment section ❻, there is a brief comment by the other analyst ❼ but none in your file. When you examine the comment, you see that it is a TODO action item that you have already done in your file.

After evaluating all of the differences between the two files, your decision is to retain your content and not accept any new content from the other binary. You accomplish this by choosing the Ignore Differences and Move icon. This takes you to the next difference. Since you already have the Diff Details window open, its contents are updated as soon as you navigate, and you see the following:

```
Diff address range 1 of 3. ❶
Difference details for address range: [ 0010081a - 0010081e ]

Reference Diffs :
  Program1 CH23:/Crypto/diff_sample1 at 0010081a :
    Reference Type: WRITE  From: 0010081a  Mnemonic  To: register:
      RAX  USER_DEFINED  Primary

  Program2 CH23:/Crypto/diff_sample1a at 0010081a :
    No unmatched references.
```

You have decreased the number of ranges containing differences by rejecting the previous difference ❶. Once again, your file has more information than the second file. This time you will navigate to the next difference by clicking the down arrow. This takes you to the following:

```
Diff address range 2 of 3. ❶
Difference details for address: 00100830

Function Diffs :
  Program1 CH23:/Crypto/diff_sample1 :
    Signature: undefined display_message()
    Thunk? : no
    Calling Convention: unknown
    Return Value :
        DataType     Storage        FirstUse Name       Size Source
        /undefined   AL:1           0x0      <RETURN>    1    IMPORTED
      Parameters:
        No parameters.
  Program2 CH23:/Crypto/diff_sample1a :
    Signature: void display_message(char * message) ❷
    Thunk? : no
    Calling Convention: __stdcall
    Return Value :
        DataType     Storage        FirstUse Name       Size Source
        /void        <VOID>         0x0      <RETURN>    0    IMPORTED
      Parameters:
        DataType     Storage        FirstUse Name       Size Source
        /char *      RDI:8          0x0      message     8    USER_DEFINED
```

Notice that the number of ranges has not changed ❶. You have just been moved to the next difference range without impacting the total number of difference ranges. Evaluating this new difference shows that the second file contains information provided by the other analyst that is not available in your file. The function signature has a return type, and a parameter has been added to the function signature ❷. You can include this in your binary by right-clicking the difference in the right-hand Listing window and choosing Apply Selection (hotkey F3), or by clicking the Apply Differences icon on the toolbar.

Navigating to the next difference, you see the following details:

```
❶ Diff address range 2 of 2.
Difference details for address range: [ 00100848 - 0010084c ]

Pre-Comment Diffs :
  Program1 CH23:/Crypto/diff_sample1 at 00100848 :
    No Pre-Comment.

  Program2 CH23:/Crypto/diff_sample1a at 00100848 :
  ❷ This is a potential vulnerability.  The parameter is being passed
    in to printf as the first/only parameter which may result in a format
    string vulnerability.
```

The number of difference ranges has decreased because you applied the differences in the previous range ❶. In this final difference, you see an interesting entry in the Pre-Comment section ❷ in the other file. The analyst has detected a potential vulnerability. To be sure this information is included in your file, you choose **Apply Differences**.

Now that you have completed the comparison of the two files, you can click the Diff View icon and confirm that you want to close the current Program Diff session. Your listing view now reflects the combined analysis from both binaries, and you can save and close your file.

The Ghidra Program Diff tool provides the ability to investigate the differences between two versions of the same file. While it will attempt to diff two unrelated files, any results are likely to reflect only coincidental similarities. Let's shift our focus to a different tool that facilitates comparisons between selected functions within the same or different programs.

Comparing Functions

If you see a function that is reminiscent of a function you have analyzed in the past, it can be helpful to directly compare the two functions so the outcome of your initial analysis can be applied to the current function when appropriate. Ghidra provides this capability through its Function Comparison window which allows you to view two functions at the same time as shown in Figure 23-7.

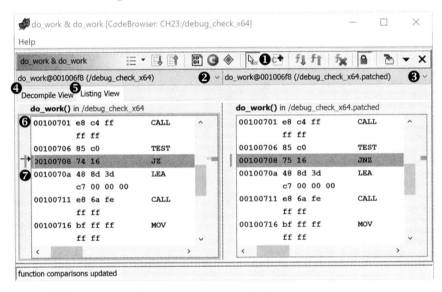

Figure 23-7: Listing view in Function Comparison window

Function Comparison Window

To use the Function Comparison window, open the one or more binaries that contain the functions in the CodeBrowser, load an initial function by highlighting a function in the active CodeBrowser tab, and select Compare Selected Functions (hotkey SHIFT-C) from the right-click context menu. The Function Comparison window shows two functions side by side with potential differences highlighted, as shown in Figure 23-7. (If you have selected only one function, it will be displayed in both windows until you load more functions.)

To add additional functions to compare, choose the Add Functions icon ❶. This will display a list of all functions in the active program in the CodeBrowser. You can select a function from the list or switch to the CodeBrowser window to change the active program by selecting another program tab in the Listing window.

To the left of the active listing (indicated by a box around the listing ❻) is a cursor arrow ❼. If the functions match, the arrow will also appear at the same location in the other window. In Figure 23-7, the instruction in the primary window does not match the instruction in the other window, so the cursor arrow is not shown in both windows.

The Function Comparison window provides the opportunity to load more than two functions from more than two binaries. You can add and remove functions from each panel when needed. A helpful pull-down menu lets you choose the function to be displayed in the associated window ❷❸.

This window lets you easily switch between Decompile View ❹ and Listing View ❺ for the two functions and change the function displayed in either window. The Decompile View for this example is shown in Figure 23-8.

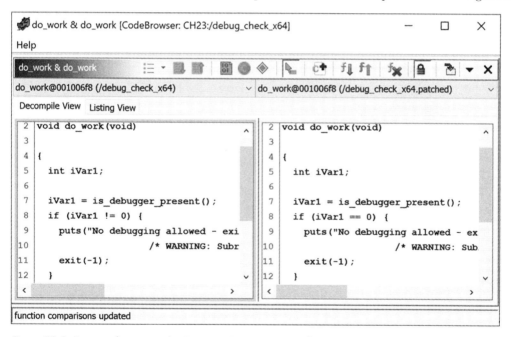

Figure 23-8: Decompile view in the Function Comparison window

The exploratory capabilities available in this window overlap significantly with the Program Diff tool, except you are comparing only two functions at a time and you can easily switch between the decompiled code and the listing. The toolbar menu for this window is shown in Figure 23-9.

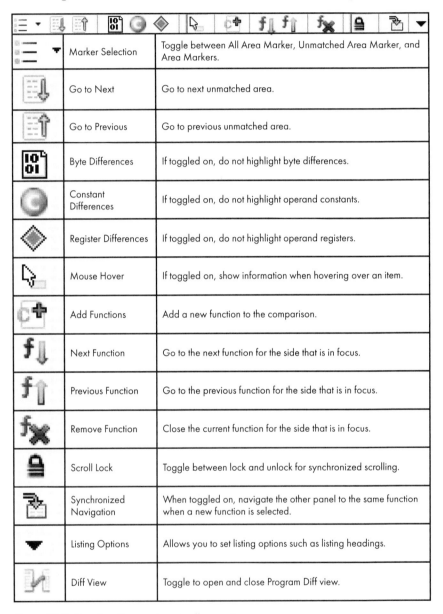

	Marker Selection	Toggle between All Area Marker, Unmatched Area Marker, and Area Markers.
	Go to Next	Go to next unmatched area.
	Go to Previous	Go to previous unmatched area.
	Byte Differences	If toggled on, do not highlight byte differences.
	Constant Differences	If toggled on, do not highlight operand constants.
	Register Differences	If toggled on, do not highlight operand registers.
	Mouse Hover	If toggled on, show information when hovering over an item.
	Add Functions	Add a new function to the comparison.
	Next Function	Go to the next function for the side that is in focus.
	Previous Function	Go to the previous function for the side that is in focus.
	Remove Function	Close the current function for the side that is in focus.
	Scroll Lock	Toggle between lock and unlock for synchronized scrolling.
	Synchronized Navigation	When toggled on, navigate the other panel to the same function when a new function is selected.
	Listing Options	Allows you to set listing options such as listing headings.
	Diff View	Toggle to open and close Program Diff view.

Figure 23-9: Function Comparison toolbar options

Let's walk through an example that demonstrates some additional Function Comparison tool capabilities.

Example: Comparing Crypto Routines

Congratulations on your promotion! Based on your successful analysis and use of the Program Diff tool for crypto routines, you have now been labeled the crypto expert in your shop. Every time one of your colleagues suspects that they have a crypto routine, they send you the binary to see if it is a crypto routine you recognize.

You now have a new file from a colleague and wish to determine whether the crypto routine used in this file is something new or is a routine you have identified in the past. Rather than loading and comparing each crypto routine against the new function, you have set up a special Ghidra project that contains all of your previously analyzed and documented crypto routines. Your goal is to load your crypto routines on one side of the Function Comparison window and then import the new file on the other side to compare against the existing crypto routines. (To simplify this example, you currently have only one analyzed crypto routine in your collection: the ROT13 routine that you merged in the previous example.)

After you load your complete collection of analyzed crypto files into the CodeBrowser and have loaded your function, `encrypt_rot13`, in the Function Comparison window, you need to load the new file into the same CodeBrowser instance (File ▸ Open) and make it the active file. At this point, you can explore the file, but it isn't necessary. You can always switch back to the CodeBrowser window if you can't find the function you need. In this case, choosing the Add Functions option from the Function Comparison toolbar, you see the complete list of functions in the new binary, and halfway down the list is a function with a name that intrigues you, `encrypt`, as shown in Figure 23-10.

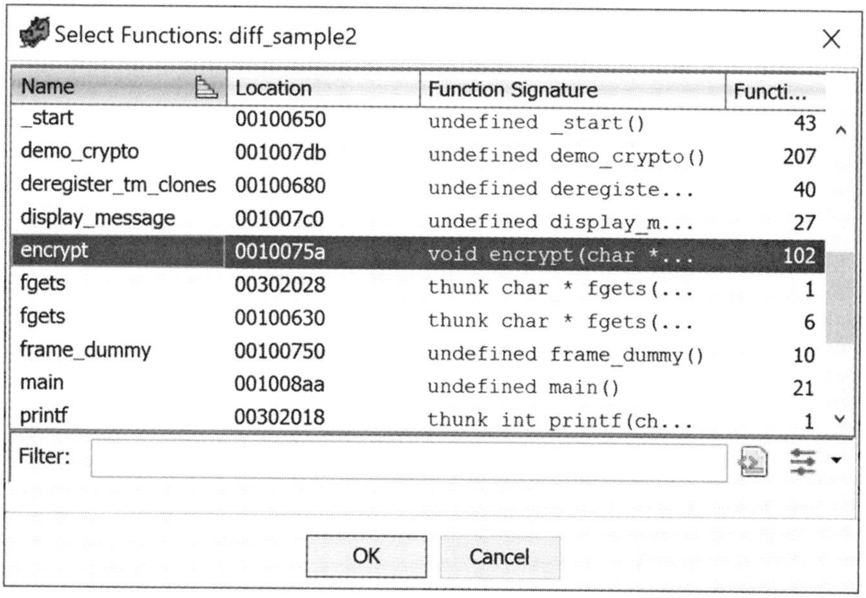

Name 📄	Location	Function Signature	Functi...
_start	00100650	undefined _start()	43
demo_crypto	001007db	undefined demo_crypto()	207
deregister_tm_clones	00100680	undefined deregiste...	40
display_message	001007c0	undefined display_m...	27
encrypt	0010075a	void encrypt(char *...	102
fgets	00302028	thunk char * fgets(...	1
fgets	00100630	thunk char * fgets(...	6
frame_dummy	00100750	undefined frame_dummy()	10
main	001008aa	undefined main()	21
printf	00302018	thunk int printf(ch...	1

Select Functions: diff_sample2 ✕

Filter: [   ]

OK   Cancel

Figure 23-10: Select Functions window with the encrypt function selected

A cursory glance at the loaded files in the Decompile View of the functions, shown in Figure 23-11, suggests that these two functions are quite different.

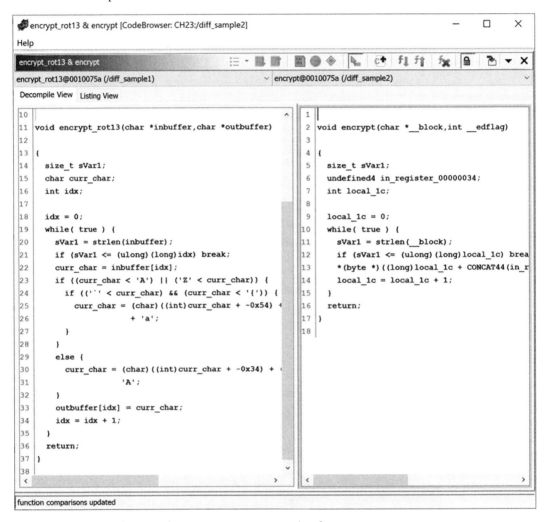

Figure 23-11: Decompile View of Function Comparison window for two crypto routines

The Listing View, shown in Figure 23-12, confirms that these two functions have significant differences.

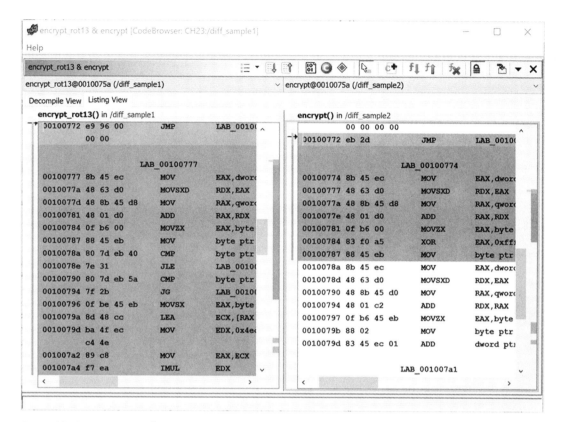

Figure 23-12: Listing View of Function Comparison window for two crypto routines with differences highlighted

On further analysis, you discover that the new routine XORs each byte with the constant value 0xa5. This is definitely different from the current crypto routine that you have, so you name and document this new function and add it to your collection (which will then have two members!). Returning to the CodeBrowser, you update the function signature and add comments to document the new crypto routine. The changes you make are reflected in the Function Comparison window as well.

As you are documenting, you notice the new binary has a function called display_message, as does the binary you are comparing it against. You recall that this function was identified as having a vulnerability in your current binary, so you decide to compare these two functions. You load them into the Function Comparison window to see if they have similarities beyond the common name. They seem different in both the Decompile and Listing Views, as shown in Figure 23-13.

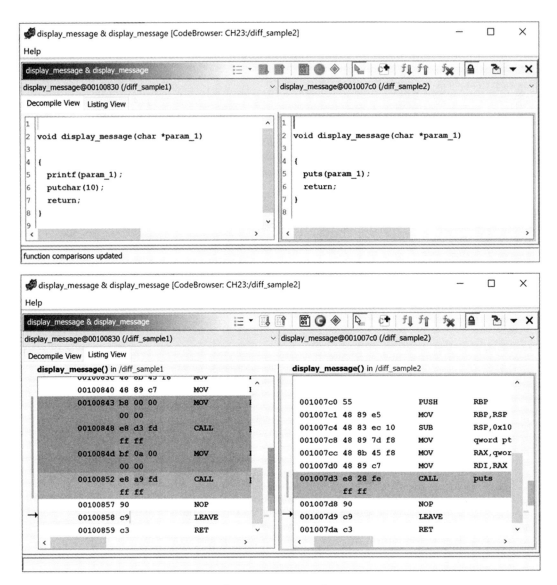

Figure 23-13: Decompile and Listing views for display_message *functions*

In the second example, param_1 is being passed to puts for output, which fixes the vulnerability.

Now that you have documented this crypto routine, you see that you have received yet another binary from your colleagues. To reset to the start of your crypto comparison process, you can use the Function Comparison toolbar icon to remove the display_message functions from the window, leaving you with your crypto routine collection, which now has two distinct members: encrypt_rot13 and encrypt_XOR_a5.

An initial exploration of this new file indicates that three functions seem to involve encryption: encrypt, encrypt_strong, and encrypt_super_strong. You load these into the Function Comparison window so you can compare them to your existing crypto routines. After comparing encrypt_rot13 against each of the new functions, you notice the following:

encrypt_rot13 vs. encrypt   Almost entirely different. The encrypt routine is just a test that may call one of the other two encryption routines.

encrypt_rot13 vs. encrypt_strong   Almost entirely the same.

encrypt_rot13 vs. encrypt_super_strong   Very different. A closer look at the differences between these two functions leads you to believe that they are not the same function.

A closer look at the differences shows that the instructions in encrypt_rot13 and encrypt_strong are identical—the differences primarily consist of address labels, as shown in Figure 23-14.

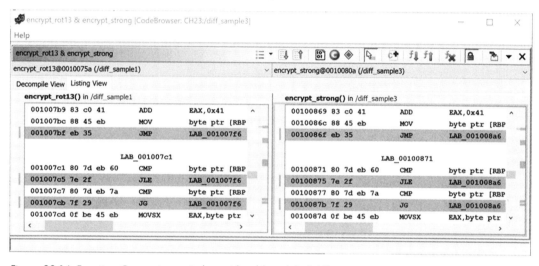

Figure 23-14: Function Comparison window with address label differences

You would not expect address labels to match perfectly in this case, as the locations of the functions within the binaries are different. The locations are consistent relative to the current address, so we are likely dealing with the same function. The only other difference is 1 byte associated with the call to strlen, as shown in Figure 23-15. This is a similar issue and can be explained by the difference in the relative positions of the encryption function and strlen in each binary.

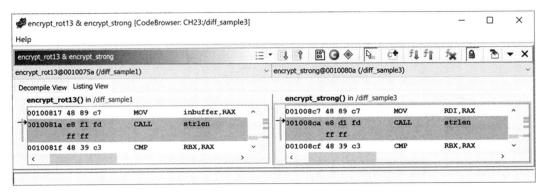

Figure 23-15: Function Comparison window with byte difference in call to strlen

After determining that these are the same function, you can right-click the previously analyzed function and choose Apply Function Signature To Other Side from the right-click context window. This will update the function signature in all needed locations, including the Listing window and Symbol Tree. Note that the Function Comparison window does not provide all of the capabilities available in the Diff View. To copy additional information (such as the detailed comments associated with the function), use the Program Diff tool.

Having completed your comparative analysis of encrypt_rot13, you turn your attention to encrypt_XOR_a5 and observe the following relationships with each of the new functions:

encrypt_XOR_a5 vs. encrypt   Almost entirely different.

encrypt_XOR_a5 vs. encrypt_strong   Very different. A closer look at the differences between these two functions also leads you to believe that they are not the same function.

encrypt_XOR_a5 vs. encrypt_super_strong   Almost entirely the same.

The identified differences between encrypt_XOR_a5 and encrypt_super_strong are also just address labels and some bytes in the call to strlen. You can handle this situation the same way you did the previous matching functions.

While this is a trivial example (and not likely consistent with the actual crypto routines you might see in the wild), it does demonstrate how Function Comparison can be used to minimize the duplication of analysis effort when you encounter familiar routines in new binaries.

The final tool for investigating two files is the most complex: the Version Tracking tool.

Version Tracking

Imagine that you have spent months analyzing a very large binary. The binary has hundreds or thousands of functions and no symbols. As part of your effort, you have provided meaningful names to the majority of the functions; renamed data, local variables, and function parameters; and added a mountain of comments that would take days or longer to re-create.

Now imagine that a new version of the binary is released, and the world stops using the version you know so much about. You could continue to analyze the old version to learn more about it under the assumption that the new version behaves similarly, but you would fail to learn about any new or modified behaviors in the updated binary. Instead, you decide to begin working on the newer version of the binary and quickly realize that you spend significant amounts of time reading the markup in the older binary to help guide you through the new binary.

Alternating back and forth between two CodeBrowser windows is not an optimal use of your time. It's time to switch from the CodeBrowser to the other default tool that Ghidra provides in the Project Tool Chest, as shown in Figure 23-16.

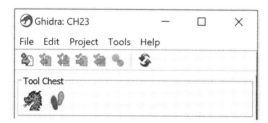

Figure 23-16: The Version Tracking tool (footprints)
in the Project Tool Chest

Ghidra's Version Tracking tool is designed to help you with precisely this situation. Through the use of various correlators, Ghidra attempts to match items, such as functions or data, in a source binary with their cor-responding versions in a destination binary. Once functions have been matched between the two binaries, Ghidra can automatically migrate infor-mation, including your labels and comments, from the source binary to the destination binary. In addition to rapidly migrating your existing analysis, the Version Tracking tool makes it easy to identify which things haven't changed, which things have only minor changes (detected by diffing), and which things are entirely new.

The Version Tracking tool is one of the most configurable tools in Ghidra, which makes it easy to adapt to a particular line of inquiry. It is also a challenging tool to present in its entirety. In the following sections, we walk you through the version tracking process at a very high level and point you to resources that can help you discover the correct settings and compo-nents to use when using the Version Tracking tool to assist you in discover-ing the relationship between two files.

Version Tracking Concepts

While Function Comparison and Program Diff tools answered specific questions about the atomic differences between two files or functions, the Version Tracking tool provides you with functionality to answer a more holistic question: how similar are these two binaries, and can you highlight and provide insight about the similarities between them? The foundational work unit is called a *session*, and each session is configured to identify and handle *correlations* between two files.

Correlators

At a high level, the Version Tracking tool is looking for correlations between two files. There are seven types of correlators that generate matches between two binaries:

- Data Match correlators
- Function Match correlators
- Legacy Import correlators
- Implied correlators
- Manual Match correlators
- Symbol Name Match correlators
- Reference correlators

Rather than just counting and compiling a list of specific differences in each of the categories, the Version Tracking tool extends correlations between the two files to identify matches with varying levels of exactness:

Exact matches   These are one-to-one matches between the two files and can match data, function bytes, function instructions, or function mnemonics (for example, when two binaries contain the exact same function).

Duplicate data match   These are exact matches that are not one-to-one matches (for example, when a string appears once in one file and seven times in the other file).

Similar matches   These are matches that pass a user-controlled similarity threshold. The matching is similar to the approach used for word models described in Chapter 13, but uses 4-grams as well as trigrams.

With the ability to introduce thresholds, and accept and reject matches, this tool offers a powerful capability to migrate your previous analysis to new versions of a binary. Further, the information associated with each session provides an effective analysis audit trail that can help capture the incremental changes of a binary or the evolution of a malware family.

Sessions

While an in-depth walk-through of a complete session would take a significant amount of time, a basic version tracking session might include the following steps:

1. Open Ghidra's Version Tracking tool.
2. Create a new session by choosing a source file and a destination file.

3. For all appropriate correlators: add to the existing session, choose the correlator, select all resulting matches, and accept all matches and apply their markup items.

4. Save the session.

5. Close the session.

The preceding workflow provides a very general overview, and the combinatorial potential associated with the correlator step is extensive. The potential of and the nuances associated with this tool cannot be covered in a single chapter. The Ghidra team has provided sample workflows (as well as significant documentation about the Version Tracking tool) in Ghidra Help. It is up to you to determine how best to apply the capabilities of this tool in your reverse engineering workflow.

Summary

In this chapter, we stepped away from a single binary to begin looking at ways to identify differences and similarities between binaries by using the Program Diff, Function Comparison, and Version Tracking tools. These tools are valuable time-savers for porting existing work to new binaries, merging annotations from your colleagues, and rapidly identifying exactly what has changed between two versions of the same program.

As we wrap up our tour of Ghidra's vast landscape of features, know that we have only scratched the surface of Ghidra's capabilities. You should now have a deeper understanding of Ghidra and how it can be applied to the reverse engineering challenges you face. When you have questions, the Ghidra community is there to help through resources like GitHub, Stack Exchange, Reddit, YouTube, and many other forums.

More importantly, you should now be in a position to contribute by answering questions and providing help to others. Ghidra is community-supported software and continually evolving. We hope you participate by posting tutorials, writing and publishing Ghidra scripts and modules, identifying and addressing issues, or perhaps even developing new functionality for Ghidra itself. The future of Ghidra will be determined by the community, and that now includes you. Welcome, and happy reversing!

GHIDRA FOR IDA USERS

If you are an experienced IDA Pro user interested in giving Ghidra a test run, either as a curiosity or as a more permanent transition, you may be familiar with many of the concepts presented in this book. This appendix is intended to map IDA terminology and usage to similar functionality in Ghidra, without providing instruction on Ghidra functionality. For specific usage of any Ghidra feature mentioned here, please refer to the relevant chapters in this book that discuss the features in far more detail.

We make no attempt to compare the performance of the two tools, nor do we argue for the superiority of one over the other. Your choice of which to use might be motivated by price or a specific feature offered by one and not the other. What follows is a whirlwind tour through the topics of the book from the perspective of an IDA user.

The Basics

As you begin your journey, you may find it useful to bring along a guide to help you learn an entirely new set of hotkeys. The *Ghidra Cheat Sheet* (*https://ghidra-sre.org/CheatSheet.html*) is a useful trifold that lists common user actions and their associated hotkeys and/or tool buttons. Shortly, we'll cover how to remap hotkeys in the event that you miss your trusted IDA favorites.

Database Creation

Whereas IDA imports one binary into one database and is inherently single user, Ghidra is project oriented, can contain multiple files per project, and can support collaborative reversing by many users working together on the same project. The concept of an IDA database most closely maps to a single *program* within a Ghidra project. Ghidra's user interface is split into two main components: *Project* and *CodeBrowser*.

Your first interaction with Ghidra is to create projects (shared or non-shared) and import "programs" (binaries) into those projects through the Project window. When you use IDA to open a new binary, and ultimately create a new database, you and IDA perform the following actions:

1. (IDA) Query every available loader to learn which loaders recognize the newly selected file.
2. (IDA) Display the load file dialog, presenting a list of acceptable loaders, processor modules, and analysis options.
3. (User) Choose the loader module that should be used to load file content into the new database, or accept IDA's default choice.
4. (User) Choose the processor module that should be used when disassembling database content, or accept IDA's default choice (which may be dictated by a loader module).
5. (User) Choose any analysis options that should be used when creating the initial database, or accept IDA's default choices. You may also elect to disable analysis altogether at this point.
6. (User) Confirm your choices by clicking **OK**.
7. (IDA) The selected loader module populates the database with byte content taken from the original file. IDA loaders generally do not load the entire file into the database, and it is generally not possible to re-create the original file from content available in the new database.
8. (IDA) If analysis is enabled, the selected processor module is used to disassemble code identified by the loader and any selected analyzers (IDA calls analyzers *kernel options*).
9. (IDA) The resulting database is displayed in IDA's user interface.

Ghidra has analogues for each of the listed steps; however, the process is broken into two distinct phases: import and analysis. The Ghidra import process is generally initiated from the Project window and includes the following steps:

1. (Ghidra) Query every available loader to learn which loaders recognize the newly selected file.
2. (Ghidra) Display the import dialog, presenting a list of acceptable formats (roughly loaders) and languages (roughly processor modules).
3. (User) Choose the format for importing the file into the current project, or accept Ghidra's default choice.
4. (User) Choose the language for disassembling program content, or accept Ghidra's default choice.
5. (User) Confirm your choices by clicking **OK**.
6. (Ghidra) The loader associated with the selected format loads byte content taken from the original file into a new "program" in the current project. The loader creates program sections and processes the binary's symbol, import, and export tables, but performs no analysis involving disassembly. Ghidra loaders generally load the entire file into your Ghidra project, though some portions of the file may not be displayed by the CodeBrowser.

Though this process is similar to IDA database creation, some steps are missing. With Ghidra, analysis takes place in the CodeBrowser. Once you have successfully imported a file, double-clicking that file in the Project view opens the file in Ghidra's CodeBrowser. When you open a program for the first time, Ghidra performs the following steps:

1. (Ghidra) Open the CodeBrowser and display the results of the import process, asking whether you would like to analyze the file.
2. (User) Decide whether to analyze the file. If you elect not to analyze the file, you are dropped into the CodeBrowser, where you can scroll through byte content but will have no disassembly. In this case, you may choose Analysis ▶ Auto Analyze to analyze the file at any time. In either case, when you decide to analyze the file, Ghidra displays a list of "analyzers" compatible with the current file format and language setting. You may choose which analyzers to run and then modify any options the analyzer utilizes before allowing Ghidra to perform its initial analysis.
3. (Ghidra) Execute all selected analyzers and drop the user into the CodeBrowser to begin working with the fully analyzed program.

For more information about the import and analysis stages, refer to the appropriate chapters in this book. IDA has neither an analogy for Project view nor any collaborative reversing capabilities other than the shared Lumina database. Project view is introduced in Chapter 4. Shared projects and support for collaborative reverse engineering are discussed in Chapter 11. The CodeBrowser is introduced in Chapter 4, with more depth beginning in Chapter 5 and continuing through the remainder of the book.

The CodeBrowser is a Ghidra *tool* and is your primary interface for analyzing programs. As such, it is the Ghidra component most similar to IDA's user interface, so we will spend some time relating IDA user-interface elements to their CodeBrowser equivalents.

Basic Windows and Navigation

In its default configuration, the CodeBrowser is a container for multiple specialty windows that display information about features of a program. Detailed discussion about the CodeBrowser begins in Chapter 5 and continues, with coverage of related data displays, through Chapter 10.

Listing View

At the center of the CodeBrowser is the Ghidra Listing window, which provides a classic disassembly similar to your IDA View in text mode. To customize the format of your listings, the Browser Field Formatter enables you to modify, rearrange, and delete individual listing elements. As in IDA, navigation within the Listing windows is primarily accomplished by double-clicking *labels* (IDA names) to navigate to the address associated with a label. Right-click, context-sensitive menus provide access to common operations associated with labels, including renaming and retyping.

Similar to IDA, each function in the listing has a header comment that lists the function's prototype, provides a summary of the function's local variables, and displays cross-references that target the function. The Ghidra equivalent of IDA's Stack view is accessible only by right-clicking in a function's header and selecting Function ▸ Edit Stack Frame.

If you enjoy IDA highlighting all occurrences of a string that you click (such as a register name or instruction mnemonic), you may be disappointed to learn that this is not a default behavior in Ghidra. To enable this behavior, visit Edit ▸ Tool Options ▸ Listing Fields ▸ Cursor Text Highlight and change Mouse Button to Activate from MIDDLE to LEFT. Another feature you may love or hate is Markup Register Variable References, which causes Ghidra to automatically rename registers that are used to hold a function's incoming parameters. To disable this behavior and have Ghidra use register name instruction operands, navigate to Edit ▸ Tool Options ▸ Listing Fields ▸ Operands Fields and uncheck Markup Register Variable References.

Finally, if you are longing for Ghidra to "do the right thing" when muscle memory causes you to use your favorite IDA hotkey sequences, you'll want to spend some time in Edit ▸ Tool Options ▸ Key Bindings to reassign default Ghidra hotkeys to match those that you use in IDA. This is such a common task for IDA users that third-party key binding files have been published to automate reassignment of all your favorite hotkey sequences.[1]

---

1. Try *https://github.com/enovella/ida2ghidra-kb/* or *https://github.com/JeremyBlackthorne/Ghidra-Keybindings/*.

Graph View

Ghidra's Listing window is a text-only view. If you prefer working in IDA's graph view, you'll need to open a separate Function Graph window in Ghidra. Like IDA's graph view, Ghidra's Function Graph window can display a single function at any one time, and you can manipulate the items in the Function Graph window just as you would in the Listing window.

By default, Ghidra's graph layout algorithm may route edges behind basic block nodes, which may make tracing the edge more difficult. You can disable this behavior by visiting Edit ▸ Tool Options ▸ Function Graph ▸ Nested Code Layout and checking Route Edges Around Vertices.

The Decompiler

Ghidra includes decompilation capability for all supported processors. By default, the Decompiler window appears to the right of the Listing window and will display decompiled C source code whenever your cursor is positioned within a function in the Listing view. If you like to add and view end-of-line comments in the generated C source, you'll need to enable them at Edit ▸ Tool Options ▸ Decompiler ▸ Display by checking Display EOL comments. On the same options tab, you'll also find Disable printing of type casts, which can improve readability in some cases by dramatically decluttering the resulting code.

The decompiler also has a tendency to aggressively optimize the code it generates. If you find yourself reading the disassembled version of a function and feel like behaviors are missing in the decompiled version, the decompiler may have eliminated what it believes to be dead code within the function. To display that code in the Decompiler window, navigate to Edit ▸ Tool Options ▸ Decompiler ▸ Analysis and deselect Eliminate dead code. The decompiler is discussed further in Chapter 19.

The Symbol Tree

The CodeBrowser's Symbol Tree window provides a hierarchical view of all symbols contained in a program. The Symbol Tree contains six top-level folders representing six classes of symbols that may exist within a program. Clicking a name in any Symbol Tree folder will navigate the Listing window to the corresponding address:

Imports   The *Imports* folder is relevant for dynamically linked binaries and provides a listing of external functions and libraries referenced by the program. This most closely correlates to IDA's Imports tab.

Exports   The *Exports* folder lists any symbols in the program that are publicly visible outside the program. The symbols in this folder are often similar to those output by the nm utility.

Functions   This folder contains an entry for each function in the program listing.

Labels   This folder contains entries for any additional nonlocal labels within the program.

Classes   This folder contains the names of any C++ classes for which Ghidra has located Runtime Type Identification (RTTI).

Namespaces   This folder contains an entry for each namespace created by Ghidra during program analysis. Refer to Ghidra Help for more information on Ghidra namespaces.

Data Type Manager

The Data Type Manager maintains all of Ghidra's knowledge about data structures and function prototypes. Each folder in the Data Type Manager is the rough equivalent of an IDA type library (*.til*). The Data Type Manager fills the role of IDA's Structures, Enums, Local Types, and Type Libraries windows and is discussed in detail in Chapter 8.

Scripting

Ghidra is implemented in Java, and its natural scripting language is Java. In addition to routine scripts, the primary Java extensions to Ghidra include analyzers, plugins, and loaders. Ghidra analyzers and plugins together take on the role that IDA's plugins fill, while Ghidra loaders perform essentially the same role as IDA loaders. Ghidra supports the concept of processor modules; however, Ghidra processors are defined using a specification language known as SLEIGH.

Ghidra includes a basic script editor for routine scripting tasks as well as an Eclipse plugin to facilitate the creation of more complex Ghidra scripts and extensions. The use of Python is supported via Jython. The Ghidra API is implemented as a class hierarchy that represents the features of a binary as Java objects, and convenience classes are provided for easy access to some of the most commonly used API classes. Ghidra scripts are discussed in Chapters 14 and 15 and extensions are discussed in Chapters 15, 17, and 18.

Summary

Ghidra's capabilities are quite clearly similar to those of IDA. In some cases, Ghidra's displays are similar enough to IDA's that the only things that will slow you down are new hotkeys, tool buttons, and menus. In other cases, information is presented in a different manner than in IDA, and your learning curve will be steeper. In either case, whether you take advantage of Ghidra's customization capabilities to make it drive like IDA or you take the time to learn a new way of doing things, you're likely to find that Ghidra meets most of your reverse engineering needs and in some cases opens up entirely new ways of getting things done.

INDEX

Archive Current Project (Ghidra), 225
archives
    creating data type archives, 269
    creating new file archives, 271
    creating new project archives, 272
    data type archives, 268
arguments. *See also* parameters, 94–113,
        453, 454, 458, 464-466
ARM, 405, 418, 491
    instructions, 94–96, 113
arrays, 140, 144
    Array type option (Ghidra), 156
    base address, 150, 152, 153, 158,
        159, 160, 170
    bounds, 151
    constant indices, 153, 154, 159, 160
    create, 139
    elements, 150–153, 156, 158, 159, 169
    globally allocated, 150, 154, 161
    heap-allocated, 157, 158
    index value, 150, 153, 156, 160,
        161, 165
    member access, 150
    reference, 150, 160
    stack-allocated, 154, 162
        example, 155
    static assignments, 156
    of structures, 164
    variable indices, 151, 153
Array type option (Ghidra), 156
articulation, 200
ASCII, 16, 28, 111, 183, 486
ASCII format export (Ghidra),
        514, 522, 523
askAddress method, 300
askDirectory method, 301
askFile method, 301
askInt method, 300
askString method, 293, 300
askYesNo method, 300
ASPack, 19, 479, 496
ASProtect, 479
assembler (Ghidra), 513, 515–518, 528
Assembler Rating, 516
assemblers, 4, 7, 9
assembly language
    directives, 4
-a strings option, 29
Attach existing FidDb, 275
attaching FidDbs, 275
authentication
    functions, 512
    Ghidra Server, 219, 221, 227, 228,
        230, 231

auto analysis, 52–53, 90, 107, 110, 261,
        265, 268, 273
    Analysis Options, 48, 49, 51
    options, 50
    results, 51
Auto Analysis Summary dialog, 50
Auto Create Structure, 439, 441
automated structure creation, 437
automatic storage class (C++), 177

B

back references, 184, 185, 195
backward navigation (Go To Previous
        Location)
    hotkey ALT-left arrow, 92, 93
    hotkey OPTION-left arrow (Mac), 93
backward slice, 435
base address, 47
base address (array), 150, 152, 153, 158,
        159, 160, 170
Base Library (FidDb), 277
base virtual address (PE files), 367, 369
basic block, 66, 67, 190, 198, 199,
        203–208, 428, 436
basic data transformations, 140
basic disassembly algorithm, 8
batch import, 226, 227, 346, 359
Batch Import dialog, 282
batch import (Ghidra), 282
batch import (headless analyzer),
        346, 347, 359
Batch mode (import), 226, 227, 282
binaries, 4
    ELF, 92
    importing, 262, 264, 276, 278
    stripped, 18, 152, 461, 465
binary differencing, 529
Binary format export (Ghidra),
        522, 523, 525
binary search, 444, 446–448
bitness, 263
breakpoints
    hardware, 477, 489
    software, 490
Browser Field Formatter, 65, 66, 133,
        134, 247, 248, 419
.bss section, 71, 150, 153
buffer overflow, 184, 330
buildLanguage.xml, 404
build options (compiler), 152, 444,
        451, 455
BuiltInTypes, 268
Burneye, 492, 493, 495, 496
byte code, 4

pointer cross-reference, 191, 192
PointerToRawData, 370
polymorphism (C++), 172, 180
Populate Fid Database, 275, 277
Populate FidDb from programs,
  275, 277
populating FidDbs
 Populate Fid Database
  Base Library, 277
  Common Symbols File, 278
  Fid Database, 275, 277
  Language, 263, 277
  Library Family Name, 277
  Library Variant, 277
  Library Version, 277
  Root Folder, 277
 Populate FidDb from programs,
  275, 277
popup method, 300, 308
Portable Executable (PE) format.
  See PE files, 8
post comments, 130, 302
-postScript (headless analyzer), 354,
  355, 357–359
pre comments, 130, 131, 302
Pre-Comment section, 537, 538
prefixes, 120, 126
-preScript (headless analyzer), 354
preventing debugging, 489
printf method, 300, 307, 309, 310
println method, 293, 300
private files (Ghidra Server), 238, 239
private headers, 24
-process (headless analyzer), 343, 348,
  351–353, 359
Process Monitor (procmon), 488
-processor (headless analyzer), 351,
  352, 359
processor manuals, 5, 58, 375, 406,
  407, 409
processor modules, 401–403, 405, 408,
  418, 426
 adding an instruction, 409
 adding a register, 424
 files
  buildLanguage.xml, 404
  README.txt, 404
  sleighArgs.txt, 404
 modifying, 407
 modifying an instruction, 415
 template (Eclipse), 323
processor name field, 263

processors
 ARM, 94–96, 113, 405, 418, 491
 MIPS, 491, 496
 SuperH, 426
 x86, 474, 476–478, 488, 490, 491,
  494, 496
processor specification language, 36
processor type, 263
processor variant/mode field, 263
process tracing. *See* ptrace, 490
procmon (Process Monitor), 488
Program API, 297, 302, 304–306
Program class, 297, 299
 getFunctionManager method, 305
 getLanguageID method, 306
 getListing method, 293, 305,
  308, 309
 getMaxAddress method, 306, 307
 getMemory method, 305
 getMinAddress method, 306, 307, 309
 getReferenceManager method, 306
 getSymbolTable method, 305, 310
Program Database (PDB), 50, 53
Program Differences, 530
Program Diff tool, 530–532, 534, 538,
  540, 541, 546, 547, 549
Program Diff toolbar (hotkey F5), 532
 Apply Differences, 534, 537, 538
Program Diff View, 532
program entry point, 8
program section, 71
program slice, 435
program stack pointer, 94, 95, 97, 98,
  101–106, 108, 111, 113, 500
program text search, 115, 508
Program Trees window, 71, 214, 519
project (Ghidra Server), 235
Project menu (Ghidra Project), 229, 231
project repository, 221, 223, 232
projects
 nonshared, 34, 224, 232, 240
 shared, 34
 shared (Ghidra Server), 225
prologue, 95, 100, 102, 104, 105, 110, 375
-propertiesPath (headless analyzer), 354
ptrace, 490
pure virtual function, 174, 175
python_basics.py, 295

Q

Quick Fix options (Eclipse), 315, 320, 321
QuickUnpack, 480

S

XML format export (Ghidra), 523
XREF, 64, 69, 185–193
XREFs Field edit window, 186
XRefs window, 193

Z

Z flag (x86), 474
zip export format (Ghidra), 522
zooming (Function Graph View),
    58, 60, 68

RESOURCES

Visit *https://nostarch.com/ghidrabook/* for errata and more information.

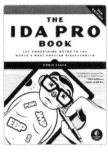
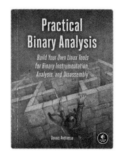

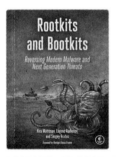

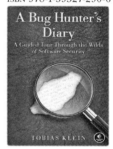

The Electronic Frontier Foundation (EFF) is the leading organization defending civil liberties in the digital world. We defend free speech on the Internet, fight illegal surveillance, promote the rights of innovators to develop new digital technologies, and work to ensure that the rights and freedoms we enjoy are enhanced — rather than eroded — as our use of technology grows.

EFF.ORG

ELECTRONIC FRONTIER FOUNDATION

Protecting Rights and Promoting Freedom on the Electronic Frontier